AILA's Guide to Worksite Enforcement and Corporate Compliance

AILA TITLES OF INTEREST

AILA'S OCCUPATIONAL GUIDEBOOKS

Immigration Options for Artists and Entertainers

Immigration Options for Physicians

Immigration Options for Nurses & Allied Health Care Professionals

Immigration Options for Religious Workers

Immigration Options for Academics and Researchers

Immigration Options for Investors and Entrepreneurs

STATUTES, REGULATIONS, AGENCY MATERIALS & CASE LAW

Immigration & Nationality Act (INA)

Immigration Regulations (CFR)

Agency Interpretations of Immigration Policy (Cables, Memos, and Liaison Minutes)

AILA's Immigration Case Summaries

CORE CURRICULUM

Navigating the Fundamentals of Immigration Law

Immigration Law for Paralegals*

AILA's Guide to Technology and Legal Research for the Immigration Lawyer

CD PRODUCTS & TOOLBOX SERIES

AILA's Immigration Practice Toolbox

AILA's Litigation Toolbox

FOR YOUR CLIENTS

Client Brochures (10 Titles)

U.S. Tax Guides for Foreign Persons and Those Who Pay Them, 4 volumes— (H-1Bs, L-1s, J-1s, B-1s)*

ONLINE RESEARCH TOOLS

AILALink Online

AILA'S FOCUS SERIES

EB-2 & EB-3 Degree Equivalency by Ronald Wada

Waivers Under the INA by Julie Ferguson

Private Bills & Pardons in Immigration by Anna Gallagher

TREATISES & PRIMERS

Kurzban's Immigration Law Sourcebook by Ira J. Kurzban

Professionals: A Matter of Degree by Martin J. Lawler

AILA's Asylum Primer by Regina Germain

Immigration Consequences of Criminal Activity by Mary E. Kramer

Essentials of Removal and Relief by Joseph A. Vail

Essentials of Immigration Law by Richard A. Boswell

Litigating Immigration Cases in Federal Court by Robert Pauw

OTHER TITLES

AILA's Guide to Worksite Enforcement and Corporate Compliance

David Stanton Manual on Labor Certification

AILA's Global Immigration Guide: A Country-by-Country Survey

Immigration & Nationality Law Handbook

The Visa Processing Guide

Ethics in a Brave New World

Immigration Practice Under NAFTA and Other Free Trade Agreements

GOVERNMENT REPRINTS

BIA Practice Manual

Immigration Judge Benchbook

Citizenship Laws of the World

CBP Inspector's Field Manual

USCIS Adjudicator's Field Manual

Tables of Contents and other information about these publications can be found at *www.ailapubs.org*. Orders may be placed at that site or by calling 1-800-982-2839.

*An AILA-distributed title

AILA's Guide to Worksite Enforcement & Corporate Compliance

Featuring a mini-primer on I-9s

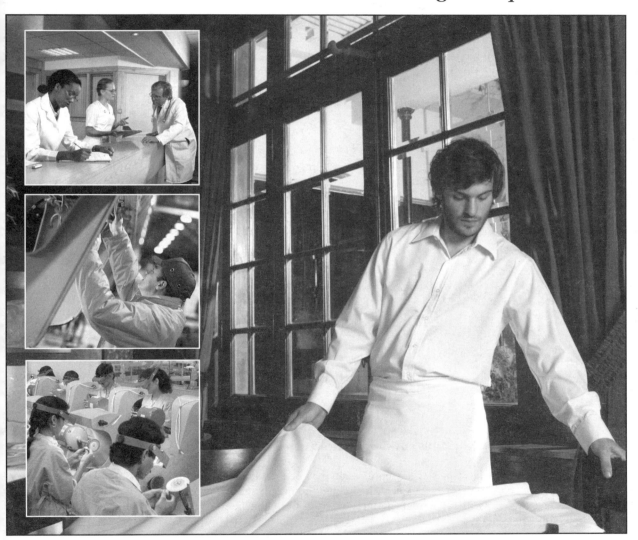

EDITOR-IN-CHIEF
Josie Gonzalez

ASSOCIATE EDITORS
Richard A. Gump, Jr.
Nancy-Jo Merritt
Howard "Sam" Myers
Mary E. Pivec
Anthony E. Weigel

MANAGING EDITORS
Tatia L. Gordon-Troy
Richard J. Link

1.800.982.2839
www.ailapubs.org

AMERICAN IMMIGRATION LAWYERS ASSOCIATION

> ## Website for Corrections and Updates
>
> Corrections and other updates to AILA publications can be found online at: *www.aila.org/BookUpdates.*
>
> If you have any corrections or updates to the information in this book, please let us know by sending a note to the address below, or e-mail us at *books@aila.org*.

This publication is designed to provide accurate and authoritative information in regard to the subject matter covered. It is distributed with the understanding that the publisher is not engaged in rendering legal, accounting, or other professional service. If legal advice or other expert assistance is required, the services of a competent professional should be sought.

—from a Declaration of Principles jointly adopted by a Committee of the American Bar Association and a Committee of Publishers

Copyright © 2008 by the American Immigration Lawyers Association

All rights reserved. No part of this publication may be reproduced or transmitted in any form or by any means, electronic or mechanical, including photocopy, recording, or any information storage retrieval system, without written permission from the publisher. No copyright claimed on U.S. government material.

Requests for permission to make electronic or print copies of any part of this work should be mailed to Director of Publications, American Immigration Lawyers Association, 1331 G Street NW, Washington, DC 20005, or e-mailed to *books@aila.org*.

Printed in the United States of America

ISBN 978-1-57370-232-4
Stock No. 52-32

ACKNOWLEDGMENTS

This book is the product of a collaborative effort by some of the leading lights in the field of immigration-related worksite enforcement and corporate compliance. The seeds for this book were sown in Scottsdale in November 2007 at AILA's worksite enforcement conference, which brought together many of the contributors to this book. I appreciate all those who attended and spoke at that conference, and those who presented materials for its accompanying handbook, which served as a starting point for developing this book. Particular recognition goes to Mel Kay, CEO of Golden State Fence, who spoke so eloquently in Scottsdale regarding the events leading up to the criminal charges that were filed against him and Golden State Fence. His description of the ICE worksite raids, the factors cited by the court in imposing a probationary sentence, and GSF's subsequent development of an "A+" corporate immigration compliance program, left an indelible impression in the hearts and minds of all the attendees.

I would like to thank editors Mary Pivec and Tony Weigel for doing a lot of the heavy lifting in getting this book off the ground, as well as editors Rick Gump, Nancy-Jo Merritt, and Sam Myers for lending their expertise. Thanks also go to all the contributing authors, each of whom covered a unique aspect of the worksite enforcement issue. I am grateful for the assistance of AILA Publications Director Tatia L. Gordon-Troy in organizing the framework for this book, and Legal Editor Richard Link at AILA for shepherding it through the editing process.

Josie Gonzalez
March 2008

TABLE OF CONTENTS

AILA'S GUIDE TO WORKSITE ENFORCEMENT AND CORPORATE COMPLIANCE

Preface xi
About the Editors xiii
Subject-Matter Index 645

REPORTS FROM THE TRENCHES: PRACTICE TIPS AND ADVICE

IRCA—TWENTY YEARS LATER
by Roger Tsai 3

EMPLOYER SANCTIONS FOR IMMIGRATION-RELATED HIRING VIOLATIONS
Congressional testimony of Stephen Yale-Loehr 35

ETHICAL ISSUES IN REPRESENTING EMPLOYERS
IN ICE WORKSITE INVESTIGATIONS
by Josie Gonzalez 49

THE NEW LOOK OF WORKSITE ENFORCEMENT
by Bo Cooper, Eileen Scofield, Doug Weigle, and Steven M. Ladik 57

DEPUTIZING—AND THEN PROSECUTING—AMERICA'S BUSINESSES
IN THE FIGHT AGAINST ILLEGAL IMMIGRATION
by Thomas C. Green, Jay T. Jorgensen, and Ileana M. Ciobanu 77

CRIMINAL PENALTIES IN WORKPLACE IMMIGRATION CASES
by Kathleen M. Brinkman 101

OF KATZ AND "ALIENS": PRIVACY EXPECTATIONS
AND THE IMMIGRATION RAIDS
by Raquel Aldana 113

THE ANATOMY OF AN ICE RAID
by Josie Gonzalez and Nancy-Jo Merritt 179

SOCIAL SECURITY "NO-MATCH" LETTERS:
CONTINUED UNCERTAINTY FOR EMPLOYERS
by Daniel Brown 187

ESTABLISHING AN EFFECTIVE FORM I-9 COMPLIANCE PROGRAM
by Scott J. FitzGerald 203

IMMIGRATION COMPLIANCE PROGRAM TOOLS:
AN ANALYSIS OF I-9 DEFENSE MECHANISMS
by Anthony E. Weigel 225

UNCOVERING THE TICKING TIME BOMB: IDENTIFYING IMMIGRATION
COMPLIANCE ISSUES IN CORPORATE DUE DILIGENCE
by Marketa Lindt 245

I-9 CONSIDERATIONS IN MERGERS AND ACQUISITIONS—
A BACK-BURNER ISSUE REQUIRING FRONT-BURNER ATTENTION
by Anthony E. Weigel 253

    Appendix A: Employer Compliance Matter
    Information-Document Request 262

    Appendix B: I-9 Review Checklist 264

    Appendix C: Immigration Matter Inventory Checklist 266

THE MUSHROOM PATCH OF STATE IMMIGRATION LAWS—
A MAD HATTER'S WONDERLAND FOR EMPLOYERS
by Nancy-Jo Merritt and Anthony E. Weigel 269

    Appendix A: Contractor Measures 287

    Appendix B: Measures Related to Public Finance 293

    Appendix C: Measures Applicable to All Employers 296

CIVIL RICO CLASS ACTION SUITS BY U.S. DOMESTIC WORKERS
by Mary E. Pivec 301

PRACTICE AIDS: CHECKLISTS AND BEST PRACTICES

CORPORATE COMPLIANCE PRACTICE AIDS
FOR THE IMMIGRATION LAWYER
by Richard A. Gump, Jr. 315

    A Perspective to Consider 317

    Best Practices: Developing an Immigration
    Corporate Compliance Program 319

    The Wal-Mart Consent Decree 333

    The Wal-Mart Model of Best Practices and
    Subcontractor Liability: Tools for the Embattled Employer 339

EMPLOYER IMMIGRATION COMPLIANCE AUDIT:
CHECKLIST OF ISSUES FOR REVIEW AND RISK ASSESSMENT
by Mary E. Pivec 341

THE I-9 GETS A MAKE-OVER, AND OTHER DEVELOPMENTS
IN EMPLOYMENT VERIFICATION
by Josie Gonzalez 349

QUESTIONS AND ANSWERS: THE NEW EMPLOYMENT ELIGIBILITY VERIFICATION FORM I-9 AND THE NEW HANDBOOK FOR EMPLOYERS by Scott W. Wright	381
SUBSTANTIVE VS. TECHNICAL/PROCEDURAL FAILURES UNDER THE GOOD-FAITH DEFENSE courtesy of Kathleen Campbell Walker	387
EMPLOYER VERIFICATION AND NO-MATCH LETTERS by Kathleen Campbell Walker and L. Edward Rios	389
EMPLOYMENT OF THE UNDOCUMENTED: CRIMINAL AND CIVIL LIABILITY RISKS by Mary E. Pivec	421
PRACTICAL POINTERS IN CONDUCTING INVESTIGATIONS AFTER ICE WORKSITE RAIDS by Josie Gonzalez	429

A MINI-PRIMER ON I-9S & RELATED RESOURCE MATERIALS

by Josie Gonzalez

Table of Contents	435
Summary of Key Issues Related to Representing an Employer in an I-9 Inspection	437
I-9 Inspections Outline	443
Ethical Considerations in Conducting Immigration Investigations	445
Questions for the Company Executive Officer	449
Questions for the Hiring Manager	453
Preliminary I-9 Inspections Instructions to Client	455
I-9 Inspections Checklist	457
I-9 Audit Report— (Attorney-Client Work Product—Privileged and Confidential)	459
Work Authorization Tracking	461
Sample ICE Notice of Inspection	463
Sample ICE Second Notice of Inspection	465
How to Prepare for an ICE Business Inspection	467
ICE Business Entity Questionnaire	469
ICE Employee Information Certification Form	471
Sample ICE Subpoena	473
Subpoena and Custody Receipt for Seized Property	475

Sample ICE Notice of Suspect Documents 479

Sample ICE Notice of Unauthorized Aliens 481

Sample Notice of Intent to Fine 483

GOVERNMENT RESOURCES AND COURT DOCUMENTS

Handbook for Employers—Instructions on
Completing the Form I-9 497

Guide to Selected U.S. Travel and Identity Documents 545

Good-Faith Guidelines Memorandum 569

E-Verify Fact Sheet 581

E-Verify Q&A for Employers 583

Social Security Number Verification Service (SSNVS) Handbook 587

Tarrasco Indictment: Inducement and False Statements 621

Wolnitzek Information: Harboring for Commercial Advantage 631

Pereyra-Gabino Order: Concealing/Shielding 635

PREFACE

Much criticism has been levied over the inadequacies of the Immigration Reform and Control Act of 1986. The goals of this legislation were laudable: legalize the pool of undocumented workers who entered the United States before January 1, 1982, and enlist the assistance of employers to screen their workforce to ensure that all workers had the right to lawfully work in the United States. Over the next 20 years, employers were told to accept work authorization documents that reasonably appeared to be genuine and record related data on a new form, the "I-9," that had to be retained for possible inspection by the government. Employers were not asked to mail the I-9s to the government to verify the accuracy of the data accepted, nor, until just recently, were they given the tools to decipher a valid document from a forged one. It should come as no surprise that many employers viewed this effort as a toothless and ineffective enforcement measure, with the result that today there are many workforces that are comprised largely of unauthorized workers. Weaning America's employers from their undocumented workforces is no easy task. Special relationships—emotional and economic—have developed between employers and their workers. There is no more important asset to a company than its trained labor pool. Lacking adequate measures to apply for work permits to legalize their foreign talent, employers are sitting on a keg of dynamite—waiting with tremor for the ICE-man (Immigration and Customs Enforcement) to cometh.

Without the passage of any new legislation, the Department of Homeland Security (DHS) decided approximately three years ago that it would use existing statutes to pursue criminal prosecutions of employers for conduct that in prior years was either largely ignored or was punished through civil penalties. Vigorous enforcement is resulting in multimillion-dollar fines and prison sentences for corporate executives, managers, and lower-level supervisors. The highly publicized prosecutions by DHS are designed to inculcate in the minds of employers that a new zero-tolerance landscape is in place and that the climate of "willful blindness" to the "real" composition of the workforce will not be tolerated.

The unfortunate group of employers caught in DHS's prosecutorial net had no idea that the government's prior laissez-faire attitude regarding an employer's immigration responsibilities had abruptly changed. These employers and many more fail to realize that fulfilling their immigration obligations requires far more than the mere completion of the I-9.

Although the government often describes the conduct of the employers it has prosecuted as "egregious, shocking, and willful," a close examination of the underlying indictment documents reveals that what is "egregious" is clearly in the mind of the beholder: the government. Certainly, not all employers were evildoers who blatantly violated the law. Had adequate education, corporate controls, and compliance measures been instituted, a criminal prosecution for some could have been avoided. For example, take the case of Mel Kay, the chief executive officer of Golden State Fence, who was criminally prosecuted in San Diego for hiring 10 or more unauthorized aliens within a 12-month period. At sentencing, Judge Moskowitz stated:

> *Of most significant interest in reviewing this case is the fact that the case agent, that is, the government agent, found that none of the undocumented workers had been exploited by Kay and/or his corporation. In fact, the undocumented workers were paid well and had health and employee benefits. They were not treated as day laborers, but were permanent, longstanding, and loyal employees. When he had to terminate his undocumented workers, Kay provided them with their last due paychecks as well as severance pay. It's hard to image that there are other companies or employers out there who would treat their undocumented employees as fairly as their eligible employees such as Kay did, and I think that is an accurate statement of the fact here.*

The U.S. attorney acknowledged that there was no evidence of Mr. Kay's direct knowledge of any criminal conduct. Mr. Kay paid a high price, not for participating in any criminal conduct, but simply for tolerating it and failing to adopt appropriate safeguards as the company's highest executive officer. Mr. Kay's minimal culpability and the corporation's subsequent rehabilitative measures contributed to the court's decision not to impose any jail time. Judge Moskowitz credited the company's efforts, saying that it "obtained expert legal advice and devised an A plus system for dealing with the situation to essentially clean up their act and make their act a model for what corporations in the construction field should do to avoid hiring illegal aliens."

The need to heighten employer awareness and to provide enhanced, practical education was the catalyst for this publication. Our authors have sought to provide a balanced, comprehensive tool that will inform employers about their legal obligations and their due process rights. Much of the material is focused on assisting employers in developing effective immigration corporate compliance policies that will avert civil and criminal liability.

This book begins with articles that trace the history of worksite enforcement and provide an excellent overview of all of an employer's responsibilities. Roger Tsai's introductory article provides a comprehensive summary of the shift from civil to criminal prosecution of employers.

Next is an article analyzing the complex ethical issues in the representation of employers in a worksite enforcement setting. Issues such as obstruction of justice, document retention requirements, conducting internal investigations, and conflict of interest dilemmas in representing the corporation, its managers, and the workforce are discussed.

Two articles are contributed by criminal defense attorneys, who describe the criminal penalties that can attach to specific employer conduct. The article authored by Jay Jorgensen, Thomas Green, and Ileana Ciobanu describes their successful representation of Tyson Foods. It discusses key defenses available to companies facing criminal investigations and suggests ways that they can avoid becoming targets of government prosecutions.

Several articles focus on one of ICE's most effective enforcement tools—the dreaded worksite raid. These articles demystify this enforcement tool by describing how the government conducts its investigations, the profile of the targeted company, and what occurs during a raid, including what due process rights an employer and worker can invoke.

Daniel Brown has contributed an article that describes the Social Security "no-match" regulations and related litigation. Although at the time of writing there was no final resolution concerning the injunction preventing the government from implementing the "no-match" regulations, Brown's analysis provides an insightful roadmap for companies to follow in the absence of definitive guidance.

Four articles address instituting corporate immigration compliance measures that should foster a climate of immigration awareness regarding the government's new zero-tolerance stance toward the employment of unauthorized workers. We provide a thorough nuts and bolts approach—including instituting defensive measures such as participating in DHS's E-Verify new-hire screening, IMAGE, or I-9 electronic programs; conducting I-9 internal audits with full awareness of antidiscrimination responsibilities; and the need for conducting I-9 due diligence stemming from corporate mergers and acquisitions.

Tony Weigel and Nancy-Jo Merritt have written an excellent article on various state immigration laws promulgated throughout the United States, aptly called "The Mushroom Patch of State Immigration Laws—A Mad Hatter's Wonderland for Employers."

When you think it's over, it isn't. In her article on the Racketeer Influenced and Corrupt Organizations Act, Mary Pivec describes the continued focus on the employer's hiring practices from civil litigants who press claims against employers for alleged racketeering activity such as harboring and transporting undocumented aliens. Notwithstanding a criminal conviction, domestic workers and businesses can sue to recover actual and treble damages and attorney's fees and costs.

The second section of the book provides a panoply of practice aids to assist the employer in the development of immigration corporate compliance measures. Rick Gump leads off by providing a PowerPoint presentation and other materials related to subcontractor liability using the "Wal-Mart Model of Best Practices" as a guide. Other helpful Power Points are contributed by Mary Pivec, Kathleen Walker, and me on the topics of criminal and civil liability, the Social Security "no-match" letter, and the newly revised I-9. I have also included an article full of practice pointers in conducting investigations after ICE worksite raids.

Assistant Secretary of Homeland Security for ICE Julie Myers recently announced a new shift in enforcement tactics and an increase in I-9 worksite audits. In order to prepare the employer for these inspections, I have provided a wealth of information on the representation of employers facing I-9 government inspections, including how to respond to ICE subpoenas, how to conduct internal investigations with sample questions for the hiring manager and corporate executives, instructions for surrendering ICE requested data, and guidance on how to correct I-9s. Sample ICE notices of inspection and related documents are included.

The last section of the book provides valuable resource materials such as the latest DHS *Handbook for Employers*, E-Verify fact sheets, and various criminal indictments.

In conclusion, there will continue to be many interesting and emotionally charged developments in the area of worksite enforcement. Government tactics are ever changing.

Today, the government focuses on immigration-related prosecutions. Perhaps in the future there will be a shift to deferred prosecution agreements, which are now being used to redefine corporate criminal liability in other areas of white collar crime. Hopefully, ameliorative legislation will be enacted that will help to preserve a company's most valuable asset—its trained and highly regarded workforce, and thus make the implementation of effective corporate compliance measures more palatable for the employer.

Josie Gonzalez
March 2008

ABOUT THE EDITORS

Josie Gonzalez (editor-in-chief) is the managing partner of Gonzalez & Harris, and has represented employers in all aspects of immigration law for more than 25 years. She recently represented a major corporation facing federal criminal charges for hiring undocumented workers. Ms. Gonzalez has published numerous articles for legal and trade journals on the topic of employer sanctions. Her background as a former criminal defense attorney and employer sanctions expert makes her uniquely qualified to address issues such as RICO and other criminal charges against employers, the future of employer sanctions, and how to develop and implement immigration corporate compliance materials. She currently chairs AILA's Worksite Enforcement Conference Committee.

Richard A. Gump, Jr. is the shareholder of the Law Offices of Richard A. Gump, Jr. Mr. Gump graduated from the University of Texas School of Law, and has been practicing business and employment-related immigration law for more than 30 years. He is a member of AILA, past chair of the AILA Texas Chapter, past chair of the AILA Texas Service Center Liaison Committee, and is a member of the AILA Worksite Enforcement Conference Committee. Mr. Gump has been named in *Texas Lawyer*'s "Go-To Guide" as one of the attorneys whom his peers would call if they needed representation in immigration law, and since 2003 has been recommended by *Super Lawyers* in the field of immigration law. He also has been recognized in *The International Who's Who of Business Lawyers 2006* and *Chambers USA: America's Leading Lawyers for Business* in 2006. Mr. Gump handled the first employer sanctions case filed in the southwestern United States under the Immigration Reform and Control Act of 1986, and was co-counsel in one of the largest civil/criminal settlements in worksite compliance history.

Nancy-Jo Merritt, a director in the Phoenix office of Fennemore Craig, P.C., has more than two decades of practice in the field of immigration law. Her practice is broad-based and includes the representation of domestic and international companies regarding visa and work authorization issues for foreign national employees. She also assists employers with federal compliance issues in the contexts of mergers and acquisitions and government audits. Ms. Merritt has been successful in challenging the federal government's interpretation of immigration law in a number of matters, and received the first award of fees in the United States from an immigration judge under the Equal Access to Justice Act. Ms. Merritt is the author of *Understanding Immigration Law: How to Enter, Work and Live in the United States*. She publishes frequently and serves as a senior editor of AILA's *Immigration & Nationality Law Handbook*, published annually. She also lectures frequently on U.S. immigration law, most frequently on issues relating to employers.

Howard S. (Sam) Myers III is a 1972 graduate of the University of Virginia Law School. His law practice focuses on business-related immigration. Mr. Myers consistently has been selected for inclusion in *Super Lawyers*, *The Best Lawyers in America*, and *The International Who's Who of Business Lawyers* for his work in the field of immigration law. He is cofounder of Minneapolis-based Myers Thompson, P.A., a law firm with a national business immigration practice. Mr. Myers cofounded the Minnesota-Dakotas Chapter of AILA. He is a permanent board director of AILA and served as AILA president in 1991–92. He organized and chaired AILA's Board of Publications, and currently serves as a member of that board. He has chaired and served on AILA's Committee on INS Reorganization and has served on many of AILA's agency liaison committees. Mr. Myers is an honorary fellow of the American Immigration Law Foundation, where he served as the chair of the board of trustees for four years.

Mary E. Pivec, a partner with Keller and Heckman, LLP, in Washington, D.C., has extensive experience in representing employers in labor, employment, and immigration matters. She lectures on issues such as union avoidance techniques for supervisors and managers, defeating union representation elections, employer sanctions and I-9 compliance, developing effective employee handbooks, investigating and defending sexual harassment claims, and complying with the Family and Medical Leave Act, the Americans with Disabilities Act, and the Fair Labor Standards Act. Prior to her legal practice, Ms. Pivec worked as a business agent and handled collective bargaining and grievance and arbitration disputes in the public sector. In 2007, she was named by *Super Lawyers* as an outstanding attorney in Washington, D.C., in the fields of employment/labor and immigration law, and has also been named in *The Best Lawyers in America* since 1990 in the area of immigration law.

Anthony E. Weigel practices immigration law at Husch Blackwell Sanders, LLP in Kansas City, MO, and is a member of AILA. His practice focuses on employer compliance and employment-based immigration. Prior to practicing law, Mr. Weigel worked in human resources and was responsible for coordinating immigration matters and a broad spectrum of employment law compliance issues, including I-9 verifications and record retention.

ABOUT AILA

The American Immigration Lawyers Association (AILA) is a national bar association of more than 11,000 attorneys who practice immigration law and/or work as teaching professionals. AILA member attorneys represent tens of thousands of U.S. families who have applied for permanent residence for their spouses, children, and other close relatives for lawful entry and residence in the United States. AILA members also represent thousands of U.S. businesses and industries who sponsor highly skilled foreign workers seeking to enter the United States on a temporary or permanent basis. In addition, AILA members represent foreign students, entertainers, athletes, and asylum-seekers, often on a pro bono basis. Founded in 1946, AILA is a nonpartisan, not-for-profit organization that provides its members with continuing legal education, publications, information, professional services, and expertise through its 36 chapters and over 50 national committees. AILA is an affiliated organization of the American Bar Association and is represented in the ABA House of Delegates.

American Immigration Lawyers Association
www.aila.org

Reports From the Trenches: Practice Tips & Advice

IRCA—Twenty Years Later
by Roger Tsai[*]

Introduction

November 6, 2006, marked the 20th anniversary of the Immigration Reform and Control Act of 1986 (IRCA).[1] Enacted in hopes of decreasing illegal immigration, IRCA has been clearly unsuccessful in stopping the tsunami of 12 million undocumented workers now in the United States. It has created a troubling situation where employers are forced to walk a fine line between scrutinizing documents too little or too much. The amount of paperwork that is generated, along with the fear among both employers and employees, has sapped the public will for stringent enforcement. Enforcement by legacy Immigration and Naturalization Service (INS) and now U.S. Immigration and Customs Enforcement (ICE) has waxed and waned depending on the political winds, and with limited resources committed to worksite enforcement ICE has become desperate to make a public example of employers who are caught.

Through these 20 years, immigration officials have unsuccessfully tried to catch up to those who would circumvent the rules. Despite changes made in 1998 to limit the number of acceptable employment eligibility verification documents, it took nine years for immigration officials to update the I-9 form to reflect those changes. Their response to the widespread problem of document fraud consists of an online verification program that forces undocumented workers to go further underground to assume the identity of others. Despite the challenges in implementing IRCA, Congress has attempted to create a nuanced law that acknowledges discrimination against lawful immigrants and the problems that employers face in compliance. Regardless of the criticism, IRCA remains in effect, and any comprehensive immigration legislation will likely increase the burdens placed on employers.

---

[*] Updated from an article appearing at *Navigating the Fundamentals of Immigration Law* 71 (AILA 2007–08 Ed.).

Roger Tsai is an immigration attorney with the Salt Lake City-based law firm of Parsons Behle & Latimer. He specializes in employment-based immigration and worksite enforcement. A graduate of the University of Houston Law Center (J.D.) and the University of Michigan (B.A.), Mr. Tsai has spoken to numerous organizations on the topic of worksite enforcement and has appeared before the Utah state legislature to discuss immigration bills on worksite enforcement.

[1] Pub. L. No. 99-603, 100 Stat. 3359. *See* Immigration and Nationality Act (INA) §§274A, 274B, and 274C; 8 USC §§1324a, 1324b, and 1324c; 8 CFR §§274a.1 to 274a.10.

The Raid on Undocumented Workers at Swift

On December 12, 2006, ICE conducted one of its largest raids in history by arresting 1,282 workers at six meat processing plants across the Midwest.[2] In February 2006, ICE began investigating Swift & Company, when immigrants who were being processed for removal confessed to identity theft and working at the Iowa Swift plant.[3] ICE also had received anonymous calls through the ICE hotline and referrals from local police.[4] Due to the arrests, Swift lost 40 percent of its labor force and temporarily suspended operations at all six of its plants. The raid on the second-largest meatpacking company in the world was part of an increased effort by ICE to target undocumented workers in low-wage industries, including restaurants, construction, and retail.

A casual observer might ask how Swift could not have suspected that much of its labor force was undocumented. In fact, Swift, fearful of being penalized for hiring undocumented workers, had intensely scrutinized the documents of its workers, so much that in 2001 Swift was forced to pay a $200,000 settlement to the Department of Justice (DOJ) Office of Special Counsel for Immigration-Related Unfair Employment Practices (OSC) for excessively scrutinizing documents of individuals who looked or sounded "foreign."[5] Federal immigration laws prohibit employers from considering foreign appearance, accents, or national origin in their hiring practices. Employers are caught between two federal agencies with opposing interests: ensuring that all workers are authorized for employment and protecting those who are lawfully here from discrimination.

Employer Responsibilities Under IRCA

The I-9 Form

IRCA requires all employers to fill out an I-9 form for all employees hired since November 6, 1986, regardless of their immigration status.[6] The purpose of the I-9 is to verify the identity and employment authorization of workers. The form consists of two portions. In the first portion, the employee attests, under penalty of perjury, that he or she is a citizen, lawful permanent resident, or alien authorized to work tempo-

---

[2] U.S. Immigration and Customs and Enforcement (ICE) Press Release, "U.S. Uncovers Large-Scale Identity Theft Scheme by Using Illegal Aliens to Gain Employment at Nationwide Meat Processor" (Dec. 13, 2006), *published on* AILA InfoNet at Doc. No. 06121379 (*posted* Dec. 13, 2006).

[3] S. Reddy, "Government Raids of Swift Plants Add to Growing Immigration Debate," *The Dallas Morning News* (Dec. 14, 2006).

[4] *Id.*

[5] "Swift Responds to Plant Raids," *The Greeley Tribune* (Dec. 22, 2006).

[6] 8 CFR §274a.2(b).

rarily.[7] Section 1 must be completed at the time of hire. In the second portion, employers are required to record that they have examined original documents from a specified list verifying the employee's identity and eligibility to work.[8] Employers must accept the documents if they appear "reasonably genuine" and relate to the person presenting the documents.

Section 2 of the I-9 must be completed within three days of the employee's start date.[9] The I-9 itself is not submitted to ICE; instead, the employer must keep the form on file for three years from the date of hire or one year after the last day of work, whichever is later.[10] The I-9 may be stored in its original form, microfilm, microfiche, or electronically.[11] The only exceptions to an employer's I-9 obligations are for independent contractors and sporadic domestic workers.[12] Employers are not required to complete an I-9 for independent contractors, but remain liable if they know that contractors are using unauthorized aliens to perform labor or services.

"Knowing" Employment

IRCA prohibits any person or entity from knowingly hiring or continuing to employ an unauthorized worker.[13] Knowledge may be either actual or constructive. Constructive knowledge is defined as knowledge that may fairly be inferred through notice of certain facts and circumstances that would lead a person, through the exercise of reasonable care, to know about a certain condition.[14] A nonexhaustive list of conditions that would establish a rebuttable presumption of constructive knowledge includes (1) an employer's failure to complete or improper completion of the I-9; (2) failure to take reasonable steps after receiving information indicating that the employee may be an alien who is not employment authorized; and (3) reckless and wanton disregard for the legal consequences of permitting another individual to introduce an unauthorized alien into the workforce.[15]

Initially, courts interpreted the doctrine of constructive knowledge fairly narrowly. Constructive knowledge was specifically found where employers ignored notices from legacy INS stating that certain employees were not authorized to work.[16] The U.S. Court of Appeals for the Ninth Circuit overruled an administrative law judge's (ALJ) finding of constructive knowledge where the employer had failed to notice that

---

[7] 8 CFR §274a.2(b)(1)(i)(A).
[8] 8 CFR §274a.2(b)(1)(i)(B).
[9] 8 CFR §274a.2(b)(1)(ii).
[10] 8 CFR §274a.2(c)(2).
[11] 8 CFR §274a.2(b)(2)(ii).
[12] 8 CFR §274a.1(j).
[13] INA §274A(a); 8 USC §1324a(a).
[14] 8 CFR §274a.1(*l*)(1).
[15] *Id.*
[16] *Mester Mfg. Co. v. INS*, 879 F.2d 561 (9th Cir. 1989); *New El Rey Sausage Co. v. INS*, 925 F.2d 1153 (9th Cir. 1991).

the employee's name was misspelled on his Social Security card and a lack of lamination of the Social Security card.[17] The court disagreed with the INS argument that constructive knowledge should be found where the employer failed to notice the delay in presentation of a Social Security card, the lamination of the card, the misspelling of Rodriguez as Rodriquez on the Social Security card, the lack of any reference to the United States of America on the card, and the use of two family names on Rodriguez's California driver's license but not on the card. In that case, the Ninth Circuit noted that "to preserve Congress' intent . . . the doctrine of constructive knowledge must be sparingly applied."[18]

More recent cases have broadened the interpretation of constructive knowledge to include instances in which an employer is in possession of an I-9, indicating that the alien is out of status, but fails to reverify.[19]

Constructive knowledge arising from "reckless and wanton disregard" may have originally been intended for employers who accept employees through recruiters, but the concept of constructive knowledge has been interpreted to include employers who recklessly entrust incompetent employees with hiring or I-9 compliance responsibilities.[20] Because whoever completes section 2 of the I-9 does so on behalf of the employer, any knowledge acquired by the agent may be imputed to the employer, regardless of that agent's actual authority to hire.[21]

The Obligation to Reverify

Knowledge acquired by the employer after the initial hire may trigger an obligation to reverify the I-9 documents. The obligation to reverify I-9 documentation is triggered when (1) the temporary employment authorization expires; (2) the employer receives information from a government agency or through other sources that an employee may not be authorized to work; or (3) the employee presents a receipt for the application of an acceptable I-9 document.[22] Expiration of list B identity documents and the permanent resident card would not warrant reverification, as they may be accepted at hire even if they are expired.[23]

Reverification procedures should mirror initial I-9 procedures. The employee may choose which documents to present. An employer should not specify which documents, nor should it specify that the document provided must be a document issued by U.S. Citizenship and Immigration Services (USCIS). If any changes are made to the I-9, the employee should initial and date any updated information. Instead of re-

---

[17] *Collins Foods International Inc. v. INS*, 948 F.2d 549 (9th Cir. 1991).

[18] *Id.* at 555.

[19] *INS v. China Wok Restaurant, Inc.*, 4 OCAHO 608, OCAHO Case No. 93A00103 (Feb. 10, 1994).

[20] *U.S. v. Carter*, 7 OCAHO 931, OCAHO Case No. 95A00164 (May 9, 1997).

[21] *Id.*

[22] 8 CFR §274a.2(b)(1)(vi).

[23] "The I-9 Process in a Nutshell" (USCIS Employer Information Bulletin 102), at 7, *available at* www.uscis.gov/files/article/EIB102.pdf.

verifying through an entirely new form, an employer may use section 3 of the I-9. Section 3 may only be used if the original I-9 form was executed within three years of the date of rehire. In all instances an employer may use a new form to reverify as well.

Social Security "No-Match" Letters

In April 2006, seven managers of IFCO Systems, the largest pallet services company in the country, were arrested on criminal charges for failing to terminate workers after being repeatedly notified that more than half of the 5,000 IFCO employees had invalid or mismatched Social Security numbers (SSNs). Nearly 1,200 illegal workers were rounded up in raids on IFCO's U.S. facilities. Employers must be aware of how they respond to "no-match" letters, because ICE has informally stated that it considers the percentage of employees who are the subject of such a letter and the employer's failure to respond in determining good-faith compliance.

When Are They Issued?

Social Security "no-match" letters are issued when the employee name and SSN provided on the W-2 form conflict with the Social Security Administration's (SSA) records. Out of the 240 million W-2s submitted, 10 percent contain nonmatching SSNs. In 2007, 140,000 letters were expected to be sent to employers who had at least 11 employees with nonmatching data, where the nonmatching data constituted at least half of 1 percent of their employees. As a side note, taxed wages that cannot be doled out to individuals due to "no-matches" are sent to the SSA Earnings Suspense file, which now totals $586 billion.[24] The SSA also issued nine million letters to employees reminding them that correcting the information is in their best interest.

SSA expects the employer to check typos and talk with employees about any discrepancies without demanding a Social Security card. If the discrepancy is unresolved, the employee should be advised to check with his or her local SSA office. The Internal Revenue Service (IRS) may penalize employers $50 for each W-2 filed with an incorrect SSN.[25]. Employers will only face fines if they fail to respond to IRS notices that employee SSN information is incorrect—not for failure to respond to Social Security "no-match" letters.[26]

How Is Information Shared Between SSA and ICE?

While there has been significant debate concerning information-sharing between SSA and ICE, currently the database of "no-match" employers is not used to target specific employers. In 1998 and 1999, legacy INS attempted to use SSA work re-

---

[24] P. Orrenius, "No Match, No Sense," *Wall St. J.* (Aug. 13, 2007).

[25] 26 USC §6721.

[26] Letter from Thomas Dobbins, IRS Small Business/Self-Employed Division, to Michael O'Neill and Connie Davis, IRS Information Advisory Reporting Program Committee (Sept. 24, 2003), *published on* AILA InfoNet at Doc. No. 03100745 (*posted* Oct. 7, 2003).

cords to identify unauthorized aliens in Operation Vanguard.[27] After significant criticism from workers, farmers, and industry leaders, SSA limited INS's ability to check employee records to instances in which INS had a "reasonable cause to believe that a worker is unauthorized."[28]

SSA and the IRS are not permitted to share the information with any other agency.[29] Tax returns and return information are confidential and may not be disclosed by the IRS and others having access to the information, with certain specific exceptions, because the confidentiality of tax data is considered crucial to voluntary compliance. ICE may receive the Social Security "no-match" data from the SSA Office of Special Counsel when there is an ongoing investigation, but it is not used to select employers to target for I-9 audits or investigations.

How Must an Employer Respond Under the Final Regulations?

On August 15, 2007, the Department of Homeland Security (DHS) issued a controversial final regulation on how employers should respond to a Social Security "no-match" letter.[30] The regulation describes "safe-harbor" procedures employers can follow after receiving a letter to avoid a constructive knowledge finding. It also effectively broadens constructive knowledge to include situations in which the employer fails to take reasonable steps in response to (1) a "no-match" letter or (2) written notice from DHS that the employment authorization document (EAD) submitted for I-9 purposes does not match DHS records.[31]

The AFL-CIO and the American Civil Liberties Union challenged the new regulation in the U.S. District Court for the Northern District of California on the basis that rulemaking procedures were not correctly followed. On October 10, 2007, the court temporarily enjoined the implementation of the "no-match" regulation.[32] The court then granted DHS's request for a stay until March 24, 2008, pending a new rulemaking process to address the court's concerns.[33] Therefore, as of this writing, the Social Security "no-match" regulation is not in effect, although it may be prudent to advise employers to follow the final regulation in the interim.

Prior to the final regulation, SSA and legacy INS had indicated that a "no-match" letter alone was not a reliable indicator of lack of employment authorization.[34] Under

---

[27] A. Siskin, *et al.*, "Immigration Enforcement Within the United States," (Congressional Research Service Report for Congress, Apr. 6, 2006), at CRS-45, *available at www.fas.org/sgp/crs/misc/RL33351.pdf.*

[28] *Id.*

[29] 26 USC §6103.

[30] 72 Fed. Reg. 45611 (Aug. 15, 2007).

[31] *Id.*

[32] Order Granting Motion for Preliminary Injunction, *AFL-CIO v. Chertoff*, No. 07-4472 (N.D. Cal. Oct. 10, 2007).

[33] *See* Motion to Stay Proceedings Pending New Rulemaking, *AFL-CIO v. Chertoff*, No. 07-4472 (N.D. Cal. Nov. 23, 2007).

[34] Letter from David A. Martin, INS, to Bruce R. Larson (Dec. 23, 1997), *reproduced in* 76 *Interpreter Releases* 203 (Feb. 9, 1998).

the final regulations, employers must: (1) attempt to resolve the discrepancy within 30 days; and (2) reverify employment authorization through the I-9 procedure within 93 days.[35] If the employer completes a new I-9 form for the employee, it should use the same procedures as it would if the employee were newly hired, except that documents presented for both identity and employment must: (1) not contain the SSN, although the alien number may be used for employment authorization; and (2) contain a photograph.[36]

There has been some disagreement as to whether this expands an employer's existing obligations. The DHS view of current obligations finds support in *Mester Mfg. Co. v. INS*,[37] a Ninth Circuit case in which an employer was found to have constructive knowledge after receiving notice that three aliens were suspected of green card fraud, but failed to follow up on that information. In *Mester*, the Ninth Circuit held that the employer must terminate an unauthorized employee within a "reasonable" time period. Determining a reasonable time period will include factors such as "the certainty of the information provided" and the steps taken by the employer to confirm it.[38] Ultimately, a two-week delay in firing an undocumented worker after an employer received a notice of intent to fine from legacy INS was found to constitute continued employment of an undocumented worker.[39]

Good-Faith Defense

If an employer has employed an undocumented worker, good-faith compliance with I-9 procedures provides a "narrow but complete defense."[40] A person or entity that has complied in good faith with the requirements of employment verification has established an affirmative defense against unlawful hiring.[41] Completion of the I-9 raises a rebuttable presumption that the employer has not knowingly hired an unauthorized alien, but the government may rebut the presumption by offering proof that the documents did not appear genuine on their face, the verification was pretextual, or that the employer colluded with the employee in falsifying the documents.[42] The good-faith defense does not apply for employers who fail to make corrections on the I-9 after being given 10 days' notice or employers who have a pattern and practice of hiring undocumented workers.[43] Therefore, setting proper policies and training employees who administer I-9 documents is critical to demonstrating good-faith compliance.

---

[35] 72 Fed. Reg. 45611 (Aug. 15, 2007) (amending 8 CFR §274.1(*l*)(2)).

[36] *Id.* (amending 8 CFR §274.1(*l*)(2)(iii)).

[37] 879 F.2d 561 (9th Cir. 1989).

[38] *Id.* at 567.

[39] *Id.*

[40] *U.S. v. Walden Station, Inc.,* 8 OCAHO 1053, at 813, OCAHO Case No. 99A00040 (Apr. 21, 2000); *see* INA §274A(b)(6)(A); 8 USC §1324a(b)(6)(A).

[41] *See* INA §274A(b)(6)(A); 8 USC §1324a(b)(6)(A).

[42] H.R. Rep. No. 99-682, at 57 (1986), as quoted in *Collins Foods, supra* note 17.

[43] INA §§274A(b)(6)(B), (C); 8 USC §§1324a(b)(6)(B), (C). "Technical or paperwork violations of the employer sanctions provisions are exempted, as long as there has been a "good faith attempt" by an

Claims of Discrimination on the Basis of National Origin or Citizenship

In ensuring employment authorization, employers with more than three employees may not discriminate on the basis of national origin or citizenship status except against unauthorized aliens.[44] The antidiscrimination provisions seek to prevent overzealous employers from excluding lawful workers who appear foreign. Knowledge that an employee is unauthorized may not be inferred from an employee's foreign appearance or accent.[45] Discriminatory practices include copying identity documents for only certain employees, and scrutinizing documents more carefully for workers who look foreign. Screening out prospective employees through the I-9 process is also considered a discriminatory practice.

On September 30, 1996, the provisions making document abuse an unfair employment practice were amended to require the intent to discriminate.[46] Document abuse involves the refusal of documents or the request for more or different documents.[47] Employers also should avoid requests for specific documents, such as the applicant's Social Security card. Any requests for an applicant's Social Security card should be made apart from the I-9 process. If employers are found to have requested more or different documents than an employee chooses to present, they may be fined $110–$1,100 for each individual determined to have suffered such document abuse.[48] Prior to the 1996 amendment, document abuse was treated as a strict liability offense. Since the amendment, employers who have rejected documents due to their lack of awareness of the receipt rule were not found to have intentionally discriminated.[49] Lastly, the date of employment authorization expiration should not be considered in the hiring process, as that could be deemed to discriminate on the basis of immigration status.[50]

Because IRCA also prohibits discrimination in employment practices on the basis of citizenship or immigration status, employers must be aware of potential pitfalls in prehiring inquiries. OSC maintains that employers may inquire in an interview or employment application as to whether an applicant is legally authorized to work in

---

employer to comply with the verification requirement. The exemption will not apply if the employer fails to cure the violations within a 10-day window or if the employer has engaged in pattern and practice violations. This section applies to violations occurring on or after September 30, 1996." Illegal Immigration Reform and Immigrant Responsibility Act of 1996, §411, 110 Stat. 3009-546, 3009-666.

[44] INA §274B(a)(1); 8 USC 1324b(a)(1).

[45] 8 CFR §274a.1(*l*)(3).

[46] INA §274B(a)(6); 8 USC 1324b(a)(6).

[47] *Id.*

[48] 28 CFR §68.52(d)(1)(xii) (offenses occurring on or after March 15, 1999); INA 274B(g)(2)(B)(iv)(IV); 8 USC §1324b(g)(2)(B)(iv)(IV).

[49] *U.S. v. Diversified Tech.*, 9 OCAHO No. 1098, OCAHO Case No. 01B00059 (June 10, 2003).

[50] OSC guide to fair employment, at 9, *available at www.usdoj.gov/crt/osc/pdf/en_guide.pdf.*

the United States.[51] Depending on the response of the applicant, the employer may not inquire any further.[52] If the applicant responds affirmatively, the interviewer should not inquire further into the basis of the employment authorization. If the applicant responds in the negative, the employer can inquire into the current immigration status of that individual. Because unauthorized workers are not protected from discrimination under IRCA, such prehiring questions pose minimal risk. If the applicant lacks employment authorization, the employer is allowed to ask whether the applicant now or in the future requires sponsorship for employment visa status, such as H-1B.[53] Pre-employment questions should focus on employment authorization rather than specific status as a citizen or permanent resident, as those questions could be later interpreted to have been the basis for discriminating on the basis of citizenship.

Claims of unlawful discrimination are handled through OSC for employers with four to 14 workers or through the Equal Employment Opportunity Commission for employers with 15 or more workers.[54] Employers may be ordered to pay civil monetary penalties of $375–$3,200 per individual discriminated against for the first offense, $3,200–$6,500 per individual discriminated against for the second offense, and $4,300–$16,000 per individual for subsequent offenses.[55] The variation in the fine imposed will be partly based on whether economic damage was done to the employee. It also should be noted that fines are discretionary, not mandatory.[56]

If a claim of an employee or prospective employee has been discriminated against, charges must be filed with OSC within 180 days of the alleged discrimination. After receipt of the discrimination charge, the OSC will inform the employer of the charges within 10 days and begin an investigation. If OSC has not filed a complaint with an ALJ 120 days after receiving a charge of discrimination, the charging party (the employee) may file a complaint with an ALJ within 90 days.

OSC recently celebrated its 20th year of operations and issued an insightful report in November 2006.[57] From 1997 until 2005, OSC secured $1,374,664 in back pay for workers, as well as $1,578,865 in civil penalties from employers. While those numbers include the $200,000 that Swift & Company was forced to pay in 2001, it is a bit misleading to say that OSC has been aggressive in pursuing discrimination charges

---

[51] E. Scofield, *et al.*, "Employment Verification Systems—Where Are We and Where Are We Going?" *Immigration & Nationality Law Handbook* 518 (AILA 2006–07 Ed.); *see* OSC Memorandum, J. Trasviña, "Pre-Employment Inquiries Regarding Sponsorship for an Employment Visa" (Aug. 6, 1998).

[52] E. Scofield et al., *supra* note 51.

[53] *Id.*

[54] "Memorandum of Understanding Between the Equal Employment Opportunity Commission and the Office of Special Counsel for Immigration Related Unfair Employment Practices" (Dec. 18, 1997), *available at www.eeoc.gov/policy/docs/oscmou.html.*

[55] 28 CFR §§68.52(d)(1)(i)–(iii) (offenses occurring on or after March 27, 2008); INA §§274B(g)(2)(B)(iv)(I)–(III); 8 USC §§1324b(g)(2)(B)(iv)(I)–(III).

[56] Upon an ALJ's finding of a violation based on the preponderance of the evidence, he or she "*may* also require" a person or entity to pay a civil penalty. 28 CFR §68.52(d)(1) (emphasis added).

[57] *OSC Update* (Nov. 2006), available at *www.usdoj.gov/crt/osc/pdf/oscupdate_nov_06.pdf.*

against employers.[58] In the three years preceding the report, out of 1,038 investigations of employer discrimination, not a single case resulted in an ALJ order or fines.[59] This is in large part due to a shift in attitude from heavy-handed penalties to educating employers through the OSC hotline and encouraging settlements.

The Extent of Personal Liability

IRCA imposes liability on a "person or other entity" who knowingly hires undocumented workers. The U.S. Court of Appeals for the Eighth Circuit held that the "person or other entity" language of IRCA can impose joint liability on both the employer and the agent.[60] An agent of a company will not escape personal liability for hiring undocumented workers simply because he or she is acting on behalf of the company and not in an individual capacity. In larger companies, executives who have control over hiring policies may arguably be held individually liable should the company hire unauthorized aliens.

Recent Developments in IRCA

Changes to the I-9 Form

For years, the I-9 form changed relatively little. Then on June 21, 2005, DHS rebranded the I-9 and eliminated outdated references to legacy INS.

In an effort to comply with the Illegal Immigration Reform and Immigrant Responsibility Act of 1996 (IIRAIRA),[61] legacy INS issued an interim rule, effective September 30, 1997, that has yet to be superseded by a final rule. The interim rule removed the following documents from the list of acceptable identity and work authorization documents: Certificate of U.S. Citizenship (list A #2), Certificate of Naturalization (list A #3), the Form I-151 Alien Registration Receipt Card (list A), Unexpired Re-entry Permit (list A #8), and the Unexpired Refugee Travel Document (list A #9).[62] The number of documents that employers could review was reduced to lessen employer confusion. On November 7, 2007, DHS released a new I-9 that reflects the decade-long change, instructing that after December 26, 2007, prior versions of the I-9 should not be used.[63] After that date, employers who fail to use the revised Form I-9 may be subject to all

---

[58] *Id.*

[59] *Id.*

[60] *Steiben v. INS*, 932 F.2d 1225, 1228 (8th Cir. 1991).

[61] Pub. L. No. 104-208, div. C, 110 Stat. 3009, 3009-546 to 3009-724.

[62] 62 Fed. Reg. 51001 (Sept. 30, 1997). Under section §412 of IIRAIRA, the certificate of naturalization, the certificate of citizenship, and foreign passports were eliminated from list A. However, legacy INS used its discretion to continue the use of foreign passports for nonimmigrants and birth certificates in list C.

[63] 72 Fed. Reg. 65974 (Nov. 26, 2007).

applicable penalties under INA §274A [8 USC §1324a], as enforced by ICE.[64] The new I-9 also adds the I-766, a new employment authorization document, to list A.

The EAD I-688B (list A #10) is no longer being issued as of October 1, 2006, although it remains acceptable as an I-9 document.[65] The EAD I-688B was issued by local USCIS field offices and contained outdated security features, and it has been phased out by the Employment Authorization Card (EAC) I-766. Legacy INS began issuing the EAC in 1997, and it contains more advanced security features, such as a fingerprint and a bar code containing biometric data.

On February 2, 1998, legacy INS issued proposed regulations that significantly reduced the number of acceptable documents and required that all documents be unexpired.[66] The proposed regulations also introduced a reverification I-9A form. Immigration officials have yet to issue a final rule either adopting or rejecting the proposed changes; therefore, the interim rule that eliminated four documents remains in force.

Shift from Civil Fines to Criminal Prosecution

Since 1986, employer compliance with IRCA has focused primarily on civil fines and a possible maximum penalty of six months and a $3,000 fine for a pattern and practice of unlawful hiring.[67] Penalties for violations of the I-9 paperwork requirements can result in a civil fine ranging from $110 to $1,100 per employee involved.[68] The fines for knowingly hiring undocumented workers can reach $16,000 for each worker.[69] In setting the proposed fine, the government must weigh five factors: (1) the size of the employer; (2) the good faith of the employer; (3) the seriousness of the violation; (4) any history of previous violations; and (5) any actual involvement of unauthorized aliens.[70] The severity of the violation takes into account whether the forms simply contained errors, if important sections or attestations were incomplete, or if the requisite form and documents were retained at all.[71]

---

[64] 72 Fed. Reg. 65975 (Nov. 26, 2007).
[65] USCIS Interoffice Memorandum, M. Aytes, "Elimination of Form I-688B, Employment Authorization Card" (Aug. 18, 2006), *published on* AILA InfoNet at Doc. No. 06090560 (*posted* Sept. 5, 2006).
[66] 63 Fed. Reg. 5287 (Feb. 2, 1998).
[67] INA §274A(f)(1); 8 USC §1324a(f)(1), 8 CFR 274a.10(a).
[68] 8 CFR §274a.10(b)(2) (offenses occurring on or after September 29, 1999).
[69] 8 CFR §274a.10(b)(1)(ii)(C); 28 CFR §68.52(c)(1)(iii).
[70] 8 CFR §§274a.10(b)(2)(i)–(v).
[71] *U.S. v. Hudson Delivery Serv., Inc.*, 7 OCAHO 945, OCAHO Case No. 97A00003 (June 6, 1997).

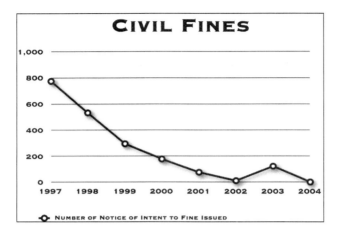

In the late 1990s, legacy INS was having significant difficulties in pursuing civil fines against companies. Often, the fine amounts were so low that employers considered them a cost of doing business, and corporate entities would simply fold, making it impossible to collect the fine. For instance, nationwide, legacy INS only collected $72,585 in 2002 using the administrative fine process.[72]

Recently, the federal government has shifted its focus from imposing civil penalties to criminal prosecution in order to punish employers who knowingly employ workers without work authorization.[73] In April 2006, ICE announced a new interior enforcement strategy as part of the Secure Border Initiative.[74] Under this strategy, ICE planned to target employers who knowingly employ unauthorized workers by bringing criminal charges against them.[75] Through a combination of criminal fines, restitutions, and civil judgments, ICE claims to have collected more than $29 million from employers in just the first half of 2007.[76]

ICE investigators have focused particularly on employers who are involved in human trafficking, smuggling, and harboring. It is a felony to knowingly: (1) bring an illegal alien into the United States; (2) transport an illegal alien in order to further his

---

[72] J. Myers, "No More Slaps on Wrist for Work-Site Violations," (June 26, 2007), *available at* www.ice.gov/doclib/pi/news/testimonies/070626KCStarOpEd.pdf.

[73] *See* Op-Ed, J. Myers, "Expect More Arrests," *USA Today* (Apr. 25, 2006), *available at* www.usatoday.com/news/opinion/editorials/2006-04-25-oppose-immigration_x.htm. Julie Myers, Assistant Secretary of DHS for ICE, stated: "The most effective way [to enforce worksite regulations] is to bolster our criminal investigations against employers hiring illegal immigrants. For many employers, fines had become just another 'cost of doing business.' More robust criminal cases against unprincipled employers are a much more effective deterrent than fines." *Id.*

[74] Government Accountability Office (GAO) "Immigration Enforcement, Weaknesses Hinder Employment Verification and Worksite Enforcement Efforts," (June 19, 2006), at 4 (GAO-06-895T, testimony of Richard M. Stana, Director Homeland Security and Justice, before the Subcommittee on Immigration, Border Security, and Citizenship, Committee on the Judiciary, U.S. Senate), *available at* www.gao.gov/new.items/d06895t.pdf.

[75] *Id.*

[76] J. Myers, *supra* note 72.

or her unlawful presence; (3) conceal, harbor, or shield an illegal alien from detection; or (4) encourage or induce an alien to illegally enter the country.[77] Congress expressly amended the statute to eliminate prior express exclusion of employers in the harboring statute. While several courts have found that unauthorized employment alone is insufficient for a harboring conviction, additional acts, such as facilitating a change in identity, willfully misrepresenting facts on the I-9,[78] assisting with the procurement of false documents, providing housing, and warning aliens about impending inspections, will constitute harboring.[79] If the harboring was "done for the purpose of commercial advantage or private financial gain," the maximum prison term increases from five to 10 years.[80] Employers who pay aliens low wages and fail to withhold taxes have been subject to the higher prison term.[81]

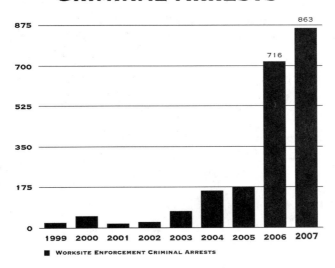

If an employer is not convicted of harboring, another provision specifically addresses employers. Any person who during any 12-month period knowingly hires for employment at least 10 individuals, with actual knowledge that the individuals are unauthorized aliens, will be fined under Title 18 or imprisoned for not more than five years, or both.[82]

Emerging Issues with Electronic Storage

On October 30, 2004, Congress passed legislation giving employers the option of completing the I-9 form electronically.[83] On June 15, 2006, DHS issued regulations

---

[77] INA §274(a); 8 USC §1324(a).

[78] *U.S. v. Kim*, 193 F.3d 567 (2d Cir. 1999).

[79] *Id.*

[80] INA §274(a)(1)(B)(i); 8 USC §1324(a)(1)(B)(i).

[81] *U.S. v. Zheng*, 306 F.3d 1080 (11th Cir. 2002).

[82] INA §274(a)(3)(A); 8 USC §1324(a)(3)(A).

[83] Pub. L. No. 108-390, 118 Stat. 2242 (2004).

giving employers guidance on how I-9s may be written and stored electronically.[84] The standards for electronic retention are fairly flexible and technology-neutral.[85] Any system employed must include an audit trail—a timestamp whenever any I-9 is accessed or altered.[86] Other requirements include backup and recovery of records to protect against information loss and a retrieval system that allows searching based on fields.

The program must be able to attach an electronic signature to the completed I-9 at the time of the creation of the records, create and preserve a record certifying the identity of the person producing the signature, and provide a printed confirmation of the I-9 to the employer.[87] If the electronic signature does not meet the requirements stated, the I-9 will be considered improperly completed in violation of INA §274a(a)(1)(B).[88] While electronic storage creates the opportunity for a streamlined I-9 process and increased accuracy when fields are skipped or improperly entered, employers must take care in adhering to the regulatory standards when implementing the electronic storage.

Verifying Employment Authorization

With widespread document fraud and the requirement that employers accept documents that reasonably appear genuine, employers are faced with difficult choices in challenging a worker's employment authorization. Despite an employer's best attempts at verifying documents, only the issuing agency will know for certain whether documents are genuine and match the individual. Due to these enormous challenges, Congress authorized a pilot verification system that would allow employers to ensure employment authorization.

The E-Verify Program

IIRAIRA authorized DHS to create an online verification system that allows registered employers to quickly verify employment eligibility. While E-Verify (formerly known as Basic Pilot) initially was available in only five states, since December 1, 2004, the program has been an option for employers nationwide.[89] In just over a year spanning most of 2007, the number of employers participating soared from 14,000 to 52,000.[90] President George W. Bush requested $100 million for fiscal year (FY) 2009 to expand and improve E-Verify.[91] Because E-Verify is a voluntary program, participa-

---

[84] 71 Fed. Reg. 34510 (June 15, 2006).

[85] *Id.*

[86] 8 CFR §274a.2(e)(8).

[87] 8 CFR §§274a.2(e), (g).

[88] 8 CFR §274a.2(h)(2).

[89] The passage of the E-Verify Program Extension and Expansion Act of 2003, Pub. L. No. 108-156, 117 Stat. 1943, expanded the program from the initial five states to all 50 states and required implementation no later than December 1, 2004.

[90] USCIS Fact Sheet, "E-Verify" (Feb. 12, 2008), *available at www.uscis.gov/files/pressrelease/ factsheeteverify12022008.pdf.*

[91] *Id.*

tion is further evidence of good-faith compliance with IRCA.[92] DHS Secretary Michael Chertoff has stated that good-faith participation in E-Verify will protect employers from civil and criminal penalties regarding the hiring of undocumented workers.[93]

Using E-Verify

In order to participate in E-Verify, an employer must sign a memorandum of understanding (MOU) with DHS and SSA.[94] Under the MOU terms, the employer must verify all new hires within the enrolled hiring site.[95] E-Verify cannot be used on prospective employees, employees who need to be reverified, or existing employees.[96] Therefore, E-Verify will not help an employer verify work authorization of existing employees. Employers who participate in E-Verify must still complete the I-9 and must only accept list B documents that contain a photograph.[97] Employers must submit the employee's information to E-Verify within three days of the employee's hire date.[98] The submission of information may only be done online, as there are no phone– or faxed-based alternatives. An employer also may choose to authorize a third party to process its employees through E-Verify.

Once the new hire's basic information has been submitted, most employers receive verification within 24 hours. While USCIS administers E-Verify, both SSA and DHS provide their databases to process the queries. If the new hire is a citizen, the name and SSN will be submitted to SSA and checked against more than 425 million SSA records. If the new hire is a noncitizen, then the name, SSN, and "A" number will be submitted to DHS and checked against 60 million DHS records. If neither

---

[92] *See* model E-Verify Memorandum of Understanding, art. II.C.6, *available at www.uscis.gov/files/nativedocuments/MOU.pdf*. "[A] rebuttable presumption is established that the Employer has not violated section 274A(a)(1)(A) of the Immigration and Nationality Act (INA) with respect to the hiring of any individual if it obtains confirmation of the identity and employment eligibility of the individual in compliance with the terms and conditions of E-Verify."

[93] DHS Press Release, Remarks by Secretary of Homeland Security Michael Chertoff, Immigration and Customs Enforcement Assistant Secretary Julie Myers, and Federal Trade Commission Chairman Deborah Platt Majoras at a Press Conference on Operation Wagon Train (Dec. 13, 2006), *available at www.dhs.gov/xnews/releases/pr_1166047951514.shtm* ("[A]s a consequence of participating in E-Verify, if you participate in that in good faith, then you are not going to be charged criminally or be held civilly liable.").

[94] Since February 2006, only electronic registration of E-Verify is available.

[95] Remarks of Gerri Ratliff, Chief of the USCIS Verification Division, during ILW I-9 telephonic seminar, February 22, 2006. Limiting the registration of E-Verify to hiring sites will prevent multinational employers from having to use E-Verify on all new hires worldwide. Hiring sites are defined as locations at which the company processes new hires.

[96] E-Verify MOU, *supra* note 92, art. II.C.8 ("Employer agrees not to use the E-Verify procedures for re-verification, or for employees hired before the date this MOU is in effect."). The limitation of E-Verify to new hires is a reflection of IRCA's requirements to verify employment authorization of new hires. Certainly, the scope of E-Verify in the future could extend to existing employees, as proposed in H.R. 4437, 109th Cong. (2005).

[97] E-Verify MOU, *supra* note 92, art. II.C.5.

[98] 8 CFR §274a.2(b)(1)(iv).

SSA nor DHS can confirm work authorization within 24 hours, the employer receives a tentative nonconfirmation response.

During this tentative nonconfirmation period, an employer may not terminate employment[99] and should check the accuracy of the information for misspellings. If an employee does not contest or resolve the nonconfirmation finding within eight days, E-Verify issues a final nonconfirmation notice, and employers are required to either immediately terminate the employee or notify DHS that they continue to employ the worker.[100] If the employee does contest the tentative nonconfirmation, the employer will refer the employee to either the local SSA or DHS office.[101] At that point, the employee has 10 days to resolve the issue with the local agency; otherwise, a final nonconfirmation will be issued.[102] If the employer continues to employ the worker after a final nonconfirmation notice, a rebuttable presumption is created that the employer has knowingly employed an unauthorized alien.[103] If the employer fails to notify DHS through E-Verify of the continued employment, the employer will face fines ranging from $550 to $1,100 for each individual with respect to whom such violation occurred.[104] The E-Verify program raises concerns as to what constitutes constructive notice of an unauthorized worker, and whether a nonconfirmed worker can continue to work if he or she provides additional non–SSN-related EADs.

Timeliness and Accuracy of E-Verify

Of the queries submitted to E-Verify in FY 2004, 92 percent were handled by SSA and only 8 percent were passed along to DHS, which is responsible for verification for noncitizens.[105] Of the 92 percent of queries handled by SSA, 13 percent required a second verification, and employers were issued a tentative or final nonconfirmation.[106]

Of the 8 percent of inquiries submitted to E-Verify and routed to DHS, 7 percent were confirmed by the DHS automated verification check. In 1 percent of DHS queries, a tentative nonconfirmation was issued and a secondary verification was required.[107] Secondary verifications were performed by 38 USCIS immigration status verifiers, who manually verified the employment authorization.[108] The majority of

---

[99] IIRAIRA Title IV, Subtitle A §403 (1996).

[100] GAO Worksite Report, *supra* note 98.

[101] E-Verify MOU, *supra* note 92, at 4.

[102] *Id.*

[103] IIRAIRA §403(a)(4)(C)(iii), 110 Stat. at 3009-662.

[104] 28 CFR §68.52(c)(6). For violations occurring before March 27, 2008, the penalty range is $500–$1,000. *Id.*

[105] GAO, *supra* note 74, at 11.

[106] *See* SSA Office of the Inspector General, "Congressional Response Report: Employer Feedback on the Social Security Administration's Verification Programs," appx. C-2 (Dec. 2006), *available at* www.ssa.gov/oig/ADOBEPDF/A-03-06-26106.pdf (hereinafter SSA E-Verify Report).

[107] GAO, *supra* note 74, at 11.

[108] *Id.* at 13.

secondary verifications by USCIS are typically resolved within 24 hours, but some queries may take up to two weeks.[109] E-Verify may have growing pains as more and more employers register, particularly in the secondary verification process. In the 2008 White House fiscal budget, an additional $30 million was set aside to support and expand the E-Verify program.[110]

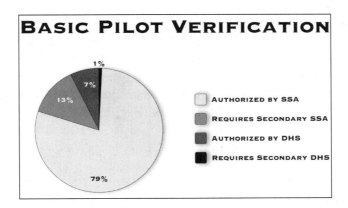

DHS has made efforts to shorten the time required to update the system data on changes in immigration status.[111] Previously, data on new immigrants was often unavailable for six to nine months.[112] Now that information is typically available for verification within 10 to 12 days of a person's arrival in the United States.[113]

In a December 2006 report by the Office of Inspector General for SSA, 49 of 50 employers using E-Verify rated their experience as good or better.[114] Ten percent of employers surveyed experienced minor problems, including: (1) periodic lack of access to E-Verify; (2) password problems; and (3) lack of a timely system response from DHS.[115] For example, a user in the food processing industry stated that DHS had taken more than 14 days to confirm the work authorization of an employee. The user notified DHS about the delay and the issue was timely resolved.[116]

---

[109] *Id.*

[110] 2008 Budget Fact Sheets (Feb. 2007), *available at* www.whitehouse.gov/infocus/budget/BudgetFY2008.pdf.

[111] Westat, *Findings of the Web Basic Pilot Evaluation* (Sept. 2007), *available at* www.uscis.gov/files/article/WebBasicPilotRprtSept2007.pdf.

[112] USCIS, Report to Congress on the E-Verify Program (June 2004), *published on* AILA InfoNet at Doc. No. 04081940 (*posted* Aug. 19, 2004).

[113] *Id.*

[114] SSA E-Verify Report, *supra* note 106.

[115] *Id.*

[116] *Id.*

Weaknesses in E-Verify

As USCIS Director Emilio Gonzalez concedes, "[T]he E-Verify system is not fraud-proof and was not designed to detect identity fraud."[117] E-Verify cannot detect when workers are using another person's name and SSN.[118] As long as an unauthorized worker presents documents containing valid information, E-Verify will report the employee as work authorized.[119] On September 25, 2007, USCIS launched photo capabilities that display the identity photo of 15 million EAD and green-card holders to assist employers in detecting fraud.[120] Despite the additional effort required for E-Verify, participation will not immunize the employer from I-9 compliance audits, nor will it preclude the possibility of a raid. Swift & Company had tried unsuccessfully to head off the raids after company records were subpoenaed by ICE in the spring of 2006.[121] In December 2006, company lawyers were denied a court injunction against the raids.

Employers who are concerned about verification data being used as a means of targeting employers for I-9 audits may have reason to worry. In 2005, employers made over 900,000 queries into E-Verify, and the Government Accountability Office (GAO) has recognized that this data potentially could be used for worksite enforcement.[122] While ICE has no direct role in monitoring the use of E-Verify,[123] it has requested and received program data from USCIS on specific employers who participate in the program and are under investigation.[124]

ICE officials also have stated that the program data could help target employers who do not follow program requirements. For instance, if the same SSN is submitted repeatedly through E-Verify, concerns may be raised about whether employees at that site are fraudulently using SSNs and whether unscrupulous employers are blindly accepting them. This usage by ICE may be considered unlawful because the information is being used not to determine whether an individual is an unauthorized alien, but to target other employees who may be associated with the same employer.[125]

---

[117] USCIS News Release, "USCIS Launches Photo Screening Tool for E-Verify Program" (Sept. 25, 2007), *available at www.uscis.gov/files/pressrelease/EVerifyRelease25Sep07.pdf*.

[118] GAO, *supra* note 74, at 11.

[119] *Id.*

[120] USCIS News Release, *supra* note 117.

[121] M. Cooper, "Lockdown in Greeley," *The Nation* (Feb. 26, 2007), *available at www.thenation.com/doc/20070226/cooper*.

[122] GAO, "Immigration Enforcement: Benefits and Limitations of Using Earnings Data to Identify Unauthorized Work," at 10 (July 11, 2006), *published on* AILA InfoNet at Doc. No. 06071362 (*posted* July 13, 2006).

[123] USCIS maintains the E-Verify Program.

[124] GAO Worksite Report, *supra* note 98, at 10.

[125] INA §274A(d)(2)(C); 8 USC §1324a(d)(2)(C). "Any personal information utilized by the system may not be made available to government agencies, employers, and other persons except to the extent necessary to verify that an individual is not an unauthorized alien."

The Future of E-Verify

Employers should take note that both comprehensive immigration bills passed in the House[126] and the Senate[127] included passages that would have made the E-Verify program mandatory for employers. States frustrated with the federal government's inability to stop undocumented hiring have taken matters into their own hands. In 2006, Colorado enacted two laws that will affect employers who do business with the state and all employers in the state.

The first law authorizes the Colorado Department of Labor and Employment (CDLE) to conduct audits of all employers in Colorado. As of January 1, 2007, all employers in Colorado are required to retain the I-9 form and copies of the identity and employment authorization documents.[128] Unlike IRCA, the state law has no good-faith defense, and requires employers to "verify" the information and documents of the employee. CDLE has interpreted "verify" to reach beyond visual inspection of I-9 documentation, to require "examining the legal work status of each newly-hired employee."[129] CDLE states that employers may "verify" by using E-Verify or the Social Security Number Verification Service (SSNVS).[130] The Colorado law also differs from IRCA by penalizing employers who have either failed to submit or submitted fraudulent documents in reckless disregard.[131]

In addition to the I-9, a one-page "Affirmation of Legal Work Status"[132] must be completed by the employer for each employee within 20 days of hire, and must be retained with the I-9.[133] Employers who fail to comply with this law face fines of $5,000 for the first offense, and $25,000 for the second or any subsequent offense.[134] This first law may be challenged on the basis that Congress has specifically preempted states from taking action in imposing civil and criminal sanctions against employers.[135]

---

[126] Border Protection, Antiterrorism, and Illegal Immigration Control Act of 2005, H.R. 4437, 109th Cong. (2005) ("Sensenbrenner Bill," unenacted).

[127] S. 2611, 109th Cong. (2006).

[128] Colo. Rev. Stat. §8-2-122(2).

[129] CDLE FAQs, at 3, *published on* AILA InfoNet at Doc. No. 07011073 (*posted* Jan. 10, 2007).

[130] The CDLE interpretation of verification may be incorrect, because under IRCA verification system has essentially referred to the I-9 and not E-Verify or SSNVS. Also, SSA has explicitly stated that SSNVS should not be used for employment authorization verification but solely to ensure correct wage reporting.

[131] Colo. Rev. Stat. §8-2-122(4).

[132] *Available at www.coworkforce.com/lab/AffirmationForm.pdf.*

[133] *See* CDLE FAQs, *supra* note 129.

[134] Colo. Rev. Stat. §8-2-122(4).

[135] INA §274A(h)(2); 8 USC §1324a(h)(2). The provisions of this section preempt any state or local law imposing civil or criminal sanctions (other than through licensing and similar laws) on those who employ, or recruit or refer for a fee for employment, unauthorized aliens. *See also* Congressional Research Service Memorandum, "Legal Analysis of Proposed City of Hazleton Illegal Immigration Relief Act Ordinance" (June 29, 2006), *available at* www.prldef.org/Civil/Hazelton/hazleton%20legal%20documents/Hazleton%20Memo.pdf.

The second Colorado law, which went into effect August 7, 2006, requires employers who have public contracts for services[136] with the state, city, or county to participate in E-Verify.[137] Because state regulations have not been issued concerning the law, it is unclear whether the law includes employees working on a state contract regardless of whether they work in Colorado.[138] Employers who have public contracts must verify that subcontractors also comply with E-Verify. When a publicly contracted employer has actual knowledge that a subcontractor has hired an undocumented worker, the employer has a duty to inform the contracting state agency within three days.[139] While there are no civil or criminal penalties for noncompliance, an employer found to be in breach will be held liable for actual and consequential damages for breach of contract.[140] A public list of noncomplying employers will be maintained by the Colorado secretary of state for two years.

Beginning July 1, 2007,[141] Georgia requires employers who have public contracts to use E-Verify.[142] It is likely that more states will take action, as nine states have introduced similar legislation. Many of these proposals contain employer verification requirements and additional penalties for employers who hire unauthorized workers.

IMAGE Program

The ICE Mutual Agreement Between Government and Employers (IMAGE) program was introduced in July 2006 as a cooperative best-practices program for employers.[143] Under the program, ICE reviews an employer's hiring practices and policies and recommends ways to correct compliance issues. The program requires nine best practices, including participation in E-Verify, as well as a mandatory ICE audit of the employer's current I-9 forms.[144] Other best practices include: (1) semiannual external audits; (2) establishing internal training on I-9s and fraudulent use of documents; (3) creating a "no-match" letter protocol; (4) establishing a self-reporting procedure for any violation; (5) assessing compliance of contractors; (6) creating a tip line; and (7) ensuring practices are not discriminatory.[145]

---

[136] ILW I-9 telephonic seminar (Nov. 22, 2006). The Colorado Dep't of Labor has interpreted "services" to include capital construction, installation of equipment, ongoing software, and computer maintenance. Services would not include pure purchases, hotel or building lease services, or catering.

[137] Colo. Rev. Stat. §8-17.5-101.

[138] CDLE FAQs, *supra* note 129. CDLE has interpreted the law to apply to out-of-state employers and employees, so long as they are performing a service under a public contract.

[139] Colo. Rev. Stat. §8-17.5-102(2)(b)(III).

[140] Colo. Rev. Stat. §8-17.5-102(3).

[141] Effective July 1, 2007, for employers with 500+ employees, effective July 1, 2008, for employers with 100+ employees, and July 1, 2009, for employers with fewer than 100 employees.

[142] Ga. Code Ann. §13-10-91.

[143] DHS Press Release, "DHS Highlights Best Practices for Maintaining Legal Workforces" (July 26, 2006), *available at www.dhs.gov/xnews/releases/press_release_0966.shtm.*

[144] *www.ice.gov/partners/opaimage/.*

[145] T. Weigel, "Thinking Twice About Partnering with ICE—An Analysis of ICE's 'Best Hiring Practices' and IMAGE," *Immigration Law Weekly, available at www.ilw.com/articles/2007,0130-weigel.shtm.*

Once an employer has registered and implemented ICE's best hiring practices, it will be deemed "IMAGE-certified." As of the writing of this article, according to ICE, there were "dozens" of companies that have taken steps toward enrollment.[146] No regulations or statutes have been issued on IMAGE, but ICE intends to release regulations on IMAGE. ICE states on its website that "participation may be considered a mitigating factor in the determination of civil fine amounts should they be levied."[147] Informally, ICE has stated that companies who undergo a civil audit as part of IMAGE will be given a two-year waiver of any additional audits.

Perhaps one of the largest benefits gained by participating in IMAGE is decreased risk of raids. If undocumented workers are found through ICE audits, a participating employer may be given more time to dismiss and transition to new workers. ICE has stated that it "will attempt to minimize disruption of business operations resulting from a company's self-disclosure of possible violations."[148] The Swift & Company raids demonstrated that civil and criminal fines may not be the most critical liability that an employer may face. Simply a day of lost production costs Swift & Company an estimated $20 million and another $10 million to quickly find replacement workers. Ultimately, this may drive Swift & Company, the world's third-largest processor of fresh beef and pork products and a company that has been in existence for 150 years, out of business.[149] However, many wonder if ICE would actually allow an employer to continue to employ unauthorized workers once they are identified as lacking valid work authorization. The current ICE practice is to identify and immediately arrest such workers.

Social Security Number Verification Service

SSA provides an online and phone-based[150] SSN verification program.[151] The online SSNVS began in December 2004 and allows registered employers to verify 10 names and SSNs online and receive results immediately.[152] The online SSNVS system also

---

[146] D. Fears & K. Williams, "In Exchange for Records, Fewer Immigration Raids," *Wash. Post,* A03 (Jan. 29, 2007), *available at www.washingtonpost.com/wp-dyn/content/article/2007/01/28/AR2007012 801172.html.*

[147] *See www.ice.gov/partners/opaimage/.*

[148] *Id.*

[149] K. Arellano & J. Dunn, "Swift & Co. Weighs a Sale," *The Denver Post* (Jan. 22, 2007), *available at www.denverpost.com/search/ci_5064270.* On July 12, 2007, Swift announced that JBS S.A., Latin America's largest beef processor, completed the acquisition of Swift from its previous owner. Swift & Company Press Release, "JBS S.A. Completes Acquisition of Swift & Company" (July 12, 2007), *available at www.jbsswift.com/media/releases/2007_07_12_JBS_Swift_closing_FINAL.pdf.*

[150] Phone-based verification can be accessed at (800) 772-6270.

[151] Social Security Act §232 [42 USC §432] authorizes SSA to collect wage and tax information and to supply it to IRS. The Privacy Act, 5 USC §552a(b)(3), provides the authority to disclose personal information without consent in certain "routine" use situations. SSA's disclosure regulations mirror the Privacy Act criteria. *See* 20 CFR §§401.25, 401.110. Finally, the SSA "Blue Book" explains the routine uses SSA will make of information under the Privacy Act authority. *See www.socialsecurity.gov/foia/bluebook/bluebook.htm.*

[152] 69 Fed. Reg. 71865 (Dec. 10, 2004).

allows employers to upload batch files of up to 250,000 names and SSNs and receive results usually the next government business day. The primary purpose of SSNVS is to ensure accurate wage reporting on W-2 wage and tax statements. The W-2 provided by the employer must match SSA's records in order for the employee's wage and tax data to be properly posted to his or her earnings record.[153]

Unlike the E-Verify program, SSNVS can be used on current employees as well as new hires. SSNVS is not intended to determine employment authorization, and employers should not take punitive action against employees on the basis of a "no-match." If an employer elects to use the system, arguably it must comply with the "no-match" regulations issued by DHS, requiring an employer to attempt to reconcile the records within 30 days, and then refile an I-9 within 93 days after notice.[154] An employer may not use the system as a new-hire screening tool for job applicants, and is subject to Privacy Act[155] sanctions for the misuse of the system.

Employee Issues

REAL ID Act and Driving Privilege Cards

The REAL ID Act of 2005,[156] which passed the House and Senate without hearings or testimony, will have a significant impact on the ability of many lawful immigrants to obtain proper employment authorization. REAL ID requires that after May 11, 2008, all states must require driver's license applicants to provide: (1) proof of an SSN or verification that the person is ineligible for one; and (2) proof that the applicant is legally present in the United States.[157] The state must then verify each of the documents with the issuing agency.[158] If a state fails to require these documents, then the state-issued identification card would not be accepted as valid identification by the federal government. The secretary of homeland security is authorized to grant extensions of the May 11, 2008, compliance date to those states that provide adequate justification for their inability to comply by the statutory deadline,[159] and has issued a final rule providing a process for states to seek an additional extension of the compliance deadline to May 11, 2011, by demonstrating material compliance with the core requirements of the REAL ID Act and the rule.[160]

---

[153] *Id.*

[154] 8 CFR §274a.1(*l*)(1)(iii)(B). Employers must respond if they receive "written notice from the Social Security Administration" that the records submitted do not match SSA records.

[155] 5 USC §552a.

[156] Pub. L. No. 109-13, div. B, 119 Stat. 231, 302–23.

[157] *Id.* §202, 119 Stat. at 312–15.

[158] *Id.*

[159] *Id.* §205(b), 119 Stat. at 315.

[160] 73 Fed. Reg. 5271 (Jan. 29, 2008). The rule also extends the enrollment time period to allow states determined by DHS to be in compliance with the REAL ID Act to replace all licenses intended for offi-

Many states are passing joint resolutions opposing REAL ID.[161] Other states have made it increasingly difficult for immigrants to obtain driver's licenses. On March 8, 2005, Utah enacted a law to limit the ability of immigrants to obtain driver's licenses.[162] Because driver's licenses are the most popular form of identification for I-9 purposes, the new law will significantly impact the ability of lawful immigrants to demonstrate employment eligibility. Prior to the passage of the Utah law, applicants were required to show only documentation of identity and residence in the state that did not include immigration status. The Utah law now requires an applicant to show U.S. citizenship, permanent residency, refugee, asylee, or parolee status in order to obtain a driver's license that may serve as identification. Other lawful temporary residents and unlawful aliens will receive a "driving privilege card."[163] Driving privilege cards for permanent residents are valid for five years, and one year for those unable to prove legal presence but able to meet the identification standards set in the statute. More importantly, the temporary license is not valid for federal identification or official purposes such as I-9 verification.[164]

Coupled with the law discussed above, Utah also enacted H.B. 223, effective July 1, 2005. H.B. 223 allows individuals with an SSN, individual taxpayer identification number (ITIN), or proof of ineligibility for an SSN, to receive a driver's license if they can show lawful status consistent with Title II §202(c)(2)(B) of the REAL ID Act.[165] Therefore, temporary lawful residents may technically receive a driver's license, but they must go through the process of obtaining an ITIN or receiving a letter from SSA showing ineligibility for a Social Security card. Applicants who have an ITIN instead of an SSN must present documents from the IRS or SSA, or a letter from the IRS to verify their ITIN.

Utah's approach[166] in determining driver's license eligibility based on an SSN is incongruent with the REAL ID Act, which requires temporary driver's licenses for aliens with nonimmigrant visa status. H.B. 223 allows an F-1 nonimmigrant student to obtain a driver's license if he or she is able to demonstrate that he or she does not qualify for an SSN, contrary to the REAL ID Act,[167] which declares that states may only issue a temporary identification card to a valid unexpired nonimmigrant visa holder, such as international students. Ultimately, both the REAL ID Act and the Utah's new driving privilege cards will create significant hurdles for lawful immigrants attempting to prove work authorization.

---

cial purposes with REAL ID-compliant cards by December 1, 2014, for people born after December 1, 1964, and by December 1, 2017, for those born on or before December 1, 1964.

[161] On Jan. 25, 2007, Maine passed a joint resolution. Georgia, Massachusetts, Montana, and Washington state may soon follow. 84 *Interpreter Releases* 352 (2007).

[162] Utah Code Ann. §53-3-207.

[163] Utah Code Ann. §53-3-207(6)(a).

[164] *Id.*

[165] *See* Utah Code. Ann. §53-3-205(9).

[166] *Id.*

[167] REAL ID Act of 2005, Pub. L. No. 109-13, div. B, §202(c)(2)(C), 119 Stat. 231, 313–14.

Misrepresentations of Citizenship Status on the I-9

There are two primary concerns when a noncitizen completes section 1 of the I-9 form. An individual must attest under the penalty of perjury that the individual is a citizen or national, permanent resident, or alien authorized to be employed.[168] If the noncitizen marks citizen/national in section 1, (1) he or she may have made a claim to U.S. citizenship for a benefit under the INA and is therefore inadmissible;[169] or (2) he or she may have made a false statement as to a material fact on a document required under the INA, or knowingly presented an application or document that "fails to contain any reasonable basis in law or fact."[170]

Claim to U.S. Citizenship

It is unclear whether checking the citizenship/national box qualifies as a false statement of U.S. citizenship to obtain "a benefit" under the INA. In an unpublished decision, the Board of Immigration Appeals (BIA) found that merely checking the "citizen or national" box on I-9 form is insufficient, without more, to support a false claim to citizenship charge.[171] Due to the ambiguity of the I-9 form, the BIA found no clear and convincing evidence demonstrating that the worker intended to represent himself as a U.S. citizen rather than a national of the United States, and decided that removal under INA §212(a)(6)(C)(ii) was not justified.[172]

All U.S. citizens are also nationals of the United States,[173] but instances of national status without U.S. citizenship are limited. U.S. nationality, but not citizenship, is bestowed on persons born in or having ties with "an outlying possession of the United States."[174] Those outlying possessions include American Samoa and Swains Island.[175] The number of applicants for noncitizen national certificates has been so low that the Department of State never created such a certificate. Instead, proof of national status would be indicated on a passport.[176]

False Statement

Prior to the passage of IIRAIRA, incorrectly marking U.S. citizen/national in section 1 of the I-9 was not regarded as a violation of INA §274C.[177] IIRAIRA made it a crime to knowingly make a false statement as to a material fact in any application or

---

[168] INA §274A(b)(2); 8 USC §1324a(b)(2).

[169] INA §212(a)(6)(C)(ii); 8 USC §1182(a)(6)(C)(ii).

[170] 18 USC §1546.

[171] *Matter of Oduor*, A75 904 456 (BIA Mar. 15, 2005), *available at* www.lexisnexis.com/practiceareas/immigration/pdfs/web887.pdf.

[172] *Id.*

[173] INA §101(a)(22); 8 USC §1101(a)(22).

[174] INA §308; 8 USC §1408.

[175] INA §101(a)(29); 8 USC §1101(a)(29).

[176] *See* INA §341(b)(1); 8 USC §1452(b)(1).

[177] *U.S. v. Remileh*, 5 OCAHO 724, OCAHO Case No. 94C00139 (Dec. 5, 1995); *reported in* 72 *Interpreter Releases* 319 (Mar. 6, 1995).

document required under the INA, or to knowingly present any such application or document that contains a false statement or that "fails to contain any reasonable basis in law or fact."[178] The Eighth Circuit has found an alien was ineligible for adjustment because when the box was marked, there was no reasonable basis in fact or law for a claim to either national or citizenship status.[179]

Adjustment of Status

Another consequence of having been employed while in unauthorized status is found in the statute governing adjustment of status. An alien, other than an immediate relative or certain special immigrants, who accepts or continues unauthorized employment is disqualified from adjustment of status,[180] as is any alien who was employed while the alien was an "unauthorized alien."[181]

Criticisms of ICE Raids

After the wave of raids, which often involved a patchwork of state and federal agencies, ICE faced considerable criticism. From nonexistent access to lawyers to seemingly unsympathetic policies toward primary child caretakers, it seemed as though the typical ICE method of dealing with fugitive immigrants was ill-suited to the humanitarian challenge of worksite raids.

Members of Congress demanded an investigation after certain raids, and the GAO released a critical report of the out-of-date process.[182] The GAO reports that the field operational manuals lack any guidance on how to deal with mass humanitarian issues. "Most Office of Investigations officers had not participated in major worksite enforcement operations since 1998 and many of the officers who participate are temporarily assigned to the operation from other duties or locations."[183] From 2003 to 2007, there was a six-fold increase in the number of new officers participating in worksite enforcement operations.[184]

ICE has been reluctant to publicize what happens to the individual immigrant workers after the raids. At one IFCO Systems pallet plant in Florida, more than a year after a raid, only three out of 38 arrested workers were actually deported.[185] An immigration judge dismissed the cases of 18 workers, suggesting that they were lawfully in the United States.[186]

---

[178] 18 USC §1546.

[179] *Ateka v. Ashcroft,* 384 F.3d 954 (8th Cir. 2004).

[180] INA §245(c)(2); 8 USC §1255(c)(2). If an immediate relative, see INA §201(b); 8 USC §1151(b).

[181] INA §245(c)(8); 8 USC §1255(c)(8). For the definition of "unauthorized alien," see INA §274A(h)(3); 8 USC §1324a(h)(3).

[182] GAO, "Immigration Enforcement: ICE Could Improve Controls to Help Guide Alien Removal Decision Making" (GAO-08-67, Oct. 15, 2007), *available at www.gao.gov/new.items/d0867.pdf.*

[183] *Id.*

[184] *Id.*

[185] E. Pera, "Polk IFCO Plant, 3 of 38 Workers Deported After Raid," *The Ledger* (Oct. 14, 2007).

[186] *Id.*

Conclusion

As a result of the congressional debates on immigration reform, worksite enforcement has continued to intensify. President George W. Bush requested in the FY 2007 budget $41.7 million in new funds and 171 additional agents to increase worksite enforcement and prosecutions.[187] As with IRCA, which legalized millions of workers while imposing new obligations on employers, any new immigration reform bill will likely impose a higher standard of due diligence required of employers.[188] With the government's renewed enforcement efforts, simple precautionary measures—such as internal audits and strict compliance with I-9-related regulations—are now more important than ever.

Frequently Asked Questions from Employers

Should an Employer Accept Documents That Have Names Swapped (John Doe and Doe John)?

Within the I-9 process, the employer must ensure that identity and employment authorization documents relate to the individual and are reasonably genuine.[189] In deciding whether the documents relate to the individual, the employer may choose to exercise reasonable business judgment in rejecting the document. Reasonable business judgment would include rejecting documents when the name on the identity document does not match the employment authorization document.

If the employer chooses not to accept the documents, the new hire may: (1) select a different document to establish identity or employment authorization; or (2) choose to obtain a new document with a name that does match. If the employee applies for a new document (*i.e.*, driver's license) within three business days of hire, he or she should present the receipt of the application for the document to the employer. The employer should record the receipt document in lieu of the actual document. The employee must present the actual document to the employer for inspection within 90 days of hire.[190]

In exercising reasonable business judgment, the employer should uniformly apply the same standard. OSC will not find this to be the basis of discrimination on the basis of ethnicity or nationality if the policy not to accept swapped documents is applied consistently. If the employer chooses not to accept two documents, one with the name John Smith, and the other document with Smith John, then it should reject all documents when the last name and first name are reversed.

---

[187] White House Press Release, "Just the Facts: President Bush's Strong Worksite Enforcement Efforts" (June 19, 2006), *available at www.whitehouse.gov/news/releases/2006/06/20060619-13.html*.

[188] New legislation may include increased civil and criminal penalties, as well as mandatory participation in E-Verify, as proposed in the Senate and House immigration bills in the 109th Congress.

[189] 8 CFR §274a.2(b)(1)(v).

[190] 8 CFR §274a.2(b)(1)(vi).

Should Employers Make Copies of the Employment Authorization and Identity Documents?

IRCA does not require employers to make copies of the supporting documentation.[191] However, if employers choose to make copies, they must do so for all new hires regardless of citizenship or national origin. If copies are made, they should be retained with the I-9.[192] Employers should be mindful that copies of supporting documentation could reveal errors in recording the document information in section 2 of the I-9. On the other hand, employers would have greater ease in conducting internal audits to ensure that documents were recorded properly and indicating when re-verification is necessary. If an employer chooses to stop copying I-9 supporting documentation, then a company-wide memo should be sent out to mark the end of the copying and ensure uniform compliance.

When Can the Verification Systems Be Used?

The E-Verify system may be used only on current hires within three days of hire. Workers who were hired before the employer entered into the memorandum of understanding with SSA and DHS may not be verified against the system, nor may prospective employees be screened through the system.

SSNVS may be used on current employees as well as new hires. Registered employees also enter into an agreement with SSA as to the proper use and disclosure of the information.

How Do the Two Verification Systems Differ?

E-Verify is administered by USCIS, and it is intended to verify employment authorization. SSNVS is only intended to verify Social Security information to provide accurate W-2 statements. A "no-match" through SSNVS alone should not prompt an employer to take punitive action against an employee. Both E-Verify and SSNVS use data provided by SSA, but E-Verify goes a step further by checking the immigration status of noncitizens.

May an Employer Continue to Employ a Worker Who Has Notified It That His or Her Past I-9 Documentation Was Invalid and That He or She Now Has Valid Documents?

It depends on whether the employer has a policy to terminate employees who have lied or committed fraud in the hiring process. If the employer has such a policy in place, it may choose to terminate the employee, but must do so consistently in similar situations.[193] The employer also may elect to continue to employ the worker once

---

[191] 8 CFR §274a.2(b)(3).

[192] *Id.*

[193] *Garcia-Contreras v. Cascade Fruit Co.*, 9 OCAHO 1090, OCAHO Case No. 02B00008 (Feb. 4, 2003). OCAHO did not find discrimination where the employee had given Cascade falsified documentation in 1994, attained legally documented status in 2000, but was fired for violating the dishonesty policy.

new I-9 documents are recorded, as the employer did not knowingly employ an unauthorized alien.

Can a Worker Without a Social Security Number Be Hired?

The new I-9 specifically notes that the employee is not required to provide a Social Security number[194] unless the employer is participating in E-Verify.[195]

Employers often raise the issue of how to pay workers who do not have a Social Security card. Neither the Internal Revenue Code nor IRCA requires that an employee possess an SSN to begin work. They simply require that an application for an SSN (Form SS-5) be made within seven days of commencing employment for taxable wages.[196] An employer may request to see a Social Security card on the first day of work.[197] However, this request should be made separately from the I-9 process, because a request to see a specific document may constitute document abuse.[198]

In lieu of a Social Security card, the employee may provide a receipt acknowledging that an application for an account number has been received[199] or a signed statement from the employee stating the employee's full name, present address, date and place of birth, father's full name, mother's full name before marriage, the employee's gender, and the date and place the employee filed the SS-5 form application.[200]

If the employee has applied for a card but has not received the card, then 000-00-000 may be entered into the payroll software to generate a paycheck. When the employee receives his or her Social Security card, he or she must present the document.[201] A Form W-2c (Corrected Wage and Tax Statement) may be filed to show the employee's correct SSN.[202]

Typically, SSA takes about a week or two to process an SS-5 application, although sometimes there may be delays lasting several months.

Should an Employer Conduct an I-9 Internal Audit?

Conducting annual internal audits is advisable for employers for several reasons. Often I-9s have been administered by a variety of managers and employees who may have limited training on how to complete them. Most importantly, an audit will provide an indication of good-faith compliance with IRCA, which will be the primary

---

[194] Privacy Act §7, 5 USC 552a note.

[195] IIRAIRA §403(a)(1), 110 Stat. 3009-661, 3009-659.

[196] 26 CFR §31.6011(b)(2).

[197] 26 CFR §31.6011(c).

[198] INA §274B(a)(6); 8 USC §1324b(a)(6).

[199] 26 CFR §31.6011(b)(2)(B)(iii).

[200] 26 CFR §31.6011(b)(2)(B)(iv).

[201] 26 CFR §31.6011(b)–.6012(b)(2).

[202] Social Security W-2 Reporting Instructions and Information, Answer ID 377, available on the SSA website (*http://employer-ssa.custhelp.com/*; search category Employer Wage Reporting; link for question "Do legal aliens need a Social Security number to work?").

defense in case of a civil fine or criminal prosecution case. Other indications of good-faith compliance would include annual training for the employer agents who consistently handle I-9s, as well as standard policies for reverification and I-9 processes. Internal audits allow employers the opportunity to review the I-9 forms at their own pace, as opposed to the 10-day notice that is provided before an ICE audit.

During the I-9 audit, at no point should employers discard or "white out" mistakes on previous I-9 forms. Any corrections or additions made should be initialed and dated. The primary focus of any internal audit should be on ensuring that all current and recent employees have a completed I-9. This can be done easily by comparing payroll records against I-9 records. Copies of identity documents that have been retained should match the recorded information. If an employee has indicated temporary work authorization in section 1, the employer should reverify when appropriate.

Must an Employer Verify the Employment Authorization of Independent Contractors or Laborers Provided by an Independent Contractor?

No. Independent contractors are one of the three categories of workers exempt from I-9 verification. Others are grandfathered employees hired before November 7, 1986, and casual domestic workers who perform sporadic, irregular, or intermittent service in private homes. While employers are not required to complete I-9 forms for independent contractors or laborers provided by contractors, employers may not use independent contractors in order to circumvent immigration laws.[203] Employers still may be held liable if they have constructive knowledge of such unauthorized employment. Constructive knowledge includes knowledge that a reasonable and prudent employer should have. For example, an employer may have a duty to investigate further if laborers provided by independent contractors are subjected to substandard working conditions or wages, as the employer may be using unlawful workers to gain a competitive advantage in contract bidding.

An argument has been made that if a company requires a contractor to complete I-9s and has the ability to inspect I-9s, then the company may have established sufficient controls over the contractor that would create direct liability for any undocumented workers hired by the contractor.[204]

What Should an Employer Do if: (1) a Worker Provides the List A Permanent Resident Card or Another Non–SSN List A Document; (2) Receives a Social Security "No-Match" Letter; and (3) the Worker Continues to Assert That the SSN Provided Is Valid?

In the context of DHS final regulations on "no-match" letters,[205] employers are placed in a difficult position, as any new I-9 filled out in compliance with the Social Security "no-match" safe-harbor provision might simply contain essentially the same

---

[203] INA §274A(a)(1); 8 USC §1324a(a)(1).

[204] J. Pearce, "The Dangerous Intersection of Independent Contractor Law and the Immigration Reform and Control Act: The Impact of the Wal-Mart Settlement," 12 *Bender's Immigr. Bull.* 9 (Jan. 1, 2007).

[205] 72 Fed. Reg. 45611 (Aug. 15, 2007).

data as the previous year's form. This remains a gray area that has not been resolved by DHS. Because the Social Security "no-match" letter is issued sometimes years after the W-2 is submitted, an employer may feel that it is on a merry-go-round when it receives annual "no-match" letters asking only that the employee reconfirm and recomplete an I-9 with no changes, provided that the SSN is not recorded as the work authorization document. Despite the conflict, employers should continue to document their efforts to follow up with the employee after a "no-match letter" is received, and reverify the I-9 form within a reasonable period of time.

What Liabilities Might a Successor Corporation Inherit?

Generally, in cases involving a corporate reorganization, merger, or sale of stock or assets, no new I-9 is necessary so long as the employer obtains and maintains the previous employer's I-9s.[206] A successor employer is exempt by regulation from completing I-9s if the predecessor employer has fulfilled that obligation.[207] An employer that has acquired a business and retains the predecessor's employees is neither expected to dispose of I-9s previously executed by its predecessor-in-interest nor required to execute all new I-9s. However, if the succeeding company chooses to retain the old I-9s rather than complete new ones, the succeeding company will be liable for any omissions and defects in the original I-9s.[208] Ultimately, the successor employer may choose to complete new I-9s for all employees to ensure proper completion.

Must a Recruiter Complete an I-9?

The recruiter must ensure that an I-9 is completed within three days of hire, not three days of referral, but a recruiter may designate the employer as an agent responsible for completing the I-9.[209] If an agent is designated, the recruiter only needs to keep a copy of the I-9 form. A temporary agency that directly pays the worker would fall under the category of an employer, as opposed to a recruiter, and would be required to complete an I-9.

Numbers for I-9 Help

E-Verify Program Help
(888) 464-4218

---

[206] 8 CFR §274a.2(b)(1)(viii)(A)(7): "An individual continues his or her employment with a related, successor, or reorganized employer, provided that the employer obtains and maintains from the previous employer records and Forms I-9 where applicable . . . ."
[207] *Id.*
[208] *U.S. v. Nevada Lifestyles Inc.*, 3 OCAHO 518, OCAHO Case No. 92A00131 (May 10, 1993).
[209] 8 CFR §274a.2(b)(1)(iv).

SSA

Tim Beard, Attorney
Northwest Oregon, Washington, Idaho, and Alaska.
Tim.beard@ssa.gov; (206) 615-2125

DOJ–Office of Special Counsel for Immigration-Related Unfair Employment Practices

Sebastian Aloot, Attorney
sebastian.aloot@usdoj.gov; (202) 616-5594
950 Pennsylvania Avenue, N.W.,
Washington, DC 20530

Electronic I-9 Storage

Dan Siciliano, Professor
Stanford Law School
siciliano@law.stanford.edu; (650) 725-9045

ICE–IMAGE

John Shofi, National Program Director; *john.shofi@dhs.gov*; (202) 353-3611

EMPLOYER SANCTIONS FOR IMMIGRATION-RELATED HIRING VIOLATIONS

Testimony of

Stephen Yale-Loehr
Adjunct Professor
Cornell University Law School

Hearing on
Problems in the Current Employment Verification and Worksite Enforcement System

Before the
Subcommittee on Immigration, Citizenship, Refugees, Border Security, and International Law

Committee on the Judiciary
U.S. House of Representatives
Washington, D.C.

April 24, 2007[*]

---

[*] **Editor's note**: Footnotes appearing in the original written testimony have been modified for style only.

Madam Chairwoman and Distinguished Members of the Subcommittee:

My name is Stephen Yale-Loehr. I teach immigration law at Cornell University Law School. I am also co-author of Immigration Law and Procedure, a 20-volume immigration law treatise. It is considered the standard reference work for U.S. immigration law. It has been cited by courts more than 400 times, including several times by the U.S. Supreme Court. I also chair the business immigration committee of the American Immigration Lawyers Association. I am testifying in my personal capacity.

Thank you for inviting me to testify about the current employer sanctions program and recommendations to improve it through an electronic employment verification system (EEVS). I have been following and writing about this issue since 1986, when Congress first enacted employer sanctions.

My testimony first provides a history of employer sanctions. I then discuss the Basic Pilot Program, which is the administration's current effort to improve employer sanctions. Next, I discuss some systemic problems in the current employer sanctions program. I conclude with some recommendations.

1. History of Employer Sanctions

A. Pre-1986: The Texas Proviso

Until 1986 no law made it illegal for an employer to hire an undocumented worker. In fact, in 1952, in passing legislation making it illegal for any American to "harbor" an undocumented individual, Congress stated that it was specifically *not* illegal to hire such an individual.[1] This came to be known as the "Texas Proviso." It meant that employers were free to hire whomever they chose, without having to verify an individual's eligibility to work. If an unauthorized worker was among the ranks of their employees, nobody questioned it and the employer was free to go on with business as usual without worry; it was simply up to the undocumented worker to avoid being caught by immigration authorities and deported.[2]

B. 1986: IRCA Enacts Employer Sanctions

As Congress considered immigration reform in the early 1980s, debate over whether to enact employer sanctions was long and intense. The theory behind employer sanctions is twofold: (1) imposing penalties on employers of undocumented workers will deter the hiring of such noncitizens; and (2) because securing employment is the primary reason for illegal entry and residence, this will reduce incentives for illegal entry.

Some members of Congress argued that an employer sanctions program might place an undue burden on employers. Not only would all employers be subject to new paperwork obligations; employer sanctions also raised the specter that employers would

---

[1] Immigration and Nationality Act of 1952, Pub. L. No. 82-414, 66 Stat. 163.

[2] *See generally* C. Gordon, S. Mailman & S. Yale-Loehr, *Immigration Law and Procedure* §7.01 (rev. ed. 2006).

have to become experts in immigration law to identify which categories of noncitizens were authorized to work.[3]

Another area of concern was what kind of documentation would suffice to establish eligibility for employment. Congress was aware of the huge market that exists in fraudulent documents. Some proponents argued that a form of counterfeit-proof documentation ought to be devised to ensure the effectiveness of any employer sanctions program. The risk that this might lead to a "national identity card," however, caused many members of Congress to shy away from such a requirement. Those opposed to an identity card won.

A third major concern was that employer sanctions would lead to discrimination against those who looked foreign or sounded foreign, and that existing fair employment laws would not provide a remedy. For example, Title VII of the Civil Rights Act of 1964[4] applied only to employers with fifteen or more full-time employees. Moreover, it barred national origin discrimination but not discrimination based solely on alienage.[5]

Congress addressed these competing concerns in the Immigration Reform and Control Act of 1986 (IRCA).[6] IRCA employed a three-pronged approach regarding the hiring of undocumented workers. First, it did away with the Texas Proviso and specifically prohibited employees from knowingly hiring undocumented workers.[7] Second, it required employers for the first time to verify, by use of the paper I-9 form still in use today, the identity and authorization to work of all their employees, including U.S. citizens.[8] For those individuals who failed to comply with or meet the new verification requirements, employers were required to refuse employment. Third, Congress included antidiscrimination provisions to prohibit employers from discriminating on the basis of national origin or citizenship status in hiring and firing employees.[9] Failure to comply with any of these provisions resulted in penalties being imposed, ranging from small monetary fines for first time, minor paperwork violations to criminal sanctions for repeat offenders, including jail time of up to six months.

To monitor whether employer sanctions would contribute to discriminatory practices, Congress asked the General Accounting Office (GAO) to prepare three annual reports on the employer sanction program's implementation. Under the statute, the employer sanctions program would terminate if: (1) the final GAO report found that a "widespread pattern of discrimination" resulted from employer sanctions; and (2) Congress enacted a joint resolution stating that it approved the GAO findings.[10]

---

[3] *See generally* M. Roberts & S Yale-Loehr, "Employers as Junior Immigration Inspectors," 21 *Int'l Law.* 1013 (1987).

[4] 42 USC §2000e-2.

[5] *See Espinoza v. Farah Manufacturing Co.*, 414 U.S. 86 (1973).

[6] Immigration Reform and Control Act of 1986 (IRCA), Pub. L. No. 99–603, 100 Stat. 3359.

[7] INA §274A(a); 8 USC §1324a(a).

[8] INA §274A(b), 8 USC §1324a(b).

[9] INA §274B, 8 USC §1324b.

[10] IRCA §101 (enacting INA §274A(j)–(n) [8 USC §1324a(j)–(n)]).

C. 1990: GAO Finds Employer Sanctions Causes Discrimination

The GAO issued its final report in March 1990.[11] It was based on a survey of over 9,400 employers, which statistically projected to a universe of about 4.6 million employers. The GAO report found that the enactment of employer sanctions had created "a serious pattern of discrimination." Overall, the GAO estimated that 19 percent of all employers began one or more discriminatory practices as a result of IRCA's enactment.[12] The GAO report concluded that IRCA's employer sanctions provisions failed to deter undocumented workers and increased discrimination against foreign-looking and -sounding workers because of: "1. lack of understanding of the law's requirements, 2. confusion and uncertainty on the part of employers about how to determine employment eligibility, and 3. the prevalence of counterfeit and fraudulent documents that contributed to employer uncertainty over how to verify eligibility."[13]

Despite the GAO report, Congress did not terminate employer sanctions. Over time, it became clear that employer sanctions was not working effectively. This was due in part to the conflicting interests that the sanctions try to satisfy and the lack of a mechanism to verify a worker's actual identity and employment eligibility. Most importantly, the government never fully committed to seeing this new employee verification program through to fruition. The appropriate and necessary resources required to run the program were never devoted to it. As a direct result of this, and as the 1990 GAO report underscored, employers were simply unequipped to properly handle the large volume of fraudulent documents. At the time of IRCA's implementation, 29 different types of documents were acceptable to verify work authorization and identity. With so many different documents allowed, this provided ample opportunity for fraud to take place. Employers, often having had little or no training in detecting fraudulent documents, were faced with the dilemma of either blindly accepting these documents or acting on a hunch and rejecting the documents but then facing penalties or lawsuits as a result of IRCA's antidiscrimination provisions. In the end, fraud and discrimination took over the system.

D. 1994: The Jordan Commission Proposes Government Verification

Employer sanctions created a paradox: a fairly high degree of supposed compliance but a relatively low degree of deterrence. Add the cost to businesses of paperwork and the documented increase in discrimination, and many people questioned the wisdom of continuing employer sanctions. One possible solution is to switch the burden of employment verification from employers to the government. The theory is that a government verification program could defeat the impact of fraudulent documents and also decrease discrimination by providing assurances to employers that the person they have hired is in fact authorized to work in the United States. The Commis-

---

[11] General Accounting Office, *Immigration Reform: Employer Sanctions and the Question of Discrimination* (1990) (testimony of Charles A. Bowsher, Comptroller General of the United States, before the Committee on the Judiciary, U.S. Sentate) [hereinafter GAO Report].

[12] *Id.*

[13] *Id.*

sion on Immigration Reform, also known as the Jordan Commission after its chair, Rep. Barbara Jordan, was a leading proponent of testing such an approach.

The Jordan Commission proposed having the government verify employment information by reviewing data from the Social Security Administration (SSA) and the immigration agency (at that time the Immigration and Naturalization Service (INS)).[14] Employers would submit employees' social security numbers to a computerized registry system. The government would then verify that the number belonged to someone authorized to work.[15]

E. 1996: IIRAIRA Changes

Congress tried to address problems in the employer sanctions regime as part of the Illegal Immigration Reform and Immigrant Responsibility Act of 1996 (IIRAIRA).[16] The 1996 law, however, did not appropriate significant and necessary resources to improve workplace enforcement. Nor did it do much to improve the existing employer sanctions provisions. And even regarding document fraud, virtually the only measure taken by Congress in IIRAIRA was to slightly reduce the number of documents allowed for the purpose of verifying work authorization and identity, from 29 to 27. However, IIRAIRA did enact three pilot projects to strengthen and improve the employee verification process. Of these three projects, only one remains: the Basic Pilot Program.[17] The Basic Pilot Program is similar in concept to the Jordan Commission's recommendation for a computerized registry system.

2. The Basic Pilot Program: Not Ready for Prime Time

The Basic Pilot Program, or the Employment Verification Pilot Program as U.S. Citizenship and Immigration Services (USCIS) now calls it, is a voluntary program whereby employers enter Form I-9 data (name; date of birth; Social Security number) into a computer within three days of an employee's hire date.[18] This information is then compared with centralized databases at the SSA and the immigration agency (originally at the INS; now in the USCIS of the Department of Homeland Security (DHS)) to verify identity and citizenship. The data is then checked against a DHS database to verify employment eligibility.[19] If eligibility cannot be confirmed immediately, employers must notify their employees of the finding. The employees have the right to contest tentative nonconfirmation findings by contacting SSA or USCIS, as appropriate, to resolve any inaccuracies in their records. This contesting process is normally limited to 10 federal workdays. During this time, employers are not permit-

---

[14] U.S. Commission on Immigration Reform, *U.S. Immigration Policy: Restoring Credibility* (1994).

[15] *Id.* at xi–xvii.

[16] Illegal Immigration Reform and Immigrant Responsibility Act of 1996, Pub. L. No. 104-208, div. C, 110 Stat. 3009, 3009-546 to 3009-724.

[17] *Id.* §403.

[18] *See generally* https://www.vis-dhs.com/EmployerRegistration/StartPage.aspx?JS=YES. [Editor's note: This URL is an update of the one appearing in the original written testimony. Basic Pilot and the Employment Verification Pilot Program are now known as E-Verify.]

[19] *See generally* USCIS, Report to Congress on the Basic Pilot Program (2004).

ted to take any adverse actions against employees based on the tentative nonconfirmation finding. When employees contest their tentative nonconfirmation findings, USCIS informs their employers of the employees' work-authorization status. When employees do not contest their findings within the allotted time, they receive final nonconfirmation findings. Employers are supposed to terminate employees in three circumstances: when employees indicate that they do not wish to contest the finding, when employees are found not to be work-authorized, or when employees receive final nonconfirmation findings.[20]

The Basic Pilot Program is not a perfect solution to the employer sanctions problem. The most fundamental problem remains the fact that for the system to work, DHS must run the identity information it receives against the SSA database, a database that is otherwise outside the Basic Pilot Program system and that is not intended to be used for immigration purposes. While the verification process now runs relatively quickly for citizens, processing times will certainly increase if all employers are required to use the system.[21] The processing times will be even longer for noncitizens. Because the DHS and SSA databases are not fully integrated and often have difficulty communicating with each other in an efficient manner, the process can take two weeks or longer for noncitizens. This is simply too long for many employers to wait.

Furthermore, a high number of errors continue to be reported, slowing the process even more. It has been estimated that about 20 percent of all initial Basic Pilot Program entries are false-negatives, meaning that the applicant is originally thought to be not work eligible, but that a later review determines him or her to be work authorized.[22] Many of these initial errors occur for simple reasons, such as the transposition of a first and last name, or a name change because the worker recently married.

With the Basic Pilot program running inefficiently and ineffectively on a voluntary basis, and with only 15,000 participants, expanding Basic Pilot in its current state and requiring participation by all 8.4 million employers would be a bureaucratic nightmare. Full scale implementation would also cost at least $11.7 billion per year, according to a 2002 study.[23]

3. Systemic Problems with the Current Employer Sanctions Regime

Several reasons exist for the failure of the current employer sanctions regime:

---

[20] *Id.* at 2–3.

[21] PowerPoint presentation by Gerri Ratliff, Chief of the U.S. Citizenship and Immigration Services (USCIS) Verification Division (June 26, 2006), *at http://myrick.house.gov/Verification%20presentation%20June%2026.ppt.*

[22] Immigrant Employment Verification and Small Business: Hearing Before the Subcomm. on Workforce, Empowerment, and Government Programs of the H. Comm. on Small Business (2006) (statement of Angelo Amador, Director of Immigration Policy, U.S. Chamber of Commerce) [hereinafter Amador testimony], *at www.uschamber.com/NR/rdonlyres/epssu7le6fzvb7aju33ys5p2fmyzvap74pqz544pn6ldmwmd4trff2nidhyfx5eyv7llftk6chqiueb7hs5d6wilxxd/060627_amador_employment_verification.pdf.*

[23] Institute for Survey Research & Westat, INS Basic Pilot Evaluation Summary Report 49 (Jan. 29, 2002), *at www.uscis.gov/files/nativedocuments/INSBASICpilot_summ_jan292002.pdf.*

- First, the political compromise that formed the basis of employer sanctions in 1986 foundered on the economic reality of the continuing need for workers and the inability of our immigration system to provide them legally. That reality continues today.

- Second, as stated above, employer sanctions has created a paradox: a fairly high degree of compliance but a relatively low degree of deterrence. Employers are checking workers' papers, as they are supposed to. But many of the verification documents may be fraudulent, or belong to a different person than the one who is presenting them. Until we solve the problem of fraudulent documents, employer sanctions will not work.

- Third, employer sanctions enforcement has not been consistent.

These themes are fleshed out below.

As recently as 2005, a Government Accountability Office study said that correcting the many problems out of the employee verification system remains the single biggest step in curtailing illegal migration and unauthorized employment.[24] But part of the problem is that we lack enough legal channels for foreign workers to come to the United States legally. Any comprehensive immigration reform bill must include temporary worker provisions if employer sanctions is to work.

Another part of the problem is inconsistent enforcement of employer sanctions. As early as 1991, for example, Doris Meissner, former INS Commissioner, and Robert Bach, former head of INS policy and planning, warned that "evidence is building that the early effort among employers to comply in response to publicity about the new law and wide-ranging INS contacts is dissolving into complacency as employers experience the low probability of an actual INS visit."[25] Their concerns proved valid. Government audits of employers to measure compliance with employer sanctions peaked at almost 10,000 in 1990, and then fell 77 percent to less than 2,200 in fiscal year (FY) 2003.[26] Notices of intent to fine companies for employer sanctions violations also dropped precipitously. From FY 1992 to FY 2004, notices of intent to fine fell 98 percent, from 1461 notices in 1992 down to just three in 2004.[27] Reflecting these trends, in 1999 the INS placed employer sanctions enforcement last in a list of five interior enforcement priorities.[28]

Employer sanctions enforcement has increased over the last two years. U.S. Immigration and Customs Enforcement (ICE) has begun what DHS Secretary Michael Cher-

---

[24] Government Accountability Office, Immigration Enforcement: Weaknesses Hinder Employer Verification and Worksite Enforcement Efforts 2 (GAO-05-813, Aug. 2005) [hereinafter GAO Report], *at* www.gao.gov/new.items/d05813.pdf.

[25] D. Meissner & R. Bach, in *The Paper Curtain: Employer Sanctions' Implementation, Impact and Reform* (M. Fix, ed., 1991).

[26] P. Brownell, "The Declining Enforcement of Employer Sanctions," *Migration Information Source*, (Sept. 2005), *available at* www.migrationinformation.org/Feature/display.cfm?id=332.

[27] GAO Report, *supra* note 11, at 35 (figure 4).

[28] Brownell, *supra* note 26.

toff calls a "strategic shift" in enforcement by focusing on employers that knowingly or recklessly hire illegal immigrants. Those employers often face criminal charges — including money-laundering charges — and seizure of assets rather than administrative fines.

"We found that [administrative] fines were not an effective deterrent," Julie L. Myers, assistant secretary for ICE, told the New York Times. "Employers treated them as part of the cost of doing business."[29] While the former INS brought 25 criminal charges against employers in 2002, ICE arrested 716 employers in 2006.[30]

"Companies that utilize cheap, illegal alien labor as a business model should be on notice. ICE is dramatically enhancing its enforcement efforts against employers that knowingly employ illegal aliens," said Ms. Myers in mid-2006. "Criminal indictments . . . are the future of worksite enforcement."[31]

That trend is continuing with some well-publicized raids. For example, just a few days before Labor Day last year, federal immigration agents descended on Stillmore, Georgia and surrounding areas just before midnight, entering homes and swarming the Crider chicken processing plant. Over three days, some 125 undocumented workers were rounded up and detained.[32]

This effort to increase worksite enforcement became even more evident on December 12, 2006, when ICE agents raided Swift & Company production facilities located in six states.[33] This was despite the fact that Swift participated in the Basic Pilot Program. While I am not here today to address the human costs of the shortcomings of our immigration system, I would like to note here that the stepped-up enforcement efforts of ICE come at the steep if not incalculable cost of the lives of hard working families being torn apart. More quantifiable is the economic price of our failed employment verification system. Swift has stated that the raids, which displaced over 1,300 of their workers, would cost the company $30 million. A third of that will go to expenses tied to hiring incentives and work-retention efforts; the rest is tied to lost operating efficiencies.[34]

Immigration raids nationwide have continued to increase this year, with recent raids in New Bedford, MA, Baltimore, MD and Santa Fe, NM, to name a few.[35] Enforce-

---

[29] J. Preston, "U.S. Puts Onus on Employers of Immigrants," *N.Y. Times*, July 31, 2006, at A6.

[30] M. Dolan, "Restaurant Owners Face Sentencing; Trio Seek to Avoid Prison in Immigration Case," *Baltimore Sun*, Mar. 28, 2007, at 1B. *See generally* S. Mailman & S. Yale-Loehr, "Criminalizing Employer Sanctions: Employers Walk a Tightrope," *N.Y. Law J.*, Aug. 25, 2006, at 3.

[31] P. Cuadros, "The New Tactics of Immigration Enforcement," *Time*, Aug. 7, *2006, available at www.time.com/time/nation/article/0,8599,1223600,00.html.*

[32] Associated Press, "Immigration Raid Cripples Georgia Town," Sept. 15, 2006.

[33] N. Gaouette, "Six Meat Plants are Raided in Massive I.D. Theft Case," *L.A. Times*, Dec. 13, 2006, at A18.

[34] R. Pore, "Swift's Beef Operation Still Feeling Effect of Immigration Raid," *Grand Island Independent*, Apr. 11, 2007, *available at www.theindependent.com/stories/041107/new_swift11.shtml.*

[35] *See generally www.ice.gov/pi/news/newsreleases/index.htm.*

ment of a broken system does not seem to be the just or economical approach that we, as a nation, should be taking. We are simply throwing good money after bad. Instead, we need to reform our employment verification system.

4. Recommendations for a Workable Electronic Employment Verification System

This much is clear: Some kind of workable, efficient, and accurate electronic employment verification system (EEVS) is necessary. The question remains, however: What steps need to be taken for this to be achieved?

- First and foremost, worksite enforcement must be part of a broader package of comprehensive immigration reform, which includes opening more—and more efficient—legal channels for foreign workers to enter the United States. Enforcement measures alone simply will not work. We must face economic reality and recognize that a labor shortage exists. For businesses to prosper and our country to remain competitive in the global economy, and to dissuade individuals from bypassing lengthy wait times and making unauthorized border crossings in search of jobs, employers need legal and efficient access to foreign workers.

- Second, the government must assist employers in making an employment verification system work, both through appropriate funding and by making all necessary resources, including money, technology, and additional training and manpower, available to them. The resources needed, while not fully identified at this point, assuredly will be great, and employers should bear some of the burden. But employers cannot be expected to comply with the law, verifying the identities and work authorization of tens of millions of potential employees fully on their own, without additional help from the government.

- Third, the government must make use of existing technology to create an efficient, workable EEVS. This includes continuing to implement and perfect biometric identification technology, possibly developing a biometric Social Security card, and simplifying the process for employers by allowing the use of a single swipe card containing information currently asked for on the I-9 form. The only documents that should be allowed to verify a noncitizen's identity, immigration status, and eligibility to work are biometric Social Security cards, legal permanent resident ("green") cards, and immigration work authorization cards.

- Fourth, once the problems with Basic Pilot or any other EEVS system are worked out--and they must be certified to have been worked out before full scale implementation—the system must require all employers to participate. Until that happens, however, the system must be phased in gradually, both to allow time for any necessary technological and/or efficiency fixes and to allow employers to acquire the tools necessary (biometric scanners, etc.) to implement and operate the system effectively. Given employers' urgent needs for foreign workers, premature full scale implementation will result in skepticism in the program and an unwillingness to participate on the part of employers, who will choose to risk penalties and operate outside of the system.

- Fifth, DHS must establish some kind of entity to monitor the progress of new measures and the efficiency and accuracy of the program in general, and to help encourage employer participation.

- Sixth, any new employment verification system must be designed to protect privacy and ensure that the discrimination caused after IRCA's enactment does not reoccur. To this end, the concerns of both employers and individual workers must be addressed. Any privacy violations or discrimination in the workplace must be quickly investigated and punished.

- Seventh, employer sanctions enforcement must be vigorous, consistent, and sustained. Employers initially complied with IRCA's employer sanctions regime, in part because of vigorous enforcement across all industries. As enforcement waned in the 1990s, however, businesses began to worry less about employer sanctions compliance. Congress must appropriate enough money every year to ensure that employers comply with the law, and that ICE actively enforces it.

It is relatively easy to state these goals. It is harder to know how to effectively implement them. For example, some people have advocated adding biometric information to Social Security cards so that they could be used as a reliable identity document for employment verification purposes.[36] The Social Security subcommittee of the House Ways and Means Committee held a hearing on this issue in March 2006.[37] That testimony deserves a careful reading. It is sobering. As Dr. Stephen T. Kent, chair of the National Research Council's Committee on Authentication Technologies and Their Privacy Implications, testified, developing identity systems is much more complex than it initially appears:[38]

> Success . . . depends not only on the card technology we use but on all of the ways the system components have to work together. The high cost of fixing or even abandoning a system makes it essential that potential ramifications are explored very thoroughly prior to making decisions about design details and deployment of a system. . . . No method of ensuring that the person presenting the card is the proper owner can be completely reliable. A key decision for any system of this sort would be determining an acceptable threshold of false rejection and false acceptances, none of which are going to be zero in any practical technology. . . . In conclusion, . . . none of the issues raised by development and deployment of large scale identity systems are simple. The questions posed . . .

---

[36] *See, e.g.*, D. Meissner & J. Ziglar, "The Winning Card," *N.Y. Times*, Apr. 16, 2007, at A19.

[37] Fourth in Series of Subcommittee Hearings on Social Security Number High-Risk Issues: Hearing Before the Subcomm. on Social Security of the H. Comm. on Ways and Means (2006) [hereinafter Social Security Hearing], at http://waysandmeans.house.gov/hearings.asp?formmode=printfriendly&id=4979.

[38] *Id.* (statement of Stephen T. Kent). *See also* Committee on Authentication Technologies and Their Privacy Implications, National Research Council, *IDs--Not That Easy: Questions About Nationwide Identity Systems* (S. Kent & L. Millett, eds., 2002), *available at* http://books.nap.edu/html/id_questions/.

should be carefully and thoroughly applied, not only from a privacy perspective but from a security, usability and effectiveness perspective as well.[39]

Frederick G. Streckewald from the Social Security Administration testified at the same hearing that it would cost over $25 per card to issue a Social Security card with enhanced security features, such as biometric identifiers.[40] The SSA estimated that the cost of replacing Social Security cards for all 240 million Social Security cardholders would be approximately $9.5 billion.[41] That would not include the startup costs to buy the equipment needed to produce and issue such a card.

Even assuming such the privacy, security, and cost issues could be worked out, other potential problems remain in using a biometric Social Security card or other national ID card. For example, such a card should not be issued to foreign nationals first. Otherwise, massive discrimination problems could result.

Similarly, it is hard to know at what point any EEVS system will be reliable enough to impose on all employers. As numerous commentators have noted, even an error rate of just 1 percent would still translate into over a million people a year being erroneously disqualified or terminated from work.[42] Most of these would be U.S. citizens.

We also need to have buy-in from employers and workers. Any system has to involve both groups to be effective. For that reason Congress should enact a provision to create an employer/worker advisory group to work with DHS in establishing an effective EEVS.[43]

Finally, Congress should carefully consider the privacy implications of any electronic system to verify work eligibility. Employers will be forced to demand the required cards so it will become impossible to work in this country without carrying an identification card. This would be a fundamental policy change, because it would mandate ID as the cost of living and working in the United States. It would represent a fundamental reorientation of the relationship between the individual and government. Instead of being free to work, with the burden on the government to intercede where illegality is suspected, it would create an America where employees must seek the affirmative permission of government to work through the construction of a complex of databases and identity papers. And once that national identity infrastructure is created, privacy advocates worry that it would inevitably be expanded to many other purposes beyond preventing undocumented labor, including the routine monitoring and control of other activities.[44] Any EEVS system must have robust procedures to allow people to quickly fix errors.

---

[39] Social Security Hearing, *supra* note 37 (statement of Stephen T. Kent).

[40] Social Security Hearing, *supra* note 37 (statement of Frederick G. Streckewald).

[41] *Id.*

[42] Amador testimony, *supra* note 22, at 7.

[43] *See* Independent Task Force on Immigration and America's Future, *Immigration and America's Future: A New Chapter* 50–52 (2006).

[44] *See* ACLU Memorandum, T. Sparapani, "Problems with Employment Eligibility Verification Legislative Proposals" (Dec. 7, 2005), *available at* www.aclu.org/privacy/workplace/22415leg200512

Many of these recommendations accord with provisions already in the Security Through Regularized Immigration and a Vibrant Economy Act of 2007 (STRIVE Act) (H.R. 1645). For example, the STRIVE Act would require ICE officials to spend at least 25 percent of their time on worksite enforcement.[45] That will help keep enforcement consistent and vigorous. Similarly, The STRIVE Act would expand existing antidiscrimination protections by applying them to the new EEVS set up under the bill.[46] The bill would make it an unfair immigration-related employment practice to terminate an individual based on a tentative nonconfirmation notice or to use the EEVS to screen an applicant before an offer of employment, among other things.[47] The STRIVE Act would also attempt to protect individuals' privacy rights by storing only limited information in the EEVSA computer system.[48] The bill would also require employers to make sure others did not have access to the system.[49]

Conclusion

Employer sanctions is a multifaceted problem. It requires a multifaceted solution. It is like a three-legged stool. I call these the three Es--Enforcement, Evaluation, and Entry:

- Enforcement: We must have consistent and vigorous enforcement of our employer sanctions laws.
- Evaluation: We must have a mechanism of properly evaluating a person's documents to know that they are not fraudulent and that they relate to the person presenting them. We must also continually evaluate any new employment verification system to make sure it is working properly and accurately, without creating adverse discrimination or privacy problems.
- Entry: We must create a temporary worker program large enough to allow most foreign workers to enter the United States legally. That will reduce the incentive to enter illegally.

The three parts must be equally strong for employer sanctions to work. Failure to adequately address any of the three legs of this stool will mean that we will back here 20 years from now, discussing the same problem.

Each of the three legs of the employer sanctions stool is a large problem itself. The overall problem cannot be corrected overnight. Congress and the American people need patience. Moreover, no one magic bullet exists for any of the legs. For example, the types of enforcement efforts may need to vary over time to keep up with new

---

07.html. See also Social Security Hearing, *supra* note 37 (statement of Marc Rotenberg); Electronic Privacy Information Center, Spotlight on Surveillance, "Expansion of Basic Pilot Would Steer Employment Verification Toward Disaster" (Apr. 2006), *at www.epic.org/privacy/surveillance/spotlight/0406/*.

[45] H.R. 1645 §305(b).

[46] *Id.* §303.

[47] *Id.* §303(c).

[48] *Id.* §301.

[49] *Id.*

trends. Congress may need to try various pilot EEVS programs and then evaluate them. And more than one temporary worker program may need to be implemented.

However, employer sanctions is a very important component of comprehensive immigration reform. It is perhaps the most important component, because it affects all Americans, not just immigrants. For that reason, it is imperative that we handle this issue carefully and thoughtfully. We may never be able to eliminate all undocumented workers, but we can work to make the problem manageable.

ETHICAL ISSUES IN REPRESENTING EMPLOYERS IN ICE WORKSITE INVESTIGATIONS
by Josie Gonzalez[*]

Some careers are known to be risky, but the practice of law typically is not one of them. Yet lawyers are exposed daily to the scary risk of criminal consequences for the practice of law. This is so because under current law, the line between laudable, ethically mandated, zealous advocacy and criminal obstruction of justice is not always clearly demarcated.[1]

This article will highlight some of the ethical concerns that can arise in U.S. Immigration and Customs Enforcement (ICE) worksite investigations. Many of these concerns are unique and have not been addressed previously in any article on immigration-related ethical concerns. However, one can apply knowledge of the basic rules of ethics and professional conduct to the challenging scenarios that one faces in representing the employer or the alien when ICE knocks on the door.

The attorney's dilemma is eloquently described by one ethics author: "Rapid-fire statutory and regulatory changes, including broadly stated federal crimes newly applied in recent years, and public perception of lawyers generally in a post 9/11 world as facilitators of fraud and illegality, have heightened concern for those seeking ethical certainty and bullet-proof defenses to civil charges, penalties, damage claims and criminal prosecution."[2]

Topics that will be discussed include document destruction related to I-9 retention requirements; conflicts arising from filing labor certification applications for workers lacking employment authorization; the need for separate counsel for the employer, the worker, and the corporate employee; when employee counseling crosses ethical boundaries and gives rise to obstruction charges; whether one can zealously preserve Fourth Amendment rights to be free of unreasonable searches and seizures in the course of an ICE raid; and when one should withdraw from representing the employer. The article is divided into various sections, starting with the early develop-

---

[*] **Josie Gonzalez** is the managing partner of Gonzalez & Harris, and has represented employers in all aspects of immigration law for more than 25 years. She recently represented a major corporation facing federal criminal charges for hiring undocumented workers. Ms. Gonzalez has published numerous articles for legal and trade journals on the topic of employer sanctions. Her background as a former criminal defense attorney and employer sanctions expert makes her uniquely qualified to address issues such as RICO and other criminal charges against employers, the future of employer sanctions, and how to develop and implement immigration corporate compliance materials. She currently chairs AILA's Worksite Enforcement Conference Committee.

[1] M. Mermelstein & C. Decker, "Walk the Line," 29 *Los Angeles Law.* 1 (Dec. 2006).

[2] R. Juceam, "Safeguarding Against Criminal Prosecution and Malpractice in Immigration Law—An Outline of Key Topics," *Ethics in a Brave New World—Professional Responsibility, Personal Accountability, & Risk Management for Immigration Practitioners* 57 (AILA 2004), available from AILA Publications, (800) 982-2839, *www.ailapubs.org*.

mental stages of an ICE investigation, progressing to an ICE inspection and/or a raid, and culminating in the ethical concerns that arise in the aftermath of the ICE raid.

Elsewhere in this publication, you will find a discussion of ethical considerations that arise when interviewing corporate executives and managerial employees while conducting in-house investigations.[3] A list of recommended articles written by white-collar criminal and corporate attorneys is appended to this article.

Why Has ICE Knocked on My Door?

A good place to begin is a discussion of one of the possible causes for ICE's focus on the employer: Has a labor certification application been filed for an alien who is out of status? The pressing ethical questions that one must resolve are: Is it a conflict of interest for one to represent the employer and the alien? Is it malpractice to fail to warn an employer that the filing of a labor certification is viewed as "constructive knowledge" that an employer is continuing the employment of an unauthorized worker under 8 CFR §274a.(*l*)(l)(iii)(a)?

It has long been known that labor certification applications for aliens lacking the right to work in the United States have been shared with ICE by the Department of Labor (DOL) and by U.S. Citizenship and Immigration Services during the I-140 petition or the adjustment of status phases. The filing of these applications can trigger an I-9 inspection or the procurement of an affidavit in support of a search warrant in order to conduct a raid at the worksite. The initial page of the new labor certification form, ETA Form 9089, states: "Employing or continuing to employ an alien unauthorized to work in the United States is illegal and may subject an employer to criminal prosecution, civil money penalties, or both." DOL has not hidden the fact that the contents of the labor certification application can be shared with other agencies.[4]

While legal authorities differ as to whether in the labor certification context one can effectively represent both the employer and the alien and whether conflict disclosures should be obtained,[5] there is no question that a grave conflict exists when the employee who is being sponsored lacks legal status. Clearly, one represents the employer when

---

[3] *See* J. Gonzalez, "Ethical Considerations in Conducting Immigration Investigations," *infra*.

[4] "Any material surrendered during the course of the submission of a labor certification can be used as evidence, as noted in the PERM instructions: 'Under routine uses for this system of records, case files developed in processing labor certification applications, labor condition applications, or labor attestations, may be released . . . in connection with administering and enforcing immigration laws and regulations . . . to such agencies as the DOL Office of Inspector General, Employment Standards Administration, the Department of Homeland Security's U.S. Citizenship and Immigration Services and Bureau of Immigration and Customs Enforcement, and Department of State.'" J. Gonzalez, "Demystifying the PERM Audit," *David Stanton Manual on Labor Certification* 13, 21 (AILA 3rd Ed.), available from AILA Publications, (800) 982-2839, *www.ailapubs.org*.

[5] *Compare* B. Hake, "Dual Representation in Immigration Practice," *Ethics in a Brave New World—Professional Responsibility, Personal Accountability, & Risk Management for Immigration Practitioners* 28 (AILA 2004) *with* C. Mehta, "Finding the 'Golden Mean' in Dual Representation," *Immigration & Nationality Law Handbook* 29 (AILA 2005–06 Ed.).

one files a labor certification.[6] However, let's assume that an employer retains an attorney to represent its interests in connection with the filing of the labor certification.[7] A prudent attorney should advise the employer that the employee should be terminated because he or she lacks the valid right to work in the United States. Misleading an employer into thinking that the employee is entitled to work while the labor certification is pending is both wrong and unethical, yet many employers say that this is exactly what the immigration attorney representing the alien has told them. This type of conduct could trigger a malpractice suit, because the attorney has failed to exercise his or her fiduciary duty to the employer and has exposed the employer to civil and criminal penalties.

What if the employer states that the "solution" for avoiding an ICE investigation is to take the employee off the payroll and pay his or her salary in cash? What if another "solution" is not recording that the employee is currently employed on part K of ETA Form 9089? Agreeing to these types of solutions may land the attorney in jail for conspiring to harbor and shield an alien from detection, for making false attestations on the ETA Form 9089, for creating a fraudulent document, and for Internal Revenue Service payroll reporting offenses.[8] An alien who agrees to cooperate with the gov-

---

[6] The declaration of preparer section of the new ETA Form 9089 states: "*I hereby certify that I have prepared this application at the direct request of the employer listed in Section C and that to the best of my knowledge the information contained herein is true and correct.* I understand that to knowingly furnish false information in the preparation of this form and any supplement thereto or to aid, abet, or counsel another to do so is a federal offense punishable by a fine, imprisonment up to five years or both under 18 U.S.C.§§2 and 1001. Other penalties apply as well to fraud or misuse of ETA immigration documents and to perjury with respect to such documents under 18 USC §§1546 and 1621." (Bold and italics in original.)

[7] DOL rules promulgated on May 17, 2007, provide new guidelines regarding who can pay the attorney for costs related to filing a labor certification. 20 CFR §656.12 states in part:

> (b) An employer must not seek or receive payment of any kind for any activity related to obtaining permanent labor certification, including payment of the employer's attorneys' fees, whether as an incentive or inducement to filing, or as a reimbursement for costs incurred in preparing or filing a permanent labor certification application, except when work to be performed by the alien in connection with the job opportunity would benefit or accrue to the person or entity making the payment, based on that person's or entity's established business relationship with the employer. An alien may pay his or her own costs in connection with a labor certification, including attorneys' fees for representation of the alien, except that where the same attorney represents the alien and the employer, such costs shall be borne by the employer. For purposes of this paragraph (b), payment includes, but is not limited to, monetary payments; wage concessions, including deductions from wages, salary, or benefits; kickbacks, bribes, or tributes; in kind payments; and free labor.
>
> (c) Evidence that an employer has sought or received payment from any source in connection with an application for permanent labor certification or an approved labor certification, except for a third party to whose benefit work to be performed in connection with the job opportunity would accrue, based on that person's or entity's established business relationship with the employer, shall be grounds for investigation under this part or any appropriate Government agency's procedures, and may be grounds for denial under §656.32, revocation under §656.32, debarment under §656.31(f), or any combination thereof.

[8] *See, e.g.*, INA §274(a)(1)(A)(iii) [8 USC §1324(a)(1)(A)(iii)] (harboring); 18 USC §1546(c) (fraud and misuse of visas, permits, and related documents).

ernment may testify against the attorney who prepared and submitted an application that contained material omissions or false information. The attorney-client privilege belongs to the client. It can be lost if the parties are engaged in criminal conduct.

Not only is the filing of a labor certification application for an unauthorized worker indicative of constructive knowledge, the mere "employee's request that the employer file a labor certification or employment-based visa petition on behalf of the employee" can also give rise to a finding of constructive knowledge.[9] What if an employer retains an attorney to interview select employees to determine if they need immigration assistance? Note that the government may attempt to use the immigration attorney as a material witness and even serve the attorney with a grand jury subpoena to testify regarding the employer's knowledge of the worker's illegal status. One might consider raising an attorney-client privilege, but what if the alien, who is cooperating with ICE, waives the privilege? Who is your client and who possesses the privilege? Payment of legal fees is not necessarily dispositive. The attorney may have to hire his or her own counsel for advice regarding his or her ethical responsibilities.

The employer who insists on filing a labor certification for an alien lacking work authorization should be notified in writing that the application may lead to an audit of the employer's workforce and the elimination of not just the target employee but the loss of other employees who also may lack work authorization.

Internal I-9 Audits and ICE I-9 Inspections

Different ethical concerns might arise during the course of an attorney's examination of the employer's I-9s. What if an attorney discovers copies of documents used in the completion of an I-9 that are not among the list of acceptable I-9 documents? For example, what if a restricted Social Security card that contains the legend "Not valid for employment without DHS authorization" was used as evidence of employment authorization and the employee lacked a DHS-issued work authorization card; or a receipt for an application for work authorization was accepted; or an approval notice for a family relative petition was recorded? In order to avoid a charge of criminal obstruction, one should not encourage the destruction of documents used to support an I-9. The solution is to counsel that the employee be terminated if he or she lacks the right to work. In due course, there will no longer be an I-9 retention requirement.[10] Additionally, if there is an official ICE I-9 inspection that is underway, document destruction should be avoided immediately on notification of the inspection.

A common scenario that can arise during the haste to present perfect-looking I-9s to ICE involves the realization that I-9s are incomplete and that an employee is sick or otherwise not available to complete his or her section of the I-9. Under no circumstances should an attorney advise an employer to complete relevant portions of the I-9,

---

[9] 8 CFR §274a.1(*l*)(1)(iii)(A).

[10] Employers must retain I-9s for a minimum of three years after the date of hire and one year after termination. 8 CFR §274a.2(b)(2)(i)(A).

such as the employee attestation of status, based on the documents recorded in section 2.

What if the I-9 needs to be corrected, or worse yet, there is no I-9 and the employer is concerned about the fines that may be assessed because of the late completion of the I-9? Any corrections to the I-9 should be conspicuously recorded, initialed, and dated with the notation, "Per audit of [x] date." An employer should be counseled strongly not to backdate but to record a current date. It is better to receive civil fines for I-9 irregularities than to be charged criminally for obstructing justice. Further, it is possible that the employer might not even be fined if the irregularity is considered a "technical" violation.[11]

What if an alien made a false claim to U.S. citizenship on the I-9 when initially hired, but has subsequently achieved a valid work permit recorded on a second I-9? The false claim to U.S. citizenship could trigger removal proceedings and be a bar to immigrating if it occurred after September 30, 1996.[12] One has an ethical responsibility to retain both I-9s, but there is a possibility that ICE will not focus on the earlier misrepresentation, as the employee now has valid work authorization.

When an employer surrenders I-9s and related documents to ICE during the course of an I-9 inspection, various attestations are made regarding the accuracy and completeness of the documentation. However, what if the employer has not provided a complete list of employees because some of them are being paid in cash off the books? If one is representing the employer and has knowledge that misrepresentations or concealment of evidence has occurred, there is an ethical responsibility to refrain from representing the employer.[13]

In the Heat of an ICE Raid

With the increase in ICE worksite raids, many unions, concerned attorneys, and civil rights organizations have advocated for the protection of the rights of the worker to be free from unreasonable searches and seizures. They have scheduled meetings with workers where "know your rights" information has been disseminated. What if an employer, sensing that a raid is imminent, requests that its attorney provide counseling to employees? Would such counseling by the employer's attorney be viewed by ICE as evidence of employer knowledge of the undocumented status of the workers? What if the counseling includes advising aliens to invoke their Fifth Amendment right to remain silent? In worksite enforcement, today's employee is tomorrow's witness for the prosecution. Most experts agree that the employees should be advised by an attorney who represents their interests solely and not those of the employer. "Ultimately, the best solution for lawyers in this situation is to ensure that another attorney is involved in the case exclusively to represent the interests of the witness. Case

---

[11] *See* INA §274A(b)(6)(A); 8 USC §1324a(b)(6)(A).
[12] *See* INA §212(a)(6)(C)(ii)(I); 8 USC §1182(a)(6)(C)(ii)(I).
[13] *See Model Rules of Prof'l Conduct*, R. 3.3 (2002) (duty to not knowingly make false statements of material facts or offer false evidence).

law protects an attorney who conveys an encouragement to invoke a Fifth Amendment right through the filter of an attorney representing the witness."[14] There is also a significant distinction between simply informing a witness of the existence of a Fifth Amendment right versus advising its invocation.[15]

Another reason to have separate counsel for employees/witnesses is to ensure that the attorney provides advice that is in their best interests. For example, such advice may be to inform the employee that ICE may give him or her a work permit and agree not to criminally prosecute if he or she becomes a government informant. Clearly, such counsel is inimical to the interests of the employer, and the corporation's attorney would be disinclined to provide it.

Some of the same considerations expressed above are present when employees are arrested and the employer seeks counsel to represent the workers. Additionally, an attorney that represents the employer, or any attorney for that matter, should not caution employees to refuse to speak with ICE investigators or suggest that false or misleading information be given.

What type of employee counseling can cross ethical boundaries and possibly trigger criminal prosecution of the attorney? Care should be taken not to cross the line from zealous advocacy to conduct that can give rise to criminal charges for obstruction of justice or attempting to conceal the presence of an unauthorized alien from government detection. An example of the latter conduct is contained in the government's indictment for attempting to shield aliens in violation of INA §274(a)(1)(A)(iii) [8 USC §1324(a)(1)(A)(iii)] against Braulio Pereyra-Gabino, a union steward for Swift & Co.[16] Swift was raided by ICE in December 2006, and it was discovered that many employees had engaged in identity theft, presenting valid documents that passed muster when verified through the E-Verify program but that did not belong to the employees. The charges against Pereyra-Gabino stemmed from a union orientation speech given to new-hire Hispanic employees, which was recorded by undercover agents. In the speech Pereyra-Gabino explained that E-Verify new-hire screening did not require the submission of the person's photo. According to the government, Pereyra-Gabino instructed the employees on how to be an illegal alien in the United States and escape detection, counseling them not to use false identification outside of work, particularly if they were ever stopped by the police.

During an ICE raid it might be advisable to have the employer videotape or carefully record the actions of ICE agents in order to note any Fourth Amendment violations and to have a record of items seized during the raid. ICE should not stop the business from operating nor prevent workers who are not known to be unauthorized aliens from leaving the premises, nor prevent personnel from making phone calls or moving freely throughout the facility. Can counseling an employer to assert its right to be free from unreasonable searches and seizures support a charge of obstructing or

---

[14] Mermelstein & Decker, *supra* note 1, at 10.
[15] *Id.*
[16] Indictment, *U.S. v. Pereyra-Gabino*, No. 4:07-CR-088 (S.D. Iowa).

interfering with the government's investigation? Failure to provide such advice could violate the attorney's obligation to zealously represent his or her client.[17] Or, as one ethics expert states: "[A]dopting a conservative approach to challenging ethical questions may result in the lawyer's representation falling below the standards of zealous advocacy. Indeed, in the context of criminalizing attorney conduct, Justice Antonin Scalia has warned of the dangers of chilling legitimate advocacy."[18]

Post Raid Ethical Considerations

In the aftermath of a raid, ICE will interview detained employees in order to decide whether to pursue criminal or civil charges and to determine if any of them will become material witnesses and testify against the employer. It's also possible that key managers might be interviewed to determine if they would cooperate in the government's investigation against the employer. A discussion of permissible, ethical advice that can be provided to corporate employees is found elsewhere in this publication.[19]

It is important that an attorney not be involved in any activity that may be construed as interfering in the government's investigation. For example, the attorney should not suborn perjury by counseling employees on how to answer questions or providing false or misleading information to the government. "Corporate counsel should be aware of the arsenal of federal statutes which are available to prosecutors. In addition to substantive charges, counsel should always be aware of obstruction of justice-related charges including statutes prohibiting obstruction of justice, perjury, false statements and witness tampering. . . . Counsel interviewing witnesses in the course of an investigation should be cognizant that attempts to encourage witnesses to recall things in a certain fashion or attempts to correct witness's recollections to match that of other witnesses or documents in the case, may run afoul of these broad federal prohibitions."[20]

Conclusion

Lastly, consider the very important question of whether one should even represent an employer in an ICE worksite investigation. First, does one have the competence or the resources to represent the employer? Representing the employer in an I-9 inspection is very labor intensive; it takes a team consisting of an attorney and one or more trained legal assistants who will pour through I-9s, recommend corrective action, and plan an effective strategy. Second, assuming one has the requisite expertise, will the employer heed one's advice regarding the necessity of coming into compliance, or is the employer instead convinced that it will go bankrupt or will be unable to operate without continued reliance on undocumented workers? Third, is the employer intent

---

[17] Model Rules of Professional Conduct, rule 1.3 comment: "A lawyer should act with commitment and dedication to the interests of the client and with zeal in advocacy upon the client's behalf."

[18] Mermelstein & Decker, *supra* note 1, at 3, *citing Hubbard v. U.S.*, 514 U.S. 695 (1995) (Scalia, J. concurring).

[19] *See* J. Gonzalez, "Ethical Considerations in Conducting Immigration Investigations."

[20] D. Purdom, "Conducting Internal Corporate Criminal Investigations," *DCBA Brief* at 9 (May 1997), available at www.dcba.org/brief/mayissue/1997/art30597.htm.

on conjuring up imaginative alternatives in order to continue employing unauthorized workers, like transferring workers to the payroll of subcontractors, paying employees off the books, moving employees to graveyard shifts or to other worksites, or knowingly allowing employees to work under false identities—"solutions" that might place the attorney in an ethically compromised position? Lastly, does one have the intestinal fortitude to work in a field with so many ethical uncertainties and such intense governmental oversight? Indeed, there are rewards to helping an employer create an effective immigration compliance program; however, that satisfaction is tempered with the unfortunate realization that it comes at the cost of eliminating jobs for talented, hardworking foreign nationals who are mired in a labyrinth of legislative indifference and callousness to their plight.

THE NEW LOOK OF WORKSITE ENFORCEMENT

by Bo Cooper, Eileen Scofield, Douglas S. Weigle, and Steven M. Ladik[*]

Trends in Investigations and Enforcement

With the passage of the Immigration Reform and Control Act of 1986 (IRCA),[1] employers became responsible for checking the identity and eligibility for employment of all hired employees. For the first time, employers were charged with the affirmative duty to check identity documents of an employee to see if he or she had the authority to work in the United States. This was required of all newly hired employees regardless of the employer size and citizenship of the prospective employee. This requirement was implemented through the completion of Form I-9 by the employee and verification of the identity and eligibility documents by the employer. Failure to complete the required documentation carried a fine of $1,000 per employee, and the hiring of an unauthorized worker carried a fine of $1,500. A pattern and practice of failing to comply could result in a six-month prison sentence.

Shortly after the implementation of the new law, immigration agents began an educational program to ensure compliance with the underlying requirements. The emphasis back then was clearly on education and compliance, and enforcement began slowly, usually resulting in a settlement requiring the employer to comply in the fu-

---

[*] A previous version of this article appeared at *Immigration & Nationality Law Handbook* 142 (AILA 2007–08 Ed.).

Steven M. Ladik updated the article for its inclusion in this work. Mr. Ladik is the managing partner of Berry Appleman & Leiden LLP in Dallas. He has served as AILA past president and is a past president of the American Immigration Law Foundation. He has also served as chapter chair of the AILA Texas Chapter and as chairman of the Board Certification Examinations Committee on Immigration and Nationality Law of the State Bar of Texas. Mr. Ladik is certified in immigration and nationality law by the Texas Board of Legal Specialization.

Bo Cooper heads the Washington, D.C., immigration practice of Paul, Hastings, Janofsky & Walker LLP. He is an adjunct faculty member and Public Interest Fellow at the University of Michigan School of Law. Mr. Cooper served as general counsel of legacy Immigration and Naturalization Service (INS) from 1999 until 2003.

Eileen Scofield is a frequent international and national public speaker and published author of numerous articles, primarily on business-related immigration. She has held numerous positions over her 22 years of practice with bar associations, including AILA. She is also a member of numerous organizations that advise Congress on business and immigration issues, such as the National I-9 Coalition. She heads a national practice with Alston & Bird.

Douglas S. Weigle practices immigration law at Bartlett & Weigle Co., LPA. An AILA member since January 1980, he served four terms as AILA's Ohio Chapter chair and three years as an AILA Board of Governors director. He was founding co-chair of the mentor program, is a co-editor of AILA's *Visa Processing Guide and Consular Posts Handbook*, and a member of the federal public defender panel in both the Eastern District of Kentucky and Southern District of Ohio.

[1] Pub. L. No. 99-603, 100 Stat. 3359. IRCA amended the Immigration and Nationality Act of 1952 (INA), Pub. L. No. 82-414, 66 Stat. 163.

ture, and negotiated reduced fines. In later years, with the concentration on the removal of criminal aliens and then preventing terrorism, employment enforcement took on a very low priority.

The New Look of Enforcement

U.S. Immigration and Customs Enforcement (ICE) began a new initiative in April 2006 to target employers engaged in the use of unauthorized workers. The emphasis was now squarely on enforcement and punishment instead of education and compliance. Whereas the former practice was to use administrative authorities to investigate and penalize violations, ICE began using criminal investigation techniques and charges far more widely.

A case in point was the May 8, 2006, ICE raid of the Northern Kentucky construction developer Fischer Homes. In this raid, ICE arrested 76 workers and four of the company's construction supervisors. The workers, mostly Hispanic, were charged with illegal entry and arraigned in the U.S. District Court for the Eastern District of Kentucky in Covington. Four supervisors were charged with the felonies of conspiracy and harboring aliens not authorized to be in the United States. Two additional supervisors were indicted later.

The significant factor in this case is that the undocumented workers were not paid "employees" of Fischer Homes. Rather, they were all employees of subcontractors used by Fischer Homes for the construction of Fischer's developments. The supervisors were charged with knowingly using subcontractors to shield Fischer Homes from the requirement of I-9s and enabling the unauthorized workers to be employed on the jobsites. Naturally enough, Fischer Homes took the position that there was never any knowing use of undocumented workers on their jobsites and that the undocumented workers were the responsibility of the subcontractors.

While I-9 regulations do not require an employer to check identity and eligibility and complete I-9s for independent contractors, the targeted workers must qualify under the law as independent contractors for the employer to escape liability. The mere designation of a worker as an independent contractor or a boilerplate paragraph in an employment contract requiring the contractor not to hire undocumented workers is not sufficient to insulate an employer from liability.

Using Internal Revenue Service (IRS) regulations as a guide, ICE relies on commonly accepted factors to determine if a worker is an independent contractor. Such factors can include whether the employer supplies the materials, is the sole employer for the independent contractor, directs the time and method of employment, and has authority to hire and discharge workers. Naturally, other factors may come into play, such as providing housing and transportation for the workers. Even if a worker is properly classified as an independent contractor, the employer still has a duty not to use undocumented workers if the employer knows that a contractor has undocumented persons as workers on the employer's worksite.

So what constitutes a knowing hire of undocumented workers by a contractor? ICE has taken a rather broad view of the employer's constructive knowledge, and of the circumstances in which an employer is under an obligation to make further inquiry of the contractor and even of the workers as to the legality of their presence in the United States. To make their case in federal court, ICE agents are often employing techniques more commonly associated with drug trafficking investigations. Wired informants are used and pressure is put on both the undocumented worker defendants and the American supervisors to plead out to lesser charges and get a reduced recommendation under sentencing guideline 5 K.1.1.[2] The undocumented workers are offered time to remain in the United States with special employment authorization, and the American defendants are offered immunity or supervised release.

In addition, IRS is getting involved by conducting a parallel criminal investigation of tax evasion and withholding employment taxes. If contractors are being paid in multiple checks just under $10,000 to avoid the cash reporting requirement, IRS is pursuing money laundering investigations. Again, contractors are offered a deal if they can provide testimony against the target company.

The pace of criminal worksite enforcement actions has risen steadily. Employers and their counsel would be well advised to monitor these cases in order to evaluate the application of specific facts to their own worksite. The following worksite enforcement actions have all taken place since the announcement of the April 2006 ICE initiative:

- Koch Foods—On August 28, 2007, in Fairfield, OH, ICE special agents executed criminal search warrants at Koch Foods. ICE identified more than 180 Koch employees working at the Fairfield plant requiring further questioning, and administratively arrested more than 160 for immigration violations. ICE agents simultaneously executed criminal search warrants at Koch's corporate office in Chicago. The enforcement actions were part of a two-year investigation based on evidence that Koch may have knowingly hired undocumented workers at its poultry processing and packaging facility.

- Fresh Del Monte Produce—A federal grand jury returned indictments on June 27, 2007, against 10 former workers of the Portland, OR facility who were arrested in conjunction with an ICE investigation. They were charged with possession of fraudulent immigration documents or Social Security fraud. The Fresh Del Monte facility was the site of a criminal search warrant executed on June 12, 2007, and a separate, court-ordered immigration enforcement action resulting in the arrest of more than 160 persons illegally present in the United States. ICE's six-month investigation into the fraudulent use of documents to illegally obtain employment at American Staffing Resources led to these indictments.

- George's Processing Inc.—On June 20, 2007, 28 employees of a southwest Missouri poultry processing plant were indicted on criminal immigration violations. They were arrested May 22, 2007, at George's Processing Inc., in Butterfield, MO, after a two-year investigation. During that action, 136 persons

---

[2] *United States Sentencing Commission Guidelines Manual* §5K1.1 (allowing the court to depart from the guidelines on "motion of the government stating that the defendant has provided substantial assistance in the investigation or prosecution of another person who has committed an offense").

were arrested and charged with administrative violations. Of those criminally charged, 27 were charged with aggravated identity theft and falsely claiming to be citizens of the United States in order to gain employment; 18 defendants were charged separately with re-entering the United States after having been deported. One was charged with Social Security fraud.

- Quality Service Integrity, Inc. (QSI)—Twelve defendants pled guilty in early May 2007 to fraud and misusing employment documents in a criminal worksite enforcement investigation against QSI in Beardstown, IL. Six remaining defendants in the case were scheduled for trial. Two of those, former managers at QSI's Beardstown operation, were charged with harboring aliens not authorized to be in the United States.

- Tarrasco Steel—On March 29, 2007, 77 aliens employed on construction projects at critical infrastructure sites in four southern states were arrested following a five-month ICE investigation. Many of those arrested worked for Greenville, MS-based Tarrasco Steel, owned by Jose S. Gonzalez. Gonzalez allegedly falsified and altered information on I-9s. Gonzalez was arrested on August 2, 2007, as part of an ongoing investigation into charges that he hired unauthorized workers from Central America.

- Jones Industrial Network (JIN)—On March 29, 2007, ICE agents executed a criminal search warrant, civil warrants, and conducted consent searches at nine business locations in the Baltimore area. ICE also seized a bank account belonging to JIN worth more than $636,000.

- Michael Bianco, Inc.—On March 6, 2007, New Bedford, MA, textile product company owner Francesco Insolia and three other managers were arrested and charged with conspiring to encourage or induce unauthorized aliens to reside in the United States and conspiring to hire undocumented workers.

- Rosenbaum-Cunningham International—On Feb. 21–22, 2007, three executives of Rosenbaum-Cunningham International, a Florida-based national janitorial services contractor, were charged with conspiracy to defraud the United States and to harbor unlawfully present aliens for profit and evading payment of federal employment taxes.

- Swift & Company—On Dec. 12, 2006, more than 1,297 workers were arrested at Swift meat processing facilities in six states during an enforcement operation that was the result of an investigation of work-related identity theft. Of those arrested, 274 were charged criminally—129 of them with federal crimes, the others with state crimes.

- HV CONNECT, Inc. (HVC)—On Oct. 12, 2006, Trun Nguyen, a naturalized U.S. citizen, pled guilty to bringing in and harboring certain aliens, mail fraud, wire fraud, conspiracy and money laundering. On March 14, 2007, ICE agents obtained a final order of forfeiture in the Northern District of Ohio. The forfeited property, which had approximately $100,000 in equity, was owned by Nguyen, a company official for HVC.

- Garcia Labor Companies/ABX Air—On Oct. 3, 2006, two temporary labor companies, as well as Maximo Garcia, the president of these companies, and two other corporate officers, pled guilty in Ohio to conspiring to provide hundreds of undocumented workers for ABX Air.

- Kentucky Limited Liability Corporations—On July 20, 2006, two corporations in Kentucky pled guilty to criminal charges of harboring aliens who were not lawfully present in the United States and money laundering in connection with a scheme that provided unauthorized workers to Holiday Inn, Days Inn, and other hotels in Kentucky. As part of the plea, Asha Ventures, LLC, and Narayan, LLC, agreed to pay $1.5 million in lieu of forfeiture and to create internal compliance programs.

- Stucco Design, Inc.—On May 2, 2006, Robert Porcisanu, the owner of an Indiana business that performed stucco-related services at construction sites in seven Midwest states, was charged with money laundering, harboring and transporting aliens unlawfully present in the United States, and making false statements in connection with an illegal employment scheme. Porcisanu was facing 40 years in prison and ICE was also seeking the forfeiture of $1.5 million.

- IFCO Systems North America—On April 19, 2006, ICE agents arrested seven current and former managers of IFCO Systems North America in Albany, NY, charging them with harboring aliens who were not legally present in the United States for financial gain. The former IFCO general manager pled guilty to conspiracy to transport and harbor them and possession of identification documents. The former corporate new market development manager also pled guilty to conspiracy to transport and harbor aliens.

Practice Tips for Employers

- Employers are faced with the often difficult-to-harmonize goals of avoiding any possible civil rights action stemming from illegal discrimination against foreign-born or foreign-looking employees, and avoiding criminal sanctions for using undocumented workers, either as employees or contractors. Therefore, an employer must have a comprehensive policy on fulfilling verification requirements for workers on its jobsites.

- Supervisors and management must be trained in the law of documenting workers and the responsibility for completing the I-9s.

- Every employer should have an explicit policy prohibiting the use of undocumented workers, and such notices should be prominently placed on every job site.

- Contractors must be put on notice and sign off on a policy that requires properly documented workers. Following a highly publicized case that it settled with an $11 million fine in 2005, Wal-Mart not only requires a signed agreement with contractors, but further requires the certification of an immigration practitioner as to the contractors' I-9 practices. While this may be more than is common for smaller employers, it obviously provides an extra layer of protection for the employer.

- The employer must train management and supervisors to use common sense and, according to the circumstances, attend to the suspected use of undocumented workers by a contractor or subcontractor. This does not mean that an employer must interrogate every employee of the contractor; on the other hand, if a supervisor observes contractor employees hiding underneath trucks or bushes whenever a police car passes, further inquiry of the contractor is appropriate. Failure by the contractor to take appropriate follow-up steps to address the employment eligibility of its employees in a circumstance like this should result in termination of the contractor's services. This duty may also extend to situations involving high-skilled contractors when an employer has reason to believe that the employees of the contractor are not in the United States on the correct visa.

- And, of course, employers should consult with immigration counsel if there are any questions or situations that need clarification. The stakes are now much higher than they used to be, and the personal exposure of company personnel is greater than it used to be. These times call for the highest standards of conduct, and employer clients should be advised to use particular caution when using contractors.

Social Security "No-Match" Letters

In recent years, it has become increasingly common for an employer to receive "no-match" letters from the Social Security Administration (SSA), indicating that certain name and Social Security number information the employer has submitted about its employees does not match the information in SSA's database. These letters have caused considerable confusion, but the way that an employer responds can have huge consequences. In particular, the U.S. Department of Homeland Security (DHS) may conclude that an employer who fails to act properly on receipt of a "no-match" letter has constructive knowledge that a particular employee is unauthorized to work in the United States.

Recently, there have been two major developments involving "no-match" letters. First, as noted above, the fact that an employer received "no-match" letters naming a large number of employees but did not take appropriate responsive action has been cited as an important factor in virtually every recent major ICE enforcement action. Second, DHS published a proposed rule on June 14, 2006, that would set out the steps that DHS considers to be appropriate when an employer receives a "no-match" letter, and providing a safe harbor for employers who follow these steps.[3] On August 15, 2007, DHS published the final rule with slight modifications from the proposed rule.[4]

Interestingly, IRS contracts with SSA to perform verifications of the accuracy of the information provided in an employee's W-2 form. The Internal Revenue Code

---

[3] 71 Fed. Reg. 34281 (June 14, 2006).
[4] 72 Fed. Reg. 45611 (Aug. 15, 2007).

prohibits the agency from sharing tax information with other government agencies such as DHS.[5] Therefore, in spite of the fact that the DHS rule purports to be utilized as an enforcement tool, SSA cannot provide DHS with information about the recipients of "no-match" letters.

This can be a tricky area, because the employer cannot conclude that an employee is unauthorized to work simply because of the "no-match" letter. It is critical that the employer not take adverse actions toward the employee on the basis of the letter alone. It can be a delicate balance to comply with both the obligation to ensure that all workers are authorized to be employed and the antidiscrimination obligations provided for in IRCA.

The final rule sets out the process in detail, and it can vary depending on the circumstances of each case. Generally, though, the rule calls for an employer first to confirm whether an error in its own records caused it to submit incorrect information to SSA. If that turns out not to be the case, the employer should have the employee deal directly with SSA (or DHS, depending on the circumstances) to resolve the discrepancy, and provide confirmation from the government agency that it has been resolved. If after 90 days the discrepancy has not been resolved, the employer would complete a new I-9 for the employee. If the employee cannot provide documents demonstrating identity and eligibility to be employed without relying on the document or documents that were called into question by the "no-match" letter, then the employer would risk a finding by DHS that it had constructive knowledge that the employee is not authorized to work.

If the discrepancy in the "no-match letter" cannot be resolved within 90 days, and the employee's employment authorization and identity cannot be verified using the I-9 procedure within 93 days, the employer is advised to terminate the employee in order to avoid a risk of DHS finding that the employer had constructive knowledge of hiring an unauthorized worker. DHS has taken the position that its rule simply codifies an employer's obligations under existing law.

In response to the publication of the final rule, a lawsuit was brought by the AFL-CIO and other plaintiffs alleging that the regulation expanded employer liability in a manner contrary to the governing statute, and that it exceeded the authority that Congress granted to DHS and SSA.[6] On October 10, 2007, the U.S. District Court for the Northern District of California granted the plaintiffs' motion for preliminary injunction preventing implementation of the DHS rule,[7] thereby ensuring that U.S. citizens and legal residents would not lose their jobs because of errors in the SSA database.

In response to the court's order, DHS Secretary Michael Chertoff stated, "President Bush made clear in August that we are going to do as much administratively as

---

[5] 26 USC §6103.
[6] Complaint, *AFL-CIO v. Chertoff*, No. 07-4472 (N.D. Cal. Aug. 28, 2007), *available at* www.aclu.org/pdfs/immigrants/aflcio_v_chertoff_complaint.pdf.
[7] Order Granting Motion for Preliminary Injunction, *AFL-CIO v. Chertoff*, No. 07-4472 (N.D. Cal. Oct. 10, 2007).

we can, within the boundaries of existing law, to further secure our borders and enforce our immigration laws. Today's ruling is yet another reminder of why we need Congress to enact comprehensive immigration reform."[8]

In November 2007, DHS "withdrew" its rule and the court granted DHS's motion to stay proceedings until March 1, 2008, pending a new rulemaking effort that DHS maintains will address the court's concerns with the regulation as originally issued in final form.[9]

In the meantime, it is crucial for employers to have a coordinated process for monitoring the receipt of "no-match" letters, and that they have clear and consistent policies to ensure follow-up when letters are received.

State Law Issues

Complicating the immigration compliance world tremendously, there is a clear new trend of state legislation affecting employment eligibility verification. In the past few years, hundreds of such laws were under consideration in legislative bodies around the country, and this pattern is sure to continue in the near term. The state laws enacted have tended to impose additional consequences on the employment of unauthorized workers, and in some circumstances impose additional procedural requirements beyond what federal law requires. To illustrate the trends at the state level and to highlight the basic requirements for employers who operate in the affected states, it is worth summarizing some of these new laws.

Georgia Senate Bill 529,[10] known as the Georgia Security and Immigration Compliance Act, is an omnibus statute that includes a wide range of immigration-related provisions. Section 2 of the act targets hiring by state and local governmental entities and by businesses contracting with state and local governments. It requires every public employer to register and participate in the E-Verify program (formerly the Basic Pilot program)[11] to verify work authorization for all new employees. It also forbids companies from entering into contracts with public employers for the "physical performance of services" unless the contractor (or subcontractor) also registers and participates in E-Verify.

The law set forth a rolling implementation schedule. As of July 1, 2007, the rules under section 2 became applicable to public employers, contractors, and subcontractors with 500 or more employees. They extend to public employers and contractors

---

[8] DHS Press Release, Oct. 10, 2007, *available at* www.dhs.gov/xnews/releases/pr_1192048059536.shtm.

[9] *See* Motion to Stay Proceedings Pending New Rulemaking, *AFL-CIO v. Chertoff*, No. 07-4472 (N.D. Cal. Nov. 23, 2007).

[10] Codified at Ga. Code Ann. §§13-10-90, 13-10-91, 16-5-46, 35-2-14, 42-4-14, 43-20A-1 to 42-20A-4, and 48-7-21.1.

[11] E-Verify is an Internet-based system operated by U.S. Citizenship and Immigration Services (USCIS) in partnership with SSA. It provides an automated link to federal databases to help employers determine employment eligibility of new hires and the validity of their Social Security numbers. *See* www.uscis.gov (E-Verify link).

with 100 or more employees on July 1, 2008, and will cover all public employers and contractors as of July 1, 2009.

Colorado also has passed laws affecting the employment verification process. Like Georgia, Colorado passed a provision requiring the use of E-Verify by companies contracting with the state. Colorado House Bill 1343, as amended by House Bill 07-1073,[12] prohibits a state agency or political subdivision from entering into or renewing a public contract for services with a contractor who knowingly employs or contracts with an "illegal alien" to perform work under the contract, or who knowingly contracts with a subcontractor who knowingly employs or contracts with an "illegal alien" to perform work under the contract. Before executing a public contract for services, each prospective contractor must certify that, at the time of the certification, it does not knowingly employ or contract with an "illegal alien" and that the contractor has participated or attempted to participate in E-Verify in order to verify that it does not employ any "illegal aliens." The term "services" is defined as the furnishing of labor, time, or effort by a contractor or subcontractor that does not involve the delivery of a specific end product other than reports that are merely incidental to the required performance. This law became effective on August 7, 2006, and applies to new contracts entered on or after that date.

Another Colorado provision, House Bill 1017,[13] is a general provision that became effective on January 1, 2007, and applies to all Colorado employers. It applies to all new employees hired on or after January 1, 2007, and requires that, within 20 days of hiring a new employee, the employer affirm that the employer (1) has examined the employment eligibility of the newly acquired employee; (2) has retained copies of the employee's work authorization and identity documents; (3) has not altered or falsified the identification documents; and (4) has not knowingly hired an unauthorized alien. This is another example of state law imposing requirements beyond those of federal law. Under the federal regulations, employers have a choice whether to retain copies of eligibility and identification documents. Now, even if they have a general policy not to retain such documents in connection with the I-9 process, employers will have to do so in Colorado.

Both the Colorado and Georgia statutes are poorly drafted and leave much for the affected employer and counsel to interpret. Georgia and Colorado presume to solve the problem of employment of undocumented workers by requiring employers who contract with the state to participate in E-Verify. However, the Colorado statute is seemingly ignorant of the fact that the provisions of E-Verify prohibit its use to screen current employees that may be destined to work on the contract. Colorado further complicated this issue by issuing a set of answers to frequently asked questions (FAQs) that seemed at one point to add a requirement for all employers, and not just contractors, to use both the SSA database and E-Verify for verification purposes.

---

[12] Codified at Colo. Rev. Stat. §§8-17.5-101, 8-17.5-102.
[13] Codified at Colo. Rev. Stat. §8-2-122.

Those FAQs appear to have been replaced by new guidance that no longer addresses the issue.[14]

Finally, the jurisdictional scope of these statutes is obscure. Although they may clearly cover an entity contracting with the state that has workers providing services in the state, what about a company that may operate a call center for the state in a completely different state? What if only 5 percent of the employees in the call center work on the state's business? There are no clear answers to these questions, but counsel can negotiate the applicability of E-Verify with USCIS so that it applies to something less than the entire corporation.

Colorado and Georgia are just two of a growing number of states that have passed or are considering laws that use state loans, contracts, licenses, and the like to impose additional penalties on employers who are found to have employed unauthorized workers. This discussion is not meant to serve as a comprehensive discussion of state law developments,[15] but instead as a reminder that this area is evolving quickly. It is critical that employers and their counsel stay abreast of legal developments in the states where they do business. It is no longer possible to consider employment verification to be solely a responsibility under federal law, or to consider that policies and practices that comply fully with federal requirements are sufficient.

The Internal Audit: Structure and Practice Tips

Given the intensification of DHS's worksite enforcement efforts, it is crucial for employers to assess their I-9 records and practices with an internal audit. As a general rule of thumb, it is wise for employers to conduct an I-9 self-audit on at least an annual basis. The I-9 form appears deceptively simple, but is fraught with potential problems. As a result, it is imperative that companies be sure first that their I-9 documentation is accurate, and second that they have no information or documentation that would require them to take additional steps.

The need for the I-9 audit is not a reflection of a company's constructive or actual knowledge of employment verification issues. Naturally, there are always potential paperwork violations and other issues when different employers or different managers actually complete the I-9, or when different employees are not comfortable or adequately prepared to fill out section 1 of the I-9, and when a company has multiple locations. These factors buttress the need for an internal audit.

The internal audit should mirror as much as possible a government compliance audit. Following such a procedure enables the company more adequately to review its I-9 documentation. In addition, the use of this process will help the company's human resources (HR) department function and compliance personnel to be better trained on I-9 procedures. Therefore, the first step is to obtain a list of employees. A sound ap-

---

[14] *See* Colorado Division of Labor, Guide to Public Contracts for Services and Illegal Aliens Law, available at www.coworkforce.com/lab/pcs/1343CompleteGuideFinal.pdf.

[15] For more information on state law developments, see N. Merritt & A. Weigel, "The Mushroom Patch of State Immigration Laws—A Mad Hatter's Wonderland for Employers," in this publication.

proach is to secure a payroll record for the company that lists all current and terminated employees. The terminated employees should be employees who were terminated within the last three years.

It is then necessary to secure the form/file for each of the current employees. The I-9 should be kept in a separate file outside of the employee's personnel file. If it appears that I-9 files are missing, this should be noted immediately.

I-9s for terminated employees should be kept for three years from the date of hire or one year after termination, whichever is longer. The I-9s that do not fall within these time frames should be destroyed. In addition, it is advisable to write a destruction date notice in that employee's file in case there are any questions about whether an I-9 was ever executed at the beginning of employment.

One approach is for two binders to be assembled, one for current employees and one for the terminated employees who fall within the retention time frame. The auditor should then systematically inspect each individual I-9 to check for errors and omissions. There are, of course, a variety of opportunities for errors and omissions to occur. Below is a list of the most common mistakes employees and employers make. The I-9 should be reviewed with these particularly in mind.

If errors or omissions are discovered during the review of the I-9s, the corrected or previously omitted information should be added to the I-9. When omitted information is added, the person adding that information to the form should initial and date that new information. He or she can also make a notation such as "corrected during self-audit, [date]", to indicate that the form was subsequently completed. If information on the form is incorrect, the information should not be deleted, but should be crossed out with a single line. Above the crossed-out information, the accurate information should be included. Again, this change should be initialed and dated, and a correction annotation such as the one above can be added to the form. Any errors or omissions amended in section 1 of the form should be completed by the employee and not the employer. All other errors and omissions can be remedied by the employer's representative. This process for correcting errors and omissions provides evidence that no one has gone back and attempted to "doctor" the forms. Moreover, in the event of a government review of the I-9s, the self-audit efforts of an employer should demonstrate diligence on the employer's part.

If, in the course of this audit, any information arises that would cause a reasonable person to be concerned about the legitimacy of the documents presented or the identity of the individual presenting those documents, further steps and action are needed. When the I-9 is initially executed, the documents must appear reasonably to relate to the person presenting them and must appear on their face to be genuine. If, for some reason, these two criteria are not satisfied, either from the I-9 review or from subsequent information (such as from a Social Security "no-match" letter and the follow-up steps that an employer should take), then there is a duty to investigate further. This further investigation could include asking the employee to meet with HR, present documentation, etc. Special care must be taken to ensure that the employer complies fully with the I-9 employment verification process but does not run afoul of the unfair immigration-related employment practice provisions.

Most Common Mistakes in Completing Form I-9

Section 1 of the form:

- The employee did not sign or date the form
- The employee did not complete section 1 on the date of hire
- The employee did not check one of the three boxes regarding status
- The employee checked the wrong box regarding status
- The employee did not list an alien number, admission number, or expiration date

Section 2:

- The employer did not sign section 2
- The employer did not date section 2
- The employer did not fill in the date of hire
- The employer did not complete section 2 within three business days of hire
- The employer photocopied the employee's documents but did not complete the form
- The employer representative who signed the form was not the person who saw the original documents
- The employer accepted unacceptable documents (hospital birth certificates, foreign birth certificates, etc.)
- The employer accepted documents that did not "reasonably relate" to the employee (different names, dates of birth, etc.)
- The employer reviewed too many documents (items on list A, B, and C), which can lead to a discrimination charge against the employer
- The employer keeps copies of documents for some employees, but not all[16]

Section 3:

- The employer did not reverify Form I-9 when required
- The employer did not complete the information required in section 3
- The employer did not sign section 3

Self-Audit Do's and Don'ts

- Do pull a current payroll list.

---

[16] There is no requirement under federal law to keep copies, but the employer's policy should be consistently applied for all employees.

- Do make an assessment of those employees, current and former, for whom the company needs to maintain an I-9.
- Do separate the I-9s for those employees who are no longer employed, but for whom an I-9 needs to be retained.
- Do destroy the I-9s for those employees who are no longer employed and for whom the company is no longer required to maintain the I-9.
- Do make a notation in the HR form file that the I-9 was executed and on what date.
- Do review the I-9 to be sure that all applicable fields are completed.
- Do be sure that all fields in section 1 are completed or a "N/A" is contained in the box if the question is not applicable.
- Do go back to the employee and have the employee complete the appropriate information in box number 1, should you discover that box number 1 is incomplete.
- Do have the employee fill in the appropriate box, preferably in a different color ink, then date and initial next to the addition. The initials should be those of the employee, and the date should be the date the additional information is included on the I-9.
- Do review section 2 of the form.
- If section 2 of the form is improperly completed, and the person who originally completed the I-9 on behalf of the employer is available, that person should ask the employee to see documents needed to properly complete section 2 of the form. That person should include the new information on the form, preferably in different color ink, and should initial and date the new information with the actual date that the new information is being added to the form.
- If the original company representative is not available to review section 2 and complete any new information that is needed, then another representative of the company should be designated to make such additions to the form. In addition, the representative may make a note on the bottom of the I-9 that on "X" date, the I-9 was reviewed and updated pursuant to an internal audit by the company.
- If the second section has incomplete documentation, the employer should not direct the employee to provide specific documents for completion. The employer should instead give the employee a copy of the list of acceptable documents that can be submitted in conjunction with the I-9, and must allow the employee to select which documents to present.
- If any of the documents listed in the A, B, or C column is in the wrong column, circle the entry and draw an arrow to where it should be. Date and initial the arrow.
- If it is determined that the validity dates of the employment authorization documents have expired, a new I-9 should be executed or section 3 of the existing I-9 should be completed on presentation of acceptable documents.

- If copies of the supporting documents were made when the I-9 was first executed and now new or additional documents are presented in conjunction with the audit, then copies of the new or additional documents should also be copied and included in the file.
- The employer must choose whether to retain copies of all documents or of no documents. Whichever choice is made, the practice must be uniform.
- Regarding copies, only copy the column A document *or* the B *and* C documents that are examined to verify employment eligibility and identity, depending upon the employee's choice. Employees often bring more documents than are necessary to present, and the employer should not simply make copies of whatever the employee happens to have in his or her possession.
- If for some reason the self-audit contains information or documentation that would cause the employer representative reasonably to conclude that the document does not appear to be genuine or to relate to the employee presenting it, the employer should conduct further investigation of the worker's legal status.
- Questions arising during the audit should be resolved with senior personnel and in a consistent manner.
- *Do not* backdate any document.

Defending a Government I-9 Audit

The following summarizes potential criminal penalties imposed on employers and their agents found violating immigration laws related to the employment of undocumented workers in the United States.

Key Issues

- How can management avoid personal liability for actions involving the employment of undocumented workers?
- What is the legal standard under which employers may be found liable for smuggling undocumented aliens into the United States?
- What is the legal standard under which corrections to an I-9 result in criminal liability?

Summary

Immigration laws authorize the government to bring criminal charges against a company and individual agents of a company. Management can avoid personal liability for the illegal actions of a company or other agents of a company by neither participating nor having any knowing involvement in the illegal activity. The knowing involvement or participation standard applies to laws related to the residency verification process in the hiring or retention of employees, to laws related to the smuggling of undocumented workers, and to changes to an I-9 that may constitute document fraud.

Discussion

The federal government's criminal suit against Tyson Foods, Inc. shed light on today's pattern of efforts to target businesses that allegedly employ illegal immigrants. It is unlawful to hire, recruit, refer an alien for a fee, or continue to employ an alien, knowing the alien is unauthorized to work in the United States.[17] Penalties imposed for violating these immigration laws include civil sanctions and criminal charges against a company and its individual agents and the threat of fines and imprisonment.[18]

The Criminal Suit Against Tyson Foods, Inc. and Individual Managers

In 2001, the federal government filed a criminal suit against Tyson Foods, Inc. and six of its managers for violating immigration laws.[19] During the course of a 2½-year investigation, legacy Immigration and Naturalization Service (INS) agents, with the cooperation of several other federal and local law enforcement agencies, tracked the company's employment practices.[20] As a result of the investigation, the government's evidence against Tyson included taped conversations in which Tyson managers allegedly arranged transportation and false documents for alien workers. The government also claimed that it had evidence that Tyson managers paid undercover INS agents, posing as smugglers, $100 to $200 for each worker brought into the United States.[21] The government alleged that the "smugglers" were paid using official Tyson corporate checks that fraudulently documented the charges as recruitment expenses.[22] In addition to the involvement of individual managers, the government argued that Tyson's top management knew that its managers were violating immigration laws, which resulted in criminal charges against the company for its alleged involvement.[23] In its defense, Tyson denied the company's involvement and contended that the individual managers were violating company policy and acting outside of the scope of their employment.[24]

A 36-count indictment charged the defendants with conspiracy to smuggle aliens into the United States, provide them with fraudulent work papers, and employ them unlawfully for the purpose of commercial advantage and private financial gain.[25] The government sought to recover more than $100 million of the profits Tyson earned during the time of the alleged incidents, and the company risked losing its government contracts.[26] In addition, each individual defendant faced a maximum sentence of

---

[17] INA §274A(a); 8 USC §1324a(a).

[18] *See* INA §274A(f); 8 USC §1324a(f).

[19] *See* S. Tanger, "Enforcing Corporate Responsibility for Violations of Workplace Immigration Laws: The Case of Meatpacking," 9 *Harv. Latino L. Rev.* 59, 74 (2006).

[20] *Id.*

[21] *Id.*

[22] *Id.*

[23] *Id.*

[24] *Id.*

[25] *Id.* at 75 (citing a press release issued by the Department of Justice).

[26] *Id.* at 78.

five years in prison and a $250,000 fine if convicted.[27] By the time the jury deliberated, however, only 12 of the 36 counts remained.[28] Although the company and three of the individual defendants were eventually acquitted of the remaining charges, the case demonstrated the government's willingness to file criminal charges against businesses.[29]

Immigration Laws Imposing Criminal Liability on Employers

Corporate Management and the Risk of Personal Liability

Agents of a corporate employer may be found personally liable for violating immigration laws while acting within the scope of employment. Regulations accompanying the Immigration and Nationality Act (INA) indicate that the term "employer" means "an individual or an entity, including an agent or anyone acting directly or indirectly in the interest thereof . . . ."[30] As the indictment in the case against Tyson illustrated, when a company and its individual agents are involved in illegal immigration and employment practices, the immigration statutes authorize civil and criminal sanctions against the company and individual managers, officers, and employees.[31]

An agent of a corporation may face criminal penalties for violating immigration laws; however, he or she will likely need to have "knowingly"[32] participated in the illegal activity to be found liable.[33] "[O]fficers, directors and agents of a corporation may be held criminally liable for their acts although performed in their official capacity[,] but where they have neither actively participated in nor directed nor authorized a violation of law by their corporation they are not liable."[34] For example, the INA provides that an employer commits a misdemeanor when it engages in a "pattern or

---

[27] *Id.*

[28] *Id.*

[29] *Id.* at 73–74.

[30] 8 CFR §274a.1(g).

[31] *See* INA §274(A)(a); 8 USC §1324a(a); 8 CFR §274a.1(g). *See also Steiben v. INS,* 932 F.2d 1225, 1228 (8th Cir. 1991) (holding that the regulations authorized legacy INS to issue civil sanctions under INA §274A(a)(1) [8 USC §1324a(a)(1)] against the chief executive officer of a corporation who exercised exclusive control over the operation of a business).

[32] "The term 'knowing' includes not only actual knowledge but also knowledge which may fairly be inferred through notice of certain facts and circumstances which would lead a person, through the exercise of reasonable care, to know about a certain condition." 8 CFR §274a.1(*l*)(1). "Constructive knowledge may include, but is not limited to," failing to comply with the employer verification system and acting with "reckless and wanton disregard for the legal consequences of permitting another individual to introduce an unauthorized alien into its workforce or to act on it behalf." *Id.*

[33] An individual charged with violating immigration laws resulting in criminal penalties may also implicate his or her employer. The government may charge a company with criminal liability when agents of the company have (1) committed a crime; (2) within the scope of their employment; and (3) with the intent to benefit the corporation. *See U.S. v. Inv. Enters., Inc.*, 10 F.3d 263, 266 (5th Cir. 1993) (stating that a corporation is criminally liable for the unlawful acts of its agents, provided that the conduct is within the scope of the agent's authority, whether actual or apparent).

[34] *U.S. v. Sherpix, Inc.* 512 F.2d 1361, 1372 (D.C. Cir. 1975).

practice" of knowingly hiring or continuing to employ unauthorized workers.[35] The penalty includes up to $3,000 in fines for each unauthorized worker, imprisonment of up to six months, or both.[36] Felony charges and a fine and/or imprisonment of up to five years apply when an employer "knowingly hires for employment at least 10 individuals with actual knowledge that the individuals are aliens" during any 12-month period.[37] With respect to the hiring, recruiting, or referral of an unauthorized worker for employment in the United States, a person or entity may assert a "good-faith defense" by establishing compliance with the requirements of the employer verification system.[38] Although the government has authorization to prosecute an individual manager of a company if he or she violates immigration laws, statutory language suggests that an individual must have a minimum level of knowledge of, or participation in, the illegal activity.

Recruiting vs. Smuggling

As Tyson and its individual managers discovered, employers may be found criminally liable for smuggling aliens into the United States.[39] Although an employer may pay a recruiter a fee in exchange for supplying employees, such action is unlawful when an employer pays a recruiter knowing that the recruiter is providing workers who are not legally present in the United States. "[A]ny person" who (1) knowingly brings or attempts to bring an alien into the United States through unauthorized channels; (2) knowingly or with reckless disregard conceals, harbors, or shields from detection an alien that has entered or remained in the United States illegally; (3) encourages or induces an alien to enter or reside in the United States, knowing or in reckless disregard of the fact that such entry or residence is in violation of the law; or (4) engages in any conspiracy to commit, or aids or abets in the commitment of those acts, may be fined or imprisoned.[40] The term "any person" includes employers.[41] A fine or imprisonment of up to 10 years may also be imposed upon "any person who, knowing or in reckless disregard of the fact that an alien has not received prior authorization to come to, enter, or reside in the United States, brings or attempts to bring [such alien] to the United States in any manner whatsoever . . . [if the] offense was done for the purpose of commercial advantage or private financial gain."[42]

---

[35] INA §274A(f)(1); 8 USC §1324a(f)(1); *see* 8 CFR §274a.10(a).

[36] INA §274A(f)(1); 8 USC §1324a(f)(1); 8 CFR §274a.10(a).

[37] INA §274(a)(3)(A); 8 USC §1324(a)(3)(A).

[38] *See* INA §274A(a)(3); 8 USC §1324a(a)(3).

[39] The grand jury indictment against Tyson included seven counts of causing undocumented workers to be brought into the United States for the purpose of commercial advantage and private financial gain, and 10 counts of causing undocumented workers to be transported into the United States for the same purpose. *See* INA §§274(a)(1)(A)(ii), (2)(B)(ii); S. Tanger, *supra* note 19, at 75–76.

[40] INA §274(a)(1)(A); 8 USC §1324(a)(1)(A).

[41] *See U.S. v. Kim*, 193 F.3d 567, 574–75 (2d Cir. 1999).

[42] INA §274(a)(2)(B)(ii); 8 USC §1324(a)(2)(B)(ii).

The I-9 and Employer Sanctions

Pursuant to IRCA, employers are required to examine certain types of identification, verify that an employee is eligible for employment in the United States, and retain the I-9 completed in the hiring process.[43] Civil penalties are imposed upon anyone who "knowingly" accepts or provides any forged or false documents to satisfy any of the hiring or employment verification requirements.[44] Penalties range from $375 to $3,200 for each forged or false document violation for first offenses occurring after March 27, 2008.[45] Criminal penalties may also be imposed upon an employer found using "(1) an identification document, knowing (or having reason to know) that the document was not issued lawfully for the use of the possessor (2) an identification document knowing (or having reason to know) that the document is false, or (3) a false attestation, for the purpose of satisfying a requirement of section 274A(b)[46] of the Immigration and Nationality Act."[47] An employer may be fined, imprisoned not more than five years, or both, if found liable for using or accepting false documents.[48]

If an employer needs to update or reverify an I-9 form for an employee who has completed a previous form, the employer may line through any outdated information and initial and date any updated information, or alternatively, the employer may fill out a new I-9.[49] An employer will not be charged with a verification violation if he or she properly complies with the I-9 form and verification requirements, and DHS subsequently discovers that an employee is not authorized to work in the United States.[50] Compliance with the I-9 requirements also establishes a "good-faith defense" against sanctions, unless the government can show that the employer had knowledge of the employee's unauthorized status.[51]

Other Issues Arising in the Context of Enforcement Actions

When involved in defending an enforcement action, it is essential that experienced litigation counsel represent the parties. Aside from the issues discussed in this article, others that can arise, include, but are not limited to, the following:

- Whistleblower Complaint

---

[43] INA §274A(b); 8 USC §1324a(b); *see supra*.

[44] INA §274C(b)(4); 8 USC §1324c(b)(4).

[45] 8 CFR §§270.3(b)(1)(ii)(A); 28 CFR §68.52(e)(1)(i).

[46] INA §274A(b) [8 USC §1324a(b)] describes the requirements of the employment verification system. "[I]n the case of a person or other entity hiring, recruiting, or referring an individual for employment in the United States," the requirements include attestation after examination of documentation that the individual is not an unauthorized alien.

[47] 18 USC §1546(b); *see* INA §274C(e) (criminal penalties for failure to disclose role as document preparer).

[48] 18 USC §1546(b).

[49] *See* USCIS, Handbook for Employers: Instructions for Completing the Form I-9 (Employment Eligibility Verification Form), at 25, *available at www.uscis.gov/files/nativedocuments/m-274.pdf*.

[50] *Id.* at 21.

[51] *Id.* at 17.

- Official Notice
- Subpoena
- Search Warrant
- Contact with Authorities
- Scope and Format of Response
- Privilege Considerations
- Elements of Corporate Culpability
- Existence of Wrongful Conduct Within Organization
- Exercise of Prosecutorial Discretion
- Entitlement to Warrant
- Instructions to Employees
- Recordkeeping
- Continuum of Perceived Culpability
- Remedial Actions
- Collateral Consequences
- Adequacy of Prosecuting Culpable Agents
- Adequacy of Noncriminal Remedies
- Steps to Impede the Quick and Effective Exposure
- Reporting Employee Misconduct
- Sanctions
- Attorney's Fees
- Compliance and Ethics Program
- Indictments for False Statements
- Corporate "*Miranda*"
- When and How to Report Questions to Expect from Authorities
- Following the Paper Trail
- Periods of Premature Presentations
- Ethical Considerations in the Conduct of Internal Investigations
- Public Companies and Their Public: How the Securities and Exchange Commission Deals with Corporate Self-Examination
- Organizing the Internal Investigation: Document Collection and Analysis
- Organizing the Internal Investigation: Preparing for and Conducting Interviews
- Reporting the Information: To Write or Not to Write

DEPUTIZING—AND THEN PROSECUTING—AMERICA'S BUSINESSES IN THE FIGHT AGAINST ILLEGAL IMMIGRATION

by Thomas C. Green, Jay T. Jorgensen, and Ileana M. Ciobanu[*]

There has been a significant upsurge in the number of federal criminal prosecutions in recent years. In fact, between fiscal years 2000 and 2004, the number of federal criminal cases increased by about one-third.[1] This upswing in federal criminal cases was largely fueled by immigration cases.[2] Indeed, the number of immigration prosecutions in those four years surged from 16,724 to 37,854, making immigration prosecutions the single largest category of federal crimes, surpassing even drug prosecutions.[3]

Given the growing number of illegal immigrants in America[4] and the corresponding political debate about how the federal government should respond,[5] it is unsur-

---

[*] **Thomas C. Green** and **Jay T. Jorgensen** are partners in the Washington, D.C., office of Sidley Austin, where **Ileana M. Ciobanu** is an associate. In 2003, Mr. Green and Mr. Jorgensen successfully defended Tyson Foods, Inc. in a case where the government alleged 36 counts of criminal conduct relating to illegal immigration. *The National Law Journal* selected the jury's verdict absolving Tyson of any wrongdoing as the most significant defense verdict in the nation for 2003. *See generally* June D. Bell, *Defense Wins of 2003: A "Less Is More" Strategy Clicks with Jury in Tyson Case*, Nat'l L.J., Mar. 26, 2004, *available at www.law.com/jsp/article.jsp?id=1080006221501* (discussing the case that led to the award). Since then, Mr. Green, Mr. Jorgensen, and their colleagues have defended a number of business clients in civil cases based on allegations of illegal hiring. An earlier version of this article was printed in the *American Criminal Law Review*. *See* Thomas C. Green & Ileana M. Ciobanu, *Deputizing—and Then Prosecuting—America's Businesses in the Fight Against Illegal Immigration*, 43 Am. Crim. L. Rev. 3 (2006).

[1] TRAC Reports, Inc., Timely New Justice Department Data Show Prosecutions Climb During Bush Years: Immigration and Weapons Enforcement Up, White Collar and Drug Prosecutions Slide (2005), *available at http://trac.syr.edu/tracreports/crim/136*.

[2] Mark Sherman, Federal Prosecutions Up Nearly a Third Under Bush, Fueled by Immigration Cases, Study Says, Associated Press, Sept. 28, 2005.

[3] TRAC Reports, Inc., *supra* note 1.

[4] *See, e.g.*, Office of Policy and Planning, U.S. Immigration and Naturalization Service, Estimates of the Unauthorized Immigrant Population Residing in the United States: 1990 to 2000, at 7, *available at www.dhs.gov/xlibrary/assets/statistics/publications/Ill_Report_1211.pdf* (estimating seven million illegal immigrants in the United States in January 2000, which was twice as many as there had been in January 1990); Ruth Ellen Wasem et al., *Unauthorized Aliens in the United States: Estimates Since 1986*, CRS Report for Congress 1 (Sept. 15, 2004), *available at www.immigrationforum.org/documents/crs/CRS_undocumented_2004.pdf* (recognizing that the Census has recorded an increase in the illegal immigrant population from 3.2 million in 1986 to 9.3 million in 2002).

[5] In 2005, the Bush administration revived its campaign to overhaul the nation's immigration system, urging, among other proposals, the creation of a guest-worker program to fill vacant U.S. jobs. June Kronholz, *Administration Renews Campaign for Guest Workers*, Wall St. J., Oct. 19, 2005, at B2. Under the administration's proposed guest-worker plan, temporary workers would be able to stay in the United States for six years but would not be able to use this residency to gain citizenship. *Id.* However, dozens of House and Senate Republicans announced their opposition to this plan, seeing it as an amnesty program that would only attract more illegal workers. *Id.* With the significant passage of time since its proposal, the president's plan appears to be dead.

prising that the Department of Justice (DOJ) and Department of Homeland Security (DHS) would place increased focus on immigration cases. What is surprising is the federal government's attempt to deputize America's business community in the fight against illegal immigration while simultaneously treating America's businesses as a favored target of the DOJ's prosecutorial efforts in immigration cases. Recent policy statements from the DOJ and DHS have made clear that the government expects America's businesses to increasingly work together with the government to curb illegal immigration or else face severe sanctions.[6] At the same time, DOJ has refused to collaborate with businesses to address any isolated problems that may arise in their hiring practices and has sought unprecedented penalties to resolve immigration investigations.[7] Indeed, at least one of the businesses that was among one of the first to volunteer for new government programs designed to stem illegal immigration was also among the first DOJ targets for investigation and prosecution when something went wrong in a part of the company. Even when those federal prosecutions have been unsuccessful, the government's charges have led to years of follow-on civil litigation, with attendant costs and distractions for the businesses involved.

In sum, the business community has never been more at risk in immigration matters. The government wants—indeed, demands—that businesses do more to assist the government's compliance efforts. Thus far, however, the government's invitation to

---

[6] For example, Homeland Security Secretary Michael Chertoff has stated that the government "owe[s] . . . employers . . . tools to verify their employees in a prompt and accurate manner." Press Release, Dep't of Homeland Security, Press Conference with Secretary Michael Chertoff, Chief of the Border Patrol David Aguilar and Acting Director of the Office of Detention and Removal John Torres on the Secure Border Initiative 7 (Dec. 1, 2005), *available at www.dhs.gov/xnews/releases/press_release_0799.shtm*. However, Chertoff also stated that once the government gives employers these tools, "they owe it to [the government] to use those tools," and if they do not use them, the government will have to sanction them. *Id.* Indeed, Chertoff announced at a news conference in 2006 that he would use everything "we have, whether it be criminal enforcement or immigration laws to break the back" of businesses that hire illegal immigrants. Terry Frieden & Mike M. Ahlers, *Companies Using Illegal Workers to be Targeted: Immigration Arrests 9 IFCO Bosses Along with 1,000 Workers*, CNN.Com, Apr. 21, 2006, www.cnn.com/2006/LAW/04/20/immigration.raids/index.html. Discussed at greater length *infra*, the government's record of using "tools" to aid businesses in verifying employment eligibility has been less than stellar. In fact, at least one company that volunteered to participate in the testing and implementation of the tools Secretary Chertoff discusses was one of the DOJ's first targets for criminal prosecution when Chertoff led the DOJ's Criminal Division.

[7] *See* Eric Rich, *Immigration Enforcement's Shift in the Workplace: Case of Md. Restaurateurs Reflects Use of Criminal Investigations, Rather Than Fines, Against Employers,* Wash. Post, Apr. 16, 2006, at C06:

> Serious criminal charges once typically reserved for drug traffickers and organized-crime figures are increasingly being used to target businesses that employ illegal immigrants, a strategy highlighted last week when three Maryland restaurateurs pleaded guilty to federal offenses and agreed to forfeit more than $1 million in cash and property.
>
> The little-publicized approach, which can include charging such employers with money laundering and seizing their assets, amounts to a strategic shift in the enforcement of immigration law in the workplace.
>
> As a result, investigations into the employment of illegal immigrants, known as worksite enforcement, resulted in 127 criminal convictions in 2005 nationwide, up from 46 the previous year . . . .

work in a closer partnership—one that many business leaders would surely like to accept—has provided businesses with few or no benefits and significant risks.

This article discusses the paradox in the federal government's attempts to invite closer cooperation with businesses while simultaneously sending the signal that cooperation with the government can be dangerous. It suggests ways that the government could achieve greater results by entering into true partnerships with American businesses. This article points out several key defenses available to businesses that are charged with failing to comply with America's complex immigration laws and ways in which companies can avoid becoming the targets of immigration investigations. Finally, this article reviews the creative civil litigation that is being filed in an attempt to capitalize on the nation's immigration problems.

The Beginning of Corporate Deputization in Immigration Affairs

The federal government's effort to deputize America's businesses in immigration matters began in 1986, when Congress passed the Immigration Reform and Control Act (IRCA).[8] That act has been amended several times as Congress has sought solutions to the nation's immigration problems.[9] Under the current form of IRCA, businesses are required to examine certain types of identification documents to verify that each job applicant is eligible for employment in the United States.[10] Employers are required to retain the I-9 forms completed in the application process, and may elect to retain copies of the identification documents presented.[11] Employing any individual without verifying the individual's identity and employment authorization can subject a business to civil penalties.[12] IRCA also makes it illegal, among other things, to knowingly hire an undocumented worker, or to retain such an individual in employ-

---

[8] Immigration Reform and Control Act of 1986 (IRCA), Pub. L. No. 99-603, 100 Stat. 3359.

[9] *See, e.g.*, Illegal Immigration Reform and Immigrant Responsibility Act of 1996 (IIRAIRA), Pub. L. No. 104-208, div. C, 110 Stat. 3009, 3009-546 to 3009-724.

[10] 8 USC §1324a(b)(1)(A) ("The person or entity must attest, under penalty of perjury and on a form designated or established by the Attorney General by regulation, that it has verified that the individual is not an unauthorized alien by examining [certain specified categories of documents]."); *see also* U.S. Citizenship and Immigration Services (USCIS), *Handbook for Employers: Instructions for Completing Form 1-9* (2007), *available at www.uscis.gov/files/nativedocuments/m-274.pdf* (explaining that the law requires employers to ensure that their employees fill out section 1 of the I-9 when they start work, to review documents establishing each employee's identity and eligibility to work, to properly complete section 2 of the I-9, to retain the I-9 the later of either three years after the date the person begins work or one year after the person's employment is terminated, and to make the I-9 available for inspection to an officer on request).

[11] 8 USC §1324a(b)(3) (discussing retention of the I-9 form); 8 USC §1324a(b)(4) ("Notwithstanding any other provision of law, the person or entity may copy a document presented by an individual pursuant to this subsection and may retain the copy, but only (except as otherwise permitted under law) for the purpose of complying with the requirements of this subsection.").

[12] 8 USC §1324a(a)(1)(B)(i) ("It is unlawful for a person or other entity . . . to hire for employment in the United States an individual without complying with the [employment verification requirements]."); 8 USC §1324a(e)(5) (discussing civil penalty for paperwork violations); 8 CFR §274a.10(b)(2).

ment after learning of his or her illegal status,[13] and businesses in violation of these provisions can be subject to both civil and criminal sanctions.[14] In passing this legislation, Congress was clearly trying to curb the flow of undocumented aliens in the United States by deputizing corporate America to reduce job opportunities for unauthorized aliens.[15]

In theory, complying with this verification process would seem to be fairly straightforward for employers and effective in combating illegal immigration. In reality, however, the process has imposed great burdens and risks on American employers, while failing to prevent the employment of unauthorized aliens. The main problem is one of counterfeit documents. While American employers are required to visually examine an applicant's identification and employment verification documents (which commonly consist of a driver's license or other photo identification, together with a Social Security card), counterfeit documents are readily available for purchase almost anywhere in America.[16]

Skeptics may say that counterfeit documents should be easily detected by prospective employers. But from our own experience with immigration-related cases, we can report that the counterfeit documents that are commonly traded on the street often appear as genuine as those issued by government agencies. In fact, in the Tyson Foods case discussed below, even the federal immigration agents and DOJ prosecutors involved in the case had difficulty determining with accuracy which of the suspected aliens were, in fact, unauthorized. Private experts hired by plaintiffs' lawyers in the immigration-related civil litigation discussed below have had similar difficul-

---

[13] 8 USC §1324a(a)(1)(A) ("It is unlawful for a person or other entity . . . to hire . . . for employment in the United States an alien knowing the alien is an unauthorized alien . . . with respect to such employment..."); 8 USC §1324a(a)(2) ("It is unlawful for a person or other entity, after hiring an alien for employment ... , to continue to employ the alien in the United States knowing the alien is (or has become) an unauthorized alien with respect to such employment.").

[14] 8 CFR §274a.10(a) (discussing criminal penalties); 8 CFR §274a.10(b)(1) (discussing civil penalties).

[15] *See, e.g., Steiben v. INS*, 932 F.2d 1225, 1227 (8th Cir. 1991) ("In an effort to deter illegal immigration, Congress designed . . . §1324a to control the unlawful employment of aliens in the United States by subjecting persons or entities who hire unauthorized aliens to civil and criminal penalties."); *Patel v. Quality Inn South*, 846 F.2d 700, 704 (11th Cir. 1988) ("Congress enacted [IRCA] to reduce illegal immigration by eliminating employers' economic incentive to hire undocumented aliens. To achieve this objective [IRCA] imposes an escalating series of sanctions on employers who hire such workers.").

[16] *See, e.g.*, Warren St. John, *In the ID War, The Fakes Gain*, N.Y. Times, Mar. 6, 2005, at 9:

> College students are becoming increasingly adept at making believable fake ID's for use at bars and clubs, using better computer technology to create better products . . . . The nation's fixation with security cards and ID systems has also been a boon for manufacturers of fake ID's. The widespread use of corporate ID's has created a large pool of people who know the inner workings of the security features in the cards. In online chat rooms dedicated exclusively to the manufacture of fake ID's, unscrupulous members of this pool—including some drivers' license bureau workers, the police say—share or sell information about security features and even run a black market in the more sophisticated components of ID's.

The Problem of Knowing Who Is Really Among Us, Tampa Trib., June 10, 2002, at 12 ("A big gap in U.S. security is the ease with which anyone can get either phony identification or authentic documents based on false information . . . . A birth certificate is easy to forge, and it can be used to get a driver's license.").

ties. Employers can spot fake identification documents that are obvious (*e.g.*, when the document has plainly been altered), but the average American businessperson is not an expert in document authentication. Moreover, under federal civil rights laws, employers must be careful not to impose higher standards of questioning or document scrutiny on applicants who do not speak English or who are of any particular national origin.[17] In sum, traditionally an employer has complied with IRCA by asking for identification and accepting IDs that reasonably appear to be genuine.[18] An employer can do no more and no less.

---

[17] 8 USC §1324a(b)(1)(A)(ii) ("If an individual provides a document or combination of documents that reasonably appears on its face to be genuine and that is sufficient to meet the requirements ... , nothing in this paragraph shall be construed as requiring the person or entity to solicit the production of any other document or as requiring the individual to produce such another document."); 8 USC §1324b(a)(1) ("It is an unfair immigration-related employment practice for a person or other entity to discriminate against any individual (other than an unauthorized alien . . .) with respect to the hiring . . . of the individual for employment or the discharging of the individual from employment—(A) because of such individual's national origin, or (B) in the case of a protected individual . . . , because of such individual's citizenship status."); 8 USC §1324b(a)(6):

> A person's or other entity's request, for purposes of satisfying the requirements of section 1324a(b) of this title, for more or different documents than are required under such section or refusing to honor documents tendered that on their face reasonably appear to be genuine shall be treated as an unfair immigration-related employment practice if made for the purpose or with the intent of discriminating against an individual in violation of paragraph (1).

In fact, shortly before the DOJ accused Tyson Foods of being too lax in its hiring practices, the federal government notified Tyson that it was investigating whether the company had been too stringent in questioning Latino applicants to ensure that they were authorized to work in the United States. *See* Scott Kilman, *The Economy: Tyson Alien-Smuggling Trial Promises To Prove a Landmark*, Wall St. J., Feb. 3, 2003, at A2.

[18] *See* 8 USC §1324a(b)(1)(A)(ii) ("A person or entity has complied . . . with respect to examination of a document if the document reasonably appears on its face to be genuine."); 8 CFR §274a.1(1)(2) (stating that employers are not permitted "to refuse to honor documents tendered that on their face reasonably appear to be genuine and to relate to the individual."); *Collins Foods Int'l, Inc. v. INS*, 948 F.2d 549, 554 (9th Cir. 1991) recognizing:

> [T]he legislative history of section 1324a indicates that Congress intended to minimize the burden and the risk placed on the employer in the verification process. The Judiciary Committee Report for the Act shows that Congress did not intend the statute to cause employers to become experts in identifying and examining a prospective employee's employment authorization documents.

H.R. Rep. No. 99-682, pt. 1, at 61 (1986) ("It is not expected that employers ascertain the legitimacy of documents presented during the verification process."); *id.* at 62 ("The 'reasonable man' standard is to be used in implementing this provision and the Committee wishes to emphasize that documents that reasonably appear to be genuine should be accepted by employers without requiring further investigation of those documents."); 2 Nat'l Law. Guild, *Immigration Law & Defense*, §12.3, at 12-7 & n.5 (2001):

> In view of the limited authority to inquire into the employee's documentation, and of the availability of the good faith verification defense, it seemed reasonable to assume that the government would be required to establish the employer's actual awareness of the employee's unlawful status rather than rely on the employer's duty to inquire more fully . . . . The *House Judiciary Report* emphasizes that employers are not required to further investigate documents which reasonably appear genuine.

Nancy-Jo Merritt & Joanne T. Stark, *The Immigration Reform & Control Act of 1986: What Employers Need To Know*, 22 Ariz. Bar J. 6, 10 (1987) ("Note that according to House Report 99-662 [sic], the

Employers' compliance with Congress' verification system is mandatory.[19] An employer who fails to comply with the employment verification requirements is subject to a civil penalty of between $110 and $1,100—for each individual violation.[20] In determining the amount of this penalty, five factors are considered: the size of the employer's business, the employer's good faith, the violation's seriousness, whether the employee in question is in fact an unauthorized alien, and the history of previous employer violations.[21] Additionally, the government often equates a company's failure to verify the employment eligibility of its employees with evidence that the company knowingly hired undocumented workers. Under IRCA, employers who knowingly hire an unauthorized alien,[22] or retain in employment an unauthorized alien after learning the alien does not have the legal right to work in the United States,[23] may be civilly fined between $275 and $2,200 for each alien so hired or retained,[24] and the range of prescribed fines increases for repeat offenders.[25] Furthermore, IRCA makes it a civil violation for anyone, including employers, to "knowingly" "accept" or "provide" any forged or false documents to satisfy any of the DHS hiring or employment verification requirements,[26] and penalties range from $250 to $2,000 for each forged document violation.[27]

Congress has also authorized criminal charges—either misdemeanor or felony—for certain violations of IRCA. If an employer is found to have engaged "in a pattern or practice" of knowingly hiring illegal immigrants (or retaining them after learning of their unauthorized status), IRCA imposes misdemeanor criminal penalties of up to

---

employer is not expected to ascertain the 'legitimacy of the documents' but only to examine them and note whether they are reasonable on their face.").

[19] There are a few exceptions based on IRCA's limited definition of "employee." "Employee" is defined as "an individual who provides services or labor for an employer for wages or other remuneration but does *not* mean independent contractors . . . or those engaged in casual domestic employment." 8 CFR §274a.1(f) (emphasis added). "Independent contractor" is, in turn, defined to include "individuals or entities who carry on independent business, contract to do a piece of work according to their own means and methods, and are subject to control only as to results." 8 CFR §274a.1(j). "Casual domestic employment" is "casual employment by individuals who provide domestic service in a private home that is sporadic, irregular or intermittent." 8 CFR §274a.1(h).

[20] 8 CFR §274a.10(b)(2). This assumes the violation took place on or after September 29, 1999. If the violation took place before such date, the penalty range is $100 to $1,000. 8 CFR §274a.10(b)(2).

[21] 8 CFR §274a.10(b)(2).

[22] 8 USC §1324a(a)(1)(A) ("It is unlawful for a person or other entity . . . to hire . . . for employment in the United States an alien knowing the alien is an unauthorized alien . . . with respect to such employment.").

[23] 8 USC §1324a(a)(2) ("It is unlawful for a person or other entity, after hiring an alien for employment..., to continue to employ the alien in the United States knowing the alien is (or has become) an unauthorized alien with respect to such employment.").

[24] 8 CFR §274a.10(b)(1)(ii). This assumes the violation took place on or after September 29, 1999. If the violation took place before such date, the penalty range is $250 to $2,000. 8 CFR §274a.10(b)(1)(ii).

[25] 8 CFR §274a.10(b)(1)(ii).

[26] 8 USC §1324c(a)(2)-(4).

[27] 8 USC §1324c(d)(3)(A). The prescribed penalty range increases to $2,000 to $5,000 for repeat offenders. 8 USC §1324c(d)(3)(B).

$3,000 in fines for each unauthorized alien and/or imprisonment of up to six months.[28] Furthermore, if the employer "knowingly hires for employment at least ten individuals with actual knowledge that the individuals are aliens" during any 12-month period, the employer has committed a felony and may be fined and/or imprisoned for up to five years.[29]

Employers may also be charged with non–employment-specific immigration violations that carry criminal sanctions. For example,

> [a]ny person who—(i) knowing that a person is an alien, brings to or attempts to bring to the United States in any manner whatsoever such person at a place other than a designated port of entry . . . (ii) knowing or in reckless disregard of the fact that an alien has come to, entered, or remains in the United States in violation of law, transports, or moves or attempts to transport or move such alien within the United States by means of transportation or otherwise . . . (iii) knowing or in reckless disregard of the fact that an alien has come to, entered, or remains in the United States in violation of law, conceals, harbors, or shields from detection, or attempts to conceal, harbor, or shield from detection, such alien in any place . . . (iv) encourages or induces an alien to come to, enter, or reside in the United States, knowing or in reckless disregard of the fact that such coming to, entry, or residence is or will be in violation of law; or (v)(I) engages in any conspiracy to commit any of the preceding acts, or (II) aids or abets the commission of any of the preceding acts[30]

may be fined, imprisoned, or even sentenced to death, depending upon the particular violation and the aggravating circumstances.[31]

---

[28] 8 USC §1324a(f)(1); 8 CFR §274a.10(a).

[29] 8 USC §1324(a)(3)(A).

[30] 8 USC §1324(a)(1)(A). In *U.S. v. Kim*, 193 F.3d 567 (2d Cir. 1999), the U.S. Court of Appeals for the Second Circuit held that employment of an undocumented worker may, in some circumstances, constitute "harboring" of unlawfully present alien under 8 USC §1324(a)(1). The defendant, who employed the alien, contended that the employment of an undocumented worker does not constitute "harboring" under §1324(a)(1) and that he should have been charged under 8 USC §1324a, which is specifically directed at employers. *Id.* at 572. (Presumably, the reason that the defendant was not charged under §1324(a)(3)(A) was that the defendant did not hire "at least ten" aliens.) The Second Circuit rejected the challenge, holding that §1324(a)(1) was "sufficiently broad on its face" to encompass the harboring of "illegal aliens" by employers. *Id.* at 574. It found that the defendant knew of or recklessly disregarded the employee's unlawful status and took steps to help her remain in his employ, such as instructing her to make a false statement to legacy INS, obtain false documentation, and submit a misleading I-9 form. *Id.* at 574–75. The court held that these facts demonstrated that the defendant attempted to facilitate the alien's unlawful presence in the United States and prevent her detection by legacy INS, and that he therefore "harbored" the alien within the meaning of §1324(a)(1). *Id.*

[31] 8 USC §1324(a)(1)(B). The death penalty is only reserved as an option when there is a violation of subparagraph (A)(i), (ii), (iii), (iv), or (v) "resulting in the death of any person." 8 USC §1324(a)(1)(B)(iv). In the case of a violation of subparagraph (A)(i) or (v)(I), or in the case of a violation of (A)(ii), (iii), or (iv) "in which the offense was done for the purpose of commercial advantage or private financial gain," the term of imprisonment may be up to 10 years. 8 USC §1324(a)(1)(B)(i). In the case of a violation of subparagraph (A)(ii), (iii), (iv), or (v)(II), the term of imprisonment may be up

Furthermore, "[a]ny person who, knowing or in reckless disregard of the fact that an alien has not received prior official authorization to come to, enter, or reside in the United States, brings to or attempts to bring to the United States in any manner whatsoever, such alien" may be fined and/or imprisoned for up to 10 years if the "offense [was] committed for the purpose of commercial advantage or private financial gain."[32] Similarly, "[a]ny person who knowingly aids or assists any alien inadmissible under [certain sections] . . . to enter the United States, or who connives or conspires with any person or persons to allow, procure, or permit any such alien to enter the United States" may be fined and/or imprisoned for up to 10 years.[33] As discussed in more detail *infra*, the government sometimes charges employers who have allegedly hired unauthorized aliens with additional, nonhiring offenses such as these,[34] and violations of 8 USC §§1324 and 1327 (but not sections 1324a or 1324c) may serve as predicate offenses for a RICO violation.[35]

The Case Studies of Tyson Foods, Wal-Mart, Golden State Fence Co., and Swift: DOJ's Efforts to Create Increased Penalties for Employers' Immigration-Related Violations

Congress has specified a myriad set of civil and criminal penalties for various violations of IRCA. As with all statutory penalties, the amounts prescribed by Congress are the product of a balance between competing interests and reflect Congress's judgment about the relative seriousness of these offenses in the federal criminal system. Since Congress deputized employers to fight illegal immigration in 1986, DOJ has applied IRCA's penalty provisions to obtain a number of convictions and settlements from employers. However, there is substantial evidence that DOJ considers the penalties that Congress authorized to be too small and that DOJ is actively seeking ways to exceed those penalties.

Until Wal-Mart's unprecedented $11 million settlement in 2005, the largest penalty that DOJ had imposed on any employer under IRCA was $2.1 million.[36] Al-

---

to five years. 8 USC §1324(a)(1)(B)(ii). In the case of a violation of subparagraph (A)(i), (ii), (iii), (iv), or (v) "during and in relation to which the person causes serious bodily injury . . . to or places in jeopardy the life of, any person," the term of imprisonment may be up to 20 years. 8 USC §1324(a)(1)(B)(iii).

[32] 8 USC §1324(a)(2)(B)(ii).

[33] 8 USC §1327.

[34] For example, several counts in the indictment against Tyson Foods alleged various violations of 8 USC §1324. Indictment 48, *United States v. Tyson Foods, Inc.*, No. CR-4-01-61 (E.D. Tenn. filed Dec. 11, 2001) (hereinafter Indictment) (counts 3 through 7 alleged violations of 8 USC §1324(a)(2)(B)(ii) and 18 USC §2); *id.* at 49 (counts 8 through 12 alleged violations of 8 USC §§1324(a)(1)(A)(ii) and 1324(a)(1)(B)(i) and 18 USC §2); *id.* at 51 (counts 14 and 15 alleged violations of 8 USC §1324(a)(2)(B)(ii) and 18 USC §2); *id.* at 52 (counts 16 through 20 alleged violations of 8 USC §§1324(a)(1)(A)(ii) and 1324(a)(1)(B)(i) and 18 USC §2).

[35] 18 USC §1961(1)(F).

[36] Lauren Coleman-Lochner, *Wal-Mart Settles Federal Complaint; Cleaning Firms Hired Illegal Immigrants, U.S. Says; Penalty Is a Record $11 Million*, Char. Observer, Mar. 19, 2005, at 1D ("The previous record fine for immigration employment violations was $2.1 million paid by Iowa egg producer DeCos-

though a former record, the $2.1 million payment was actually not far in excess of the well-established level of fines that had been levied in immigration cases.[37] In fiscal year 2001 the government levied 292 sanctions against employers for a total of about $1.6 million in fines; in fiscal year 1999, there were 890 sanctions for a total of about $3.7 million in fines.[38] However, in contrast to this established level of punishment for immigration-related offenses, DOJ sought to establish a dramatic new precedent in its investigation and prosecution of Tyson Foods.

The Tyson Foods investigation began in 1997.[39] As part of the investigation, undercover federal agents posed as smugglers of aliens, gathered supposed undocumented aliens at the Texas-Mexico border, and transported them to various Tyson facilities, where the agent tried to lure local managers into hiring the aliens.[40] At the

---

ter Farms, said Manny Van Pelt, a spokesman for the Bureau of Immigration and Customs Enforcement."); *see also* Chris Strohm, *DHS Calls on Corporations to Come Clean on Hiring Illegal Immigrants*, Am. Renaissance, Mar. 18, 2005, ("So far this fiscal year, however, ICE has reached a settlement with DeCoster Farms for hiring illegal workers, under which the company agreed to pay $2.1 million . . . ."), *available at* www.amren.com/mtnews/archives/2005/03/dhs_calls_on_co.php.

[37] In 1999, legacy INS collected the largest fine ever imposed at that time ($1.9 million) in a worksite enforcement investigation. *Restaurant Owners Fined $1.9 Million for Illegal Hiring Practices*, INS Communiqué, July 1999, at 10. The settlement resulted from the arrest of nearly 200 aliens working at 15 different restaurants owned by Filiberto's, an Arizona-based chain of Mexican eateries. *Id.* In 1998, ConAgra Poultry Co. paid $223,000 to settle an allegation that the company hired undocumented workers at its former Glasgow plant. *ConAgra Poultry Will Pay U.S. $223,000*, Louisville Courier-J., Apr. 21, 1998, at B6. The settlement included a $123,000 civil fine and a $100,000 payment toward investigation and prosecution costs. *Id.* The case originated when legacy INS removed 24 aliens from the plant in 1996, and the settlement came on the heels of guilty pleas by a plant manager, personnel manager, payroll manager, and line supervisor. *Id.* These employees pled guilty to various charges, including harboring aliens not authorized to be in the United States and providing false documents. *Id.* In 1997, Pappas Partners, a Texas-based restaurant chain, paid a $1.75 million fine after a three-year investigation uncovered evidence that undocumented workers were knowingly hired and, in some instances, were concealed during immigration raids. William Branigin, *Texas Restaurant Chain to Pay Record $1.75 Million Fine for Harboring Illegal Aliens*, Wash. Post, Aug. 14, 1997, at A10. The case against the 54-restaurant chain resulted from several raids in which more than 120 arrests of aliens were made. *Id.* As part of the plea bargain, the company also agreed to plead guilty to four felony counts of shielding unauthorized aliens. *Id.* In 1996, a New York cleaning service was assessed a $1.5 million civil fine for knowingly hiring undocumented workers. Celia W. Dugger, *Federal Agency Fines Company a Record $1.5 Million for Hiring Illegal Immigrants*, N.Y. Times, Mar. 22, 1996, at B6. Legacy INS levied the fine after determining there were more than 150 instances of the knowing hiring and continued employment of undocumented workers, and 2,500 instances of failing to maintain proper employee records. *Id.* In 1992, legacy INS fined a Georgia peach harvester $1.1 million because company employees engaged in a scheme to smuggle aliens into the United States. Peter Applebome, *Georgia Harvester Is Fined $1 Million in Alien Smuggling*, N.Y. Times, Feb. 8, 1992, at A1. Legacy INS alleged four employees, including one supervisor, of Lane Packing Company smuggled about 2,000 aliens into the country. *Id.*

[38] Strohm, *supra* note 36.

[39] Sherri Day, *Jury Clears Tyson Foods in Use of Illegal Immigrants*, N.Y. Times, Mar. 27, 2003, at A14 (hereinafter Day, *Jury*); Editorial, *Justice Department Fowl*, Wall St. J., Mar. 28, 2003, at A12.

[40] *See* Sherri Day, *Prosecutors in Smuggling Case Against Tyson Contend Trial Is About "Corporate Greed,"* N.Y. Times, Feb. 6, 2003, at A26 [hereinafter Day, *Prosecutors*] ("The government's case is based almost entirely on findings by I.N.S. agents who posed as transporters of immigrants from the Mexican border to various Tyson factories in several states, including Tennessee, Virginia, North Carolina and Arkansas."); *see also* Day, *Jury*, *supra* note 39 ("The government . . . us[ed] undercover agents

close of the investigation DOJ claimed that the company had hired 136 undocumented aliens to work among its thousands of employees at plants in six states.[41] DOJ obtained a 36-count indictment against the company in 2001, alleging various violations of IRCA.[42] The indictment also alleged that Tyson Foods had created a "corporate culture" that condoned the hiring of undocumented workers.[43] Although the government claimed that Tyson had hired 136 undocumented aliens, the indictment only named 15 alleged illegal workers.[44]

Tyson Foods acknowledged that its hiring process was not foolproof, but it denied that upper management had conspired to break the immigration laws. In fact, the company emphasized to DOJ (and later to the judge and jury) that management had worked hard to ensure that IRCA's requirements were followed at each of Tyson's various facilities by, among other things, voluntarily using a computer-based employment document verification program offered by the government that was designed to increase the likelihood of catching unauthorized aliens seeking employment.[45] Only 1 percent of employers had assisted DOJ by volunteering for this program, and Tyson was among the first to do so.[46] The district judge dismissed 24 charges related to immigrant smuggling; and Tyson went to trial in Chattanooga, TN

---

posing as labor recruiters to track the company's employment practices."); Kilman, *supra* note 17 ("As part of the 2½-year undercover investigation, agents transported about 130 illegal aliens from the Mexican border to Tyson's poultry plant in Shelbyville.").

[41] *Justice Department Fowl, supra* note 39 ("An undercover agent posing as a smuggler said the company was importing workers from south of the border to staff plants in six states. He counted 136 undocumented cases in total.").

[42] Indictment, *supra* note 34; *see also* Day, *Jury*, *supra* note 39 (reporting that there were originally 36 counts); *Justice Department Fowl, supra* note 39 (reporting that Tyson was acquitted of 36 counts).

[43] Indictment, *supra* note 34, at 10; *see also* Editorial. *The Forfeiture Precedent*, Wall St. J., Jan. 24, 2002, at A18 ("The indictment adds that Tyson management created a 'corporate culture' that condoned the hiring of illegals.").

[44] *The Forfeiture Precedent, supra* note 43 ("Yet despite two years, and a complicated string operation, the indictment names only 15 actual illegal hires."); *Justice Department Fowl, supra* note 39 ("The eventual indictment named 15 people.").

[45] *See* Day, *Jury, supra* note 39 ("Tyson was in the 1 percent of employers who volunteered to go on a computerized identification checking system. Tyson was cooperating with the government every time there was the slightest wrinkle or knowledge of a hiring problem."); Day, *Prosecutors, supra* note 40 ("Tyson also said that its co-defendants were innocent and offered voluntarily to participate in the testing of the I.N.S. computer program that was designed to ferret out fake identification documents as proof the company's innocence."); Kilman, *supra* note 17 ("Tyson was one of the first companies to voluntarily adopt an INS computer system for verifying the identification documents presented by prospective employees."); Brian Lazenby, *Tyson Foods, Managers Acquitted on All Charges: Prosecutors Attempted To Show Corporate Conspiracy*, Chattanooga Times Free Press (Tennessee), Mar. 27, 2003, at A1 ("Mr. Hopson said the corporation's voluntary implementation of government programs to prevent illegal aliens from being hired is proof Tyson did everything in its power to hire only legal workers"). This program is discussed in more detail *infra*.

[46] Day, *Jury, supra* note 39; *see also* Kilman, *supra* note 17 ("Tyson was one of the first companies to voluntarily adopt an INS computer system for verifying the identification documents presented by prospective employees.").

on the remaining counts in 2003.[47] The jury—after a mere five hours of deliberation, despite a four-year investigation and seven-week trial—acquitted Tyson of the remaining 12 counts that alleged conspiracy, transportation of illegal workers, and document falsification[48] In sum, the case established that Tyson Foods was innocent on all counts.

As noted below, there are a number of reasons why DOJ's investigation and prosecution of Tyson Foods never should have occurred and why DOJ must change its practices if it wants to encourage closer partnerships with American businesses. For current purposes, it is important to note DOJ's settlement demands in the Tyson case and the theory that prosecutors used in justifying those demands. Prior to the indictment, prosecutors wanted $140 million to settle the case; by the start of the trial, their demand decreased to about $30 million,[49] still more than 15 times the amount of the previous record settlement in a similar case.[50]

The difference between DOJ's previous record settlements and the amounts it demanded from Tyson Foods is striking. No application of IRCA's penalty provisions could support the government's demands. Accordingly, the government advanced a novel theory to justify its position. The government claimed that undocumented aliens are presumably willing to work for substandard wages and that, by allegedly employing 136 undocumented workers in six plants, Tyson Foods was able to pay a below market wage. In other words, DOJ claimed that hiring a handful of undocumented workers allowed Tyson to "suppress" the wages that it otherwise would have been required to pay to obtain an all-legal workforce.[51] The government demanded that Tyson forfeit (to the government) the difference between the allegedly sup-

---

[47] *Justice Department Fowl, supra* note 39; *see also* Day, *Jury, supra* note 39 (reporting that the judge dismissed twenty-four of the thirty-six counts); Lazenby, *supra* note 45 (reporting that the judge dismissed twenty-four counts, nine before the start of the trial and fifteen after the prosecution had rested).

[48] *Justice Department Fowl, supra* note 39; *see also* Day, *Jury, supra* note 39 (reporting a jury acquittal after five hours of deliberation); Lazenby, *supra* note 45 (reporting that the jury had acquitted Tyson Foods of all charges after a seven-week trial).

[49] *Justice Department Fowl, supra* note 39 ("Prior to the indictment prosecutors wanted $140 million to go away .... By the start of the trial, the government had reduced its demand to around $30 million.").

[50] *See* Strohm, *supra* note 36 (referring to the previous record fine of $2.1 million paid by Iowa egg producer DeCoster Farms).

[51] *See* Day, *Prosecutors, supra* note 40 (stating, "Federal prosecutors told jurors today that corporate greed caused Tyson Foods, the nation's largest meat producer and processor, to conspire to suppress its workers' wages by smuggling illegal immigrants from Mexico to work in the company's chicken plants in the United States"); *see also* Gary Young, *Tyson May Face More Litigation: Wage-Scheme Allegation To Be Renewed with New Type of Civil Claim*, Nat'l L.J., Mar. 31, 2003, at A7:

> Now that a jury has acquitted Tyson Foods Inc. of criminal violations of immigration law, federal prosecutors can no longer insist, as they had throughout the trial, that the food processing giant forfeit some $24 million that it allegedly saved by hiring illegal aliens. But the acquittal hasn't persuaded Howard W. Foster . . . that Tyson is blameless.... Foster represents four former Tyson employees who claim that their wages, and the wages of a whole class of Tyson employees similarly situated, were driven down by Tyson's alleged scheme.

pressed wages that Tyson paid the workers at the six plants over the course of five years and what it allegedly "should" have paid them.[52]

Because Tyson was found innocent of the government's charges, the myriad problems with the government's theory were never tested as part of DOJ's case. However, this did not end DOJ's quest for markedly higher payments from companies whose workers may have violated IRCA. The government's investigation of Wal-Mart provides another example of DOJ's continued efforts to impose significantly higher penalties on employers who are suspected of immigration violations.

From 1998 to 2003, DOJ conducted a probe of Wal-Mart's cleaning contractors and concluded that Wal-Mart's contractors knowingly hired undocumented workers at more than 1,000 stores.[53] In October 2003, federal agents raided 61 Wal-Mart stores in 21 states and arrested about 245 illegal immigrants who had been employed by the contractors.[54] Following the raids, Wal-Mart entered into an $11 million settlement agreement.[55] Although Wal-Mart did not admit to any wrongdoing in the agreement and stated that it was not aware that its contractors were hiring illegal workers, the company did acknowledge that it had failed to have proper procedures in place to identify whether its contractors were complying with immigration laws in hiring cleaning contractors.[56] It also agreed to implement a compliance and training program to establish a means to verify that its independent contractors were taking "reasonable steps" to comply with immigration laws and to provide all current and future store managers with training on immigration employment laws.[57] The 12 cleaning service companies used by Wal-Mart that actually hired the undocumented workers forfeited an additional $4 million and pled guilty to criminal immigration charges.[58]

The government's $11 million settlement with Wal-Mart is by far the largest civil settlement ever in a case involving alleged hiring of illegal immigrants.[59] Because DOJ said that it suspected violations of IRCA at 1,000 stores, the higher amount

---

[52] *See* Day, *Jury, supra* note 39 (stating, "[T]he government said it would seek to enact a rarely used forfeiture claim to seek millions of dollars of Tyson's profits that the company earned during the time that the incidents were said to have occurred"); Day, *Prosecutors, supra* note 40 (stating, "If the company is found guilty, prosecutors are seeking to invoke a forfeiture claim, usually reserved for illegal drug cases, that would allow the government to seize profits that the company made during the time that the reported offenses were committed"); *Justice Department Fowl, supra* note 39 (stating, "Justice also abused its power by trying to apply forfeiture law, under which a guilty defendant must give the government any ill-gotten gains. The tactic is usually reserved for drug dealers, and it recalls other efforts to expand criminal statutes—like RICO—into areas where they were never intended."); Kilman, *supra* note 17 (stating, "Instead of seeking fines, prosecutors say that if the company is found guilty, they will demand that it forfeit any ill-gotten gains, a tactic more commonly used on drug dealers").

[53] Coleman-Lochner, *supra* note 36.

[54] *Id.*

[55] *Id.*

[56] Strohm, *supra* note 36.

[57] *Id.*

[58] *Id.*

[59] *Id.*; *see also* Coleman-Lochner, *supra* note 36.

could have reflected simply an application of IRCA's penalty provisions to a broader set of facts. Yet DOJ went out of its way to rebut this conclusion, and clarified that settling with Wal-Mart for this record sum is indicative of DOJ's intent to secure higher payments from employers in immigration investigations. The spokesman for U.S. Immigration and Customs Enforcement (ICE) at the Department of Homeland Security, Manny Van Pelt, stated of the Wal-Mart settlement: "It shows we're going after bigger, bigger money."[60] Van Pelt elaborated: "We may have smaller investigations, but we're going for a larger breadth of investigations and bigger civil settlements and criminal fines."[61]

The case studies of Wal-Mart and Tyson Foods set the precedents for later ICE investigations and prosecutions. In 2006 alone, "ICE worksite investigations resulted in 127 criminal convictions and a total of 1,145 arrests, up from 46 criminal convictions and 845 arrests the previous year."[62] As Julie L. Myers, Assistant Secretary of Homeland Security for ICE, stated, "In 2006, ICE tripled the number of arrests made in conjunction with worksite-related investigations and we will be expanding our focus in this arena further in the year ahead."[63] Myers later reaffirmed, "We will pursue egregious violators by seeking criminal charges . . . ."[64]

Although there are numerous examples of ICE investigating and prosecuting businesses since Tyson Foods and Wal-Mart,[65] two case studies deserve brief special mention: those of Golden State Fence and Swift & Company.

---

[60] Chris Strohm, *On the Line*, GOVEXEC.COM, July 1, 2005, *http://govexec.com/features/0705-01/0705-01s1.htm*.

[61] *Id.*

[62] ICE News Release, Recent ICE Worksite Enforcement Cases (May 9, 2006), *www.ice.gov/pi/news/newsreleases/articles/060509worksite.htm*.

[63] ICE News Release, Corporate Executives Plead Guilty to Illegal Hiring Practices: California Company Forfeits $4.7 Million in Profits, Executives Fined (Dec. 15, 2006), *www.ice.gov/pi/news/newsreleases/articles/061215sandiego.htm*.

[64] ICE News Release, ICE Executes Federal Criminal Search Warrants at Koch Foods and Arrests More Than 160 on Immigration Charges: Simultaneous Criminal Search Warrant Executed at Koch Corporate Office in Chicago, IL (Aug. 28, 2007), *www.ice.gov/pi/news/newsreleases/articles/070828cincinnati.htm*.

[65] *See, e.g.*, ICE News Release, QSI Supervisor, Employee Sentenced for Knowingly Hiring Illegal Aliens (Nov. 19, 2007), *www.ice.gov/pi/news/newsreleases/articles/071119springfield.htm*; ICE News Release, N. Kentucky Contractor, Supervisors Sentenced for Harboring Illegal Aliens (Nov. 15, 2007), *www.ice.gov/pi/news/newsreleases/articles/071115covington.htm*; ICE News Release, ICE Probe of Alleged Illegal Hiring Practices Leads to Criminal Charges Against Owner of Oakland Carpentry Business (Nov. 7, 2007), *www.ice.gov/pi/news/newsreleases/articles/071107sanfrancisco.htm*; ICE News Release, ICE Investigation Leads to the Arrest of 23 Workers with Unauthorized Access at O'Hare Airport: Two Others Face Federal Charges as the Result of Multi-Agency Partnership (Nov. 7, 2007), *www.ice.gov/pi/news/newsreleases/articles/071107chicago.htm*; ICE News Release, Owner of Tarrasco Steel Arrested in ICE Probe for Hiring Illegal Alien Workers at Critical Infrastructure Construction Sites (Aug. 3, 2007), *www.ice.gov/pi/news/newsreleases/articles/070803jackson.htm*; ICE News Release, President and Managers of New Bedford Manufacturer Indicted on Charges of Conspiring to Harbor and Hire Illegal Aliens To Fulfill Lucrative Government Contracts (Aug. 2, 2007), *www.ice.gov/pi/news/newsreleases/articles/070802boston.htm*; ICE News Release, Centerville Business

In December 2006, the president and vice-president of Golden State Fence Company, which builds fences for residential, commercial, and military projects in California, pled guilty to the hiring of unauthorized alien workers.[66] As part of the guilty plea, the company agreed to forfeit $4.7 million, and the company's president and vice-president agreed to pay fines of $200,000 and $100,000 respectively.[67] Assistant Secretary Myers lauded the settlement and plea agreement, stating that they were proof that "employers . . . will pay dearly for such transgressions."[68]

Owner Sentenced to Prison for Harboring Illegal Aliens (July 23, 2007), www.ice.gov/pi/news/newsreleases/articles/070723dayton.htm; ICE News Release, Guilty Plea in Government's Probe of Immigration Violations at IFCO Systems (July 16, 2007), www.ice.gov/pi/news/newsreleases/articles/070716albany.htm; ICE News Release, Owners of El Pollo Rico Restaurant Charged with Employing and Harboring Aliens, Money Laundering and Structuring Deposits to Avoid Reporting Requirements: Over $7 Million Deposited in Small Amounts Allegedly To Avoid Reporting over Four Years (July 12, 2007), www.ice.gov/pi/news/newsreleases/articles/070712greenbelt.htm; ICE News Release, Operator of Bay Area Pizza Parlors Charged in ICE Probe for Harboring Illegal Alien Workers from Brazil (June 19, 2007), www.ice.gov/pi/news/newsreleases/articles/070619sanfrancisco.htm; ICE News Release, Roofing Companies Indicted for Money Laundering, Conspiring to Hire Illegal Aliens (June 18, 2007), www.ice.gov/pi/news/newsreleases/articles/070618kansascity.htm; ICE News Release, Company President, Ten Others, Charged in Worksite Probe of Arizona Drywall and Stucco Firm: Case Is First Arizona Worksite Investigation Resulting in Criminal Charges (Mar. 9, 2007), www.ice.gov/pi/news/newsreleases/articles/070309tucson.htm; ICE News Release, New Bedford Manufacturer and Managers Arrested on Charges of Conspiring: ICE to Process Hundreds for Removal (Mar. 6, 2007), www.ice.gov/pi/news/newsreleases/articles/070306boston.htm; ICE News Release, President of Garcia Labor Companies Sentenced to 15 Months in Prison for Conspiring to Provide Illegal Workers to a National Air Cargo Firm: Companies Ordered to Forfeit $12 Million, the Largest Such Forfeiture Ever (Mar. 2, 2007), www.ice.gov/pi/news/newsreleases/articles/070302cincinnati.htm; ICE News Release, Three Executives of National Cleaning Company Indicted for Harboring Illegal Aliens and Evading Taxes: Employees Arrested at 63 Locations in 17 States and D.C. (Feb. 22, 2007), www.ice.gov/pi/news/newsreleases/articles/070222grandrapids.htm; ICE News Release, Owners of Japanese Steakhouse Plead Guilty to Harboring Illegal Aliens (Jan. 18, 2007), www.ice.gov/pi/news/newsreleases/articles/070118hotsprings.htm; ICE News Release, Fairfield Restaurant Owner Pleads Guilty to Employing, Housing Illegal Aliens (Jan. 11, 2007), www.ice.gov/pi/news/newsreleases/articles/070111cincinnati.htm; ICE News Release, Business Owner Must Forfeit $1.5 Million for Conspiring To Harbor Illegal Aliens: Romanian Illegal Alien Also Sentenced to 18 Months in Prison (Dec. 1, 2006), www.ice.gov/pi/news/newsreleases/articles/061201fargo.htm; ICE News Release, Hillman Shrimp and Oyster Company and Five Employees Indicted for Hiring and Recruiting Undocumented Aliens (Oct. 13, 2006), www.ice.gov/pi/news/newsreleases/articles/061013houston.htm; ICE News Release, Business Owner Indicted for Harboring, Transporting Illegal Aliens and Money Laundering in Illegal Employment Scheme: Suspected Faces Possible 40 Years in Prison and Forfeiture of $1.5 Million, (May 2, 2006), www.ice.gov/pi/news/newsreleases/articles/060502dc.htm; ICE News Release, ICE Agents Arrest Seven Managers of Nationwide Pallet Company and 1,187 of the Firm's Illegal Alien Employees in 26 States: Roughly 53 Percent of the Firm's Employees During 2005 Had Invalid/Mismatched Social Security Numbers (Apr. 20, 2006), www.ice.gov/pi/news/newsreleases/articles/060420washington.htm.

[66] ICE News Release, Corporate Executives Plead Guilty to Illegal Hiring Practices: California Company Forfeits $4.7 Million in Profits, Executives Fined (Dec. 15, 2006), www.ice.gov/pi/news/newsreleases/articles/061215sandiego.htm.

[67] Id.

[68] Id.

Less than a year later, in July 2007, ICE arrested 18 employees at Swift & Company, one of the nation's largest processors of pork and beef, on charges related to identity theft and administrative immigration violations. ICE also charged one human resources employee with harboring aliens not authorized to be in the United States and misprision of a felony and charged one union official with harboring such aliens.[69] Harboring aliens who are not authorized to be in the United States can result in up to a five-year prison sentence, while misprision of a felony carries up to a three-year sentence.[70] These recent arrests were in addition to the 1,297 administrative arrests of aliens for immigration violations in December 2006, of which 274 resulted in criminal arrests for identity theft or use of fraudulent documents.[71] As ICE aptly stated in its news release regarding the most recent arrests at Swift, as part of ICE's new strategy "to combat the unlawful employment of illegal aliens in the United States," ICE is "seeking to initiate criminal prosecutions and cause asset forfeitures" of "employers of illegal aliens."[72]

The Government Proposes Increased Cooperation with American Employers

Undoubtedly, the vast majority of American businesses want to avoid employing undocumented workers and would be glad to work cooperatively with the federal government (as long as the government does not unduly shift the costs of immigration enforcement from tax coffers to the expense ledgers of private businesses). As noted above, DOJ and DHS officials have recently made a number of statements about seeking an improved working relationship between government and business in fighting illegal immigration. Commenting on the Wal-Mart settlement, Michael Garcia, then the assistant secretary of homeland security for ICE, stated:

> This case breaks new ground not only because this is a record dollar amount for a civil immigration settlement, but because this settlement requires Wal-Mart to create an internal program to ensure future compliance with immigration laws by Wal-Mart contractors and by Wal-Mart itself. *ICE is committed to not only bringing charges against companies that violate our nation's immigration laws, but also working with them to ensure that they have programs in place to prevent future violations.*[73]

DHS Secretary Michael Chertoff has made similar statements and has overtly recognized the concern that employers have in further investigating employees who were hired with what reasonably appeared to be authentic employment documents

---

[69] ICE News Release, ICE Makes Additional Criminal Arrests at Swift & Company Plants (July 11, 2007), *www.ice.gov/pi/news/newsreleases/articles/070711washingtondc.htm*.

[70] *Id.*

[71] *Id.*

[72] *Id.*

[73] ICE News Release, Walmart Stores, Inc. Agrees To Pay a Record $11 Million to ICE to Settle Nationwide Worksite Enforcement Investigation (Mar. 18, 2005), *www.ice.gov/pi/news/newsreleases/articles/walmart031805.htm* (emphasis added).

when at the same time they are also required to obey the nondiscrimination laws.[74] Because of the problem of forged identification cards, Chertoff has proposed that the government provide employers with "tools" to more accurately verify the actual employment status of each job applicant.[75] That way an employer could know with certainty whether the documents that an applicant presents are genuine.

But the government's actions have contradicted these statements. In fact, as noted above, DOJ has been testing a prototype of the "tool" that Chertoff mentions for a number of years, but thus far DOJ has not worked in partnership with the companies that volunteered to develop that tool. Starting in 1997, the government encouraged employers to volunteer to participate in what was called the "Basic Pilot."[76] Each company that volunteered was given computer equipment that would allow its human resources personnel to check the Social Security numbers provided by applicants against the federal government's databases.[77] Accordingly, job applicants were required to present a photo ID and a Social Security card or alien registration card with a number that matched the information on the photo ID. The government hoped that this would make the process of producing fake documentation much more difficult, since a counterfeiter would need to duplicate an existing person's correct identity rather than simply generate a fake name and a relatively random Social Security

---

[74] Dep't of Homeland Security, *supra* note 6, at 7:

> I think I've testified publicly about my concern that some employers feel that they can't—when they get a no-match letter from the Social Security Administration, they feel they can't pursue any further investigation about why there's a problem with the number. I think we're looking to see what we can do to address that problem.

See also The Forfeiture Precedent, supra note 43 ("Tyson is obligated to check identification, but fakes are common and rigorous inquiry can cause employers to run afoul of anti-discrimination statutes.").

[75] Dep't of Homeland Security, supra note 6, at 7 ("We owe the employers . . . tools to verify their employees in a prompt and accurate manner."); *see also* ICE News Release, ICE Executes Federal Criminal Search Warrants at Koch Foods and Arrests More Than 160 on Immigration Charges: Simultaneous Criminal Search Warrant Executed at Koch Corporate Office in Chicago, IL (Aug. 28, 2007), www.ice.gov/pi/news/newsreleases/articles/070828cincinnati.htm (statement of Julie L. Myers, Assistant Secretary of Homeland Security for ICE) ("We will . . . continue to deploy tools such as the new social security no match guidelines to help businesses comply with the law.").

[76] *See* www.uscis.gov (E-Verify links) (noting that "E-Verify is a re-branding of its predecessor, the Basic Pilot/Employment Eligibility Verification Program, which has been in existence since 1997," and emphasizing that "[a]n employer's participation in E-Verify is voluntary and is currently free . . . .").

[77] *See* U.S. Gov't Accountability Office, Immigration Enforcement: Weaknesses Hinder Employment Verification and Worksite Enforcement Efforts 10–11 (2005), www.gao.gov/new.items/d05813.pdf.

> After completing the [I-9] forms, . . . employers query the pilot program's automated system by entering employee information provided on the forms, such as name and Social Security number, into the pilot Web site within 3 days of the employees' hire date. The pilot program then electronically matches that information against information in SSA and, if necessary, DHS databases to determine whether the employee is eligible to work . . . . The Basic Pilot Program electronically notifies employers whether their employees' work authorization was confirmed.

number.[78] Employers volunteering for Basic Pilot bore their own start-up and operating costs.[79]

Tyson Foods was one of the first companies to volunteer for Basic Pilot.[80] Tyson's management provided training for human resources managers throughout the company and made compliance with the program mandatory. Tyson included the Basic Pilot program in its award-winning[81] corporate compliance program.

When Tyson's compliance program independently uncovered evidence that some local employees in an Alabama plant were trafficking in false documents, Tyson alerted the government and worked with the government to investigate. (This investigation was independent of DOJ's then-secret undercover investigation of Tyson.)[82] In sum, Tyson could not have done more at the level of senior management to embrace the government's invitation to enter into a cooperative partnership to prevent and detect the employment of illegal immigrants. While all of this was occurring, however,

---

[78] *See id.* at 20–29 (discussing the strengths and weaknesses of the Basic Pilot program). However, even the government recognizes that this program was not foolproof. *Id.* at 22–23 (explaining that the Basic Pilot program does not help employers detect identity fraud in verifying employees' work eligibility).

[79] *See* Institute for Survey Research, Temple University, Findings of the Basic Pilot Program Evaluation 166–69 (June 2002), *www.uscis.gov/files/article/5[1].f%20C_X.pdf* (finding that the mean start-up cost per employer was $777, while the mean operating cost per employer was $1,800. It is estimated that a mandatory dial-up version of the Basic Pilot program for all employers would cost the country about $11.7 billion per year, with employers bearing most of the annual costs. *See* U.S. Gov't Accountability Office, *supra* note 77, at 29.

[80] Kilman, *supra* note 17 ("Tyson was one of the first companies to voluntarily adopt an INS computer system for verifying the identification documents presented by prospective employees."); Ken Kimbro, *No Corporate Conspiracy to Smuggle Illegal Aliens*, ST. LOUIS POST-DISPATCH (Missouri), Jan. 9, 2002, at B7 ("Tyson Foods was one of the first and largest voluntary participants in the INS's computerized employment document verification program, known as Basic Pilot."); Tyson Foods, Inc., *Justice Department Letters Contradict Conspiracy Allegations* (July 25, 2000), *available at www.cyperus.com/cgi-bin/stories.pl?ACCT=105&STORY=/www/story/01-24-2002/0001654727* ("Tyson . . . was one of the first and largest participants in the voluntary INS Basic Pilot Program.").

[81] In 1999, the Compliance Department developed a poster campaign on ethics and compliance issues using characters developed for Tyson's modified Corporate Code publication. These posters—which dealt with topics such as food safety, Tyson's drug policy, and government relations—were distributed to Tyson facilities on a monthly basis throughout 1999, and earned the Company a 1999–2000 "Citation of Excellence" from the American Advertising Federation.

[82] Kilman, *supra* note 17, at A6 ("Tyson also told the 'government in 1998 of suspicions that some personnel employees in an Alabama plant were trafficking in false documents."); Kimbro, *supra* note 80:

[A]t about the time the DOJ was initiating its investigation, we learned of some potential activity involving false documents in one of our Alabama plants. We immediately and voluntarily self-reported this information to INS and worked with it to see if we could catch any employees engaging in the suspected illegal activity.

In December 1998, Tyson Foods suspected that clerical employees in its Ashland, Alabama, plant might be participating in a scheme to produce and market fraudulent identification records to enable the employment of undocumented workers. Tyson immediately notified the INS and began working with the government to conduct a full investigation. The company worked with the INS on this matter for six months before concluding that no wrongdoing had occurred.

DOJ prosecutors and undercover immigration agents were simultaneously trying to lure a handful of Tyson's local managers into violating IRCA.

When the facts of the government's investigation came to light, counsel for Tyson requested a meeting with Assistant Attorney General Michael Chertoff, who then headed DOJ's Criminal Division. Counsel reviewed Tyson Foods' record of partnership in Basic Pilot, the efforts of senior management to prevent violations of company hiring policy at the local level, and the disparity between the allegations of 136 alleged illegal hires (among tens of thousands) and the government's demand for $140 million. In this context, all of the company's efforts and expense to implement Basic Pilot and the company's compliance program came to nothing. Chertoff rebuffed the presentation of Tyson's counsel, endorsed DOJ's novel "wage suppression" theory, and authorized Chattanooga's U.S. Attorney's Office to proceed to trial against the company based on the actions of a few local employees.

In light of this history, how can the government convince employers that increased partnership with the government in programs similar to Basic Pilot will be advantageous (or at a minimum not harmful) to the company? The authors believe there are some concrete assurances that DOJ and DHS can and should offer and that business leaders should demand.

First, the government should expressly commit to working in partnership with companies that adopt new and more effective measures to avoid hiring undocumented workers. This commitment would include reassurances that the government will recognize the efforts of senior management to implement new policies and procedures company-wide and will look primarily to those company-wide efforts, rather than to any local violations of company policies, in deciding whether a company is complying with immigrations laws.

Second, the government should reassure its partners that it will not play "gotcha" with companies who voluntarily adopt additional policies and practices to prevent the hiring of undocumented workers. The fact that DOJ was attempting, as part of an undercover investigation, to lure Tyson's local managers into hiring undocumented workers while the company was volunteering for the Basic Pilot program obviously deters businesses from helping the government.[83]

Finally (and perhaps most importantly), the government can commit to communicating with its business partners about any suspected local breakdowns in the hiring process, rather than opening a covert investigation in response to hiring issues.[84] In

---

[83] Relatedly, even officials at USCIS have "stated that they have concerns about providing ICE with broader access to Basic Pilot Program information for [ICE's] worksite enforcement program . . . [because] if ICE has access to pilot program information for worksite enforcement purposes, that access might create a disincentive for employers to participate in this voluntary program." U.S. Gov't Accountability Office, *supra* note 77, at 22. These officials explained that "employers may be less likely to join or participate in the program because the employers may believe that they are more likely to be targeted for worksite enforcement investigation as a result of program participation." *Id.*

[84] Indeed, even ICE has recognized that costs spent on enforcing compliance are less than the costs spent on investigation. U.S. Gov't Accountability Office, *supra* note 77, at 34 ("According to ICE,

the trial of the Tyson case, defense counsel put the most senior government investigator on the stand in part to make the point that the expense and disruption of investigations and prosecutions are unnecessary when a company's management is committed to resolving any lapses or violations of hiring policy. The following is an excerpt of the testimony:

> Q: (Mr. Green): And if you had called someone at Tyson Foods to tell them that you on behalf of the Immigration Service felt that there may be some problems or issues at [a local Tyson plant], do you have any reason to believe that Tyson Foods would not have immediately attended to your message, would not immediately have entered into a cooperative effort with you to figure out what was going on there and solve it?
>
> A: (The federal immigration agent): No sir.
>
> Q: You could have gone to a pay phone and put in two quarters and made that call to Tyson Foods, right?
>
> A: True.
>
> Q: What do you think this investigation has cost the citizens of the country, the taxpayers of the country? More than the 50 cents?
>
> A: Definitely more than 50 cents.
>
> Q: Millions and millions, right?
>
> A: A couple of million.
>
> Q: [It could] have been avoided with a phone call to the company, isn't that right?
>
> A: True.[85]

Partnership is a two-way street, and governmental cooperation with companies can be much more effective and efficient in stemming the employment of unauthorized workers than covert investigations.

Plaintiffs' Lawyers Join in: Immigration Offenses Are Added to RICO

The government's mischief with its "wage suppression" theory did not die when the jury acquitted Tyson Foods. Plaintiffs' lawyers have adopted variants of the theory and are attempting to extract massive payments from American businesses.

The Racketeer Influenced and Corrupt Organizations Act (RICO)[86] includes a private enforcement tool used by plaintiffs' lawyers that provides for severe penalties

---

compliance enforcement officers are less costly than investigative agents. ICE estimates that each investigative agent would cost the agency approximately $167,000 to $176,000 in fiscal year 2006, while one compliance enforcement officer would cost about $76,000.").

[85] Trial Tr. 5130–31, Mar. 21, 2003, *United States v. Tyson Foods, Inc.*, No. CR-4-01-61 (E.D. Tenn. filed Dec. 11, 2001).

[86] 18 USC §§1961–68.

for persons who engage in a "pattern of racketeering activity,"[87] and the list of illegal acts that constitute a "racketeering activity" is a long one.[88] For our purposes, what is important is that in 1996, Congress amended the definition of "racketeering activity" to include, among other things, "any act which is indictable under the Immigration and Nationality Act, section 274 (relating to bringing in and harboring certain aliens),[89] section 277 (relating to aiding or assisting certain aliens to enter the United States),[90] or section 278 (relating to importation of alien for immoral purpose)[91] if the act indictable under such section of such Act was committed for the purpose of financial gain."[92]

In particular, it is important to reiterate that section 274, among other things as discussed *supra*, makes it illegal for "[a]ny person . . . , during any 12-month period, [to] knowingly hire[] for employment at least 10 individuals with actual knowledge that the individuals are [unauthorized] aliens."[93]

With this 1996 amendment to RICO, Congress further raised the financial stakes for corporate America with respect to certain immigration violations. Besides RICO's severe criminal penalties,[94] RICO's civil penalties are a financial trap for the unwary company, allowing private plaintiffs to collect treble damages, plus the cost of the suit and attorneys' fees.[95] Furthermore, the court can order the defendant to divest itself of any interest in the enterprise, impose restrictions on future investments or activities, and even order the "dissolution or reorganization" of the enterprise.[96] In short, the losing corporate defendant in a RICO case can be forced to provide high levels of compensation to the plaintiff, be restricted from engaging in future business activities, and even lose its business completely.

With the addition of these immigration offenses to RICO, plaintiffs' lawyers have, not surprisingly, begun to file RICO suits against employers in which they have alleged knowing employment of undocumented workers. In one case, a competitor of a janitorial service filed suit alleging that the defendant's practice of hiring undocumented workers enabled it to underbid competing firms. This case subsequently settled after the U.S. Court of Appeals for the Second Circuit held that the cleaning service had alleged a direct proximate relationship between its injury and the

---

[87] 18 USC §1962(a).

[88] 18 USC §1961(1).

[89] 8 USC §1324.

[90] 8 USC §1327.

[91] 8 USC §1328.

[92] 18 USC §1961(1)(F).

[93] 8 USC §1324(a)(3)(A).

[94] 18 USC §1963(a) (authorizing fines, imprisonment, and forfeiture).

[95] 18 USC §1964(c).

[96] 18 USC §1964(a).

competitor's alleged pattern of racketeering activity.[97] At least four other cases involve classes of current and/or former employees alleging that their employers' practice of hiring undocumented workers depressed the wages of legal employees. One of those cases ended in an affirmance of the district court's dismissal of the complaint.[98] Plaintiffs' lawyers brought a class action against Tyson Foods following up on the government's allegations against Tyson Foods, discussed above.[99] As of this writing, summary judgment motions are pending in that case, with trial scheduled for early 2008. Yet another case was brought on behalf of an alleged class of undocumented workers claiming that their employer, Wal-Mart, conspired with outside contractors to deprive class members of fair wages. The plaintiffs filed an amended complaint after the court dismissed the initial complaint.[100] Finally, a local county government filed suit against a number of employers alleging that the companies conspired with employment agencies to recruit and hire undocumented workers. The county government sought to recover costs related to health services and law enforcement from the employers.[101] These cases demonstrate the real risks arising from privately brought RICO suits.

Avoiding Court: Practical Pointers to Keep the Federal Government and Plaintiffs' Lawyers Away

An ounce of prevention is worth a pound of cure. It is obviously better for employers to take affirmative steps now to avoid having to defend themselves later against federal investigations and prosecutions, as well as private lawsuits.

Consequently, the most important preventive measure that employers can undertake is to ensure that their employees' I-9 forms confirming employment eligibility are timely completed and on file for the appropriate time frames. Employers should conduct regular audits at a random sample of facilities to review a sufficient number of forms to measure the thoroughness of their overall compliance and then take further remedial steps based on the results of the audit. Furthermore, employers should not do a comprehensive reverification of all I-9 forms because demanding a new I-9 when one was already lawfully completed—or demanding documentation beyond the

---

[97] *Commercial Cleaning Servs. v. Colin Serv. Sys.*, 271 F.3d 374, 381 (2d Cir. 2001). To bring a RICO suit, the plaintiff must plead: "(1) the defendant's violation of §1962, (2) an injury to the plaintiff's business or property, and (3) causation of the injury by the defendant's violation." *Id.* at 380 (citation omitted).

[98] *Compare Baker v. IBP*, 357 F.3d 685, 691–92 (7th Cir. 2004) (finding that employee complaint failed to adequately specify enterprise under RICO), *with Williams v. Mohawk Indus.*, 411 F.3d 1277, 1292, 1294 (11th Cir. 2006) (upholding district court denial of 12(b)(6) motion to dismiss employee RICO complaint), *Trollinger v. Tyson Foods*, 370 F.3d 602 (6th Cir. 2004) (reversing dismissal of employee complaint in RICO action), *and Mendoza v. Zirkle Fruit Co.*, 301 F.3d 1163 (9th Cir. 2002) (same). *Mendoza* settled. Lawyers from the authors' firm, Sidley Austin, have represented defendants in all but the *Mendoza* and *Zavala* cases.

[99] *Trollinger v. Tyson Foods*, No. 4:02-cv-23, (E.D. Tenn.).

[100] *Zavala v. Wal-Mart Stores*, 393 F. Supp. 2d 295, 300 (D.N.J. 2005).

[101] *Canyon County v. Syngenta Seeds*, No. CV05-306-S-EJL, slip op. (D. Idaho Dec. 14, 2005). This case has been dismissed.

requirements of the law—can result in allegations of unfair immigration-related employment practices and document abuse.

In addition, although managers in charge of corporate hiring do not need to become experts in the recognition of fake identification documents, they should be mindful of obviously fake or altered cards. Relatedly, employers should have thorough training in I-9 compliance. Many employers run afoul of the immigration laws not because of any purposeful malfeasance but because applicants fail to complete or inaccurately complete their I-9 forms. Employers should also deal promptly with reports of suspected incidents of illegal status, and make sure that their managers and supervisors are fully conversant with the proper steps and chain of communication necessary if and when such reports come to their attention.

Employers also should establish a periodic review of the status of noncitizen employees to verify that they remain in legal status, check for expiring visas, ensure that their job duties are substantially the same as those stated on the visa petition, and review whether the employees, if in nonimmigrant status, should be sponsored for residence. These reviews should be done at least annually, and they can be tied temporally to performance reviews or be done during tax time. However, employers must remain mindful that subjecting noncitizen employees to special scrutiny, or running special checks on the documentation of noncitizens who are current legal employees, may expose employers to the risk of civil rights violations, as discussed *supra*.

In addition to adopting these preventive measures, when using independent contractors, employers should insert language in any contract with them prohibiting the contractors from using unauthorized labor. Some companies have used the Wal-Mart case as an opportunity to issue a timely reminder to vendors about their obligations to comply with employment and immigration laws. Furthermore, when restructuring, merging, or acquiring, due diligence reviews and checklists should always include items of inquiry regarding the immigration status and employment eligibility of the parties' workforces as part of an overall examination of employee matters. After the merger, the new employer should be sure to retain and store the employees' I-9 forms from the previous employer. The new employer also should make a determination of how much sample auditing it needs to do of the I-9 forms for the newly acquired employees. How much sampling to do post-merger can be determined by the results of the company's preliminary investigation of I-9 forms that occurred during the due diligence period (prior to acquisition).

Conclusion

There has been a marked upsurge in prosecutions related to illegal immigration in the last few years. But the government is not merely prosecuting illegal immigrants for immigration offenses; it is reinvigorating its investigation and prosecutorial efforts against corporate America as well. The case studies of Tyson Foods, Wal-Mart, Golden State Fence, and Swift & Company show the high stakes that corporate America currently faces in confronting federal prosecutions. Congress first deputized corporate America into controlling the flow of illegal immigration at our nation's borders in 1986—by making it illegal for employers to knowingly hire, or knowingly retain after hiring, illegal immigrants, as well as to fail to comply with the employment verification requirements—and then subjecting employers to stiff civil and criminal penalties for noncompliance. Congress further deputized corporate America in 1996, and subjected corporate America to even higher financial stakes, when it made certain immigration offenses predicate offenses in RICO, and thereby opened the doors to suits from plaintiffs' lawyers for treble damages for having knowingly hired at least 10 undocumented workers in a 12-month period. Given the increasingly high stakes for employers, it is imperative that they expend the resources now to take the preventive measures outlined in this article. To do less will only perpetuate exposure to unnecessary and costly risk.

CRIMINAL PENALTIES IN WORKPLACE IMMIGRATION CASES
by Kathleen M. Brinkman[*]

Employers looking among federal statutes for the crimes they might commit if they hire an employee who is not authorized to work in the United States could be seriously misled about what statutes U.S. Immigration and Customs Enforcement (ICE) special agents and federal prosecutors are using to prosecute such cases these days.

In the past, ICE, and its predecessor, legacy Immigration and Naturalization Service, told employers little or nothing about the felony "harboring" and related offenses in Immigration and Nationality Act (INA) §274(a) [8 USC §1324(a)], and instead stressed INA §274A [8 USC §1324a], which sets forth the misdemeanor offense for *hiring* unauthorized aliens.

But the government is not limited to charging the misdemeanor offense when it prosecutes an employer who hires illegal aliens. Clearly, the government can charge felony "harboring" if the elements are present. It is doing so with greater frequency. It is even prosecuting companies and individuals who do not hire unauthorized workers directly but who use contractors that employ unauthorized workers. When charging a felony, the government increasingly does not make any distinction between one who knows or recklessly disregards the fact that his or her employee is unauthorized to work in the United States and one who knows or recklessly disregards the fact that his or her contractor's employee is unauthorized to work in the United States.

Harboring

The maximum penalty for felony "harboring" in violation of INA §274(a)(1)(A)(iii) [8 USC §1324(a)(1)(A)(iii)] is five years *for each alien harbored*,[1] unless the crime is committed for commercial advantage or private financial gain, in which case the maximum penalty is 10 years.[2]

The elements of the typical felony "harboring" offenses by an employer in violation of INA §274(a)(1)(A)(iii) [8 USC §1324(a)(1)(A)(iii)] are:

---

[*] **Kathleen M. Brinkman** is of counsel to Porter Wright Morris & Arthur LLP in its Cincinnati office. She does white-collar criminal defense, including immigration violations and asset forfeiture litigation. She was an assistant U.S. attorney for almost 25 years in the Southern District of Ohio, where she specialized in prosecuting fraud and environmental crimes and public corruption, and in litigating civil and criminal asset forfeiture. She is a retired adjunct professor at the University of Cincinnati College of Law, where she taught trial practice. She is the author of *Federal Criminal Procedure Litigation Manual* and a coauthor of *Sixth Circuit Practice Manual*, both published by LexisNexis. Among her many honors is the 2005 Nettie Cronise Lutes Award from the Ohio State Bar Association. She is a fellow of the American College of Trial Lawyers.

[1] INA §274(a)(1)(B)(ii); 8 USC §1324(a)(1)(B)(ii).

[2] INA §274(a)(1)(B)(i); 8 USC §1324(a)(1)(B)(i).

1. While knowing or recklessly disregarding that a person has come to, entered, or remains in the United States in violation of law,
2. "harboring," concealing, or shielding from detection,[3]
3. a person who has come to, entered, or remains in the United States in violation of law.

One district court judge under the jurisdiction of the U.S. Court of Appeals for the Sixth Circuit has said that to convict of "harboring," the government must prove that the defendant intended to help the illegal alien[4] avoid detection by law enforcement officials. In *U.S. v. Belevin-Ramales*,[5] Judge Karen Caldwell addressed the government's burden of proof beyond a reasonable doubt in the context of a requested jury instruction from the government on the definition of "harbor" in INA §274(a)(1)(A)(iii) [8 USC §1324(a)(1)(A)(iii)]. The government requested the following instruction:

> The term "harbor" means to afford shelter to, and includes any conduct tending to substantially facilitate an alien's remaining in the United States illegally. The government does not have to prove that the Defendant harbored the alien with the intent to assist the alien's attempt to evade or avoid detection by law enforcement.

Rejecting the second sentence of the proposed government instruction, Judge Caldwell determined that a defendant *did* have to act with intent that the alien evade or avoid detection by law enforcement before he or she could be guilty of "harboring."[6] After examining scant precedent from three other circuits, which she determined was inconclusive on the issue,[7] Judge Caldwell based her decision on the old,

---

[3] For simplicity, this article uses the term "harboring" to mean "harboring, concealing, or shielding from detection" as expressed in the statute.

[4] The term "illegal alien" is used throughout this article in the context of the felony harboring statute, as it is the most accurate shorthand for an alien "who has come to, entered, or remains in the United States in violation of law," the focus of the harboring statute. Use of this term is necessary to distinguish between "illegal alien" in the felony harboring offense and "unauthorized alien" in the misdemeanor hiring offense.

[5] 458 F. Supp. 2d 409 (E.D. Ky. 2006).

[6] *Id.* at 411. While Judge Caldwell's decision explicitly rejected the government's proposal, which would have lessened the burden of proof, it does not indicate how the instruction should read, stating instead that any definition of "harbor" must be consistent with *Susnjar v. U.S.*, 27 F.2d 223 (6th Cir. 1928). *Id.*

[7] *Id.* at 410. See *U.S. v. You*, 382 F.3d 958, 966 (9th Cir. 2004) (holding that defendants must intend to violate the law and holding adequate an instruction that required the jury to find that a defendant acted "with the purpose of avoiding [the aliens'] detection by immigration-authorities . . . ."); *U.S. v. Varkonyi*, 645 F.2d 453, 456 (5th Cir. 1981) (stating that "[i]mplicit in the wording 'harbor, shield, or conceal,' is the connotation that something is being hidden from detection . . . ."); *but cf. U.S. v. Acosta DeEvans*, 531 F.2d 428 (9th Cir. 1976) (rejecting the *Susnjar* definition because of a nonrelated U.S. Supreme Court decision and a 1952 statutory amendment, also not germane), and *U.S. v. Lopez*, 521 F.2d 437, 441 (2d Cir. 1975) (not addressing specific "avoidance" issue, but listing acts of "harboring" that encompass "avoidance").

but still applicable, definition of "harboring" determined by the Sixth Circuit in *Susnjar v. U.S.*[8] In *Susnjar*, the Sixth Circuit found that the natural meanings of the terms "shield" and "conceal" must be applied to "harboring" offenses:

> [W]e conceive the natural meaning of the word "harbor" to be to clandestinely shelter, succor, and protect improperly admitted aliens, and that the word "conceal" should be taken in the simple sense of shielding from observation and preventing discovery of such alien persons.[9]

Therefore, based on *U.S. v. Belevin-Ramales*, an employer could argue that the government's burden is to prove a fourth element beyond a reasonable doubt: acting with intent to help the alien avoid detection by law enforcement.

Judge Caldwell's conclusion on the "harboring" definition/intent element is also supported by two recent U.S. district court decisions in civil Racketeering Influenced and Corrupt Organizations Act (RICO)[10] cases. In *Zavala v. Wal-Mart Stores*,[11] a complaint was deemed insufficient in its allegation of facts to support predicate acts of "harboring," conspiracy to "harbor," and aiding and abetting "harboring." The court stated that a Wal-Mart contractor's knowing employment and housing of undocumented aliens "falls short of alleging that Wal-Mart sheltered undocumented aliens for the purposes of concealing them and avoiding their detection by immigration authorities."[12] Thus, there must not only be the knowing or reckless employment or sheltering of undocumented aliens, but it must be done with an aim that they avoid detection.[13]

In *Trollinger v. Tyson Foods, Inc.*,[14] the court determined that a civil RICO allegation met the *Susnjar* standard because it alleged facts showing that the defendants warned illegal aliens about raids, thus shielding them from law enforcement detection. *Trollinger* is further support for the requirement in the Sixth Circuit that to prove the crime of "harboring," the government must establish beyond a reasonable doubt that the defendant acted with intent that an unauthorized worker avoid detection.

In *U.S. v. Khanani*,[15] the court upheld the lower court's refusal to give the defendants' requested "mere employment" jury instruction. The defendants requested that the court instruct the jury that "[t]he employment of an illegal alien in and of itself does not constitute encouraging or inducing such alien to remain in the United States.

---

[8] 27 F.2d 223 (6th Cir. 1928).

[9] *Id.* at 224.

[10] 18 USC §§1961–68.

[11] 393 F. Supp. 2d 295, 306 (D.N.J. 2005).

[12] *Id.*

[13] *Id.*

[14] 2007 U.S. Dist. LEXIS 38882, 2007 WL 1574275 (E.D. Tenn. 2007).

[15] 502 F.3d 1281 (11th Cir. 2007).

..."[16] The court found that the instructions that the trial court had given implicitly acknowledged this theory of defense. The instructions included a statement that:

> To conceal, harbor, or shield from detection includes any knowing conduct by the defendant tending to substantially facilitate an alien's escaping detection as an illegal alien, thereby remaining in the United States illegally.[17]

So, What Is Harboring?

"Harboring" can mean, among other acts, hiring and continuing to employ a person while knowing or recklessly disregarding the fact that he or she is an illegal alien. "Harboring" can also mean paying a contractor while knowing or recklessly disregarding the fact that the contractor is an illegal alien or that the contractor is employing an illegal alien.

"Harboring" can mean renting housing to, or acquiring housing for, or otherwise providing housing for, a person while knowingly or recklessly disregarding the fact that the person is an illegal alien.

In each case, a defendant is guilty of "harboring" if the defendant does such things with intent to help the alien avoid detection by law enforcement authorities.

Attempting, Aiding and Abetting, and Conspiring to Harbor

To prove an employer guilty of "harboring" under INA §274(a)(1)(A)(iii) [8 USC §1324(a)(1)(A)(iii)], the government must prove beyond a reasonable doubt that the defendant knew or recklessly disregarded the fact that a particular person was an illegal alien. The government can also convict an employer of harboring if, while knowingly or recklessly disregarding the fact that a person was an illegal alien, the employer helped ("aided or abetted") the harboring by someone else of an illegal alien,[18] or tried ("attempted") to harbor an illegal alien, even unsuccessfully.[19]

An employer can be guilty of "conspiring to harbor" an illegal alien even if the employer is not guilty of actually "harboring" that person.[20] To "conspire to harbor," an employer must agree with at least one other person (not a government agent) to harbor an illegal alien. Because the statute making conspiracy to harbor a felony offense contains no requirement that the government prove an overt act, it is unlikely that the government needs to prove that one of the conspirators caused an act to be done during the course of the conspiracy to further the goal of the conspiracy to harbor. Nonetheless, opinions often refer to an overt act being an element of the conspiracy offense, and evidence usually shows that an overt act was committed in addition to the agreement.

---

[16] *Id.* at 1288 n.3.

[17] *Id.* at 1287.

[18] INA §274(a)(1)(A)(v)(II); 8 USC §1324(a)(1)(A)(v)(II).

[19] INA §274(a)(1)(A)(iii); 8 USC §1324(a)(1)(A)(iii).

[20] INA §274(a)(1)(A)(v)(I); 8 USC §1324(a)(1)(A)(v)(I).

The maximum penalty, for each alien with respect to whom "conspiring to harbor" in violation of the statute applies, is 10 years.[21]

And You Thought Money Laundering Was a Fraud and Drug Crime

Money laundering crimes can be committed with the proceeds of felony immigration offenses.

In general, money laundering means using proceeds from a "specified unlawful activity" in a financial transaction knowing that the money came from some kind of criminal conduct. Money laundering does not mean necessarily that the defendant was in the business of laundering money for other people, knowing that the money came from crime. Money laundering can mean using money derived from your own specified unlawful activity in a financial transaction knowing that the money was the proceeds of some crime.

Money laundering requires that the financial transaction be conducted in the proceeds of "specified unlawful activity." The crimes that constitute "specified unlawful activity" are listed in 18 USC §1956(c)(7), incorporating most of 18 USC §1961(1). Specified unlawful activity includes violations of INA §274(a) [8 USC §1324(a)], including harboring, attempting to harbor, aiding and abetting harboring, and conspiracy to harbor an alien. Specified unlawful activity does not include the misdemeanor violation of INA §274A [8 USC §1324a].

What are the "proceeds" of felony "harboring" or "conspiring to harbor" or "aiding and abetting" the harboring of an illegal alien? The U.S. Court of Appeals for the Eleventh Circuit has upheld a trial court's finding that the profits or revenue indirectly derived from an illegal alien's labor or from the failure to remit taxes cannot be "proceeds" for money laundering purposes.[22] The court held that the government's theory that tax and costs savings from hiring illegal aliens are "proceeds" is not valid and that monies received from the sale of goods or services are not "proceeds" of the labor used to produce those goods.[23] But this question is a hot one when it comes to employing illegal aliens, and case law is still developing.

Just as in the "harboring" crime, the government can convict a defendant of aiding and abetting a completed money laundering crime by someone else[24] or attempting to launder money without ever completing that crime.[25]

The maximum penalty for felony money laundering is 10 years for a violation of 18 USC §1957 or 20 years for a violation of 18 USC §1956, for each offense. Each monetary transaction that constitutes money laundering is a separate offense.

---

[21] INA §274(a)(1)(B)(i); 8 USC §1324(a)(1)(B)(i).
[22] *U.S. v. Khanani*, 502 F.3d 1281, 1296 (11th Cir. 2007).
[23] *Id.*
[24] *See* 18 USC §3 (accessory after the fact).
[25] 18 USC §§1956, 1957.

Prosecutors charge money laundering because it allows them to introduce evidence of the gain to the defendant that otherwise might not be admitted, often including evidence of how the defendant used the money after it was laundered. It makes the defendant look and sound more criminal. It increases the sentencing guidelines calculation upon conviction and may result in a stiffer sentence. It can increase the amount of property that is forfeitable by the defendant upon conviction. All property "involved in" a money laundering violation is forfeitable, not just the illegal proceeds that are laundered.[26]

Types of Money Laundering

To be guilty of any of the following money laundering offenses, a defendant must know that the property involved in the transaction is the proceeds of some form of unlawful activity.

The crime of money laundering under 18 USC §1956(a)(1)(A)(i) requires a financial transaction conducted in the proceeds of a specified unlawful activity with intent to promote specified unlawful activity, with the knowledge that the proceeds came from some form of unlawful activity.

Money laundering under 18 USC §1956(a)(1)(A)(ii) requires a financial transaction conducted in the proceeds of specified unlawful activity with intent to violate 26 USC §7201 (tax evasion) or 26 USC §7206 (false statement on a return or other tax document).

Money laundering under 18 USC §1956(a)(1)(B)(i) requires a financial transaction designed in whole or part to conceal or disguise the nature, the location, the source, the ownership, or the control of proceeds of specified unlawful activity.

Money laundering under 18 USC §1956(a)(1)(B)(ii) requires a financial transaction designed in whole or part to avoid a transaction reporting requirement under state or federal law.

Money laundering under 18 USC §1957 requires that a monetary transaction as defined in the statute be conducted in more than $10,000 in proceeds of specified unlawful activity.

Conspiring to Launder Money

Just as a defendant can be convicted of conspiring to harbor, he or she can be convicted of conspiring to launder. The defendant can be convicted even if no money was ever laundered. Conspiracy to commit money laundering is a crime when the offense is a violation of 18 USC §§ 1956 or 1957.[27] The penalty for conspiracy is the same as that for the money laundering offense that is the object of the conspiracy, either 20 years for crimes under 18 USC §1956 or 10 years for crimes under 18 USC §1957.

---

[26] See the discussion of forfeiture, *infra*.
[27] 18 USC §1956(h).

Fines

The maximum fine for felony harboring or conspiracy to harbor is the greater of $250,000 or twice the gain to the defendant.[28] For a 18 USC §1956 money laundering violation, it is the greater of $500,000 or twice the amount laundered.[29] For a 18 USC §1957 money laundering violation, the court may impose a fine of up to twice the amount laundered.[30]

Forfeiture

Harboring

Asset forfeiture can provide the government with larger financial penalties than fines against a defendant convicted of harboring and the related offenses.

Civil Asset Forfeiture: The government may seize and forfeit civilly any conveyance, including any vessel, vehicle, or aircraft, that has been or is being used in the commission of a harboring offense, the gross proceeds of such an offense, and any property traceable to such conveyance or proceeds.[31] Note that the statute allows forfeiture of "gross proceeds" and not just "profits."[32]

Criminal Asset Forfeiture: On conviction of a harboring offense, the court must order the forfeiture to the government of

(1) any conveyance used in the commission of the offense,

(2) any property, real or personal, that constitutes or is derived from or is traceable to the proceeds obtained directly or indirectly from the commission of the offense, and

(3) any property, real or personal, that is used to facilitate, or is intended to be used to facilitate, the commission of the offense.[33]

Note, again, that the statute allows the forfeiture of "proceeds," not just "profits" of the offense.[34]

Money Laundering

Money laundering forfeiture, whether civil[35] or criminal,[36] authorizes the forfeiture of all property "involved in" the money laundering offense, arguably a broader category of property than the "gross proceeds" or "proceeds" of the harboring offense.

---

[28] *See* 18 USC §§3571(b)(3), (d). Organizations can be fined up to $500,000. 18 USC §3571(c).

[29] 18 USC §1956(a).

[30] 18 USC §1957(b)(2).

[31] INA §274(b); 8 USC §1324(b).

[32] INA §274(b); 8 USC §1324(b).

[33] 18 USC §982(a)(6)(A).

[34] *Id.*

[35] *See* 18 USC §981(a)(1)(A).

[36] *See* 18 USC §982(a)(1).

Using criminal forfeiture, the government can obtain a money judgment in the amount of the property that is forfeitable because it was involved in the offense of which the defendant was convicted, and execute against any of the defendant's property in order to satisfy the judgment.[37] In satisfying a criminal forfeiture judgment, codefendants are jointly and severally liable.

Prosecutors are increasingly demanding forfeiture of very significant amounts of property when they negotiate guilty pleas and indict defendants for felony conduct relating to illegal aliens.

What a Difference an "A" Makes: The Misdemeanor in INA §274A [8 USC §1324a]

The statute prohibiting unlawful employment of aliens, INA §274A [8 USC §1324a], contains a misdemeanor criminal penalty provision:

Any person who engages in a pattern or practice of violations of [INA §§274A(a)(1)(A) or (2) (8 USC §§1324a(a)(1)(A) or (2)] shall be fined not more than $3,000 for each unauthorized alien with respect to whom such a violation occurs, imprisoned for not more than six months for the entire pattern and practice, or both, notwithstanding the provisions of any other Federal law relating to fine levels.[38]

The violations that will lead to the misdemeanor penalty are:

[T]o hire, or to recruit or refer for a fee, for employment in the United States an alien knowing the alien is an unauthorized alien (as defined in [INA §274A(h)(3) (8 USC §1324a(h)(3)]) with respect to such employment.[39]

and

[A]fter hiring an alien for employment in accordance with [INA §274A(a)(1) (8 USC §1324a(a)(1)]), to continue to employ the alien in the United States knowing the alien is (or has become) an unauthorized alien with respect to such employment.

The statute defines "unauthorized alien" to mean:

with respect to the employment of an alien at a particular time, that the alien is not at that time, either (A) an alien lawfully admitted for permanent residence, or (B) authorized to be so employed by this chapter or by the Attorney General.[40]

The statute provides a good-faith defense to an employer who complies with the employment verification system set forth in INA §274A(b) [8 USC §1324a(b)].[41]

---

[37] See 18 USC §853.
[38] INA §274A(f)(1); 8 USC §1324a(f)(1).
[39] INA §274A(a)(1)(A); 8 USC §1324a(a)(1)(A).
[40] INA §274A(h)(3); 8 USC §1324a(h)(3).
[41] INA §274A(a)(3); 8 USC §1324a(a)(3).

It is a misdemeanor under the statute to use a contract, subcontract, or exchange to obtain the labor of an alien knowing that the alien is an unauthorized alien.[42]

There is no forfeiture provision associated with the misdemeanor offense. The government is using the misdemeanor provision far less frequently, largely because it contains no forfeiture provision and the fines are less significant than those obtainable under the felony provision.

Prosecution of Business Organizations

Federal prosecutors presented with evidence of a business organization's "harboring" are supposed to be guided in deciding whether to charge the organization criminally by the "McNulty Memo," a Department of Justice memorandum on principles of federal prosecution of business organizations issued by Deputy Attorney General Paul McNulty on December 12, 2006.[43] To get maximum favorable consideration from a federal prosecutor in his or her exercise of discretion whether to prosecute, a business organization needs a strong screening process in hiring its employees and procedures that are rigorously observed to follow up and take action on information that an employee may not be authorized to work in the United States. The employer needs similar controls to prevent it from being accused of knowingly or recklessly disregarding the fact that employees of its contractors are illegal aliens.

Employer Good-Faith Efforts

Employers can improve their chances of avoiding criminal prosecution for workplace-related immigration violations by making good-faith efforts to ensure that their own workforces and those of their contractors consist of employees authorized to work in the United States. Employers should document such good-faith efforts.

What kinds of efforts by an employer would a prosecutor likely consider to be good-faith efforts? It is important to have a written hiring policy that implements I-9 requirements in a meaningful way and to ensure adequate staff training about the policy, to do internal auditing of immigration compliance efforts, and to impose sanctions for failure to follow strictly the written immigration compliance policy. Similarly, it is important to have a written policy about how to handle information that an employee or contractor may be an illegal alien or that a contractor may be employing illegal aliens. Again, it is essential to train effectively on such a policy, to do internal auditing of compliance with the policy, and to sanction for noncompliance. One can also employ a qualified third-party immigration law specialist to audit and certify that the employer's I-9 procedures are effective and that the employer has corrected any significant compliance deviations. It is also advisable to require that contractors certify that they enforce strict immigration policies and to require them to submit satisfactory third-party audit results.

---

[42] INA §274A(a)(4); 8 USC §1324a(a)(4).

[43] *Available at www.usdoj.gov/dag/speeches/2006/mcnulty_memo.pdf.*

A few red flags about contractors that an employer might encounter are (1) the contractor has not been paying federal, state, or local taxes; (2) the contractor pays workers in cash; (3) the contractor employs its workers not as W-2 employees but as 1099 independent contractors; and (4) the contractor's employees do not go to work or flee from the worksite when an ICE raid occurs in the area.

Good-faith efforts do not inoculate an employer against criminal prosecution if the government's evidence shows that the employer's controls were a sham because the employer knowingly or recklessly harbored illegal aliens despite having such controls in place.

Bottom Line

In a worksite enforcement fact sheet dated October 15, 2007, ICE stated:

In the past, administrative fines often proved to hold little deterrence value for violators. Many employers came to view these fines as simply the "cost of doing business." Administrative fines were ignored, not paid in a timely matter [sic] or mitigated down over several years. ICE has dramatically increased the amounts of criminal fines and forfeiture over previous years of administrative fines alone. Administrative fines in FY 2001 totaled $1,095,734, $72,585 in FY 2002, $37,514 in FY 2003, $45,480 in FY 2004, and $6,500 in FY 2005. However, during the three quarters of FY 2007, ICE has obtained criminal fines, restitutions, and civil judgments in WSE investigations in excess of $30 million.

In criminal cases, ICE is often pursuing charges of harboring illegal aliens, money laundering and/or knowingly hiring illegal aliens. Harboring illegal aliens is a felony with a potential 10-year prison sentence. Money laundering is a felony with a potential 20-year prison sentence. ICE has found these criminal sanctions to be a far greater deterrent to illegal employment schemes than administrative sanctions.[44]

Assistant Secretary of Homeland Security for ICE Julie L. Myers has stated:

Of course, we can never forget the true target in these [worksite enforcement] cases—the employer. I'm proud of the fact that ICE is taking a much tougher stance against the employers in these cases. For far too long, employers were simply fined for their hiring practices, even if it could be shown that they were knowingly hiring illegal aliens. These fines were relatively small—often no more than an average traffic ticket—and routinely paid. The entire process was viewed as the cost of doing business and the magnet these employers provided for illegal immigrants to enter the country in search of jobs grew stronger. But this is no longer the case. Employers who are targeted and arrested in these worksite enforcements now face jail time and risk significant asset forfeiture

---

[44] *www.ice.gov/pi/news/factsheets/worksite.htm.*

for knowingly and deliberately building their companies on the hard work of undocumented immigrants who have come to the United States illegally.[45]

ICE increasingly targets otherwise legitimate employers whose conduct is not egregious but whose actions meet the elements of the felony harboring and money laundering crimes. ICE pursues felony harboring and money laundering prosecutions of such employers to obtain general deterrence among all employers. And increasingly, the employer conduct under scrutiny is the employer's use of a contractor who supplies illegal aliens to work the employer's job and the employer's turning a blind eye to the fact that illegal aliens are working the job.

---

[45] Remarks delivered by Julie L. Myers, Assistant Secretary of DHS for ICE, at the AILA annual conference, June 14, 2007, *available at www.ice.gov/doclib/pi/news/testimonies/070614aila.pdf.*

This article, copyright 2008 by Raquel Aldana, is reprinted from the original that appeared as UNLV William S. Boyd School of Law Legal Studies Research Paper No. 07-02. The article is published at 41 *U.C. Davis L. Rev.* 1081 (2008), copyright 2008 by The Regents of the University of California. All rights reserved. Reprinted with permission.

Of *Katz* and "Aliens: Privacy Expectations and the Immigration Raids
Raquel Aldana [+]

Immigrants and their families across the United States live in fear as Immigration and Customs Enforcement ("ICE") agents raid their neighborhoods, shopping centers, worksites, and homes in a nationwide hunt targeting millions of undocumented persons.[1] In the last two years, during which raids have intensified, ICE has rounded up tens of thousands of persons, detained them, charged hundreds with immigration crimes, and returned most to their countries of origin.[2] These raids wreak havoc on families and communities as children are left without parents and communities without workers.[3]

These raids are taking place when the United States as a nation is fiercely divided on how to address the presence and future flow of millions of unauthorized immigrants.[4] Because the raids seek to enforce U.S. immigration laws against persons who broke the law by unauthorized entry into the U.S., some see the raids as neither illegal nor immoral. Especially to persons who view undocumented immigration as the cause of U.S. economic and social ills, ICE is finally doing its job of repairing the consequences of a

---

[+] Professor of Law, William S. Boyd School of Law. I thank Professor Jennifer Chacón for inviting me to speak about privacy and immigrants at the Symposium, "Katz v. U.S: 40 Years Later," and the panel participants who gave me great insight. The law review students were exceptional hosts. I am also grateful to my research assistants Barbara McDonald and Nadin Cutter, as well as to James Rogers for generously supporting my scholarship. I also thank the editors of the U.C. Davis Law Review, especially Nick Vidargas for his rigorous editing.
[1] The Associated Press, High Profile Raids Leave Immigrants Across U.S. Living in Fear, INT'L HERALD TRIBUNE, Feb. 20, 2007, *available at* http://www.iht.com/articles/ap/2007/02/21/america/NA-GEN-US-Immigration-Raids-Fear.php.
[2] *See infra* Part I.
[3] *See infra* Part II.
[4] A December 2006 Washington Post-ABC News Poll reveals that 29 % of respondents called immigration bad and the same number called it good. About 39 % said it makes no difference. Anthony Faiola, *Looking the Other Way on Immigrants: Some Cities Buck Federal Policies*, WASH. POST, April 10, 2007, at A1.

porous border, including loss of jobs, increased crime, and the rising costs of public spending.[5]

The counterstory to anti-immigrant sentiment is vastly different and challenges the legality and morality of U.S. immigration policy. The thorny history of the U.S.-Mexico border reconfiguration at the turn of the century and noncompliance with the Treaty of Guadalupe-Hidalgo is part of this narrative.[6] As well, an explanation of mass migration, particularly from Latin America into the U.S., rooted in U.S. foreign and economic policies with sending nations, shifts the lens away from the individual agency of the immigrant towards a more complex story of responsibility of U.S. multinationals and employers who cause and profit from mass migration.[7] The complicit factors of under-enforced immigration law and economic gain to U.S. employers and consumers have allowed the creation of immigrant communities, which are now at stake.[8] The human rights angle of the story thus emphasizes the stakes of family, property, and community.

---

[5] *See, e.g.*, Steven A. Camarota, Director of Research of the Center for Immigration Studies, *Use Enforcement to Ease Situation*, available at http://www.thinkaz.org/documents/Useenforcementtoeasesituation_000.pdf . (urging DHS to adopt policy of immigration attrition through enforcement, that is, forcing immigrants out by making U.S. less hospitable). *See generally* Center for Immigration Studies, Illegal Immigration, http://www.cis.org/topics/illegalimmigration.html (last visited Sept. 24, 2007) (containing links to several articles discussing the social ills created by undocumed migration).

[6] *See* RICHARD GRISWOLD DEL CASTILLO, THE TREATY OF GUADALUPE-HIDALGO: A LEGACY OF CONFLICT 173 (Univ. of Okla. Press 1990).

[7] Consider, for example, agriculture. The United States' yearly farm subsidies in the billions to U.S. farmers, combined with free trade agreements with most Latin American nations and a cheap supply of foreign agricultural workers on U.S. farms, have slowed down farm production in Latin America, displaced farmers from their homes and into the United States, and increased produce importation and profits for U.S. farmers. *See, e.g.*, Bert R. Pena & Amy Henderson, *U.S.-Mexico Agricultural Trade and Investment After NAFTA*, 1 U.S.-MEX. L.J. 259, 275 (1993); Calvin Terbeek, Comment, *Love in the Time of Free Trade: NAFTA's Economic Effects Ten Years Later*, 12 TUL. J. INT'L & COMP. L. 487, 504-07 (2004).

[8] *See* BILL ONG HING, DEPORTING OUR SOULS, VALUES, MORALITY, AND IMMIGRATION POLICY 208-09 (Cambridge Univ. Press 2006); BILL ONG HING, DEFINING AMERICA THROUGH IMMIGRATION POLICY 106 (Temple Univ. Press 2004).

The prominence of the immigration issue in public discourse in 2007 forced Congress to seriously consider comprehensive immigration reform.[9] Ultimately, Congress did not act. Consequently, undocumented immigrants' hope of a path to legalization probably will have to wait until after the 2008 presidential election.[10] In the meantime, immigration raids have intensified and become a political battleground for anti-immigrant sentiment. Since 2002, the Department of Homeland Security ("DHS") has made inside-the-border enforcement of immigration a priority, particularly targeting undocumented workers, incarcerated immigrants, suspected gang members, and persons with a final order of removal.[11]

In this battle, not unlike the "war on drugs," which disproportionately targeted Blacks,[12] a casualty has been noncitizens' Fourth Amendment rights. In the 1970s, the U.S. Supreme Court declared that the Fourth Amendment applied to immigration enforcement, even if with increased tolerance for racial profiling.[13] However, as discussed in this Article, through a subsequent series of sweeping decisions, the Fourth Amendment has become moribund, barely able to grant any privacy protections to noncitizens, particularly in the realm of immigration enforcement.

---

[9] Robert Pear & Jim Rutenberg, *Senators in Bipartisan Deal on Immigration Bill*, N.Y. TIMES, May 18, 2007, at A1; Saul Ewing, *Comprehensive Immigration Reform Bill Introduced in U.S. House of Representatives,* March 2007 STAYING AHEAD WITH SAUL EWING: IMMIGR. REFORM BILL BULL. 1 (Saul Ewing LLP, Del., Md., N.J., Pa., D.C.), *available at* http://www.saul.com/common/publications/pdf_1263.pdf.

[10] Gail Russell Chaddock & Faye Bowers, *Immigration Bill Stalls Amid Calls for 'Enforcement First,'* CHRISTIAN SCI. MONITOR, June 29, 2007, at 1.

[11] *See infra* part II.

[12] *See* Olatunde C.A. Johnson, *Disparity Rules*, 107 COLUM. L. REV. 374, 406 (2007); Dorothy E. Roberts, *The Social and Moral Cost of Mass Incarceration in African American Communities,* 56 STAN. L. REV. 1271, 1301 (2004); David Rudovsky, *The Impact of the War on Drugs on Procedural Fairness and Racial Equality*, 1994 U. CHI. LEGAL F. 237, 239 (1994).

[13] *See* United States v. Martinez-Fuerte, 428 U.S. 543, 545 (1976); United States v. Brignoni-Ponce, 422 U.S. 873, 884 (1975).

One significant explanation for this Fourth Amendment exceptionalism is the Court's early treatment of immigration as a matter of civil as opposed to criminal enforcement.[14] The characterization of immigration enforcement as administrative has colored the evolution of Fourth Amendment doctrine. In particular, by characterizing removal proceedings as non-penal, the Court has, since 1984, precluded the Fourth Amendment's exclusionary remedy, except within the narrow "egregious violations" exception.[15] Moreover, the application of the consent doctrine in immigration enforcement under the most coercive circumstances increasingly defies the fictional premise that reasonable people feel free to walk away from law enforcement encounters. In immigration encounters, Fourth Amendment doctrine assumes the reasonable person is free to refuse questions of immigration agents at immigration checkpoints.[16] That same assumption applies during unannounced workplace raids conducted by dozens of armed immigration agents, some of whom question workers while others guard the exits;[17] or even during the execution of administrative warrants in an immigrant's home while she is handcuffed for more than two hours.[18] The resulting picture is that when immigration agents target immigrants inside the border, the Fourth Amendment offers little protection. Immigrants are unprotected because either the exclusionary rule has no application in removal proceedings, or even when the exclusionary rule applies, as in criminal proceedings, most of those encounters are deemed non-seizures and non-searches.

---

[14] *See* Daniel Kanstroom, *Deportation, Social Control, and Punishment: Some Thoughts About Why Hard Laws Make Bad Cases,* 113 HARV. L. REV. 1889, 1894 (2000).

[15] INS v. Lopez-Mendoza, 468 U.S. 1032, 1050 (1984); Joseph J. Migas, *Exclusionary Remedy Available in Civil Deportation Proceedings for Egregious Fourth Amendment Violations,* 9 GEO. IMMIGR. L.J. 207, 209 (1995).

[16] *Martinez-Fuerte,* 428 U.S. at 557.

[17] INS v. Delgado, 466 U.S. 210, 218 (1984).

[18] Muehler v. Mean 544 U.S. 93, 100-01 (2005).

But what if this "reasonable" noncitizen learns to walk away from the immigration agent and refuses to answer his questions? This is a likely scenario because immigrant rights groups advise their clients to maintain a code of silence when they encounter *"la migra."*[19] Would immigrants then have a privacy expectation to refuse questions and even to walk away from ICE? Unfortunately, the answer appears to be no. Except in very limited circumstances, ICE is conducting this latest wave of raids with easy access to civil warrants in a way that expands the scope of its law enforcement power, compelling mandatory compliance.

Today, DHS's regulatory arm reaches into employer hiring practices,[20] university requirements for foreign students,[21] the government's distribution of public benefits,[22] and driver's licenses,[23] among other areas. In turn, this preoccupation has caused the proliferation of databases that, in most cases, grant ICE easy access to information about a person's immigration status as a worker,[24] student,[25] or driver.[26] With easy access to such information in these databases, ICE can arm itself with civil warrants even where

---

[19] *See* Anna Gorman, *Immigrants Advised About Their Rights*, L.A. TIMES, Mar. 4, 2007, at B1.
[20] *See infra* Part I.A.
[21] *See* Michael A. Olivas, *IIRIRA, The Dream Act, and Undocumented College Student Residency*, 25 IMMIGR. & NAT'LITY L. REV. 323, 325 (2004) (discussing immigration laws' regulation of foreign students); Ty S. Wahab Twibell, *The Road to Internment: Special Registration and Other Human Rights Violations of Arabs and Muslims in the United States*, 29 VT. L. REV. 407, 445, 455-56, 461-643 (2005);.
[22] Richard A. Boswell, *Restrictions on Non-Citizens' Access to Public Benefits: Flawed Premise, Unnecessary Response*, 42 UCLA L. REV. 1475, 1476 (1995); Bill Ong Hing, *Don't Give Me Your Tired, Your Poor: Conflicted Immigrant Stories and Welfare Reform*, 33 HARV. C.R.-C.L. L. REV. 159, 159 (1998).
[23] Raquel Aldana & Sylvia Lazos, *"Aliens" in Our Midst Post-9/11: Legislating Outsiderness Within the Borders*, 38 UC DAVIS L. REV. 1683, 1711-22 (2005).
[24] *See infra* Part I.A.
[25] Victor C. Romero, *Noncitizen Students and Immigration Policy Post-9/11*, 17 GEO. IMMIGR. L.J. 357, 361 (2003) (describing adoption and implementation of Student and Exchange Visitor Information Service (SEVIS) database, which tracks foreign student compliance with visa conditions).
[26] *See* Kris W. Kobach, *The Quintessential Force Multiplier: The Inherent Authority of Local Police to Make Immigration Arrests*, 69 ALB. L. REV. 179, 180, 189 (describing that immigration violations, including persons holding expired visas and persons who did not comply with removal orders, are now listed in National Crime Information Center (NCIC) database, which is available to squad cars enforcing traffic laws).

there's no particularized probable cause, to conduct raids in private or quasi-private spaces without having to seek the information directly from immigrants themselves. These warrants name no suspects. Rather, they are issued precisely to allow ICE to identify and arrest persons for removal or to charge them for criminal immigration violations. Indeed, ICE agents have employed this strategy in the latest wave of workplace raids.[27]

Moreover, ICE has easy access to over 600,000 civil warrants to enforce against persons with prior removal orders who are labeled absconders or fugitives and who appear in their outdated databases.[28] While such "absconder warrants" target a particular suspect, their execution is no different than the indiscriminate targeting of immigrants that occurs in workplace raids. For example, despite the fact that the target often no longer lives at the address that appears in the database, no oversight occurs to protect third parties from privacy invasions. Not surprisingly then, ICE strategically enforces these warrants in people's homes to arrest as many persons who may be in the country without authorization, often relying on racial profiling and intimidating tactics in the process.[29]

In addition, recent inside-the-border enforcement is occurring with the collaboration of local law enforcement, in places such as prisons but also in routine traffic enforcement and other policing.[30] More disturbing, however, is the proliferation

---

[27] *See infra* Part I.A.
[28] *See infra* Part I.B.
[29] *Id.*
[30] Kobach, *supra* note 26, at 197-99; *see also* Michael Hethmon, *The Chimera and the Cop: Local Enforcement of Federal Immigration Law*, 8 D.C. L. REV. 83, 89 (2004); Michael J. Wishnie, *State and Local Police Enforcement of Immigration Laws*, 6 U. PA. J. CONST. L. 1084, 1085 (2004). *But see* Orde F. Kittrie, *Federalism, Deportation, and Crime Victims Afraid to Call the Police*, 91 IOWA L. REV. 1449, 1463-80 (2006) (discussing local sanctuary policies that protect immigrants seeking police assistance from

of local anti-immigrant ordinances that make it illegal for undocumented immigrants to loiter in public spaces, occupy housing, procure employment, or conduct business transactions.[31] These ordinances could also expand the administrative policing arm of local law enforcement against noncitizens not just in public, but also into quasi-private spaces, such as workplaces, and even into private spaces, such as homes. Further, these ordinances may encourage the proliferation of databases and database information sharing to assist law enforcement in identifying immigration violations for reporting them to ICE. Subsequently, like the use of housing and zoning ordinances to police the poor,[32] the traditionally private spaces that persons occupy would become so heavily regulated by immigration restrictions that local police, like ICE, might be able to easily obtain civil warrants to arrest immigrants in the workplace, businesses, or universities, or even in private homes without probable cause.[33]

These civil immigration warrants are neither very different nor less offensive to liberty values than the general warrants that originally inspired the Fourth Amendment. The infamous general search warrants in early U.S. history were issued by executives and legislators, without judicial intervention, with neither a probable cause requirement or oath, nor a description of the particular places to be searched and persons or things to be

---

federal immigration enforcement); Huyen Pham, *The Constitutional Right Not to Cooperate? Local Sovereignty and the Federal Immigration Power*, 74 U. OF CIN. L. REV. 1373, 1381-84 (2006).
[31] Raquel Aldana, *On Rights, Federal Citizenship, and the "Alien,"* 46 WASHBURN L.J. 263, 270-85 (2007).
[32] *See* Robert C. Ellickson, *Controlling Chronic Misconduct in City Space: Of Panhandlers, Skid Rows, and Public-Space Zoning*, 105 YALE L.J. 1165, 1202-1219 (1996); Nicole Stelle Garnett, *Relocating Disorder*, 91 VA. L. REV. 1075, 1088-98 (2005);; Lorne Sossin, *The Criminalization and Administration of the Homeless: Notes on the Possibilities and Limits of Bureaucratic Engagement*, 22 N.Y.U. REV. L. & SOC. CHANGE 623, 640-46 (1996).
[33] *See infra* Part I.C.

seized.[34] Today, immigration laws and codes authorize the compelled collection of information on ever-expanding databases over which persons retain no expectation of privacy and that become the basis for the issuance of warrants. Moreover, the *Camara*[35] legacy of balancing government regulatory powers against individual liberty interests[36] has validated the use of indiscriminate warrants to conduct immigration raids for decades.[37] The principle mischief of the Fourth Amendment balancing doctrine is that it has redefined the probable cause requirement as one of a flexible inquiry of reasonableness, rather than requiring probable cause to fulfill the prerequisite of reasonableness.[38] Judicial pre-approval becomes a mere procedural formality when warrants do not require particularized suspicion based on probable cause.

In the immigration context particularly, the Fourth Amendment scale has tilted heavily in favor of the state. The trend towards eliminating noncitizens' expectations of privacy in the spaces they occupy inside the border cannot be detached from the ongoing war against undocumented migration. Local governments' interests in protecting the economy or the federal government's interest in controlling immigration or national security weigh heavily against the privacy interests of undocumented immigrants to hide their "illegality." Increasingly, local and federal laws have sought to make the mere presence of undocumented immigrants in U.S. spaces illegal, rendering them neither

---

[34] Geoffrey G. Hemphill, *The Administrative Search Doctrine: Isn't This Exactly What the Framers Were Trying to Avoid?*, 5 REGENT U. L. REV. 215, 218-20 (1995).
[35] Camara v. Mun. Court, 387 U.S. 523, 536 (1967).
[36] *See* Scott E. Sundby, *A Return to Fourth Amendment Basics: Undoing the Mischief of Camara and Terry*, 72 MINN. L. REV. 383, 392 (1988).
[37] Int'l Molder's & Allied Workers' Local Union No. 164 v. Nelson, 799 F.2d 547, 553 (9th Cir. 1986) (agreeing with D.C. Circuit that immigrant workplace warrants require only reasonable belief unauthorized workers may be present and not that each be particularly named); Blackie's House of Beef, Inc. v. Castillo, 659 F.2d 1211, 1213 (D.C. Cir. 1981), *cert. denied*, 455 U.S. 940 (1982) (upholding constitutionality of immigration workplace warrant lacking particularized suspicion).
[38] Sundby, *supra* note 36, at 393-94.

deserving nor reasonably expectant of privacy's protection.[39] Like cars[40] or certain "heavily regulated" businesses,[41] immigrants have become so regulated that any *Katz*[42] expectation of privacy to occupy spaces in silence without detection becomes unreasonable.

Worse yet, immigrants are treated like drugs or hazardous waste, which is precisely the imagery Justice O'Connor evoked in 1984 in *INS v. Lopez-Mendoza* to deny immigrants the exclusionary rule as a remedy:

> Presumably no one would argue that the exclusionary rule should be invoked to prevent an agency from ordering corrective action at a leaking hazardous waste dump if the evidence underlying the order had been improperly obtained, or to compel police to return contraband explosives or drugs to their owner if the contraband had been unlawfully seized.[43]

Thus, despite violation of their privacy by INS, immigrant workers can still be seized and discarded because of their illegality. Paraphrasing Justice Cardozo's famous quote, Justice O'Connor concludes: "[t]he constable's blunder may allow the criminal go free . . . but he should not go free within our borders."[44]

The latest example of denying undocumented immigrants all expectation of privacy occurred in February 2007 when the U.S. Department of Justice ("DOJ") announced a plan to collect DNA evidence from all undocumented persons arrested for any reason to include in the DNA database.[45] Before the announcement, DNA evidence

---

[39] *See infra* Part I.
[40] David A. Harris, *Car Wars: The Fourth Amendment's Death on the Highway*, 66 GEO. WASH. L. REV. 556, 556 (1998).
[41] Hemphill, *supra* note 34, at 233-37; Lynn S. Searle, Note, *The "Administrative" Search from Dewey to Burger: Dismantling the Fourth Amendment*, 16 HASTINGS CONST. L.Q. 261, 273-88 (1989).
[42] Katz v. United States, 389 U.S. 347, 353 (1967).
[43] 468 U.S. 1032, 1046 (1984).
[44] *Id.* at 1047.
[45] Julia Preston, *U.S. Set to Begin a Vast Expansion of DNA Sampling*, N.Y. TIMES, Feb. 5, 2007, at A1.

had been collected solely from convicted felons,[46] a practice that perpetually erases any privacy expectations. Congress authorized this ample expansion of power "in a little-noticed amendment"[47] to the January 2006 renewal of the Violence Against Women Act,[48] purportedly to protect victims of sexual crimes.[49] The FBI anticipates that this new law would mean an anticipated increase of as many as 250,000 to one million new DNA samples per year.[50]

In this Article, I analyze the privacy implications of ICE's recent workplace and home raids. I also examine the furthering erosion of privacy expectations for noncitizens through the local regulation of the spaces they occupy in this country. I focus specifically on the town of Hazleton's anti-immigrant ordinances restricting housing for undocumented immigrants.[51] On July 26, 2007, U.S. federal district court judge James Munley of Pennsylvania struck down Hazleton's ordinances based on due process concerns and federal preemption in immigration matters.[52] This ruling will halt, at least temporarily, Hazleton's implementation of the ordinances and may stall hundreds of other towns from implementing similar measures.[53] However, Hazleton's Mayor, Louis Barletta, vowed to appeal the case all the way to the U.S. Supreme Court, if necessary.[54] This issue, then, is not disappearing anytime soon and its privacy implications remain relevant.

---

[46] *Id.*
[47] *Id.*
[48] Violence Against Women and Department of Justice Reauthorization Act of 2005, §§ 1003-1004, Pub. L. No. 109-162, 119 Stat. 2960, 3085-86 (codified at 42 U.S.C. § 1435(a) (2007); 18 U.S.C. 3142 (2007)).
[49] Preston, *supra* note 46, at A1.
[50] *Id.*
[51] See *infra* Part II.C.
[52] Lozano v. City of Hazleton, 496 F. Supp. 2d 477, 554 (M.D. Pa. 2007).
[53] Peter Elstrom, *Small-Town Quarrel, Big Implications*, BUS. WK., July 26, 2007, *available at* http://www.businessweek.com/bwdaily/dnflash/content/jul2007/db20070726_264512.htm.
[54] *Id.*

Through these case studies, I reveal the trend to construct a *Katz* doctrine that excludes or undermines the expectation of privacy of noncitizens in a bounded construction of nationality to the detriment of the Fourth Amendment. In this construct, law enforcement abuses of power are tolerated, ignored, or worse yet, rationalized through law, on the faulty premise that "privacy" should not allow "illegality" to hide. The origins of the Fourth Amendment, however, dictate otherwise. The King's aim for general warrants was to find and arrest those who refused to pay legally mandated taxes.[55] Trumping the legitimacy of the King's laws, and today, immigration laws, the Fourth Amendment's purpose has always been to limit the state's abuses of privacy.

Immigration raid abuses include the issuance of civil warrants that are not substantiated on particularized probable cause. Instead, the warrants are often issued based on flawed information contained in databases whose information was never intended to have a law enforcement purpose.[56] These abuses also include the dragnet-like and intimidating execution of warrants in people's homes and in the workplace with devastating effects on families and communities.[57] Still more abuses include the racially charged nature that has always characterized immigration law enforcement.[58] Yet, courts have mostly turned a blind eye to these abuses by pretending that removal is not punishment, ignoring the fact that raids carry criminal consequences for many, or, worse yet, allowing the "illegality" of those arrested to justify law enforcement's wrongdoing.

PART I

---

[55] Thomas K. Clancy, *The Fourth Amendment's Concept of Reasonableness*, 2004 UTAH L. REV. 977, 978-82 (2004); *see also* Scott E. Sundby, *Protecting the Citizen "Whilst He Is Quiet": Suspicionless Searches, "Special Needs" and General Warrants*, 74 MISS. L.J. 501, 506-08 (2004).
[56] *See infra* Part I.
[57] *See infra* Part I.
[58] Kevin R. Johnson, *Race Profiling in Immigration Enforcement*, 28 HUM. RTS. 23, 23 (2001).

A. *"Operation Wagon Train" and the Swift & Co. Workplace Raids*

In December 2006, ICE agents, armed with civil search warrants procured by the DOJ and dressed in riot gear, stormed six Swift & Co. meat packing plants in various cities to carry out Operation Wagon Train.[59] According to ICE, an investigation lasting ten months uncovered substantial evidence of Swift workers using stolen identities of U.S. citizens, namely their Social Security numbers ("SSN") and dates of birth.[60] The investigation began when former Swift workers, who had been arrested for other violations, admitted to using other people's SSNs to procure employment at Swift & Co.[61] Tips also came from anonymous calls to ICE and by local police referrals.[62]

The civil warrants allowed ICE agents to search for and apprehend any undocumented worker encountered during those raids.[63] In order to identify those workers not authorized to work, ICE conducted onsite interviews of all employees, including legal residents and U.S. citizens.[64] ICE claims it did not prevent any workers from leaving the area during the interviews. Moreover, ICE claims that its agents did not frisk employees and limited interview questions to ascertaining the worker's immigration status, allowing them to make calls to family members if they needed to go home to verify their work eligibility.[65]

---

[59] Press Release, Dep't. of Homeland Sec., Remarks by Sec'y of Homeland Sec., Michael Chertoff, Immigration & Customs Enforcement Assistant Sec'y, Julie Myers, and Fed. Trade Comm'n Chairman, Deborah Platt Majoras at a Press Conference on Operation Wagon Train (Dec. 13, 2006), *available at* www.dhs.gov/xnews/releases/pr_1166047951514.shtm [hereinafter DHS Press Release]; *see also* Nicole Gaouette, *Six Meat Plants are Raided in Massive I.D. Theft Case; Swift & Co. Workers Are Accused of Immigration Violations and Using Stolen Social Security Numbers*, L.A. TIMES, Dec. 13, 2006, at A18.
[60] DHS Press Release, *supra* note 59.
[61] *Id.* at 3.
[62] *Id.*
[63] On December 8, 2006, ICE "applied for and was granted a civil administrative warrant by U.S. District Court Judge Figa." Respondent's Memorandum of Law in Response to the Order to Show Cause at 2, Yarrito v. Myers, No. 06-CV-2494 (D. Colo. Dec. 18, 2006).
[64] *Id.* at 3-4.
[65] *Id.*

The workers, however, tell a much different story. At one plant, for example, workers describe that at early in the morning a half-dozen buses arrived with dozens of heavily armed federal agents accompanied by local police dressed in riot gear. Some ICE agent shut all the entrances and exits and surrounded the factory, while others entered the factory and gathered the entire workforce.[66] Some of the workers who tried to run were wrestled to the ground.[67] Some even allege that ICE agents used chemical sprays to subdue those who did not understand the orders barked at them in English.[68]

As a result of the raids, ICE arrested 1,282 workers on immigration violations and some existing criminal warrants.[69] Most workers arrested were placed in immigration removal proceedings. About 240 workers were charged criminally, mostly for the use of false or stolen SSNs.[70] The Swift & Co. raids are the largest worksite raid to date, with the largest before that executed in April 2006 against a company called IFCO Systems North America, during which 1,187 workers were arrested at forty locations nationwide.[71] As of July 2007, targeted arrests of Swift employees have continued, whether documented or undocumented, based on allegations of document fraud or harboring of undocumented workers.[72]

---

[66] Marc Cooper, *Lockdown in Greeley*, NATION, Feb. 26, 2007, at 11.
[67] *Id.*
[68] *Id.*
[69] DHS Press Release, *supra* note 59.
[70] Cooper, *supra* note 66, at 11; *see also* Julia Preston, *Illegal Worker, Troubled Citizen and Stolen Name*, N.Y. TIMES, Mar. 22, 2007, at A1 (reporting 148 workers were charged with identity theft).
[71] DHS Press Release, *supra* note 59.
[72] Jean Hopfensperger, *2 Illegal Immigrants Seized at Swift's Worthington Plant: Federal Officials Arrested 15 Other People at Swift & Co. Meatpacking Plans around the Country as Part of an Investigation into Identity Theft*, STAR TRIB. (Minneapolis-St. Paul), July 12, 2007, at 4B.

Immigration worksite raids have occurred for decades.[73] In the past, complaints by government, employers, and civil rights groups of economic disruption and violations of civil liberties had convinced immigration officials to shift their efforts to immigration enforcement near the border and at checkpoints.[74] Recently, however, the landscape for worksite immigration enforcement has changed. In 2006, DHS Secretary Michael Chertoff made worksite enforcement a priority, announcing in April 2006 a nationwide immigration enforcement strategy that would aggressively target employers who knowingly or recklessly hire undocumented workers.[75]

ICE's new worksite enforcement strategy, begun in eleven major U.S. cities, adopts a comprehensive approach focusing on how undocumented workers enter the country and obtain identity documents, as well as targeting employers who knowingly hire such workers.[76] As a result of this strategy, the number of persons arrested in the workplace for being unable to prove legal immigration status jumped nearly tenfold since 2002 to 4,385 in fiscal year 2006.[77]

---

[73] Note, *Reexamining the Consitutionality of INS Workplace Raids After the Immigration Reform and Control Act of 1986*, 100 HARV. L. REV. 1979, 1979 (1987); *see also* Alfredo Mirandé, *Is There a "Mexican Exception" to the Fourth Amendment?*, 55 FLA. L. REV. 365, 370-72 (2003) (documenting case law involving workplace raids in 1970s).

[74] *See* Gaouette, *supra* note 59.

[75] DHS requested $41 million in funds and 200 more ICE agents for fiscal year 2007 to implement a worksite enforcement strategy. Jerry Seper, *Agents Raid Job Sites for Illegals*, WASH. TIMES, Dec. 13, 2006, at A3.

[76] DHS Press Release, *supra* note 59.

[77] The following ICE table illustrates the number of arrests arising from ICE raids in worksite enforcement investigations. ICE, Worksite Enforcement, http://www.ice.gov/pi/news/factsheets/worksite.htm (last visited Sept. 24, 2007).

In addition, an increasing number of persons arrested during workplace raids are criminally prosecuted and face felony criminal charges with a real threat of jail time for violating immigration or other U.S. laws principally related to identity theft. In 2006, for example, that number was 716 of the total arrests (16%), up from only twenty-five in 2002 (5%).[78] In fact, ICE today is effectively, even if deceivingly,[79] appealing to identity theft concerns, as well as to the image of foreigners as potential terrorists. This appeal increases the level of tolerance for civil rights erosions, especially of privacy interests. Consider, for example, Chertoff's remarks in defense of worksite raids:

> [Document fraud] is a serious problem not only with respect to illegal immigration, but with respect to national security. And that's precisely the point made by the 9/11 Commission a couple of years ago, because illegal documents are not only used by illegal migrants, but they are used by terrorists who want to get on airplanes, or criminals who want to prey on our citizens. And so, as part of this overall strategy of worksite enforcement, we've gotten very focused on the question of those who exploit illegal documents and identity theft in order to pursue illegal acts. So yesterday's enforcement action [in the Swift Co. raids] demonstrates another step in this work site enforcement strategy. A tough stance against worksites that employ illegal aliens and against individuals and organizations that commit or facilitate identity theft or fraud.[80]

---

[78] DHS Press Release, *supra* note 59.
[79] Chertoff mischaracterizes the undocumented workers' use of fake SSNs or even real ones (often inadvertently) because workers are not, for example, running up someone else's credit card bill or pushing someone into financial ruin. Rather, as Mark Grey, director of the Iowa Center for Immigrant Leadership and Integration, describes, these workers are embroiled in "an elaborate choreography among the employers who need the immigrant workers, the immigrants who want these jobs, the communities who need them, the cattlemen who depend on them and the government whose basic motto has been: Don't ask, don't tell." Cooper, *supra* note 66, at 12.
[80] DHS Press Release, *supra* note 59.

These workplace immigration raids are representative of Fourth Amendment exceptionalism for immigrant workers in the U.S. It is not that the Fourth Amendment has no application in this context, but rather that privacy expectations about immigration status in the workplace have been eroded. Such erosion occurs through statutes authorizing the creation of databases from which ICE has easy access to obtain civil warrants to conduct raids without particularized suspicion. Unions representing some of the workers arrested during the Swift & Co. raids have filed complaints alleging, inter alia, Fourth Amendment violations when ICE arrested a large group of workers without a warrant and without reasonable suspicion.[81] The likely success of the litigation, however, is quite narrow even for workers who may have a remedy in criminal proceedings. Fourth Amendment violations will be difficult to establish under current Fourth Amendment doctrine. The threshold for a *Katz* reasonable expectation of privacy in a worker's immigration status is likely quite high in light of the heavily regulated nature of workplace immigration enforcement that allows unregulated databases, compels employer "collaboration," and sanctions general warrants.

1. On IRCA, Databases, and Employer "Collaboration"

With the passage of the Immigration Reform and Control Act of 1986 ("IRCA"),[82] employers are required to have their employees complete a government-

---

[81] Class Action Request for Injunctive and Declaratory Relief and Damages, United Food and Commercial Workers Int'l Union, et. al v. Chertoff, et. al, No. 07-00188 (N.D. Tex. Sept. 2007), *available at* http://www.ailf.org/lac/clearinghouse_122106_ICE.shtml. In addition, United Food & Commercial Workers Union filed a petition for habeas corpus and complaint for declaratory relief based on ICE's due process violations in conducting the raids. Petition for Writ of Habeas Corpus, Yarrito v. Meyers, No. 06-CV-2494 (D. Colo. Dec. 2006), *available at id.*. That case, however, was closed when the district court judge considered that ICE has sufficiently corrected any constitutional deficiencies. Final Judgment, Yarrito v. Myers, No. 06-CV-2494 (D. Colo. Jan. 2007), *available at id.*
[82] Immigration Reform and Control Act of 1986, Pub. L. No. 99-603, 100 Stat. 3359, (1986) (codified as amended at 8 U.S.C. § 1324a).

issued Employment Eligibility Verification Form ("Form I-9") to establish that the employee is authorized to work in the United States.[83] The employee must complete and sign Form I-9 and present work authorization and identification documents, which employers must examine, copy, and retain for three years after the date of hire or one year after employment ends, whichever comes later.[84] The accepted documents that establish work authorization include a U.S. passport, social security card, or DHS-issued immigration documents such as a permanent residency card or a work authorization card, while identity documents are mostly U.S.-issued and include driver licenses and voter or military identification cards.[85] Employers retain these documents expressly to enforce the immigration restrictions on unauthorized employment against employers and workers in the workplace.[86]

To this end, Congress created the Basic Pilot Employment Verification Project ("Basic Pilot"), an electronic employment eligibility verification program, initially to operate in a few states.[87] Created in 1996, Basic Pilot permits employers to match employee Form I-9s against U.S. Bureau of Citizenship and Immigration Services ("CIS") and Social Security Administration ("SSA") databases for verification.[88] Congress set forth a limited list of employers required to participate in Basic Pilot. This

---

[83] Immigration and Nationality Act of 1990, § 8 U.S.C. 1324a(b) (2000); 8 C.F.R. § 274a.2 (2000); *see also* NAT'L EMPLOYMENT LAW PROJECT, EMPLOYMENT WORK AUTHORIZATION VERIFICATION & REVERIFICATION: FACT SHEET FOR WORKERS (2002), *available at* www.nelp.org/docUploads/pub147%2Epdf [hereinafter Fact Sheet for Workers].
[84] 8 C.F.R. § 274a.2(b)(2).
[85] *Id.* § 274a.2(b)(1)(v)(A)-(B).
[86] *Id.* § 274a.2(b)(4).
[87] Illegal Immigration Reform and Immigrant Responsibility Act of 1996, § 401(b), Pub. L. No. 104-208, 110 Stat. 3009, 3009-655 to 3009-656 [hereinafter IIRIRA]. The original states included California, Florida, Illinois, New York, and Texas, and extended in 1999 to cover Nebraska. Nat'l Immigration Law Ctr., *"Basic Pilot" Employment Eligibility Verification Program Expanded Nationwide*, IMMIGRANTS' RTS. UPDATE, Dec. 22, 2004, *available at* http://www.nilc.org/immsemplymnt/ircaempverif/irca060.htm.
[88] Nat'l Immigration Law Ctr, *Basic Information Brief, DHS Basic Pilot Program* (revised March 2007), *available at* http://www.nilc.org/immsemplymnt/ircaempverif/basicpilot_infobrief_brief_2007-03-21.pdf.

included federal employers and other employers that an administrative law judge has required to participate as part of a cease and desist order issued under 8 U.S.C. § 1324a ("Unlawful Employment of Aliens.")[89] Congress also specifically provided, however, that the government "may not require any person or other entity to participate in a pilot program."[90]

Through Basic Pilot, employers should be able to detect false or made-up SSNs or those whose names and numbers do not match. Both the immigration and SSA databases are notoriously inaccurate, however, and significantly undermine Basic Pilot's utility.[91] In 2002, DHS hired Temple University and Westat to conduct an independent evaluation of Basic Pilot. The team identified several problems and recommended against larger-scale implementation.[92] These problems included CIS's failure to provide timely data; employer misuse of the database to prescreen applicants seeking employment; adverse employer action against workers who receive a tentative non-confirmation in the first phase of verification; and employer failure to institute appropriate privacy safeguards.[93]

Nevertheless, Congress expanded employer use of Basic Pilot in 2003 to operate in all fifty states, subject to review and monitoring.[94] In 2004, DHS submitted a report to Congress to address the concerns outlined in the Temple/Westat report. This report noted

---

[89] IIRIRA, § 402(e).
[90] *Id.* § 402(a).
[91] The SSA itself estimates that 17.8 million of its records contain discrepancies related to name, date of birth, or citizenship status. OFFICE OF THE INSPECTOR GEN., SOC. SEC. ADMIN, CONGRESSIONAL RESPONSE REPORT: ACCURACY OF THE SOCIAL SECURITY ADMINISTRATION'S NUMIDENT FILE ii (2006), *available at* http://www.ssa.gov/oig/ADOBEPDF/A-08-06-26100.pdf. The same report also notes that 4.8 million of the approximately 46.5 million noncitizen records contained in the SSA's databas contain discrepancies. *Id.* at 11. The GAO also found that over 111,000 A-files were lost. GOV'T ACCOUNTABILITY OFFICE, IMMIGRATION BENEFITS: ADDITIONAL EFFORTS NEEDED TO HELP ENSURE ALIEN FILES ARE LOCATED WHEN NEEDED 4 (2006), *available at* http://www.gao.gov/new.items/d0785.pdf.
[92] TEMPLE UNIV. INST. FOR SURVEY RESEARCH & WESTAT, INS BASIC PILOT EVALUATION SUMMARY REPORT 41 (2002), *available at* www.nilc.org/immsemplymnt/ircaempverif/basicpiloteval_westat&temple.pdf.
[93] *Id.* at 41-42.
[94] Basic Pilot Program Extension and Expansion Act of 2003, Pub. L. No. 108-156, 117 Stat. 1944, ¶ 3(a).

that SSA's databases are currently able to automatically verify employment eligibility of less than fifty percent of the work-authorized noncitizens and recommended against expanding Basic Pilot into a large-scale national program until DHS and SSA addressed the databases' inaccuracies.[95] Basic Pilot, moreover, is unable to detect fraud when workers have appropriated another person's valid identification and work authorization documents.[96] Despite these shortcomings, approximately 12,000 employers across the United States today use Basic Pilot.[97]

Meanwhile, in July 2006, DHS instituted a program called ICE Mutual Agreement between Government and Employer ("IMAGE"), a collaborative agreement between government and businesses to reduce the hiring of undocumented workers.[98] For some companies, joining IMAGE, particularly after what happened to Swift & Co., is a way of avoiding ICE raids.[99] Under the program, businesses receive training on and must adhere to a series of "best practices," including using Basic Pilot, arranging for annual Form I-9 external audits, and establishing a procedure for reporting any violations or deficiencies to ICE.[100] Companies that comply with the terms of IMAGE become "IMAGE certified," a distinction that ICE believes will become an industry standard.[101]

---

[95] U.S. CITIZENSHIP AND IMMIGRATION SERVS., REPORT TO CONGRESS ON THE BASIC PILOT PROGRAMS 4-5 (2004), *available at* www.nilc.org/immsemplymnt/ircaempverif/basicpilot_uscis_rprt_to_congress_2004-06.pdf; *see also* GOV'T ACCOUNTABILITY OFFICE, IMMIGRATION ENFORCEMENT: WEAKNESSES HINDER EMPLOYER VERIFICATION AND WORKSITE ENFORCEMENT EFFORTS 5-6 (2005), *available at* www.gao.gov/new.items/d05813.pdf.
[96] GOV'T ACCOUNTABILITY OFFICE, *supra* note 95, at 6.
[97] NAT'L IMMIGR. LAW CTR., THE BASIC PILOT PROGRAM: NOT A MAGIC BULLET 1 (rev. ed. 2007), *available at* http://www.nilc.org/immsemplymnt/ircaempverif/basicpilot_nomagicbullet_2007-06-26.pdf.
[98] Stinson Morrison Hecker LLP, *A New "IMAGE" for Immigration Compliance*, LAW AT WORK, Aug. 2, 2006, http://www.lawatwork.com/news/2006/08/02/a_new_image_for_immigration_compliance.html.
[99] Darryl Fears & Krissah Williams, *In Exchange for Records, Fewer Immigration Raids: Businesses Skeptical of New Federal Program*, WASH. POST, Jan. 29, 2007, at A03.
[100] *Id.*
[101] *Id.*

Companies participating in the program have already yielded results for ICE. For example, ICE arrested several employees at the Smithfield Packing Company's hog slaughterhouse after the company handed over employee records to ICE in compliance with the IMAGE program.[102]

Additionally, the SSA has been sending so-called No-Match letters, about 130,000 every year,[103] which provide employers with a list of employees whose names or SSNs on their Wage and Tax Statement (Form W-2) do not match SSA records.[104] The SSA's stated purpose for this letter is to correct errors in its database, not to provide employers grounds for firing an employee or reporting him to immigration authorities.[105] However, some employers fire employees or report them to ICE out of fear that not doing so could make them liable for knowingly hiring undocumented workers or subject to IRS fines.[106]

In reality, employers face neither IRS[107] nor IRCA liability for receiving SSA No-Match letters.[108] However, in June 2006, ICE issued proposed rules regarding an employer's legal obligations upon receiving a No-Match letter.[109] The rule would allow

---

[102] *Id.* As of January 2007, 541 of the 5000 Smithfield employees faced the prospect of job termination or arrest based on document discrepancies detected in their job applications through company audits. *Id.*
[103] N.C. Aizenman, *Bush Moves to Step Up Immigration Enforcement*, WASH. POST, Aug. 11, 2007, at A1.
[104] Fact Sheet for Workers, *supra* note 83.
[105] *See* SOC. SEC. ADMIN., RETIREMENT, SURVIVORS, AND DISABILITY INSURANCE: REQUEST FOR EMPLOYER INFORMATION (2004), *available at* http://policy.ssa.gov/poms.nsf/lnx/0101199028?opendocument; *see also* SOC. SEC. ADMIN., SOCIAL SECURITY NUMBER VERIFICATION SERVICE HANDBOOK 19 (rev. ed. 2007), *available at* www.ssa.gov/employer/ssnvs_handbk.htm.
[106] *See* Lee Sustar, *Feds Greenlight Firing of Immigrant Workers: Bosses Take Aim at the Undocumented*, COUNTER-PUNCH, Sept. 15, 2006, http://www.counterpunch.org/sustar09152006.html.
[107] Letter from Thomas B. Dobbins, Dir., P'ship Outreach, IRS to Michael O'Neill and Connie Davis, Infor. Reporting Program Advisory Comm. (Sept. 24, 2003) (on file with author).
[108] NAT'L EMPLOYMENT LAW PROJECT, SSA "NO MATCH" LETTERS: TOP TEN TIPS FOR EMPLOYERS: FACT SHEET FOR IMMIGRANT WORKER ADVOCATES (2006), *available at* http://www.nelp.org/docUploads/top_ten_tip2009060final.pdf.
[109] NAT'L IMMIGRATION LAW CTR., SUMMARY OF DHS-PROPOSED RULES: "SAFE HARBOR PROCEDURES FOR EMPLOYERS WHO RECEIVE A NO-MATCH LETTER" (July 2006), *available at* http://www.nilc.org/immsemplymnt/ssa_related_info/ssanomatch_fedregs_summary.pdf.

ICE to use an employer's failure to act after receipt of these letters as evidence that the employer had "constructive knowledge" of an employee's work ineligibility.[110] Under the proposed rules, an employer must fire a worker with a No-Match SSA letter if within 90 days that worker has failed to rectify the mistake.[111] Failure to do so could lead to stiff civil sanctions, $10,000 per violation, or prosecution.[112] On August 10, 2007 DHS Secretary Michael Chertoff and Commerce Secretary Carlos M. Gutierrez in a joint press conference presented a new immigration enforcement plan that includes the new SSA No-Match rule, which took effect in September of 2007.[113] This move is very likely to provoke employers to fire even more, or report immediately to ICE, employees identified in SSA No-Match letters.[114]

Through Basic Pilot, IMAGE, and SSA No-Match letters, the federal government has institutionalized significant information sharing between DHS and employers to facilitate immigration laws' workplace enforcement. Essentially, IRCA delegated immigration oversight to private employers.[115]

2. On ICE's Scope of Enforcement Powers

Given the degree of access to a company's employee records that ICE currently enjoys, ICE's use of civil search warrants to raid the meatpacking plants is not

---

[110] *Id.*
[111] Aizenmann, *supra* note 103.
[112] *See id.*
[113] *See id.*
[114] Press Release from Migration Policy Institute, *No-Match Letter Could Affect 1.5 Million Workers*, *ImmigrationProfBlog*, available at http://lawprofessors.typepad.com/immigration/2007/10/no-match-letter.html. On October 10, 2007, U.S. District Court Judge Charles R. Breyer of the Northern District in California issued an injuctive order against the regulation based on its conflict with the 1980 Regulatory Flexibility Act, as well as because the SSA databases' discrepancies could result in the firing of lawfully employed workers. Order Granting Motion for Preliminary Injunction, American Federation of Labor, et al., v. Chertoff, et. al. No. C 07-04472 CRB (U.S. Dist. Northern CA Oct. 10, 2007).
[115] *See generally* Gillian E. Metzer, *Privatization as Delegation*, 103 COLUM. L. REV. 1367 (2003) (discussing trend to muddle private/public divide when government privatizes public functions).

surprising.[116] Getting the civil warrants was actually quite easy. Post-IRCA, employers have all the incentive to cooperate with ICE in order to limit their own liability. Swift & Co., for example, participated in Basic Pilot for at least a decade before the raids.[117] Moreover, DHS regulations on IRCA enforcement leave employers that are subject to an investigation little room to refuse to cooperate. IRCA expressly authorized DHS access to examine evidence of any person or entity under investigation for immigration violations and to compel such participation by subpoena.[118] Moreover, IRCA mandated DHS to establish investigative procedures to enforce IRCA, even when DHS received complaints from individuals or entities.[119]

In this case, ICE leads regarding possible identify theft by workers employed at Swift & Co. initially came from interviews of former Swift & Co. employees convicted for unrelated crimes.[120] Tips also came from anonymous individuals who, pursuant to IRCA, are able to report to ICE when they believe undocumented workers have been employed.[121] Based on these interviews, ICE allegedly discovered at least one "criminal ring" of persons supplying Swift & Co. workers with genuine U.S. birth certificates of individuals from Puerto Rico, as well as Social Security cards.[122]

Not surprisingly, in March 2006, ICE subpoenaed Swift & Co. employee records as part of its investigation into the alleged ring of SSN fraud connected to Swift & Co.

---

[116] ICE applied for and was granted a civil administrative search warrant by United States District Court Judge Figa to assess the citizenship and immigration status of the Swift employees on December 8, 2006. *See* Respondent's Memorandum of Law, *supra* note 63 at 2, Yarrito v. Meyers.
[117] Complaint for Declaratory and Injunctive Relief at 1-2, Swift & Co. v. ICE, No. 2-06CV-314-J (N.D. Tex. Nov. 28, 2006) [hereinafter Swift & Co. Complaint].
[118] Immigration and Nationality Act, 8 U.S.C. § 1324a(e)(2)(C) (2007).
[119] *Id.* § 1324a(e)(1).
[120] DHS Press Release, *supra* note 59.
[121] *Id.*
[122] *Id.* at 7.

workers.[123] Swift & Co. quickly complied with ICE and allowed it to review the Form I-9s.[124] Had Swift & Co. refused, ICE had the statutory authority to seek enforcement of the subpoena through a federal district court order.[125] Failure to comply with an ICE audit request or subpoena would also likely have had even more adverse practical consequences for Swift & Co., including raising ICE's suspicion of potential wrongdoing.

ICE's March 2006 subpoena request was for all Form I-9s and supporting identity documents of all employees working at Swift's plant in Marshalltown, Iowa.[126] In this initial request, Swift & Co. provided 1300 records, 665 of which ICE retained for further review.[127] In summer 2006, ICE issued similar subpoenas to the company's six other plants across the U.S.[128] In addition, Swift & Co. also conducted an internal audit of any suspect document identified by ICE and identified a number of workers who, according to Swift & Co., "appear to have deliberately defeated the Basic Pilot verification program."[129] All of this readily available information permitted ICE to establish grounds for the civil immigration warrants.

Notably, Swift & Co. disagreed with ICE over the planned raids. In their place, Swift & Co. proposed a phased enforcement action that would allow it to identify and incrementally dismiss unauthorized workers from its plants.[130] In fact, Swift & Co. initially responded to the investigation without notifying ICE by interviewing approximately 450 suspect employees at several of its plants and found that ninety to

---

[123] Swift & Co. Complaint, *supra* note 117, at ¶ 5.
[124] DHS Press Release, *supra* note 59.
[125] Immigration and Nationality Act, 8 U.S.C. § 1324a(e)(2)(B) (2007).
[126] Swift & Co. Complaint, *supra* note 117, at ¶ 5.
[127] *Id.*
[128] *Id.* at ¶ 7.
[129] *Id.* at ¶ 11.
[130] *Id.* at ¶ 11-12.

ninety-five percent were ineligible to work.[131] The result was that 400 of these workers were terminated, quit, or did not show up for the scheduled interviews and were fired.[132] Swift and Co. also sought an injunction to stop the raids in late November 2006, arguing that the raids would place an unnecessary financial and operational burden on the company.[133] The federal district court judge denied the relief, however, reasoning that an injunction would "harm the public's interest in quickly catching such criminals, swiftly breaking up any rings which cause or contribute to [identify theft] harm, and minimize continuing damages to innocent citizens."[134]

Swift & Co.'s actions angered ICE because it now had no way of knowing how to find those workers and remove them or criminally charge them. Seizing on such examples, in fact, Chertoff faulted ICE's failure to curb more SSN fraud on SSA's inability to refer all instances where the same SSN is used on multiple occasions in multiple workplaces to ICE.[135] As a result, Chertoff is now seeking to have direct access to the SSA database, a move now proscribed by statute:[136]

> If we were able to get the legal authority to do this kind of review of information, we could much more readily identify the kind of identity theft and identity fraud that we discovered in this case . . . I call on Congress . . . to take up this issue of revising the Social Security rules so we can further protect Americans from identity theft, and protect our borders against illegal immigration.[137]

---

[131] Injunctive Order at 7, Swift & Co. v. ICE, Civ. Action 2:06-CV-314-J (N.D. Tex. Dec. 7, 2006) [hereinafter Injunctive Order].
[132] *Id.*
[133] Motion for Preliminary Injunction and Expedited Hearing, Swift & Co. v. ICE, Civ. Action 2:06-CV-314-J (N.D. Tex. Nov. 28, 2006).
[134] Injunctive Order, *supra* note 131, at 9.
[135] DHS Press Release, *supra* note 59.
[136] *See* Privacy Act of 1974, Pub. L. 93-579, 88 Stat 1896, 1897-99 (protecting data from SSA use in absence of statute or regulation requiring verification of identity of individual).
[137] DHS Press Release, *supra* note 59.

Already, there have been several proposals to grant DHS such authority. Senator Wayne Allard, Republican of Colorado, has introduced legislation to authorize the SSA to share No-Match notices with DHS.[138]

3. Of General Warrants and the Swift & Co. Raids

During the Swift & Co. raids, ICE interviewed hundreds of present workers and reviewed each employee's Form I-9 records.[139] These actions were authorized by the warrants.[140] Even prior to IRCA, however, the courts had largely sanctioned similar questioning of workers to ascertain immigration eligibility when immigration agents possessed civil warrants lacking particularized suspicion.[141]

At the end of the raids, ICE found thousands of SSNs that it believed were being misused at Swift & Co. ICE then turned the numbers over to the Federal Trade Commission ("FTC"). The FTC runs the National Security Theft Clearinghouse ("Clearinghouse") and takes in consumer complaints about identity theft that it shares with more than 1,400 law enforcement partners.[142] The FTC ran these numbers through the Clearinghouse and found that some identities were being misused not only to procure employment, but also for credit card fraud, student loan fraud, and tax evasion.[143] About the Swift & Co. raids, Chairman Deborah Platt Majoras of the FTC remarked:

> These arrests today demonstrate the power of interagency coordination. They show how enforcers from across the government, working together,

---

[138] M.E. Sprengelmeyer, *Bill Aims at Data Loophole: Immigration Raids Prompted Allard Proposal*, ROCKY MTN. NEWS, Mar. 1, 2007, at 12.
[139] Respondent's Memorandum of Law, supra note 63 at 3-4 Yarrito v. Meyers.
[140] THE ASSOCIATED PRESS, *36 Arrested in Mishawaka Immigration Raid*, Mar. 7, 2007, *available at* http://www.thetimesonline.com/articles/2007/03/07/updates/breaking_news/doc45eee114b4138808006704.txt.
[141] *See*, Blackie's House of Beef, Inc. v. Castillo, 659 F.2d 1211, 1211 (D.C. Cir. 1981); Int'l Molder's & Allied Workers' Local Union No. 164 v. Nelson, 799 F.2d 547, 547 (9th Cir. 1986).
[142] DHS Press Release, *supra* note 59.
[143] *Id.*

can uncover and stop a scheme that harmed hundreds of U.S. citizens who simply were going about their lives.

Despite such rhetoric, fewer than sixty-five of the 1,200 persons arrested, about five percent, during the Swift & Co. raids were actually charged with identity theft.

4. Pretextual Raids?

The sixty-five defendants facing criminal charges could have challenged their arrests and any evidence seized on the ground that ICE abused its administrative investigative powers for the purpose of conducting law enforcement.[144] Assertions by Chertoff and Myers of uncovering identity theft during Swift & Co. raids lends strong support for this claim,[145] as does the fact that during the raid, ICE specifically asked the workers specific questions about how they obtained their identifications.[146] In addition, ICE agents denied union representatives' access to the workers during the interviews for the stated reason that a criminal investigation was ongoing.[147] Ironically, however, the relatively low yield in criminal prosecutions is likely to preclude a plausible Fourth Amendment argument based on ICE's abuse of its broad immigration investigative authority for criminal law enforcement purposes.

In parallel cases, where the argument has been that the administrative function is only a pretext for criminal law enforcement, motions to suppress have not succeeded.[148] The Court's position is generally to avoid trying to guess the real intent or motivation of law enforcement officers when acting, approving the action as long as officers have

---

[144] *See, e.g.*, Michigan v. Tyler, 436 U.S. 499 (1978) (requiring probable cause when government officials sought access to commercial establishment to gather evidence for criminal prosecution).
[145] *See supra* notes 80-82 and accompanying text.
[146] Petition for Habeas Corpus at 6, Yarrito et al., v. Myers, No. 06-CV-2494 (D. Colo. Dec. 13, 2006).
[147] *Id.* at 5.
[148] See, e.g., Whren v. U.S., 517 U.S. 806 (1996).

"objective" Fourth Amendment grounds.[149] Courts are likely to consider *Whren v. United States* controlling in this regard.[150] There, the Court refused to consider whether the true motives of police officers who detained a group of young men for a minor traffic infraction was to investigate them for drug possession.[151] The Court held that "[s]ubjective intentions play no role in ordinary, probable-cause Fourth Amendment analysis."[152]

One important distinction between *Whren* and the Swift & Co. raids, however, is that ICE lacked particularized probable cause to conduct the administrative function. Obtaining warrants to conduct workplace immigration raids, unlike traffic stops, however, have not required particularized suspicion.[153] In this regard, the raids are doctrinally more comparable to suspicionless vehicular checkpoints where other standards, such as randomness of stops and notice to drivers, rather than probable cause or reasonable suspicion, have satisfied the Fourth Amendment's requirement of reasonableness.[154] However offensive generalized warrants are to privacy, their judicial sanction in the immigration context would preclude a pretextual doctrine claim as long as ICE is conducting the administrative function as permitted by law.

Pretextual claims have been used to successfully challenge vehicle checkpoints, but only when the government's stated primary purpose cannot be justified as

---

[149] *See* Craig M. Bradley, *The Reasonable Policeman: Police Intent in Criminal Procedure*, 76 MISS. L.J. 339, 340 (2006).
[150] *See* 517 U.S. 806 (1996).
[151] *Id.* at 818-19.
[152] *Id.* at 813.
[153] Int'l Molder's & Allied Workers' Local Union No. 164 v. Nelson, 799 F.2d 547, 553 (9th Cir. 1986) (agreeing with D.C. Circuit that immigrant workplace warrants require only reasonable belief unauthorized workers may be present and not that each be particularly named); Blackie's House of Beef, Inc. v. Castillo, 659 F.2d 1211, 1213 (D.C. Cir. 1981), *cert. denied*, 455 U.S. 940 (1982) (upholding constitutionality of immigration workplace warrant lacking particularized suspicion).
[154] *See* Michigan Dep't of Police v. Sitz, 496 U.S. 444, 453 (1990) (upholding sobriety checkpoint where officers stopped vehicles without reasonable suspicion when police used neutral guidelines for carrying out roadblock and its purpose was to protect public from drunk drivers).

administrative. For example, in *City of Indianapolis v. Edmond*,[155] which involved random stops at a checkpoint to investigate drug crimes, police conceded that the checkpoint was primarily for the detection of drugs, which the Court considered primarily a criminal law enforcement purpose.[156] The *Edmond* facts differ from workplace immigration raids, however, given that immigration enforcement is still their principal function, at least in terms of results. In these, the majority of persons arrested are solely being removed, rather than criminally charged, which may make the raids constitutionally permissible. Even after *Edmond*, drug enforcement at immigration or sobriety checkpoints is constitutionally permissible so long as the checkpoints remain primarily for an administrative purpose.[157]

5. Exceeding the Scope of the Warrant Execution or Consent?

A narrower challenge is not to the unparticularized warrant itself but to its execution. Specifically, the challenge is that while civil immigration warrants authorize ICE to enter worksite premises to conduct an investigation, they do not authorize it to seize and search the workers to discover their immigration status, much less to question them about possible criminal identity theft charges. In fact, this challenge is the principal basis for the union's Fourth Amendment challenges filed on behalf of Colorado workers ensnared in the Swift & Co. raids.[158]

Indeed, some early federal district court decisions preceding IRCA affirmed that particularized probable cause was not required for immigration workplace warrants, but

---

[155] 531 U.S. 32, 32 (2000).
[156] *Id.* at 50-51.
[157] *See* Susan Lentz & Robert Charis, *Full Speed Ahead:* Illinois v. Lidster *and Suspicionless Vehicle Stops,* CRIM. L. BULL., Mar.-Apr. 2007, at Part IV.
[158] Class Action and Injunctive Relief, *supra* note 81, at ¶¶ 33-6 and Petition for Habeas Corpus, *supra* note 81, at 18-19..

also held that INS could not execute such warrants to seize large numbers of workers and conduct dragnet-style questioning without reasonable suspicion or probable cause.[159] These early cases, however, also recognized that Fourth Amendment doctrine offered ICE some flexibility to investigate once inside the premises, including acting within the reasonable scope of the warrant to identify the workers, if any, named in the warrant[160] or to engage in consensual encounters with the workers,[161] which could lead to reasonable grounds to detain or arrest.

Unfortunately, the *INS v. Delgado*[162] precedent involving consensual encounters during workplace raids still offers ICE significant flexibility to question the workers and ascertain reasonable suspicion, even if workers refuse to answer questions. The problem with general warrants is precisely their undefined scope; thus, what constitutes its reasonable execution remains vague but is likely to lie somewhere between consensual encounters and indiscriminate seizures. In the early cases involving workplace raids with general warrants, courts drew the line when INS agents specifically targeted Hispanics, or persons who simply looked foreign, for more than brief questioning, which led to their arrests.[163]

In *Delgado*, the INS moved systematically through a garment factory, asked employees to identify themselves, and asked them one to three questions about their

---

[159] Int'l Molders' and Allied Workers' Local Union No. 164, v. Nelson, 643 F. Supp. 884, 894 (N.D. Cal. 1986), *remanded* 799 F.2d 547 (9th Cir. 1986) (remanding to modify injunction); Ill. Migrant Council v. Pilliod, 531 F. Supp. 1011, 1019-21 (N.D. Ill. 1982).

[160] Those early warrants named half a dozen or so workers and listed "others" who were believed to be working without authorization. *See Int'l Molders*, 643 F. Supp. at 889-90.

[161] *See id.* at 891-97. Notably, the California district court in this case rejected the plain view doctrine as an alternative theory, reasoning the illegality of undocumented workers, unlike contraband, is not immediately apparent. *Id.* at 893.

[162] 466 U.S. 210 (1984).

[163] *Int'l Molders*, 643 F. Supp. at 893-95; *Pilliod*, 531 F. Supp. at 1020-21.

citizenship.[164] During the survey, armed INS agents were stationed near the exits while other agents moved throughout the factory and questioned workers at their work areas.[165] The agents showed badges, had walkie-talkies, and carried arms, though they never drew their weapons.[166] ICE's factual description of the events in the Swift & Co. litigation is intended to suggest consent:

> Swift management then brought approximately 700 people in groups to the beef plant cafeteria . . . *no workers were prevented from leaving the area.* Upon entry into the cafeteria, an announcement was made by ICE (in both English and Spanish) *requesting* that all employees who were born in the United States move to one side of the cafeteria, and the remaining employees were asked to move to a different area . . . ICE agents then conducted interviews, limited to eliciting background information on each Swift employee to determine each employee's nationality and immigration status . . . If certain employees needed immigration documents outside the facility to confirm their lawful status, these employees were allowed to contact family and friends . . . *There were no locked doors, and no one was prevented from leaving the area . . . Officers did not frisk the employees or act in anything but a calm and courteous manner so as to facilitate the safest environment possible.*[167]

The workers, of course, tell a much different story of intimidation, including an inability to contact family or lawyers and compelled detention leading to the arrests.[168] Even if a fact finder were to embrace ICE's version of the raids, the *Delgado* facts and the raids at Swift & Co. differ sufficiently enough that an argument for consent may still be precluded.

In the Swift & Co. raids, ICE agents also surrounded the plants and covered each entrance and exit.[169] One significant difference in the Swift & Co. raids, however, is that ICE agents removed workers from their workstations and ordered them to the cafeteria

---

[164] 466 U.S. at 212.
[165] *Id.*
[166] *Id.*
[167] Respondent's Memorandum of Law, supra note 63 at 2-5, Yarrito v. Meyers (*emphasis added*).
[168] *See supra* notes 66-68 and accompanying text.
[169] *See* Yarrito et al., Petition for Writ of Habeas Corpus, *supra* note 81.

for questioning and document verification.[170] Other factors courts may consider in distinguishing the Swift & Co. raids from *Delgado* is the number of ICE agents present during the raids, the length of detention during questioning, and discrepancies in testimony regarding ICE instructions to workers about the nature of the interviews.[171]

An unanswered question is how the courts will handle the apparent refusal of some workers to collaborate with ICE during the interviews at Swift & Co. In *Florida v. Royer*, the Court held that refusal to cooperate cannot alone be grounds to substantiate reasonable suspicion.[172] In *Illinois v. Wardlow*, however, the Court narrowed *Royer* and held that such refusal could be grounds if other factors exist that in combination could lead a reasonable law enforcement agent to conclude that a crime has or is about to be committed.[173] Here, Swift & Co. was armed with information that hundreds of Form I-9s did not match either SSA or CIS records. In light of this fact, a court could hold that refusal to answer a question on immigration status or identity along with other information possessed by ICE could be used to satisfy the reasonable suspicion standard laid out in *Wardlow*.

Another remaining question is whether, during these raids, ICE could have compelled workers to disclose their identity for purposes of locating persons actually named in the warrant, as was ICE's practice with the early warrants. ICE could argue that finding the workers named in the warrant requires engagement of workers in brief questioning. Interestingly, ICE, in the Swift & Co. raids, shifted

---

[170] U.S. District Judge Mary Lou Robinson noted as much when denying the Swift's injunction request. Injunctive Order, *supra* note 131, at 10.
[171] *See supra* notes 167-68.
[172] 460 U.S. 491, 497-98 (1983).
[173] 528 U.S. 119, 125 (2000).

away from a model of indiscriminate questioning of workers into one resembling an administrative checkpoint where all workers, including citizens and lawful permanent residents, are subjected to brief questioning under standardized procedures. In permanent immigration car checkpoints near the border, courts have considered the suspicionless questioning of drivers about their immigration status reasonable under the Fourth Amendment.[174] Of course, workplaces are not like immigration checkpoints. They are not required to be permanent, fixed locations; they may not be near the border; workers do not have prior notice of the raids; and, unlike, public highways, workplaces comprise a greater zone of privacy.

In summary, IRCA's delegation of immigration enforcement to private employers, with the ensuing proliferation of databases, and interagency information sharing about workers' immigration status have combined with preexisting doctrines permitting unparticularized warrants and flexible consensual encounters in immigration raids to significantly erode workers' expectations of privacy. The recent workplace immigration raids, exemplified by the Swift & Co. experience, closely resemble the general warrants that inspired the adoption of the Fourth Amendment.

B. *Home ICE Raids: "Operation Return to Sender"*

Since 2002, ICE has put in place various enforcement programs designed to apprehend persons it labels as fugitives or absconders, terms that refer mostly to persons

---

[174] United States v. Martinez-Fuerte, 428 U.S. 543, 545-46 (1976).

who did not comply with removal orders against them.[175] The National Fugitive Operations Program ("NFOP") was officially established on February 25, 2002, under the auspices of ICE's Office of Detention and Removal.[176] DHS estimates that more than 623,000 absconders live in the U.S.[177] In response, ICE has deployed fifty-two Fugitive Operations Teams nationwide to apprehend these so-called fugitives by conducting raids in people's homes.[178] ICE expects that this number will increase to 75 teams in 2007.[179]

In its initial stages, INS specifically targeted "priority" absconders, a category that included persons with removal orders from countries with an Al Qaeda presence and subsequently persons with a criminal history.[180] In May 2006, however, DHS launched "Operation Return to Sender," which casts a wider net and targets all persons with a preexisting removal order.[181] Since the program's inception, ICE has identified over 25,000 persons who are in the United States in violation of immigration law.[182] Of these, more than one-third were not the people ICE originally targeted.[183]

1. Of Katz, Unreliable Data, and the Merging of Immigration and Criminal Databases

---

[175] *See* Kevin Lapp, *Pressing Public Necessity: The Unconstitutionality of the Absconder Apprehension Initiative*, 29 N.Y.U. REV. L. & SOC. CHANGE 573, 574 (2005).
[176] U.S. Immigration and Customs Enforcement, National Fugitive Operations Program, http://www.ice.gov/pi/dro/nfop.htm [hereinafter NFOP].
[177] DEP'T. OF HOMELAND SEC., OFFICE OF INSPECTOR GEN., AN ASSESSMENT OF UNITED STATES' IMMIGRATION AND CUSTOMS ENFORCEMENT'S FUGITIVE OPERATIONS TEAMS 3 (2007), *available at* http://www.dhs.gov/xoig/assets/mgmtrpts/OIG_07-34_Mar07.pdf.
[178] Press Release, U.S. Immigration & Customs Enforcement, More than 300 Arrested in ICE Operation Targeting Illegal Alien Fugitives and Immigration Violators in San Diego and Imperial Counties (Apr. 2, 2003), *available at* http://www.ice.gov/pi/news/newsreleases/articles/070403sandiego.htm [hereinafer ICE Press Release].
[179] Nina Bernstein, *Hunts for "Fugitive Aliens" Lead to Collateral Arrests*, N.Y. TIMES, July 23, 2007, at B1.
[180] Lapp, *supra* note 175, at 574-75.
[181] ICE Press Release, *supra* note 178.
[182] Ernesto Londoño, *Database Is Tool in Deporting Fugitives: Police Officers Find Illegal Immigrants in Warrant Searches*, WASH. POST, June 12, 2003, at A1.
[183] THE ASSOCIATED PRESS, Elliot Spagat, *Immigration Raids Net Many Not on the Radar*, Apr. 6, 2007, *available at* http://www.dailybreeze.com/news/regstate/articles/6901022.html.

The implementation of the absconder initiatives involved several preliminary steps. First, the NFOP prepared the cases of immigration fugitives for entry into the National Crime Information Center Database ("NCIC"),[184] an FBI-operated federal criminal database containing individuals' criminal histories that is also available to local law enforcement. In 1996, Congress authorized the inclusion of deported "felons" records in the NCIC[185] to help authorities identify and prosecute persons for illegal reentry.[186] Until then, the long-standing policy had been to keep immigration law enforcement information separate from that of criminal law enforcement. Now, the NCIC contains records of persons with civil immigration removal orders, whether or not they also have a criminal history. The database contains around 247,500 ICE warrants, more than half of which are for people with old removal orders, while the rest are records of persons removed for the commission of crimes.[187] To date, the few court challenges to the inclusion of civil immigration records in the NCIC database have failed.[188]

Subsequently, the NFOP divided the immigration fugitives by judicial district based on the most current address available. Then, the relevant portion of each file was transmitted to the appropriate field office and assigned to an apprehension team.[189] The NFOP also became the clearinghouse for all leads on immigration fugitives gleaned from

---

[184] Memorandum from Larry Thompson, Deputy Att'y Gen. to the INS Comm'r, FBI Dir., U.S. Marshall Serv. Dir., and U.S. Att'ys, § A, at 1 (Jan. 25, 2002), *available at* http://news.findlaw.com/hdocs/docs/doj/abscndr012502mem.pdf [hereinafer Thompon Memorandum].

[185] Under the INA, felons are persons removed for the commission of an aggravated felony as defined in the Act, which is not necessarily a felony under federal or state criminal law. Immigration and Nationality Act, 8 U.S.C. § 1101(a)(43) (2007)

[186] A person previously removed who re-enters or attempts to re-enter is punishable with up to two years imprisonment. *Id.* § 1326(a) (2007). This sentence can increase up to ten years if the person who re-enters or attempts to enter was removed because of the commission of three or more misdemeanors or one non-aggravated felony. The sentence can increase up to twenty years if the removal was for the conviction of an aggravated felony. *Id.* § 1326(b).

[187] Londoño, *supra* note 182.

[188] *Id.*

[189] Thompson Memorandum, *supra* note, 184 at 2.

information received from law enforcement or other sources vaguely referred to as "intelligence assets."[190]

The apprehension teams arresting "priority" absconders comprised both immigration and FBI agents,[191] though ICE alone has conducted the most recent raids. The apprehension teams procured warrants to execute the raids based on information compiled on each absconder from their immigration records. At least some of the information gathered from the arrests was then entered into a criminal database.[192] Unfortunately, much of the information that forms the basis for these fugitive warrants is unreliable. Immigration agencies have been notorious for atrocious record keeping and faulty databases, including errors in removal order files.[193]

Several other factors also result in incorrect records. First, many of the removal orders date back years,[194] which increases the probability other persons other than the person subject to the removal order live at the address when the warrant is finally executed. Second, DHS relies on the addresses provided by non-complying immigrants,

---

[190] ICE Press Release, *supra* note 178.
[191] *Id.*
[192] The Thompson Memorandum did not specify whether this database is the NCIC or a different one. Instead there is a reference to entry into a "Computerized Reporting System." Thompson Memorandum, note 184, at 4.
[193] Memorandum from Glenn A. Fine, Inspector Gen., U.S. Dep't of Justice on Immigration and Naturalization Service's Removal of Aliens Issued Final Orders (Feb. 25, 2003), *available at* http://www.usdoj.gov/oig/reports/INS/e0304/memo.pdf [hereinafter Fine Memorandum]. "Our interviews and recent reports prepared by GAO and the INS Office of Internal Audit confirm that the INS continues to face significant data accuracy problems. During this review, we compared data from the INS's and EOIR's alien case tracking and management systems and found name, nationality, and case file number discrepancies, as well as cases missing from the electronic files . . . . According to INS, data discrepancies are caused by data entry errors, incompatibilities between the systems, and the lack of a system for correcting data inconsistencies." *Id. See generally* Thomas W. Donovan, *The American Immigration System: A Structural Change with a Different Emphasis*, 17 INT'L J. REFUGEE L. 574 (2005) (discussing how INS's administrative disarray led to its replacement with Department of Homeland Security in 2002); Catherine Etheridge Otto, *Tracking Immigrants in the United States: Proposed and Perceived Needs to Protect the Borders of the United States*, 28 N.C. J. INT'L L. & COM. REG. 477 (2002) (discussing series of proposed databases and technological improvements to track immigrants inside United States).
[194] Ruth Morris, *U.S. Adding Fugitive Squads that Target Immigrants Who Ignore Expulsion Orders*, S. FLA. SUN SENTINEL, Feb. 26, 2007, *available at* http://oneoldvet.com/?page_id=281.

who often move to avoid immigration authorities. Third, address changes reported to immigration agencies often are not recorded in the databases.[195] In addition, many persons in the databases are not even aware of their removal orders because notice was sent to the incorrect address or because DHS never gave the immigrant notice of her removal order.[196] As a result, the administrative warrants are often issued on the basis of incorrect information about the person's place of residence,[197] or against people who do not know they have a removal order at all.

Consider the story of Elizabeth Pozada, a Peruvian national, who did not know she had a four-year old removal order against her when ICE showed up at her door in late 2006. She thought her case for political asylum was on appeal since her initial denial in 2001. In fact, Elizabeth had been living in the United States for fifteen years when ICE agents came knocking and arrested her and her husband in their South Florida home.[198] Two weeks after her arrest, Pozada was released to settle her "affairs," including having to leave behind a house in foreclosure and her eight-year-old, U.S.-born son, who would live with her brother, a naturalized U.S. citizen.[199]

Unfortunately, even knowing that an administrative warrant could contain the wrong address, ICE's strategic practice in conducting these raids has been to round up every person living in the home, ask for proof of immigration status, and arrest those unable to provide it. ICE acts in the hope, not under reasonable suspicion much less probable cause, that some of the current residents in the home are also undocumented.

---

[195] Michelle Wucker, *The Top Ten Ways America Gets Immigration Wrong*, AM. IMMIGRATION L. FOUND., June 19, 2006, http://www.ailf.org/ipc/wucker_topten.shtml.
[196] DHS and immigration courts are authorized to issue removal orders in absentia. Immigration and Nationality Act, 8 U.S.C. § 1229a(b)(5) (2007).
[197] THE ASSOCIATED PRESS, *supra* note 1.
[198] Morris, *supra* note 194.
[199] *Id.*

For example, during an East Hampton, New York, raid in March 2007, ICE executed ten warrants to arrest twenty-eight persons "discovered" to be in the country without authorization during the raid.[200] As is standard practice, several armed ICE agents came to the door before dawn, knocked and yelled to open up. Once inside, the agents inquired about every occupant's immigration status, allegedly for officer safety.[201]

Not surprisingly, when ICE shows up to execute warrants, those living in the home are not always undocumented immigrants. Regardless, if the residents are Brown, they will experience the same terror and intimidation. Consider the story of Christina Ramos, a U.S. citizen and student at the University of Colorado, her U.S. citizen brother, a friend living with them, and her parents who are lawful permanent residents from El Salvador. On March 13, 2007, at about 7:30 a.m., ICE agents jumped out of their van and pulled out their guns, blocked the Ramos's driveway with another vehicle and screamed at Ramos who was outside her home.[202] When Ramos ran inside to take shelter, ICE officers refused to identify themselves, chased her, tackled another resident, searched everyone residing in the home for weapons, and repeatedly screamed at them to verify their immigration status.[203]

Immigration raids also affect mixed-status families — families comprising both documented and undocumented citizens or residents. The Pew Hispanic Center has found that there are 6.6 million unauthorized families in the United States, where at least

---

[200] *See* Taylor K. Vecsey, *Clergy Calls for Investigation of Federal Raid: Did Immigration Agents Violate Civil Rights?*, E. HAMPTON STAR, Mar. 1, 2007, *available at* http://www.easthamptonstar.com/DNN/Default.aspx?tabid=1448.
[201] *Id.*
[202] Katie Kerwin McCrimmon, *Citizen Wants Apology for Raid: Immigration Agents Search Legal Residents*, ROCKY MTN. NEWS (Denver), Mar. 24, 2007, at 4.
[203] *Id.* For a similar story involving a home raid against an immigrant family with legal status, see Samuel G. Freedman, *Immigration Raid Leaves Sense of Dread in Hispanic Students*, N.Y. TIMES, May 23, 2007, at B1.

one head of household is undocumented, comprising a total of 14.6 million people, most of them U.S. citizens or lawful residents.[204] In fact, 3.1 million U.S.-born citizen children have at least one parent who is undocumented.[205] As a result, ICE has raided homes with U.S. citizen children. One such child is Kebin Reyes, who at seven years old was taken into custody along with his father, Noe Reyes, who had been ordered deported in 2000.[206] Whether ICE even had a warrant is unclear.[207] Nonetheless, the child was taken into custody so as not to leave him alone, despite requests by his father to allow him to call relatives.[208] The child allegedly remained locked in a cell with his father for about ten hours until picked up by an uncle.[209] During the ordeal, Kebin was given only bread and water, while agents repeatedly denied his father's requests to make calls.[210]

2. The Litigation

In the Bay Area, where ICE has arrested more than 800 people in house raids conducted mostly during four months in early 2007, the American Civil Liberties Union of Northern California and the Lawyer's Committee for Civil Rights filed a Freedom of Information Act ("FOIA") request with ICE. The FOIA request lists serious concerns about aspects of the raids, including ethnic profiling and misuse of warrants.[211] Other immigration rights groups have filed suits seeking injunctive relief and compensatory

---

[204] JEFFREY S. PASSEL, PEW HISPANIC CTR., THE SIZE AND CHARACTERISTICS OF THE UNAUTHORIZED MIGRANT POPULATIONS IN THE U.S. 11-12 (2007), *available at* http://pewhispanic.org/files/reports/61.pdf.
[205] *Id.*
[206] Mark Prado, *ACLU Files Suit on Behalf of Child Taken in Immigration Raid,* OAKLAND TRIBUNE, Apr. 27, 2007, *available at* http://findarticles.com/p/articles/mi_qn4176/is_20070427/ai_n19063631.
[207] *Id.*
[208] *Id.*
[209] *Id.*
[210] *Id.*
[211] Melissa McRobbie, *ACLU Seeks Records On Raids; Group Wants ICE Training Materials Among Other Things,* THE PALO ALTO DAILY NEWS, Mar. 7, 2007, *available at* http://www.paloaltodailynews.com/article/2007-3-7-03-07-07-smc-immigration.

damages on behalf of immigrants arrested during fugitive raids.[212] A key example is Central Legal, Inc.'s lawsuit on behalf of more than fifty immigrants arrested in their homes during an April 2007 raid in Willmar, Minnesota. Their complaint alleges that the raids were conducted without a warrant and that ICE agents identified themselves as police before storming into homes to arrest the residents.[213] The ACLU also filed a civil lawsuit challenging Kebin's detention on Fourth and Fifth Amendment grounds,[214] while the Ramos are simply waiting for an apology.[215] More recently, immigrant rights groups filed a lawsuit challenging the New Haven raids, which occurred two days after the city adopted a program to issue identification cards to all residents, including undocumented immigrants, to allow access to banking, library and other public services..[216]

Hundreds of similar newspaper stories echo the concerns detailed in these lawsuits. It is difficult to conceive how the Fourth Amendment could reasonably allow law enforcement to execute dragnets on people's homes without obtaining any warrant or by obtaining warrants based on flawed databases. Nevertheless, here too, like with challenging workplace raids, actual Fourth Amendment violations are difficult to establish. Some immigrants are removed immediately without a hearing and thus without an opportunity to raise a Fourth Amendment challenge.[217] Similarly, those in removal proceedings also lack a remedy because the exclusionary rule is unlikely to protect them

---

[212] The American Immigration Law Foundation, Litigation Relating to ICE Raids, available at http://www.ailf.org/lac/clearinghouse_122106_ICE.shtml,
[213] Complaint for Declaratory and Injunctive Relief and Damages, Carlos Arias, et al. v. ICE & DHS, No. 07CV1959 (C.D. Minn. Apr. 19, 2007) (on file with author).
[214] Complaint for Violations of the Fourth and Fifth Amendments to the United States Constitution, Kebin Reyes v. Nancy Alcantar (N.D. Cal. 2007), *available at* http://www.aclunc.org/cases/cases_to_watch/asset_upload_file318_5387.pdf.
[215] McCrimmon, *supra* note 202.
[216] *Immigrant advocacy groups sue over New Haven raids*, HARTFORD COURANT, Aug. 11, 2007, at B7.
[217] Preexisting removal orders are enforced without a hearing. Immigration and Nationality Act §240(d) (2007).

in the hearing, even if a violation is found.[218] Immigrants who face criminal charges or motions to enjoin will encounter Fourth Amendment doctrines that are quite favorable to ICE as explored below. Additionally, civil suits for damages must overcome liability shields for government agencies and their officials, including the doctrine of qualified immunity.[219]

a. Defective Warrants?

ICE's primary reliance on information from immigration databases as a basis for issuing warrants could be grounds for a Fourth Amendment challenge, at least when the information in the warrants contains errors. Specifically, the challenge would be that ICE's knowing and exclusive reliance on inaccurate immigration databases to certify the existence of removal orders, the person's identity, or his address, is insufficient for substantiating probable cause.

There are several considerations that could undermine this challenge. First, courts have not required foolproof evidentiary reliability in finding probable cause and may tolerate some degree of database inaccuracy.[220] Second, courts may tolerate immigration inaccuracies even more when they result from an immigrant's own failure to accurately report her residence change to immigration authorities. Finally, the good faith exception

---

[218] The violation must rise to the level of egregiousness for the exclusionary remedy to apply. *See generally* Migas, *supra* note 15 (analyzing the narrow Fourth Amendment challenges that meet the egregiousness standard).

[219] Civil lawsuits to challenge immigration agents' abuses are difficult to win in part because of doctrines, such as qualified immunity, but also because of immigrants' diminished constitutional protections. Officers are only civilly liable when their conduct violates clearly established constitutional rights of which a reasonable person should have known. *See generally* Steve Helfand, *Desensitization to Border Violence & the Bivens Remedy to Effectuate Systemic Change*, 12 LA RAZA L.J. 87 (2001) and Stephen A. Rosenbaum, *Keeping an Eye on the I.N.S.: A Case for Civilian Review of Uncivil Conduct*, 7 LA RAZA L.J. 1 (1994).

[220] *See* Arizona v. Evans, 514 U.S. 1, 16-17 (1995) (upholding the use of evidence obtained from a false arrest record that was the product of a clerical error); United States v. Hines, 564 F.2d 925, 928 (10th Cir. 1977) (finding that reliance upon FBI's NCIC database to substantiate probable cause for an arrest was acceptable).

to the exclusionary rule could provide ICE with an excuse if its reliance on the warrants, despite errors, is viewed as executed in good faith.

A 2003 study of immigration removal records revealed that discrepancies in identity and address information occurred in seven percent of the 308 cases of immigrant files with final orders, and eleven percent of the 470 aliens from states that sponsor terrorism.[221] Whether this statistic is sufficient for courts to invalidate warrants that rely solely on immigration data is an open question. However, parallel challenges to the FBI's NCIC database, which is also known for its inaccuracies,[222] have not been successful.[223] In those challenged cases, however, there existed corroborating information thus the databases and were not the sole basis for substantiating probable cause.[224] This fact could distinguish the immigration raid cases from those challenging reliance on the NCIC during traffic stops.

Were courts to accept probable cause challenges to immigration warrants based on erroneous data, ICE could still rely on the good faith exception to the exclusionary rule. The good faith doctrine as established in *U.S. v. Leon* excuses errors, including computer errors, as long as law enforcement believes in "good faith" that the warrant was valid.[225] In essence, this doctrine has excused inadvertent or even negligent disregard of

---

[221] U.S. Department of Justice of the Inspector General, The Immigration and Naturalization Services' Removal of Aliens Issues Final Orders, Report No. 1-2003-004 (Feb. 2003), at 6, *available at* http://www.npr.org/documents/2005/mar/doj_alien_removal.pdf [hereinafter OIG 2003 Removal Report]..
[222] *See* Office of the Inspector General, REVIEW OF THE TERRORIST SCREENING CENTER: EXECUTIVE SUMMARY, AUDIT REPORT: 05-27 (June 2005), *available at* http://www.usdoj.gov/oig/reports/FBI/a0527/exec.htm.
[223] United States v. Davis, 568 F.2d 514, 515 (6th Cir. 1978); United States v. Hines, 564 F.2d 925, 928 (10th Cir. 1977), *cert. denied*, 434 U.S. 1022 (1978).
[224] *Id.*
[225] 468 U.S. 897, 919-21 (1984).

warrant inaccuracies by police, except when that disregard is "substantial and deliberate."[226]

In *Arizona v. Evans*, for example, the Court applied the good faith exception to deny the suppression of a marijuana joint discovered during police execution of an arrest warrant that, unbeknownst to the officer, had been quashed.[227] *Evans* is distinguishable from the ICE database errors, however, because in *Evans* the error was attributable to a justice court clerk who failed to inform the warrant section of the Sheriff's Office that a judge had ordered the warrant quashed.[228] However questionable the premise that the deterrence purpose of the exclusionary rule is intended to curtail police misconduct not that of the courts,[229] ICE warrant errors are attributable to DHS recordkeeping and data entry, except for those based on an immigrant's own failure to provide accurate information. Errors attributable to law enforcement entities as a whole could exempt the application of the good faith rule since good faith is measured against the collective knowledge of law enforcement officers, not solely those who execute the warrant.[230]

b. *Unconstitutional Warrant Execution?*

ICE's dragnet strategy when enforcing individual removal order warrants may also exceed the reasonable scope of the warrants' execution. Several questions arise here. The first question involves the constitutional knock and announce requirement

---

[226] *Id.* at 908-09 (quoting Franks v. Delaware, 438 U.S. 154, 171 (1978)). *See generally* Andrew E. Taslitz, *The Expressive Fourth Amendment: Rethinking the Good Faith Exception to the Exclusionary Rule*, 76 MISS. L.J. 483, 490-93 (2006) (explaining the holding in U.S. v. Leon).
[227] 115 S. Ct. 1185, 1188 (1995).
[228] *Id.*
[229] *Id.* Similarly, in *Illinois v. Krull*, 480 U.S. 340, 350-53 (1987), the Court applied the good faith exception when police relied on a statute later declared unconstitutional to conduct a search. There, the Court similarly concluded that the exclusionary rule deterrence was not intended for the legislature.
[230] *See* Taslitz, *supra* note 226, at 502-04.

before the execution of warrants.[231] Immigrant rights groups have advised their clients not to open the door when ICE arrives. Does ICE have authority to force entry into the home? If so, how long must ICE wait? With criminal warrants, the knock and announce requirement only requires law enforcement to wait a reasonable time for occupants to respond to their knock, after which they may enter by force.[232] What is a reasonable waiting period, furthermore, is partly up to the discretion to law enforcement, particularly in cases where evidence might be easily disposed or destroyed.[233]

Unlike drugs, however, immigrants are not disposable, though they admittedly can hide. In fact, in contrast to criminal warrants, ICE's administrative warrants do not require immigrants to answer the door or allow entry.[234] Were a pattern of refusal to develop, however, courts might be more willing to create similar exceptions to the knock and announce rule as have developed in criminal cases.[235] ICE has reportedly announced themselves as police rather than as immigration agents.[236] Even if courts recognize this practice as a violation of the knock and announce rule, a remedy may not exist. Of note is the Court's recent holding that knock and announce violations would not require suppression of all related evidence.[237]

---

[231] *See* Wilson v. Arkansas, 514 U.S. 927, 927(1995) (holding that a factor for considering the reasonableness of a search is whether officers knock and announce their presence and authority before entering dwelling, as required by common law).
[232] WILLIAM E. RINGEL, EXECUTION OF WARRANTS, SEARCHES AND SEIZURE, ARRESTS, AND CONFESSIONS § 6:10 (2007).
[233] United States v. Banks, 540 U.S. 31, 31(2003) (approving forceful entry after officers knocked, announced, and waited for 15-20 seconds and evidence sought involved cocaine).
[234] *See* Bernstein, *supra* note 179 (reporting on DHS Secretary Chertoff's explanation that civil immigration warrants do not permit ICE to force entry) Jerry Seper, *Outnumbered in a Hunt for Aliens: Force of 200 Charged with Tracking 400,000 Criminals, "Absconders,"* THE WASH. TIMES, July 20, 2004, at A1 (describing the same practice).
[235] U.S. v. Banks, 540 U.S. at 31.
[236] *Bay Area Communities in Uproar Over Raids*, EL TECOLOTE ONLINE, Mar. 22, 2007, http://news.eltecolote.org/news/view_article.html?article_id=268824dad47cb14d56fe4eced7a0a113.
[237] Hudson v. Michigan, 126 S. Ct. 2159, 2167 (2006).

The second issue raised by ICE's warrant execution practices is the reasonableness of the scope of warrant's execution once ICE gains home entry: May ICE reasonably seize and question all the occupants in the home about their immigration status? Unfortunately, under some circumstances, the answer may be yes. In *Muelher v. Mena*,[238] police officers, armed with a criminal search warrant based on probable cause that Raymond Romero had been involved in a gang-related drive-by shooting, executed the warrant and detained respondent Iris Mena in handcuffs and then asked her about her immigration status.[239] The Court considered the handcuffing a reasonable seizure under the Fourth Amendment as a necessary measure to protect officer safety.[240] The officers, however, then proceeded to ask Mena about her immigration status, and the Court reversed the Ninth Circuit on the immigration status questioning issue, holding that there is no requirement of particularized reasonable suspicion for purposes of inquiring into citizenship status.[241] Instead, the Court expanded the legal fiction of consent. Even though Mena had been handcuffed for more than two hours, the Court sanctioned ICE's questioning into her immigration status without reasonable suspicion.[242] In essence, the Court did not consider inquiry into Mena's immigration statuts as an additional seizure under the Fourth Amendment requiring independent justification.

Mena may be read narrowly to hold that a person otherwise legally detained may be asked "consensually" about her immigration status without an additional need for reasonable suspicion. It is unclear, however, whether Mena could have been compelled to answer the questions if she had refused to answer.

---

[238] 544 U.S. 93, 95-96 (2005).
[239] *Id.*
[240] *Id.* at 100.
[241] *Id.* at 95.
[242] *Id.*

In other words, can the residents of a home who are not the targets of an arrest warrant refuse to answer questions about their immigration status? Generally, in nonconsensual encounters, the Court has required reasonable suspicion to compel a person to disclose their identity.[243] Here, however, we return to the question of what ICE officers can reasonably do during warrant execution, beyond consensual inquiries, a question also relevant to workplace raids.[244]

Unlike workplace raids, home raids may offer ICE agents broader discretion to compel residents to disclose their identity. First, ICE could argue that asking residents their name and even, perhaps, requiring identification may be necessary to identify whether the person is the one named in the warrant. Second, ICE may argue that officer safety compels identification.

The safety justification is less convincing, however, when, unlike *Mena*, the case does not involve a violent precedent. Despite the rhetorical force of words like "fugitives" and "absconders," the ICE warrants enforce the law against persons who failed to comply with a removal order, not violent criminals. The requirement to force disclosure of a person's immigration status is even less reasonable. The reality is that, in most cases, ICE is likely to claim to possess reasonable suspicion to make the inquiry based on factors such as foreign appearance, language, and identity documents, and even the refusal to answer questions.[245]

c. *Pretextual Enforcement*

---

[243] Hiibel v. Sixth Judicial Dist. Court of Nevada, Humbolt County, 542 U.S. 177, 181-83 (2004).
[244] *See supra* notes 158-74 and accompanying text.
[245] Illinois v. Wardlow, 528 U.S. 119, 125 (2000) (refusing to cooperate can be one of several factors to establish reasonable suspicion).

The absconder initiative has a clear criminal law enforcement nature. Especially in its initial stages, an independent aim of the raids was to investigate terrorist leads and arrest persons with a criminal history.[246] But even outside these categories, absconders are not solely immigration violators but also criminals *per se*, as they could face up to four years incarceration for failure to depart after a removal order.[247] The entry of absconder's names into the NCIC, moreover, indicates immigration agencies' shift to treat absconders as criminals and not solely as immigration violators. That all the specific targets of the absconder initiative are *per se* criminals under the law distinguishes absconder raids from the workplace raids because working without authorization in the United States is not yet a federal crime, unless the person engages in identify theft.[248]

This distinction between the absconder home raids and workplace raids could bar ICE from relying on the pretextual doctrine to justify reliance on its administrative powers to conduct criminal enforcement. The pretextual doctrine confers broad discretion on ICE to conduct criminal law enforcement,[249] but courts might be more willing to draw the line where all the targets of the arrests could face criminal liability.[250] Ironically, ICE could argue in its defense that, as executed, the absconder ICE raids primarily serve an administrative immigration function: to detect and remove immigration violators, and not to criminally charge them. In fact, ICE retains discretion to treat all absconders as immigration violators rather than as criminals. Moreover, ICE

---

[246] *See supra* note 180 and accompanying text.
[247] Immigration and Nationality Act, 8 U.S.C. § 1253 (2007).
[248] Working without authorization in the United States continues to constitute solely a civil immigration violation, despite recent legislative efforts to impose criminal sanctions. *See* Enic Trucios-Haynes, *Civil Rights, Latinos, and Immigration: Cybercades and Other Distortions in the Immigration Reform Debate*, 44 BRANDEIS L. J. 637, 652 (2006).
[249] *See supra* notes 148-52 and accompanying text.
[250] *See, e.g.*, City of Indianapolis v. Edmond, 531 U.S. 32 (2000) (striking down car drug checkpoint because primary purpose of narcotics-interdiction could not be rationalized in terms of highway safety but for scourge of illegal drugs).

arrests not only the absconders but also co-residents who are immigration violators but not criminals, as mere unlawful presence is not yet criminal under the immigration laws. Thus, to the extent that ICE is primarily opting to pursue removal for the persons arrested, courts might still be willing to justify the program under the pretextual doctrine.

d. Racial Profiling

When ICE instituted the "priority" absconder program to target primarily Muslims and persons of Arab descent, equal protection violations were explicit.[251] With the expansion of the "fugitive initiatives" to include the more than 600,000 persons with removal orders, the program is now at least facially neutral. Its disparate targeting of Latino immigrants, however, is documented in nearly all media stories detailing the raids.[252] Courts are unlikely to consider these challenges at least in the context of Fourth Amendment doctrine. For example, the Court has directed defendants in "driving while Black" cases to raise charges of disparate law enforcement in civil rights lawsuits rather than in the context of the Fourth Amendment.[253]

Moreover, the Court has tolerated racial targeting in immigration enforcement, at least at immigration checkpoints and as a factor in the determination of reasonable suspicion in traffic enforcement.[254] These cases are nominally distinguishable on the basis of how invasive the practices are in the context of home searches. Yet, to the extent

---

[251] *See* Lapp, *supra* note 175, at 586-89.

[252] The disparate targeting of Latino workers is also evident in workplace raids, which primarily occur in segregated workspaces, occupied primarily by Brown or Latino workers. *See* Leticia M. Saucedo, *The Employer Preference for the Subservient Worker and the Making of the Brown Collar Workplace*, 67 OHIO ST. L.J. 961, 965-66 (2006).

[253] *See* David Harris, *"Driving While Black" and Other Traffic Offenses: The Supreme Court and Pretextual Traffic Stops*, 87 J. CRIM. L. & CRIMINOLOGY 544, 550-51 (1997). Unfortunately, a remedy for selective immigration enforcement may not be available under equal protection grounds. *See* DAVID COLE, ENEMY ALIEN: DOUBLE STANDARDS AND CONSTITUTIONAL FREEDOMS IN THE WAR ON TERRORISM 204 (2003). *But see* Lapp, *supra* note 175, at 592-600.

[254] *See* Mirandé, *supra* note 73, at 372-73.

that warrants allow such searches, courts may not view the presence of ICE in the home as offensive to the Fourth Amendment.

In summary, even though ICE executes defective warrants to conduct dragnet raids in people's homes and disproportionately targets Latinos, current Fourth Amendment jurisprudence offers little protection to immigrants.

C. The Future of Local Immigration Raids: The Hazleton Anti-Immigrant Ordinances

Since the events of 9/11, anti-immigrant groups like the Federation of American Immigration Reform (FAIR) and the U.S. English-Only, Inc. have been supporting or promoting local efforts to pass anti-immigrant ordinances or include them as propositions in key local elections.[255] In 2006 alone, at least seventy-eight state immigration-related bills were approved in thirty-three states.[256] These ordinances range from denying the undocumented basic worker protections to restricting their access to higher education and other state benefits, such as denying them driver's licenses, barring them from congregating as day laborers, and prohibiting them from speaking Spanish.[257] The ordinances also include housing and employer restrictions, such as the 2006 Hazleton, Pennsylvania anti-immigrant ordinances that sought to bar the undocumented from taking jobs, renting apartments, or engaging in other commercial transactions. These housing and employer ordinances would have required employers, landlords, and businesses to monitor the immigration status of workers and tenants. They also sought to impose both

---

[255] *See* Edward Sifuentes, *FAIR Could Join Escondido to Defend Rental Ban*, THE NORTH COUNTY TIMES, Oct. 28, 2006, *available at* http://www.nctimes.com/articles/2006/10/29/news/top_stories/22_03_2810_28_06.txt; Howard Witt, *It's Official: English-only movement Gains Traction: Hispanic Leaders Alarmed*, CHI. TRIB., Oct. 15, 2006, at 4.

[256] Summer Harlow, *Small Towns Play Big Role on Immigration: Fear of Persecution Forces Many to Move*, THE NEWS J. (Wilmington, DE), Oct. 15, 2006, *available at* http://www.ijjblog.org/2006/10/small_towns_big_role_immigrati.html.

[257] Aldana, *supra* note 31, at 270-85.

civil and criminal penalties on employers, landlords or businesses that violated the restrictions.

1. The Hazleton Ordinances

Beginning in July 2006, the City of Hazleton passed a series of four anti-immigrant ordinances designed to target and expel undocumented immigrants from the town.[258] On July 13, 2006, Hazleton passed the Illegal Immigration Relief Act Ordinance, which it subsequently replaced in September 2006 with Ordinance 2006-18, in response to litigation challenging the July ordinance's constitutionality.[259] On December 28, 2006, also in response to the litigation, the Hazleton City Council amended Ordinance 2006-18 by adopting Ordinance 2006-40, which added Section 7 dealing with the ordinances' procedures and implementation.[260] In addition, in August 2006, Hazleton passed Ordinance 2006-13, titled "Establishing a Registration Program for Residential Rental Properties."[261] On December 28, 2006, Hazleton also enacted Ordinance 2006-35 with the same title.[262]

Under section 4, Ordinance 2006-18 prohibits any entity doing business in the city of Hazleton to hire or continue to employ any worker who is not authorized to work under U.S. immigration laws.[263] Every business entity that applies for a business permit to engage in any type of work in Hazleton must sign an affidavit "affirming that they do

---

[258] Not discussed in this Article is Hazleton, Pa., Ordinance 2006-10, (July 13, 2006), which is an English-only provision, *available at* http://clearinghouse.wustl.edu/chDocs/public/IM-PA-0001-0003.pdf.
[259] *See infra* Part I.C.3.
[260] Memorandum of Law in Support of Plaintiffs' Opposition to Plaintiff's Motion to Dismiss and Cross Motion for Summary Judgment at 1-2, Lozano v. Hazleton, 496 F. Supp. 2d 477 (M.D. Pa. 2007) (No. 3:06cv01586) [hereinafter Memorandum of Law].
[261] *Id.*
[262] *Id.*
[263] Hazleton, Pa., Ordinance 2006-18, §§ 4, at A (Sept. 8, 2006), *available at* http://www.aclu.org/pdfs/immigrants/hazleton_secondordinance.pdf.

not knowingly utilize the services of an unlawful worker."[264] Ordinance 2006-18 also seeks to deny "illegal alien[s[", defined as persons "not lawfully present in the United States" the ability to obtain housing in Hazleton based on their immigration status.[265] Specifically, the ordinance prohibits the harboring of "illegal aliens," which includes "to let lease, or rent a dwelling unit to an illegal alien, knowing or in reckless disregard of the fact that an alien has come to, entered, or remains in the United States in violation of the law.".[266] Violation of these terms by employers, businesses, or landlords could result, *inter alia*, in civil penalties and denial of licenses.[267]

To enforce both the employment and housing restrictions, the Hazleton ordinances rely on existing federal databases or else try to establish citywide registration records.[268] In regards to the employment restrictions, for example, a complaint by any city official or entity to the Hazleton Code Enforcement Office would trigger an investigation that would require an employer to provide the identity of the alleged undocumented workers within three days.[269] In turn, the Code Office would seek to verify the worker's authorization to work through Basic Pilot.[270] Ordinance 2006-18, in fact, mandates that all city agencies enroll and participate in the Basic Pilot Program, and conditions the award of city contracts or business grants exceeding $10,000 to the business entity's participation in Basic Pilot.[271] Even when Ordinance 2006-18 does not require such enrollment, those employers that do not enroll risk exorbitant penalties.[272]

---

[264] *Id.*
[265] *Id.* §§ 3(D), and 5(A).
[266] *Id at 5(A)(1).*
[267] *Id.* §§ 4(B)(3)-(4), 5(B)(8).
[268] Memorandum of Law, *supra* note 260, at 13-16.
[269] *Id.* § 4(B)(1)-(3).
[270] *Id.* § 4(B)(5); *See supra* Part I.A.1.
[271] Ordinance 2006-18, § 4(C), (D).
[272] *Id.* §§ 4(B)(5), (E).

The housing provisions go even further by requiring the creation of a tenant registration system. Ordinance 2006-13 requires all occupants of rental units to obtain an "occupancy permit."[273] To obtain the permit, an applicant must provide "[p]roper identification showing proof of legal citizenship and/or residency."[274] Under the ordinance, Hazleton's Code Office officials determine whether each tenant presented proof of legal immigration status. Tenants who allow additional tenants in the rental unit must first obtain written permission from the landlord. In turn, those additional occupants must obtain their own permits.[275] Further, tenants must inform the city when they move or when members of their family move out.[276] Thus, all tenants who do not own their home must disclose, in addition to their immigration status, their place of residence, as well as information about their associations.

All Hazleton landlords are barred from renting to unregistered tenants.[277] The housing restrictions would be enforceable upon receipt by the Code Office of any complaint by a city official, business entity, or resident.[278] Hazleton's Code Office then has the responsibility of using the identity information provided by the landlord[279] or tenant upon registration[280] to verify the person's immigration status with the federal government. Though the process for immigration verification is not specified in the ordinances, Hazleton officials have clarified in documents submitted in the litigation challenging the ordinances that verification would consist of seeking authority from the

---

[273] Hazelton, Pa., Ordinance 2006-13, § 7b (Aug. 15, 2006), *available at* http://www.aclu.org/pdfs/immigrants/hazleton_firstordinance.pdf.
[274] *Id.*
[275] *Id.* § 10(b).
[276] *Id.*
[277] Hazelton, Pa., Ordinance 2006-18, § 5(A) (Sept. 8, 2006), *available at* http://www.aclu.org/pdfs/immigrants/hazleton_secondordinance.pdf.
[278] *Id.* § 5(B)(1).
[279] *Id.* § 5(B)(3).
[280] Ordinance 2006-13, § 7(b)(1)(g).

federal government to use or access the Systematic Alien Verification for Entitlements ("SAVE") program.[281]

SAVE administers and controls access to information contained in the Verification Information System ("VIS") database.[282] This database is nationally accessible and contains selected immigration status information compiled from more than sixty million records.[283] SAVE allows federal, state, and local government agencies and licensing bureaus to obtain immigration status information in order to determine a non-citizen applicant's eligibility for public benefits.[284] To join the SAVE program and acquire access to VIS to perform immigration status verification, an agency must first establish a Memorandum of Understanding ("MOU") with the SAVE Program, then establish a purchase order with the SAVE Program contractor to pay for VIS transaction fees. Access to SAVE is subject to CIS resource limitations and other legal or policy criteria.[285] SAVE was actually designed primarily to permit federal and local entities to determine an applicant's eligibility to receive certain public benefits. It was never intended to provide a final finding of fact or conclusion of law about the applicant's immigration status in the U.S.[286]

2. The Litigation on Privacy

---

[281] Ordinance 2006-18, § 5(B)(3).
[282] *See* ICE, Systematic Alien Verification for Entitlements (SAVE) Program, http://www.uscis.gov/portal/site/uscis (search for "SAVE"; follow top hyperlink for "Systematic Alien Verification for Entitlements (SAVE) Program").
[283] *Id.*
[284] *Id.*
[285] *Id.*
[286] *See* Responsibility of Certain Entities To Notify the Immigration and Naturalization Service of Any Alien Who the Entity "Knows" Is Not Lawfully Present in the United States, 65 Fed. Reg. 58,301-01, 58,302 (Sep. 28, 2000) ("A Systematic Alien Verification for Entitlements (SAVE) response showing no Service record on an individual or an immigration status making the individual ineligible for a benefit is not a finding of fact or conclusion of law that that individual is not lawfully present.").

In September 2006, the ACLU, joined by several law firms and nonprofits, filed a complaint in the U.S. District Court for the Middle District of Pennsylvania against the City of Hazleton challenging the ordinances on behalf of several named plaintiffs, including several undocumented noncitizen adults and children and U.S. citizen children of the undocumented.[287] The ACLU also filed for a temporary restraining order, which the district court granted on October 31, 2006.[288] Trial began on March 12, 2007.[289] On July 26, the district court invalidated the ordinances on preemption and due process grounds, but it dismissed the privacy allegations based on lack of factual information that would allow the court to balance the individuals' with the government's privacy interests.[290] Despite this outcome, the issue may resurface on appeal and the challenge is worth considering in this Article.

The complaint alleged, *inter alia*, violations of privacy rights based on the ordinances' housing registration and immigration verification provisions. In addition to these provisions, Ordinance 2006-40 would have required landlords to cure violations of the housing restrictions either by initiating eviction proceedings, giving notice to quit, or extracting additional identifying information from the tenant or occupant.[291] Thus, under the ordinance, the onus fell on the landlord to obtain highly confidential documents proving lawful status. The complaint protested that the ordinances did not impose any

---

[287] First Amended Complaint at 5-19, Lozano v. Hazleton, 496 F. Supp. 2d 477 (M.D. Pa. 2007) (No. 3:06cv1586).
[288] Temporary Restraining Order at 12-13, *Lozano*, 496 F. Supp. 2d 477 (No. 3:06cv1586).
[289] Press Release, ACLU, Trial Begins in Landmark Challenge to Anti-Immigrant Laws in Hazleton, PA: Laws Would Legitimize Discrimination against Immigrant Community, Groups Charge (Mar. 12, 2007), *available at* http://www.aclu.org/immigrants/discrim/28976prs20070312.html.
[290] Lozano v. Hazleton, 496 F. Supp. 2d 477, 554 (M.D. Pa. 2007).
[291] Hazleton, Pa., Ordinance 2006-40, § 7(D) (Dec. 26, 2006), *available at* http://www.aclu.org/pdfs/immigrants/hazleton_thirdordinance.pdf.

confidentiality obligation on the landlords who receive such information.[292] Moreover, under the ordinances, this information would then be provided to the Hazleton Code of Enforcement Office for purposes of verification, and in the case of a complaint, the information must be retained.[293]

Even worse, because the ordinances did not provide any prohibition against subjecting tenants to searches, private or public officials could have conducted unlimited searches. With respect to the latter, the ordinances specified that the following persons were authorized to enforce them: "The Chief of Police, any police officer, Code enforcement Officer, the Fire Chief, the Deputy Fire Chief, a Health Officer, and the Director of Public Works."[294] Further, in the course of the litigation, Hazleton officers participating in the litigation clarified that "police powers" could be used to "preserv[e] the public health, safety and morals" of Hazleton, as well as to abate public nuisances.[295] In the "Findings and Declaration of Purpose" in Ordinance 2006-18, the city stated that the presence of undocumented immigrants in Hazleton is *per se* a public nuisance and "a harm to the health, safety, and welfare of authorized U.S. workers and legal residents in the city."[296] It it therefore reasonable to presuppose that the ordinances sought to authorize searches to uncover immigration violations

3. Local Immigration Raids?

---

[292] Memorandum of Law, supra note 260, at 73.
[293] *Id.* at 78.
[294] Hazelton, Pa., Ordinance 2006-35, § 8 (Dec. 13, 2006), *available at* http://www.aclu.org/pdfs/immigrants/hazleton_ordinance_200635.pdf; Hazleton, Pa., Ordinance 2006-13, § 8 (Aug. 15, 2006), available at h http://www.aclu.org/pdfs/immigrants/hazleton_firstordinance.pdf.
[295] Memorandum of Law, *supra* note 260, at 79.
[296] Hazelton, Pa., Ordinance 2006-18, § 2 (Sept. 8, 2006), *available at* http://www.aclu.org/pdfs/immigrants/hazleton_secondordinance.pdf.

At the same time that Congress and federal immigration agencies seek to increase local enforcement collaboration with immigration enforcement,[297] local governments are passing their own ordinances to control or restrict undocumented immigration. What are the implications of these ordinances for future immigration raids conducted by local law enforcement? Some local police are already enforcing immigration laws during traffic stops, in prisons, and, at times, even when responding to other local policing duties.[298] The Hazleton and similar ordinances throughout the country, which seek to impose employment and housing restrictions, open the door wider to questions about how and whether local police will also regulate workplaces and homes. Here too, there is a trend to employ federal databases containing information on immigration for purposes of local immigration enforcement.

One thing is certain: like federal enforcement, local immigration enforcement will be characterized as regulatory in nature, particularly when the consequences continue to be non-penal. In Hazleton, undocumented tenants and workers will be forced out of workplaces and homes, and possibly reported to immigration agencies, but not prosecuted *per se*. Nevertheless, these consequences are all extremely harsh, and criminal prosecution, as in the federal immigration enforcement context, for such crimes as identity theft and fraud remains a strong possibility.

An interesting parallel exists between these new anti-immigrant ordinances and attempts by local police to regulate disorder among the homeless and poor. For many generations, local police enforced laws criminalizing public order offenses, such as vagrancy, loitering, and public drunkenness, until the courts stepped in to declare them

---

[297] *See* Pham, *supra* note 30, at 1374.
[298] *See, e.g.*, Kobach, *supra* note 26 (describing local enforcement of immigration laws).

unconstitutional under doctrines such as the prohibition against status crimes.[299] These legal challenges, however, encouraged the proliferation of order-maintenance policies that replaced criminal with administrative enforcement, namely through property regulation tools like zoning laws.[300] Here again, the relaxed criminal safeguards in the context of administrative law enforcement has made it possible for these measures to survive judicial scrutiny at a significant "cost of rights."[301] Local anti-immigrant ordinances, such as those in Hazelton, if successful, have the potential to exponentially multiply the number of law enforcement officers involved in immigration raids, and are likely to suffer from similar "costs of rights," including to the Fourth Amendment.

PART III

In immigration law, reliance on the characterization of immigration raids as administrative to allow for more flexible law enforcement has becoming increasingly difficult to justify. In other administrative law contexts, the Supreme Court's adoption of a balancing test that pairs the government's interest against that of the individual has led to the erosion of privacy interests.[302] Professor Scott Sundby cautioned almost two decades ago against *Camara's* unlimited application beyond so-called administrative searches, given that terms like "administrative search" or "inspection" are neither self-defining nor self-limiting.[303] This observation is particularly pertinent in the immigration context where, increasingly, what were once civil immigration violations have now been criminalized, resulting in an unprecedented cooperation between criminal and

---

[299] Nicole Stelle Garnett, *Relocating Disorder*, 91 VA. L. REV. 1075, 1077-78 (2005).
[300] *Id.* at 1078-79.
[301] *Id.* at 1078.
[302] *See* Clancy, *supra* note 55, at 1003-15, 1023-36; Hemphill, *supra* note 34, at 218-220; Searle, *supra* note 41, at 273-88; Sundby, *supra* note 36, at 392; Steven T. Wax, *The Fourth Amendment, Administrative Searches and the Loss of Liberty*, 18 ENVTL. L. 911, 917-927 (1988) (arguing that the expansion of the administrative search has led to a loss of liberty).
[303] Sundby, *supra* note 36, at 406-07.

immigration law enforcement. Indeed, immigration and other law enforcement agencies have pretextually relied on the more flexible immigration law enforcement power to conduct criminal investigations to also charge persons with non-immigration crimes, including allegations of identity theft, terrorism, and drugs. Yet, the civil sanctions and procedures of immigration enforcement are dire, and the liberty interests no less substantial than in the criminal context. Immigrants linger in mandatory detention centers. Deportation separates them from family and destroys their stakes in property, community, and jobs. To insist, therefore, on the legal fiction of punitive vs. non-punitive consequences to justify fewer constitutional protections for immigrants, including privacy, is not only illogical but disingenuous. It undermines the pain experienced by the "other," whose constructed "illegality" strips them even of rights intended to protect against governmental overreach and abuses.

Several scholars have documented, especially in the last twenty years, how immigration control has increasingly adopted the practices and priorities of the criminal justice system.[304] Congress has created a host of new immigration crimes, ranging from illegal reentry to the most recent attempt to criminalize simple immigration presence.[305] Further, criminal prosecution for immigration violations has increased rapidly, as have criminal penalties for such violations.[306] This trend is even more disturbing because, in most cases, an immigrant's tenuous connection to a crime is constructed solely based on

---

[304] *See, e.g.*, Stephen H. Legomsky, *The New Path of Immigration Law: Asymmetric Incorporation of Criminal Justice Norms*, 64 WASH. & LEE L. REV. 469 (2007); Teresa A. Miller, *Citizenship and Severity: Recent Immigration Reforms and the New Penology*, 17 GEO. IMMIGR. L.J. 611 (2003); Juliet Stumpf, *The Crimigration Crisis: Immigrants, Crimes, and Sovereign Power*, 56 AM. U. L. REV. 367 (2006)
[305] In 2005, the House of Representatives passed a bill that would have created several additional crimes, including criminalizing the presence of the undocumented. *See* Border Protection, Antiterrorism, and Illegal Immigration Control Act of 2005, H.R. 4437, 109th Cong.
[306] *See* Legomsky, *supra* note 304, at 476-82, Miller, *supra* note 304, at 639-40; Stumpf, *supra* note 304, at 384.

their attempt to flee from economic and sometimes political repression. These so-called criminals who falsify their immigration documents include asylum seekers and workers who cross the border or overstay their visas and falsify documents in order to work.[307] As a result of workplace raids more than 700 persons are facing criminal charges for identity theft or other immigration violations, while some employers have been criminally charged for knowingly hiring the undocumented.[308] The Swift & Co. raids alone yielded at least 65 persons who are facing serious identity theft charges.[309] Several of them have already pled guilty to fraud charges and face a possible maximum sentence of 10 years in prison and a $250,000 fine.[310]

Civil immigration enforcement, moreover, has become more punitive and difficult to distinguish from criminal enforcement. Mandatory immigration detention, previously reserved for the most dangerous persons, is now broadly applied in almost all removal cases.[311] Indeed, immigration detainees are currently the fastest growing segment of the jail population in the United States.[312] Most persons picked up in the latest wave of immigration raids have been detained. Only a few have been released for humanitarian reasons or because they were eligible for some other type of immigration relief. In fact, those charged with any immigration crime or those with a criminal history will not be eligible for bond or any other avenue of relief from detention.[313]

---

[307] *See* Miller, *supra* note 304, at 649-50.
[308] THE ASSOCIATED PRESS, *supra* note 1; *see also* Jerry Seper, *Janitor-Service Chiefs Charged in Illegal Ring*, WASH. TIMES, Feb. 23, 2007, at A1 (discussing criminal indictments of IFCO Systems North America and Rosenbaum-Cunnningham International Inc. employers).
[309] Sprengelmeyer, *supra* note 138.
[310] THE ASSOCIATED PRESS, *Six More Plead Guilty in Aftermath of Immigration Raid*, Apr. 18, 2007, *available at* http://oneoldvet.com/?page_id=1037#25.
[311] Miller, *supra* note 304, at 614-15; Stumpf, *supra* note 304, at 391.
[312] *See* Miller, *supra* note 304, at 648-49.
[313] *Id.* at 635-36.

The criminal justice parallels in immigration enforcement, however, have not resulted in correspondingly greater constitutional protections for immigrants. As Stephen H. Legomsky explains, the criminal justice system has been asymmetrically imported into the immigration control context.[314] The enforcement aspects of criminal justice have been imported, without the bundle of procedural and substantive rights recognized in criminal cases.[315] This asymmetry has meant that decision-makers are left with no incentive to balance immigrants' interests against the government's interest to control immigration.[316]

In the Fourth Amendment context, the asymmetry applies even when the immigrant is charged criminally rather than placed in removal proceedings. Again, pretextual doctrines permit prosecutors to rely on the significantly more relaxed immigration-related Fourth Amendment doctrines to justify the reasonableness of searches and arrests.[317] In addition, at times, even when a Fourth Amendment violation is recognized, there is no remedy. Such is the case, for example, with the most common federal immigration crime charged, illegal reentry.[318] There, exclusion of any unlawfully seized evidence does not remedy the Fourth Amendment violation because the defendant's identity is never suppressible as the fruit of an unlawful arrest and the government can prove its case simply by providing proof of a prior removal order and the defendant's renewed presence in the United States.[319]

---

[314] Legomsky, *supra* note 304, at 472.
[315] *Id.*
[316] *Id.* at 473.
[317] *See supra* Part I.
[318] *See generally* James P. Fleissner & James A. Shapiro, *Sentencing Illegal Aliens Convicted of Reentry After Deportation: A Proposal for Simplified and Principled Sentencing*, 8 FED. SENT'G REP. 264 (1996)
[319] Daniel P. Blank, Note, *Suppressing Defendant's Identity and Other Strategies for Defending Against a Charge of Illegal Reentry After Deportation*, 50 STAN. L. REV. 139, 140-41 (1997).

Of course, when the immigrant does not face criminal charges for his immigration transgressions, his privacy right is even less meaningful, given the tendency of courts to undervalue the liberty interest of persons not in criminal proceedings. In the immigration context, the courts' insistence that deportation is not punishment has translated into an unjustifiable legal tolerance for the pain that immigrants experience from their, at times, permanent expulsion from the United States, despite their long term residence and vested stakes in this country.

The recent immigration raids leave us with stories that document the devastation of deportation on families as well. In Massachusetts, for example, Governor Deval Patrick called immigration raids' effect on families a "humanitarian crisis," when the state had to make childcare arrangements for at least thirty-five children, ranging from infants to age sixteen, whose parents were among at least 361 workers, mostly women, who were arrested during a raid at the Michael Bianco, Inc. leather factory.[320] Additionally, in Massachusetts, ICE denied social workers attempting to advocate on behalf of the children access to the detainees because it was a law enforcement issue.[321] When DHS complied with Governor Patrick's plea to halt flights to detention centers in other states, DHS released 60 persons, who identified themselves as the primary parent, on humanitarian grounds.[322] In some cases, their children had stayed with family and friends, while community groups stepped in to locate other children and provide them with care.[323] At least one seven-month-old child, however, who breastfed, required a

---

[320] Monica Rhor, *Immigration Raids Can Divide Families*, WASH. POST, Mar. 12, 2007, *available at* http://www.washingtonpost.com/wp-dyn/content/article/2007/03/11/AR2007031100762.html; David Weber, *Mass. Protests Feds' Immigration Flights*, WASH. POST, Mar. 9, 2007, *available at* http://www.washingtonpost.com/wp-dyn/content/article/2007/03/08/AR2007030800181.html.
[321] *Id.*
[322] Weber, *supra* note 320.
[323] *Id.*

feeding tube after being separated from his mother for two days during the raid.[324] The degree of harm caused to children, many who happened to be U.S. citizens, in the Massachusetts raids has prompted a congressional investigation by the House Subcommittee on Immigration.[325]

To improve the plight of immigrants and to claim greater constitutional protection on their behalf, scholars have argued that deportation should be treated as punishment given the emphasis on retribution, deterrence, and incapacitation that bear on theories of deportation.[326] However, privacy interests should not depend on the type of consequences the persons might experience when they are invaded. Privacy interests are intended to protect, among other things, "freedom of thought," "solitude in one's home," "control of information about oneself," and "protection of one's reputation," harms that occur regardless of whether a person is criminally charged or faces no "criminal" consequences.[327]

Beyond these personal autonomy conceptions of privacy, there is also the notion of privacy's relationship to antitotaliatarianism. In his influential article, "The Right to Privacy," Jed Rubenfeld suggested that privacy should be defined as "the fundamental freedom not to have one's life too totally determined by a progressively more normalizing state."[328] Thus, to Rubenfeld, privacy should protect against a "creeping

---

[324] David Weber, *Delahunt Says Congress Will Investigate Immigration Raid*, ASSOCIATED PRESS, Mar. 11, 2007, *available at* http://www.boston.com/news/local/massachusetts/articles/2007/03/11/delahunt_says_congress_will_investigate_immigration_raid/.
[325] *Id.*
[326] Legomsky, *supra* note 304, at 511-15; *see also* Kanstroom, *supra* note 14, at 1893-94. *See generally* Robert Pauw, *A New Look at Deportation as Punishment: Why at Least Some of the Constitution's Criminal Procedure Protections Must Apply*, 52 ADMIN. L. REV. 305 (2000) (discussing deportation as punishment).
[327] *See* Daniel J. Solove, *Conceptualizing Privacy*, 90 CAL. L. REV. 1087, 1088 (2002).
[328] Jeb Rubenfeld, *The Right to Privacy*, 102 HARV. L. REV. 737, 784 (1989).

totalitarianism, an unarmed occupation of individuals' lives."[329] In this regard, the consequences to the individual should matter less in assessing the reasonableness of law enforcement action. This again illustrates of the fallacy of the balancing approach. The reasonableness of privacy invasions by the state should not be judged against the relative interest of the state or the individual. Rather, they should be guided by the application of the original reasonableness principles of the Fourth Amendment, including the requirements for particularized warrants and probable cause.

Finally, privacy rights for immigrants should be recognized, despite their constructed illegality, because there are compelling policy reasons for protecting privacy in certain spaces.[330] In the workplace, for example, immigration raids have devastated employers, the well-being of small towns, and the economic well-being of the entire nation.[331] The reality is that immigrant workers dominate certain industries, including agriculture and meatpacking plants like that of Swift & Co. "Ridding" the country of twelve million undocumented workers through raids is not only unrealistic but incredibly disruptive.

These raids also significantly undermine the rights of all workers. Unfortunately, the vulnerability of undocumented workers and their diminished labor protections render them vulnerable to employers or even employees who might report them to immigration in order to undermine efforts to improve their working conditions.[332] Further, these raids and the ensuing dearth of workers in certain communities have been so disruptive that

---

[329] *Id.*
[330] *See* Solove, *supra* note 327, at 1142-43 (arguing that privacy should be constructed by law to safeguard important societal interests, even if these would not be protected under reasonable expectation of privacy analysis).
[331] *See* Jennifer Talhelm, *Senators Question Immigration Raids Against Meatpacker*, POST-INDEP., Jan. 22, 2007, *available at* http://cbs4denver.com/politics/local_story_023102531.html.
[332] *See* Lori A. Nessel, *Undocumented Immigrants in the Workplace: The Fallacy of Labor Protection and the Need for Reform*, 36 HAR. C.R.-C.L. L. REV. 345, 346-48 (2001).

communities have devised ill-conceived strategies that further undermine workplace rights. In Colorado, for example, as immigrant workers are arrested or leave because of the state's anti-immigration ordinances, the state has instituted a program to permit low risk inmates to harvest the crops, replacing migrant workers in the fields.[333] Under the program, farmers pay a fee to the states in exchange for the work of volunteer inmates, who are paid about sixty U.S. cents a day.[334] This prison program has precedents in Arizona where last year, about sixty prisoners worked in watermelon fields, replacing migrant workers.[335] Other states facing similar labor shortages, including Iowa, are considering similar measures.[336] The cynicism embodied these proposals is that the very same undocumented workers arrested by the immigration raids and subsequently charged with identity theft crimes could end up being the very ones who fill these jobs as prisoners, especially given the rising statistics of immigrants imprisoned for immigration crimes.

Likewise, home raids invade the most intimate sphere of privacy protection under the Fourth Amendment. In the home, privacy is conceptualized as a form of intimacy; the home is a space where privacy is not just essential to individual self-creation, but also to human relationships, including families.[337] The immigration raids executed in people's homes during the early hours of the day purposefully target entire families and small enclaves of immigrant communities that have chosen to share the intimate space of mutual residence.

---

[333] Dan Frosch, *Inmates Will Replace Migrants in Colorado Fields*, N.Y. TIMES, Mar. 4, 2007, at A1.
[334] *Id.*
[335] *Id.*
[336] *Id.*
[337] Solove, *supra* note 327, at 1121.

Here, citizens and non-citizens coexist and relate to one another in the most intimate of spaces. There is no ongoing criminal activity inside the home, other than the constructed illegality of a one or a few of the residents. During the raids, most residents are getting up, preparing to commence their days, to have breakfast, to go to school, or to work. True, some arrests must occur in the home. However, these should be restricted in scope to safeguard intimacy by only allowing for the arrest of the warrant's actual target and only when immigration agents have reasonable grounds for believing the target still lives in the home.

CONCLUSION

The U.C. Davis School of Law's Symposium titled "*Katz v. U.S.*: 40 Years Later," for which I write this Article turned out to be more a reflection about the failing of *Katz* or its unfulfilled promise, rather than a celebration. Part of the explanation lies in *Katz*'s inherent doctrinal flaws, but also in the subsequent distortion of the doctrine.

We can blame technological advancements, for example, for some of the distortion, but beyond that, this immigration case study reveals the intolerance for recognizing the privacy expectations of "undesirable" persons or activities. Such has been the case in the constructed "illegality" of immigrants, which has had a corrosive effect on privacy, including in spaces such as the home, where citizens still receive heightened privacy protection. The web of Fourth Amendment doctrines that undermine privacy protections for immigrants is more complex than the effect of *Katz* alone. However, *Katz* plays a central role. Immigrants' attributed "blame" for crossing the border or overstaying their visas render them undeserving of an expectation of privacy in the spaces they occupy in the United States. This blame justifies the proliferation of immigration databases, the issuance of general and defective warrants based on such databases, and the dragnet-like and discriminatory enforcement of administrative warrants. But is this right? Was the Fourth Amendment intended to protect solely the so-called innocent? Or was its purpose to curtail abuses of policing powers, particularly against vulnerable groups? Courts must reconsider these questions as they examine the legality of the current raids.

THE ANATOMY OF AN ICE RAID
by Josie Gonzalez and Nancy-Jo Merritt[*]

In the minds of employers, the most feared enforcement event is the U.S. Immigration and Customs Enforcement (ICE) raid. A raid is feared not only because it will be the product of a lengthy preliminary investigation that may result in charges of criminal violations of federal statutes, but the chaos and disruption and the ensuing unpleasant media attention create a great deal of instability. This article will attempt to demystify some aspects of the enforcement process that culminate in a raid and provide direction for preparation for—and, to the extent possible, management of— the process. Of course, life would be easier if employers followed the regulatory requirements carefully and avoided activities that result in investigations and enforcement events, but a quick look at recent ICE press releases indicates that elements of the employment community have not gotten that message and will inevitably need the help of legal counsel.

The Investigation

It is important to understand that ICE is nothing like the investigations division of legacy Immigration and Naturalization Service (INS). ICE is a powerful, well-funded, effective enforcement agency. Its investigations are well managed, in partnership with such disparate agencies as the U.S. Attorney's Office, state police departments and security agencies, the Social Security Administration (SSA), the Internal Revenue Service (IRS), the Department of Labor (DOL), the Department of Homeland Security's (DHS) Office of Inspector General (OIG), and the Federal Bureau of Investigation (FBI), as necessary. It is important to note that Immigration and

---

[*] **Josie Gonzalez** is the managing partner of Gonzalez & Harris, and has represented employers in all aspects of immigration law for more than 25 years. She recently represented a major corporation facing federal criminal charges for hiring undocumented workers. Ms. Gonzalez has published numerous articles for legal and trade journals on the topic of employer sanctions. Her background as a former criminal defense attorney and employer sanctions expert makes her uniquely qualified to address issues such as RICO and other criminal charges against employers, the future of employer sanctions, and how to develop and implement immigration corporate compliance materials. She currently chairs AILA's Worksite Enforcement Committee.

Nancy-Jo Merritt, a director in the Phoenix office of Fennemore Craig, P.C., has more than two decades of practice in the field of immigration law. Her practice is broad-based and includes the representation of domestic and international companies regarding visa and work authorization issues for foreign-national employees. She also assists employers with federal compliance issues in the contexts of mergers and acquisitions and government audits. Ms. Merritt has been successful in challenging the federal government's interpretation of immigration law in a number of matters, and received the first award of fees in the United States from an immigration judge under the Equal Access to Justice Act. Ms. Merritt is the author of *Understanding Immigration Law: How to Enter, Work and Live in the United States*. She publishes frequently and serves as a senior editor of AILA's *Immigration & Nationality Law Handbook*, published annually. She also lectures frequently on U.S. immigration law, most often on issues relating to employers.

Nationality Act (INA) §287(g) [8 USC §1357(g)], which authorizes delegation to state and local law enforcement officials of the power to investigate, apprehend, and detain aliens, has become a very popular tool. Many local enforcement agencies now have "embedded" local immigration agents, extending the breadth and reach of enforcement activities.

When ICE initiates an investigation against a target company, it will take advantage of traditional criminal investigative techniques, including confidential informants, cooperating witnesses, body wiretaps, and statements from former and current employees. In addition, any investigation will take advantage of ICE's ability to obtain data from other government agencies, such as SSA, DOL's Wage and Hour Division, and the DHS OIG, to name a few. ICE also has the ability to obtain evidence through a routine I-9 inspection. Although for several years I-9 inspections were an infrequently used tool, today, with increased personnel and funding, ICE is once again conducting numerous I-9 audits throughout the United States. It uses the fruits of these investigations to secure affidavits in support of search warrants. A raid will frequently be the result of many months of prior investigation and a carefully coordinated gathering of evidence.

What are the danger signs of a targeted company?

- Company executives fail to understand the culture at the worksite and may be the last to know that problems are brewing.
- Hiring decisions made by individuals with mixed loyalties who have strong sympathies toward job seekers who are desperate for employment, or by individuals who see their role as having the possibility for personal enrichment.
- I-9s are maintained, but without attention to detail, substance, or both.
- Companies are reluctant to question the authenticity of employee documents for fear of discrimination claims, or fear of an inability to find sufficient workers.
- The pool of new hires comes mainly from the existing workforce—their relatives and friends.
- Management assumes that long years of residence in the United States and U.S.-born children equate to legal status for the employee, or that a worker can get a green card easily and quickly, and thus is careless about documentation.
- The company has received Social Security "no-match" letters, and believes it has no responsibility to question employees over discrepancies, or doesn't want to know what it doesn't know.
- Management allows employees to change their identities and present new and different documents without questioning their authenticity.
- The company fails to realize that supervisors and lower-level managers' actions can be imputed to management—that their sins are the sins of the company.
- The company ignores complaints and rumors that employees are undocumented or are using the valid documents of another person.

- State benefits agencies have frequently contacted the company about employees who are using the Social Security cards of others who are trying to apply for benefits, but are being denied because IRS records show that the holder of the card is employed.

Bases for Investigation

The following scenarios describe ways in which ICE may be alerted to alleged immigration violations by employers:

- An employee is arrested, perhaps for speeding, and is grilled by a city police officer (authorized under INA §287(g)) regarding his immigration status. The officer determines that the employee should be turned over to ICE, which then questions him about his employment, how he became employed with the company, whether any company representatives assisted in procuring false documents, whether the company has actual or constructive knowledge of his undocumented status, how many other undocumented workers work at the facility, and so on. The employee may, in exchange for temporary work authorization, agree to work as a confidential informant.

- If the information provided by the employee suggests to ICE that further investigation is warranted, ICE will obtain a subpoena under 26 USC §6103(i)(1) to secure information from SSA regarding any "no-match" letters sent to the employer under investigation. If the SSA information indicates that the company has received letters over several years, that the same names appear each year, and that the subjects of the letters constitute a substantial percentage of the workforce, the investigation will continue.[1]

- The former HR manager (or an unhappy HR specialist, or a recently demoted supervisor) believes that the company is not in compliance with federal law governing employment verification, feeling that the company workforce is riddled with unauthorized workers. She begins sending letters to ICE, naming names.

- A company worker is terminated, and while applying for unemployment insurance tells the state clerk that his former employer didn't withhold Social Security payments and federal income tax and that other employees did not complain because they were here illegally and preferred to be paid in cash anyway. This triggers an investigation by the state revenue agency, which also informs IRS. The U.S. attorney on that investigation notifies ICE, and they begin a joint investigation and prosecution of the company for tax violations and money laundering.

- A dishwasher in a Chinese restaurant is fired and complains to ICE that all of his coworkers were in the United States illegally and lived free of charge in

---

[1] *See* www.ice.gov/pi/news/newsreleases/articles/070716albany.htm. ICE indicted six managers of IFCO Systems North America for conspiracy to transport and harbor, conspiracy to possess identification documents, unlawful employment, and conspiracy to unlawfully employ.

houses provided by the restaurant owner. ICE investigates and charges the owners with illegally employing unauthorized aliens and harboring.[2]

- ICE receives information on its toll-free tip line and investigates via SSA records. The 16-month investigation results in criminal charges filed against the owner of the business, who is undocumented, and the placing of all eight employees in deportation proceedings.[3]

- ICE conducts an I-9 inspection and discovers that many of the workers are using false documents or documents that belong to a deceased person, or a child or someone of the opposite sex, or of a different age. ICE may also request or subpoena Social Security "no-match" letters that contain data regarding discrepancies between employee numbers and names. In lieu of providing a list of the employees with suspect documents, ICE may use this information to easily obtain a search warrant.

- The employer has submitted to DOL's Employment and Training Administration an application for labor certification or has submitted an immigrant petition (Form I-140) to DHS for an unauthorized employee. These agencies may share these applications with ICE, which views such filings for workers who are currently employed without authorization as knowingly continuing the employment of an unauthorized worker on a constructive knowledge basis.[4]

The Next Step

ICE makes an application for a search warrant before a federal magistrate or judge for permission to search the employer's worksite for the presence of undocumented employees and property that will be used as evidence that specific crimes have been committed.

What are the components of a criminal search warrant?

- The order from the court will authorize a search to be conducted within 10 days, during daylight hours, before a specific date.

- It may contain a description of the premises to be searched. ICE agents will have conducted surveillance of the premises, noting all entrances and exits, in order to determine how to secure the premises. Sometimes, in advance of a raid, an agent may ask for a tour of the premises, often using various false pretenses such as wanting a tour to ensure that the company is running a clean operation.

- A description of items to be searched for and seized. The list may include such items as:
  – employee identification documents;

---

[2] *See www.ice.gov/pi/news/newsreleases/articles/071114louisville.htm.*

[3] *See www.ice.gov/pi/news/newsreleases/articles/071107sanfrancisco.htm.*

[4] As to constructive knowledge, see 8 CFR §274a.1(*l*).

- payroll records;
- documents generated by SSA indicating irregularities with Social Security numbers;
- I-9 forms and copies of documents in support of the I-9;
- bank records showing payroll and cash ledgers, and any notes or other bookkeeping data that may contain information about paying undocumented workers (sometimes on sticky notes);[5]
- financial records, tax records, letters of credit, escrow documents, money orders, cashier checks, bank checks;[6]
- "records" or "information" in whatever form and by whatever means created or stored, including in electrical, electronic, or magnetic form: hard disks, zip disks, CD-ROMs, optical disks, backup tapes, etc.

- An affidavit in support of the search warrant drafted by the supervisory ICE agent that describes his or her background and experience in these investigations and chronicles the evidence collected that supports the agent's belief that crimes have been committed.

The Raid

The elements of surprise, intimidation, and shock are successfully employed by ICE to catch the unprepared company off guard and to create chaos. The disruption is compounded when the company is unaware that it has rights that it can assert.

How does a raid proceed?

- Armed ICE agents surround the premises, effectively sealing all exits and routes of escape. The supervising agent serves the search warrant on either a receptionist or other company representative and alerts other agents via radio transmitters that entry has been made, thus allowing their entry.
- ICE may demand that all machinery be shut down, that no one leave the premises without their permission, and that employees be corralled into contained areas such as the cafeteria room for questioning.
- While some ICE agents are questioning employees, others are going through drawers and seizing documents and computer equipment.
- Employees may not have their immigration documents on them. Human resources personnel can retrieve copies of the documents from the I-9 files, provided backup copies were made, or family can be contacted to bring the original documents to the company.

---

[5] Such evidence may relate to violations of INA §274(a)(1)(A)(iv) [8 USC §1324(a)(1)(A)(iv)], encouraging an unauthorized alien to come to or remain in the United States; 18 USC §1028(a)(7), aggravated identity theft; or 42 USC §408(a)(6), misuse of Social Security numbers.

[6] Such evidence might indicate the transfer of funds in furtherance of the employment of unauthorized aliens.

How should the company respond?

There may be informal contact indicating an investigation is under way, but often the initial notice will come from service of a federal or state search warrant.

Employers should be prepared by planning ahead and providing clear instructions to staff in presenting a calm and orderly response. Implementation of a crisis management plan that identifies a response team and specific response management procedures is a "best practice." The team should include one or more employees to serve as the designated company representative for acceptance of service of the warrant and management of the visit. Employees who might first encounter officers serving the warrant, such as the receptionist or security guards, should be instructed specifically to immediately call the company representative, who will contact corporate officers and in-house or outside counsel before meeting with the officers.

The company representative should introduce him- or herself, obtain identification of the lead agent, and determine which government agencies are involved. The next step is to carefully review the warrant and any other documentation and obtain a copy, while being courteous and helpful. The agents should be advised that the company does not consent to the search, but will not impede execution of the warrant.

The company representative, along with other individuals directed by the company, should accompany the agents as long as they are on the property, and carefully monitor and record the search in a convenient and unobtrusive way, such as with portable dictating equipment, pen and paper, or a camera or video recorder. The record should include the names and titles of the agents conducting the search, the location and identification of any files or equipment searched or seized, and any communication between any agent and company employees.

If the warrant is for a named person or persons who are present at the worksite, the company representative should offer to locate the individuals and have them brought to the officers to avoid having government agents wandering through the property looking for employees, possibly causing further disruption and chaos. If there are safety or security considerations that prevent unaccompanied persons on site, the agents should be informed.

As much as possible, the involved company employees should be prepared to present a calm and reassuring presence, and should not chat with the agents, especially about anything related to the warrant, company employees, or company policies. However, if employees are approached by an agent, the company representative must not direct employees not to speak to the agent. Employees may be advised that they may choose to speak, but are not required to speak or answer questions. A company representative should request to be present during any employee interview.

When the search is concluded, the company should obtain a receipt and copy of the inventory of any property seized, signed and dated by the agent in charge. He or she should not sign or in any manner concur in the inventory, or permit any other employee to do so. After the agents have left, company representatives should meet with and debrief any search monitors or employees present during the visit. If the company is a prominent business, it will be important to be prepared to manage media coverage, and to the extent possible, limit employee contact with media representatives.

Lessons To Be Learned

Management procedures and policies that integrate the requirements of the work authorization rules are the wise way to protect the company from unexpected liability for improper hires and the intense level of enforcement activity aimed at employers today. There is no better protection than a strong, well-managed corporate compliance program, no matter the size of the business.

Social Security "No-Match" Letters: Continued Uncertainty for Employers

*by Daniel Brown**

Introduction

The Department of Homeland Security's (DHS)[1] focus on Social Security "no-match" letters, part of the agency's reinvigorated worksite enforcement strategy, has caused a great deal of anxiety for many employers and has increased the need for employers to have sound compliance practices and procedures in place. The government has pursued criminal prosecutions of employers believed to be knowingly employing unauthorized workers, and has alleged the existence of "no-match" letters in support of its criminal allegations in a number of cases.[2] It is critical that employers have policies in place to track the receipt of "no-match" letters and resolve any mismatches that are identified.

But what exactly are employers supposed to do when they receive a "no-match" letter? Dealing with Social Security mismatch issues has always been tricky. It can often be difficult to determine just when a Social Security "no-match" issue implicates an employee's immigration status or work eligibility. This hasn't been helped by the fact that, historically, the various agencies involved have provided conflicting guidance regarding the potential ramifications of a "no-match" letter. DHS has been trying to provide what it believes to be the guidance that employers have been looking for, but has been stymied in that effort by litigation. Thus, although the stakes have been raised dramatically for employers who become subject to DHS enforcement actions, there may be more uncertainty than ever as to how "no-match" issues should be handled.

DHS, believing that "no-match" letters should be regarded as a potential indicator that one or more employees may be unauthorized, has been struggling to issue (and

---

* **Daniel Brown** is an attorney with Paul, Hastings, Janofsky & Walker LLP in the firm's Washington, D.C. office. He counsels clients on compliance and enforcement matters. Mr. Brown previously served in a number of senior positions in the Department of Homeland Security. From May 2005 to August 2006, he served as the counselor to the assistant secretary of ICE and as the director of the Office of Policy and Planning. Prior to that time, he served as deputy associate general counsel for immigration in the DHS general counsel's office.

[1] References to DHS in this article are meant to encompass U.S. Immigration and Customs Enforcement (ICE), the component of DHS that is responsible for worksite enforcement investigations.

[2] *See* Second Declaration of James Spero, *AFL-CIO v. Chertoff*, No. 07-4472-CRB (N.D. Cal.) ("ICE has consistently viewed failure by such employers to take any action to address the no-match as possible evidence that the employers know that the employees in question are not authorized to work in the United States."). DHS also has added Social Security "no-match" information to its standard subpoena for I-9 information.

make effective) its regulation on "no-match" letters.[3] The DHS rule provides that employers who fail to follow up and resolve Social Security mismatches may, depending on the totality of the relevant circumstances, be considered to have constructive knowledge that one or more workers (who are the subject of the "no-match" letter) are ineligible for employment.[4] However, the rule also establishes "safe-harbor" procedures for employers to utilize in response to "no-match" letters, and promises employers who use those procedures immunity from constructive knowledge allegations regarding the employees who are the subject of the "no-match" letter.[5] The rule imposes no affirmative requirements on employers, and the rule commentary recognizes that the new steps detailed in the rule are not the only means for taking reasonable steps to resolve a "no-match."[6] The rule commentary states that should an employer decline to follow the safe-harbor procedures but choose to respond to a "no-match" letter in other ways, the reasonableness of that response will be viewed under the "totality of relevant circumstances."[7]

Although DHS in its media and outreach efforts has tried to portray the regulation as simply providing needed guidance to the business community, the rule has come under widespread criticism from business and trade organizations, labor unions, and immigrant rights advocates. The agency received approximately 5,000 comments in response to the proposed rule.[8] The rule has never taken effect. When DHS finally published the final regulation on August 15, 2007, it was quickly challenged in the U.S. District Court for the Northern District of California by a group of employer and labor organizations, and DHS was preliminarily enjoined from implementing the rule.[9] DHS appealed the court's preliminary injunction decision, but, in the interim, obtained a stay of the litigation while it revised the rule to address the district court's concerns.[10]

Particularly as of this writing, when the regulation has still not taken effect and the outcome of the litigation over the regulation is uncertain, it is difficult to advise em-

---

[3] 72 Fed. Reg. 45611 (Aug. 15, 2007). A proposed regulation was published on June 14, 2006. *See* 71 Fed. Reg. 34281.

[4] 72 Fed. Reg. 45611, 45623 (amending 8 CFR §274a.1(*l*)(1)). DHS is able to obtain access to previous "no-match" letters issued to an employer in a criminal investigation. *See* 26 USC §6103(i). The agency has used evidence of an employer's failure to follow up on "no-match" letters to support constructive knowledge allegations against the employer in certain cases, including its prosecution of IFCO Systems, North America, Inc. *See* www.ice.gov/pi/news/newsreleases/articles/060420washington.htm.

[5] 72 Fed. Reg. 45611, 45624 (amending 8 CFR §274a.1(*l*)(2)).

[6] *Id.* at 45618.

[7] *Id.* at 45614.

[8] *Id.* at 45611.

[9] Order Granting Motion for Preliminary Injunction, *AFL-CIO v. Chertoff*, No. 07-4472 (N.D. Cal. Oct. 10, 2007).

[10] According to the website of the Office of Management and Budget (OMB), *www.reginfo.gov* (RIN: 1653-AA50), the rule was received from DHS for review on February 5, 2008. Normally OMB reserves the right to a 90-day review period for regulations. According to OMB, the revised rule was a new proposed rule, meaning there would be an additional comment period.

ployers on how they should be handling "no-match" letters.[11] Employers need to have clear and consistent procedures in place for dealing with "no-match" letters that are uniformly applied to all employees. It probably makes sense for many employers to model their procedures fairly closely on the "safe-harbor" procedures provided in the DHS rule, even if it is not in effect. The procedures represent the best view of what the government believes to be a prudent response to a notification of a Social Security "no-match." With the preliminary injunction in place and the rule not yet in effect, however, the government may proceed cautiously before adding "no-match"-related allegations in criminal cases, although it is actively gathering the information in its investigations and audits. Until the regulation takes effect and the litigation is resolved, employers should consult with counsel, even if they have adopted the DHS safe-harbor procedures, before taking any adverse action (at the end of the process) against employees who have been unable to resolve Social Security mismatches. This is particularly true in the context of a unionized workforce, where an employer's right to terminate is typically circumscribed by the "just cause" provision of a collective bargaining agreement. This is not to suggest that an employer is free to take no action if it obtains information that would place a reasonable person on notice that the employee is not authorized to work in the United States.

What Are Social Security "No-Match" Letters?

"No-match" letters are a written notification sent out by the Social Security Administration (SSA) to notify an individual, or his or her employer, that the Social Security number (SSN) information reported by the employer does not match the information in the agency's databases. Employers report wage information for each employee to SSA on Internal Revenue Service (IRS) Form W-2. SSA collects the information for IRS but also uses the information to ensure that earnings are credited correctly to each worker for Social Security benefits purposes. When the name and SSN on a W-2 wage report does not match the records in SSA's databases, those earnings cannot be allocated to an individual and instead are posted to the agency's Earnings Suspense File (ESF). According to SSA, approximately 4 percent (8–11 million) of all W-2 reports go into the ESF each year.[12]

SSA uses a number of methods to resolve "no-match" discrepancies in order to reduce the totals in the ESF and allocate them to the individuals to whom they belong. One of these methods is to send out "no-match" letters. SSA actually sends out two different types of "no-match" letters. One is sent to employers and is known as an Employer Correction Request or Educational Correspondence (EDCOR) letter. The other

---

[11] As of this writing, it is not even clear when the Social Security Administration (SSA) will resume mailing out "no-match" letters to employers. The agency delayed mailing out "no-match" notices in 2007 in anticipation of the DHS final regulation taking effect. SSA had planned to enclose a notice from DHS with each "no-match" letter advising employers of their obligation to follow up on Social Security mismatches. Ultimately however, as a result of the litigation, SSA eventually decided not to issue any employer "no-match" letters in 2007.

[12] Government Accountability Office, *Social Security: Better Coordination Among Federal Agencies Could Reduce Unidentified Earnings Reports* (GAO-05-154, Feb. 2005).

is sent to the individual worker and is referred to as a Decentralized Correspondence (DECOR) letter.[13] The "no-match" letter sent out to employers is the focus of the DHS "no-match" rule.[14] It is very important to remember that mismatches can occur for any number of reasons that have nothing to do with an employee's immigration status. Mismatches frequently are caused by clerical error, name changes after marriage or divorce that have not been reported to SSA, and naming conventions and misordering of multiple surnames. One additional reason that may be the cause for a mismatch, of course, and the reason that DHS has focused so much attention on the issue, is that an unauthorized alien worker has submitted a false name or SSN or is using someone else's SSN to obtain employment.

Historically (at least prior to the publication of the final rule), SSA has explicitly warned employers—on the "no-match" letter itself—that a mismatch does not indicate anything about an individual's immigration status, and no adverse action should be taken against any employee simply because a "no-match" letter has been received. With the publication of the final rule in August 2007, the government had intended to include an insert from DHS with each "no-match" letter explaining to employers the potential liability for ignoring a "no-match" letter and the steps they should take to resolve the mismatch discrepancies. Because of the litigation, SSA did not send out employer EDCOR "no-match" letters in 2007.

The DHS Regulation

The DHS final rule expands the definition of "constructive knowledge" to include an employer's failure to take reasonable steps after receiving a "no-match" letter from SSA.[15] Section 274A of the Immigration and Nationality Act (INA) prohibits employers from knowingly hiring or continuing to employ unauthorized workers. The term "knowing" includes both actual knowledge as well as the concept of constructive knowledge. The DHS rule explains that "constructive knowledge is knowledge that may fairly be inferred through notice of certain facts and circumstances that would lead a person, through the exercise of reasonable care, to know about a certain condition."[16] The U.S. Court of Appeals for the Ninth Circuit has examined the issue of constructive knowledge in the context of the worksite verification process in several cases. In *New El Rey Sausage Co. v. INS*,[17] the Ninth Circuit held that an employer who ignored legacy Immigration and Naturalization Service (INS) warnings

---

[13] See www.ssa.gov/legislation/nomatch2.htm; The Migration Policy Institute has also published a useful reference article regarding Social Security "no-match" issues. See Bergeron, Terrazas & Meissner, *Immigration Backgrounder, Social Security "No-Match" Letters: A Primer*, The Migration Policy Institute (Oct. 2007).

[14] To confuse the issue just a bit more, SSA will sometimes send the employee letter to the employer's attention when it does not have accurate address information for the employee.

[15] 72 Fed. Reg. 45611, 45623–24 (amending 8 CFR §274a.1(*l*)(1)(iii)).

[16] *Id.* at 45623 (amending 8 CFR §274a.1(*l*)(1)); *see also U.S. v. Jewell*, 532 F.2d 697, 704 (9th Cir. 1976) (*en banc*) (stating that constructive knowledge is a "mental state in which the defendant is aware that the fact in question is highly probable but consciously avoids enlightenment").

[17] 925 F.2d 1153 (9th Cir. 1991).

regarding paperwork deficiencies for particular employees had at least constructive knowledge that the employees were unauthorized. The court held that the employer was on constructive notice because he had been told "whom the INS considered unauthorized and why," but failed to acquire independent corroboration of work eligibility other than the employees' self-serving representations.[18]

In addition to expanding the constructive knowledge definition to encompass receipt of "no-match" letters, the DHS regulation also provides a set of "safe-harbor" procedures that employers can follow when they receive a "no-match" letter.[19] The safe-harbor protocol outlines a series of steps for employers to follow over a 93-day timeframe to try to resolve the Social Security discrepancy. Employers are promised immunity from a constructive knowledge charge premised on a "no-match" letter if they follow the procedures exactly as laid out in the rule.

DHS Safe-Harbor Procedures

The following is a step-by-step outline of the safe-harbor protocol provided in the DHS "no-match" regulation.[20]

- **To Be Completed Within 30 Days of Receiving a "No-Match" Letter**
    1. CHECK FOR CLERICAL ERRORS
        A. Check personnel and payroll records to determine whether the mismatch discrepancy was caused by a clerical or typographical error when the employee's SSN was recorded or reported to SSA.
        B. If the mismatch was caused by a clerical error, correct the error by filing a corrected W-2 with SSA, and verify that the corrected information now matches the agency's records. Use SSA's Social Security Number Verification Service (SSNVS) to verify that Social Security information is now correct.
        C. Make a record of the manner, date, and time that the corrected information was verified with SSA, and retain the record with the employee's I-9 form.
    2. CHECK WITH EMPLOYEE TO ENSURE THAT HIS OR HER SOCIAL SECURITY NUMBER INFORMATION IS CORRECT

---

[18] *Id.* at 1158; *see also Mester Mfg. Co. v. INS*, 879 F.2d 561, 567 (9th Cir. 1989) (finding that the constructive knowledge requirement is satisfied even where the employer has no "actual specific knowledge of the employee's unauthorized status" so long as the employer receives specific information that an employee is likely to be unauthorized but the employer makes no further inquiry). *But see Collins Foods Int'l v. INS*, 948 F.2d 549 (9th Cir. 1991) (finding that employer did not have constructive knowledge even though the employer may have determined that a Social Security card presented by an employee was fraudulent by comparing the card to an example in the INS *Handbook for Employers*).

[19] 72 Fed. Reg. 45611, 45624 (amending 8 CFR §274a.1(*l*)(2)).

[20] Although as of this writing DHS is currently revising the "no-match" regulation published in August 2007, it is unlikely that significant changes, if any, will be made to the safe-harbor procedures and the timelines that were established in that final rule.

A. If the "no-match" discrepancy was not the result of a clerical error, promptly check with the employee to confirm that the SSN information in the company's records is correct.

B. If the employee indicates that the SSN information in the company's records is incorrect, then correct the records and verify, using SSNVS, that the corrected information now matches SSA's records.

C. Make a record of the manner, date, and time that the corrected information was verified with SSA, and retain the record with the employee's I-9 form.

D. If the employee confirms that the SSN information in the company's records is correct, promptly ask the employee to resolve the discrepancy with SSA. Advise the employee of the date that the company received the "no-match" letter, and advise the employee that he or she has 90 days from that date to resolve the issue with SSA.

- **To Be Completed Within 90 Days of Receiving the "No-Match" Letter**
  3. THE EMPLOYEE RESOLVES THE SOCIAL SECURITY "NO-MATCH" DISCREPANCY

      A. The employee has 90 days from the company's receipt of the "no-match" letter to resolve the discrepancy with SSA. In almost all cases this will require the employee to personally visit the local SSA office and bring his or her identity document and records to resolve the "no-match" issue. If the "no-match" discrepancy is resolved, the employee may receive a new Social Security card or a receipt from the SSA office.

      B. If within the 90-day period the employee indicates that he or she has resolved the mismatch discrepancy and presents a new Social Security card with a different name or number, file a corrected W-2 form with SSA, if necessary, and verify, using SSNVS, that the new information matches SSA's records.

      C. Make a record of the manner, date, and time that the corrected information was verified with SSA, and retain the record with the employee's I-9. If necessary (if the employee presented a Social Security card as proof of employment eligibility when the I-9 was completed and the employee now has a new Social Security card with a different name or number), correct the employee's I-9 (or complete a new one) to reflect the updated Social Security information.

- **To Be Completed Within 93 Days of Receiving the "No-Match" Letter**
  4. THE EMPLOYEE IS UNABLE TO RESOLVE THE "NO-MATCH" DISCREPANCY WITHIN THE 90-DAY PERIOD

      A. If the employee cannot resolve the "no-match" discrepancy with SSA within 90 days of receiving the "no-match" letter, the employer must attempt to reverify his or her employment eligibility by completing a new I-9 form within 93 days of receiving the "no-match" letter.

B. The employer should use the same procedures as when completing an I-9 at the time of hire, with the following exceptions:

(i) The employee must complete section 1 of the new I-9, and the employer must complete section 2 of the new I-9, by the end of the 93rd day after receiving the "no-match" letter.

(ii) The employer cannot accept any document (or a receipt for a document) to establish identity or work eligibility that contains the SSN that is the subject of the "no-match" letter.

(iii) The employee must present a document that contains a photograph in order to establish identity or both identity and work eligibility.

(iv) The new I-9 should be retained with the original I-9.

C. If a new I-9 cannot be completed because the employee cannot provide acceptable documentary evidence of identity and work eligibility (without the questionable SSN), then the employer must decide whether to terminate the employee or risk, in any subsequent DHS enforcement action, being determined to have constructive knowledge and being penalized for the continuing employment of an unauthorized worker.

The final rule provides that whether an employer will be found to have constructive knowledge in any particular case will depend on "the totality of the relevant circumstances."[21] An employer should not terminate an employee because of the mismatch until the entire process is completed, unless the employer obtains additional knowledge (such as through an admission by the employee) that the employee is not eligible for employment in the United States. In the final rule, DHS attempted to provide assurance that applying the safe-harbor protocol in a uniform manner for all employees who are the subject of a "no-match" letter would not subject an employer to liability for claims of document abuse or unlawful discrimination on the basis of national origin or citizenship status.[22] However, as will be discussed in the context of the litigation over the rule, DHS may have exceeded its authority in making that assurance, because INA §274B, which governs immigration-related discrimination, falls within the authority of the Department of Justice.

Litigation Against the Regulation

Almost immediately after the final rule was published on August 15, 2007, a collection of business organizations, labor unions, and immigrant rights groups filed a legal challenge to the regulation on both substantive and procedural grounds in the

---

[21] 72 Fed. Reg. 45611, 45623 (amending 8 CFR §274a.1(*l*)(1)).

[22] *See id.* at 45613–14, 45624 (amending 8 CFR §274a.1(*l*)(3)).

U.S. District Court for the Northern District of California.[23] The plaintiffs were successful in keeping the DHS regulation from taking effect. First, a temporary restraining order was issued on August 31, 2007, prohibiting DHS from implementing the rule.[24] On October 10, 2007 the district court granted the plaintiff's request for a preliminary injunction.[25] The court found that the plaintiffs had raised serious questions on several of their claims and that the balance of harms tipped sharply in favor of the injunction.[26]

In granting the preliminary injunction, the court found that the plaintiffs raised serious questions regarding three of their claims. First, the court found that there was at least a serious question whether the DHS rule was "arbitrary and capricious," and in violation of the Administrative Procedure Act (APA)[27] because it failed to provide a reasoned analysis for its change in position regarding the impact of "no-match" letters. The court determined that historically, DHS and legacy INS had taken the position that a Social Security "no-match" letter, by itself, could not constitute notice to an employer that an employee is not authorized to work in the United States, and thus by itself could not be sufficient to establish constructive knowledge on the part of the employer. The discussion in the preamble to the rule is consistent with the agency's historical guidance.[28] However, the court determined that in the actual text of the regulation DHS had departed from the agency's historical position by providing that receipt of a "no-match" letter by itself can be sufficient to impart knowledge that the identified employees are unauthorized.[29] According to the court's decision, the government even confirmed this point during oral argument.[30] The district court determined that because there was no reasoned analysis for the change of position in the

---

[23] Complaint, *AFL-CIO v. Chertoff*, No. 07-4472 (N.D. Cal. Aug. 29, 2007), *available at* www.aclu.org/pdfs/immigrants/aflcio_v_chertoff_complaint.pdf.

[24] Temporary Restraining Order and Order to Show Cause Re: Preliminary Injunction, *AFL-CIO v. Chertoff*, No. 07-4472 (N.D. Cal. Aug. 31, 2007).

[25] Order Granting Motion for Preliminary Injunction, *AFL-CIO v. Chertoff*, No. 07-4472 (N.D. Cal. Oct. 10, 2007).

[26] *See id.* at 1. The American Civil Liberties Union and the National Immigration Law Center have many of the pleadings in the litigation, as well as a great deal of useful background information on Social Security "no-match" issues in general, available on their websites. *See* www.nilc.org/immsempl ymnt/SSA_Related_Info/index.htm#suit; www.aclu.org/immigrants/workplace/31643res20070829.html.

[27] 5 USC §§7062(A), (C).

[28] "[A]n SSA "no-match" letter by itself does not impart knowledge that the identified employees are unauthorized aliens." 72 Fed. Reg. 45611, 45616.

[29] In its appeal brief, DHS takes issue with the district court's assessment of the record. According to DHS, "the government has consistently explained to employers in guidance letters that while the mere receipt of a 'no-match' letter is not a sufficient basis for inferring constructive knowledge, an employer's failure to undertake any inquiries may, depending on all the circumstances, form the ground for imputing such knowledge." Appellants' Brief, *AFL-CIO v. Chertoff*, No. 07-17241 (9th Cir. Feb. 19, 2008), at 17.

[30] In its appeal brief, DHS denies that any such concession was made at oral argument before the district court. *Id.* at 21 n.5.

regulation, a serious question had been raised whether the agency had "casually ignored prior precedent in violation of the APA.[31]

The court also agreed with the plaintiffs that DHS may have overstepped its authority by interpreting INA §274B in the final rule. Section 274B contains the prohibitions against immigration-related discrimination. However, the authority to enforce and interpret those provisions belongs to the Office of Special Counsel for Immigration-Related Unfair Employment Practices within the Civil Rights Division of the Department of Justice, and not DHS.[32]

The third basis for the court's decision was the claim that the DHS rule was promulgated in violation of the Regulatory Flexibility Act (RFA).[33] Under the RFA, federal agencies generally must conduct an analysis of the potential costs and compliance burdens imposed by a final regulation on small businesses and organizations, unless the agency head certifies that the rule will not have a significant economic impact on a substantial number of small entities. DHS elected not to conduct an analysis under that exception.[34] In its decision, the court strongly disagreed with the agency's assertions that the "no-match" rule will not impose any additional costs or burdens on employers.[35]

As of this writing, the legal challenge against the rule has successfully frustrated the government's efforts to implement the "no-match" regulation. However, in spite of issuing the preliminary injunction, the district court did not find that the plaintiffs raised serious questions with regard to their more substantive claims against the regulation. The court did not agree that the rule is inconsistent with its governing statute, and did not find that the rule improperly amended the statutory meaning of "knowing." All three of the issues that formed the basis for granting the preliminary injunction can be

---

[31] *See* Order Granting Motion for Preliminary Injunction, *AFL-CIO v. Chertoff*, No. 07-4472 (N.D. Cal. Oct. 10, 2007), at 13–14.

[32] *Id.* at 15–16.

[33] *See* 5 USC §§604–05.

[34] In support of DHS Secretary Chertoff's certification that the rule would not significantly impact small entities, DHS stated, "The rule does not mandate any new burdens on the employer and does not impose any new or additional costs on the employer, but merely adds specific examples and a description of a 'safe harbor' procedure to an existing DHS regulation for purposes of enforcing the immigration laws and providing guidance to employers." 72 Fed. Reg. 45611, 45623.

[35] *See* Order Granting Motion for Preliminary Injunction, *AFL-CIO v. Chertoff*, No. 07-4472 (N.D. Cal. Oct. 10, 2007), at 17–19 ("The rule as good as mandates costly compliance with a new 90-day timeframe for resolving mismatches. Accordingly there are serious questions whether DHS violated the RFA by refusing to conduct a final flexibility analysis."). In the district court, DHS argued alternatively that the RFA did not apply because the new rule is interpretive, not legislative, which the district acknowledged to appear to be correct. *Id.* at 18 and n.2. The district court nonetheless held that DHS was required to defend its decision not to conduct a flexibility analysis on the justification provided in the rule. On appeal, DHS maintains the district court erred as a matter of law in so ruling, citing Ninth Circuit precedent for the proposition that the interpretive rule exception may be raised in the context of an APA challenge even though the agency did not rely on it when it promulgated the rule. As such, DHS argued that "it would be senseless to vacate a rule because the agency offered the wrong reason for declining to undertake a duty that does not apply." *See* Appellants' Brief, *AFL-CIO v. Chertoff*, No. 07-17241 (9th Cir. Feb. 19, 2008), at 28.

corrected, and the rule can likely be reissued without changes to any of its substantive provisions. DHS obtained a stay of the district court litigation to allow time to revise the regulation to address the district court's concerns.[36]

"No-Match" Resolution Issues

A number of issues can and will arise when trying to resolve Social Security mismatches. Interacting with employees over "no-match" issues can potentially lead to additional information that could also constitute actual or constructive notice regarding an employee's lack of immigration status. Employers need to ensure that employees follow up and resolve mismatches. However, they need to act carefully and uniformly with all employees over Social Security mismatches and in other situations in which constructive knowledge issues may arise. Having comprehensive policies in place will help employers deal with these situations and limit exposure to potential discrimination claims that employees may raise. Employers with unionized workforces, in particular, will want to consult with counsel before taking any adverse action against employees because of Social Security mismatches. A number of unions have sought to include provisions covering Social Security "no-match" issues in the collective bargaining agreement, and "no-match" issues have been the subject of a number of union grievances.[37]

Discrimination Concerns

The DHS rule has come under significant criticism due to concerns that implementation of the rule will lead to increased immigration-related and worksite discrimination on the part of overzealous or mistaken employers afraid of DHS enforcement after receipt of Social Security "no-match" letters. Although it is fairly unusual for one federal agency to comment publicly on another agency's regulation,[38] the Equal Employment Opportunity Commission publicly commented on the regulation and indicated that it had serious concerns that the proposed DHS rule created "circumstances in which employers have incentives to take actions that violate Title VII and/or IRCA's applicable nondiscriminatory provisions."[39]

It is important that employers develop and apply any Social Security "no-match" policies and procedures uniformly for all employees. Employers should not take precipitous adverse action against employees merely because they are the subject of a

---

[36] *See* Motion to Stay Proceedings Pending New Rulemaking, *AFL-CIO v. Chertoff*, No. 07-4472 (N.D. Cal. Nov. 23, 2007).

[37] *See, e.g., In re Tysons Foods, Inc. and Retail, Wholesale and Department Store Union Mid-South Council*, 2006 WL 4122899 (Dec. 8, 2006). Some additional examples of arbitration decisions are available at *www.nilc.org/immsemplymnt/SSA_Related_Info/index.htm#decisions*.

[38] The interagency review process managed by the Office of Management and Budget provides agencies an opportunity to review and comment on regulations prior to their publication.

[39] *See* Letter Comment from Peggy Mastroianni, Associate Legal Counsel, Equal Employment Opportunity Commission, to Richard Sloan, Director, Regulatory Management Division (Aug. 14, 2006), *available at www.eeoc.gov/foia/letters/2006/vii_national_immigration.html*. Title VII is Title VII of the Civil Rights Act of 1964, codified at 42 USC §2000e *et seq.*

"no-match" letter. While the ultimate outcome of the regulation may be unclear, it makes little sense for an employer to adopt a stricter policy for resolving the "no-match" discrepancies (by giving employees less than 90 days to resolve a "no-match," for example) than the safe-harbor procedures outlined in the DHS rule. The rule serves as the best indication of DHS's view of what constitutes a reasonable response to "no-match" letters. An employer should follow all of the steps of the procedures in order, and take adverse action (if any) only after all of the procedures have been completed.

Actual or Constructive Knowledge

When interacting with employees regarding Social Security "no-match" issues, it is very likely that an employer may become aware of additional information, beyond the "no-match" discrepancy, that may constitute constructive or even actual knowledge that the worker in question is not eligible for employment. In these situations the employer cannot simply continue to follow the "no-match" resolution process, but may need to take more immediate action. When confronted with new or additional information regarding an employee calling into question that worker's employment eligibility, the employer will have a duty to inquire further, beyond any "no-match" issue, to avoid a potential knowing employment charge.

For instance, it may be necessary to question an employee whether he or she has any idea why a Social Security mismatch has occurred. It is entirely possible, once an employee has been informed that he or she is the subject of a "no-match" letter, that the employee returns to the employer with new information or documentation that contradicts information he or she has previously provided. The employee may present a new Social Security card that contains a name or SSN different than the one previously provided in section 1 (and section 2 if the employee presented a different Social Security card as evidence of employment eligibility) of the I-9. In this situation it is difficult for the employer to know which information is accurate, or even be sure of the employee's true identity. The employer will likely need to inquire further or review additional documentation in order to be assured that the employee is eligible for employment or that the documents he or she presents appear genuine and to relate to the employee.[40] There may well be an explanation for the discrepancy, one that does not necessarily require any adverse action against the employee. It may be possible that the employee presented a false SSN at the time he or she was hired, but has since obtained legal status and is now eligible for employment. Constructive knowledge questions, even when they don't involve Social Security mismatch issues, can be

---

[40] The employee in this situation clearly may have originally submitted false information or documentation to the employer at the time of hire. Many employers have honesty policies, and the employee may be subject to termination for violation of such a policy. Termination for violation of such a policy has been held not to constitute immigration-related discrimination. *See Contreras v. Cascade Fruit Company*, 9 OCAHO 1090, at 22 (2003) (stating "an employer who discharges an employee for having presented false documents does not thereby violate [INA §274B, 8 USC §1324b]"); *Simon v. Ingram Micro, Inc.*, 9 OCAHO 1088, at 15 (2003). If the employer has such a policy, it should, of course, be applied uniformly to all employees.

tricky. Employers need to be sensitive to the need to follow up on any information that may cause the employer to doubt an employee's work authorization.

Social Security Number Verification Service (SSNVS)

At several points in the commentary to the final rule establishing the safe-harbor protocol, DHS recommends that employers use SSNVS.[41] SSNVS is provided by SSA to allow employers to check their records of employee names and SSNs against the agency's records.[42] It provides several access methods, including over both the Internet and telephone, to check employee SSN information. Some employers regularly use SSNVS to verify their employee's SSN information.

There is no requirement that employers use SSNVS. SSA states that the service should be used solely to ensure that the records of current or former employees are correct for tax reporting purposes.[43] According to SSA, it must not be used to screen applicants for employment before they are hired, and should be used uniformly for the entire workforce. In other words, if it used for newly hired workers, then it should be used for all newly hired workers.[44] SSA guidance also explicitly instructs employers not to take punitive action against employees because of a mismatch identified through SSNVS, and states that a mismatch does not make any statement about an individual's immigration status.[45]

Employers should carefully choose whether to use the program outside of the DHS "safe-harbor" procedures. Using SSNVS amounts essentially to soliciting a "no-match" letter from SSA for some portion of the company's workforce. A mismatch identified through SSNVS is functionally equivalent to one indicated in a "no-match" letter from the agency and should not be ignored without risk of being charged with constructive knowledge that an individual is unauthorized. While the final rule only addresses the situation in which an employer has received a "no-match" letter from SSA, and the safe-harbor procedures technically do not apply to discrepancies revealed through the use of SSNVS,[46] an employer who ignores or fails to resolve such discrepancies does so at its own peril. There are, however, potential benefits to using SSNVS. Using SSNVS will very likely help an employer improve the accuracy of its tax and wage reporting, and may help to identify potential Social Security mismatch problems before they come to the government's attention.[47] Employers may want to consider implementing the same procedures to follow up and

---

[41] *See* 72 Fed. Reg. 45611, 45618–19.

[42] Information about SSNVS is available from SSA's website at *www.ssa.gov/employer/ssnv.htm*.

[43] SSA, Business Services Online, *Social Security Number Verification Service (SSNVS) Handbook*, available at *www.ssa.gov/employer/ssnvs_handbk.htm*.

[44] *Id.*

[45] *Id.*

[46] 72 Fed. Reg. 45611, 45618.

[47] Using SSNVS to check the Social Security information of the entire workforce, along with submitting to an audit by ICE, is one of the prerequisites to joining the IMAGE program. *See www.ice.gov/partners/opaimage/index.htm*.

resolve SSNVS mismatches as are adopted for dealing with actual "no-match" letters, with the same cautions and safeguards. Any procedures implemented should be applied uniformly for all employees.

Soliciting Social Security Number Information from Employees

Given the heightened concern regarding Social Security mismatches, employers should understand the rules for soliciting Social Security information from employees at the time of hire. Although an unrestricted Social Security card can serve as acceptable evidence of employment eligibility, a new employee is not required to fill in the field for his or her SSN in section 1 of the I-9. According to instructions to the most recent version of the form, this section is optional.[48] There is actually no statutory or regulatory requirement that a job applicant possess or provide an SSN at the time of application or at the time he or she begins employment.[49] SSA and IRS guidance clearly contemplates that not all new employees will have SSNs assigned when employment begins.[50] The employer does have an obligation to solicit an employee's SSN at the time of hire.[51] If the employee does not have a number, the IRS regulations require that the employee apply for one within seven days of commencing employment.[52] IRS Form W-4 can be used as the employer's initial solicitation of the employee's SSN. It is generally a good practice to separate the solicitation of an employee's Social Security information from the I-9 process.

Compliance Steps for Employers

Employers should consider taking the following steps to improve their compliance posture with regard to "no-match" letters:

---

[48] Provision of an SSN is not optional if the employer participates in E-Verify. See USCIS, "I am an Employer . . . How Do I . . . Use E-Verify" (M-655, Sept. 2007), reprinted in this book and available at *www.uscis.gov/files/nativedocuments/E4_english.pdf* (stating that E-Verify cannot be used for employees who do not yet have an SSN).

[49] There also doesn't appear to be a statutory or regulatory prohibition against an employer requiring a job applicant or new employee to provide an SSN. In fact, there have been several decisions by the Office of the Chief Administrative Hearing Officer concluding that there is no prohibition under the immigration laws against an employer requiring SSNs as a precondition of employment. *See Toussaint v. Tekwood*, 6 OCAHO 892, at 803 (1996) ("Nothing in the logic, text, or legislative history of the Immigration Reform and Control Act limits an employer's ability to require a Social Security number as a precondition of employment."); *Winkler v. Timlin*, 6 OCAHO 912 (1997); *Lewis v. McDonald's Corp.*, 2 OCAHO 383 (1991). Interestingly, the complainants in each of these cases were not very sympathetic. All of these decisions deal with claims of national-origin and citizenship status discrimination made by U.S. citizens who were either not hired or terminated shortly after hire because they were tax protesters. They had refused to provide an SSN to their employer in order to try to avoid payment of income tax.

[50] *See* IRS Publication 15, Circular E, *Employer's Tax Guide*. For the filing of the W-2, where the employee has requested an SSN and has not received it, the employer may write "SSN applied for" (or 000-00-0000 if filing electronically) in the SSN space. Once the SSN is received, the employer should then file Copy A of Form W-2c to correct the wage statement so it reflects the employee's SSN.

[51] 26 CFR §31.6011(b)-2(c)(2).

[52] 26 CFR §31.6011(b)-2(a)(2).

1. Conduct an internal I-9 audit. This will allow the company to make an assessment of its overall I-9 compliance posture and to correct any errors or omissions upfront, before a government audit. Determine, if possible, whether the company has been the recipient of SSA "no-match" letters in previous years. If so, take steps to resolve any discrepancies revealed in those letters. Even if the deadlines in the safe-harbor protocol have passed long ago, this will demonstrate good faith on the employer's part in the case of any future DHS audit.

2. Review and update personnel and I-9 compliance policies and procedures to incorporate "no-match" concerns. These should include policies to assign responsibility for the receipt of and follow-up on "no-match" letters, and the resolution of "no-match" discrepancies. Employers should consider incorporating the DHS safe-harbor procedures into these policies. These documents should make clear the employer's policy against discrimination, and the policies must be applied uniformly to all employees, not just those with foreign appearance or names. No adverse action should be taken against any employee until the employer has completed every step of the "no-match" resolution process, unless the employer otherwise comes to know the employee is unauthorized.

3. Provide training on I-9 compliance to supervisors and HR personnel, including training on "no-match" resolution and the prohibitions against immigration-related discrimination.

Conclusion

Some of the current uncertainty surrounding the question of Social Security "no-match" letters will be clarified, but there are no guarantees. At the time of this writing, the revised version of the DHS rule was under review for publication. Interestingly, the OMB website[53] indicates that the revised rule would be reissued as a proposed, rather than a final regulation. Thus, it is likely, even without the legal challenge to the rule, that it will take some time before a final rule is published and can take effect. It is impossible to predict the ultimate outcome of the legal challenge to the rule. Although the district court in San Francisco preliminarily enjoined DHS from implementing the rule, its decision was based primarily on procedural issues rather than finding a legal flaw with the substantive provisions of the rule. It appears that there is still a good chance that the rule will go into effect at some point in the future. While these issues are playing out, employers should take a conservative approach to dealing with any "no-match" letters they may receive.

Given the increased pace of worksite enforcement and the potential extreme consequences of a DHS investigation, "no-match" letters cannot be ignored. Employers need to check their records, tell employees to resolve any mismatches with SSA, and follow up with employees to check on the progress of their efforts. There is no need for an employer to overreact simply because it receives a "no-match" letter. The employer should follow its "no-match" policy or procedure and give the employee suffi-

---

[53] *www.reginfo.gov* (RIN: 1653-AA50).

cient time to resolve the "no-match" letter. The timeline provided in the DHS safe-harbor procedures seems like a reasonable place to start. Regardless of whether the regulation takes effect any time soon, the stakes are simply too great for any employer and its management officials to ignore or delay dealing with Social Security "no-match" issues when they arise.

ESTABLISHING AN EFFECTIVE FORM I-9 COMPLIANCE PROGRAM

by Scott J. FitzGerald*

Introduction

The daunting employment verification procedures introduced by the Immigration Reform and Control Act (IRCA) of 1986,[1] amending the Immigration and Nationality Act (INA) of 1952,[2] still challenge many employers today. In 1986, as a means of controlling the problem of illegal immigration into the United States,[3] Congress for the first time charged employers with the responsibility of systematically verifying that their new hires and existing employees are eligible to work in the United States. The statute applies not only to aliens authorized to work, but also to lawful permanent residents and U.S. citizens.[4] To facilitate the employment verification process, IRCA's employer sanctions provisions introduced Form I-9 (Employment Eligibility Verification), the document on which all employees hired after November 6, 1986, must verify under penalty of perjury that they are authorized to work in the United States. Form I-9 currently includes a list of 24 qualifying documents that employers may accept as proof of the employee's identity and authorization to work.[5]

---

* Updated from an article that originally appeared at 1 *Immigration & Nationality Law Handbook* 609 (AILA 1999–2000 Ed.).

Scott J. FitzGerald is the managing partner of the Boston office of Fragomen, Del Rey, Bernsen & Loewy LLP, and a managing director of Fragomen Global Immigration Services, LLC, with specific responsibility for the firm's India operations. Mr. FitzGerald has previously served as the managing partner of the firm's Washington, D.C. and Vienna, VA offices, as well as an associate in the firm's New York office. He is admitted to practice law in New York, Connecticut, and Washington, D.C., and is a member of the Labor Relations Committee of the U.S. Chamber of Commerce and of the U.S. India Business Council. He is also a member of the American Bar Association, the Federal Bar Association, the Association of the Bar of the City of New York, and the American Immigration Lawyers Association. Mr. FitzGerald also serves on the board of the Council for Emerging National Security Affairs (CENSA). He is a graduate of the Johns Hopkins University (B.A., International Studies, 1989) and Fordham University School of Law (J.D., 1992). He would like to thank Sophia M. Goring for her assistance in the preparation of this article. He also would like to thank Christina B. LaBrie, an associate in the New York office of Fragomen, Del Rey, Bernsen & Loewy LLP, for her assistance in updating the article for this publication.

[1] Pub. L. No. 99-603, 100 Stat. 3359.

[2] Pub. L. No. 82-414, 66 Stat. 163.

[3] H.R. Rep. No. 682, 99th Cong., 2d Sess., pt. 1, at 46 (1986).

[4] For a comprehensive listing of what constitutes an alien authorized to work, *see* A. Lamdin, "Employment Authorization and I-9 Compliance," 96-09 *Immigration Briefings* (Sept. 1996); 8 CFR §274a.12.

[5] As discussed later in this article, Congress enacted the Illegal Immigration Reform and Immigrant Responsibility Act of 1996 (IIRAIRA), Pub. L. No. 104-208, div. C, 110 Stat. 3009, 3009-546 to 3009-724, which in part reduced the number of acceptable documents in Form I-9. The Department of Homeland Security (DHS) issued a revised Form I-9 on November 7, 2007, reflecting IIRAIRA's reduction

Under IRCA, employers face civil penalties, including hefty fines, for noncompliance with IRCA's employment eligibility verification procedures.[6] Employers may also face civil penalties for having knowingly hired or continuing to employ an unauthorized worker.[7] In addition, employers that engage in a pattern or practice of violations may incur civil and even criminal penalties. Initially the law seemed harsh, because even technical infractions committed by the employer when completing the Form I-9 could expose it to substantial civil monetary penalties.[8]

Congress also incorporated provisions into IRCA prohibiting discrimination against employees in the verification process based on citizenship or national origin, and prohibited employers from specifying which documents could be presented.[9] In addition, IRCA prohibited retaliation against any employee by an employer against whom a claim of such discrimination had been made.[10] Although these provisions were a necessary deterrent against discriminatory practices that would inevitably arise out of the employment verification requirements, IRCA seemed to place employers in a hopeless position. If an employer unnecessarily questioned the validity of a document presented, or requested a specific document from an employee, such an action could be construed as discriminatory. In such circumstances, the employer in question would then have to defend itself against a claim brought by the Office of Special Counsel for Immigration-Related Unfair Employment Practices (OSC) of the Department of Justice.[11] However, at the same time, if an employer failed to determine the fraudulent nature of a document presented, and in fact accepted a facially fraudulent document as proof of the individual's identity and employment eligibility, the employer could be fined.[12] In addition, if the employer made a technical error when completing the Form I-9, it could be fined. In essence, IRCA seemed intent on penalizing employers more than it aimed to curb illegal immigration.

---

in the number of acceptable documents. USCIS also published a notice in the *Federal Register* mandating use of the new Form I-9 starting on December 26, 2007. 72 Fed. Reg. 65972 (Nov. 26, 2007).

[6] INA §274A(e)(5); 8 USC §1324a(e)(5).

[7] INA §274A(e)(4); 8 USC §1324a(e)(4).

[8] INA §§274A(f)(1), (2); 8 USC §§1324a(f)(1), (2).

[9] INA §274B(a)(6); 8 USC §1324b(a)(6).

[10] INA §274B(a)(5); 8 USC §1324b(a)(5).

[11] OSC has jurisdiction to process certain charges of employment discrimination on the basis of national origin or citizenship status, under §102 of IRCA. See A. Gallagher, *Immigration Law Service 2d*, §12:95 *et seq*. OSC is responsible for receiving and investigating discrimination charges and, when appropriate, filing complaints with specially designated administrative law judges. 63 Fed. Reg. 19515 (Apr. 20, 1998). OSC also initiates independent investigations of possible section 102 violations. *Id.*

[12] In addition, it is often difficult for employers to cull legal workers from illegal ones. "Most illegal immigrants work for bona fide businesses and are hired and paid like other workers on the payroll …. When the illegal immigrants are hired, their employers don't know whether the documents are authentic." M. Jordan, "Firms Brace for Crackdown on Illegal Labor," *Wall St. J.* (Oct. 1, 2007), *available at* http://online.wsj.com/article/SB119119705298544271.html?mod=hpp_us_whats_news (subscription required).

Faced with these difficulties, through passage of the Illegal Immigration Reform and Immigrant Responsibility Act of 1996 (IIRAIRA),[13] Congress proposed to lessen the procedural burdens on employers presented by IRCA. Specifically, through IIRAIRA, Congress introduced the "good-faith compliance" defense, allowing employers a means of correcting technical and procedural violations on Form I-9, and allowing the employer 10 days in which to cure the violation.[14] Moreover, IIRAIRA contained provisions that made it easier for employers to comply with the sanctions requirements by reducing the number of documents that may be presented for employment eligibility verification.[15] IIRAIRA also imposed a more stringent burden of proof upon claimants of employment discrimination when employers requested more documents to comply with the Form I-9 completion requirement. This section held the employer liable for unlawful discrimination only if the action was taken with the intent of discriminating against the individual.[16]

In August 2007, U.S. Immigration and Customs Enforcement (ICE) published a regulation establishing rules for responding to Social Security Administration (SSA) "no-match" letters.[17] Employers who receive "no-match" letters, which indicate that a name and Social Security number do not match SSA records, must take specific steps in order to receive "safe harbor" from a finding that the employer had knowledge that an employee was not authorized to work in the United States. The same procedures apply to letters sent by the Department of Homeland Security (DHS) indicating that an immigration status or employment authorization document (EAD) used in completing a Form I-9 was not assigned to the employee. The "no-match" regulation was originally scheduled to take effect on September 14, 2007, but on October 10, 2007, a federal judge issued a preliminary injunction in response to a lawsuit challenging the ICE regulation.[18] The injunction prevents ICE from implementing the "no-match" regulation, and halts SSA from sending some 140,000 "no-match" letters that were to include new, more stringent language and instructions on complying with the regulation. DHS filed a motion requesting that the lawsuit be adjourned until the regulation is rewritten.[19] At the time of publication of this article, the "no-match" regulation remains suspended until further notice.

---

[13] Pub. L. No. 104-208, div. C, 110 Stat. 3009, 3009-546 to 3009-724.

[14] IIRAIRA §411, 110 Stat. at 3009-666; INA §274A(b)(6); 8 USC §1324a(b)(6).

[15] IIRAIRA §412, 110 Stat. at 3009-666 to 3009-668; INA §274A(b)(1)(B); 8 USC §1324a(b)(1)(B); J. Osuna, "The 1996 Immigration Act: Employer Sanctions, Antidiscrimination and Work Verification," 73 *Interpreter Releases* 1749, 1751 (Dec. 20, 1996).

[16] IIRAIRA §421, 110 Stat. at 3009-670; INA §274B(a)(6), 8 USC § 1324b(a)(6); J. Osuna, "The 1996 Immigration Act: Employer Sanctions, Antidiscrimination and Work Verification," 73 *Interpreter Releases* 1749, 1752 (Dec. 20, 1996).

[17] 72 Fed. Reg. 45611 (Aug. 15, 2007).

[18] Order Granting Motion for Preliminary Injunction, *AFL-CIO v. Chertoff*, No. 07-4472 (N.D.Cal. Oct. 10, 2007).

[19] Motion to Stay Proceedings Pending New Rulemaking, *AFL-CIO v. Chertoff*, No. 07-4472 (N.D.Cal. Nov. 23, 2007).

Despite these changes, much controversy remains over the effectiveness of the employment eligibility verification process in general. Particularly, the continuing rise of illegal immigration into the United States places more doubt than ever on the effectiveness of the program.[20] Given this dilemma, many have questioned whether employers should really be burdened with such ministerial and penalty-driven procedures as a means of solving the nation's illegal immigration problem.[21] In the meantime, however, immigration practitioners and employers are required to keep abreast of changes in the law pertaining to employment eligibility verification to meet their continuing obligations. To facilitate this effort, this article will track the effect of the IIRAIRA amendments, the continuing difficulties employers face as they attempt to comply with IRCA's employment verification provisions, and will recommend ways in which employers may circumvent potential problems to ensure a high level of compliance.

Overview of the Form I-9 Compliance Requirements

Basic Requirements

Under IRCA, a Form I-9 must be completed by every employee who has been hired after November 6, 1986.[22] In 2004, legislation was enacted that allows the Form I-9 to be completed, signed, and stored electronically.[23] ICE issued an interim rule in June 2006 that conformed the regulations to the new law.[24] The interim rule also set performance standards for the electronic completion, storage, and signing of Forms I-9.[25] In addition, the interim rule permits employers to electronically scan and store existing Forms I-9.[26]

An "employee" is defined as an individual who provides services or labor for an employer for wages or other remuneration, other than an independent contractor.[27] To determine whether an individual is an "independent contractor," several factors must be examined, including: whether the individual supplies the tools or materials; makes his or her services available to the general public; works for a number of clients simultaneously; has an opportunity for profit of loss as a result of the services provided; invests in the facilities for work; directs the order or sequence in which the work is performed; and determines the hours during which the work is done.[28] If the

---

[20] *See* J. Preston, "Immigration at Record Level, Analysis Finds," *N.Y. Times* (Nov. 29, 2007), *available at www.nytimes.com/2007/11/29/us/29immig.html?_r=1&oref=slogin* ("Immigration over the past seven years was the highest for any seven-year period in American history, bringing 10.3 million new immigrants, more than half of them without legal status . . . .").

[21] *Id.*

[22] 8 CFR §274a.2(a).

[23] Pub. L. No. 108-390, 118 Stat. 2242 (2004).

[24] 71 Fed. Reg. 34510–17 (June 15, 2006).

[25] 8 CFR §§274a.2(e)–(i).

[26] 8 CFR §274a.2(e).

[27] 8 CFR §274a.1(f).

[28] 8 CFR §274a.1(j).

majority of these factors do not apply, the individual in question is likely an employee, and must complete a Form I-9.

The employee is required to complete section 1 of the Form I-9 at the time of hire.[29] The employee must indicate in section 1 whether he or she is a U.S. citizen, a lawful permanent resident, or an alien authorized to work until a specific date. By signing section 1, the employee attests under penalty of perjury that the information provided is accurate. The employee may complete section 1 prior to the time of hire, but in no circumstances later than the first date of hire. If the employee is physically unable to complete section 1, or requires that it be translated, the preparer or translator must complete the "Preparer/Translator Certification" section of the form.[30]

Within three business days of the date of hire, the employer must physically examine documentation that establishes the identity and employment authorization of the employee, and must complete section 2 of the Form I-9. (The lists of acceptable documents are printed on the back of the Form I-9.)[31] To meet the documentation requirement, the employee must present one original document (no photocopies) from list A on the back of the Form I-9 that establishes identity and employment authorization (*e.g.*, a U.S. passport), or one original document from list B that establishes identity (*e.g.*, a driver's license), and one original document from list C that establishes employment authorization (*e.g.*, an "unrestricted" Social Security card—one that does not indicate, for instance, "not valid for employment without DHS authorization").[32] Once presented, the document name, identification number, and expiration date (if any) must be recorded in the appropriate space in section 2.[33] Documents are considered to be acceptable if they appear genuine on their face and relate to the employee who presents them.[34] In addition, an employer may not specify which document or documents an individual is to present.[35]

Receipts for Lost Documents

If the employee is unable to provide the required documentation within three days of hire because a document is lost, stolen, or damaged, the employee may present a receipt for the application for a replacement document by the third day of employment.[36] The employee then has 90 days from the date of hire to produce the original replacement document.[37] The employer must follow up with the employee to ensure

---

[29] 8 CFR §274a.2(b)(1)(i)(A).
[30] *Id.*
[31] 8 CFR §274a.2(b)(1)(ii).
[32] 8 CFR §274a.2(b)(1)(v).
[33] *Id.*
[34] 8 CFR §274a.2(b)(1)(v)(A).
[35] 8 CFR §274a.2(b)(1)(v).
[36] 8 CFR §274a.2(b)(1)(vi)(A).
[37] *Id.*

that the original document is presented within that 90-day period, and the Form I-9 should be notated to reflect such presentation.

The receipt is acceptable for verification purposes only if it has been issued for a lost, stolen, or damaged document (*e.g.*, lost unrestricted Social Security card). Therefore, in a scenario in which an employee has presented a receipt for the filing of an application for either an initial or the extension of an EAD issued by U.S. Citizenship and Immigration Services (USCIS), the receipt rule would not apply.[38]

Reverification

If the employee checks box 3 in section 1 of the Form I-9 indicating that he or she is an alien authorized to work until a specific date,[39] the employee must present documentation confirming continued employment authorization on or before that expiration date.[40] Such documentation consists of either one document from list A or one document from list C, since the identity of the employee (list B) need not be reverified. On receipt of the documentation, the employer must complete section 3 of the Form I-9 and record the new expiration date. The employer may sign the attestation by hand or with an electronic signature. Failure to complete section 3 could result in the continued employment of an unauthorized alien, which could lead to substantial civil and even criminal penalties, as outlined below.

Transfers

When an employee transfers from one distinct unit of an employer to another distinct unit of the same employer in a different geographic location, the employer may transfer the individual's Form I-9 to the receiving unit without completing a new one.[41] However, as discussed below, there may be distinct advantages to centralizing all responsibility for Form I-9 storage at one location for the entire company nationwide.

Retention and Inspection

The employer must retain Forms I-9 for all employees for a period of three years after the date of hire or one year after the date the individual's employment is terminated, whichever is later.[42] Any person or entity required to retain Forms I-9 must be given three days' notice prior to a DHS inspection of the Forms I-9.[43] At the time of inspection, Forms I-9 must be made available in their original paper or electronic form, a paper copy of the electronic form, or on microfilm or microfiche at the location where the request for production was made.[44] A recruiter or referrer for a fee

---

[38] *Id.*

[39] This rule also applies to a lawful permanent resident who presents an unexpired foreign passport with an I-551 stamp indicating temporary employment authorization (list A, #4).

[40] 8 CFR §274a.2(b)(1)(vii).

[41] 8 CFR §274a.2(b)(1)(viii)(A).

[42] 8 CFR §274a.2(b)(2)(i).

[43] 8 CFR §274a.2(b)(2)(ii).

[44] *Id.*

who has designated an employer to complete the employment verification procedures may present a photocopy or printed electronic image of the Form I-9 in lieu of presenting the Form I-9 in its original form.[45]

Any refusal or delay in presentation of the Forms I-9 for inspection is a violation of the retention requirements.[46] No subpoena or warrant is required for such inspection, but the use of such enforcement tools is not precluded.[47]

Electronic Collection and Storage

Employers are not required to follow electronic collection and storage procedures; all prior rules for paper collection and storage of Forms I-9 remain in place. If, however, an employer chooses to use an electronic I-9 system, it must follow minimum standards. Specifically, an employer must use an electronic collection or storage system that includes: (1) reasonable controls to ensure integrity, accuracy, and reliability; (2) reasonable controls designed to prevent and detect the unauthorized or accidental creation of, addition to, alteration of, deletion of, or deterioration of an electronically completed or stored Form I-9; (3) an inspection and quality assurance program; (4) an indexed retrieval system; and (5) the ability to produce legible hard copies.[48]

Employers using electronic Form I-9 systems must also maintain and make available to any U.S. agency upon request documentation of the business processes that: (1) create the retained Forms I-9; (2) modify and maintain the retained Forms I-9; and (3) establish the authenticity and integrity of the Forms I-9.[49] The security program for an employer's electronic Form I-9 system must: (1) ensure that only authorized personnel have access to electronic records; (2) provide for backup and recovery of records; (3) ensure that employees are trained to minimize the risk of unauthorized or accidental erasure of electronic records; and (4) ensure that whenever an electronic record is accessed, a secure and permanent record is created, showing the date of access, the identity of the individual who accessed the record, and the action taken.[50]

If a Form I-9 is completed electronically, the attestations must be completed using a system that includes a method to acknowledge that the attestation has been read by the signatory.[51] The system must also affix the electronic signature at the time of the transaction, create and preserve a record verifying the identity of the signatory, and provide printed confirmation (*e.g.*, a "receipt") to the signatory.[52]

---

[45] *Id.*
[46] *Id.*
[47] *Id.*
[48] 8 CFR §274a.2(e)(1).
[49] 8 CFR §274a.2(f)(1).
[50] 8 CFR §274a.2(g)(1).
[51] 8 CFR §274a.2(h)(1).
[52] *Id.*

Photocopying or Making Electronic Images of Documentation

An employer may, but is not required to, photocopy or make an electronic image of documents presented by an employee for the purpose of complying with the verification requirements.[53] If such a photocopy or electronic image is made, it must be retained with the Form I-9.[54] However, the photocopying or electronic imaging of any such document and retention of the photocopy or electronic image do not relieve the employer of the requirement to fully complete section 2 of the Form I-9.[55] Employers should also be sure to photocopy or make an electronic image of the front and back of original documents presented. When passports are presented, the employer need only capture those pages on which the passport holder's name, photograph, country of issue, date of birth, and passport expiration date are provided.

When IRCA was first enacted in 1986, many practitioners recommended not photocopying documents presented for fear that such photocopies would be used by legacy Immigration and Naturalization Service (INS) as evidence that an employer knowingly hired an unauthorized alien. However, due to the fact that such photocopies or electronic images are critical to the efficient review and correction of Forms I-9 during an internal audit, and the fact that the quality of fraudulent documents today is extremely high, it is recommended that such photocopies or electronic images be retained. Conversely, if you or your client is using an electronic I-9 completion system that does not allow the user to accept an incompatible document, such photocopying of supporting documents should not be necessary.

Rehires

If an employee is rehired within three years of the date of the initial execution of the Form I-9, it is possible for the employer to use that Form I-9 to complete the verification process.[56] Upon inspection of the Form I-9, the employer must confirm that the Form I-9 relates to the employee and that the employee is still eligible to work. The employer updates section 3 of the Form I-9 to reflect the date of rehire.[57] Alternatively, if the employer determines that the employee's employment authorization has expired, the employee must present evidence of current work authorization and the employer must complete the reverification portion of section 3.[58]

"Knowing" Hiring Violations Through Contract

Any person or entity who knowingly uses a contract, subcontract, or exchange entered into, renegotiated, or extended after November 6, 1986, to obtain the labor services of an alien in the United States knowing that the alien is unauthorized to work will be considered to have hired the alien for employment in violation of INA

---

[53] 8 CFR §274a.2(b)(3).
[54] *Id.*
[55] *Id.*
[56] 8 CFR §274a.2(c).
[57] Id.
[58] *Id.*

§274A(a)(1)(A).[59] Therefore, an employer is not allowed to use the existence of a written contract for labor services to protect itself if the employer is aware that the laborers provided through that contract are not authorized to work.

Criminal and Civil Penalties

Any person or entity that engages in a pattern or practice of violations of INA §§274A(a)(1)(A) or (2) may face criminal penalties.[60] Such person or entity will be fined not more than $3,000 for each unauthorized alien, imprisoned for not more than six months for the entire pattern or practice, or both, notwithstanding the provisions of any other federal law relating to fine levels.[61]

As mentioned above, Congress incorporated provisions for substantial monetary penalties to encourage compliance with IRCA. Specifically, any person or entity may face civil penalties for a violation of INA §274A. Civil penalties may be imposed by DHS or an administrative law judge for violations of INA §274A.[62] For purposes of determining the level of penalties that will be imposed, a finding of more than one violation in the course of a single proceeding or determination will be counted as a single offense.[63] However, a single offense will include penalties for each unauthorized alien who is determined to have been knowingly hired or recruited or referred for a fee.[64]

A respondent determined by ICE (if a respondent fails to request a hearing) or by an administrative law judge to have failed to comply with the employment verification requirements is subject to a civil penalty in an amount of not less than $100 and not more than $1,000 for each individual with respect to whom such violation occurred before September 29, 1999, and not less than $110 and not more than $1,100 for each individual with respect to whom such violation occurred on or after September 29, 1999.[65] In determining the amount of the penalty, consideration will be given to the following mitigating factors: (i) the size of the business of the employer being charged; (ii) the good faith of the employer; (iii) the seriousness of the violation; (iv) whether the individual was an unauthorized alien; and (v) the history of previous violations of the employer.[66]

If the U.S. attorney general has reasonable cause to believe that a person or entity is engaged in a pattern or practice of employment, recruitment or referral in violation of INA §§274A(a)(1)(A) or (2), the attorney general may bring a civil action in the appropriate U.S. district court requesting relief, including a permanent or temporary

---

[59] 8 CFR §274a.5.
[60] 8 CFR §274a.10(a).
[61] *Id.*
[62] 8 CFR §274a.10(b).
[63] *Id.*
[64] *Id.*
[65] 8 CFR §274a.10(b)(2).
[66] *Id.*

injunction, restraining order, or other order against the person or entity, as the attorney general deems necessary.[67]

A respondent found by ICE or an administrative law judge to have knowingly hired, or to have knowingly recruited or referred for a fee, an unauthorized alien for employment in the United States or to have knowingly continued to employ an unauthorized alien in the United States is subject to either an order to cease and desist from such behavior, or to pay a civil fine.[68] The civil fine is set by a predetermined schedule, such that for the first offense, the respondent would be fined not less than $275 and not more than $2,200 for each unauthorized alien with respect to whom the offense occurred before March 27, 2008, and not less than $375 and not exceeding $3,200 for each unauthorized alien with respect to whom the offense occurred on or after March 27, 2008.[69] For a second offense, the fine charged would be not less than $3,200 ($2,200 for offenses prior to March 27, 2008) and not more than $6,500 ($5,500 for offenses prior to March 27, 2008) for each unauthorized alien.[70] For more than two offenses, the fine would be not less than $4,300 ($3,300 for offenses prior to March 27, 2008) and not more than $16,000 ($11,000 for offenses prior to March 27, 2008) for each unauthorized alien.[71] In addition, the respondent would be responsible for complying with the requirements of 8 CFR §274a.2(b), and to take such other remedial action as is appropriate.[72]

The Effect of the 1996 Amendments on Employer Sanctions and Employment Verification

Bono Amendment

The Bono Amendment,[73] introduced by the late Congressman Sonny Bono (R-CA), grants employers charged with employment eligibility verification violations under IRCA on or after September 30, 1996, a period of 10 days to correct technical or procedural paperwork infractions. The Bono Amendment also provides employers with a "good-faith compliance" defense before such infractions are deemed to be violations of the INA.[74] Specifically, it provides that a person or entity that has made a good-faith attempt to comply with an employment verification requirement of INA §274A(b) will be considered to have complied with the requirement, notwithstanding a technical or procedural failure to meet such a requirement.[75] However, this provision is subject to

---

[67] 8 CFR §274a.10(c).

[68] 8 CFR §274a.10(b)(1).

[69] 8 CFR §274a.10(b)(1)(ii)(A); 28 CFR §68.52(c)(1)(i).

[70] 8 CFR §274a.10(b)(1)(ii)(B); 28 CFR §68.52(c)(1)(ii).

[71] 8 CFR §274a.10(b)(1)(ii)(C); 28 CFR §68.52(c)(1)(iii).

[72] 8 CFR §274a.10(b)(1)(iii); *see* 28 CFR §68.52(c)(3).

[73] IIRAIRA §411, 110 Stat. at 3009-666; INA §274A(b)(6); 8 USC §1324a(b)(6).

[74] INA §274A(b)(6); 8 USC § 1324a(b)(6); *see* "INS Proposes Rule Limiting Liability for Certain Violations of Paperwork Requirements," 75 *Interpreter Releases* 509 (Apr. 13, 1998).

[75] INA §274A(b)(6)(A); 8 USC § 1324a(b)(6)(A); "INS Proposes Rule Limiting Liability for Certain Violations of Paperwork Requirements," 75 *Interpreter Releases* 509, 510 (Apr. 13, 1998).

two exceptions. First, INA §274A(b)(6)(B) provides that a person or entity will be considered not to have complied with the requirement if: (1) DHS has explained to the person or entity the basis for the failure; (2) the person or entity has been provided a period of not less than 10 business days, beginning after the date of the explanation, within which to correct the failure; and (3) the person or entity has not corrected the failure within such period.[76] Under the second exception, provided by INA §274A(b)(6)(C), a person or entity will be considered not to have complied with the requirement if the person or entity is engaging in a pattern or practice of knowing-hire or continuing-to-employ violations of INA §§ 274A(a)(1)(A) or 274A(a)(2).[77]

In April 1998, legacy INS issued a proposed rule explaining the effective date of the good-faith compliance provisions and comprehensively defining the meaning of "technical" and "procedural" violations.[78] The proposed rule closely follows the language of the March 1997 legacy INS policy memorandum implementing the Bono Amendment.[79] Although the rule has never been finalized, it serves as a useful tool for employers to more carefully avoid noncompliance allegations. Immigration practitioners and employers should note that the Bono Amendment applies to failures occurring on or after September 30, 1996, even if the failures first occurred on a Form I-9 prepared before the date of enactment.[80] Therefore, except for timeliness failures, failures to meet a verification requirement continue from the first day the requirement must be met until: (1) the day that the failures are corrected; (2) the day that the failures can no longer be corrected, such as when DHS inspects the employer's Forms I-9; or (3) the day that the duty to meet the requirement ceases.[81] Moreover, the rule states that for failures associated with timely completion of the Form I-9, the Bono Amendment will not apply if the requirement to complete the Form I-9 should have been met before September 30, 1996.

The proposed rule distinguishes between employment eligibility verification failures that are not considered to be technical and procedural, and those that represent technical and procedural infractions that the employer may correct within the 10-day grace period.[82] For example, the rule explains that a technical or procedural violation

---

[76] *Id.*

[77] *Id.*

[78] 63 Fed. Reg. 16909–13 (Apr. 7, 1998); *see* "INS Proposes Rule Limiting Liability for Certain Violations of Paperwork Requirements," 75 *Interpreter Releases* 509 (Apr. 13, 1998).

[79] INS Memorandum, P. Virtue, "Interim Guidelines: Section 274A(b)(6) of the Immigration & Nationality Act Added by Section 411 of the Illegal Immigration Reform & Immigrant Responsibility Act of 1996" (Mar. 6, 1997), *published on* AILA InfoNet at Doc. No. 97030691 (*posted* Mar. 6, 1997), and reprinted in this book. For a detailed explanation of the memorandum, *see* "INS Issues Important Instructions on Employer Sanctions Provisions of 1996 Act," 74 *Interpreter Releases* 706 (Apr. 28, 1997).

[80] *Id.*

[81] 63 Fed. Reg. 16910 (Apr. 7, 1998).

[82] For a detailed summary of the examples of technical and procedural violations and substantive violations, *see* 63 Fed. Reg. 16910–12; *see also* "INS Issues Important Instructions on Employer Sanctions Provisions of 1996 Act," 74 *Interpreter Releases* 706, 707 (Apr. 28, 1997).

falling the Bono Amendment may include failure of a person or entity to ensure that an individual provides his or her maiden name, address, or birth date in section 1 of the Form I-9.[83] A technical or procedural violation may also be failure of an entity or person to provide the document title, identification number(s) and/or expiration date(s) of a proper list A document or proper list B and list C documents in section 2 of the Form I-9, but only if a legible copy of the document(s) is retained with the Form I-9 and presented at the Form I-9 inspection.[84] However, substantive violations not covered under the Bono Amendment may include the employer's failure to ensure that: (1) the employee provides his or her printed name; or (2) the individual checks the box attesting to whether he or she is a citizen or national of the United States, a permanent resident, or an alien authorized to work until a certain date.[85] Moreover, in section 2 of the Form I-9, a substantive violation will be deemed to have occurred if the employer fails to: (1) review and verify a proper list A document or proper list B and C documents; (2) provide the document title, identification number or expiration date of a proper list A, B, or C document, unless a copy is retained and presented at the I-9 inspection; (3) sign the attestation; or (4) date section 2 of the I-9 within three business days of the hire.[86]

The rule also recognizes that in some circumstances the employer's ability to correct technical or procedural failures is impossible. The rule states that when the employer's explanation of an inability to correct a technical or procedural failure is reasonable, the employer will be deemed to have complied with the requirement, notwithstanding the inability to correct the failure.[87] Such explanations may be warranted based on the nature of the failure, such as a timeliness failure, or to the inability of the employer to access the necessary information, such as when the information has been independently destroyed or is inaccessible due to termination of the individual's employment.[88]

An unimplemented ICE regulation published in August 2007[89] establishes specific rules for responding to SSA "no-match" letters. Employers who receive "no-match" letters from SSA, or letters from DHS indicating that an immigration status document presented by an employee does not belong to the employee, would be required to follow specific procedures during a 93-day period in order to receive "safe harbor" protection from a finding of knowingly hiring or continuing to employ an unauthorized worker. First, the employer would check its own records for clerical errors. If an error is discovered, the employer would confirm the corrected information with SSA. If a check of the employer's own records does not resolve the discrepancy, the regulation recom-

---

[83] 63 Fed. Reg. 16910–11 (Apr. 7, 1998).

[84] *Id.*

[85] "INS Issues Important Instructions on Employer Sanctions Provisions of 1996 Act," 74 *Interpreter Releases* 706, 707 (Apr. 28, 1997).

[86] *Id.*

[87] 63 Fed. Reg. 16911-12 (Apr. 7, 1998).

[88] *Id.*

[89] 72 Fed. Reg. 45611 (Aug. 15, 2007). See the introduction to this article, *supra*.

mends that the employer "promptly" ask the employee to confirm its records. If the employer's records are correct according to the employee, the employer must request that the employee resolve the discrepancy with SSA within 90 days of the date the employer received the "no-match" letter. If the discrepancy cannot be resolved within 90 days, the employer and employee must complete a new Form I-9 within an additional three days, using documents other than those subject to the original SSA notification. If the repeated I-9 process is not successful and the employee's identity and work authorization still cannot be verified, the employer must terminate the worker's employment or risk a finding that it had constructive knowledge that the employee was not authorized to work in the United States. As of this writing, the regulation has not yet taken effect because an injunction has been issued by a federal court.

Reduction in Number of Required Documents on Form I-9

Section 412(a) of IIRAIRA,[90] amending INA §274A(b)(1)(B), reduced by half the number of documents listed on the back of Form I-9 that employers are allowed to accept, while giving the attorney general discretion to amend the list by regulation.[91] Legacy INS also issued proposed rules on Form I-9 changes that were never finalized, with the purpose of making the regulation easier to understand and use.[92] The proposed rule explains that employers may complete the Form I-9 before the time of hire or at the time of hire, so long as they have made a commitment to hire and provided that the employer completes the Form I-9 at the same point in the employment process for all employees.[93] In addition, the proposed rule details reverification requirements and includes a proposal for a new employment eligibility reverification form (Form I-9A).[94]

---

[90] Pub. L. No. 104-208, div. C, §412(a), 110 Stat. 3009, 3009-666 to 3009-667.

[91] *Id.*; *see also* 63 Fed. Reg. 5287, 5289 (Feb. 2, 1998) (proposed rule).

[92] 63 Fed. Reg. 5287 (Feb. 2, 1998). Also note that an interim rule had been published at 62 Fed. Reg. 51001 (Sept. 30, 1997). The interim rule was a stopgap measure, required by the effective date provision for §412(a) of IIRAIRA. The amendments to the list of documents were to take effect "with respect to hiring (or recruitment or referral) occurring on or after such date (not later than 12 months after the enactment of IIRAIRA as the Attorney General shall designate)". Since 12 months after the date of enactment of IIRAIRA was September 30, 1997, the interim rule designated September 30, 1997, as the effective date for the amendments. The goal of the interim rule was to maintain the status quo to the extent possible under the IIRAIRA document provision. On October 6, 1997, President Bill Clinton signed legislation (Pub. L. No. 105-54) extending the deadline for the designation of the effective date from 12 months to 18 months. Legacy INS withheld enforcement of violations related to the changes while the interim rule was in place. 63 Fed. Reg. at 5289.

[93] 63 Fed. Reg. at 5289. USCIS's recently revised instructional handbook for employers on how to complete Form I-9 reflects this guidance: "Q. If someone accepts a job with my company but will not start work for a month, can I complete the Form I-9 when the employee accepts the job? A. Yes. The law requires that you complete the Form I-9 only when the person actually begins working. However, you may complete the form earlier, as long as the person has been offered and has accepted the job. You may not use the I-9 process to screen job applicants." USCIS, *Handbook for Employers: Instructions for Completing the Form I-9 (Employment Eligibility Verification Form)* (M-274, rev. Nov. 1, 2007), at p. 21.

[94] 63 Fed. Reg. at 5289.

On November 7, 2007, USCIS announced the release of a revised Form I-9.[95] The new form, which contains a revision date of June 5, 2007, in the lower right-hand corner, was issued to reflect the reduction in the number of documents employers may accept as verification of employment eligibility brought about by IIRAIRA. USCIS also published a notice in the *Federal Register* mandating use of the new Form I-9 starting on December 26, 2007.[96] Employers who fail to use the revised Form I-9 on or after December 26, 2007, may be subject to fines and penalties. Employers are not required to complete new Forms I-9 for existing employees unless the employees are subject to reverification. For example, on or before the date that a current employee's work authorization expires, that employee's work authorization must be confirmed, either on section 3 of the original I-9 that the employee completed at the time of hire, or on the new I-9 form.

Immigration practitioners and employers are encouraged to familiarize themselves with these changes to ensure compliance with employment eligibility verification obligations. Employer familiarity with the documents included in lists A, B, and C on the back of the Form I-9 fosters more careful detection of obviously fraudulent documents, but more importantly, protects them from rejecting genuine documents—rejection that could easily lead to penalties for "document abuse." With regard to specific changes to the categories of acceptable documents, §412(a) of IIRAIRA eliminated the Certificate of Naturalization, the Certificate of U.S. Citizenship, and the unexpired foreign passport with an endorsement that indicates eligibility for employment.[97] The remaining list A includes: (1) a U.S. passport; (2) a Permanent Resident Card (Form I-551); (3) An unexpired foreign passport with a temporary I-551 stamp; (4) an unexpired EAD that contains a photograph (Form I-766, I-688, I-688A, or I-688B); and (5) an unexpired foreign passport with an unexpired Form I-94 Arrival-Departure Record showing nonimmigrant status and authorization to work for the employer. IIRAIRA also restricted the attorney general's authority to add documents to list A.[98] Each document designated by the attorney general must meet three conditions.[99] The document must: (1) bear a photograph and personal identification information; (2) constitute evidence of employment authorization, and (3) contain security features to make it resistant to tampering, counterfeiting, and fraudulent use.[100]

IIRAIRA made no statutory changes to Form I-9 list B documents establishing identity.[101] Section 412(a) of IIRAIRA amended INA §274A(b)(1)(C) by removing

---

[95] *See* USCIS Update, "USCIS Revises Employment Eligibility Verification Form I-9" (Nov. 7, 2007), *available at www.uscis.gov/files/pressrelease/FormI9Update110707.pdf*.

[96] 72 Fed. Reg. 65972 (Nov. 26, 2007).

[97] INA §274A(b)(1)(B); 8 USC §1324a(b)(1)(B); 63 Fed. Reg. 5292 (Feb. 2, 1998); *see also* J. Osuna, "The 1996 Immigration Act: Employer Sanctions, Antidiscrimination and Work Verification," 73 *Interpreter Releases* 1749, 1751 (Dec. 20, 1996).

[98] 63 Fed. Reg. at 5292.

[99] *Id.*

[100] INA §§274A(B)(ii)(I)–(III); 8 USC §§1324a(b)(ii)(I)–(III); 63 Fed. Reg. at 5292.

[101] 63 Fed. Reg. at 5293.

the certificate of birth in the United States (or other certificate acceptable by the attorney general as establishing U.S. nationality at birth) from list C, the list of acceptable documents that may be used to establish employment authorization for compliance with the employment verification requirements.[102] Acceptable list C documents are a Social Security account number card (other than one that specifies on its face that the issuance of the card does not authorize employment in the United States) or other documentation found acceptable by the attorney general that evidences employment authorization.[103] Under the proposed rule, DHS proposes to limit acceptable list C documents to the following: (1) a Social Security account number card; (2) a Native American tribal document; and (3) in the case of a nonimmigrant alien authorized to work only for a specific employer, an Arrival-Departure Record, Form I-94, containing an endorsement of the alien's nonimmigrant status and the name of the approved employer with whom employment is authorized, so long as the period of endorsement has not yet expired and the proposed employment is not in conflict with any restrictions or limitations identified on the Form I-94.[104] However, the new Form I-9, with a revision date of June 5, 2007, does not include any changes to list C, so an employer may continue to accept those list C documents that were slated for elimination in the proposed rule.

New Burden of Proof: Intent to Discriminate

Section 421 of IIRAIRA,[105] amending INA §274B(a)(6) regarding charges of prohibited discrimination[106] based on national origin or citizenship status, made it more difficult for individuals to bring discrimination charges against employers. Claimants must now show that the employer had a discriminatory intent.[107] Specifically, the law states that a person's or other entity's request, for purposes of satisfying the requirements of INA §274A(b) [8 USC §1324a(b)], for more or different documents tendered, that on their face reasonably appear to be genuine, will be treated as an unfair immigration-related employment practice only if made for the purpose or with the intent of discriminating against an individual in violation of the statute.[108]

---

[102] *Id.* at 5295.

[103] *Id.*

[104] *Id.*

[105] IIRAIRA §421, 110 Stat. at 3009-670; INA §274B(a)(6), 8 USC §1324b(a)(6).

[106] *See* USCIS, *Handbook for Employers, supra* note 93, at pt. 4. Although all employers must comply with IRCA's employment verification procedures and the general prohibition against knowingly hiring unauthorized alien workers, IRCA's discrimination provisions only apply to employers with four or more employees. By contrast, Title VII of the 1964 Civil Rights Act, 42 USC §2000e *et seq.*, bars employers of 15 or more employees from engaging in discrimination on the basis of national origin, among other prohibited bases. To enhance the coverage of Title VII, IRCA sweeps within its jurisdiction those employers of between four and 14 employees who previously were not subject to national origin discrimination claims, and subjects all employers of four or more employees to "citizenship-status" discrimination claims for the first time.

[107] INA §274B(a)(6); 8 USC §1324b(a)(6).

[108] INA §274B(a)(6); 8 USC §1324b(a)(6).

According to the Department of Justice, the discriminatory intent standard encompasses more than just cases in which employers have made bigoted remarks or have openly engaged in facially disparate treatment.[109] Facially neutral policies, such as "English-only" rules, lengthy residence requirements, or a hierarchy of preferred documents for employee verification, which are intended to discriminate on prohibited bases and have that effect, are also prohibited, as is a facially neutral policy that is neutrally applied, but was adopted for the purpose of discriminating on a prohibited basis and has that effect.[110] Legacy INS indicated that the following situations may indicate such a pattern of discrimination: (1) application of the employment eligibility verification requirements more harshly or only to one ethnic group over another, or only to authorized aliens rather than U.S. citizens; (2) discharge of present employees or refusal to hire new employees based on their foreign appearance or accent; (3) adoption of "U.S. citizens only" policies, in circumstances under which such policies cannot be justified under the INA; and (4) imposition of a requirement that all aliens produce "green cards" in order to establish their employment eligibility.[111]

Employers most likely will have benefited from IIRAIRA's "intent to discriminate" provision. The provision attempts to alleviate the burden on employers who feel they are between a rock and a hard place when it comes to employer sanctions and antidiscrimination provisions.[112] Those employers attempting to comply with IRCA's employment eligibility verification requirements who have erred toward requesting more or different documents than required will only be liable if the employee can prove intentional discrimination.[113]

Practice Pointers

The following are practice pointers that the author recommends when developing an effective Form I-9 compliance program:

Centralization of Authority

It is important to limit the number of employees who are authorized to complete the employment eligibility verification process on behalf of the employer. There are a few employment positions in the United States in which mistakes can lead to substantial civil monetary penalties. Placing this responsibility in the hands of a low-level, untrained administrative person may result in a high number of mistakes. This responsibility instead should be placed in the hands of a human resources representative who has been trained in the proper compliance procedures.

---

[109] A. Gallagher, Immigration Law Service 2d, §12:80.
[110] *Id.*
[111] *Id.*
[112] J. Osuna, "The 1996 Immigration Act: Employer Sanctions, Antidiscrimination and Work Verification," 73 *Interpreter Releases* 1751, 1752 (Dec. 20, 1996).
[113] *Id.*

Centralization of Storage

Forms I-9 should be stored alphabetically, and separated between current and former employees. Some employers choose to store Forms I-9 for employees with temporary work authorization separately from other Forms I-9 to allow for easy retrieval and docketing. For large corporations, the Form I-9 storage procedure can be divided further by geographic location, year of hire (for current employees) and year of termination (for former employees). Some large corporations also centralize all of their Form I-9 storage in one location. This allows the company to place its best Form I-9 compliance managers in one location to review all Forms I-9 before filing them away. Because all companies are entitled to three business days before presenting Forms I-9 to ICE for inspection, forwarding Forms I-9 in a timely manner to the geographic location being audited should not be problematic.

Independent Contractors

As previously mentioned, a Form I-9 should be completed for every employee of a company, except for independent contractors. However, an employer's attempt to bypass the employment eligibility verification process by mislabeling employees as independent contractors, when in fact such employees should be classified differently, is clearly prohibited.

In addition, employers should not classify foreign national employees as independent contractors while those individuals are in the process of applying for the necessary employment authorized status, such as the H-1B or L nonimmigrant visa status. For example, in a situation in which a management consulting firm needs to immediately place a foreign national employee at a U.S. worksite, it is not allowed to bring such an employee into the United States in B-1/B-2 (or Visa Waiver Pilot Program) visitor status. The B-1/B-2 visitor is not authorized to provide services that benefit a U.S. source.[114] In such instances, not only does the employer run the risk of being fined for a knowing hire violation, but the employee may be charged with committing entry fraud by misrepresenting the purpose of his or her entry.

Reverification

Temporary I-551 Stamps

When a person enters the United States with an immigrant visa or adjusts status to lawful permanent residence in the United States, an Alien Documentation and Identification Telecommunications System (ADIT) stamp is provided as temporary evidence of permanent residence status.[115] The ADIT stamp is typically valid for one year.[116] Permanent Resident Cards ("green cards") are mailed to most individuals before the ADIT stamp expires.[117] Delays in issuance of the green card can present sub-

---

[114] 9 *Foreign Affairs Manual* 41.31 N4.

[115] Department of Justice Memorandum, "Processing Inquiries Regarding Unreceived Permanent Resident Cards When Initial ADIT Stamp is About to Expire" (Oct. 22, 1998).

[116] *Id.*

[117] *Id.*

stantial problems for employers who are required to reverify the employment eligibility of any employee who has previously presented an ADIT stamp that is expiring, and who has not yet received his or her green card. In such instances, the employee will need to obtain a new ADIT stamp, which can be a lengthy process.

In such a scenario, a possible solution is for the employee to present another document from list C of the Form I-9. Specifically, every lawful permanent resident is entitled to an unrestricted Social Security card. Therefore, in such circumstances the employee may present this document as evidence of his or her continued authorization to work in the United States, even though his or her ADIT stamp has expired. If the Social Security card is restricted with the legend, "Not valid for work without DHS authorization," the employee must go to the nearest Social Security office with proof of permanent resident status in order to have the legend removed.

Interim Employment Authorization: 240/90-Day Rules and H-1B Portability

If an employer files a petition to extend certain nonimmigrant visa status (*e.g.*, H-1B or L-1) on behalf of one of its employees, at least one day prior to expiration, the employee is granted 240 days of interim employment authorization while the petition is pending.[118] In addition, if an alien files an application for an initial grant or extension of an EAD (Form I-766 or I-688B), USCIS must adjudicate the application within 90 days of receipt.[119] However, possession of a USCIS Form I-797 Notice of Action reflecting receipt of the filing of an application for an EAD is not evidence of employment authorization. In light of this fact, and because delays occur in the adjudication of EAD applications, it is strongly recommended that employers remind their employees who have presented EADs of their responsibility to present evidence of continued employment authorization prior to expiration. The author recommends providing such a reminder up to 120 days in advance of expiration.

H-1B nonimmigrants are also afforded interim employment authorization when changing employers. An individual in H-1B status may commence work for a new employer once the new employer has filed an H-1B petition on behalf of the individual.[120] In this situation, an employer will typically attach a copy of the receipt notice for the new H-1B petition along with the employee's I-94 to the Form I-9. Although there is no time limit on interim work authorization after a change of H-1B employers, the employer must reverify work authorization when a decision is issued on the new H-1B petition.

Discriminatory Intent—Pre-Employment Inquiries Regarding Sponsorship for an Employment Visa

Many employers have struggled with the appropriate language to use regarding employment eligibility when interviewing a prospective employee. In a memo addressed to Arnold Eagle, President of American Council on International Personnel,

---

[118] 8 CFR § 274a.12(b)(20).

[119] 8 CFR § 274a.13(d).

[120] INA §214(n)(1); 8 USC §1184(n)(1).

Inc., dated August 6, 1998, OSC Special Counsel John D. Trasviña provided a helpful suggestion.[121] He advised that the employers' use of the following questions, either orally or on the employment application, would not expose them to discrimination liability under INA §274B:

1. Are you legally authorized to work in the United States?
   __ YES __ NO
2. Will you now or in the future require sponsorship for employment visa status (*e.g.*, H-1B visa status)?
   __ YES __ NO

Trasviña also recommended that employers not ask applicants to specify their citizenship status in the context of the employment application process. The OSC takes this position because a rejected applicant may rely upon such an inquiry later to allege that the employer considered the information in making the hiring decision, and discriminated against him or her based on citizenship status.[122] In this regard, the OSC does *not* recommend use of the questions below, which may cause the employer to inquire into specific citizenship categories, a prohibited action:

1. Are you one of the following?
   - U. S. citizen
   - Lawful permanent resident
   - Temporary resident
   - Asylee
   - Refugee
   __ YES __ NO
2. If no, are you currently authorized to work in the United States?
   __ YES __ NO

Employment Verification Issues Arising From Getahun v. DuPont Merck Pharmaceutical Co.

A federal court decision indicates that an employer may be subject to civil liability for document abuse under INA §274B for not accepting proof of political asylee status alone as evidence of an alien's employment authorization. In *Getahun v. OCAHO and DuPont Merck Pharmaceutical Co.*,[123] the U.S. Court of Appeals for the Third Circuit held that an employee who has been granted political asylum and who can prove that he or she has applied for employment authorization is entitled to work in the United States.

The court reached this decision by interpreting two regulations in conjunction. The court focused on the "automatic" language of a prior version of 8 CFR §208.20, which stated that "employment authorization is *automatically* granted or continued for persons granted political asylum." The court read this statute in conjunction with

---

[121] *See* OSC Memorandum, J. Trasviña, "Pre-Employment Inquiries Regarding Sponsorship for an Employment Visa" (Aug. 6, 1998).
[122] *Id.*
[123] 124 F.3d 591 (3d Cir. 1997).

the prior version of 8 CFR §274a.12, which at the time provided that an alien granted asylum "who seeks to be employed in the United States must apply to the INS for a document evidencing such employment authorization." The court appears to have treated the requirements of 8 CFR § 274a.12 as a routine post-employment authorization procedure, rather than as a prerequisite to employment authorization.

The court specifically chose not to address the issue of whether proof of political asylee status alone is sufficient documentation for an alien to prove eligibility to work in the United States. However, the court stated that the petitioner had argued this exact position "with considerable persuasiveness."[124] Therefore, employers should be cautioned that, in the future, proof of political asylee status alone may be sufficient to prove work authorization, and that employers who discriminate against aliens who provide only this proof may be liable for document abuse.

It should be noted that the scope of this decision is limited to the applicable regulations as they existed in 1991. Specifically, the language of 8 CFR §208.20 as it existed at the time of the filing of the underlying complaint in *Getahun* (October 1993) has since been revoked. Therefore, it appears that the current provisions under 8 CFR §274a.12(a)(5), requiring that asylees must apply for an EAD issued by USCIS, may control. However, the ability for asylees to obtain unrestricted Social Security cards may provide a quick solution for any asylee who lacks documentary evidence of employment authorization.

Internal Audits

It is highly recommended that employers conduct periodic internal audits of their Form I-9 compliance efforts. Ideally, such audits should take place no less frequently than once per year. If the employer is a large entity, reviewing a sample of Forms I-9 (*e.g.*, 100 to 500) should suffice. However, if there are large numbers of mistakes, a more extensive review should be initiated.[125]

In addition, it is critical that the employer devise some follow-up strategy to ensure future compliance. Specifically, once a pattern of repeated mistakes has been determined, a timetable should be set up for future review of such issues. If the employer was consistently requesting too many documents from its employees (*e.g.*, one from list A and one from list C), practitioners should follow-up three months later and spot-check for compliance with this issue. Failure to do so will likely lead to a substantial amount of additional work during the next annual audit.

Electronic Verification

The federal E-Verify program, one of three pilot programs authorized by IIRAIRA, provides an automated link to government databases to help employers determine the eligibility of hew hires. The other two pilot programs have been terminated. E-Verify was originally known as the Basic Pilot program. It was re-named E-

---

[124] *Id.* at 595.

[125] For a comprehensive discussion on conducting internal audits, *see* A. Lamdin, "Employment Authorization and I-9 Compliance," 96-09 *Immigration Briefings* (Sept. 1996).

Verify in 2007 but continues to be commonly referred to as Basic Pilot. In July 2005, Basic Pilot was converted to an entirely internet-based verification program.

Under the terms of E-Verify, the authenticity of information provided by an employee is verified after the employee has been hired and the Form I-9 completed. Specifically, E-Verify involves computerized verification checks of the new employees' Social Security numbers and alien identification numbers through SSA and DHS databases. If the information matches, the employer records the match. If it does not, the employee is referred to SSA or DHS to resolve his or her record. Participation in E-Verify does not provide "safe harbor" from worksite enforcement, but does create a rebuttable presumption that the employer has not knowingly hired an unauthorized alien.

Employers may also participate in the ICE Mutual Agreement Between Government and Employers (IMAGE) program, which is designed to facilitate compliance with employment verification laws and regulations.[126] Employers participating in the IMAGE program are required to use E-Verify, submit to an I-9 audit conducted by ICE, and follow certain best practices. ICE provides IMAGE participants with training and education on proper hiring procedures, fraudulent document detection, and antidiscrimination laws.[127]

Some practitioners have taken issue with these programs because of the additional burdens they present. In addition, over the years many practitioners have encountered inaccuracies in information provided by SSA and DHS from their databases. According to a 2005 report of the Government Accountability Office, about 15 percent of all DHS database queries required secondary verification or follow-up by an agency official after the initial query failed to confirm employment authorization.[128] On the other hand, some employers view the electronic verification programs as a way of showing good-faith hiring practices to the government.

Conclusion

Although on its face the Form I-9 appears relatively simple, its correct completion has proven to be an arduous task for many employers. This problem has only been compounded by the additional factor of civil monetary and even criminal liability for noncompliance and the recent introduction of new, voluntary electronic Form I-9 verification programs offered by the government. In light of this fact, Form I-9 compliance has become an important practice area for many immigration practitioners.

Unfortunately, it is difficult for practitioners to provide effective representation in this area unless they have spent sufficient time reviewing the forms and working with employers to develop effective Form I-9 compliance systems. Although the electronic Form I-9 verification programs are currently voluntary, there is no better time than

---

[126] *See* www.ice.gov/partners/opaimage/.

[127] *Id.*

[128] U.S. Government Accountability Office, Immigration Enforcement: Weaknesses Hinder Employment Verification and Worksite Enforcement Efforts (GAO 05-813, Aug. 2005), *available at* www.gao.gov/new.items/d05813.pdf.

the present for practitioners to familiarize themselves with these issues so that they can effectively assist their clients.

IMMIGRATION COMPLIANCE PROGRAM TOOLS: AN ANALYSIS OF I-9 DEFENSE MECHANISMS

by Anthony E. Weigel[*]

Introduction

Across the United States, employers are being subjected to increased government enforcement efforts, state and local government legislative incursions, and public pressure from politicians and vigilante groups. In light of the offensive, it continues to become more difficult to develop a corporate immigration compliance program. Many employers, both rationally and irrationally, are scurrying about, seeking the right mix of tools to ensure compliance.

The purpose of this article is to analyze various compliance tools, evaluate the benefits and disadvantages of each, and provide employers and their representatives with useful guidance.

Corporate Compliance Program Basics

Elements of a Compliance Program

Prior to focusing on use of E-Verify/Basic Pilot, electronic I-9s, or other tools, every employer should establish a corporate compliance program. Regardless of the size or type of business, an employer's program should provide solutions for the following questions:

1. What are the employer's relevant legal requirements under federal, state, and local laws?
2. How will the employer's requirements be satisfied?
   a. What tasks need to be performed?
   b. When do they need to performed?
   c. Who will have responsibility for these tasks and how will they be trained?
3. How will the employer periodically review that these requirements are being satisfied?
4. How will I-9 related records be maintained and, when possible, destroyed?
5. How will the employer respond to inquiries about employment eligibility verification matters from the government and other third parties?

---

[*] **Anthony E. Weigel** practices immigration law at Husch Blackwell Sanders, LLP in Kansas City, MO, and is a member of the American Immigration Lawyers Association. His practice focuses on employer compliance and employment-based immigration. Prior to practicing law, Mr. Weigel worked in human resources and was responsible for coordinating immigration matters and a broad spectrum of employment law compliance issues, including I-9 verifications and record retention.

Basic I-9 Compliance Requirements

At a minimum, an employer should establish the following procedures:

1. Require every new employee to complete the top portion (Section 1) of the I-9 form on the first day—*no exceptions*! If the person refuses to do so, he or she should not be permitted to resume working until this is completed. Please note, the employee should not complete any other part of the form.

2. In most cases, the new employee must provide documents that show his or her employment eligibility by the end of the third day of work.[1] If the person fails to do so, he or she should not return to work until such documents are provided.

3. The employee should be permitted to provide any acceptable document or acceptable combinations of documents listed on the form for compliance with I-9 rules. Requesting specific documents can be considered discriminatory "document abuse." Likewise, an employer must treat all employees in a consistent manner and not discriminate on the basis of citizenship status or national origin in employment eligibility matters.

4. If the employer decides to make copies of the documents presented, the employer should make two-sided copies *and* should make copies of documents for all new hires going forward. If the process is done in a remote location, one can use a portable, PC-powered scanner to capture images of documents to be printed later. There are advantages and disadvantages—the employer must make a decision here.[2]

5. If an employee is not a U.S. citizen or permanent resident, the employer must note when that person's employment eligibility expires and calendar to re-verify employment eligibility about 90 days prior to that date. This can be done in Microsoft Outlook or by some other simple method.

6. All I-9 forms should be kept separate from all other personnel or payroll records. One can simply three-hole punch these completed forms and place them in a binder.

7. Designate specific individuals to handle these functions with trained backups. There are serious consequences for failing to comply with the law, so it is well worth the trouble. Even if an employer only employs authorized workers, it can still be liable for significant fines for failure to maintain adequate paperwork.

---

[1] 8 CFR §274a.2(b)(1) specifies that an employee must present documents *within the time limits* set forth in paragraphs (b)(1)(ii) through (b)(1)(v) of that section. According to 8 CFR §274a.2(b)(1)(ii), the employer is required to examine documents within three days, but the regulation does not state that the employee has this amount of time to comply with an employer's request. If, as a matter of discretionary policy, an employer requires documents to be provided in less than three days, all employees should be treated in a consistent manner under this policy.

[2] See discussion of the decision whether to copy, *infra*.

Immigration Compliance Program Tools

8. An employer should train its hiring managers on I-9 requirements and periodically review these requirements with its hiring managers. These initial and subsequent efforts should be documented.

9. Develop a plan for responding to government inquiries, including in-person visits by government agents, and designate a company official with authority to respond.
   a. Any written inquiries should be reviewed as soon as possible, because a government agency may demand surrender of the I-9s *within three days*.
   b. In the event of an unannounced, in-person visit by a government agent, ask the agent to wait until the designated company official is available. If the agent has no search warrant or subpoena, the employer should contact an attorney immediately. Immigration agents might make unannounced visits without a search warrant and attempt to obtain consent to enter the premises or to secure I-9 forms without the requisite regulatory notice of three days.

10. An employer should not ignore letters from the Social Security Administration (SSA) that state that a particular employee's Social Security number (SSN) does not match its records. These are often referred to as "no-match" letters. The receipt of such a letter might raise suspicions that an employee is not authorized to work. An employer should follow up on these matters after consulting with counsel.

To Copy or Not to Copy?

One of the critical choices an employer has to make is whether it will make copies of identity and employment eligibility documents. The relevant statute and regulation state:

> **Copying of documentation permitted.**—Notwithstanding any other provision of law, the person or entity may copy a document presented by an individual pursuant to this subsection [INA §274A(b)] and may retain the copy, but only (except as otherwise permitted under law) for the purpose of complying with the requirements of this subsection.[3]

> *Copying of documentation.* An employer, or a recruiter or referrer for a fee may, but is not required to, copy or make an electronic image of a document presented by an individual solely for the purpose of complying with the verification requirements of this section [8 CFR §274a.2]. *If such a copy or electronic image is made, it must be retained with the Form I-9.* The copying or electronic imaging of any such document and retention of the copy or electronic image does not relieve the employer from the requirement to fully complete section 2 of the Form I-9. An employer, recruiter or referrer for a fee should not, however, copy or electronically image only the documents of individuals of certain national origins or citizenship statuses. To do so may violate section 274B of the Act.[4]

---

[3] INA §274A(b)(4).
[4] 8 CFR §274a.2(b)(3) (emphasis added).

If an employer's representatives accurately complete the I-9, there is generally no need for copies. However, retaining copies of identity and employment eligibility documents may clearly assist in conducting self-audits or preparing for an audit by U.S. Immigration and Customs Enforcement (ICE). As a practical matter, making and retaining copies of identity and employment eligibility documents might help to administer and monitor a corporate compliance program.

Without proper I-9 training, a company may make copies of unacceptable documents, such as restricted Social Security cards that are unacceptable list C documents, or immigration approval notices or receipt notices that do not reflect a grant of work authorization. Such copies may support fines for the improper completion of I-9s.

There are a couple of instances in which copies of documents are required to be retained. Users of the E-Verify/Basic Pilot system must now compare certain U.S. Department of Homeland Security (DHS) photos against the photo on immigration documents presented by the new hire. If an employee presents an I-551 "green card" or employment authorization document, a copy must be maintained pursuant to the E-Verify memorandum of understanding signed by DHS, SSA, and the employer.[5] In addition, a recently enacted Colorado statute[6] requires an employer to complete a state affirmation form for each new employee and to retain file copies of identity and/or employment eligibility documents presented for purposes of the federal government's Form I-9. Other state and local laws may have requirements similar to Colorado's.

The decision whether to retain copies can be made on a case-by-case basis. In the absence of rock-solid I-9 procedures, an employer should probably make and retain copies of documents.[7]

Electronic I-9s: A Tool Worth Consideration

In the past year or so, a growing number of vendors have introduced electronic I-9 products that are utilized to create and retain I-9 records. These products can assist many employers and are worthy of consideration.

---

[5] Model E-Verify Memorandum of Understanding, art. II.C.5, *available at www.uscis.gov/files/nativedocuments/MOU.pdf*.

[6] Colo. Rev. Stat. §8-2-122.

[7] In response to the public outcry that the Illegal Immigration Reform and Immigrant Responsibility Act of 1996 (IIRAIRA), Pub. L. No. 104-208, div. C, 110 Stat. 3009, 3009-546 to 3009-724, elevated form over substance and penalized employers who were attempting in good faith to comply with their verification responsibilities, the late Congressman Sonny Bono successfully included a provision in IIRAIRA that mandates that DHS provide a notice of deficiency with a 10-day opportunity to cure the deficiencies for procedural and technical I-9 violations that occurred after September 30, 1996. This provision is codified at INA 274A(b)(6) [8 USC §1324a(b)(6)]. Although a proposed rule interpreting the good-faith defense, 63 Fed. Reg. 16909-13 (Apr. 7, 1998), has never been finalized, in the interim, implementation of the good-faith compliance provision has been governed by interim guidelines issued by legacy Immigration and Naturalization Service. *See* INS Memorandum, P. Virtue, "Interim Guidelines: Section 274A(b)(6) of the Immigration & Nationality Act Added by Section 411 of the Illegal Immigration Reform & Immigrant Responsibility Act of 1996" (Mar. 6, 1997), *published on* AILA InfoNet at Doc. No. 97030691 (*posted* Mar. 6, 1997), and reprinted in this book.

Legal History

On October 30, 2004, legislation was enacted that permitted employers to retain Forms I-9 in an electronic format beginning on April 29, 2005, or upon the effective date of implementing regulations.[8] On June 15, 2006, DHS issued an interim rule on the electronic signature and storage of I-9 forms.[9] Comments were received by DHS through August 14, 2006. If an employer created electronic I-9 forms after April 29, 2005, those electronic records do not need to comply with the interim rule.[10] However, records created after June 15, 2006, must comply with the new requirements.[11] Please note, as they were established by an *interim* rule, requirements for electronic I-9 storage may change upon issuance of a final rule.

Requirements

In adopting its interim rule, DHS utilized existing Internal Revenue Service (IRS) standards for electronic recordkeeping.[12] An electronic I-9 storage system under the interim rule must include:

- Reasonable controls to ensure the integrity, accuracy, and reliability of the electronic storage generation or storage system;
- Reasonable controls to prevent and detect unauthorized use or the accidental deletion or alteration of completed and electronically stored I-9 forms;
- Training programs to minimize unauthorized or accidental alteration or erasure of records;
- Creation of a secure and permanent record establishing date of access, identity of person accessing a particular record, and action taken;
- Backup and recovery of records to protect against information loss, such as power interruptions;
- Inspection and quality assurance program evidenced by regular evaluations of the electronic generation or storage system, including periodic checks of the electronically stored Form I-9, including the electronic signatures;
- Retrieval system that includes an indexing system that permits searches by any data element; and
- The ability to reproduce legible and easily readable print copies.

Additionally, electronic signatures must be attached to or logically associated with an electronic I-9, and the system must:

- Affix the electronic signature at the time of the transaction;

---

[8] Pub. L. No. 108-390, 11 Stat. 2242 (2004), amending INA §274A(b) [8 USC §1324a(b)].

[9] 71 Fed. Reg. 34510 (Jun. 15, 2006).

[10] *Id.* at 34512.

[11] *Id.*

[12] *Id.* at 34510–11.

- Create and preserve a record verifying the identity of the person producing the signature; and
- Provide a printed confirmation of the transaction to the person providing the signature.

Basically, an employer must utilize a highly secure database that demonstrates to the government that it really completed its I-9 forms.[13]

Potential Benefits

Organizations with multiple worksites spread out across large geographic regions could benefit significantly by maintaining I-9 records electronically. Ideally, an employer should maintain all of its I-9 records separately from personnel records in a location or locations where they can be quickly produced for inspection. Although the government generally requires records to be available within three days, an employer will want them consolidated and organized in a central location for review in advance of a government inspection. Perhaps the single greatest benefit of electronic storage to certain employers is minimizing the effort required to accomplish these two critical tasks with its I-9 forms.

Another significant benefit of an electronic system would be minimizing or eliminating the risk of accumulating incomplete I-9 forms. An electronic system with appropriate features could prompt the employee and employer's representative to complete all of the required items. One of the more common problems with I-9 forms is that some may not be completely filled out on the front-end. If the employer catches these omissions in the course of a self-audit, it can attempt to tie up these loose ends. If the government identifies these incomplete forms, it can lead to administrative fines or, even worse, the basis for allegations of "knowing" violations of the law.[14]

Use of an electronic I-9 system could also make providing data to other parties more efficient, which can be either a detriment or a benefit. In the event of a government inquiry, an employer could theoretically burn a disc and turn it over for review to the agency, which would then be able to review and use the data quite efficiently. Similarly, if an employer's counsel used a compatible system, an employer could send the data to its counsel for a more efficient review of I-9 records.

Considerations in Going Electronic

A significant consideration in adopting an electronic I-9 storage system is that the guidance comes only in the form of an interim, not final rule. DHS may issue a final rule and change the requirements with little notice. On the other hand, DHS agencies often issue interim rules that are not finalized for many years.

Many anticipated that 2007 would be a year in which visions of comprehensive immigration reform would materialize. It is still possible that the current I-9 related

---

[13] *Id.* at 34515–16 (system requirements); *id.* at 34516 (signature requirements).
[14] *See* 8 CFR §274a.1(*l*)(1).

statutes may undergo major transformations. If that happens, the requirements set forth in the interim rule may be affected.

Regardless of any potential changes to the interim rule, an employer must consider cost/benefit issues. Like many new technology-related products, the costs of acquisition and implementation go down over time. Many companies have and are in the process of implementing systems to comply with the interim regulation. A by-product of these efforts is that more reasonably priced products that are easier to implement are being developed.

Once an employer decides to adopt an electronic I-9 system, it should consider important elements like training, support, and future information technology transitional needs. These records will likely need to be maintained for long periods of time, in some cases for longer periods of time than IRS or other company records. For example, IRS laws may require that certain financial records only be maintained for a certain number of years. However, under current law, an I-9 is required to be maintained for at least three years after the date of hire or one year after the date of termination, whichever is later.[15] This means that if an employee is hired today and works for an employer for 30 years, that employee's I-9 record must be available until 31 years from now!

There are also seemingly trivial legal questions that go beyond the technical and practical aspects of electronic I-9 storage. For example, when will an electronic record truly be deleted and unavailable for review? Other legal questions are sure to arise after DHS examines the records of a few employers who have electronic systems.

Finally, an employer should fully understand that use of an electronic system is merely a tool to create and retain records—it is no substitute for substantive compliance with the law.

E-Verify/Basic Pilot

Overview

The E-Verify system was originated in 1996 under the name Basic Pilot.[16] It is a no-cost, Internet-based system that provides a means for employers to perform a secondary verification of a newly-hired employee's work authorization. The system has also added DHS photos to add an extra measure of certainty or uncertainty to the process, depending upon the ability of DHS to accurately match photographs with the right record.

To participate, an employer must register online, agree to the terms of an E-Verify memorandum of understanding with DHS and SSA,[17] and designate a program ad-

---

[15] INA §§274A(b)(3)(B)(i), (ii); 8 USC §§1324a(b)(3)(B)(i), (ii).
[16] References to E-Verify and Basic Pilot are to the same system.
[17] E-Verify Memorandum of Understanding, *supra* note 5. There is no opportunity to negotiate terms of acceptance; an employer must adhere to its contractual terms, but DHS may modify the terms of use, in essence, at its discretion.

ministrator.[18] The administrator and any other users must review a user training manual and receive approximately 45 minutes of training and testing. An employer must also post DHS-provided notices alerting potential new hires that it uses the system.

After completing a new hire's I-9 form, a participating employer must submit an electronic query via the Internet. The query tool uses automated systems to verify Social Security account numbers and work authorization. Employers must verify all newly hired employees at the registered hiring location without exception, and make verification inquiries within three days of the hiring. A copy of the system confirmation and other documentation associated with the inquiry must be kept with the completed I-9 form.

If an electronic query does not result in a confirmation, the system generates a "Tentative Nonconfirmation" response for failure to clear either the SSA or DHS portions of the query. At this point, the following requirements apply to employers and affected employees:

- Employer must print and provide the system-generated referral notice of the Tentative Nonconfirmation to the employee (unless employee opts not to contest).

- Employer must provide the employee an opportunity to contest the response.

- Employer must input a referral in the system and direct the employee to contact the appropriate agency to resolve information discrepancies.

- Employer then resubmits the query to receive a final confirmation or the system will generate a notice of final confirmation.

- If the employer receives a final nonconfirmation, it may terminate the employment relationship and arguably should not be civilly or criminally liable for the termination, as long as the action was taken in good faith reliance on information provided through the confirmation system. *If the employer does not terminate an employee after final nonconfirmation, the employer must notify the government.* Failure to notify the government of continued employment after receiving final nonconfirmation will be deemed a violation of the law and may result in a civil monetary penalty of between $550 and $1,100 for each individual with respect to whom such violation occurred.[19] This fine may be in addition to a fine or criminal penalties for knowingly hiring an unauthorized worker.

---

[18] E-Verify also permits designation of a "Corporate Administrator" to perform oversight and supervisory duties, or "Designated Agents," who are permitted to perform E-Verify queries on behalf of an employer. *See* USCIS's website, *www.uscis.gov*, and the *E-Verify User Manual* for more detailed information. The *Manual* is available through a user's E-Verify web access and at *www.uscis.gov/files/nativedocuments/E-Verify_Manual.pdf*.

[19] 28 CFR §68.52(c)(6). For violations occurring before March 27, 2008, the penalty range is $500–$1,000. *Id.*

State-Law Specific E-Verify Provisions

There are a growing number of state-level requirements for employers mandating the use of E-Verify, including:

Government Contractors

Colorado	Effective June 2006
Georgia	Phased-in effective dates:
500+ employees	July 1, 2007
100+ employees	July 1, 2008
All others	July 1, 2009
Oklahoma	Effective July 1, 2008

All Employers

Arizona	Effective January 1, 2008

Ironically, Illinois passed a law that prohibits employers from using E-Verify until the system reaches an almost impossible performance standard. The federal government has sued to strike this law on the basis that it conflicts with federal law. As of the date of this writing, the outcome of this lawsuit is uncertain.

Two state laws offer various protections if the employer uses E-Verify:

Oklahoma	Effective July 1, 2008
Tennessee	Effective January 1, 2008

E-Verify requirements are significant components of state legislative proposals across the country, so this list may likely grow in 2008.

One question yet to be tested in the courts is what protection, if any, is offered by federal law and the terms of the E-Verify program against alleged violations of state or local laws. Under federal law, proper use of the system creates a rebuttable presumption that the employer has *not* violated the Immigration Reform and Control Act of 1986 (IRCA).[20] If federal law presumes an employer has not violated the law, an employer that has adopted use of E-Verify/Basic Pilot could arguably claim protection from any type of state enforcement action. Also, according to the employer's agreement with the federal government, proper use of the system might serve as a protection from state and local laws. The model E-Verify Memorandum of Understanding expressly states that *no person or entity participating in E-Verify shall be civilly or criminally liable **under any law** for any action taken in good faith on information provided through the confirmation system.*[21]

Push for Enrollment

Many in the government have a strong desire for all employers to use E-Verify. Almost every major immigration reform proposal in Congress has incorporated mandates to use the E-Verify/Basic Pilot system, including a proposal to require use of

---

[20] Pub. L. No. 99-603, 100 Stat. 3359.

[21] E-Verify Memorandum of Understanding, *supra* note 5, at art. II.C.6(5).

the system to reverify the entire U.S. workforce.[22] Absent congressional action, the Bush Administration is pursuing expanded use by regulation and persuasion.[23] In addition, more state and local governments will continue to pursue parochial efforts to mandate use of the system by employers.

---

[22] *See* H.R. 4088, 110th Cong. §201(b) (2007):

SEC. 201. MANDATORY EMPLOYMENT AUTHORIZATION VERIFICATION.

(b) Mandatory Use of E-Verify System—

(1) IN GENERAL— Subject to paragraphs (2) and (3), every person or other entity that hires one or more individuals for employment in the United States shall verify through the E-Verify program, established as the basic pilot program by section 403(a) of the Illegal Immigration Reform and Immigrant Responsibility Act of 1996 (division C of Public Law 104-208; 8 U.S.C. 1324a note), that each such individual is authorized to work in the United States. The Secretary of Homeland Security shall ensure that verification by means of a toll-free telephone line is an available option in complying with the preceding sentence.

(2) SELECT ENTITIES REQUIRED TO USE E-VERIFY PROGRAM IMMEDIATELY— The following entities must satisfy the requirement in paragraph (1) by not later than one year after the date of the enactment of this Act:

(A) FEDERAL AGENCIES— Each department and agency of the Federal Government.

(B) FEDERAL CONTRACTORS— A contractor that—

(i) has entered into a contract with the Federal Government to which section 2(b)(1) of the Service Contract Act of 1965 (41 U.S.C. 351(b)(1)) applies, and any subcontractor under such contract; or

(ii) has entered into a contract exempted from the application of such Act by section 6 of such Act (41 U.S.C. 356), and any subcontractor under such contract; and

(C) LARGE EMPLOYERS- An employer that employs more than 250 individuals in the United States.

(3) PHASING-IN FOR OTHER EMPLOYERS—

(A) 2 YEARS FOR EMPLOYERS OF 100 OR MORE— Entities that employ 100 or more individuals in the United States must satisfy the requirement in paragraph (1) by not later than two years after the date of the enactment of this Act.

(B) 3 YEARS FOR EMPLOYERS WITH 30 OR MORE EMPLOYEES— All entities that employ 30 or more individuals in the United States must satisfy the requirement in paragraph (1) by not later than three years after the date of the enactment of this Act.

(C) 4 YEARS FOR ALL EMPLOYERS— All entities that employ one or more individuals in the United States must satisfy the requirement in paragraph (1) by not later than four years after the date of the enactment of this Act.

(4) VERIFYING EMPLOYMENT AUTHORIZATION OF CURRENT EMPLOYEES— Every person or other entity that employs one or more persons in the United States shall verify through the E-Verify program by not later than four years after the date of the enactment of this Act that each employee is authorized to work in the United States.

[23] DHS Fact Sheet, "Improving Border Security and Immigration Within Existing Law" (Aug. 10, 2007), *available at* www.dhs.gov/xnews/releases/pr_1186757867585.shtm; Office of Management and Budget Memorandum, S. McMillin, "Verifying the Employment Eligibility of Federal Employees" (Aug. 10, 2007) (restating existing federal requirements for agencies to have already registered for E-Verify/Basic Pilot and request for voluntary participation by government contractors), *available at* www.whitehouse.gov/omb/memoranda/fy2007/m07-21.pdf.

Several companies in the private sector also are facilitating the increased used of E-Verify. Companies in the background check/pre-employment screening and third-party I-9 service industries are, to a certain extent, encouraging employers to use the system in connection with services provided. In some instances, these companies benefit from an employer's election to participate in E-Verify because it limits exposure of the service provider.

An Employer's Considerations

Whether it is the government or a private company that prompts an employer to consider E-Verify, there are significant factors that every employer should first consider. The most critical consideration is the state of the employer's current I-9 practices. If an employer is having difficulty getting its paper-based I-9s done consistently within the one-day and three-day requirements, it will have difficulties with the requirements of E-Verify.

In general, there are advantages and disadvantages with use of E-Verify. Advantages include a potential reduction in the risk of employing unauthorized workers and additional legal defenses if the system is used properly. Disadvantages include taking on additional administrative work and providing additional information to the government not otherwise required. Further, there is also the risk of failing to hire an applicant based on potentially incorrect information in the DHS database. Lastly, E-Verify often does not detect use of a false identity by a worker, although the implementation of a photo tool to match the worker's identity with the photos in the DHS database will help to deter instances of identity theft.

In some industries, use of E-Verify has become the standard of care, such as in the meat processing sector. Even though the law does not require use of the system, the government may view negatively the employer that fails to use it. An employer should be aware of the use of E-Verify within its industry and factor that information into any decision regarding use of the system.

Emerging Issues

New E-Verify users in search of a basis for nocturnal slumber should seek alternate sleep aids. Unfortunately, when an employer adopts this system, it also adopts the "ghosts" of E-Verify's past, present, and future. There are several open questions about E-Verify at present, and more that may emerge over 2008. Many of these raise very significant concerns.

—Employer's Agreement to Waive Rights

There has been extensive discussion and analysis of whether the use of E-Verify grants unfettered permission to the government to inspect the I-9 records it collects. Specifically, the current model memorandum of understanding includes the following terms:

> The Department of Homeland Security agrees to safeguard the information provided to the Department of Homeland Security by the Employer, and to limit access to such information to individuals responsible for the verification of alien employment eligibility and for evaluation of E-Verify, or to such other

persons or entities as may be authorized by applicable law. *Information will be used only to verify the accuracy of Social Security Numbers and employment eligibility, to enforce the INA and federal criminal laws, and to ensure accurate wage reports to the SSA.*[24]

The Department of Homeland Security reserves the right to conduct Form I-9 compliance inspections during the course of E-Verify, as well as to conduct any other enforcement activity authorized by law.[25]

The Employer agrees to allow the Department of Homeland Security and SSA, or their authorized agents or designees, to make periodic visits to the Employer for the purpose of reviewing E-Verify-related records, *i.e.*, Forms I-9, SSA Transaction Records, and Department of Homeland Security verification records, which were created during the Employer's participation in the E-Verify Program. In addition, *for the purpose of evaluating the E-Verify, the Employer agrees* to allow the Department of Homeland Security and SSA or their authorized agents or designees, to interview it regarding its experience with E-Verify, to interview employees hired during the E-Verify concerning their experience with the pilot, and *to make employment and E-Verify related records available to the Department of Homeland Security and the SSA, or their designated agents or designees.*[26]

It is unclear whether these provisions could be used to circumvent any requirements for subpoenas, search warrants, or even a three-day notice requirement to review records. DHS or ICE could certainly argue that these sections of the memorandum grant it the authority to conduct suspicionless, electronic searches of an employer's E-Verify/Basic Pilot records, which could generate information that then meets legal standards for obtaining warrants and subpoenas. Another unanswered question is whether this review would only be limited to the I-9s of those hired through E-Verify/Basic Pilot, or expand to all of the company's I-9s.

—Phantom Minders and the Machine

In September of 2007, Westat released its report entitled *Findings of the Web Basic Pilot Evaluation.*[27] This 254-page report makes repeated, negative references about both employers who fail to follow the E-Verify rules and employees who utilize fraudulent documents that clear the system to obtain employment. These are the ghosts of E-Verify's past and present. In response to these types of improprieties, U.S. Citizenship and Immigration Services (USCIS) has created and is implementing a compliance and monitoring program. The Westat report lists specific monitoring "indicators" or data queries that USCIS could perform to identify employers that are failing to comply with the system. These indicators include:

---

[24] E-Verify Memorandum of Understanding, *supra* note 5, at art. II.B.6 (emphasis added).
[25] *Id.* at art. II.C.6.
[26] *Id.* at art. II.C.15 (emphasis added).
[27] *Available at www.uscis.gov/files/article/WebBasicPilotRprtSept2007.pdf.*

- A high rate of duplicate SSNs and A- (alien) numbers submitted by an employer in one work location;
- A high overall rate of duplicate SSNs and A-numbers used in disparate locations within a limited period of time;
- An unusually low percentage of employees not clearing the system the first time through;
- A variety of indicators that indicate otherwise improper usage of the system (prescreenings, reverifications, etc.); and
- Other indicators identifying failures to comply with technical requirements mandated by use of the system, such as failure to enter follow-up resolution data.

E-Verify-registered employers can expect the government to mine E-Verify/Basic Pilot data. Audits of I-9 records and ICE follow-up on suspect data and persons of interest may become the ghost of E-Verify/Basic Pilot future for an unwary user.

E-Verify/Basic Pilot is just a tool with multiple uses. It can aid an employer in reducing the risk of employing unauthorized workers and offer some additional legal protections. However, it can also be used as an effective investigative tool by the government to facilitate enforcement actions that would otherwise be more difficult to pursue. The best way for an employer to minimize the risk of improprieties is to have solid, basic I-9 practices in place performed by quality people, and to fully commit to the hiring of only workers with a valid right to work in the United States.

Analysis by Courts

The number of courts analyzing E-Verify/Basic Pilot will continue to grow.

At the federal level, courts have issued decisions in litigation involving the interplay between state and local ordinances and E-Verify/Basic Pilot in states like Pennsylvania, Arizona, and Oklahoma. The main focus of these cases has been whether these state laws are preempted by federal law or are otherwise unconstitutional. E-Verify/Basic Pilot has also been analyzed in Racketeer Influenced and Corrupt Organizations Act cases involving private plaintiffs. These cases include allegations that employers knowingly hired individuals who provided false documents that cleared E-Verify/Basic Pilot. In connection with enforcement actions, ICE's challenge to defeat good-faith compliance claims by E-Verify/Basic Pilot employers will likely be litigated in the future, too.

State courts will become the situs for litigation flowing from Arizona-styled laws. Employers and their representatives will be challenged to defend employers caught up in these state processes, while pursuing claims of federal preemption and attempts to remove cases to federal court.

In some respects, judicial review will provide more clarity in certain areas. On the other hand, interpretations may vary across jurisdictions, making the lawyer's job more challenging.

Extension of E-Verify

In November 2008, the statutory authority for E-Verify expires. In order to continue the program, Congress will have to act in the heat of an election year. In 2003, the last time the system was extended, there was significant controversy within the Republican-controlled U.S. House of Representatives. At the end of the day, the Senate's less controversial proposal extending the system for five years was adopted.[28]

One leading proposal introduced in 2007[29] grants E-Verify eternal and everlasting life. Specifically, it provides:

> Section 401(b) of the Illegal Immigration Reform and Immigrant Responsibility Act of 1996 (8 U.S.C. 1324a note) is amended by adding before the period at the end of the last sentence the following ', except that the basic pilot program described in section 403(a) shall be a permanent program'.[30]

It is difficult to predict whether Congress will extend the program indefinitely, or will simply pass a three- to five-year lease on life. However, it is highly doubtful that the program will be allowed to lapse, despite the shortcomings highlighted in the Westat report.

The bigger question will be what further employer obligations will be attached to the extension of E-Verify. There is sizable support for a bill[31] that mandates usage of the program by all employers within four years and reverification of the country's approximately 140 million workers. Given the dynamic political climate, the outcome is unpredictable.

Concluding Thoughts on E-Verify

Overall, E-Verify is viewed by many as some sort of mystical elixir that will solve the country's illegal immigration—but it isn't. Upon closer review, it can be a useful tool for employers, but it can also be a useful, efficient tool for the government to target employers. Employers should carefully consider whether to enroll in the program and once registered, whether there is an impact withdrawing from the system. E-Verify is a lot like IRCA in that it has several inherent flaws. If the system's life is extended beyond 2008, one can anticipate the number and complexity of considerations and issues to grow.

IMAGE: Is It for You (Or Only for a Very Few)?

In July of 2006, ICE announced two measures billed as "voluntary partnerships with the government." The first was a list of what the agency considers to be "Best Hiring Practices." The second was a voluntary program entitled the ICE Mutual Agreement Between Government and Employers, also referred to as IMAGE. As of

---

[28] Basic Pilot Program Extension and Expansion Act of 2003, Pub. L. No. 108-156, 117 Stat. 1943.

[29] H.R. 4088, 110th Cong. (2007).

[30] *Id.* at §201(a).

[31] *Id.*

this writing, ICE continues to offer IMAGE, but the list of requirements[32] has become more invasive and even more unattractive.

Analysis of IMAGE

Employers seeking to participate in IMAGE must first agree to submit to an I-9 audit by ICE. In order to ensure the accuracy of their wage reporting, employers must use the Social Security Number Verification System (SSNVS) to verify the SSNs of their existing labor force. An employer must then commit to the "Best Hiring Practices" listed below. ICE will then provide training and education to IMAGE partners on proper hiring procedures, fraudulent document detection, and antidiscrimination laws. ICE has also stated it will share data with employers on the latest illegal schemes used to circumvent legal hiring processes. One of the primary benefits of being an IMAGE partner is confidence that an employer will have a legal workforce and not suffer a loss of workers in the event of an ICE investigation or raid.

"Best Hiring Practices"

Basic Measures

1. Establish a protocol for Social Security "no-match" letters, and
2. Ensure that I-9 processes are nondiscriminatory.

Reasonable Measures

1. Arrange for semiannual I-9 audits by an external auditing firm or a trained employee not otherwise involved in the I-9 process; and
2. Use the Basic Pilot Program for all hiring.

Questionable Measures

1. Establish an internal training program with annual updates on how to manage completion of Form I-9 and how to detect fraudulent use of documents in the I-9 process and in the use of E-Verify. Note that although IRCA doesn't require that employers be document experts, IMAGE purports to provide fraudulent documentation expertise.
2. Permit the I-9 and E-Verify process to be conducted only by individuals who have received this training—and include a secondary review as part of each employee's verification, to minimize the potential for a single individual to subvert the process. Note: The secondary review requirement is based upon ICE's inherent mistrust of only one employee handling the I-9 process. The I-9 is signed under the penalty of perjury, and the data obtained must be entered into E-Verify, which in effect serves as a secondary review.
3. Establish a protocol for assessing adherence to the best-practices guidelines by the company's contractors/subcontractors. Note: If the employer's implementation of all ICE-recommended practices seems unreasonable, an employer

---

[32] *See www.ice.gov/partners/opaimage/.*

cannot in turn reasonably require its contractors to follow the full set of practices.

Highly Questionable Measures

1. Establish a self-reporting procedure to report to ICE any violations or discovered deficiencies, including a requirement to immediately report to ICE the discovery or allegations of any substantive criminal violations.

2. Establish a "tip line" for employees to report activity relating to the employment of unauthorized aliens, and a protocol for responding to employee tips; and designate an IMAGE compliance officer if an employer has more than 50 employees.

3. Submit an annual report to ICE to track the results and assess the effect of participation, to include: number of employees removed and denied employment as a result of IMAGE participation, organizational changes, and updated points of contact.

Given ICE's aggressive disposition and ICE's inspection powers under IMAGE, an employer should seriously consider the consequences of implementing these practices.

ICE's stated goal is to "help restore the integrity of the immigration system of the United States by utilizing industry outreach and self-policing."[33] ICE states that it has developed IMAGE "as a new concept for employer self-compliance within the worksite enforcement program."[34] As of December 2007, only nine of approximately 6 million U.S. employers were IMAGE-certified, with about 350 even expressing interest in the program. One of the reasons for failing to attain ICE's goal may be that IMAGE represents an effort to impose a regulatory scheme on employers beyond the legislative intent of IRCA, other statutes, or the associated regulations. As unattractive as IMAGE appeared when it was introduced, it appears to have grown extra warts. Absent a more employer-friendly, "real world" restructuring, willing IMAGE participants will likely remain limited.

Additional Tools

There is no doubt that the government's zero-tolerance enforcement approach has placed employers and their representatives under intense pressure to go beyond basic I-9 compliance. Two main things many employers would like to avoid are employing workers who have presented false identities and avoiding the receipt of Social Security "no-match" letters.

Many companies in the background check/pre-employment screening, human resources consulting, and third-party I-9 service industries are attempting to offer employers solutions to address these concerns. In many cases, these companies retain legal counsel to ensure that recommended practices and products or services offered

---

[33] IMAGE FAQs at *www.ice.gov/partners/opaimage/image_faq.htm.*
[34] *Id.*

are legitimate. However, as in any industry or profession, there may be a few who utilize or encourage questionable practices.

Employers should be aware that certain tools can be accessed directly without the aid of third-party vendors. However, other tools are better implemented by such vendors.

Social Security Number Verification Service (SSNVS)

Overview

SSNVS can be used to reduce the risk of receiving Social Security no-match letters. SSA provides SSNVS to employers and to third-party companies to verify the names and SSNs of employees against SSA records. According to the *Social Security Number Verification Service (SSNVS) Handbook*,[35] SSA limits use of SSNVS to ensuring that the records of current or former employees are correct for the purpose of completing IRS Form W-2 (Wage and Tax Statement). These verifications can be done by phone for up to 10 numbers at a time, or an employer can register for online access to SSA's system to verify all of the employer's payroll data.

An employer can utilize SSNVS *after* a new employee is hired, but the confirmation of the SSN must be made apart from the I-9 process. For SSA's purposes, the relevant definition of an "employment" is contained in the Federal Insurance Contributions Act (FICA)[36] and means any service of whatever nature by an employee for the purpose of employing him or her.[37] An "employee" is "any individual who, under the usual common law rules applicable in determining the employer-employee relationship has the status of employee.[38] An employer should perform this verification across the board in its new hire setup process, or not at all. Some employers verify all of their employees' SSNs on a periodic basis.

The dilemma for some employers is that this process can yield the same data as SSA's "no-match" letters. Prudent employers should undergo the same procedures they have established for "no-match" situations, especially in light of ICE and SSA's more recent enforcement actions for false reporting of wage data.

SSNVS Limitations of Use and Penalties for Misuse

The *Handbook* lists certain restrictions on the use of SSNVS and SSA data. Specifically, it states it is illegal to use the service to verify SSNs of potential new hires or contractors. It also states that third-party use of SSNVS is strictly limited to organizations that contract with employers to either handle the wage reporting responsibilities or perform an administrative function directly related to annual wage reporting responsibilities of hired employees. *It is not proper to use SSNVS for non-wage reporting purposes such as identity checks.*

---

[35] *Available at www.ssa.gov/employer/ssnvs_handbk.htm.*

[36] 26 USC §§3101–28.

[37] 26 USC §3121(b).

[38] 26 USC §3121(d)(2).

The *Handbook* refers to penalties for improper use of SSNVS. Anyone who knowingly and willfully uses SSNVS to request or obtain information from SSA under false pretenses violates federal law and may be punished by a fine, imprisonment, or both. SSA may also ban a company or a third-party service from use of SSNVS if SSA determines there has been a misuse of the service.

In the event SSA provides a "no-match" result, the *Handbook* states that such a response is not a basis, in and of itself, to take any adverse action against the employee, such as laying off, suspending, firing, or discriminating against the employee.

Alternative Practices

Both E-Verify and SSNVS restrict the use of each tool to screening prospective employees. In light of those limitations, background check/pre-employment screening and human resources consulting companies have attempted to fill the void. Again, it is critical to note that most advertised services and practices are legitimate and have been reviewed by legal counsel. However, certain practices may cross the line and result in an outcome that creates additional legal problems. The buyer should definitely ask questions of service providers and determine the legitimacy of a vendor's practices.

Social Security Number Trace Searches—Many background/pre-employment screening companies offer SSN trace search services. These companies can search commercial databases maintained by major credit reporting companies and SSA's death claim database. These searches can yield the following data regarding the SSN: the state of issue, the year of issue, whether the number is in a valid range, and whether a death claim has been filed with SSA. These searches do not verify the individual's identity or that the information is 100 percent accurate. The results of a trace search are only an indicator that an applicant may have provided inaccurate information.

Background Checks—Pre-employment background checks offer a more complete picture about an applicant's identity. These checks utilize public records and other means of verifying information provided by an applicant. One of the core requirements to a valid background check is the provision of a valid SSN. The main problem with using background checks is that an employer may not want to request one for each potential employee. Generally, an employer cannot utilize background checks selectively. If an employer desires to require it for only certain positions, it should have a business justification for such a requirement. If utilized in accordance with employment law requirements, background checks can provide employers with a higher level of certainty that they are not hiring someone who is using another's identity.

Citizenship Requirements—Certain employers may be required by law, regulation, executive order, or government contract to hire only U.S. citizens or nationals, permanent residents, or other protected individuals. These employers are protected against charges of an unfair immigration-related employment practice.[39] There are two major points employers must keep in mind, however.

---

[39] INA §§274B(a)(2)(c), (3); 8 USC §§1324b(a)(2)(C), (3).

First, an employer may not utilize blanket practices that extend citizenship discrimination restrictions for all positions. An employer must look at the express restriction at issue, the position in question (type of work done, location, etc.) and employ reasonable restrictions. If the U.S. Department of Justice, Office of Special Counsel received claims of discrimination on this basis, an employer should expect that its facility will be physically inspected and its practices scrutinized to ensure the restriction is no broader than required.

Second, an employer should phrase and document its query appropriately to determine whether or not a prospective or new employee is qualified to work in the relevant position. An employer can satisfy this requirement by providing a brief questionnaire in the following format:

Citizenship Status Questionnaire

Please answer the following question, and then sign and date the form below:

Are you a U.S. citizen or national, asylee, refugee, or lawful permanent resident?

Yes or No

Signature:

Name:

Date:

Please note, this information is being collected solely for governmental contract compliance purposes and will not be used to unfairly discriminate in any employment action.

The employer can then maintain this information for future reference in a binder or file separate from the personnel file or I-9 file.

Other Practices—There are other practices being advertised and promoted to employers as short-hand methods to avoid employing unauthorized workers and receiving Social Security "no-match" information. For example, some parties are advocating the view that an employer does not even have to consider an applicant for employment if the person fails to provide an SSN on an application. Given that the federal government does not require an SSN for the I-9 Form (except for E-Verify) or for initial wage reporting, this practice is questionable. Employers and their representatives should keep in mind the old adage that if something seems too good to be true, it probably is. Employers should contact legal counsel before adopting employment practices that have the potential to create significant employment law problems.

Conclusion

There are a variety of tools that can be used in connection with a corporate compliance program. Each tool has advantages and disadvantages that should be carefully considered. Additionally, an employer should adopt tools it can realistically utilize and be prepared to adapt to constant change in the law. One of the most critical things an employer should keep in mind is that tools in and of themselves are just that—

tools. Without the right people, doing the right things, at the right time, tools can quickly lose their value.

Index of Compliance Tools Covered
- Basic I-9 compliance
- Electronic I-9s
- E-Verify/Basic Pilot
- IMAGE
- Social Security Number Verification Service (SSNVS)
- Background checks
- "Citizen only" policies

UNCOVERING THE TICKING TIME BOMB: IDENTIFYING IMMIGRATION COMPLIANCE ISSUES IN CORPORATE DUE DILIGENCE

*by Marketa Lindt**

Historically, the corporate lawyers driving the process of mergers and acquisitions (M&A) often failed to consider the impact of the corporate transaction on a target company employing professional foreign nationals in nonimmigrant status. Fortunately, in recent years this topic has received increased attention within the immigration bar and consequently among M&A attorneys. Anecdotal experience indicates that buyers conducting due diligence are now more frequently requesting information from the target company to identify employees who will be affected by the corporate transition and proactively taking steps to ensure their seamless transition. For example, a buyer and seller now more frequently collaborate to begin the process of amending nonimmigrant status before the deal closes, or work to place successor-in-interest language in the purchase agreement so that the buyer can assume the immigration-related liabilities for the eligible immigration processes.

However, an area that has not received as much consideration is identification of immigration-related compliance issues, including the target's compliance with the I-9, H-1B, and Program Electronic Review Management (PERM) rules.[1] In the past, if immigration compliance was in fact addressed in a corporate deal, the tendency was to include these issues in the form of blanket representations and warranties, rather than including specific immigration issues in the due diligence process and addressing any resulting problems directly in the negotiations.

However, given the current enforcement landscape, buyers can no longer afford to ignore the potential exposure of the target's immigration compliance violations. A company that completes an acquisition without conducting due diligence with respect to immigration-related compliance areas risks inheriting significant potential liability. Substantial failure to comply with the Department of Labor's (DOL) regulations for H-1Bs and labor condition applications[2] may result in substantial fines[3] and potentially in

---

* **Marketa Lindt** practices business immigration law at Sidley Austin LLP in Chicago, where she primarily advises employers regarding immigrant workforce planning, temporary and permanent visa processing, I-9 compliance, and employer sanctions. She currently serves on AILA's ICE Liaison Committee and the Interior Enforcement Committee. In the past, she has served as the chair of AILA's Chicago Chapter and as national AILA liaison to the Department of Labor, USCIS Nebraska Service Center, and the Social Security Administration. She is a previous recipient of AILA's Joseph Minsky Young Lawyer Award. Ms. Lindt is also past chair of the Chicago Bar Association Immigration & Nationality Law Committee. Ms. Lindt frequently speaks and writes about business immigration practice and provides pro bono immigration counsel to a number of community and cultural organizations.

[1] The PERM rules can be found at 20 CFR Parts 655 and 656.

[2] *See* 20 CFR §§655.700 to 655.760.

[3] *See* 20 CFR §655.810(b).

the company's debarment from the H-1B program.[4] Failure to comply with the requirements of the PERM program may result in increased scrutiny of the employer's recruitment requirements[5] or the company's debarment from the program.[6] Perhaps most significantly, a target's past failure to comply with its I-9 obligations under the Immigration Reform and Control Act of 1986 (IRCA)[7] can result in civil[8] and criminal[9] penalties and, in serious cases, vulnerability to a worksite raid, which can result in substantial civil and criminal penalties, disruption of operations, loss of workforce, and substantial harm to reputation with customers, investors, and the public. Even if the company is not subjected to a raid, a buyer should not underestimate the value of the workforce and the effort and cost that will be required to replace an undocumented workforce, including recruitment and training, and potentially outsourcing product lines or even moving to a different locale with a more adequate workforce.

In an era where the government has significantly stepped up its enforcement of employers it suspects employ undocumented workers, a company that unknowingly acquires a target with a record of past I-9 hiring violations has just purchased a ticking time bomb. Therefore, a thorough pre-purchase due diligence investigation must include inquiries that will permit the interested buyer to analyze any potential problem issues relating to the target's professional foreign national workforce, as well as its compliance with its obligations relating to I-9s, H-1Bs and PERM filings.

Definition and Purpose of Due Diligence

In its most general sense, due diligence is the measure of prudence that can properly be expected from a reasonable person under the circumstances.[10] In current business parlance, due diligence is most typically used as a term of art to describe the buyer's analytical process for performing an in-depth and systematic scrutiny of the buyer during the course of a merger or acquisition.

As a general matter, due diligence serves to test the assumptions on which the transaction is based. As the buyer and seller move deeper into the negotiations, the buyer must put into place an effective due diligence process to obtain the details of all of the essential characteristics of the seller's operations and business that affect its value (assets and liabilities), as well as the less tangible "fit" of the two entities. A robust due diligence process assists the buyer to assess the seller's strategic, financial, legal and operational position. Effective due diligence confirms or contradicts management's depiction of the seller's business and helps the buyer to better focus its estimate of the value and synergy that would result from the transaction. Failure to

---

[4] 20 CFR §655.810(d).
[5] *See* 20 CFR §656.21.
[6] *See* 20 CFR §656.31(f).
[7] Pub. L. No. 99-603, 100 Stat. 3359.
[8] *See* 8 CFR §274a.10(b).
[9] *See* 8 CFR §274a.10(a).
[10] *Black's Law Dictionary* (8th Ed. 2004) (entry for *diligence*).

conduct effective due diligence can have adverse consequences for the buyer, including overpayment for the target entity, mismatched business models or corporate culture, or unanticipated civil or criminal liability for the successor entity.

The due diligence process is invariably expensive and labor intensive for both parties. In addition, it is typically a frustrating process, as it almost always reveals undisclosed problems in the seller's business. During the initial stages of negotiations, due to confidentiality reasons and the seller's attempt to market its business, information flow about the essential details of the seller's business is inherently limited. Often, during the due diligence process the buyer uncovers deficiencies the existence or scope of which the seller is unaware.

After the due diligence concludes, the buyer reviews the initial valuation and offer price for the target. At that point, the parties use the information gained in the due diligence process to renegotiate the price or other terms of the deal, or when the due diligence raises insurmountable issues in the negotiation, to terminate the deal.

Statutory and Regulatory Framework for Due Diligence

Sarbanes-Oxley Act

While the Sarbanes-Oxley Act of 2002[11] did not specifically create standards for the merger and acquisition process, its existence has made a dramatic impact on due diligence in corporate transactions. Sarbanes-Oxley creates significantly heightened standards for accountability in corporate governance of U.S. public companies, including more objectivity for board members, increased autonomy for auditors, stronger control over financial reporting processes and stiffer penalties for abuse of corporate governance and financial reporting rules. Sarbanes-Oxley requires U.S. public corporations to conduct specific review of the internal controls and financial reporting procedures of its companies, including any recently acquired businesses. Since the passage of Sarbanes-Oxley and the resulting shift in the culture of corporate deals, many potential buyers consider a public or nonpublic company's weak internal controls and lack of adequate compliance mechanisms to be significant deal-breakers.

Other Federal and State Statutes

In addition to the Sarbanes-Oxley Act, a number of other federal and state laws affect a buyer's potential liabilities in acquiring another company. An extensive body of law at the federal and state levels regulates a company's obligations to disclose the presence of hazardous material and other environmental concerns. Under federal antitrust rules, some companies must request permission to enter into large corporate transactions, and the Department of Justice (DOJ) and the Federal Trade Commission have the authority to block acquisitions that they deem will likely significantly lessen competition. Also, there are a number of federal and state laws in the employment and labor law area that can appreciably affect the valuation of a target company's value and liabilities. Examples include a company's past compliance, or lack of com-

---

[11] Pub. L. No. 107-204, 116 Stat. 745.

pliance with the leave requirements of the Family Medical Leave Act, the disability accommodations of the Americans with Disabilities Act and the layoff and retraining protections of the Worker Adjustment and Retraining Notification Act. Employers are potentially liable for past employment practices that violated state and federal employment laws regarding discrimination, sexual harassment, and benefit, retirement, and pension rules, including the Employee Retirement Income Security Act. For companies operating in an organized environment, potential target companies may have liabilities stemming from obligations under the National Labor Relations Act and a collective bargaining agreement.

Federal and State Immigration Statutes and Regulations

While it is standard practice to incorporate Sarbanes-Oxley, antitrust laws, environmental rules, and employment and labor law obligations into the due diligence processes, corporate lawyers often overlook critical immigration-related visa and compliance issues. Immigration-related assets, liabilities, and obligations arising out of federal and state law that should be considered in the due diligence process of every corporate transaction include the following:

- Whether key personnel at the company hold nonimmigrant visas or are pursuing permanent residence processing, and whether those processes could be transferred to the new company.

- Whether the company has historically complied with DOL's employer obligations and document retention requirements for the H-1B and PERM processes.

- Whether the company has historically complied with IRCA's rules for properly completing I-9s, verifying work authorization for its employees, and retaining required I-9 documentation

- Whether the company has a robust I-9 compliance program moving forward, including I-9 written policies and practices, training for staff, I-9 self-audits, and protocols for dealing with actual and constructive knowledge situations, such as Social Security Administration (SSA) "no-match" letters and allegations of unauthorized workers.

- Whether the company has ever been the subject of a DOL, Department of Homeland Security (DHS), or DOJ investigation, inspection, proceeding, or enforcement action related to the employment of foreign-national workers.

- Particularly in certain industries employing low-skilled workers, whether the company's industry, workforce, and past I-9 practices make it vulnerable to a raid by U.S. Immigration and Customs Enforcement, and whether corrective measures need to be instituted.

- In the event of a raid, whether the company has a contingency plan in place to ensure that it can continue its operations in the short and long term.

- Whether the company's industry, workforce, and past I-9 practices make it vulnerable to being named as a defendant in a civil suit alleging violations of the Racketeer Influenced and Corrupt Organizations Act.

- Whether the company operates in a state or municipality that has enacted laws to impose additional immigration-related obligations on employers, and whether the company is in compliance with such state laws.

Parties and Roles in the Due Diligence Process

Clearly, the two most important parties in the transaction, and in the due diligence process, are the buyer and the seller. Typically, each of the parties retains an outside law firm as "deal counsel" to represent it in the negotiation. The role of the buyer's team is to structure the due diligence inquiries to address its primary concerns, and the seller's team organizes the information and documentation in response to the inquiries. A thorough due diligence process typically involves written inquiries and requests for documents followed up with more in-depth investigation, including interviews of key staff.

In addition, depending on the size of the deal, the nature of the companies, and the expertise of deal counsel, any number of specialized experts may be retained to analyze the information, including industry experts, independent accountants, auditors, human resources consultants, and payroll consultants. In situations in which immigration issues arise, the parties would be well advised to bring in an immigration attorney with a thorough understanding of the particular issues that arise from the documentation, whether those pertain to retention of professional workers, H-1B compliance issues, I-9 obligations and liability, or defense from government or third-party litigation on immigration issues.

Integrating Critical Immigration Inquiries into Effective Due Diligence

By its nature, due diligence is more of an art than a science, as the analysis seeks to integrate issues that range from the highly objective (*e.g.*, figures from audited financial statements) to deeply subjective (*e.g.*, assessments of market conditions or compatibility of corporate cultures). However, the due diligence process can be grouped into four broad categories of inquiry: (1) strategic, (2) financial, (3) legal, and (4) operational. There are a number of important immigration inquiries that should be added to a buyer's checklist of questions, particularly in the legal and operational due diligence categories.

Legal Due Diligence Issues

In the legal aspect of the due diligence inquiry, the buyer seeks information pertaining to the seller's ability to comply with the necessary regulatory clearances for the transaction, as well as to assess the company's existing and potential exposure to legal liabilities. As such, the buyer typically requests documentation related to the seller's:

- legal standing and governance documents
- key operating contracts
- employment contracts with key employees
- pending lawsuits, patent filings, and trademarks
- tax filings

- potential product liability claims
- potential employment law claims
- environmental cost and liability
- real estate

In addition, the buyer should conduct an immigration audit to determine the seller's potential legal liabilities under its H-1B, PERM, and I-9 obligations. The buyer should ask for the following as part of its legal due diligence checklist:

- full copy of all I-9 documentation for current and for terminated employees whose I-9s fall within the document retention requirements
- all written policies and procedures regarding the company's I-9 compliance program
- description of all unwritten I-9 procedures and processes, including completion, training, document storage and retention, and resolution of problem issues
- information about any additional procedures in place to comply with state or local immigration obligations
- copy of all "no-match" letters received from SSA
- copy of all documentation regarding any DOL, DOJ, or DHS investigation, inspection, proceedings, or enforcement actions relating to foreign-national workers
- list of all H-1B workers and copy of all H-1B public access files
- copy of PERM files for all employees who were sponsored under this process over the past five years, including all DOL PERM audits and employer's responses[12]
- list of employees to whom the company has promised permanent residence sponsorship at some point in the future

Unless deal counsel has substantial expertise in I-9 and immigration issues, the buyer should retain an immigration attorney with experience in these areas to provide support on the immigration issues, including conducting a liability assessment and conducting a more in-depth investigation, such as interviewing hiring staff to determine whether hiring occurs with actual knowledge of undocumented status.

Operational Due Diligence Issues

In performing due diligence on the target's operational capabilities, the buyer seeks to assess the seller's capacity to perform its day-to-day activities in carrying out its core business. The operational inquiry typically covers a wide range of issues, including:

- the corporate culture
- competence of management

---

[12] Particular attention should be paid to whether the company filed PERM applications for any undocumented workers.

- the philosophy and personality of key executives
- capacity of the workforce
- the morale of the workforce
- the methods of production and delivery of its core goods or services
- ability to sustain sales and earnings growth
- personnel policies, contracts, wage scale, and benefits
- cost of potential layoffs
- feasibility and cost of bringing statutory and regulatory compliance up to standard

Certainly, a company that relies on foreign-national employees who serve as executives, managers, and professionals will need to ensure that its employees will be able to work seamlessly through a corporate transaction. Similarly, a company that appears to rely on undocumented labor should be requested to demonstrate that it can develop and implement a cost-effective I-9 compliance program and "clean up" its workforce to replace undocumented workers with authorized ones as quickly as possible to mitigate the liability. With respect to immigration compliance, there are a significant number of important operational items to ask for as part of the due diligence checklist:

- a list of all foreign-national employees and their job titles who hold E-1, E-2, E-3, F-1 OPT, H-1B, J-1, L-1A, L-1B, O-1, TN, or any other work-authorized visa status
- a list of all foreign nationals currently in the permanent-residence process
- a list of employees who would require amendments and corresponding legal and filing fees
- a list of employees who would not be eligible to amend status after corporate change, and costs of replacing them

The operational checklist should further include:

- consideration of the impact of any layoffs resulting from the transaction on PERM cases in process
- if the legal analysis shows that the existing I-9 compliance program is deficient, an inquiry to demonstrate that the company can bring it to standard in a timely and cost-effective manner
- if the legal analysis shows that the company is employing workers with insufficient work authorization, an inquiry to demonstrate the timely remedy of that deficiency, and that any resulting staff turnover will be managed in an orderly fashion
- if the legal analysis shows defects in the H-1B public-access file methodology, an inquiry to confirm that the methodology will be corrected, and that the company will comply with the required obligations, including raising the employee wages if necessary

- if the company operates in a state or municipality that has enacted laws to impose additional immigration-related obligations on employers, an inquiry as to whether the company's operations in that locality will be adversely affected

Strategic Due Diligence Inquiries

Through the strategic component of due diligence, the buyer seeks to understand the seller's market position and the way in which its business model fits into the characteristics and trends of the market, and its potential synergies with the buyer. Based on public information and industry-insider knowledge, the buyer conducts research into the market in which the buyer operates and performs a general inquiry into its ability to compete. As the strategic inquiry pertains primarily to the seller's product and marketing strategy, any immigration issues relating to its workforce are not likely. However, if the company heavily relies on unskilled labor, it may be important to take into account any potential impact on the employer's industry and business caused by an increase in DHS enforcement and worksite raids. Similarly, if the company relies heavily on foreign professional workers, it may be relevant to consider whether limits on certain visa categories (such as the H-1B specialty occupation or fast-track permanent residence for nurses) will have an adverse impact on the company's core business model.

Financial Due Diligence Inquiries

The inquires relating to verifying the seller's financial statements and accounting standards, while extremely important for the overall due diligence analysis, do not typically implicate immigration issues.

Conclusion

In conducting due diligence, the buyer and its deal counsel cannot underestimate the potential liabilities of the employer's immigration-related compliance obligations. A buyer's failure to conduct due diligence regarding I-9, H-1B, and PERM-related compliance issues leaves it vulnerable to purchasing a company that is a ticking time bomb. Therefore, so that the buyer is able to make a complete, informed assessment of its target, it is critical that deal counsel include immigration-related inquiries on its due diligence checklist for an M&A deal.

I-9 CONSIDERATIONS IN MERGERS AND ACQUISITIONS—
A BACK-BURNER ISSUE REQUIRING FRONT-BURNER ATTENTION
by Anthony E. Weigel[*]

Introduction

In today's worksite enforcement environment, all parties to merger or acquisition transactions should make room on the front burner for consideration of employment eligibility verification (Form I-9) compliance. Overall, federal worksite enforcement charges increased by almost 400 percent from 2005 to 2007.[1] U.S. Immigration and Customs Enforcement (ICE) has also dramatically increased the amounts of criminal fines and asset forfeitures it has collected. In fiscal year (FY) 2007, ICE obtained criminal fines, restitutions, and civil judgments in worksite enforcement actions in excess of $30 million, dwarfing the $6,500 it obtained FY 2005.[2] ICE has targeted businesses of all sizes in a variety of industries across the country.[3]

To illustrate the importance of this issue, consider the following examples:

Example #1. An investment group acquired an employer's business assets with the intent to operate the enterprise on an ongoing basis, but failed to focus on how well the prior employer maintained its Form I-9 records and associated processes. If ICE conducts a raid of the successor employer's business and removes a significant portion of the workforce, the value of the buyer's investment may be greatly diminished as it attempts to salvage the situation.

Example #2. A party agreed to merge her company into another company. In the transaction, she surrendered her ownership interest in her business entity for an ownership interest in the surviving business entity. Neither she nor her counsel inquired about the surviving business entity's I-9 practices. If ICE subsequently pursues criminal charges for violations of immigration law against the management of the successor company based on premerger activities, the value of her shares may also be greatly diminished.

---

[*] **Anthony E. Weigel** practices immigration law at Husch Blackwell Sanders, LLP in Kansas City, MO, and is a member of the American Immigration Lawyers Association. His practice focuses on employer compliance and employment-based immigration. Prior to practicing law, Mr. Weigel worked in human resources and was responsible for coordinating immigration matters and a broad spectrum of employment law compliance issues, including I-9 verifications and record retention.

[1] ICE Fact Sheet, Worksite Enforcement (Oct. 15, 2007), *available at www.ice.gov/pi/news/factsheets/worksite.htm*. Statistics on this Fact Sheet show that the number of criminal and administrative arrests in worksite enforcement actions increased from 1,292 in 2005 to 4,940 in 2007.

[2] *Id.*

[3] ICE Fact Sheet, Worksite Enforcement (Sept. 27, 2007), *available at www.ice.gov/pi/news/factsheets/worksite_cases.htm*.

The bottom line: the failure to adequately inquire into I-9 compliance can lead to financial losses. In example #1, the investment group could have discovered that the target business had received over the last few years a large number of Social Security "no-match" letters to which it never responded. In example #2, the party to the transaction may have been able to discover that ICE had requested all of its I-9 records for review a few months prior to closing and that there were lingering questions about immigration compliance in the workplace. If neither did, they will ask why their counsel failed to do so and react accordingly.

In cases in which the ability to employ existing workers is an issue, all parties to the transaction should have a handle on the other's I-9 compliance early to avoid surprises later.[4] The timing of immigration-related inquires is critical, because this information could significantly impact the acquiring party's options to manage this issue.

Background Information: Transaction Basics

Generally, corporate transactions take the form of business entity mergers, one party's acquisition of another company's ownership shares (*i.e.*, stock), or the acquisition of assets.

Merger transactions—The term "merger" is often used to describe a variety of business transactions. In any merger, there are predecessor entities and surviving entities. Ownership interests in predecessor entities are typically exchanged for ownership interests in a surviving entity. *The main concept relating to I-9 liabilities is that all of the liabilities of the entities involved in the transaction are poured into the same pot.* Parties to merger acquisitions can and often do negotiate for the owners of predecessor entities to indemnify other parties for certain liabilities that might arise after closing.

Stock acquisitions typically involve the purchase of an entity's ownership interests held by another party. The acquiring party assumes all liabilities that the previous owners of such ownership interests have accumulated over time. Parties to stock transactions can and often do negotiate for the seller to indemnify the buyer for certain liabilities that might arise after closing.

Asset acquisitions differ because *they normally do not involve the broad assumption of liabilities*. Parties normally negotiate assumption of liabilities, but some are fixed by state "bulk sales" laws. Other legal duties may attach by virtue of other controlling legal authority.

---

[4] The main focus of this article is employment eligibility verification requirements of parties involved in corporate transactions. There are several excellent articles primarily focusing on the impact of corporate transactions on immigration sponsorship. *See, e.g.,* A. Paparelli, "Assuage Therapy: Enticing M&A Lawyers to Help with Immigration Sponsorship," *Immigration & Nationality Law Handbook* 43 (AILA 2007–08 Ed.); N. Chu, "Avoiding a Potential Show Stopper: Verification of Employment Eligibility," *Immigration Options for Artists & Entertainers* 101 (AILA 2007).

I-9 CONSIDERATIONS IN MERGERS AND ACQUISITIONS

Question #1—Will Existing Employees Have a Place at the Table?

Corporate transactions are driven by a variety of factors. Much of the time, the continued operation of the business and employment of its workforce are critical factors. An acquiring party often must keep much of the target's workforce in place in order to fully realize the value of a transaction. Thus, it is worth the investment of time and resources to investigate I-9 records, processes, and history with enforcement agencies. *Counsel to the acquiring party should identify early on the importance of keeping the target's employees on board.* There are transactions, such as pure asset deals, in which employees will not be retained. In such transactions, determining the I-9 compliance of the target is not as critical.

Question #2—Will There Be a Continuing Employer in the Kitchen?

Under current law, a "continuing employer" is not required to complete new I-9 forms on behalf of newly acquired employees if such employees have a reasonable expectation of employment at all times.[5] In the merger or acquisition context, a "continuing employer" is defined broadly as an "employer who continues to employ some or all of a previous employer's workforce in cases involving a corporate reorganization, merger, or sale of stock or assets."[6]

In order to determine whether a post-closing employer would be considered a "continuing employer," one must evaluate whether employees expect to resume employment (post-closing) and whether the employees' expectations are reasonable.[7] The reasonable expectations of employees affected by the transaction are determined on a case-by-case basis, taking into consideration several factors, including:

(1) Whether the employees in question were employed by the predecessor employer on a regular and substantial basis. A determination of a regular and substantial basis is established by a comparison of other workers who are similarly employed by the employer;

(2) Whether the positions held by the employees in question have not been taken permanently by other workers after closing;

(3) Whether the financial condition of the successor employer indicates the ability of such employer to permit the employees in question to resume employment within a reasonable time after closing; or

(4) Whether the oral and/or written communication between the predecessor employer, such employer's supervisory employees, and the employees in question indicates that it is reasonably likely that they will resume employment with the employer within a reasonable time after closing.[8]

---

[5] INA §§274A(a)(1)(A), (B), (2); 8 USC §1324a(a)(1)(A), (B), (2); 8 CFR §274a.2(b)(1)(viii).

[6] 8 CFR §274a.2(b)(1)(viii)(A)(7)(ii).

[7] 8 CFR §274a.2(b)(1)(viii)(B).

[8] 8 CFR §§274a.2(b)(1)(viii)(B)(1), (4), (6), and (7).

Assuming these criteria are satisfied, the successor employer can claim to be a "continuing employer" under the law and will not be required to have its post-closing workforce complete new I-9 forms.

Conducting Due Diligence—Finding Out What Is in the Cupboard

Parties to corporate transactions are keenly focused on financial data, obligations to creditors, and pending litigation. If real estate is involved, the environmental state of such properties is usually on the front burner as well. Other potential liabilities, like those associated with I-9 compliance, are often put on the back burner or even left in the pantry. Given that new I-9 forms in many cases are not required, regardless of the form of the transaction, investigating these potential liabilities might have even been left off the due diligence menu.

The risks for failing to act or in acting too late are great. If employees will be retained after closing, proposed transactions involving businesses in ICE-targeted industries (construction, food processing, restaurant, and agricultural production) or businesses that are the subject of a publicized ICE enforcement action should include I-9 inquiries in the *first* due diligence requests of other parties. Proposed transactions involving companies in other industries should still make I-9 inquiries a high priority.

Appendix A to this article contains a list of items a party to a transaction may use to inquire about another party's I-9 compliance practices. Once counsel to an acquiring party has this basic information, it can make an assessment of a target's I-9 compliance practices. In some cases, the information obtained may impact the nature of the entire transaction. Often, the nature of the transaction is not fixed at the onset. An acquiring party may have a merger, stock deal, or asset acquisition all on the table.

Follow-Up on "Normal" Responses

In transactions involving nontargeted industries (those other than construction, food processing, restaurant, and agricultural production), one may find that a target company has policies in place and seems to have paid adequate attention to I-9-related matters. At that point, an acquiring party can request a random sample of current and former employees' I-9s for review.[9] This can be accomplished by:

- Requesting a complete list of active employees and employees terminated within the last year
- Randomly identifying employees on each list (*e.g.*, every 15th name) and requesting those I-9 forms

This sample of I-9 forms can then be evaluated using the checklist set forth in appendix B to this article. At this point, counsel will be able to advise the acquiring party of two things: (1) whether assuming the target company's I-9s may be an op-

---

[9] INA §274A(b)(3)(B) [8 USC §1324a(b)(3)(B)] requires an employer to maintain I-9 forms for former employees for three years after the date of hire or one year from the last date of employment, whichever is later. If a target company is unable to readily produce I-9 forms for former employees whose employment ended within the previous year, its records are probably inadequate. This would contribute to a decision to "re-I-9" the entire workforce after closing.

tion; and (2) whether the target company's I-9s are so deficient that any consideration of a merger or stock deal may be put in question due to potential liabilities.

Follow-Up for Targeted or Distressed Companies

In transactions involving targeted industries, one should exercise caution in obtaining information regarding existing I-9 practices and records. If the target company has been the subject of a recent immigration raid or criminal charges relating to immigration, one should exercise similar caution. Counsel to the acquiring party should maintain a balance between conducting adequate due diligence to assess the state of I-9 practices and records, and obtaining too much knowledge of the current workforce's immigration status. This is by no means an effort to skirt the law because a potential acquiring party has no legal duty to a target company's workforce prior to closing.[10] Regardless of the form of a transaction, the acquiring party should be advised to obtain new I-9 forms from all continuing employees after closing. The information obtained will assist with identifying risks associated with the structure of the transaction and determining terms of the transaction.

Post–Due Diligence—Outlining Options and Considerations

"Normal Transactions"

After due diligence has been conducted in "normal" transactions involving non-targeted industries, counsel should be able to advise on the following:

- The state of the target company's I-9 compliance and related records;
- The advisability of accepting inherent liabilities associated with a stock or merger transaction;
- The advisability of accepting the target's I-9 records as a "continuing employer"; and
- Options to minimize and mitigate risks flowing from the form of transaction or assuming the target's I-9 records.
  - *General Rule*—As a general rule, an acquiring party should obtain new I-9s from all employees after closing to minimize I-9-related liabilities. However, if a target company's records and processes appear to be in good condition, an acquiring party may choose to forego verifying the identity and employment eligibility of the acquired workforce.

Asset Transactions—In terms of I-9-related liabilities, an acquiring party can minimize these risks by only acquiring assets of the target company and requiring all "acquired" employees to complete new I-9 forms. If the existing I-9 forms will be

---

[10] INA §274A(a)(2) [8 USC §1324a(a)(2)] prohibits the continuing employment of an employee knowing the person is unauthorized to work. By limiting the examination of individual I-9 records, the acquiring party should not be charged with the knowledge of the prior employer. Instead, the acquiring party is advised to perform its own I-9 verifications in these situations and utilize the government's optional electronic verification system, E-Verify (formerly known as Basic Pilot).

accepted, the acquiring party should consider an indemnification provision and possibly an associated escrow arrangement.

Stock or Merger Transactions—If the transaction goes forward as a stock or merger transaction, there are inherent liabilities regardless of whether the acquiring party completes new I-9 forms after closing. To minimize legal exposure, an acquiring party should require all acquired employees to submit new I-9s. To further mitigate financial risk, one can negotiate for indemnification of realized liabilities relating to I-9 practices. For example, part of the purchase price for the target company's shares or ownership interest might be put in escrow. The maximum term of the escrow period may be set at five years, as that is the statute of limitations for criminal violations of the I-9 related laws. In addition, portions of the escrow may be released over a three-year period as the statute of limitations for civil violations of I-9-related laws runs.

Targeted/Distressed Situations

In transactions involving companies in targeted industries or in distressed situations, counsel should be able to advise on the following:

- The risks associated with accepting inherent liabilities associated with a stock or merger transaction;
- The risks associated with accepting the target's I-9 records as a "continuing employer";
- Options to mitigate the risk of inheriting the target company's potential I-9-related liabilities, and
- General expectations and considerations regarding the ability to continuously employ a high percentage of the existing workforce after closing.

General Rule—As a general rule, an acquiring party should obtain new I-9s from all employees after closing to minimize I-9-related liabilities, regardless of the state of a target company's records and processes. Additionally, an acquiring party should seriously consider the use of E-Verify to verify the work authorization of all newly acquired employees.

Asset Transactions—In terms of minimizing I-9-related liabilities, an acquiring party should be advised to only acquire assets of the target company and require all new employees to complete I-9s. For good measure, the acquiring party may also want to negotiate for indemnification of any I-9-related claims it may have to defend based on the target's past actions.

Stock or Merger Transactions—If the transaction goes forward as a stock or merger transaction, the acquiring party should be fully aware of the inherent liabilities. To mitigate risk, one should negotiate for indemnification of realized liabilities relating to I-9 practices. Part of the purchase price for the target company's shares or ownership interest may be put in escrow in a manner as indicated above.

Post-Closing Expectations and Considerations, Targeted Industries—If the acquiring party only requires new I-9 forms, it is likely that a high percentage of the workforce will satisfy the basic I-9 process. However, if the acquiring party utilizes

E-Verify, on average about 7 percent of the workforce will not clear the system the first time through, and the employer will need to work through the "tentative nonconfirmation" process with affected employees. In some industries, the percentage of "tentative nonconfirmation" results might be higher. It is possible that the status of a high percentage of these employees ultimately may not be resolved after this nonconfirmation process.

Therefore, an acquiring party might go into the deal fully expecting to lose 10 percent of the existing workforce. If that is the case, there will be costs associated with recruiting and staffing the balance of the open positions. In addition, there might be higher wage costs associated with retaining the existing workforce, especially if the market rate for new workers is higher than the target company had to pay before closing. There may also be reduced revenue streams if fewer workers are immediately available. The acquiring party will probably want to factor increased costs and decreased revenue into its purchase price considerations.

Post-Closing Expectations and Considerations, Distressed Situations—If a target company has been the subject of an ICE raid, an acquiring party should utilize E-Verify to verify the work authorization of all acquired employees after closing. The reasonable expectations of an acquiring party will vary depending on the timing of the raid.

If the raid occurred recently, the percentage of workers unable to clear the system should be fairly low, but the need to staff positions may be great. If the prior employer had difficulty finding an adequate number of authorized workers, the acquiring party may face the same situation. If workers are available, there will be costs associated with recruiting new workers and retaining the existing ones.

If some time has passed since the raid, it is possible that the target employer may have inadvertently hired unauthorized workers, which would result in a higher "tentative nonconfirmation" rate. Similar recruiting and retention costs would apply, as would a loss of revenue.

The acquiring party will probably want to factor in increased costs and decreased revenue into its purchase price considerations under either scenario.

Closing Considerations

Prior to closing, the acquiring party should make appropriate arrangements to ensure I-9 compliance. If it will accept the target company's I-9 forms, it should be advised of the location of all I-9 records in advance of closing. If the acquiring company will "re-I-9" the entire workforce, it should plan in advance to have an adequate number of people available trained in the I-9 process for timely completion of all forms. Larger companies with significant human resources staff may be able to assemble a crew to accomplish this task. Otherwise, third-party I-9 service providers may be of great value in processing a large number of new employees in multiple work locations. If the logistics are such that it is impossible to complete all I-9s on day one, an acquiring party may look at options to stagger start dates of new employment and continue employment under the target company's employ temporarily.

Special arrangements will need to be made if the acquiring employer will use E-Verify. Prior to closing, the entity that will employ the target company's employees must register with U.S. Citizenship and Immigration Services to use the system and set up all users who will perform electronic verifications.

Subcontractor Issues

In light of the government's current enforcement priorities, an acquiring party should make reasonable inquiries to ensure that contractors critical to the operation of the business are complying with immigration laws. *Prior to closing, an acquiring party should identify the target company's critical contractors and make queries of the ones it intends to utilize after closing.* The acquiring party should query each contractor by requesting answers to questions 9 through 13 in appendix A of this article. Based on the responses, informed decisions can be made regarding continued use of these contractors.

Other Immigration-Related Obligations

Appendix C to this article contains a list of questions to identify information regarding sponsored workers and related obligations. An acquiring party should make this inquiry at the time it requests information about I-9 compliance. The acquiring party should take necessary actions to ensure continued work authorization of necessary employees. The buyer can assume certain sponsorship obligations and minimize the amount of time and expense on transitioning work authorization and even permanent residence sponsorship—both of which can result in significant value.[11]

Representing a Target Company

If counsel represents a target company, the structure of the deal will drive the importance of the I-9 issue for your client. In some instances, your client may not have a vested interest in the surviving business operation. If your client will walk away from the deal with cash, he or she may express little interest in I-9 compliance of the parties involved.

There are, however, instances in which your client should pay close attention to these matters. First, if the target company will be merged into another entity *and* the target company's owners will own an interest in the surviving entity, the I-9 compliance of the other party should be of interest. The target company's interests and recommended due diligence will be very similar to that described above for acquiring parties. Second, if the target company's owners will be paid out over time from the surviving business' income, they should have an interest in the acquiring party's continuing ability to pay. And third, if the acquiring party is negotiating to have funds escrowed based on I-9 compliance concerns, the target company will be interested in minimizing the amounts withheld. Demonstrating the target company's good I-9 compliance can aid with these types of negotiations.

---

[11] See A. Paparelli, *supra* note 4, at 45, for model language for use in selective assumption of a target company's immigration sponsorship obligations.

Making the Most of Leftovers

In the event an acquiring party contacts immigration counsel right before or after closing, it may be too late in the game to conduct due diligence, restructure transactions, or renegotiate escrow or indemnification arrangements. If counsel is contacted prior to closing, a couple of options may be left on the table. Depending on the acquiring party's relative bargaining power, it may be able to delay closing to provide time for an adequate review of the target company's records. Also there may be time still to require each continuing employee to complete a new I-9 after closing. Otherwise, an acquiring party's options will be limited.

Presuming the target company's I-9s will serve as evidence of an authorized workforce, one option may be to conduct a post-closing self-audit of the I-9 records. During this process, the acquiring employer can attempt to correct as many deficiencies as possible. It can also implement sound corporate compliance policies and procedures to ensure prospectively hired employees provide proper documentation.

Sometimes, time just may not be on your side.

Conclusion

I-9 compliance has become and will remain an important consideration in corporate transactions. Due diligence associated with this issue should be a staple on any transactional checklist. Parties to transactions can identify potential issues and manage them to minimize legal liability and mitigate potential financial losses. In order to effectively obtain these results, parties must address the issue early in the process, make the right inquiries, evaluate available options, and execute appropriately.

Appendix A
EMPLOYER COMPLIANCE MATTER
INFORMATION-DOCUMENT REQUEST

1. Name of Entity/Business: _____
2. a. Number of employees: _____
   b. Are any employees unionized? _____
   c. Prospects for unionization? _____
3. Cities and states of work locations, plus Gov. Contractor/State Aid (tax credits, grants, loans, etc.)

City	State	Gov. Contractor?	State Aid Recipient?
		Yes or No	Yes or No

4. Type of business entity:
   ___ Corporation ___ Partnership ___ Limited Partnership
   ___ Limited Liability Company ___ Sole Proprietor ___ Other
5. Date of Incorporation/Organization: _____
6. Business entity history—any mergers, acquisitions or reorganizations? If so, when?
7. Who are the owners of the business entity (shareholders/partners/members/etc.)?
8. Who manages the business entity (board of directors/officers/upper management)?
9. Please summarize the following regarding the employer's current I-9 procedures and policies:
   a. How are I-9 forms handled now?
      (i) Completion for new hires?
      (ii) Retention/storage of forms?
      (iii) Reverification (where required)?
      (iv) Document destruction (when permitted)?
   b. Are there any policies or procedures in place regarding I-9 completion and storage? Please provide copies of such policies.
10. Does the employer use independent contractors? If so, please summarize how much control the employer has over these contractors and what efforts have been taken to ensure contractors comply with I-9 laws.
11. Has the employer ever been the subject of review or investigation by any government agency, such as the U.S. Department of Labor? If so, please provide dates of inquiries and summary of action.
12. With respect to immigration-related compliance:

a. Has employer sponsored workers for temporary work visas and/or permanent residence? If yes, please summarize sponsorship activity.

b. Has employer ever received one of the following by immigration authorities?

   i. Educational Visit—Immigration authorities visit the employer and inform the employer of its responsibilities and encourage compliance.

   ii. Warning Letter—Issued by immigration authorities for failure to complete I-9 forms or for technical/procedural errors.

   iii. Notice of Technical/Procedural Failures—Issued by immigration authorities to give an employer an opportunity to correct I-9 forms, as directed.

   iv. Notice of Intent to Fine—Issued by immigration authorities after finding violations of I-9 requirements.

c. Has employer or any of its owners, members of management, or employees ever been the subject of a criminal action regarding I-9 compliance?

d. Has employer ever entered into a civil settlement agreement with immigration authorities for I-9 violations?

IF THE EMPLOYER ANSWERED "YES" TO ANY ITEM IN QUESTIONS 11 OR 12, PLEASE PROVIDE COPIES OF DOCUMENTS RELATING TO THE CURRENT STATUS OR FINAL DISPOSITION OF SUCH ACTIONS.

13. Social Security "No-Match" Letters

    a. Has the employer received "no-match" letters from the Social Security Administration?

    b. If yes, please summarize how many letters the employer has received and what actions, if any, have been taken to resolve these inquiries.

    c. Does the employer have any policies or procedures regarding "no-match" letters?

Appendix B

Employee Name: _____ **Date of Hire:** _____
Review Date: _____ **Reviewed By:** _____

SECTION 1				
Employee Information	Complete/Yes	Incomplete/No	Correct	Incorrect
Employee name				
Date of birth				
Social Security number				
Address				
Citizenship/Immigration Status				
Status indication				
If perm. resident (PR), Alien#				
If not PR, A# or Admission #				
Expiration date (if applicable)				
Employee's Attestation				
Signature			N/A	N/A
Date of signature				
Signed on first day?			N/A	N/A
Preparer/Translator Certification				
Signature				
Name				
Address				
SECTION 2				
Employer Review & Verification	Complete/Yes	Incomplete/No	Correct	Incorrect
List A				
Appropriate document/receipt			N/A	N/A
Document title				
Issuing authority				
Document #				
Expiration date				
Document #				
Expiration date				
List B				
Appropriate document/receipt			N/A	N/A
Document title				
Issuing authority				
Document #				
Expiration date				

List C				
Appropriate document/receipt			N/A	N/A
Document title				
Issuing authority				
Document #				
Expiration date				
Employer Verification				
Date of hire				
Signature of employer representative			N/A	N/A
Name of employer representative				
Title of employer representative				
Employer name				
Employer address				
Date of signature				
Signed within three days of first day?			N/A	N/A
SECTION 3				
Updating & Reverification	Complete/Yes	Incomplete/No	Correct	Incorrect
Employee name				
Date of rehire (if applicable)				
Document title				
Document #				
Expiration date (if any)				
Signature of employer representative				
Date of signature			N/A	N/A

Appendix C
Immigration Matter Inventory Checklist

COMPANY NAME: _____ (the "Company")

Item	Question—Does the Company:	Yes or No	If Yes, How many? (est.)
1.	currently employ any workers in H-1B visa status? (temporary, professional work visa status)		
2.	currently employ any workers in TN visa status? (temporary work visa status for Canadians and Mexicans)		
3.	currently employ any workers in L-1 visa status? (temporary work visa status for intracompany transferees)		
4.	currently employ any workers in E-3 visa status? (temporary work visa status for Australians)		
5.	currently employ any workers in H-1B1 visa status? (temporary work visa status for professionals from Singapore or Chile)		
6.	currently employ any workers (including managers) in an E visa status? (treaty-based temporary work visa status)		
7.	currently employ any workers in F-1, Optional Practical Training status? (recent graduates who are issued work authorization for up to 12 months)		
8.	have either outstanding offers to, or accepted offers of employment from, foreign nationals who will require employer sponsorship? (H-1B transfers, F-1 visa holders, or other new hires)		
9.	currently sponsor foreign national employees for permanent residence based on employment with the Company?		
10.	currently employ any workers whose work authorization is based on existing employment-based permanent residence cases ("portability")?		
11.	currently sponsor any workers in any other visa category, such as H-2A or H-2B? (seasonal agricultural or nonagricultural workers)		

A. FOR CURRENT EMPLOYEES

General Employee Immigration Information

Name	Position	Date of Hire	Present Status	In Permanent Residence Process?
			H-1B; TN; L-1A or L-1B; E-1, 2 or 3; H-1B1; or Adjustment Applicant	Yes or No—Include description/status of case

B. FOR CANDIDATES WITH EITHER OUTSTANDING OR ACCEPTED OFFERS OF EMPLOYMENT/NOT YET WITH THE COMPANY

General Candidate Immigration Information

Name	Position	Proposed Start Date	Present Status	Required Immigration Filings in Process?
			H-1B; TN; L-1A or L-1B; E-1, 2 or 3; H-1B1; or Adjustment Applicant	Yes or No—Include description/status of case

THE MUSHROOM PATCH OF STATE IMMIGRATION LAWS—
A MAD HATTER'S WONDERLAND FOR EMPLOYERS
by Nancy-Jo Merritt and Anthony E. Weigel[*]

In the Lewis Carroll classic, *Alice's Adventures in Wonderland*, the story's main character, Alice, journeys down a rabbit hole and ends up in a place where logic, reason, and any semblance of order no longer exist.[1] As the story progresses, Alice nibbles a bit of mushroom, takes a seat at a table with an odd lot of characters, and is presented with answerless riddles, the likes of which she had never before heard.[2]

Anyone examining state-level employment eligibility verification laws and policies that place additional requirements on government contractors, recipients of government funding, and multistate employers has good reason to feel that he or she, too, has journeyed to another realm. For more than 20 years, employers have based employment eligibility policies and procedures around the federal government's "I-9" requirements set forth by the Immigration Reform and Control Act of 1986 (IRCA).[3] Over the last several years, states have begun to create their own schemes and plans to monitor or control the hiring practices of employers.[4] Some now require govern-

---

[*] **Nancy-Jo Merritt,** a director in the Phoenix office of Fennemore Craig, P.C., has more than two decades of practice in the field of immigration law. Her practice is broad-based and includes the representation of domestic and international companies regarding visa and work authorization issues for foreign national employees. She also assists employers with federal compliance issues in the contexts of mergers and acquisitions and government audits. Ms. Merritt has been successful in challenging the federal government's interpretation of immigration law in a number of matters, and received the first award of fees in the United States from an immigration judge under the Equal Access to Justice Act. Ms. Merritt is the author of *Understanding Immigration Law: How to Enter, Work and Live in the United States*. She publishes frequently and serves as a senior editor of AILA's *Immigration & Nationality Law Handbook*, published annually. She also lectures frequently on U.S. immigration law, most frequently on issues relating to employers.

Anthony E. Weigel practices immigration law at Husch Blackwell Sanders, LLP in Kansas City, MO, and is a member of AILA. His practice focuses on employer compliance and employment-based immigration. Prior to practicing law, Mr. Weigel worked in human resources and was responsible for coordinating immigration matters and a broad spectrum of employment law compliance issues, including I-9 verifications and record retention.

[1] A directory to the full text of Alice's Adventures in Wonderland is *available at www.cs.indiana.edu/metastuff/wonder/wonderdir.html*.

[2] *www.cs.indiana.edu/metastuff/wonder/ch6.html*.

[3] Pub. L. No. 99-603, 100 Stat. 3359.

[4] For purposes of this article, the focus is only on state-level measures. According to the Fair Immigration Reform Movement's listing maintained on their website, *www.fairimmigration.org*, as of July 23, 2007, the following jurisdictions have enacted employment eligibility verification requirements: **Contractor/Public Finance**—Apple Valley, CA; Mission Viejo, CA; Cape Coral, FL; Lawrenceville, GA; O'Fallon, MO; and Lincoln County, NC. **All Employers**—Athens, AL; Lake Havasu City, AZ; Payson, AZ; Apple Valley, CA; Lancaster, CA; Santa Clarita, CA; Valley Park, MO; Suffolk County, NY; Bellaire, OH; Inola, OK; Oologah, OK; Tulsa, OK; Altoona, PA; Bridgeport, PA; Gilberton, PA; Hazelton, PA; Mahoney City, PA; West Hazelton, PA; Beaufort County, SC; Pickens County, SC; and Green

ment contractors to use U.S. Citizenship and Immigration Services' "E-Verify" program, formerly known as the "Basic Pilot" program, to verify their employees' work authorization status. Other states have added an extra level of punishment to employers with improperly hired foreign-national employees. Employers will be as dismayed as Alice as they attempt to map a compliance strategy to bridge the widely varying provisions established by state governments.

The challenge: How do affected employers subject to both federal and state laws governing employment verification consistently comply in a way that minimizes the risk of running afoul of widely varying laws?

Familiar Ground—Federal Requirements

Until recently, not many would have imagined the need to examine state-specific employment eligibility verification requirements. Employers needed only to focus on compliance with the familiar federal I-9 requirements.

Verification and Documentation Requirements

The core statutory requirements covering employment eligibility verification and retention requirements, the antidiscrimination rules, and limitations on use of the I-9 forms and data are as follows:

- An employer cannot hire, recruit, or refer for a fee an individual[5] knowing the person is not authorized to work in the United States.[6]

- Employees and employers must comply with employment verification requirements, using the I-9 form.[7]

- An employer may not continue to employ an individual in the United States knowing he or she is (or has become) unauthorized to work.[8]

- An employer may not attempt to contract or otherwise agree with another party to obtain the labor of an individual knowing that he or she is not authorized to work in the United States.[9]

Bay, WI. These types of ordinances typically duplicate the federal prohibition on employing unauthorized workers, but penalties range from suspension or revocation of business licenses to monetary fines. In many cases, applications for business licenses and permits require an employer's certification that it complies with the law and does not employ unauthorized workers.

[5] The statute uses the term "alien." INA §274A(a)(1)(A); 8 USC §1324a(a)(1)(A). The term "alien" means any person not a citizen or national of the United States. INA §101(a)(3); 8 USC §1101(a)(3). In this article, an "alien" in the statutory sense will be referred to as a person or individual, unless he, she, or it entered the United States through the atmosphere via spacecraft.

[6] INA §274A(a)(1)(A); 8 USC §1324a(a)(1)(A).

[7] INA §274A(a)(1)(B)(i); 8 USC §1324a(a)(1)(B)(i).

[8] INA §274A(a)(2); 8 USC §1324a(a)(2).

[9] INA §274A(a)(4); 8 USC §1324a(a)(4).

- An employer must attest, under the penalty of perjury, that it has verified that an individual is authorized to work in the United States after examining the appropriate documents.[10]

- Each newly hired employee must attest, under penalty of perjury, he or she is either: (1) a citizen or national of the United States, (2) a person lawfully admitted for permanent residence, or (3) a person who is otherwise authorized to work in the United States.[11]

- An employer complies with federal law if the document or documents presented by the employee reasonably appear to be genuine, and an individual complies if he or she provides a document or combination of documents that reasonably appear to be genuine and meet the I-9 form requirements.[12]

- Federal law limits the use of I-9 forms, and any information contained therein or appended thereto, to the enforcement of IRCA and for enforcement of other specific sections of federal law. *The I-9 and its associated information may not be used for any other purpose.*[13]

To a great extent, the associated federal regulations mirror the specific text of the statute. Significant regulations relating to prohibited activities and employment verification procedures are:

- *Employee* means an individual who provides services or labor for an employer for wages or other remuneration, *but does not mean independent contractors* or those engaged in casual domestic employment.[14]

- *Employer* means a person or entity, including an agent or anyone acting directly or indirectly in the interest thereof, who engages the services or labor of an employee to be performed in the United States for wages or other remuneration. In the case of an independent contractor or contract labor or services, the term employer means the independent contractor or contractor *and not the person or entity using the contract labor*.[15]

- *Independent contractor* includes individuals or entities that carry on independent business, contract to do a piece of work according to their own means and methods, and are subject to control only as to results. Whether an individual or entity is an independent contractor, regardless of what the individual or entity calls itself, will be determined on a case-by-case basis.[16]

- *Knowing* includes not only actual knowledge but also knowledge that may fairly be inferred through notice of certain facts and circumstances that would

---

[10] INA §274A(b)(1)(A); 8 USC §1324a(b)(1)(A).

[11] INA §274A(b)(2); 8 USC §1324a(b)(2).

[12] INA §274A(b)(1)(D); 8 USC §1324a(b)(1)(D).

[13] INA §274A(b)(5); 8 USC §1324a(b)(5).

[14] 8 CFR §274a.1(f) (emphasis added).

[15] 8 CFR §274a.1(g) (emphasis added).

[16] 8 CFR §274a.1(j).

lead a person, through the exercise of reasonable care, to know about a certain condition. The regulation contains several examples.[17]

- *Knowledge that an employee is unauthorized may not be inferred from an employee's foreign appearance or accent.* An employer may not request more or different documents than are required or to refuse honor documents tendered that on their face reasonably appear to be genuine and to relate to the individual.[18]

Anti-Discrimination Provisions—As a counterbalance to the employment eligibility verification procedures, Congress enacted measures to prevent discriminatory treatment against those who "looked or sounded foreign."

- *General rule*—It is an unfair immigration-related employment practice for an employer to discriminate against any individual (other than an "unauthorized alien") with respect to the hiring, or recruitment or referral for a fee, of the individual for employment or the discharging of the individual from employment because of: (1) an individual's national origin, or (2) a protected individual's citizenship status.[19]

- *Document Abuse*—An employer's request, for purposes of satisfying the I-9 requirements, for more or different documents than are required or refusing to honor documents tendered that on their face reasonably appear to be genuine is treated as an unfair immigration-related employment practice if made for the purpose or with the intent of discriminating against an individual.[20]

Optional Measures—In addition to the 1986 IRCA provisions, the federal government enacted provisions in 1996 that created the optional "Basic Pilot" program, now known as E-Verify.[21] Other optional programs include the government's IMAGE program,[22] an extensive set of measures available to employers that has not been widely utilized.[23]

Federal Enforcement Procedures—The federal statutes and regulations also set forth specific procedures for making complaints and to determine whether or not an employer has violated IRCA. The statute requires the federal government to investigate complaints that, on their face, have a substantial probability of validity.[24] After

---

[17] 8 CFR §274a.1(*l*).

[18] 8 CFR §274a.1(*l*)(2).

[19] INA §274B(a)(1); 8 USC §1324b(a)(1).

[20] INA §274B(a)(6); 8 USC §1324b(a)(6).

[21] For information about E-Verify, follow the link to E-Verify from the website of U.S. Citizenship and Immigration Services, at *www.uscis.gov*. *See* R. Tsai, "IRCA—Twenty Years Later," in this publication.

[22] IMAGE is an acronym for ICE Mutual Agreement between Government and Employers. *See www.ice.gov/partners/opaimage*.

[23] *See* T. Weigel, "Thinking Twice About Partnering with ICE—An Analysis of ICE's Best Hiring Practices and IMAGE," *available at www.ilw.com/articles/2007,0130-weigel.shtm*.

[24] INA §274A(e)(1); 8 USC §1324a(e)(1); *see also* 8 CFR §274a.9(a):

investigation, U.S. Immigration and Customs Enforcement (ICE) may issue a warning notice or a notice of intent to fine.[25] The notice of intent to fine contains the basis for the notice, a designation of the charges against the employer, the statutory provisions alleged to have been violated, and the penalty that will be imposed.[26]

Additionally, for investigations conducted after September 30, 1996, ICE should defer issuance of a notice of intent to fine until the employer has been given notice of technical or procedural I-9 verification failures and is provided with at least 10 business days to cure the deficiencies.[27] There is also a specific appeals process set forth under IRCA.[28]

Varying Degrees of Madness—State Measures Related to Employment Eligibility Verification

The following states currently have laws, executive orders, and policies that include state-level employment eligibility verification provisions: Arizona, Arkansas, Colorado, Georgia, Idaho, Illinois, Louisiana, Missouri, Oklahoma, Pennsylvania, Tennessee, Texas, and West Virginia. This list is by no means exhaustive and one should periodically review state law requirements to stay up to date.

As prospects for significant congressional action fade, one can expect efforts further regulating employment eligibility verification to mushroom across the country. The level to which each current or prospective measure imposes additional, conflicting burdens on employers varies from mild to mad. These measures also vary greatly in their triggers for investigations and violations, from those that penalize only employers that have violated federal law, to those that penalize an employer based upon state-based processes, or even penalize employers in the absence of any coherent process at all.[29]

Procedures for the filing of complaints. Any person or entity having knowledge of a violation or potential violation of section 274A of the [INA] may submit a signed, written complaint in person or by mail to the [Department of Homeland Security (DHS)] office having jurisdiction over the business or residence of the potential violator. The signed, written complaint must contain sufficient information to identify both the complainant and the potential violator, including their names and addresses. The complaint should also contain detailed factual allegations relating to the potential violation including the date, time and place of the alleged violation and the specific act or conduct alleged to constitute a violation of the [INA]. Written complaints may be delivered either by mail to the appropriate[DHS] office or by personally appearing before any immigration officer at a [DHS] office.).

---

[25] 8 CFR §§274a.9(c), 1274a.9(c).

[26] 8 CFR §§274a.9(d)(1), 1274a.9(d)(1).

[27] INA §274A(b)(6); 8 USC §1324a(b)(6).

[28] INA §274A(e)(7); 8 USC §1324a(e)(7).

[29] *State or Local Inquiries and Determinations of Employment Authorization*—Arizona's and Oklahoma's legislation provides for state determinations about an employee's immigration status. However, both of these states have incorporated a particular section of federal statute, 8 USC §1373, to aid in these determinations. Arizona's law attempts to authorize state officials the power, pursuant to 8 USC §1373, to verify work authorization to determine violations of the employer sanctions law. Ariz. Rev. Stat. §23-212(B). Oklahoma's law is similar in that it claims that

The following sections are intended to highlight and analyze certain aspects of various state measures. Please refer to appendices A, B, and C of this article for summaries of state-level employment eligibility verification measures in place as of the date of this writing affecting government contractors, recipients of public financing, and all employers within a particular state.

Government Contractors

The policy goal of measures affecting government contractors is that state governments should not do business with companies who violate immigration laws. Few would disagree with this policy goal, but the measures to ensure this outcome vary.

Minimally Intrusive

Arkansas and Idaho have minimally invasive measures that mildly affect a targeted employer's federal immigration compliance program.

Arkansas' law[30] adds conditions to contracts, including subcontracts, for provision of services to the state and covers any person contracting with a state agency for professional, technical, or general services or construction for contracts of $25,000 or

---

8 USC §1373 delegates an exercise of authority to verify citizenship or immigration status, primarily for purposes of state contractor compliance. H.B. 1804, §7 (Okla. 2007) (codified at Okla. Stat. tit. 25, §1313, applicable to contracts entered into after July 1, 2008).

The text of 8 USC §1373 reads (emphasis added):

(a) **In general.** Notwithstanding any other provision of Federal, State, or local law, a Federal, State, or local government entity or official *may not prohibit, or in any way restrict*, any government entity or official from sending to, or receiving from, the Immigration and Naturalization Service information regarding the citizenship or immigration status, lawful or unlawful, of any individual.

(b) **Additional authority of government entities.** Notwithstanding any other provision of Federal, State, or local law, *no person or agency may prohibit, or in any way restrict*, a Federal, State, or local government entity from doing any of the following with respect to information regarding the immigration status, lawful or unlawful, of any individual:

(1) Sending such information to, or requesting or receiving such information from, the Immigration and Naturalization Service.

(2) Maintaining such information.

(3) Exchanging such information with any other Federal, State, or local government entity.

(c) **Obligation to respond to inquiries.**

The Immigration and Naturalization Service shall respond to an inquiry by a Federal, State, or local government agency, seeking to verify or ascertain the citizenship or immigration status of any individual *within the jurisdiction of the agency* for any purpose *authorized by law*, by providing the requested verification or status information.

The text of this statute suggests two things. One, it does not explicitly authorize a state or local government to take action. Instead, the text suggests that Congress intended to prevent state and local governments from placing limits on their employees from contacting the immigration service. And two, the state or local agency must have legal authority to make a query regarding status for employment authorization purposes. If, for example, Arizona's law is struck by the courts, there would be no explicit authorization for employment authorization queries.

[30] Ark. Code Ann. §19-11-105.

greater in value. Contractors may not knowingly employ "illegal immigrants" or knowingly use subcontractors who employ or contract with "illegal immigrants." There are certification requirements in place for contractors and subcontractors, and contractors are provided with a 60-day cure period for potential violations. Potential penalties are actual damages to the state. Arkansas' law is unique because of the $25,000 threshold and 60-day cure period.

Idaho's Executive Order 2006-40 adds conditions to contracts for provision of services to the state. The order requires a contractor to warrant: (1) it does not knowingly hire or engage any "illegal aliens" or unauthorized workers; and (2) it takes steps to verify work authorization of new hires and otherwise to engage persons authorized to work in the United States. Misrepresentation or employment of unauthorized workers is a material breach and cause for termination. There is some uncertainty as to whether the unknowing employment of an unauthorized worker would trigger sanctions, so the reasonableness of this measure depends upon enforcement.

An affected employer should be able to comply with these measures if it has a solid, basic compliance program in place with respect to its employees and use of subcontractors.

Significantly Intrusive

Colorado and Georgia have intrusive measures that may significantly affect a targeted employer's federal immigration compliance program and require modifications to the I-9 process.

Colorado's House Bill 06-1343, as amended by House Bill 07-1073,[31] requires contractors who provide services to any level of state or local government to use E-Verify to verify the work authorization of all employees newly hired in the United States. In addition, contractors may not knowingly employ "illegal aliens" or knowingly contract with a subcontractor who knowingly employs or contracts with an "illegal alien" to perform work under the contract. Prior to executing a state/local contract for services, the contractor must certify: (1) it does not knowingly employ or contract with an "illegal alien"; and (2) it has participated (or attempted to do so) in Basic Pilot/E-Verify to verify the work authorization of all employees newly hired in the United States. If a contractor obtains actual knowledge that a subcontractor has employed "illegal aliens" on the project, it must give the subcontractor three days to prove it has not done so and terminate the relationship if proof is not available. A contractor must provide documentation of its employees' immigration/work authorization status, if requested. Penalties include termination of the contract, actual and consequential damages, and listing of the contractor's name as a violator of state immigration law on the Colorado secretary of state's website for a period of two years.

Georgia's law[32] includes a phased-in requirement for contractors and subcontractors to register and use E-Verify, based upon size of the employer.[33] The law covers

---

[31] Codified at Colo. Rev. Stat. §§8-17.5-101, 8-17.5-102.

[32] Ga. S.B. 529 (2006), *available at www.legis.ga.gov/legis/2005_06/fulltext/sb529.htm*. Codified at Ga. Code Ann. §§13-10-90, 13-10-91, 16-5-46, 35-2-14, 42-4-14, 43-20A-1 to 42-20A-4, and 48-7-21.1.

contractors providing physical performance of services within the state to any level of government.[34] Penalties include loss of the contract based upon a presumption of misrepresentation, and loss of the ability to contract with state or local governments.

The questionable aspects of both laws are the extent to which each applies to an employer's operations outside of the state and the legal basis for the right of state government to request or inspect I-9 forms, in light of IRCA's explicit restrictions. To date, there have been no legal challenges to either state's laws.

Just Plain "Mad as a Hatter"

Missouri, Oklahoma, and Tennessee have measures that may drastically affect a targeted employer's federal immigration compliance program, and so require special attention.

The Missouri statute[35] attempts to authorize state agencies to determine whether a contractor or subcontractor has violated IRCA and to punish contractors. A state agency contracting for the work may make a determination based on "reasonable evidence" that a contractor hired at least one unauthorized worker. If such a determination is made, the agency can attempt to cause the contractor to fire the unauthorized workers. In addition, the agency may withhold up to 20 percent of the total contract. The statute also states if a state agency, based on "reasonable evidence," determines that a contractor has engaged a subcontractor to complete work required by the contract with knowledge that the subcontractor violated or *intended* to violate IRCA, the state agency may withhold from the contractor up to double the amount caused to be withheld from payments to the subcontractor. A contractor or subcontractor may be barred for up to two years from state contracts for violating this statute. Two of the more troubling aspects of this statute are the ambiguous standard of "reasonable evidence" as applied by any state agency, and punishing a party for *intended* violations of IRCA.

Missouri Executive Order 07-13[36] adds conditions to contracts for the provision of services to the state. Contractors doing business with the state must make various certifications to the state. They must certify that *all current employees* are authorized to work in the United States. Future contract holders must certify they do not knowingly employ unauthorized workers. And all contract holders must certify that any employee assigned to perform services under the contract is eligible to work in the United States. The form of certification also requires the ambiguously phrased "use of personnel" will be in accordance with applicable federal and state laws. Penalties include termination of contracts and possible debarment from state contracts.

Given the structural deficiencies within the executive order and the nature of the state's enforcement actions, it is very difficult to discern any set processes or stan-

---

[33] Ga. Code Ann. §13-10-91.

[34] *See id.*

[35] Mo. Rev. Stat. §8.283.

[36] *Available at www.gov.mo.gov/eo/2007/eo07_013.htm.*

dards. The executive order contains internally inconsistent certification requirements, and the form of certification sent out by the state's Office of Administration for current contractor certification is overly broad in its reference to "use of personnel," which may or may not include subcontractors.

Based on reports of two enforcement actions, the state provides minimal due process. In March 2007 in Jefferson City, MO, an enforcement action was taken against a contractor that had been doing business with the state for nearly nine years. On the basis of a rumor, the state contacted ICE to investigate the rumor, which resulted in an ICE raid. The company's contract was immediately terminated. When the contract was terminated, there had been no finding that the employer violated federal law, and there was no belief it violated state law. On October 25, 2007, the contractor filed suit against the Missouri and its governor, alleging wrongful termination of the contracts.[37]

In May 2007, George's Processing, a Butterfield, MO, poultry processing plant, was the subject of an ICE raid. Governor Matt Blunt immediately revoked the employer's contracts and barred it from doing any future business with the state.[38] When the contracts were terminated, there had been no charge or finding that the employer violated federal immigration law. Additionally, the state disregarded the rebuttable presumption created by use of E-Verify/Basic Pilot, under which an employer is presumed not to have violated federal law.[39]

In Oklahoma, the law[40] mandates that state contractors and subcontractors use a "Status Verification System." The law covers contractors and subcontractors, *including contract employees and staffing agencies*, that provide physical performance of services within the state to any level of government. As of July 1, 2008, targeted employers must register and utilize E-Verify or another "Status Verification System" to verify the work eligibility status of all new employees. Based on a legal presumption that the employer is in breach of contract for misrepresentation, an employer failing to comply faces loss of the contract and of the ability to contract with state or local governments.

---

[37] "Lawsuit Claims Race Discrimination, Abuse of Power by Blunt," *available at www.wibw.com/home/headlines/10806191.html*.

[38] "Governor Cancels Contract with Poultry Plant," *available at http://ozarksfirst.com/content/fulltext/?cid=7704*.

[39] According to the employer's agreement with the federal government, proper use of the Basic Pilot/E-Verify system should serve as a protection under state and local laws. Specifically, the model E-Verify memorandum of understanding signed by DHS, SSA, and the employer states: *no person or entity participating in E-Verify is civilly or criminally liable under any law for any action taken in good faith on information provided through the confirmation system.* Model E-Verify Memorandum of Understanding, art. II.C.6(5), *available at www.uscis.gov/files/nativedocuments/MOU.pdf*. An employer that has adopted use of E-Verify in Missouri could claim this protection in response to any type of state enforcement efforts.

[40] H.B. 1804, §§6, 7 (Okla. 2007) (codified at Okla. Stat. tit. 25, §§1312, 1313; applicable to contracts entered into after July 1, 2008).

The "red flag" affected employers should note is that the Oklahoma law incorrectly lists the Social Security Administration's Social Security Number Verification Service (SSNVS) as a valid means of verifying work authorization.[41] In fact, SSNVS is only to be used to confirm information for payroll purposes, and it is illegal to use it to verify work authorization. *No negative employment action can be taken against a worker whose number cannot be verified through SSNVS!*

In Tennessee, House Bill 111[42] and Executive Order 41 add conditions to contracts for provision of services *and goods* to the state or any state entity. Contractors cannot knowingly utilize the services of "illegal immigrants" or of a subcontractor utilizing "illegal immigrants" in the performance of contracts for goods or services. If an affected employer is discovered to have knowingly utilized the services of "illegal immigrants" in performance of the contract, the following penalties apply: (1) the inability to contract or bid on state contracts for one year from date of discovery; and (2) the possible termination of the contract and monetary penalties.[43] Contractors must provide an initial attestation that they comply with this law and obtain similar certifications from subcontractors.[44] These certifications must be retained along with semi-annual updates of the attestation for inspection by the state. Contractors must also agree to comply with random state audits, *which include the contractors' and subcontractors' personnel records!*

There are maddening aspects of Tennesee's measures that require special attention. The inclusion of "goods" is uncommon for these types of laws, as it arguably attempts to regulate an employer's activities beyond the state's borders. The utilization of suspicionless audits is troubling, especially the extension of searches to personnel records.

Government-Aid Recipients

The policy goal of measures affecting government-aid recipients is similar to that for measures targeting government contractors: state governments should not aid companies who violate immigration laws. Again, few would disagree with this policy goal, but the measures to ensure this outcome vary.

Minimally Intrusive

Pennsylvania and Texas have minimally invasive measures that mildly affect a targeted employer's federal immigration compliance program.

Pennsylvania House Bill 2319[45] prohibits use of "illegal immigrant" labor on a project financed with any state loan or grant money. The Pennsylvania law incorporates a couple of employer-friendly features. One, an employer can attain an "affirmative defense" if: (a) it obtains certification from a contractor that it complies

---

[41] Okla. Stat. tit. 25, §1312.1.d.

[42] Codified at Tenn. Code Ann. §12-4-124.

[43] *Id.* §12-4-124(b).

[44] *Id.* §12-4-124(a)(3).

[45] Codified at 43 Pa. Con. Stat. §§166.1 to 166.5.

with IRCA, and (b) notifies the federal government if its contractor uses "illegal alien" labor. And two, penalties under the law, repayment of grant or loan, with penalty interest, only apply if the person is sentenced under federal law for knowingly employing an "illegal alien" on a project using state grant or loan money.

Texas House Bill 1196[46] restricts the granting of public subsidies to employers convicted of more severe violations of federal immigration law. The law applies to the broad spectrum of an employer's business structure, including any business, branch, division, or department of that business that applies for a public subsidy (any public program, benefit, or assistance) from any level of government within the state. An employer is required to certify that it and its affiliates do not and will not knowingly employ an "undocumented worker." Penalties include repayment of the subsidy, plus interest, but are only triggered if the employer is convicted under federal law for criminal or pattern/practice violations.[47]

Just Plain "Mad as a Hatter"

Colorado and Missouri have measures that may drastically affect a targeted employer's federal immigration compliance program and require special attention.

Colorado House Bill 06-1001[48] adds conditions regarding immigration compliance for employers seeking state government money (grants, loans, etc.) administered by the Colorado Economic Development Commission. The conditions are: (1) employers must only employ authorized workers and comply with IRCA in order to receive and retain state government money; (2) employers must provide proof to the state that each employee in the United States is authorized to work in the United States; and (3) the commission is granted discretion to verify compliance with IRCA. Penalties include repayment of state money and a bar to receipt of state government money for a period of five years following the date of repayment. The two troubling aspects of this law are the requirements to require proof that an employer's entire U.S. workforce is authorized, and the provision regarding the state's ability to request or inspect I-9 forms.

Missouri has two measures that are worthy of "*Wonderland*" status. One is a statute that prohibits employers in receipt of state economic incentives from the "knowing" and "negligent" employment of "illegal aliens."[49] Affected employers are to provide certification that they only employ authorized workers (no "illegal aliens"). The statute requires any applicant for such aid to affirm it "employs no illegal aliens." The penalty for "negligent" violations of the law is a five-year bar to any state aid, unless the employer is a first-time offender and eligible for a waiver of the penalty. For a "knowing" violation, an employer may be subject to *criminal prosecution* by the Missouri attorney general.

---

[46] *Available at www.capitol.state.tx.us/tlodocs/80R/billtext/pdf/HB01196F.pdf*. This bill was codified at Tex. Gov't Code §§2264.001 to 2264.101 (but note that two other laws have been codified at those sections).

[47] *See* INA §274A(f); 8 USC §1324a(f).

[48] Codified at Colo. Rev. Stat. §24-46-105.3.

[49] Mo. Rev. Stat. §285.025.

On November 16, 2007, the Missouri Housing Development Commission (MHDC) adopted an I-9 workforce eligibility policy[50] that imposes onerous requirements on developers, general contractors, and subcontractors working on state-assisted projects.[51] These requirements will become a condition to participation in future MHDC loans to developers of affordable, residential housing and financing provided through the sale of MHDC-issued tax-exempt notes and bonds. Once the state's MHDC program is up and running, based upon public statements, there are plans to expand this scheme to projects involving any funding from the Missouri Department of Economic Development (DED), which affects an even greater number of employers.[52]

The MHDC I-9 workforce eligibility policy provides:

- Developers, general contractors, and subcontractors must use E-Verify and provide written certification of current and future use the system for all new hires
- Copies of all I-9s of developers, general contractors, and subcontractors must be maintained on the construction site

---

[50] *Available at www.mhdc.com/rental_production/workforce_policy/Workforce_Eligibility_Policy.pdf.*

[51] See T. Weigel, "I-9 Compliance and Missouri State-Assisted Housing Construction—A Brave New World Of Regulation," *available at www.ilw.com/articles/2007,1204-weigel.shtm.*

[52] See "Illegal Immigration Stirs Debate During Special Session," *http://mochamber.com/mx/hm.asp?id=083107immigration;* see also Minutes of the MHDC August 17, 2007 Regular Meeting (Sept. 21, 2007), *available at www.mhdc.com/about/commission_meetings/2007_09_21_Regular_Meeting_Book_u1.pdf,* noting that Ed Martin, Governor Blunt's Chief of Staff, stated that "the Department of Economic Development was going to come up with a policy, even if it is legislatively done, that across the board, if illegal workers are used in the state of Missouri you will not receive tax credits."

The State of Missouri has already attempted to "shoot first and ask questions later" in one instance involving immigration enforcement and DED funding. On September 13, 2007, at 7:00 am, Missouri highway patrolmen arrived at a Missouri business' premises and requested to check the identities of 19 Hispanic employees of a contractor's 180 employees on site. The names were sent to ICE to verify the status of the workers. The basis for such an inquiry was an anonymous tip from a former employee through a local state legislator. The substance of the complaint was that there were possibly some illegal immigrants working there. According to reports, the business (using a contractor for a kiln project) received DED funds to train its own workers, but no state funds were involved in the kiln project. In spite of the attenuated relationship between the state funds and the alleged activities of an independent contractor, the DED immediately began investigating whether the training funds could be in jeopardy if unauthorized workers were employed by the contractor for work on the business' premises. On October 29, 2007, it was reported that ICE did not investigate this matter further because there wasn't enough evidence of wrongdoing. The damage, however, has been done to the reputations of the Missouri business and the subcontractor. If one does an Internet search of either company's name and the word "illegal," dozens of hits surface that repeat the allegations. One has to search and read a little closer to find that neither employer was prosecuted by the federal government for violations of federal law. *See, e.g.,* A. Pierceall, "Troopers Checking on Status of Contracted Workers at Hannibal Plant," *Quincy Herald Whig,* Sept. 13, 2007, *available at www.whig.com/289818622230489.php*; "State Investigating Whether Construction Workers are Illegal Immigrants," *St. Louis Post-Dispatch,* Sept. 13, 2007; R. Hart & A. Pierceall, "State Troopers Detain Contracted Workers at Hannibal Plant," *Quincy Herald Whig,* Sept. 12, 2007, *available at www.whig.com/358120106054601.php*; D. Henley, "MSHP: One Illegal Immigrant Found Working at Continental Cement," *The Hannibal Courier-Post,* Sept. 14, 2007; and C. Leonard, "Immigration Plan Worries Some Businesses," Oct. 29, 2007.

- General contractors must verify the employment eligibility of subcontractors' employees
- Mandatory notification of multiple law enforcement entities in cases in which there are "*concerns*" that unauthorized workers are on a construction site
- The developer is assigned the burden of proof to show compliance with the policy
- MHDC must be provided with contractors' and subcontractors' I-9 records, payroll, benefits, tax, and employee information

The policy's penalty provisions are:

- Developers, general contractors, and subcontractors may be barred from MHDC programs for one year to life. This includes the legal entity, key principals, *and any individual who had or should have had knowledge of a violation of the policy.*
- Sanctions may also include fines and penalties (including *criminal* penalties) set forth by Mo. Rev. Stat. §285.025.
- In cases involving MHDC tax credits, collection of liquidated damages against the developer and a bar to approval of new money for a project subject to sanctions above the amounts initially agreed upon.

Employers affected by these measures in Colorado and Missouri clearly have to take into account employment eligibility verification requirements that drastically depart from IRCA.

All Employers

In an effort to "do something" about illegal immigration, several states have responded with measures that impact every employer within state lines.

Significantly Intrusive Measures

Colorado, again, has an intrusive measure that may significantly affect a targeted employer's federal immigration compliance program and require modifications to the I-9 process. Colorado's House Bill 06-1017[53] requires the completion of an "Affirmation of Work Status" form[54] to be completed by every Colorado employer with respect to each new employee within 20 days of hiring the new employee. The law also requires an employer to make copies of the documents used to satisfy the federal government's I-9 form, even though federal law does not require that copies of such documents be made or retained.[55] One questionable aspect of this law is that federal

---

[53] Codified at Colo. Rev. Stat. §8-2-122.

[54] The form is available at *www.coworkforce.com/lab/AffirmationForm.pdf*.

[55] INA §274A(b)(4); 8 USC §1324a(b)(4): **Copying of documentation permitted.**—Notwithstanding any other provision of law, the person or entity may copy a document presented by an individual pursuant to this subsection and may retain the copy, but only (except as otherwise permitted under law) for the purpose of complying with the requirements of this subsection.

law limits the use of I-9 forms, any information contained therein, or appended thereto, to the enforcement of IRCA and other specific sections of federal law.[56] The form and its associated information may not be used for any other purpose.[57] Another questionable aspect of the law is the fines of $5,000 for a first offense and up to $25,000 for subsequent offenses.

While one may question the incursion Colorado has made into the area of federal immigration law, there are much more onerous laws.

Just Plain "Mad as a Hatter"

Arizona, Illinois, Louisiana, Tennessee, and West Virginia all have measures that may drastically affect a targeted employer's federal immigration compliance program. These measures require special attention. Some states have adopted provisions that may well be preempted by federal law, while others have attempted to skirt the contours of IRCA and make the most out of the apparent ambiguity surrounding the preemption exemption "loophole" of INA §274A(h)(2) [8 USC §1324a(h)(2)]:

> **Preemption**.—The provisions of this section [INA §274A; 8 USC §1324a] preempt any State or local law imposing civil or criminal sanctions (other than through licensing and similar laws) upon those who employ or recruit or refer for a fee for employment, unauthorized aliens.

Arizona has attempted to take advantage of this provision by requiring employers to comply with a complex, complaint-driven process directed by the attorney general or county attorney.[58] The process involves state and local inquiries of the federal government to verify an employee's work authorization, well after an employer has completed its I-9 process. Penalties include suspending the employer's business licenses for a first offense and permanently revoking all licenses held by the employer at the employer's primary place of business for a second offense.[59] "Licenses" are defined broadly to include:

> any agency permit, certificate, approval, registration, charter or similar form of authorization that is issued by any agency for the purposes of operating a business in this state.[60]

Thus, among the licenses to be revoked are articles of incorporation, partnership, any transaction privilege, tax license, or grant of authority to operate a business. The only licenses excluded are professional licenses and those dealing with two critical public resources, the environment and water. The punishment set forth by the statute has been called the "business death penalty."

---

[56] INA §274A(b)(5); 8 USC §1324a(b)(5).
[57] INA §274A(b)(5); 8 USC §1324a(b)(5).
[58] *See* Ariz. Rev. Stat. Ann. §§23-211 to 23-214, 41-2505.
[59] *Id.* §23-212(F).
[60] *Id.* §23-211(7)(a).

Of note, Arizona is the first state to require all employers to use E-Verify,[61] although there is no penalty for failing to enroll. Instead, the statute extends a carrot: use of E-Verify provides a rebuttable presumption that the hire decision did not violate the statute.[62] Although efforts to stop the implementation of the law failed, the litigation challenging this law continues and the outcome remains uncertain.

Tennessee has taken a similar approach to Arizona, but does not require employers to use E-Verify. Senate Bill 903[63] adds a duplicative state requirement that employers may not knowingly employ, recruit, or refer for a fee an "illegal alien" (someone lacking working authorization in the United States). Complaints may come from any state or local agency or associated party with "reason to believe" an employer is in violation of the state's law. The complaint-driven process is directed by the commissioner of labor and workforce development. After notice and a hearing, an employer can be found in violation of the state's law. The penalty for the first offense is suspension of business licenses until employer evidences it no longer employs "illegal aliens." If an employer is found to have violated law within three years of first offense, then employer's business licenses will be suspended for one year. However, the state does offer limited "safe harbor" protection if the employment authorization of the employee in question was confirmed using E-Verify.

There are two questionable aspects of Tennessee's law. One is the duplicative prohibition on employing unauthorized workers. The second is the creation of the state-level processes and penalties in the absence of a federal finding that an employer violated IRCA.

On the other end of the spectrum, Illinois's House Bill 1744[64] prohibits employers from using E-Verify until the system reaches an almost impossible performance standard. Interestingly enough, in September 2007, the U.S. Department of Homeland Security (DHS) sued to have the Illinois law struck down on the basis of federal preemption.[65] As of this writing, the State of Illinois and DHS have reached an agreement that the state will not attempt to enforce this law until the conclusion of the lawsuit.[66]

If there were a Mad Hatter's Award for the most perplexing state-level immigration law, the laws of Louisiana and West Virginia would be among the top nominees.

The first runner-up would be Louisiana Senate Bill 753,[67] which creates state-level offenses and penalties for employing unauthorized workers for employers with more than 10 employees. Under this law, employers may not knowingly employ an "undocumented alien." If an agency somehow determines a violation of the law, it may

---

[61] *Id.* §23-214.

[62] *Id.* §23-212(I).

[63] Codified at Tenn. Code Ann. §§50-1-101, 50-1-103.

[64] Codified at 820 Ill. Comp. Stat. 55/12.

[65] The complaint can be accessed at *www.dhs.gov/xlibrary/assets/US_v_Illinois_Complaint_092407_to_File.pdf*.

[66] Notice for Illinois Employers about E-Verify, *www.dhs.gov/ximgtn/programs/gc_1199120920203.shtm*.

[67] Codified at La. Rev. Stat. Ann. §23:996.

notify the Louisiana attorney general or district attorney of a violation. Also, investigations may be initiated by an agency or by a private party's written statement. Penalties include the issuance of a "cease and desist" order to end the employment. If failure to comply with an order, and a court subsequently finds a violation of the order, an employer is subject to a fine up to $10,000 and/or suspension or revocation of business licenses.

The winner of the Mad Hatter's Award would be West Virginia Senate Bill 70.[68] It creates state-level offenses and penalties for employing unauthorized workers, *but most critically provides for confinement of employers for violating the state law*![69] West Virginia's law covers any person who employs *or seeks to employ* an individual within West Virginia.[70] It prohibits an employer from knowingly employing, hiring, recruiting, or referring an unauthorized worker.[71] Additionally, employers must verify a prospective employee's legal status or authorization to work *prior to employing the individual, or "contracting with the individual for employment services."*[72] Also in West Virginia's favor is a provision that subjects employers to state investigations by the labor commissioner, who may be able to request I-9 forms.[73]

Without a doubt, the centerpiece of West Virginia's law is the penalties.

- For a knowing violation for employing unauthorized workers, the penalties are:
    - First offense—fine ranging from $100 to $1,000, per violation
    - Second offense—fine ranging from $500 to $5,000, per violation
    - Third or subsequent offense—fine ranging from $1,000 to $10,000 per violation and/or confinement in jail from 30 days to one year
    - Conviction of a third or subsequent offense—an employer may have its business licenses (state and local) revoked or suspended, after notice and a hearing
- The penalties for knowingly providing false records about an employee's status or work authorization (a misdemeanor) are up to one year of confinement and/or a fine of up to $2,500.
- The penalties for the knowing and willful sale/transfer of business assets to avoid liability (a misdemeanor) are up to one year of confinement and/or a fine of up to $10,000.

The law does not specify exactly how to confine an employer beyond the scope of a sole proprietor, but in Wonderland anything is possible.

Conclusion

---

[68] Amending W.Va. Code §§21-1B-2, 21-1B-3, and 21-1B-5, and adding W. Va. Code §§21-1B-6, 21-1B-7.
[69] *Id.* §§21-1B-5(a)(3), (b), and (c).
[70] *Id.* §21-1B-2(a).
[71] *Id.* §21-1B-3(a).
[72] *Id.* §21-1B-3(b).
[73] *Id.* §21-1B-3(d).

The Mushroom Patch of State Immigration Laws

Outlining a compliance strategy to cover measures like Colorado's questionable "affirmation" requirement, Arizona's mandated use of E-Verify, and Illinois's bar against using E-Verify is troubling. Most distressing are the hostile and overly-punitive tactics employed in certain states, where the calling to "do something" far exceeds reason. In these states, ignorance of congressional mandates, like IRCA, and constitutional protections from unreasonable government actions should be cause for great concern.

Affected employers and their lawyers are being forced to grapple with answerless riddles. The following is a parody of an inquisitorial portion of *Alice's Adventures in Wonderland*.[74]

> The Hatter opened his eyes very wide during the immigration enforcement hearing but all he *SAID* was, "Can you explain why you can't comply with this state's law and all other applicable laws, federal and state?"
>
> "Come, we shall have some fun now!" thought Alice the Employer. "I'm glad they've begun asking riddles. —I believe I can guess that," she added aloud.
>
> "Do you mean that you think you can find out the answer to it?" said the March Hare.
>
> "Exactly so," said the Employer.
>
> "Then you should say what you mean," the March Hare went on.
>
> "I do," the Employer hastily replied; "at least—at least I mean what I say—that's the same thing, you know."
>
> "Not the same thing a bit!" said the Hatter. "You might just as well say that 'You I-9 your new employees in Colorado the same as you I-9 your new employees in Kansas' is the same thing as 'You I-9 your new employees in Kansas the same as you I-9 new employees in Colorado'!"
>
> "You might just as well say," added the March Hare, "that 'You I-9 your new employees in West Virginia the same as you I-9 your new employees in Arkansas' is the same thing as 'You I-9 your new employees in Arkansas the same as you I-9 your new employees in West Virginia'!"

---

[74] The original text, in chapter 7, reads:

> The Hatter opened his eyes very wide on hearing this; but all he *SAID* was, "Why is a raven like a writing-desk?" "Come, we shall have some fun now!" thought Alice. "I'm glad they've begun asking riddles. —I believe I can guess that," she added aloud. "Do you mean that you think you can find out the answer to it?" said the March Hare. "Exactly so," said Alice. "Then you should say what you mean," the March Hare went on. "I do," Alice hastily replied; "at least—at least I mean what I say—that's the same thing, you know." "Not the same thing a bit!" said the Hatter. "You might just as well say that 'I see what I eat' is the same thing as 'I eat what I see'!" "You might just as well say," added the March Hare, "that 'I like what I get' is the same thing as 'I get what I like'!" "You might just as well say," added the Dormouse, who seemed to be talking in his sleep, "that 'I breathe when I sleep' is the same thing as 'I sleep when I breathe'!" "It IS the same thing with you," said the Hatter, and here the conversation dropped, and the party sat silent for a minute while Alice thought over all she could remember about ravens and writing-desks, which wasn't much.

"You might just as well say," added the Dormouse, who seemed to be talking in his sleep, "that 'You I-9 your new employees in Arizona the same as you I-9 your new employees in Illinois' is the same thing as 'You I-9 your new employees in Illinois the same as you I-9 your new employees in Arizona'!"

"It *IS* the same thing with you," said the Hatter, and here the conversation dropped, and the panel sat silent for a minute, while the Employer's lawyer, sitting by her side, thought over all he could remember about federal preemption and the Fourth, Fifth, and Fourteenth Amendments, which wasn't as much as he would have liked.

Inquisitions, like the parody above, are likely to become more factual, less fictional, and on full display in a state near you. An employer that fully complies with federal law may find itself stuck in more than a few rabbit holes for violating state immigration laws.

As more state-level immigration laws are passed, the level of compliance companies face increases, especially for employers with multistate operations. All employers must, without a doubt, continue to follow all federal I-9 requirements. Additionally, government contractors should identify state-specific requirements and coordinate efforts between human resources, affected managers, and contracting personnel to ensure compliance. Employers receiving any government aid should identify any immigration-related strings that may be attached and identify compliance needs. Finally, affected employers should consider litigation as a means to close the book on laws that disregard the borderline of sanity.

Appendix A—Contractor Measures

Arkansas—House Bill 1024[75] adds conditions to contracts for provision of services to the state.

Who is covered?	Any person contracting with a state agency for professional, technical, or general services or construction for contracts $25,000 or greater in value. Includes subcontractors.
What is required?	• Contractors may not knowingly employ "illegal immigrants" or knowingly use subcontractors who employ or contract with "illegal immigrants" • Contractors must certify before executing the contract that they do not employ or contract with an "illegal immigrant" • Subcontractors must submit certification that they do not employ or contract with an "illegal alien" within 30 days of executing the contract. • Contractors have 60 days to remedy violations or face termination of the contract • A contractor can terminate the relationship with a subcontractor in violation of the law
Penalties:	Actual damages to the state
Effective Date:	Enacted on 02/14/2007.

---

[75] Codified at Ark. Code Ann. §19-11-105.

Colorado—House Bill 06-1343, as amended by House Bill 07-1073,[76] adds conditions to contractors who provide services to any level of state or local government, and requires use of E-Verify.

Who is covered?	All persons holding a public contract for services with a state or local government
What is required?	• Contractors may not knowingly employ "illegal aliens" to perform work under the contract • Contractors may not knowingly contract with a subcontractor who knowingly employs or contracts with an "illegal alien" to perform work under the contract • Prior to executing a state/local contract for services, the contractor must certify: (1) it does not knowingly employ or contract with an "illegal alien," and (2) it has participated (or attempted to do so) in Basic Pilot/E-Verify to verify the work authorization of all newly hired employees in the United States. • If a contractor obtains actual knowledge that a subcontractor has employed "illegal aliens" on the project, it must give the subcontractor three days to prove it has not done so and terminate the relationship if proof is not available • A contractor must provide documentation of its employees' immigration/work authorization status, if requested
Penalties:	• Termination of the contract • Actual and consequential damages • Listing of the contractor's name as a violator of state immigration law on the secretary of state's website for a period of two years
Effective Date:	06/06/2006

---

[76] Codified at Colo. Rev. Stat. §§8-17.5-101, 8-17.5-102.

Georgia—Senate Bill 529[77] added a phased-in requirement for contractors to register and use Basic Pilot/E-Verify.

Who is covered?	Contractors and subcontractors providing physical performance of services within the state to any level of government.
What is required?	• Registration and participation in E-Verify
Penalties:	• Loss of ability to contract with state or local governments • Presume contractor or subcontractor would be in breach of contract for misrepresentation and face loss of contract
Effective Date:	• 500+ employees—07/01/2007 • 100+ employees—07/01/2008 • All others—07/01/2009

Idaho—Executive Order 2006-40,[78] among other things, adds conditions to contracts for provision of services to the state.

Who is covered?	Any employer contracting with the state for services.
What is required?	Contractor must warrant: • It does not knowingly hire or engage any "illegal aliens" or unauthorized workers • It takes steps to verify work authorization of new hires and to otherwise engage persons authorized to work in the United States.
Penalties:	Misrepresentation or employment of unauthorized workers is a material breach and cause for termination
Effective Date:	12/31/2006

---

[77] Codified at Ga. Code Ann. §§13-10-90, 13-10-91, 16-5-46, 35-2-14, 42-4-14, 43-20A-1 to 42-20A-4, and 48-7-21.1.

[78] *Available at http://gov.idaho.gov/mediacenter/execorders/eo06/eo_2006-40.html.*

Missouri—Mo. Rev. Stat §8.283 attempts to authorize state agencies to determine whether a contractor or subcontractor has violated IRCA and to punish contractors financially and by means of debarment.

Who is covered?	Contractors and subcontractors engaged to complete work for the state
What is required?	Contractors cannot violate IRCA, based upon the state agency's determination of "reasonable evidence," and cannot engage a subcontractor with knowledge that the subcontractor violated or *intended* to violate IRCA.
Penalties:	• Debarment from state contracts for up to two years • Contractors and subcontractors may have up to 20 percent of the total contract value withheld • Contractors may also lose up to two times the amounts withheld from subcontractors
Effective Date:	1998

Missouri—Executive Order 07-13[79] adds conditions to contracts for provision of services to the state.

Who is covered?	Contractors "doing business" with the state.
What is required?	• (1) current contractors must certify *all current employees* are authorized to work in the United States; (2) future contract holders must certify they do not knowingly employ unauthorized workers (an acceptable form of certification); and (3) all contract holders must certify that any employee *assigned to perform services under the contract* is eligible to work in the United States. • The form of certification also requires that the "use of personnel" will be in accordance with applicable federal and state laws
Penalties:	Termination of contracts and possible debarment from state contracts
Effective Date:	March 6, 2007

---

[79] *Available at www.gov.mo.gov/eo/2007/eo07_013.htm.*

Oklahoma—House Bill 1804,[80] among other things,[81] mandates that state contractors and subcontractors use a "Status Verification System."

Who is covered?	Contractors and subcontractors (to include contract employees and staffing agencies) providing physical performance of services within the state to any level of government.
What is required?	• Contractors and subcontractors must register and utilize E-Verify or other "Status Verification System" to verify the work eligibility status of all new employees
Penalties:	• Loss of ability to contract with state or local governments • Presume contractor or subcontractor would be in breach of contract for misrepresentation and face loss of contract
Effective Date:	Applicable to contracts entered into after 07/01/2008

---

[80] H.B. 1804, §§6, 7 (Okla. 2007) (codified at Okla. Stat. tit. 25, §§1312, 1313, applicable to contracts entered into after July 1, 2008).

[81] Section 4 of H.B. 1804, codified at Okla. Stat. tit. 21, §1550.42, imposes certain requirements upon *federal*, state, and local government employers to essentially "re-I-9" employees, if they issue ID documents. Additionally, public schools and state or *private* educational institutions that issue ID documents to administrators, faculty, or other employees will also have to re-I-9 these people, unless such ID documents are restricted to use on campus. Both requirements became effective Nov. 1, 2007.

Tennessee—House Bill 111[82] and Executive Order 41[83] add conditions to contracts for provision of goods or services to the state or any state entity.

Who is covered?	Any person who provides goods or services to the state or any state entity
What is required?	• Contractors cannot knowingly utilize the services of "illegal immigrants" in the performance of contracts for goods or services • Contractors cannot knowingly utilize a subcontractor who will utilize the services of an "illegal immigrant" in the performance of contracts for goods or services • Contractors must provide an initial attestation that they comply with this law and maintain semiannual updates of the attestation for inspection by the state • Contractors must obtain similar certifications from subcontractors and maintain semiannual updates of the attestations for inspection by the state • Contractors must comply with random audits
Penalties:	If the employer is discovered to have knowingly utilized the services of "illegal immigrants" in performance of the contract, the following penalties apply: • Inability to contract or bid on state contracts for one year from date of discovery • Possible termination of contract and monetary penalties
Effective Date:	January 1, 2007

---

[82] Codified at Tenn. Code Ann. §12-4-124.

[83] The state provides information regarding Exec. Order 41 at *www.tennessee.gov/finance/Exe_Order/index.html*.

Appendix B—Measures Related to Public Finance

Colorado—House Bill 06-1001[84] adds conditions to the receipt of state government money (grants, loans, etc.).

Who is covered?	Employers seeking state government money administered by the Colorado Economic Development Commission
What is required?	• Employers must only employ authorized workers and comply with IRCA in order to receive and retain state government money • Employers must provide proof to the state that each employee *in the United States* is authorized to work in the United States. • The commission is granted discretion to verify compliance with IRCA
Penalties:	• Repayment of state government money • Bar to receipt of state government money for five years following date of repayment
Effective Date:	10/01/2006

Missouri—Mo. Rev. Stat. §285.025 covers employment of "illegal aliens," receipt of state economic incentives, and criminal penalties.

Who is covered?	Employers seeking state money administered by a state agency
What is required?	• An employer may not "knowingly" or "negligently" employ an "illegal alien" • Certification that the employer only employs authorized workers (no "illegal aliens") and an affirmation that the employer "employs no illegal aliens"
Penalties:	• Negligent employment violation—Ineligibility for any state aid for five years, unless the employer is a first-time offender (penalty may be waived) • Knowing employment violation—Attorney general may bring *criminal charges* for violation of state statute
Effective Date:	1999

---

[84] Codified at Colo. Rev. Stat. §24-46-105.3.

Missouri—The Missouri Housing Development Commission (MHDC) has an "I-9 Workforce Eligibility Policy"[85] that imposes requirements related to its state-assisted projects.

Who is covered?	Developers, general contractors and subcontractors on state-assisted projects
What is required?	• Developers, general contractors and subcontractors must use E-Verify and provide written certification of current and future use the system for all new hires • Copies of all I-9s of developers, general contractors, and subcontractors must be maintained on the construction site • General contractors must verify the employment eligibility of subcontractors' employees • Mandatory notification of multiple law enforcement entities in cases in which there are "*concerns*" that unauthorized workers are on a construction site • Developer is assigned the burden of proof to show compliance with the I-9 policy • MHDC must be provided with contractors' and subcontractors' I-9 records, payroll, benefits, tax, and employee information
Penalties:	• Developers, general contractors, and subcontractors may be barred from MHDC programs for one year to life (includes the legal entity, key principals, *and any individual who had or should have had knowledge of a violation of the I-9 policy*) • Sanctions may also include fines and penalties (including criminal penalties) set forth by Mo. Rev. Stat. §285.025. • In cases involving MHDC tax credits, collection of liquidated damages against the developer and a bar to approval of new money for a project, subject to sanctions above the amounts initially agreed upon
Effective Date:	December 2007

---

[85] *Available at* www.mhdc.com/rental_production/workforce_policy/Workforce_Eligibility_Policy.pdf; *see* MHDC Memorandum, P. Ramsel, "Enforcement of I-9 Workforce Eligibility Policy" (Nov. 16, 2007), *available at* www.mhdc.com/about/commission_meetings/2007_11_16_Regular_Meeting_Book.pdf; M. Franck, "Mo. Panel Demands Builders Act as Immigration Cops," *St. Louis Post-Dispatch*, Nov. 17, 2007.

Please note, MHDC adopted amendments to three sections of the I-9 policy memorandum cited above: (1) Item 18 was amended to require MHDC staff to notify MHDC commissioners, DHS, the attorney general, and local law enforcement of any "concerns" of the presence of any unauthorized workers; (2) Item 20.c. was amended to change the sanction of "damages" to "liquidated damages," specifically to eliminate the need for the courts to determine damage amounts; and (3) Item 20.e. was added to the list of sanctions and prevents a developer from asking for additional assistance if it is subjected to I-9 policy sanctions.

Pennsylvania—House Bill 2319[86] prohibits use of "illegal immigrant" labor on a project financed with any state loan or grant money. Penalties result from knowing violations of federal immigration law.

Who is covered?	Any person who uses labor in the state utilizing any state grant or loan money
What is required?	• No person may knowingly employ or knowingly permit the employment of an "illegal alien" on any project using state grant or loan money • An employer has an affirmative defense if: (1) it obtains certification from a contractor that it complies with IRCA, and (2) notifies the federal government if its contractor uses "illegal alien" labor
Penalties:	Repayment of grant or loan (with penalty interest) if the person is sentenced under federal law for knowingly employing an "illegal alien" on a project using state grant or loan money
Effective Date:	07/2006

Texas—House Bill 1196[87] restricts the granting of public subsidies to businesses that are convicted of more severe violations of federal immigration law.

Who is covered?	Any business, branch, division or department of that business that applies for a public subsidy (any public program, benefit, or assistance) from any level of government within the state.
What is required?	The business must certify that it and its affiliates do not and will not knowingly employ an "undocumented worker"
Penalties:	Repayment of subsidy, plus interest, if convicted under federal law[88] for criminal or pattern/practice violations
Effective Date:	09/01/2007

---

[86] Codified at 43 Pa. Con. Stat. §§166.1 to 166.5.

[87] *Available at www.capitol.state.tx.us/tlodocs/80R/billtext/pdf/HB01196F.pdf.* This bill was codified at Tex. Gov't Code §§2264.001 to 2264.101 (but note that two other laws have been codified at those sections).

[88] INA §274A(f); 8 USC §1324a(f).

Appendix C—Measures Applicable to All Employers

Arizona—House Bill 2779[89] adds provisions to police all employers through state/county-level determinations and processes. It also requires all employers to use E-Verify.

Who is covered?	All employers that transact business in Arizona
What is required?	• All employers are required to use E-Verify for all new hires after 01/01/2008 (but no penalty for not enrolling) • Employers may not intentionally or knowingly employ unauthorized aliens (as defined by federal law) • Employers must comply with a complex, complaint-driven process directed by the attorney general or county attorney that involves state/local inquiries with the federal government to verify an employee's work authorization well after an employer has completed its I-9 process
Penalties:	Suspension of charters and any state and local business licenses required to do business in Arizona with permanent revocation for a second offense
Effective Date:	01/01/2008

---

[89] Codified in relevant part at Ariz. Rev. Stat. Ann. §§23-211 to 23-214, 41-2505.

Colorado—House Bill 06-1017[90] requires the completion of a state affirmation form[91] by every Colorado employer with respect to each new employee.

Who is covered?	All employers who transact business and have employees in Colorado
What is required?	Within 20 days of hiring a new employee: • Affirm that the employer has examined the legal work status of each newly hired employee • Affirm that the employer has retained file copies of identity and/or employment eligibility documents presented for purposes of the I-9 • Affirm that the employer has not altered or falsified the employee's identification documents • Affirm that the employer has not knowingly hired an unauthorized worker
Penalties:	Fines: Up to $5,000 for a first offense Up to $25,000 for subsequent offenses
Effective Date:	01/01/2007

Illinois—House Bill 1744[92] *prohibits* employers from using E-Verify until the system reaches an almost impossible performance standard. The law also adds a state attestation requirement regarding strict compliance with the terms of this optional verification system, once an employer is authorized to use it.

Who is covered?	All employers that transact business in Illinois
What is required?	• No employer may enroll in E-Verify until the system nears perfection (99 percent of problem cases able to be resolved within three days) • Once nirvana is attained, employers must attest to strict compliance under the penalty of perjury
Penalties:	
Effective Date:	Approved 08/2007; effective 01/01/2008

---

[90] Codified at Colo. Rev. Stat. §8-2-122.

[91] *www.coworkforce.com/lab/AffirmationForm.pdf.*

[92] Codified at 820 Ill. Comp. Stat. 55/12.

Louisiana—Senate Bill 753[93] creates state-level offenses and penalties for employing unauthorized workers.

Who is covered?	Employers with more than 10 employees
What is required?	• Employers may not knowingly employ an "undocumented alien" • Any government agency may notify the attorney general or district attorney of a violation—after an agency determines the state law has been violated • Investigations may be initiated by an agency or by a private party's written statement
Penalties:	• Cease and desist order • If there is a failure to comply with an order, and a court subsequently finds a violation of the order, an employer is subject to a fine up to $10,000 and/or suspension or revocation of business licenses
Effective Date:	06/23/2006

---

[93] Codified at La. Rev. Stat. Ann. §23:996.

Tennessee—Senate Bill 903[94] adds provisions to police all employers through state-level determinations and processes, with punishment reserved until *after notice and a hearing*. It also provides for a "safe-harbor" for those who use E-Verify.

Who is covered?	All employers that transact business in Tennessee
What is required?	• Employers may not knowingly employ, recruit, or refer for a fee an "illegal alien" (someone lacking working authorization in the United States) • Employers must comply with a complaint-driven process directed by the commissioner of labor and workforce development • Complaints must come from a state or local agency or associated party with "reason to believe" an employer is in violation of the law • After notice and a hearing, employer must terminate any "illegal alien" workers and provide evidence of compliance
Penalties:	• First offense: Suspension of business licenses until employer evidences it no longer employs "illegal aliens" • Second offense: For violations of law within three years of first offense, employer's business licenses will be suspended for one year • Use of E-Verify/Basic Pilot provides employers a "safe harbor" *if used for the employee(s) in question*
Effective Date:	01/01/2008

---

[94] Codified at Tenn. Code Ann. §§50-1-101, 50-1-103.

West Virginia—Senate Bill 70[95] creates state-level offenses and penalties for employing unauthorized workers.

Who is covered?	Any person who employs or seeks to employ an individual within West Virginia
What is required?	• Employers may not knowingly employ, hire, recruit, or refer an authorized worker • Employers must verify a prospective employee's legal status or authorization to work prior to employing the individual or "contracting with the individual for employment services" • Employers will be subjected to state investigations by the labor commissioner, who may be able to request I-9s
Penalties:	Knowing violation for employing unauthorized workers: • First offense—fine ranging from $100 to $1,000, per violation • Second offense—fine ranging from $500 to $5,000, per violation • Third or subsequent offense—fine ranging from $1,000 to $10,000, per violation, and/or confinement in jail for 30 days to one year • Conviction of a third or subsequent offense—an employer may have its business licenses (state and local) revoked or suspended, after notice and a hearing • Any wages over $600 paid to an unauthorized worker may not be deducted as a business expense, following a conviction (eff. 01/01/2008) Knowingly providing false records about an employee's status or work authorization: • Misdemeanor resulting in up to one year of confinement and/or a fine of up to $2,500 Knowing and willful sale/transfer of business assets to avoid liability: • Misdemeanor resulting in up to one year of confinement and/or a fine of up to $10,000
Effective Date:	06/2007

---

[95] Amending W.Va. Code §§21-1B-2, 21-1B-3, and 21-1B-5, and adding W. Va. Code §§21-1B-6, 21-1B-7.

CIVIL RICO CLASS ACTION SUITS BY U.S. DOMESTIC WORKERS

*by Mary E. Pivec**

Almost 40 years ago, domestic farm workers filed a series of class action lawsuits seeking relief for deprivation of employment benefits and depressed wages brought about by the defendant growers' alleged employment of illegal workers. Plaintiffs theorized that the criminal harboring provisions of the Immigration and Nationality Act of 1952 (INA)[1] provided grounds for a private right of action to sue for economic injuries suffered by native workers who suffered job and wage losses as a result of immigration law violations. These suits were part of a broad civil rights campaign to improve the wages and working conditions of American farm workers. The courts uniformly rejected plaintiffs' claims,[2] relying principally upon the Texas proviso, previously codified at 8 USC §1324(a)(4), which specifically exempted mere employment from the definition of "harboring" aliens not legally in the United States.

The Texas proviso was repealed with passage of the Immigration Reform and Control Act of 1986 (IRCA),[3] in which Congress substantially revised the harboring provisions of the INA. However, under IRCA, the sanctions against employers for knowingly hiring and continuing to employ undocumented workers were largely civil, with the exception of the misdemeanor "pattern or practice" violation codified at 8 USC §1324a(f). Congress expressly rejected calls to create a private right of action for domestic workers who claimed to have been injured by competition from illegal immigrants.

---

* **Mary E. Pivec**, a partner with Keller and Heckman, LLP, in Washington, D.C., has extensive experience in representing employers in labor, employment, and immigration matters. She lectures on issues such as union avoidance techniques for supervisors and managers, defeating union representation elections, employer sanctions and I-9 compliance, developing effective employee handbooks, investigating and defending sexual harassment claims, and complying with the Family and Medical Leave Act, the Americans with Disabilities Act, and the Fair Labor Standards Act. Prior to her legal practice, Ms. Pivec worked as a business agent and handled collective bargaining and grievance and arbitration disputes in the public sector. In 2007 she was named by *Super Lawyers* as an outstanding attorney in Washington, D.C., in the fields of employment/labor and immigration law, and has also been named in *The Best Lawyers in America* since 1990 in the area of immigration law.

[1] Pub. L. No. 82-414, 66 Stat. 163.

[2] *See Chavez v. Freshpict Foods, Inc.*, 456 F.2d 890, 893 (10th Cir. 1972); *Flores v. George Braun Packing Co.*, 482 F.2d 279, 280 (5th Cir. 1973); *Lopez v. Arrowhead Ranches*, 523 F.2d 924, 926 (9th Cir. 1975).

[3] Pub. L. No. 99-603, 100 Stat. 3359.

Ten years later, Congress changed its mind. As part of the Illegal Immigration Reform and Immigrant Responsibility Act of 1996 (IIRAIRA),[4] Congress amended the Racketeer Influenced and Corrupt Organizations Act of 1970 (RICO)[5] to permit private individuals to sue for injuries to their business or property resulting from a pattern of racketeering activity perpetrated through an interstate or foreign enterprise based on criminal violations of the INA committed for the purpose of financial gain.[6] Thus was born a cause of action for domestic workers and businesses allowing recovery for actual and treble damages, attorneys' fees and costs. The specific INA provisions that constitute predicate crimes for RICO purposes include the antismuggling, transporting, and harboring provisions codified at 8 USC §1324(a)(1)(A), and the felony hiring provision codified at 8 USC §1324(a)(3)(A). The elements of these predicate crimes differ substantially.

Felony Harboring Claims

Of the five subparts of 8 USC §1324(a)(1)(A), subpart (iii), dealing with felony harboring, is the one most often cited in civil RICO immigration cases. To be guilty of felony harboring, a jury must conclude that a defendant concealed, harbored, or shielded an individual from detection by law enforcement, or attempted to take such action, knowing or in reckless disregard of the fact that the individual is in the United States in violation of law.[7] In the employment context, the courts have always required more than mere proof that an employer employed workers with knowledge that they were not legally present in the United States. However, even prior to removal of the Texas proviso, the government successfully prosecuted an employer who took action to help illegal workers avoid arrest by immigration offers under the harboring clause.[8] Post-IIRAIRA, courts have upheld harboring charges against employers who engaged in a pattern of conduct designed to help illegal workers remain in the United States, including providing housing and transportation to such workers.[9] In *U.S. v. Rubio-Gonzalez*,[10] the United States Court of Appeals for the Fifth Circuit approved a jury charge defining harboring as "any conduct tending to substantially facilitate an alien's remaining in the United States illegally." More recently, the Fifth Circuit upheld the conviction of an employer who provided undocumented workers with false identity documents and failed to submit record-keeping paperwork to the

---

[4] Pub. L. No. 104-208, div. C, 110 Stat. 3009, 3009-546 to 3009-724.

[5] Codified at 18 USC §§1961–68.

[6] *See* 18 USC §1961(1)(F).

[7] *See Susnjar v. U.S.*, 27 F.2d 223 (6th Cir. 1928).

[8] *See U.S. v. Cantu*, 557 F.2d 1173 (5th Cir. 1977) (employer defendant successfully prosecuted for harboring based on evidence that he arranged for alien employees to leave his restaurant under the guise of being customers to avoid detection by authorities).

[9] *See, e.g., U.S. v. Zheng*, 306 F.3d 1080, 1086 (11th Cir. 2002) (affirming conviction where the defendant provided housing and employment to aliens); *accord, U.S. v. Singh*, 261 F.3d 530 (5th Cir. 2001).

[10] 674 F.2d 1067, 1073 (5th Cir. 1982).

Social Security Administration (SSA) with respect to their employment, holding such conduct tantamount to concealment.[11]

Because the "reckless disregard" standard permits admission of circumstantial evidence that the defendant knew of illegal status, and because of the absence of any limitation as to the types of conduct that might prove a harboring charge, RICO plaintiffs appear free to make a broad variety of charges against employers, including charges of hiring workers who cannot speak English while claiming to be citizens or permanent residents; hiring workers who present authorization documents that are invalid on their face because the pictures are of a different person, are upside down, or are of poor quality; hiring workers known to be in the United States illegally and using fake documents; hiring workers who were previously employed under different identities; hiring workers who do not have housing; and failing to investigate Social Security "no-match" letters. Although defendants have argued that using an applicant's inability to speak English as a basis for according them different treatment would violate the unfair immigration employment practices provisions of 8 USC §1324b, the U.S. Court of Appeals for the Ninth Circuit has recognized that it may be considered as a relevant factor in determining a defendant's knowledge that a person is in the United States illegally in the context of a harboring prosecution.[12] Notwithstanding these liberal pleading rules, the U.S. District Court for the Eastern District of California recently granted a motion to dismiss a RICO felony harboring suit, with leave to amend, based on the absence of sufficient factual allegations that the defendant employer concealed, harbored, or shielded from detection alien workers using a blind-eye hiring theory and lax I-9 practices.[13]

Felony Hiring Violations Distinguished

For purposes of establishing civil liability for unlawful hiring in violation of 8 USC §1324a, the government may make its case based on actual or constructive knowledge of unauthorized status at the time of hiring or in continuing employment beyond an authorized date. Constructive knowledge also will suffice to sustain a misdemeanor count for a pattern or practice violation under §1324A(f). However, mere constructive knowledge or reckless disregard on the part of defendants as to the undocumented status of particular workers is not enough to establish criminal liability under the felony hiring statute, 8 USC §1324(a)(3). Neither is it sufficient to allege that the workers became unauthorized after the onset of employment. As a result, certain courts have held that plaintiffs, in order to establish liability for a felony hiring violation, must plead that defendants possessed actual knowledge of the undocu-

---

[11] *U.S. v. Shum*, 496 F.3d 390, 392 (5th Cir. 2007); *cf. U.S. v. Acosta de Evans*, 531 F.2d 428, 430 (9th Cir. 1976) (holding that the word "harbor" means "to afford shelter to" and does not require the intent to avoid detection).

[12] *U.S. v. Holley*, 493 F.2d 581, 582–83 (9th Cir. 1974).

[13] *See* Memorandum Opinion and Order Granting in Part and Denying Part Defendant Salyer's Motion to Dismiss (May 16, 2007), *Brewer v. Salyer*, No. 06-01324 (E.D. Cal.).

mented status of specific workers as of the time of hire and actual knowledge that the workers were "brought into" the United States in violation of the immigration laws.[14]

Zirkle Fruit Company Litigation

From 1997 to 1999, legacy Immigration and Naturalization Service (INS) conducted a series of highly publicized raids and I-9 audits in Washington State's Yakima Valley. Zirkle Fruit Company was among the employers who were targeted for audits and raids. In the aftermath of these raids, a group of legal immigrants sued Zirkle and Selective Employment Agency, Inc. in 2000 for conspiring to keep farm wages down by supplying Zirkle with an illegal workforce. Plaintiffs sought back pay for the wages they purportedly lost as a result of the alleged criminal violations of immigration law, as well as treble damages under the RICO's penalty provisions. The district court dismissed the complaint at the pleading stage, holding that plaintiffs lacked standing to sue and that their lost-wages theory was too speculative to support a RICO action.

On appeal in 2002, the Ninth Circuit reinstated the lawsuit, holding that plaintiffs had satisfied the liberal pleading requirements of the Federal Rules of Civil Procedure with respect to damage causation and standing. The Ninth Circuit was influenced by the 2001 decision of the U.S. Court of Appeals for the Second Circuit in *Commercial Cleaning Servs. v. Colin Serv. Sys., Inc.*,[15] which upheld the standing of a janitorial contractor to sue a competitor for allegedly engaging in an illegal immigrant hiring scheme in order to undercut business rivals, finding the plaintiff's damage theory to be sufficiently direct to satisfy RICO requirements. The Ninth Circuit panel observed "[W]e are unable to discern a more direct victim" of an illegal immigration hiring scheme than domestic workers who allege that the defendants' scheme was to gain an illegal commercial advantage over them in the negotiation of employment contracts.[16] The court held that the plaintiffs should have the opportunity "to make their case [as to lost wages] through presentation of evidence, including experts who will testify about the labor market, the geographic market, and the effects of the illegal scheme."[17]

Following remand to the district court, the parties engaged in heated discovery involving class and merits issues. Along the way, plaintiffs amended their complaint to add as defendants Zirkle's chief financial officer, chief executive officer, and human

---

[14] *See Valenzuela v. Swift Beef Company, Inc.*, No. 3:06-CV-2322 (N.D. Tex. Dec. 20, 2007), slip op. at 7–8 (*citing Commercial Cleaning Services, L.L.C. v. Collin Service Sys., Inc.*, 271 F.3d 374, 387 (2d Cir. 2001)); *Zavala v. Wal-Mart Stores, Inc.*, 393 F. Supp. 2d 295, 309 (D.N.J. 2005); *Sys. Mgmt., Inc. v. Loiselle*, 91 F. Supp. 2d 401, 408 (D. Mass. 2000). *But see Trollinger v. Tyson Foods, Inc.*, 370 F.3d 602 (6th Cir. 2004) (reinstating a felony hiring claim based on judicial notice that a substantial portion of illegal immigrants are smuggled into the country, negating the need for plaintiffs to plead specific facts establishing that defendants possessed actual knowledge that specified workers entered the country illegally as of their hire date).

[15] 271 F.3d 374 (2d Cir. 2001).

[16] *Mendoza v. Zirkle Fruit Co.*, 301 F.3d 1163, 1170 (9th Cir. 2002).

[17] *Id.* at 1171.

resources director—all of whom allegedly conspired along with unnamed co-conspirators to staff Zirkle with large numbers of unauthorized workers in violation of the INA and RICO. In 2004, the district court approved certification of two sub-classes of authorized workers employed directly by Zirkle and indirectly through defendant Selective Employment Agency, Inc. from November 1999 onward. According to plaintiffs' trial brief, plaintiffs were prepared to present evidence that roughly 70 percent of Zirkle's employees proffered Social Security numbers that did not correspond to SSA records, that the company had mass-produced thousand of pre-signed I-9 forms certifying that a company agent had examined employment identity and eligibility documents and found them to be genuine, that company officials had disregarded and destroyed SSA "no-match" letters and destroyed incriminating I-9 forms during discovery, and that Selective had accepted visibly fake documents and sent them to work for Zirkle. Shortly prior to the January 2006 trial date, the parties reached agreement on a $1.3 million settlement.

Tyson Foods' Legal Battle

The same legal team that sued Zirkle sued Tyson Foods, Inc. in April 2002 in the U.S. District Court for the Eastern District of Tennessee under civil RICO on behalf of a class of domestic workers currently or previously employed in six different Tyson plants across the south and central United States. Not surprisingly, the suit was filed while Tyson and several of its managers were defending themselves in the same district against criminal harboring charges. In the original complaint, plaintiffs alleged that Tyson had conspired with a network of recruiters and temporary employment agencies to transport illegal workers to the United States, obtain housing for them, and provide them with false identification documents so Tyson could employ them. Plaintiffs alleged that as a result of these practices, their wages were depressed, notwithstanding the fact the Retail, Wholesale and Department Store Union (RWDSU), AFL-CIO, had negotiated the wages and working conditions plaintiffs alleged to be noncompetitive.

Tyson fought back with a preliminary dismissal motion, asserting that plaintiffs' claims were preempted under a judicially created rule blocking RICO claims that draw their essence from a collective bargaining agreement. The rule provides that such disputes should be resolved in the first instance by the National Labor Relations Board, which has primary jurisdiction when it comes to labor disputes covered under the National Labor Relations Act.[18] Tyson also argued that plaintiffs lacked standing to assert injuries to wages and benefits since they were represented by the RWDSU, and that in any event, the injuries were too speculative to proceed beyond the pleading stage.

The district court granted Tyson's dismissal motion based on an apparent lack of standing and speculative causation,[19] but the U.S. Court of Appeals for the Sixth Circuit reversed[20] and ultimately rejected all of Tyson's arguments as either lacking le-

---

[18] Codified at 29 USC §§151–69.

[19] *Trollinger v. Tyson Foods, Inc.*, 214 F.Supp.2d 840 (E.D. Tenn. 2002).

[20] *Trollinger v. Tyson Foods, Inc.*, 370 F.3d 602 (6th Cir. 2004).

gal merit or premature. The Sixth Circuit ruled that the union's involvement in bargaining the disputed wages and working conditions was merely collateral to the central issues in the case, and that RICO provides independent federal remedies to U.S. workers who are potentially injured by employers who violate the nation's immigration workers in recruiting and hiring the undocumented. And while the U.S. Supreme Court has made clear the need to establish actual injury in order to prove standing, the Sixth Circuit rejected the notion that individual workers could not establish an injury in fact notwithstanding the union's role as collective bargaining representative. Lastly, the Sixth Circuit held that the plaintiffs must be given the opportunity to prove the contentions contained in the complaint, *e.g.*, that illegal workers impacted legal employees' wages; that each additional illegal worker hired into the bargaining unit by Tyson had a measurable impact on the bargained-for wage scale; that the illegal worker allegedly brought into the country through Tyson's efforts allowed Tyson to avoid competing with other businesses for unskilled labor; and that Tyson's legal workers were compelled to remain with Tyson because of diminished opportunities.

On remand, plaintiffs amended their complaint to add allegations that Tyson and high ranking executives were associating in a RICO enterprise with immigrant rights groups such as the League of United Latin American Citizens (LULAC) and the National Council of La Raza (NCLR) through contributions intended for the improper purpose of recruiting illegal workers from within these organizations. The Tyson defendants objected that this new theory was reckless and offensive, but the district court permitted plaintiffs to depose representatives of LULAC and NCLR, as well as four senior Tyson executives responsible for directing the company's federal and community relations policies, to pursue evidence of the alleged scheme.

In October 2006, over the objection of Tyson Foods, the court certified a class of over 800 domestic workers allegedly injured as a result of the Tyson defendants' illegal conduct. In the fall of 2007, following completion of discovery, Tyson moved for summary judgment, arguing variously that plaintiffs could establish neither liability nor damages. Plaintiffs named as an expert witness a former INS special agent, who testified that Tyson either knew or should have known that approximately 91 workers were illegal at the I-9 hiring stage based upon their inability to speak English despite purported lengthy residence in the United States. The agent deduced these "facts" from an inspection of Tyson's I-9 paperwork alone—without having interviewed any workers or I-9 preparers. Plaintiffs also employed a labor economist as an expert witness on damages. He opined that the presence of the 91 alleged illegal workers depressed the wages of U.S. workers at the Tyson plants at issue. Tyson moved to disqualify the foregoing expert testimony as speculative and insufficiently reliable under *Daubert v. Merrell Dow Pharmaceuticals*.[21]

---

[21] 509 U.S. 579 (1993).

Mohawk Industries Tries a Different Tack

After the Sixth Circuit revived the civil RICO action against Tyson Foods, Mohawk Industries, Inc. became the next target for a civil RICO action. As in the Tyson Foods case, the class plaintiffs alleged that the company had conspired with recruiters and temporary help agencies, in this case to locate and transport large numbers of undocumented workers from the Brownsville, TX area to Mohawk's plants in Georgia for the purpose of driving down the wages of its U.S. workers. The complaint recited violations of various immigration crimes taking place over a five-year period, including knowingly hiring more than 10 illegal workers in 12-month increments, harboring those workers though employment, shielding them from detection by federal authorities, and accepting fraudulent documents to satisfy I-9 requirements. Mohawk publicly denied these allegations and responded legally with a preliminary dismissal motion. Therein, Mohawk's legal team argued that plaintiffs had failed to plead facts sufficient to demonstrate the existence of a cognizable "association-in-fact" RICO enterprise—one in which the co-conspirators pursued an objective that was separate and distinct from the normal business affairs of Mohawk Industries.

Mohawk reasoned that since employee recruitment and hiring are routine corporate functions, an enterprise formed for the purpose of carrying out such functions could never form the basis of a RICO claim—regardless of whether predicate crimes were alleged to have been committed. The U.S. Court of Appeals for the Seventh Circuit had dismissed similar RICO claims in a 2004 decision ending a RICO action brought by U.S. workers against IBP, Inc., holding that the objectives of the recruiters and the corporation were too diverse to satisfy the "common purpose" element of a racketeering case.[22]

Unfortunately for Mohawk, the district court in Georgia denied its motion.[23] However, Mohawk did succeed in convincing the court to stay proceedings and approve the company's request for interlocutory review based upon the different views expressed in the Seventh Circuit's decision. The U.S. Court of Appeals for the Eleventh Circuit agreed to hear the appeal, but ultimately rejected Mohawk's argument.[24] Siding with the Second and Ninth Circuits, the Eleventh Circuit held that in the context of a civil RICO case based upon immigration crimes in the workplace, factual allegations of a "loose or informal association of distinct entities," formed to supply an employer with undocumented workers, constituted a cognizable enterprise for RICO purposes when the defendant employer is alleged to have played some role in carrying out the purpose of the enterprise.

The Supreme Court Agrees to Hear Mohawk's Case

Mohawk petitioned for certiorari from the order of the Eleventh Circuit, asking the U.S. Supreme Court to determine a slightly broader question than the one raised below,

---

[22] *Baker v. IBP, Inc.*, 357 F.3d 685 (7th Cir. 2004).

[23] *Williams v. Mohawk Industries, Inc.*, 314 F. Supp. 2d 1333 (N.D. Ga. 2004).

[24] *Williams v. Mohawk Industries, Inc.*, 411 F.3d 1252 (11th Cir. 2005).

namely whether it is settled law that a corporate defendant must "conduct" or "participate" in the affairs of some larger separate enterprise in order to be susceptible to RICO liability. The Supreme Court agreed to accept the case[25] and to decide whether a corporate defendant, in combination with nonemployee recruiters and temporary help agencies, may constitute a RICO enterprise if formed to locate and place undocumented aliens for employment with Mohawk. The U.S. Chamber of Commerce, the National Federation of Independent Business Legal Foundation, the Society for Human Resource Management, the National Association of Manufacturers, Associated Builders and Contractors, Inc., the Carpet and Rug Institute, and the American Staffing Association signed on to amici curiae briefs supporting Mohawk's appeal.

In their respective briefs, Mohawk and the business community argued for a strict construction of the statutory definition of "enterprise" found in the RICO statute, asserting that Congress intentionally excluded corporations from the exclusive list of "individuals" that could enter into a de facto racketeering arrangement known as an "association-in-fact." Mohawk's alternative defense derives from the Supreme Court's 1993 decision in *Reves v. Ernst & Young*.[26] Therein, the Court held that a RICO conspirator must have a separate and distinct identity from the RICO enterprise in which it is alleged to have participated, regardless of the alleged criminal wrongdoing. Mohawk argued that absent allegations in the complaint of conspiratorial acts directed at achieving goals that are outside the scope of Mohawk's routine business activity, the complaint must be dismissed for failure to state a claim.

Plaintiffs attracted support from interest groups opposed to liberalizing the country's immigration laws and insistent upon using RICO to enforce the employer sanctions laws. These include the Immigration Political Action Committee, U.S., Inc., the Federation for American Immigration Reform, the Center for American Unity, the American Unity Legal Defense Fund, Negative Population Growth, Inc., and the U.S. Immigration Reform Political Action Committee. Mohawk's attempt to limit the scope of corporate RICO liability attracted the opposition of the U.S. Department of Justice, which has used RICO to prosecute corporate defendants for alleged participation in a broad range of criminal conspiracies. Plaintiffs and these amici argued that Congress intended to hold corporations liable for workplace immigration crimes under the 1996 RICO amendments and that the government's failure to enforce employer sanctions has left domestic workers with no remedies for unlawful competition from undocumented workers. For these advocates, corporate hiring of the undocumented is not "a routine business function," but one that involves a serious crime against American workers within the legitimate scope of civil RICO prosecution.

The Remanded Action

Ultimately, the Supreme Court ignored the corporate liability argument and remanded the case to the Eleventh Circuit for determination whether the alleged injury to domestic workers flowing from a criminal conspiracy to employ illegal workers

---

[25] *Mohawk Industries, Inc. v. Williams*, 546 U.S. 1075 (2005) (granting certiorari).
[26] 507 U.S. 170 (1993).

alleged a sufficiently direct injury for RICO purposes to survive a motion to dismiss.[27] The Eleventh Circuit soon responded in the affirmative, remanding the case to the trial court for class discovery.[28] As of this writing, the parties are in the midst of a briefing schedule on plaintiffs' motion for class certification under both the federal and state (Georgia) RICO statutes, to which defendants have not yet responded. Plaintiffs cite Mohawk's failure to use available government databases to verify Social Security numbers, failure to train hiring personnel to complete I-9 forms, and ignoring inability to speak English as evidence of willful blindness supportive of their claim that defendants engaged in a widespread conspiracy to harbor undocumented workers through the employment process. In addition, plaintiffs have proffered the testimony of current and former Mohawk supervisors and workers supporting the claim that Mohawk had actual knowledge that many employees were not legally authorized to work when they were hired. Plaintiffs rely upon the same labor economist used in the Tyson Foods case to support their wage suppression-damage theory. Should Mohawk prevail in excluding this expert witness from testifying in summary judgment proceedings or at trial, it may influence the district court in Georgia to deny class certification due to absence of a common injury.

Postscript

Approximately four weeks prior to the scheduled start of the Tyson trial, the district court issued a decision granting Tyson's summary judgment motion and dismissing the complaint in its entirety.[29] The court held that plaintiffs had failed to produce admissible, probative evidence at the summary judgment stage that Tyson knowingly hired any illegal workers. Notably, the court rejected the conclusion of plaintiffs' counsel that a lack of English language proficiency despite possession of documents evidencing several years of permanent resident status establishes illegal status. The court also rejected hearsay testimony and inconclusive anecdotal evidence offered by plaintiffs to establish the knowledge element essential to proof of both the felony hire offense and the RICO damage claim.

The court pointedly rejected plaintiffs' "willful blindness" theory as a substitute for admissible evidence of the actual knowledge element and faulted plaintiffs for failing to offer any evidence that Tyson possessed actual knowledge that at least 10 of their employees were brought to the United States for purposes of illegal employment.[30]

---

[27] *Mohawk Industries, Inc. v. Williams*, 547 U.S. 516 (2006).

[28] *Williams v. Mohawk Industries, Inc.*, 465 F.3d 1277 (11th Cir. 2006).

[29] *Trollinger v. Tyson Foods, Inc.*, No. 4:02-CV-23, 2008 WL 413635 (E.D.Tenn. Feb. 13, 2008).

[30] It is notable that during *Daubert* proceedings, plaintiffs withdrew the former INS agent's expert report. In opposition to Tyson's summary judgment motion, plaintiffs continued to rely on the expert's conclusion that completing an I-9 in Spanish despite alleged longstanding U.S. residence constituted evidence of illegal status. Plaintiffs previously served a subpoena on the Department of Homeland Security (DHS) seeking the immigration records of the 91 individuals identified by the expert as unauthorized workers, and when DHS failed to comply (citing, among other reasons, Privacy Act prohibitions), plaintiffs sued to compel enforcement in the U.S. District Court for the District of Columbia. *Trollinger*

Although the court credited plaintiffs with producing some admissible evidence of concealment in support of the alternative harboring offense theory for one of the eight facilities at issue in the suit (a former plant employee in Corydon, IN testified she personally observed a Tyson supervisor warn illegal workers of impending legacy INS inspections), the court dismissed the RICO harboring claims at the remaining seven facilities for lack of evidence. However, to avoid summary judgment, the court held that plaintiffs had to provide evidence to establish a direct causal relation between their claimed injury (lost wages) and the predicate offense (concealing illegal workers from legacy INS inspections). To do so, plaintiffs first had to establish that Tyson was actually paying wages lower than the market wage at the Corydon, IN facility, and that Tyson was able to do so because it was retaining illegal workers through a pattern of concealment.

Next, plaintiffs had to provide evidence of a direct causal link between Tyson's lower wages and Tyson's retention of some illegal workers at the Indiana facility. The court observed: "Even if a jury accepts Plaintiffs' arguments that their wages were depressed and Tyson retained unauthorized employees, that is not a sufficient basis for the jury to determine one caused the other—only that both occurred." The court ruled that the testimony of plaintiffs' labor economist, that in general the employment of illegal immigrants can cause a depression of wages, was insufficient to establish actual injury to the plaintiffs absent expert testimony establishing predicate facts, such as (1) the percentage of undocumented workers in the plant workforce; (2) whether the plant was unionized and the membership and influence of undocumented workers in the bargaining unit; (3) the overall tenure of particular illegal workers at the plant, and (4) a host of factors impacting a worker's decision to work for Tyson rather than another employer.

Without considering the impact of such factors, the court held that the plaintiffs had no more than a speculative chain of causation plagued by the possibility of intervening causes impacting wage determination decisions. Significantly, the court agreed with Tyson that the plaintiffs had failed to account for the impact of the union wage negotiations predating the alleged acts of concealment, further contributing to the speculative nature of plaintiffs' claimed RICO injury.

The Tyson Foods victory is highly significant. It is the first decision analyzing and rejecting many prevalent theories supporting claims of illegal status, as well as the theories offered by the plaintiffs' expert labor economist, at least in the context of a civil RICO case. In short, these theories fail to meet the requirements of the Federal Rules of Evidence. The court's decision may indeed herald the demise of copycat domestic worker cases. On the other hand, the government's decision to prosecute more employers for criminal harboring and aiding and abetting document fraud may yield stronger types of evidence to support civil RICO cases. Because of this uncer-

---

et al. v. Tyson Foods, Inc., No. 1:07-MC-341. On January 11, 2008, the court issued a decision denying enforcement. The court record includes copies of the exchange of correspondence between plaintiffs' counsel and DHS.

tainty, cautious employers are well advised to adopt strict immigration-compliance policies and procedures that would serve the twin purposes of defeating governmental enforcement actions and civil class-action suits.

Practice Aids: Checklists & Best Practices

CORPORATE COMPLIANCE PRACTICE AIDS FOR THE IMMIGRATION LAWYER

*by Richard A. Gump, Jr.**

Table of Contents

1. A Perspective to Consider 317
2. Best Practices: Developing an Immigration Corporate Compliance Program 319
3. The Wal-Mart Consent Decree (which set the stage for a world class model of best practices) 333
4. The Wal-Mart Model of Best Practices and Subcontractor Liability: Tools for the Embattled Employer 339

These practice aids are intended as a quick "go to" reference for immigration attorneys to assist clients in developing appropriate compliance programs.

---

* **Richard A. Gump, Jr.** is the shareholder of the Law Offices of Richard A. Gump, Jr. Mr. Gump graduated from the University of Texas School of Law, and has been practicing business and employment-related immigration law for more than 30 years. He is a member of AILA, past chair of the AILA Texas Chapter, past chair of the AILA Texas Service Center Liaison Committee, and is a member of the AILA Worksite Enforcement Conference Committee. Mr. Gump has been named in *Texas Lawyer*'s "Go-To Guide" as one of the attorneys whom his peers would call if they needed representation in immigration law, and since 2003 has been recommended by *Super Lawyers* in the field of immigration law. He also has been recognized in the *International Who's Who of Business Lawyers 2006* and *Chambers USA: America's Leading Lawyers for Business* in 2006. Mr. Gump handled the first employer sanctions case filed in the southwestern United States under the Immigration Reform and Control Act of 1986, and was co-counsel in one of the largest civil/criminal settlements in worksite compliance history.

A PERSPECTIVE TO CONSIDER
by Richard A. Gump, Jr.

Over 20 years ago, I poured over the newly minted piece of legislation called the Immigration Reform and Control Act of 1986 (IRCA),[1] and came to the conclusion that immigration law would be forever changed. Once employers were placed at the forefront of enforcement, history indicated there would be no turning back. I had observed the transitions of the Environmental Protection Agency, the Occupational Safety and Health Administration, and the Securities and Exchange Commission from agencies charged with regulating respectively the environment, safety at the worksite, and securities into monolithic enforcement agencies that required employers to set high standards and stick to them.

Over the past 20 years, a rollercoaster ride of enforcement has occurred. First, education of employers was the focus; second, high-profile raids and fines were the hallmark; third, a pause in enforcement occurred after a rose garden was raided on Mother's Day; and finally, we have seen the recent two-year steady increase of criminal enforcement. Indecision over funding and lack of trained personnel led to poor judgment on the part of government enforcement in the early days. In the late 1980s, a manufacturing plant was raided in Lewisville, TX, with vans, helicopters, and guns blazing in an effort to find unauthorized aliens and to check out the I-9 verification documents. The tips proved to be false, very few unauthorized aliens were located, and the I-9s were in decent shape. The public affairs officer for legacy Immigration and Naturalization Service (INS) issued the following statement: "I judge the success of the operation by the fact that no one was hurt." INS had not learned the difference between enforcing corporate compliance of a new regulatory scheme and deporting unauthorized aliens.

The emergence of an effort to utilize criminal sanctions in lieu of civil fines is the result of a sense that employers considered paying civil fines a mere added cost of doing business. The interesting aspect of the rise in criminal enforcement is that most of the criminal laws being used have been available since IRCA was passed in 1986, but were sparingly used in the first 20 years. I had expected the use of criminal sanctions to be used much earlier and much more frequently after the first three years of IRCA, but politics, funding, and indecision prevented enhanced enforcement. Thus, employers treated worksite compliance as if it were a truck traveling over the speed limit on the highway—if the highway patrol was not on the horizon, speeding was permissible, and even if they got caught, they could pay the fine and move on.

Perhaps the most surprising change to some employers has been the imposition of a responsibility to have a watchful eye on all workers at a given worksite, whether they are independent contractors or direct employees. However, IRCA, from the beginning, indicated that an employer could not use a contract or subcontract to violate

---

[1] Pub. L. No. 99-603, 100 Stat. 3359.

the law. The legal ramifications of imposing a duty on employers who have no obligation or ability to control a separate company other than by contract will be revealed through future litigation.

Legislation is proliferating at the state and local level, yet silence exists at the federal level. Will this be a trend, a "push-down" of enforcement by the federal government, which is not without precedent? Will federal comprehensive immigration reform legislation emerge to assist in balancing enforcement with benefits? I would suggest the following for any legislation to be successful:

1. A new, technologically driven system of identification of individuals entering the United States
2. A balanced system of benefits (supply meets demand) and enforcement (fair, constant, and consistent)
3. A workable, funded, and timely administration of benefits and enforcement policies
4. Availability of visas for new workers at the low and high ends of the pay scale
5. A process of earned citizenship for aliens illegally in the United States
6. Assimilation tools (English, civics, cultural adaptation, etc.) for new and current aliens as they work their way toward legal status and U.S. citizenship
7. Development of a culture of compliance by employers and aliens alike (a culture of compliance for payment of federal income tax, for example, came only after decades of education and consistent enforcement)

No one knows the future, but the steady march toward prohibiting illegal immigration is upon us, and the days of turning a blind eye are forever gone.

Best Practices: Developing an Immigration Corporate Compliance Program

BEST PRACTICES: DEVELOPING AN IMMIGRATION CORPORATE COMPLIANCE PROGRAM

Richard A. Gump, Jr.
Law Offices of Richard A. Gump, Jr., P.C.
One Galleria Tower, Suite 1940
13355 Noel Drive
Dallas, Texas 75250-6834
(972) 386-9544
www.rickgump.com

BEST PRACTICES: DEVELOPING AN IMMIGRATION CORPORATE COMPLIANCE PROGRAM
Richard A. Gump, Jr.

Outline
- Historically Speaking....
- Four Critical Steps to Risk Assessment and Avoidance
- Best Practices Checklist
- Best Compliance Practices
- No Match Letters
- Final "No-Match" Regulations
- Legal Counsel
- Training for use of Independent and Subcontractors
- Who is an employee? New I-9 Required?
- Actual knowledge
- Constructive knowledge
- Electronic Verification Programs
- IMAGE
- IMAGE's Best Hiring Practices
- Compliance Audit
- I-9 Forms
- When does a Compliance Audit become the best practice?

Audit and Act
Change the Corporate Culture

Historically Speaking...

- Employer sanctions created in 1986
- In 1996, IIRIRA stiffened penalties, broadened definition of fraud
- Sarbanes-Oxley (2002) and the amendment of the Federal Sentencing guidelines (2004) focus on corporate compliance and governance
- The Wal-Mart case – liability for independent contractors
- All proposed immigration reform legislation highlight need for increased enforcement

Four Critical Steps to Risk Assessment and Avoidance

- Comprehensive Compliance Policy

- Training

- Internal Audits

- Change the corporate culture

Best Practices Checklist

1. Immigration Issues
2. Players
3. Policy Purpose Statement
4. Audit
5. Policy Compliance Manual
6. Verification Procedures
7. Contracts and Sub-contracts
8. Electronic Management Programs
9. Non-discriminatory Practices
10. Management Acceptance
11. Training
12. Periodic Review
13. Internal Investigations

Best Compliance Practices

- Written Employer Compliance Policy
    - Verification and record keeping provisions
    - H-1B posting, benching and record keeping
    - Anti-discrimination provisions
- Employer No-Match Policy
- Training
- How is your company's IMAGE?
    - When do you advise your client to join IMAGE versus adopting IMAGE's Best Practices cafeteria-style?
    - Compliance Audit versus I-9 Audit?

No-Match Letters

- Sent 1st to each individual employee whose name and number do not match
- Sent to employers who:
  - Report more than 10 mismatches, *and* number exceeds 0.5% of total W-2s in report
  - Please file any W-2Cs within 60 days

Final "No-Match" Regulations

- ICE issued regulations on August 14, 2007 to become effective September 14, 2007

- As of February 2008, effective date postponed pending new regulation from DHS

- Primary Concern: flawed SSA database

- DHS intends to use SSA "no match" letters as evidence of actual or constructive knowledge
- Employers need firm policy regarding procedure and timing for handling "no match" letters

Legal Counsel

- Develop auditing compliance safeguards
- Develop indemnification provisions against the use of unauthorized labor when negotiating or renewing contracts involving independent contractors or subcontractors.
- Develop contracts for independent contractors and subcontractors with DHS compliance standards and reporting requirements
- Employer should contact legal counsel prior to an immigration-related hiring or firing
- Develop and implement contractor termination policies based on civil or criminal law compliance issues

Training for use of Independent and Subcontractors

- Train employees and managers in the permissible use of independent and subcontractors.
- Teach them to report the suspected use of unauthorized labor by contractors.

Who is an employee?

- Independent Contractors: Look at who controls the work
- Treat the same for immigration and tax purposes
- Cannot use a contract (leasing, independent contractor status) to avoid compliance with regulations

New I-9 Required?

- Continuing employment
  - Employee returning from leave of absence
  - Seasonal employment
  - Reasonable expectation of employment
- Merger & Acquisitions
  - New I-9s not required; employer liable for errors

Actual knowledge

- Employee confession
- Employee says I do not have documents. Can you help me?
- Work authorization document has expired and the employer knows it

Constructive knowledge

- Prior regulations and case law provide insight
- Final "No-Match" regulations add two examples – (i) receipt of "no-match" letter; and (ii) DHS letter saying I-9 does not match USCIS records
- Now employer with new final regulations is to look at the totality of the circumstances
- In the case of investigations, ICE is talking to the employee using its investigative tools

Electronic Verification Programs

E-VERIFY

- Verification of SSA and DHS databases
- Voluntary program
- Employers must sign agreement and meet requirements
- Permit DHS/SSA audits/visits
- Proposed legislation may make mandatory

IMAGE
ICE Mutual Agreement between Government and Employers

- "To assist employers in **targeted sectors** to develop a more secure and stable workforce" and to
- "enhance fraudulent document awareness through education and training program"
- Will "IMAGE Certified" become an industry standard?

IMAGE: Employers must agree to

- Submit to an ICE I-9 audit
- Verify the Social Security numbers of current employees with the Social Security Number Verification System (SSNVS).
- Use E-Verify for all new hires
- Implement IMAGE's best hiring practices

IMAGE's *Best Hiring Practices*

- Use **E-Verify** for all hiring
- I-9 training program
- Trained employees with quality supervision
- Annual I-9 audits by external auditing firm or independent company auditor
- Self-reporting procedure for deficiencies
- No-match letter response protocol
- Tip Line with protocol
- Anti-discrimination
- Contractor adherence to **IMAGE** Best Practices
- Annual Report

Compliance Audit

- Has due diligence expanded from the restructuring employer situation to an annual compliance audit?
- I-9s
- LCAs
- Public access file
- PERM retention files
- H-1B dependency
- Anti-discrimination
    - *Getahun v. OCAHO,* 124 F.3d 591(3rd Cir. 1997)
- No-Match, constructive knowledge and contractor compliance

I-9 Forms

- Check for all employees against payroll records and No-Match letters
- Substantive versus technical or procedural
- Mitigation by internal audit
- Retention
- Past enforcement effect
- Assess the potential civil and criminal penalties

When does a Compliance Audit become the best practice?

- When a public company discloses potential enforcement liability on an SEC filing?
- As a condition of a civil or criminal settlement?
- For due diligence in mergers and acquisitions?
- As contract requirements for contractors and subcontractors?
- IMAGE requires external or independent I-9 audit
- May be best practice compliance for enforcement features found in proposed legislation
    - e.g. Certifications of compliance COMPREHENSIVE IMMIGRATION REFORM ACT OF 2007 S.1348, § 301(b).
    - Enhanced responsibility for Government Contractors

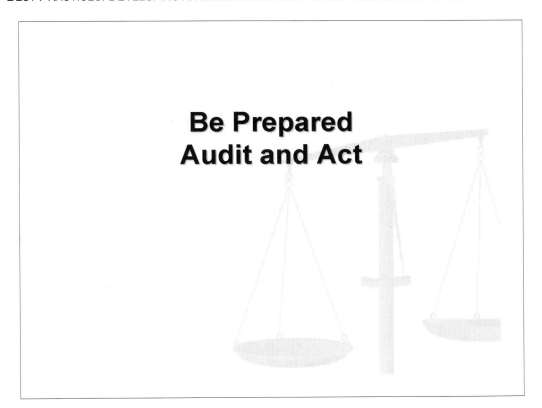

WAL-MART CONSENT DECREE AND ORDER

ORIGINAL

IN THE UNITED STATES DISTRICT COURT
FOR THE MIDDLE DISTRICT OF PENNSYLVANIA

UNITED STATES OF AMERICA

v.

WAL-MART STORES, INC.

Civil No.
1:CV-05-0525
(Judge   )

CONSENT DECREE AND ORDER

AND NOW, the Court finds as follows:

1. This action is brought by the United States of America, on behalf of its agency, Immigration and Customs Enforcement, seeking equitable relief pursuant to Title 8, United States Code, Section 1324a(f)(2), to enjoin, prevent, and deter the employment of unauthorized aliens by contractors employed by the defendant, **WAL-MART STORES, INC.**, its subsidiaries, divisions, and affiliates (hereinafter referred to as "**WAL-MART**").

2. Title 8, United States Code, Section 1324a prohibits persons and entities from knowingly hiring, recruiting, or continuing to employ aliens who are not legally authorized under federal law to work within the United States. See 8 United States Code, Section 1324a(a)(1)-(2); and

3. The defendant, **WAL-MART**, is a Delaware corporation headquartered in Bentonville, Arkansas, which operates more than 3,000 retail stores, 500 SAM'S Wholesale Clubs, 50 Neighborhood

Markets, and distribution centers throughout the United States and around the world, including stores within the Middle District of Pennsylvania, and directly employs world-wide approximately 1,600,000 associates.

4. In addition to its own employees, from 1998 through 2003, **WAL-MART**, acting through its store managers, used independent contractors to provide floor cleaning services to many of its stores in the Middle District of Pennsylvania and elsewhere.

5. At various times between 1998 and 2003, as many as 1,000 **WAL-MART** stores used independent contractors to provide cleaning services to the stores which **WAL-MART** operated in the Middle District of Pennsylvania and elsewhere. By October 2003, approximately 700 **WAL-MART** stores used independent contractors to provide these store cleaning services.

6. Beginning in 1998 and continuing through October 2003, enforcement actions undertaken by Special Agents of the Immigration and Naturalization Service and its successor agency, Immigration and Customs Enforcement, against floor cleaning contractors performing cleaning services at various **WAL-MART** stores in the Middle District of Pennsylvania and elsewhere documented that independent contractors used by **WAL-MART** to provide floor cleaning services were knowingly hiring,

3
recruiting, and employing unauthorized aliens in violation of Title 8, United States Code, Section 1324a.

7. These enforcement actions culminated on October 23, 2003, when Immigration enforcement actions at approximately 61 **WAL-MART** stores in the Middle District of Pennsylvania and elsewhere apprehended approximately 245 unauthorized, undocumented aliens employed by independent cleaning service contractors at **WAL-MART** stores located in 21 states.

8. Following this enforcement action, **WAL-MART** notified the United States of its intention to take steps, including, but not limited to, a series of corrective actions to ensure that independent contractors working for **WAL-MART** comply with all aspects of federal laws governing the employment of illegal aliens.

9. Following a thorough investigation, the United States concluded that federal criminal proceedings against **WAL-MART**, its directors, officers, or employees would not be appropriate.

10. The United States and **WAL-MART** entered into a Stipulation in Compromise dated the 14th day of March, 2005, which is a global settlement resolving all criminal, civil, and administrative actions and is binding on all components of

4

the United States Department of Justice and the Department of Homeland Security.

11. In accordance with the Stipulation in Compromise executed by the parties, it is ordered as follows:

A. **WAL-MART**, acting either directly or through independent contractors used by **WAL-MART**, is permanently enjoined from knowingly hiring, recruiting, and continuing to employ aliens who are not legally authorized to work within the United States.

B. **WAL-MART** is directed to continue to cooperate with the United States in its investigation of alleged illegal employment practices by independent cleaning contractors previously used by **WAL-MART**. **WAL-MART** understands and agrees that complete and truthful cooperation is a material condition of this Agreement. Cooperation shall include providing all information known to **WAL-MART** regarding any criminal activity, involving employment of illegal aliens, including but not limited to the matters described in this Agreement. Cooperation will also include complying with all reasonable instructions from the United States, regarding interviews of **WAL-MART** personnel by investigators and attorneys at such reasonable times and places to be determined by counsel for the United States and to testifying fully and truthfully before any grand juries,

5
hearings, trials, or any other proceedings where this testimony is deemed by the United States to be relevant.

C. **WAL-MART** is directed to maintain its own established, on-going and pre-existing program of taking reasonable steps to ensure that associates employed by **WAL-MART** are authorized to work within the United States, while continuing to ensure Wal-Mart's compliance with pertinent anti-discrimination laws.

D. **WAL-MART** is directed to establish as part of its compliance programs a means to verify that independent contractors used by **WAL-MART** are also taking reasonable steps to comply with immigration laws in their employment practices and cooperate truthfully with any investigation of these matters. **WAL-MART** shall have eighteen months from the date of this Agreement and Decree to develop compliance guidelines for independent contractors.

E. **WAL-MART** is directed to provide all of its store managers and future store managers with training regarding their legal obligations to prevent the knowing hiring, recruitment, and continued employment of unauthorized aliens while complying with pertinent anti-discrimination laws. Such training will be provided to all **WAL-MART** store managers within eighteen months of

6

the filing of the Complaint and the entry of this Court Order pursuant to the terms of the Stipulation in Compromise.

F. **WAL-MART** is directed to make a payment of $11,000,000 through the United States Attorney's Office to the Treasury Forfeiture Fund for the purpose of promoting future law enforcement programs and activities in this field by Immigration and Customs Enforcement.

G. That the Consent Decree and Order entered approving this Stipulation in Compromise is a global settlement binding all components of the United States Department of Justice and Department of Homeland Security, relating to the matters set forth in Paragraph G of the Stipulation in Compromise filed in this case.

H. That the Consent Decree and Order entered in this matter terminate on the fifth anniversary of the date the Order is entered by the United States Court for the Middle District of Pennsylvania.

I. This court retains jurisdiction to enforce this agreement, Consent Decree, and injunction.

7

SO ORDERED this 15th day of March, 2005.

_____
UNITED STATES DISTRICT JUDGE

The Wal-Mart Model of Best Practices and Subcontractor Liability: Tools for the Embattled Employer
by Richard A. Gump, Jr.

In an effort to be compliant with immigration related verification requirements, most employers have historically been concerned only with their direct employees. It has become increasingly important for employers to also consider indirect employees, or workers performing services through a contact agreement. Although subcontractor workers will not have all the same requirements of direct employees, it is important for employers to establish procedures to remain compliant with respect to indirect workers.

Wal-Mart has created among the most conservative approaches to dealing with both direct and indirect employees. This approach was created in response to Wal-Mart receiving government scrutiny because of subcontractor employees working on Wal-Mart locations.

Other employers are adopting similar approaches to meet immigration related verification requirements for subcontractor employees. In establishing such a policy, Wal-Mart focused on certain themes which other employers may consider:

- INA §274A(a)(4) discusses labor through contract, and does not allow an employer to circumvent U.S. immigration law by employing foreign nationals through a contractor agreement knowing that the workers do not have employment authorization.

  In an agreement between a general contractor and subcontractor, the verification of employment eligibility of the subcontractor's employees would be the responsibility of the subcontractor, provided that the general contractor does not have knowledge of the unauthorized employment of any workers.

- The agreement between Wal-Mart and the U.S. government imposed additional duties on Wal-Mart to verify the employment authorization of the employees of subcontractors at any tier.

- Wal-Mart passes this liability on to its general contractors, who must then impose additional requirements of its subcontractors. These requirements do not arise out of law, but by contract with Wal-Mart.

- A Wal-Mart model of best practices, particularly involving subcontractor employees, could include the following:
  - Language in the contractor agreement that the contractor is responsible for employee verification and compliance with immigration laws. Examples of desired language would depend on the parties. Wal-Mart requires its general contractors to implement an immigration related compliance plan containing

specific elements. Additionally, any subcontractors used are required to implement their own compliance polices containing the same elements.

- Language in the contractor agreement indemnifying the general contractor of any penalties or liabilities assessed due to violations of the subcontractor.
- Language in the contractor agreement providing for the possible termination of the contract due to immigration related violations of the subcontractor.
- Requirement that the contractor have a properly completed Form I-9 for each employee who will perform work on the project.
- Requirement that the contractor maintain photocopies of all supporting employment eligibility and identity documentation for all employees.
- Requirement for the contractor to provide copies of the Form I-9 and supporting employment eligibility and identity documentation for each employee.
- Requirement that the contractor provide a certification letter stating that the contractor has complied with the verification requirements as described in the agreement.
- Willingness of the contractor to cooperate in the event that an audit is requested by the general contractor or the government of the contractor's Forms I-9 and copies of the employment eligibility and identity documentation, which creates privacy concerns.

Other Possibilities/Issues Arising in Subcontractor Scenario:

- Requirement that the contractor name a third party auditor who is familiar with U.S. immigration law and employee verification process to audit the contractor's compliance plan, review I-9s and provide certification letter.
- Requirement that the contractor participate in government verification program such as E-Verify or IMAGE.
- Badge Requirements: No employee can begin work on a project until receiving a badge from the general contractor or owner after employment authorization is verified and/or certified.
- Ability of the owner or general contractor to terminate the contractor or remove contractor from the worksite for non-compliance with contractual requirements.
- Subcontractors need to carefully review agreements and be familiar with the immigration related requirements imposed by a general contractor. Subcontractors can be surprised to discover that working on certain projects may require additional steps related to employee verification that were not previously required.

EMPLOYER IMMIGRATION COMPLIANCE AUDIT: CHECKLIST OF ISSUES FOR REVIEW AND RISK ASSESSMENT

by Mary E. Pivec[*]

The purpose of this briefing is to provide a checklist of issues to be covered in an immigration compliance audit. The audit should be conducted under the supervision and direction of a licensed attorney so as to preserve all applicable evidentiary privileges, thus avoiding the obligation to produce potentially incriminating information in civil enforcement proceedings or a private Racketeering Influenced and Corrupt Organizations Act (RICO)[1] action. The goals of a thorough compliance audit are to (1) identify areas of potential civil and criminal liability and to develop recommendations to cure existing violations and prevent future violations; (2) preserve evidence of good faith compliance that may be useful in deterring state and federal officials from pursuing civil or criminal prosecution of the employer, and/or mitigate fines and penalties if such action does occur; and (3) control the risk of liability in civil RICO actions predicated on worksite immigration felonies.

Experience teaches that there is not a "one size fits all" formula for conducting an immigration compliance audit. Employers in targeted industries such as food processing, construction, landscaping, restaurant operations, parts manufacturing, mining, and agriculture may require a more thorough audit, particularly if other risk factors are present. These factors include high concentrations of non–English-speaking workers in low-level jobs working directly or indirectly for the employer; prior I-9 or employer sanctions violations and warning letters; a record of foreign workers who have been arrested and detained and interrogated by police or immigration officers; sponsorship of out-of-status foreign workers for immigration benefits; a history of wage and workplace safety violations; and adverse publicity for hiring foreign workers and picketing by anti-immigration groups. Such compliance audits typically require a review of all I-9s, I-9 policies and procedures, wage and safety practices and enforcement history, in-depth interviews with managers involved in the recruitment, hiring, and I-9 process, and assistance in correcting I-9 forms and resolving Social Security "no-match" reports.

---

[*] **Mary E. Pivec**, a partner with Keller and Heckman, LLP, in Washington, D.C., has extensive experience in representing employers in labor, employment, and immigration matters. She lectures on issues such as union avoidance techniques for supervisors and managers, defeating union representation elections, employer sanctions and I-9 compliance, developing effective employee handbooks, investigating and defending sexual harassment claims, and complying with the Family and Medical Leave Act, the Americans with Disabilities Act, and the Fair Labor Standards Act. Prior to her legal practice, Ms. Pivec worked as a business agent and handled collective bargaining and grievance and arbitration disputes in the public sector. In 2007, she was named by *Super Lawyers* as an outstanding attorney in Washington, D.C., in the fields of employment/labor and immigration law, and has also been named in *The Best Lawyers in America* since 1990 in the area of immigration law.

[1] 18 USC §§1961–68.

Some employers request immigration compliance audits in order to satisfy procurement requirements imposed by clients. The time and intensity of the audit may be more limited, but sufficient to allow the attorney to certify that the employer's I-9 practices and procedures meet client specifications. Other employers who are foreign-worker dependent, such as computer-consulting firms, may seek legal counsel to confirm that their compliance systems meet the standards imposed by the U.S. Department of Labor (DOL) and U.S. Citizenship and Immigration Services with respect to the H-1B and Program Electronic Review Management (PERM) programs, particularly when contemplating sale, merger, or public financing. Lastly, large corporate employers in white-collar industries such as banking and finance, engineering, medicine, research, and academia have greater risks of being audited by DOL for violations of the H-1B and PERM sponsorship programs. These employers also may be seeking a clean bill of health with respect to foreign workers employed in the E, L, and J categories.

I. <u>Audit Review Information and Documentation Request.</u> A preliminary requirement of any immigration compliance audit is a review of the relevant document trail. Depending on the circumstances, counsel may determine that it is important to review the following information and documentation to preliminarily assess client risk levels and identify areas for further inquiry in the interview process:

   A. Background Information
      1. Latest annual report or other documentation providing overview of the business, nature of governance structure, key executives and managers, number and types of employees
      2. History of the business: founders, mergers and acquisitions
      3. Identification of owners and shareholders and their immigration status
      4. Biographies and job descriptions of senior corporate executives
      5. Identification of board members and their affiliations and committee responsibilities
      6. Organizational charts: headquarters, regional, plant/facility
      7. Description of products or services offered at each facility outside headquarters

   B. Business and Compliance Culture
      1. Mission statement
      2. Business code of ethics
      3. Budget for risk management, corporate compliance, program auditing and training
      4. Internal complaint system/tip hotline procedures
      5. Procedures for investigating complaints alleging immigration law violations
      6. Policies and procedures for auditing existing immigration compliance policies
      7. Disciplinary records resulting from immigration compliance violations

Employer Immigration Compliance Audit

8. Honesty-only policy
9. Governmental compliance agreements: E-Verify/Basic Pilot memorandum of understanding (MOU)
10. Internal monitoring procedures to ensure compliance with MOU
11. Lists of employees terminated based on final non-confirmation notice, dates of hire, dates of termination, related I-9 forms and documents, and E-Verify notification

C. Internal Communications re: Immigration Compliance
   1. Management memoranda and directives
   2. Statements of corporate officials with respect to immigration issues, including amnesty, immigration reform, legalization, the Department of Homeland Security/Social Security "no-match" rule
   3. E-mail traffic regarding immigration compliance issues, "no-match" letters, I-9s, and employee status questions

D. Public Relations
   1. Adverse newspaper articles or other adverse publicity dealing with immigration issues
   2. Community outreach programs—jobs, housing, English-language training

E. Government Contract Relationships
   1. List of government contracts: federal and state
   2. Security clearance obligations

F. Workforce Composition, Recruitment, Labor Relations, and Human Resources
   1. Recruitment practices and procedures
   2. EEO-1 diversity reports (prior three years)
   3. List of individuals with hiring authority—and for what positions
   4. Provisions of collective bargaining agreements—immigration issues
   5. Provisions of employee handbooks—I-9s, "no-match" letters, Social Security numbers, compliance investigations, terminations
   6. Representative sampling of personnel files

G. Wage Payment and Safety Issues
   1. Method of wage payment
   2. Wage payment/overtime policies and procedures
   3. List of positions deemed overtime exempt
   4. Local market analyses of employee wages
   5. Off-the-books wage payments
   6. Wage violation history—state, federal, and private audits and litigation

7. Safety policies
8. Safety violation history and record of injuries

H. Social Security Issues
1. Records of Social Security Number Verification Service checks
2. "No-match" letters
3. Records of resolution of "no-match" letters
4. Document fraud policies
5. Safe-harbor policy for resolving "no-match" letters

I. Potential Labor-Through-Hire Issues
1. Agreements with temporary employee leasing firms
2. Subcontractor/independent contractor agreements
3. Past citation of contractor employees for immigration violations
4. Internal complaints that contract workers are not legally authorized to work
5. Reports on audits and worksite inspections of contractors
6. Policies for maintaining independent contractor status and avoiding formation of joint employment relationship

J. Potential Harboring Issues
1. Records of employer leases for properties housing foreign workers
2. Records of wage deductions for employee housing and transportation
3. Local employee arrest records
4. Local police investigations involving rowdy conduct at employer-owned properties

K. I-9 Compliance
1. Standard I-9 completion procedures
2. Procedures for completing and processing I-9s at nonheadquarters facilities
3. Procedures for updating I-9s
4. I-9 storage and retention procedures
5. Documentation evidencing that employer has an I-9 for all current employees and terminated employees covered by the retention period
6. Deterrence procedures for rogue employee activity—document/identity fraud, illegal hires
7. Results of past internal I-9 audits
8. List of individuals authorized to execute I-9 forms
9. I-9 training materials and records of training sessions
10. Representative sampling of I-9 forms (original forms and attached documents)

L. Past Immigration Enforcement Activity
   1. Legacy Immigration and Naturalization Service/U.S. Immigration and Customs Enforcement warning letters and documentation of resolution
   2. Notices of intent to fine
   3. Employer sanctions settlement agreements
   4. Immigration-related discrimination settlement agreements
M. Immigration Sponsorship Policies and Procedures
   1. Conditions of sponsorship
   2. List of employees in sponsorship process
N. H-1B Compliance
   1. If H-1B dependent, recruitment and attestation policies and procedures
   2. Methodology for determining H-1B required wage, including job classification mapping policies and procedures
   3. Policy governing payment of legal and filing fees
   4. Policies and procedures governing wage deductions
   5. Copies of H-1B employment agreements
   6. Copies of voluntary agreements authorizing deductions
   7. Copies of noncompete agreements and enforcement actions
   8. Policies and procedures governing early termination of employment and employer cost recoupment
   9. Policies and procedures governing filing of notice of withdrawal upon H-1B termination of employment; sampling of withdrawal letters
   10. List of all outstanding labor certification applications, effective dates, covered workers, and corresponding I-129B petitions
   11. Representative sampling of public access files
   12. Representative sampling of I-129 petitions, resumes, and support letters
O. PERM Compliance Issues
   1. List of all PERM applications filed within preceding two years, including names of beneficiaries, position and wage offered, and dates of internal and external recruitment
   2. All PERM applications filed within preceding two years, including evidence that PERM beneficiaries remain in the position offered through approval of the related I-140 petition
   3. All I-140 petitions filed based on approved PERM applications
   4. All required documentation supporting the PERM applications filed within the preceding two years, including state workforce agency prevailing wage determinations, internal postings, newspaper advertisements,

other forms of recruitment, statements of interest in jobs offered, resumes submitted by U.S. workers, and documentation supporting business necessity job requirements

5. Results of interviews of U.S. workers for each PERM application
6. Policies governing legal fees and recruitment expenses
7. Evidence that the PERM beneficiaries accepted employment with the sponsor following grant of permanent resident status
8. Evidence that the required wage has been paid to I-140 beneficiaries

P. State Immigration Compliance Documentation
1. Listing of states where employer maintains facilities and employees
2. Individual state compliance documentation

II. Interviews and Site Visits

A. Headquarters Interviews—The purpose of conducting interviews is to gather additional information for use in the risk assessment report, supplementing and clarifying information derived from a review of the client's documents. Additional record review may be necessary. During the interview process, counsel should discuss the business issues driving the compliance audit, explore problem areas, and seek suggestions to practically manage risk. Depending on the scope and intensity of the audit, counsel may seek to interview each of the following executives during the headquarters' interview process:

1. Chief executive officer
2. Senior legal officer
3. Chief financial officer
4. Senior risk management/compliance officer
5. Senior human resources director/payroll administrator
6. Senior labor relations officer

B. Site Visits—The ability to tour the employer's production or service facilities, to observe the workforce, and to speak with local management officials and employees regarding immigration compliance issues is essential to identifying weaknesses in implementation of the existing immigration compliance plan. At each facility, counsel should attempt to interview:

1. Plant or facilities manager—for purposes of discussing local recruitment methods, the I-9 screening process, community relations issues, and subcontractor selection and oversight

2. I-9 preparers—regarding their routine procedures, understanding of document requirements, thoroughness in reviewing documents, and antidiscrimination regulations. Counsel should observe the employment verification process. If E-Verify is being used, observe data entry process and

follow-up procedures. Review of the location's I-9s may be in order to detect problems if not previously produced in the document review stage.

3. Supervisors—to explore known or suspected violations of sanctions laws and document fraud issues, if any

4. Cross section of employees—regarding unresolved I-9 issues and concerns and other potential violations of immigration laws

III. <u>Audit Report and Recommended Compliance Plan</u>

A. Audit Report. Certain employers may require counsel to prepare an audit report setting forth findings with respect to the client's pre-existing practices and procedures and steps taken to correct past violations. Other employers may prefer an oral briefing.

B. Suggested Compliance Plan Elements. An effective immigration compliance plan should meet the requirements of the federal sentencing guidelines with respect to corporate ownership and control of business systems subject to criminal abuse. In this regard, an employer should seriously consider inclusion of the following elements:

- Promulgation of a policy by the president or chief executive officer stating the employer's commitment to full compliance with federal and state immigration laws
- Designation of a senior immigration compliance officer responsible to the president (and/or board) for managing and enforcing the employer's immigration compliance policies and procedures, supported by an adequate budget and personnel
- Mandated immigration compliance training of all officers, managers, and employees on a recurring basis, with supplemental training provided to all I-9 verifiers
- Creation of a "hotline" for anonymous reporting of suspected violations by managers, employees, or contractors
- Prompt investigation and resolution of all reports of suspected immigration law violations by knowledgeable personnel reporting to the senior immigration compliance officer
- Threat of disciplinary sanctions, up to and including discharge, for managers and employees found to have knowingly violated company policy with respect to immigration compliance
- Verification of all Social Security account numbers at the time of hire, or participation in E-Verify system
- Creation of a system of secondary review of all I-9s and documentation to ensure proper completion of all newly hired workers
- Requirement that all employee leasing and temporary help agencies attest to compliance with I-9 verification requirements, subject to third-party verification at the election of the employer
- Regular financial auditing to ensure compliance with all wage payment and payroll tax requirements with respect to local hires

- Periodic third-party audits to ensure plan compliance at all levels of the organization

THE I-9 GETS A MAKE-OVER, AND OTHER DEVELOPMENTS IN EMPLOYMENT VERIFICATION
*by Josie Gonzalez**

The I-9 Gets a Make-Over and Other Developments in Employment Verification

A Presentation by Josie Gonzalez

---

* **Josie Gonzalez** is the managing partner of Gonzalez & Harris, and has represented employers in all aspects of immigration law for more than 25 years. She recently represented a major corporation facing federal criminal charges for hiring undocumented workers. Ms. Gonzalez has published numerous articles for legal and trade journals on the topic of employer sanctions. Her background as a former criminal defense attorney and employer sanctions expert makes her uniquely qualified to address issues such as RICO and other criminal charges against employers, the future of employer sanctions, and how to develop and implement immigration corporate compliance materials. She currently chairs AILA's Worksite Enforcement Committee.

Why is the proper completion and maintenance of an I-9 important?

- Affirmative defense against a charge of knowingly hiring or continuing to employ an unauthorized worker
- Requires good faith compliance and no actual knowledge
- Defense against a charge of Constructive Knowledge ("CK") based on "totality of the circumstance"
  - 8 CFR 274a.1 (1)(i), example of CK: Fails to complete or improperly completes I-9
  - Missing I-9s for just the unauthorized workers
  - Employer and employee failure to sign the I-9 and attest to status
  - Continued employment of worker with expired documents
- Demonstrates adherence to regulations and helps establish corporate immigration compliance

What are the most significant changes to the I-9?

- Publication changes date – 06/05/07 – VIP: use version as of 12/26/07 or penalties
- Reduced list of documents
- Revised instruction sheet
- New M274 Handbook for Employers

FORMER I-9: DOCUMENTS ELIMINATED FROM LIST A

1. Certificate of U.S. Citizenship (USCIS Form N-560 or N-561)
2. Certificate of Naturalization (USCIS Form N-550 or N-570)
3. Form I-151, outdated Alien Registration Receipt Card
4. Unexpired Reentry Permit (USCIS Form I-327)
5. Unexpired Refugee Travel Document (USCIS Form I-571)

LIST OF ACCEPTABLE DOCUMENTS
CURRENT I-9: LIST A

1. U.S. Passport (unexpired or expired) *(I-9, Section 1, Box 1)*
2. Permanent Resident Card or Alien Registration Receipt Card (*Form I-551*) *(I-9, Section 1, Box 2)*
3. An unexpired foreign passport with a temporary I-551 stamp *(I-9, Section 1, Box 2, Considered a "receipt" for actual card")*
4. An unexpired Employment authorization document that contains a photograph (*Form I-766—New Document, I-688, I-688A, I-688B*) *(I-9, Section 1, Box 3)*
5. An unexpired foreign passport with an unexpired Arrival-Departure Record, Form I-94, bearing the same name as the passport and containing an endorsement of the alien's nonimmigrant status, if that status authorizes the alien to work for the employer. *(I-9, Section 1, Box 3)*

Resident Alien Card
Form I-551 (Jan. 1977)

The **RESIDENT ALIEN CARD**, Form I-551, was introduced in January 1977 and phased in over a period of time. In addition to the photograph, the I-551 contains the bearer's signature and fingerprint. As with the older I-151 cards, this version I-551 generally does not contain an expiration date.

Form I-551

Resident Alien Card

The **RESIDENT ALIEN CARD**, Form I-551, was revised in August 1989. This version was the first Alien Registration Card to contain an expiration date on every card. These cards were usually valid for ten years from the date of issue. The expiration date indicates when the card expires and must be renewed. It does **NOT** indicate that the alien's status has expired. The card was modified in January 1992 when a white box was added behind the fingerprint.

Form I-551 (January 1992)

Reverse

Form I-551 (August 1989)

Permanent Resident Card – Form I-551 (Dec. 1997)

The **PERMANENT RESIDENT CARD**, Form I-551, was introduced in December 1997. Noticeable differences on the front of the card include a change of card title from **RESIDENT ALIEN CARD** to **PERMANENT RESIDENT CARD**, a three-line machine readable zone and the addition of a hologram.

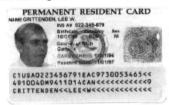

PHOTO SIDE

REVERSE

The Optical Memory Stripe on the reverse contains encoded cardholder information as well as a personalized etching which depicts the bearer's photo, name, signature, date of birth, alien registration number, card expiration date and card number.

Permanent Resident Card Form I-551 (Nov. 2004)

The latest version of the **PERMANENT RESIDENT CARD**, Form I-551, was introduced in November 2004. It retains many of the same features of the previous version while updating the design. The card now shows the seal of the Department of Homeland Security and contains a more detailed hologram on the front of the card.

PHOTO SIDE

REVERSE

The Optical Memory Stripe on the reverse retains the same features as the previous card version. The stripe contains encoded cardholder information on the card bearer. Each card is personalized with an etching showing the bearer's photo, name, signature, date of birth, alien registration number, card expiration date and card number.

Unexpired Foreign Passport with I-551 Stamp

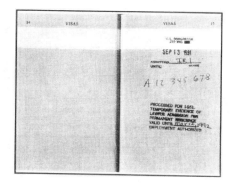

Employment Authorization Card (Form I-766)

An updated **EMPLOYMENT AUTHORIZATION CARD**, Form I-766, was introduced in May 2004. The new card is similar in appearance to the previous revision, with some modifications to the card design. The front of the document continues to show the photograph, fingerprint and signature of the bearer beneath a holographic film, but now displays the DHS seal. The reverse has a standard bar code, magnetic strip, and a two-dimensional bar code containing encoded data.

Form I-766 (May 2004)

Employment Authorization Card (Form I-688A)

 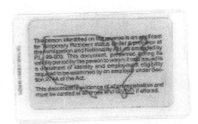

Employment Authorization Document (Form I-688B)

This **EMPLOYMENT AUTHORIZATION DOCUMENT**, Form I-688B, was introduced in November 1989 and is issued to aliens who have been granted permission to be employed in the U.S. for a specific period of time. The card was produced originally with a Polaroid process and has interlocking gold lines across the front.

Form I-688B

Unexpired Foreign Passport with an Unexpired Arrival-Departure Record, Form I-94

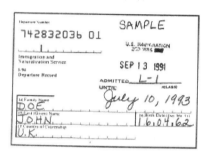

Form I-94 for Asylum Grantee

I-9 Section 1
Employee Information & Verification

[Image of Form I-9, Employment Eligibility Verification, Department of Homeland Security, U.S. Citizenship and Immigration Services, Section 1]

I-9 Basics: Section 1 Employee Information and Verification

- ☐ All employees hired on or after 11/7/86 must complete an I-9.
- ☐ Make sure that employee **fully completes** Section 1.
- ☐ The employee <u>must check **one** of the boxes</u> and provides the information requested if checking box 2 or 3. If checking box 3, generally one provides an expiration date. *(exception: certain asylees/refugees)*
- ☐ Always verify that the employee has **signed and dated** Section 1, **NO LATER** than the date of hire. Ensure the <u>birth date</u> is not mistakenly entered for the signature date.
- ☐ **Do not use** the Preparer/Translator section **unless** the employee cannot complete Section 1 without assistance.

I-9 Section 2
Employee Review & Verification

Section 2. Employer Review and Verification. To be completed and signed by employer. Examine one document from List A OR examine one document from List B and one from List C, as listed on the reverse of this form, and record the title, number and expiration date, if any, of the document(s).

List A	OR	List B	AND	List C
Document title:				
Issuing authority:				
Document #:				
Expiration Date (if any):				
Document #:				
Expiration Date (if any):				

CERTIFICATION - I attest, under penalty of perjury, that I have examined the document(s) presented by the above-named employee, that the above-listed document(s) appear to be genuine and to relate to the employee named, that the employee began employment on *(month/day/year)* _____ and that to the best of my knowledge the employee is eligible to work in the United States. (State employment agencies may omit the date the employee began employment.)

Signature of Employer or Authorized Representative | Print Name | Title

Business or Organization Name and Address *(Street Name and Number, City, State, Zip Code)* | Date *(month/day/year)*

GONZALEZ & HARRIS
A PROFESSIONAL CORPORATION

I-9 Basics: Section 2
Employer Review and Verification

- ☐ Record **ALL** of the required document information in Section 2: Document Title, Issuing Authority, Document #, Expiration Date, if any. **Accept original documents only**. (Acceptance of Receipts is discussed separately)

- ☐ Do not attach document copies to the I-9 <u>in lieu of</u> recording the information.

- ☐ The <u>List of Acceptable Documents</u> is on the back of the I-9. Do not accept any documents that do not establish employment eligibility, e.g., USCIS approval notices of preference classification that do not state employment authorization, consular notifications, attorney letters, etc.

- ☐ The employee must provide **either**.

  A <u>List A</u> document, **OR** <u>List B</u> + <u>List C</u>
  Do Not <u>Over</u>document!

GONZALEZ & HARRIS
A PROFESSIONAL CORPORATION

I-9 Basics: Section 2
Employer Review and Verification
(continued)

- ☐ Always record expiration dates, especially for work authorization documents.

- ☐ Insert the employees's date of hire (start date) in the "**CERTIFICATION**" box in Section 2.

- ☐ **You** must **sign and date** Section 2 **NO LATER** than the third business day from the employee's start date. Best practice is to complete all paperwork on or before the start date.

I-9 Section 3
Updating & Reverification

Section 3. Updating and Reverification. To be completed and signed by employer.

A. New Name (if applicable) B. Date of Rehire (month/day/year) (if applicable)

C. If employee's previous grant of work authorization has expired, provide the information below for the document that establishes current employment eligibility.

Document Title Document #: Expiration Date (if any):

I attest, under penalty of perjury, that to the best of my knowledge, this employee is eligible to work in the United States, and if the employee presented document(s), the document(s) I have examined appear to be genuine and to relate to the individual.

Signature of Employer or Authorized Representative Date (month/day/year)

Form I-9 (Rev. 06/05/07) N

Q **What do I do when an employee's work authorization noted in either Section 1 or 2 of the I-9 expires?**

A The employee must present a List A or C document that shows either an extension of the initial work authorization or new work authorization.

- Record the document title, number and expiration date, if any, in Section 3 of the I-9; sign and date.

- If you used a version of the I-9 that predated the June 5, 2007 version for the original verification, you must complete Section 3 of the latest Form I-9 to reverify.

Handbook Question #33

Q **Expired work authorization - continued**

- You may want to establish a calendar call-up system for those with temporary work authorization.

- You should not reverify an expired U.S. Passport, an Alien Registration Receipt/Permanent Resident Card (Form I-551), or a List B Document that has expired.

- You cannot refuse to accept a document because it has a future expiration date, as long as it is one of the acceptable documents, appears to be genuine and relates to the presenter.

Handbook Question #33

Q **What should I do if I <u>rehire</u> a person who previously filled out a Form I-9?**

A If you used a version of the I-9 dated <u>before</u> June 5, 2007 when you initially verified the employee, you must complete a new I-9 upon rehire.

(Editor's Note: For rehires where new version of the I-9 is used for initial hire, use Section 3 to reverify)

Q **My employee's DHS-issued employment authorization document expired and the employee now wants to show me a Social Security card. Do I need to see a current DHS document?**

A No. During initial verification and reverification, an employee may choose what documentation to present from the list of acceptable documents. If the employee presents an <u>unrestricted</u> Social Security card, he does not also need to present a current DHS document.

Handbook Question #24

Q **Can I avoid reverifying an employee on the I-9 by not hiring persons whose employment authorization has an expiration date?**

A You cannot refuse to hire persons solely because their employment authorization is temporary. The existence of a future expiration date does not preclude continuous work authorization for an employee, and does not mean that subsequent work authorization will not be granted.

In fact, consideration of a future work authorization expiration date in determining whether an alien is qualified for a particular job may be an unfair immigration-related employment practice in violation of the anti-discrimination provision of the INA – Immigration and Nationality Act.

Handbook Question #34

GONZALEZ & HARRIS.
A PROFESSIONAL
CORPORATION

How To Update Employment Authorization Expirations For Certain Non-immigrants?

Employees with temporary work authorization for H-1B, L, J, O, E or TN status who have filed extensions may present a USCIS extension receipt. This receipt (USCIS Form I-797C for filing of I-129, Petition of Nonimmigrant Worker) is valid for 240 days beyond the current expiration. Section 3 of the I-9 should be updated as follows:

- Document Title - Form I-797C
- Issuing Authority – USCIS
- Document # - Insert the USCIS receipt number located in the upper left corner of the document
- Expiration Date - Insert the date that is 240 days (8 months) beyond the current expiration date and note (8CFR 274a.12(b)(20)) in the margin.
- Once the extension of status is approved, USCIS issues a new form I-797 and I-94 with the new expiration date. A new I-9 or Section 3 of the I-9 should be completed and attached to the existing I-9.

H-1B TRANSFERS: PORTABILITY

- A worker who <u>currently</u> holds H-1B status may <u>change jobs upon the filing of a new petition</u>, or "port" to a new employer, under the following conditions:
  - The individual is in lawful status, and;
  - Has not engaged in unauthorized employment since last lawful admission.

H-1B TRANSFERS: I-9 COMPLETION

- The USCIS filing receipt Form I-797C can be used to complete the I-9. Section 2, List C of the I-9 should be completed as follows:
  - <u>Document Title</u> - Form I-797C (I-129). In margin – "Proof of H-1B petition filing with USCIS, pursuant to Section 105 AC21"
  - <u>Issuing Authority</u> – USCIS
  - <u>Document #</u> - Insert the USCIS receipt number located in the upper left corner of the document
  - <u>Expiration Date</u> – "N/A" - Currently CIS hasn't provided guidance regarding what date to use as an expiration date - the date of current H-1 petition, or the requested expiration date of new petition. If petition denied, employment must cease. Once approved, update I-9 or complete new I-9 with new expiration date.

Q Do I need to fill out forms I-9 for independent contractors or their employees?

A No. The contractor is responsible for completing Forms I-9 for its own employees. However, you must not knowingly use contract labor to circumvent the law against hiring unauthorized aliens.

Handbook Question #6

Q If someone accepts a job with my company but will not start work for a month, can I complete the Form I-9 when the employee accepts the job?

A Yes. You may complete the form earlier, as long as the person has been offered and has accepted the job. You may not use the I-9 process to prescreen job applicants.

Handbook Question #4

Q **May I specify which documents I will accept for verification?**

A No. You must accept any List A document provided by the employee or combination of documents from Lists B & C that are listed on the Form I-9. They must reasonably appear on their face to be genuine and to relate to the person presenting them.

- **NOTE**: An employer participating in the E-Verify Program can only accept a List B document with a photo.

Handbook Question #10

Q **If an employee writes down an Alien Number or Admission Number when completing Section 1 of the I-9, can I ask to see a document with that number?**

A No. To complete Section 2, you may not ask to see a document with the employee's Alien or Admission Number or otherwise specify which document(s) an employee may present.

Handbook Question #11

Q **An employee has attested to being a U.S. Citizen or national on Section 1 of the I-9, but has presented a DHS Form I-551 "green card". Another employee has attested to being a Permanent Resident but has presented a U.S. passport. Should I accept these documents?**

A First ensure that the employee understands the attestation of status and make corrections if necessary. You cannot accept documents that are directly inconsistent with the status attested to.

Handbook Question #14

Q May I accept an expired document?

A Expired documents can be accepted in limited Circumstances:
- Expired U.S. passport or any List B identity document
- Expired Employment Authorization Document (EAD) from a Temporary Protected Status (TPS) recipient where DHS has granted an automatic extension.

Handbook Question #15

Temporary Protected Status (TPS): Automatic Extensions

- Eligible TPS recipients will have an I-688B or an I-766 EAD with notation "A-12" or "C-19" on front

- El Salvador: Automatic extension through 3/9/08 & EADs to be issued through 3/9/09. Current EAD should have expiration of 7/5/06 or 9/9/06 with DHS 9/07 extension sticker on back, or expiration of 9/30/07 on front of EAD.

- Honduras & Nicaragua: Had an automatic extension through 1/5/08 & EADs to be issued through 1/5/09. Current EAD should have expiration of 7/5/06 with DHS 7/07 extension sticker on back, or expiration of 7/31/07 on front of EAD.

Q **What should I do if an employee presents a Social Security card marked "NOT VALID FOR EMPLOYMENT," but states that he or she is now authorized to work?**

A For I-9 purposes, you cannot accept this card or one that states "VALID FOR WORK ONLY WITH DHS AUTHORIZATION". If the employee has gained permanent residence, he can go to the local SSA office with proof of lawful status and request a replacement card with the restriction removed.

Handbook Question #19

Q When can employees present receipts for documents establishing employment eligibility?

A When an employee is authorized to work at the time of hire or reverification, a document receipt may be accepted in the following situations:

- A receipt for a replacement document, where the original has been lost, stolen or damaged. The replacement document must be presented within 90 days of hire.

- An I-94 card with an I-551 stamp & photo. The I-551 card must be presented by the expiration of the stamp or within one year from the date of issuance of the I-94 card if the stamp does not contain an expiration date.

Handbook Question #23

Q When can employees present receipts *(continued)* :

- An I-94 containing an unexpired refugee admission stamp. This is considered a receipt for either an EAD (Form I-766 or I-688B) or combination of an unrestricted SS card and List B document. The employee must present acceptable documentation to complete the I-9 within 90 days of hire or, in the case of reverification, the date employment authorization expires.

- Receipts showing application for initial grant of work Authorization, or for renewal of work authorization, are not acceptable.

  Note: Individuals under TPS whose EADs are subject to an automatic extension may continue to work with expired EADs during the automatic extension period.

Handbook Question #23

Recording a Receipt for a Document

- ☐ Record the document title in Section 2, e.g., Resident Alien Card, Driver License, Social Security Card

- ☐ Note the word "Receipt" after the document title, & record issuing authority, e.g., USCIS, CA DMV, SSA

- ☐ Record any document number provided

- ☐ Update the I-9 within 90 days (see exceptions for I-551 stamp and Refugees): Line out "receipt", enter the document number, if different, expiration date, if any, initial and date

- ☐ Attach document copy to I-9

Recording an I-551 Stamp as a Receipt

A Form I-94 arrival card with a photo attached, or an I-551 stamp on a foreign passport, are treated as receipts and can be accepted as <u>temporary evidence</u> of permanent residence for I-9 purposes. If no expiration date is indicated, it must be reverified no later than one year from the I-94 date of issuance.

Under List A, record:

- Document Title & Issuing Authority - Passport and country issuing passport
- Document Number – Passport number
- Expiration Date - Passport expiration date
- Document # -- I-94 or I-551 A#
- Expiration Date, if any – DHS document expiration date

Q What should I do if an employee presents a Form I-20 and says the document authorizes her to work?

A The Form I-20 is evidence of employment eligibility outside of the school in two situations: *(Ed.'s Note: On-campus employment is authorized)*

- At an off-campus location educationally affiliated with the school's established curriculum or related to funded research projects at the post-graduate level where the employment is an integral part of the student's program
- An F-1 student authorized by the Designated School Official (DSO) to participate in a Curricular Practical Training (CPT) program as part of an established curriculum (e.g., internship, co-op, etc., offered by sponsoring employers).
    - The I-20 is endorsed by the DSO and lists the employer, dates of employment, and whether full-time or part-time.
- In both situations, the Form I-20 must accompany a valid Form I-94 or I-94A indicating F-1 status. When combined with an unexpired foreign passport, these documents are acceptable for List A of the I-9.

Handbook Question #27

Q **What is my responsibility concerning the authenticity of document(s) presented to me?**

A If the documents reasonably appear to be genuine and to relate to the person presenting them, you must accept them.

If not "genuine" looking, you must <u>not</u> accept them.

Handbook Question #12

Successor Liability

Q If I acquire a business, can I rely on I-9 forms completed by the previous owner/employer?

A Yes. However, you also accept full responsibility and liability for all Forms I-9 completed by the previous employer relating to individuals who are continuing in their employment.

Handbook Question #42

I-9 Retention

- After employee termination, I-9s must be retained for:
  - Three (3) years after the date of hire **or**
  - On Year after the date employment ends, **whichever is later**.
- <u>Example #1</u>:
  Hired: 3/1/99
  Left: 5/1/00
  Retain until: 3/1/02
- <u>Example #2</u>:
  Hired: 3/1/99
  Left: 8/5/02
  Retain until: 8/5/03
- Simple approach: Retain all I-9s for three years from termination. Store I-9s in binders per year of termination; discard binder contents after three years.
- I-9s for current employees should be stored separately from personnel files, organized alphabetically and easily retrievable.
- I-9s for terminated employees should be stored separately and organized according to your retention schedule.

I-9 Corrections

- It's never too late to complete or correct an I-9. If I-9 is missing, complete a new form using the current date. **Do not backdate**.
- All changes to the form should be clearly acknowledged to avoid the appearance of an attempt to hide or disguise information. **Initial and date all additions or corrections and note "per audit."**
- Do not use "white-out" or black out the original information. Draw a line through the incorrect information and update the I-9.
- In Section 1, any changes to the <u>attestation area</u> (Box 1, 2 or 3) and <u>signature and date areas</u> **must be made by the employee**.

Civil Penalties for offenses occurring on or after March 27, 2008

- **Paperwork**
  - Not less than $110 and not more than $1,100 per individual
  - Good-Faith Exception for Paperwork Violations
    - Available for technical or procedural failures to properly complete I-9
    - Unless employer fails to correct within 10 days after DHS notice
    - Unless there is a pattern and practice of violations
    - No regulations yet defining a "technical or procedural" error
      - Is the use of the older I-9 a procedural error?
      - Is the acceptance of newly eliminated documents for an authorized worker a procedural error?
- **Civil**
  - First offense: not less than $375, and not to exceed $3,200, for each unauthorized worker.
  - Second offense: not less than $3,200, and not to exceed $6,500, for each unauthorized worker.
  - More than 2 offenses: not less than $4,300, and not to exceed $16,000, for each unauthorized worker.

Social Security No-Match Letters and Status of Current Litigation

- DHS Final Rule – August 15, 2007 (effective 9-14-07)
- August 31, 2007 – U.S. District Judge Breyer granted temporary restraining order:
  - Prohibited DHS from implementing final rule
  - Prohibited SSA from mailing No-Match letters with DHS "no match" guidance
- October 15, 2007 – Judge Breyer issued preliminary restraining order against DHS
- November 2007 – DHS announced it will re-write the regulations addressing specific deficiencies, including:
  - Conduct Regulatory Flexibility Analyses to assess impact on small businesses, particularly the 90 day time frame
  - Provide more clarity regarding its safe harbor guidance and its relationship to constructive knowledge

GONZALEZ & HARRIS
A PROFESSIONAL
CORPORATION

Social Security No-Match continued

- December 2007 – DHS announces it will also appeal and issues press release:
  - Employers have been given guide map; fail to follow it at your peril.
  - *"When employers receive such No-Match letters, they are on notice that the employees in question may not be authorized to work. Under our No-Match Rule, no employer should terminate an employee based upon a no-match letter alone. But no employer should ignore such a letter or the discrepancy it reveals. The No-Match Rule gives employers and employees 90 days – a full three months – to correct the mistake. When the mismatch shows fraud, however, appropriate steps should be taken. Businesses that follow the procedures in the rule will have a safe harbor from enforcement action. Those that ignore no-match letters place themselves at obvious risk and invite suspicion that they are knowingly employing workers who are here illegally."*
    (Secretary Michael Chertoff, December 5, 2007)

Constructive Knowledge

- Constructive Knowledge Defined
  - 8 CFR §274a.1(l)(1) The term *knowing* includes not only actual knowledge but also knowledge which may fairly be inferred through notice of certain facts and circumstances which would lead a person, through the exercise of reasonable care, to know about a certain condition.
  - Depends on the totality of the circumstances
- Constructive knowledge includes failure to take reasonable steps to address the following situations:
  - An employee's request for the employer's sponsorship for a labor certification or visa petition;
  - Receipt of a no-match letter from the Social Security Administration ("SSA")

Safe Harbor Steps

1) Within 30 days of receipt of SSA No-Match Letter:
   - Check records to determine if clerical error; correct the error with SSA; and verify that corrected name and social security number now match SSA's records.
   - Retain verification.
   - Update the I-9 or complete a new I-9 (retaining the original)
2) If not clerical error, request that the employee confirm that name and social security number in records are correct.
   - If information is incorrect, employer makes corrections;
   - Informs SSA of correction
   - Verifies a match
   - Retains a record.

Safe Harbor Steps continued

3) If employee confirms information is correct, the employer tells employee to resolve the discrepancy with SSA no later than 90 days after the SSA receipt date.
    - *Note: If within 90 days, employee cannot resolve due to unauthorized status, employee is terminated.*

4) Within 93 days of Receipt of Notice from SSA, if employee affirms valid right to work but SSA discrepancy cannot be resolved, the employer must re-verify the worker's employment eligibility by completing a new I-9:
    - Do not accept any document (or receipt for such a document) that contains the questionable SSN
    - Employee must present a document with photo
    - The new I-9 must be retained with original I-9

No Safe Harbor

☐ Employee requests employer sponsorship for a labor certification or visa petition and the employee is unauthorized.

☐ Employee admits unauthorized status (Actual Knowledge)

Worksite Enforcement

☐ April 16, 2006 – Washington Post, "Immigration Enforcement's Shift in the Workplace"

"...If you're blatantly violating our worksite enforcement laws, we'll go after your Mercedes and your mansion and your millions. We'll go after everything we can, and we'll charge you criminally."

–Asst. Sec. of ICE, Julie Myers

Worksite Enforcement Investigations Ice Statistics

☐ First half of FY 2007: ICE obtained criminal fines, restitutions, and civil judgments in excess of $29 Million

☐ Administration's FY 07 budget: $41.7 million for worksite enforcement and 171 additional ICE agents

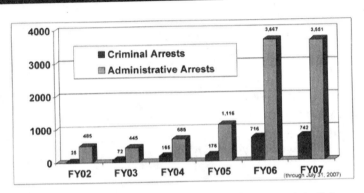

Source: Immigration & Customs Enforcement, *Fact Sheets: Worksite Enforcement* (Aug. 16, 2007) (http://www.ice.gove/pi/news/factsheets/worksites.htm.)

Criminal Charges

- 8 USC §1324 and 18 USC §371 – Conspiracy to Transport and Harbor Unlawful Aliens

- 18 USC §1546 – Fraud and Misuse of Immigration Documents

- 18 USC §§1956 and 1957 – Money Laundering

- 8 USC § 1324(a) – Unlawful Employment of Aliens

E-Verify Employment Verification

- Program Summary
  - Automated link to federal databases – DHS & SSA
  - Employers can register online for E-Verify at http://www.vis-dhs.com/EmployerRegistration
  - Memorandum of Understanding (MOU) is signed by employer, DHS and SSA
  - Staff members using E-Verify must complete tutorial online
  - Electronic query submitted once I-9 is completed: no prescreening; no verifying existing workforce – not even Section three re-verifications.
  - Automated response regarding employment eligibility
  - Follow-up required for "tentative non-confirmations"

E-Verify Employment Verification – continued

- Participation in E-Verify: Right Choice for All Companies?
  - Willingness to hire only those with valid documents even if competitors are not
  - Controversy as to accuracy of databases
  - Nonconfirmation resolution might be time consuming. Must hire and later fire if not resolved
  - MOU agreement gives ICE broad access to company records
  - De-centralized hiring or remote hiring sites present special challenges

Basic Pilot/E-Verify

- ☐ States with some form of Basic Pilot/E-Verify Requirement
  - Arizona – Effective January 1, 2008
  - Colorado – Effective June 2006
  - Georgia – Phased in effective dates:
    - ☐ 500+ employees – July 1, 2007
    - ☐ 100+ employees – July 1, 2008
    - ☐ All others – July 1, 2009
  - Oklahoma – Effective July 1, 2008

QUESTIONS AND ANSWERS: THE NEW EMPLOYMENT ELIGIBILITY VERIFICATION FORM I-9 AND THE NEW HANDBOOK FOR EMPLOYERS

by Scott W. Wright[*]

In the fall of 2007, the federal government issued a formal notice in the *Federal Register* obligating all U.S. employers to use a newly revised version of Form I-9, Employment Eligibility Verification, for all employees hired on or after Wednesday, December 26, 2007.[1] Form I-9 is used by employers to verify the identity and employment eligibility of new hires. To aid in the preparation of I-9s, U.S. Citizenship and Immigration Services (USCIS) has issued a revised 47-page *Handbook for Employers: Instructions for Completing the Form I-9* (publication M-274).[2]

The following discussion, in question-and-answer (Q&A) format, helps explain the significance of the new I-9 and *Handbook for Employers*.

1. What's new on the I-9?

Not much. Employers will find that the new I-9 looks almost exactly like the Form I-9 they had been using for years. What has changed the most is list A—the list of acceptable documents that employees can present to establish both identity and employment eligibility. The primary reason for the release of the new I-9 was to bring that list into compliance with a law that went into effect in 1997 and reduced the acceptable number of list A documents.[3] But the Form I-9 was not changed at that time to reflect these changes in the law.

2. What documents were taken off the list of acceptable documents?

Five documents were taken off of the list, while one was added. The new *Handbook for Employers* provides a good summary of these documents. The five documents that can no longer be accepted as proof of employment eligibility and identity are:

- Certificate of U.S. citizenship (Form N-560 or N-561)
- Certificate of naturalization (Form N-550 or N-570)
- Alien registration receipt card (I-151)

---

[*] **Scott W. Wright** is a partner in Faegre & Benson's Minneapolis office, where he manages the firm's business immigration law practice. He is listed in *The Best Lawyers in America* for work in immigration law. Mr. Wright is a graduate of the University of Minnesota Law School and was a Fulbright research scholar in Panama. He is a frequent author and lecturer on I-9 and immigration compliance issues.

[1] 72 Fed. Reg. 65972 (Nov. 26, 2007).

[2] *Available at www.uscis.gov/files/nativedocuments/m-274.pdf* and reprinted in this book.

[3] *See* Illegal Immigration Reform and Immigrant Responsibility Act of 1996, Pub. L. No. 104-208, div. C, §412(a), 110 Stat. 3009, 3009-666 to 3009-667; 62 Fed. Reg. 51001 (Sept. 30, 1997) (corresponding interim rule designating acceptable documents for employment verification).

- Unexpired re-entry permit (Form I-327)
- Unexpired refugee travel document (Form I-571)

The government said these documents were taken off of the list because they lacked features to prevent fraud or tampering. The one immigration document that was added to list A is an unexpired employment authorization document (Form I-766).

3. Must employers use the new I-9?

Yes. Employers are legally obligated to use the new I-9 for all employees hired on or after Wednesday, December 26, 2007.

4. Are there advantages to the new I-9?

The list of acceptable documents on the new version of the I-9 is shorter, cleaner, and accurate as to current law. For the past decade, the government has advised employers not to accept the five list A documents that were removed from the new form, even though they continued to appear on the list of acceptable documents. Most employers followed that guidance and long ago trained their staff accordingly. For them, the new Form I-9 is helpful, as it helps avoid confusion and inconsistency. Others beg to differ. For example, the re-entry permit, now off of the list, is arguably as tamper- and fraud resistant as a passport. Likewise, newly naturalized U.S. citizens are unfairly inconvenienced by not being able to use their hard-earned certificates of naturalization in the I-9 process. These are just two examples of how the streamlining of the I-9 process for employers has shifted some burdens to legal immigrants and citizens. They may encounter delays or complications in securing new employment by having fewer document options.

5. What are the consequences of accepting a document that was off the list?

Once the new I-9 formally went into effect, employers (1) were legally barred from using prior versions of the I-9 form, and (2) face liability if they accept one of the five documents that were removed from the list of acceptable documents for purposes of documenting an employee's identity and employment eligibility. Allowing a new hire to go to work based on one of the "de-listed" documents will constitute a substantive I-9 violation.

6. How do I know if I'm using the correct, new Form I-9?

The new Form I-9 bears a revision date of June 5, 2007 in the lower right-hand corner of each page.

7. There are nongovernment services that have sent notices saying I could purchase I-9 forms from them. Should my company do that?

No. The I-9 form and the new *Handbook* are both available free of charge and can be printed directly from the USCIS website. The instructions from USCIS confirm that employers can make their own copies of the I-9 form.

8. Why didn't USCIS take this opportunity to make more comprehensive changes to the I-9 form and process?

This new I-9 is essentially a product of general housekeeping. USCIS admits that its objective in this release was quite modest—bringing the form into compliance with changes in the law from 11 years ago. USCIS acknowledges that it has plans to make more profound changes in the overall I-9 process. But doing more to tinker with the system would have required even more delays, as formal rulemaking and broader changes to federal regulations would have been required. Rather than delay these basic changes any further, USCIS decided to make the modest changes now. USCIS has advised that we should expect to see more changes to the I-9 in the future.

9. Can an employer require a Social Security number in the I-9 process?

The *Handbook* contains numerous reminders that providing a Social Security number (SSN) in section 1 of the I-9 is voluntary for all employees unless the employer participates in E-Verify, which requires an SSN. An employee must, of course, provide his or her SSN and original Social Security card if that document is being used in section 2 to confirm employment eligibility. But if the employee is presenting another acceptable document to prove employment eligibility (such as a U.S. passport under list A or a U.S. civil birth certificate under list C), the employer cannot obligate the employee to provide an SSN in section 1 as part of the I-9 process. *Note: An employer will typically confirm the SSN or taxpayer ID number during the W-4/payroll process.*

10. Does the updated *Handbook for Employers* include new information?

Yes. The new M-274 *Handbook* includes some badly needed, long-overdue clarifications that many employers have welcomed. Some of the *Handbook*'s new features include:

- **E-Verify.** The *Handbook* explains exceptions to standard I-9 procedures for companies that use the USCIS E-Verify system (formerly known as the Basic Pilot/Employment Eligibility Verification Program), in addition to information about how a company can voluntarily enroll in E-Verify. Entities that use E-Verify must secure an SSN in the I-9 process, as that number is one of the mandated data fields in the E-Verify electronic verification process. In addition, the list of acceptable list B identity documents is shortened for E-Verify users. This system limits list B to documents that include a photograph (such as a state driver's license or government-issued identification card).

- **Electronic Retention of I-9s.** The *Handbook* has been updated to provide details on federal requirements for completing and storing I-9s electronically, including a list of the security features that must be implemented. These are important reminders for employers, as some converted to scanning I-9s in recent years without attention to the security requirements.

- **Sample I-9s.** The *Handbook* includes new sample I-9s that are filled out to illustrate some I-9 rules. Examples include completion of the translation certification and completing an I-9 for an employee under age 18.

- **Office of Special Counsel.** There are more references to the U.S. Department of Justice, Office of Special Counsel (OSC), the agency charged with enforcing the provisions of the immigration laws that guard against discrimination based on citizenship status and national origin in the I-9 process. The *Handbook* now provides a better summary of how the Equal Employment Opportunity Commission and OSC share jurisdiction for certain national origin discrimination claims, and provides more details on procedures for filing charges of employment discrimination with these agencies.

- **Penalties.** Employers will find more details and updates about potential penalties for immigration law violations in the new *Handbook*.

- **More Answers to Common Questions.** In updating the *Handbook*, USCIS expanded the Q&A section. Most of the information in this section is designed to explain how to implement the I-9 process correctly under the law (*e.g.*, explaining that an employer can complete an I-9 before a new employee actually starts work). However, some of the new material is clearly the result of the government recognizing that the I-9 rules can be hard to understand (*e.g.*, the *Handbook* provides more details about when an employee can present a receipt for documents in lieu of actual documents to prove employment eligibility).

- **Unique Immigration Classifications Addressed.** Employers will find the *Handbook* much more helpful for understanding how to meet I-9 documentation requirements for certain employees who indicate they are "aliens authorized to work" under different immigration classifications. There are, for example, helpful references to foreign nationals who have been granted (1) temporary protected status; (2) curricular practical training or optional practical training pursuant to F-1 foreign student visa status; (3) TN status under the North American Free Trade Agreement; (4) refugee or asylee status; and (5) J-1 exchange visitor visa status.

- **Sample Identity and Employment Eligibility Documents.** Employers will especially welcome the expanded and updated display and description of documents that are acceptable for identity and employment eligibility verification.

11. What went missing in the *Handbook for Employers*?

Despite getting a thorough revision, the *Handbook* will still frustrate employers, especially those new to the I-9 process. Employers looking for a resource to help in distinguishing between genuine and fake documents will be greatly disappointed with the new *Handbook*. In fact, its samples of the "latest version" of the permanent resident card (Form I-551) and employment authorization card (From I-766) do not show the correct, current type of photo that should appear on those documents. The *Handbook* examples include photos of the document bearers with a side-view pose, which has been phased out by the government in recent years. Without adding any pages to the *Handbook*, the government could have presented sample documents with both the side-view pose and photo format that is now required, which is a straight fontal view (as used for passports). Likewise, it would have been more accurate and helpful to employers if the *Handbook* included correctly annotated I-94 cards with the special documents (Forms I-20 and DS-2019) that are issued to F-1 foreign students and J-1 exchange visitors. A few more sample I-9s would certainly be warranted to help show exactly how to document some of the common and more complex I-9 scenarios. It would have been especially helpful to expand the discussion of how to properly complete I-9s for refugees and asylees.

USCIS also failed to recognize that the I-94 card is the least understood document that employers must contend with in the I-9 process, in large part because I-94 cards are annotated in so many different ways to confirm the many different types of immigration authorization. USCIS would have been wise to include a summary of immigration classifications with corresponding samples of work authorization documents, especially as they relate to the multitude of I-94 annotations. The *Handbook* does not adequately educate employers on the fact that many I-94 card annotations do not provide any evidence of employment authorization. Some I-94 annotations authorize employment, but are specific to only one employer. Others provide proof of employment eligibility with virtually any employer.

U.S. immigration authorities also missed an opportunity with this new *Handbook* to address a number of areas of confusion. For example:

- There is no sample document provided for conditional permanent residents.
- The sample foreign passport in the *Handbook* is insufficient, as it fails to illustrate any information on the issuing authority, validity date, or different formats used by foreign countries in extending passport validity (the key data points that need to be documented on the I-9).
- More details could have been provided to clarify characteristics of valid documents to prevent legal immigrants from being denied employment. For example, the sample of the employment authorization card (Form I-766) shows the cardholder's fingerprint. However, many employers would not be aware that the majority of valid I-766 cards are now issued without fingerprints.
- The new *Handbook* will keep employers guessing about the often contradictory rules that apply to extensions or changes in an employee's temporary work visa status. A few of those scenarios are addressed, but most are not. For example, the next generation *Handbook* would serve employers well by providing examples of how to complete section 3 reverifications based on employer-based filings on extension of nonimmigrant visa status for foreign workers (*e.g.*, H-1B, L-1, and O-1). Federal regulations provide these workers with up to 240 days of legal status with work authorization while timely filed extension of status requests are pending with USCIS. The *Handbook* could contrast these scenarios, under which continued work authorization is permissible, with other types of USCIS filings for work authorization renewal that do not provide proof of employment eligibility while the foreign worker awaits a decision.

- The *Handbook* fails to "connect the dots" between the 1980s-era I-9 process and legal developments of the last 20 years. One example is the absence of any reference to H-1B or I-485 "portability," two new-hire scenarios that are not adequately addressed for employers in the *Handbook*. The immigration laws were amended several years ago to permit foreign workers to move from one employer to another in certain settings.[4] This allows an H-1B professional worker to start working for a new H-1B employer when that company files an H-1B petition on the worker's behalf. The employment with the second company is fully authorized by that filing, even though it may be weeks or months before USCIS issues an approval notice in connection with that change in employment. Similarly, a foreign national who has had an I-485 adjustment of status application pending with USCIS for more than six months may be able to change jobs without the new employer ever having to file any application or immigration benefits petition on that worker's behalf. The government would do a great service to employers and foreign workers alike by having these rules explained in the *Handbook*, as there is often confusion on how the I-9 is to be completed in these "portability" scenarios.

Conclusion

The government is to be commended for clarifying more issues in the updated *Handbook*. It's unfortunate that it took so many years for this expanded version to be released. Likewise, as the comments above illustrate, this is a resource that warranted greater input from I-9 users. More collaboration on USCIS's part with business groups and human resources professional associations would have resulted in a more comprehensive tool. But as it stands, employers certainly welcome the update and will benefit from the improvements.

---

[4] *See* American Competitiveness in the Twenty-First Century Act of 2000, Pub. L. No. 106-313, §§101–16, 114 Stat. 1251, 1251–62.

SUBSTANTIVE VS. TECHNICAL/PROCEDURAL FAILURES UNDER THE GOOD-FAITH DEFENSE

Courtesy of Kathleen Campbell Walker

SUBSTANTIVE VERSUS TECHNICAL/PROCEDURAL FAILURES UNDER THE GOOD FAITH DEFENSE CREATED BY § 411 OF IIRAIRA *

	Substantive Failures		Technical or Procedural Failures
I.	Failure to prepare or present the I-9 form.		
II.	In Section One of the I-9, failure of the employer to ensure that the individual: A. Enters his or her printed name. B. Checks a box for citizen, lawful permanent resident alien, or alien authorized to work until a specified date. C. Gives his or her A number as to one of the latter two checked boxes and the A number is NOT provided in Section 2 or 3, or on a legible copy of the document which is retained with the I-9. D. Signs the attestation. E. Dates the attestation at the time of hire, if the date of hire occurred before September 30, 1996.	I.	In Section One of the I-9, failure of the employer to ensure that the individual: A. Provides his or her maiden name, address, or date of birth. B. Provides his or her A number on the line provided next to the box for "Lawful Permanent Resident" or "Alien authorized to work until" if either of the two boxes is checked, and provides the A number in Section 2 or 3, or a legible copy of the document is retained with the I-9 and submitted at the audit. C. Dates Section One. D. Dates Section One at the time of hire if the time of hire occurred on or after September 30, 1996. E. Failure of the employer to ensure that a preparer and/or translator provides his or her name, address, signature, or date on the space provided.
III.	In Section Two of the I-9, failure to: A. Review and verify a proper List A document or proper List B and C documents. B. Provide the document title, identification number(s), and/or expiration date(s) of a List A or Lists B and C documents (unless a legible copy of the document is retained with the I-9 and provided at the audit). C. Sign the attestation. D. Date the attestation within three business days of the date of hire, or, if the individual is hired for three business days or less, at the time of hire, if the date that Section Two was to be completed occurred before September 30, 1996.	II.	In Section Two of the I-9, failure of the employer to: A. Provide the document title, identification number(s), and/or expiration date(s) of a List A or Lists B and C documents provided that a legible copy of the document is retained with the I-9 and provided at the audit. B. Provide the title, business name, and business address. C. Provide the date of hire in the attestation portion. D. Date the section. E. Date the section within three business days of the date of hire, or if the individual is hired for three business days or less, at the time of hire, <u>if the date on which Section Two had to be completed occurred on or after September 30, 1996.</u>
IV.	In Section Three of the I-9, failure to: A. Review and verify a proper List A or proper List B and C documents. B. Provide the document title, identification number(s), and/or expiration date(s) of a List A or Lists B and C documents (unless a legible copy of the document is retained with the I-9 and provided at the audit). C. Sign the section. D. Date the section. E. Date the section not later than the date that the work authorization of the individual expires.	III.	In Section Three of the I-9, failure to: A. Provide the document title, identification number(s), and/or expiration date(s) of a List A or Lists B and C documents provided that a legible copy of the document is retained with the I-9 and provided at the audit. B. Provide the date of rehire.

*Applies to Inspections and Audits Conducted On or After September 30, 1996.

EMPLOYER VERIFICATION AND NO-MATCH LETTERS

by Kathleen Campbell Walker and L. Edward Rios[*]

---

[*] **Kathleen Campbell Walker** is the 2007–08 president of the American Immigration Lawyers Association (AILA). She heads the immigration department of Kemp Smith LLP in El Paso. She is also board-certified in immigration and nationality law by the Texas Board of Legal Specialization (TBLS) and serves as chair of the TBLS exam committee on immigration and nationality law. She has testified for AILA multiple times before Congress on issues regarding border security, US VISIT, and immigration reform. In addition, she has testified before Texas House and Senate committees on immigration issues. She is also a previous four-year chair of the AILA State Department Liaison Committee. Ms. Walker has been named as one of five "go-to" lawyers in Texas on immigration law by *Texas Lawyer* in its "Go-To Guide," and as a recommended immigration law attorney in Texas by *Super Lawyer*. Ms. Walker has been recognized as one of the top 50 women lawyers in Texas, and as one of the top 50 lawyers in Central and West Texas, by *Texas Monthly*. In addition, she is recognized in *Chambers USA: America's Leading Lawyers for Business*, the *International Who's Who of Business Lawyers*, and *Best Lawyers in America* as a leading immigration lawyer.

L. Edward Rios is a partner in Kemp Smith LLP's immigration law department in El Paso. Mr. Rios practices exclusively in the areas of immigration and related cross-border business formation, and import/export issues. Mr. Rios is an active member of AILA, previously serving three years on the National Customs and Border Protection Liaison Committee. He currently serves on the AILA National Admissions and Border Security Committee. Mr. Rios is invited regularly to speak at both chapter and national conferences on immigration matters involving various aspects of business immigration, practice before U.S. consulates abroad, and security screening procedures, as well as various aspects of business immigration.

April 2006: The Criminal Card in Worksite Enforcement

April 16, 2006 - Washington Post, "Immigration Enforcement's Shift in the Workplace"

"...*If you're blatantly violating our worksite enforcement laws, we'll go after your Mercedes and your mansion and your millions. We'll go after everything we can, and we'll charge you criminally.*" --Asst. Sec. of ICE, Julie Myers

KEMP SMITH
SINCE 1866

ICE STATISTICS

- Criminal Arrest in Worksite Enforcement – 25 in FY 2002, 716 in FY 2006 and 588 in the beginning of FY 2007 (as of May 23, 2007)

- Administration's FY 07 budget requests $41.7 million in new funds for worksite enforcement and 171 additional ICE agents

KEMP SMITH
SINCE 1866

ICE STATISTICS

- Michael Chertoff requested $3 billion for Fiscal Year 2009 for immigration enforcement, including raiding work sites and increasing the number of beds to detain those suspected of being in the country unlawfully

KEMP SMITH
SINCE 1866

ICE STATISTICS

- Number of individuals arrested in worksite cases on administrative immigration violations – 485 in FY02 to 3,667 in FY 06

- For FY 2007, ICE secured fines and judgments of more than $30 Million while making 863 criminal arrests and 4,077 administrative arrests

KEMP SMITH
SINCE 1866

Playing Hard Ball

- 8 USC §1324 and 18 USC §371– Conspiracy to Transport and Harbor Unlawful Aliens

- 18 USC §1546 – Fraud and Misuse of Immigration Documents

- 18 USC §§1956 and 1957 – Money Laundering

- 8 USC § 1324(a) – Unlawful Employment of Aliens

- Constructive Knowledge – ICE Final Rule, 72 Fed. Reg. 45611 (8/15/2007) (Proposed 6/14/2006)

KEMP SMITH
SINCE 1866

DEMISE OF THE TEXAS PROVISO

- Act of 7/12/1951 (65 State 119) – Creates Basic Bracero Framework

- Act of 3/20/1952 (66 Stat 26) – Amends Immigration Act of 1917 making it a felony to bring in or willfully induce an alien to enter or reside in the U.S. unlawfully (Texas Proviso exempts usual and normal practices incident to employment.)

KEMP SMITH
SINCE 1866

DEMISE OF THE TEXAS PROVISO

- INA 6/27/52 (66 Stat 163) – Creates comprehensive immigration statute

- Immigration Reform and Control Act (IRCA) 1/26/1986 (100 Stat 3359) – Creates Employer Sanctions and Anti-Discrimination Provisions and Removes Texas proviso to expose certain willful employment to criminal harboring charges

KEMP SMITH
SINCE 1866

Harboring Caselaw Examples

- U.S. v Matousek 131 Fed. Appx. 541 (CA 10 Kan) (May 17, 2005) - D played essential role in conspiracy transporting workers from airport to worksite, paid for lodging, and received and distributed paychecks.

- U.S. v Kim 193 F.3d 567 (2d Cir. 1999) – Conduct of employer taking steps to conceal identity of alien and instructing alien to obtain false documentation for I-9.

KEMP SMITH
SINCE 1866

Harboring Caselaw Examples

- U.S. v. Winnie Mae Mfg. Co., 451 F. Supp. 642 (DC Cal 1978) – Texas Proviso does not offer blanket immunity to all employers – applies only if normal practices of employment followed.

- U.S. v. Lopez, 521 F.2d 437 (2d Cir 1970), cert. denied, 423 US 995 (1975) – providing illegal aliens with housing, transport, employment, and sham marriages constituted harboring.

KEMP SMITH
SINCE 1866

Recent ICE Actions

- August 28, 2007 – Koch Foods – ICE special agents administratively arrested 160 Koch employees for immigration violations and executed criminal search warrants at Koch's corporate office in Chicago

- May 2007 – Quality Service Integrity, Inc. – Twelve defendants pleaded guilty in early May to fraud and misuse of employment documents. Two former managers, who are awaiting trial, have been charged with harboring illegal aliens

KEMP SMITH
SINCE 1866

Recent ICE Actions

- March 2007 – Golden State Fence Co. - Melvin Kay, 3 years probation, 180 days of home confinement and a $200,000 fine. Michael McLaughlin, 3 years probation, 180 days of home confinement and a $100,000 fine. Corporation must forfeit $4.7 million of its proceeds.

- March 2007 – Sun Drywall and Stucco, Inc. - Company president charged with harboring.

KEMP SMITH
SINCE 1866

Recent ICE Actions

- March 2007 – Michael Bianco, Inc. - Company owner and 3 managers arrested on criminal charges related to knowingly hiring illegal workers.

- March 2007 – Garcia Labor Companies - Company president sentenced to 15 months in prison followed by two years of supervised release, fined $25,000. Companies required to forfeit $12 million.

KEMP SMITH
SINCE 1866

State Legislative Efforts

Colo - HB 06S – 1017 requires businesses to comply with federal immigration law by only hiring those who are legally authorized to work in the US. As of January 1, 2007, businesses must confirm in writing within 20 days of hiring a new employee that they have examined the legal work status of the employee and kept copies of documents presented by an employee to establish legal work status.

KEMP SMITH
SINCE 1866

State Legislative Efforts

- GA - The Georgia Security and Immigration Act (SB529) requires state employers and companies that do business with the state as of 7/1/07 to verify the legal status of employees through the DHS Basic Pilot Program.

- ID - Governor of Idaho signed an Executive Order on 12/13/2006 requiring all state agencies and contractors and subcontractors with the state to use the Basic Pilot program to verify new hires.

KEMP SMITH
SINCE 1866

State Legislative Efforts

- OK – The Oklahoma Taxpayer and Citizen Protection Act of 2007 – requires every public employer to register with and utilize a Status Verification System to verify the federal employment authorization status of all new employees. After July 1, 2008 no contractor or subcontractor may enter into a contract with a public employer unless the contractor or subcontractor registers and participates in the Status Verification System.

KEMP SMITH
SINCE 1866

State Legislative Efforts

- NV – Requires the Director of the Department of Business and Industry to include on the Department's website a link to the Social Security Administration for employer's to verify employee social security numbers; provides for an administrative fine for a person with a state business license who willfully, flagrantly, or otherwise egregiously engages in the unlawful hiring or employment of an unauthorized alien.

- WV – Requires employers to verify prospective employee's legal status or authorization to work in the U.S. before hiring the individual or contracting with them for services; provides for fines and possible revocation of business license for multiple offenses.

KEMP SMITH
SINCE 1866

State Legislative Efforts

TN – Prohibits an employer, including any contractor, from accepting an Individual Taxpayer Identification Number as a form of identification by a potential employee or subcontractor. Effective January 1, 2008.

AZ – After December 31, 2007 requires every employer, after hiring an employee, to verify the employee's employment eligibility using the basic pilot program. Enforcement has been delayed until March 1, 2008 pending District Court Judge Wake's ruling on a motion to permanently bar its enforcement. District Court Judge Wake dismissed the actions and denied the motion for preliminary injunction on February 7, 2008.

KEMP SMITH
SINCE 1866

State Legislative Efforts

- IL – Law prohibiting employers from enrolling in any employment eligibility program until the SSA and DHS databases are able to make a determination of 99% of the tentative non-confirmation notices within 3 days. Effective January 1, 2008. On December 14, 2007, District Court Judge Scott granted a stipulated joint motion to stay DHS's lawsuit to enjoin the law to allow the IL General Assembly time to consider new legislation, which may moot DHS's lawsuit.

- The government is suing Illinois to declare this legislation invalid and permanently enjoin Illinois from execution or enforcement of this legislation.

KEMP SMITH
SINCE 1866

Constructive Knowledge

- Constructive Knowledge Defined
    - 8 CFR §274a.1(l)(1) The term *knowing* includes not only actual knowledge but also knowledge which may fairly be inferred through notice of certain facts and circumstances which would lead a person, through the exercise of reasonable care, to know about a certain condition. (May not be inferred from an employee's foreign appearance or accent.)

- Depends on the totality of the circumstances

KEMP SMITH
SINCE 1866

Constructive Knowledge and Subcontractors

- Under 8 C.F.R. §274a.5, any person or entity knowingly using a subcontract after November 6, 1986 to obtain the labor or services of an alien in the U.S. knowing that the alien is an unauthorized alien with respect to such labor or services, is considered as the employer for purposes of INA §274A(a)(1)(A) violations concerning the unlawful employment of unauthorized aliens.

KEMP SMITH
SINCE 1866

Constructive Knowledge Before September 14, 2007

- Constructive Knowledge Examples
  - Constructive knowledge may include, but is not limited to, situations where an employer:
    - (i) Fails to complete or improperly completes the Employment Eligibility Verification Form, I-9;
    - (ii) Has information available to it that would indicate that the alien is not authorized to work, such as Labor Certification and/or an Application for Prospective Employer; or
    - (iii) Acts with reckless and wanton disregard for the legal consequences of permitting another individual to introduce an unauthorized alien into its work force or to act on its behalf.

KEMP SMITH
SINCE 1866

Constructive Knowledge Case Examples

U.S. v. Mester Manufacturing Co., OCAHO Case No. 87100001, (June 17, 1988), aff'd Mester Manufacturing Co. v. INS, 879 F.2d 561 (9th Cir. 1989) – knowing includes "should have known" in the context of knowingly continuing to employ; employer is liable if fails to take steps necessary to learn the status of an employee.

U.S. v. Valdez, OCAHO Case No. 89100014, (September 27, 1989) – applies the constructive knowledge standard to a "knowing hiring" – Respondent's failure to prepare an I-9 Form, when coupled with her conscious avoidance of acquiring knowledge as to the identification and status of her employees, provide believable circumstantial evidence of her knowledge of an employee's unauthorized status. "Deliberate ignorance cannot reasonably be a defense." at 11.

KEMP SMITH
SINCE 1866

Constructive Knowledge Case Examples

U.S. v. New El Rey Sausage Co., OCAHO Case No. 88100080, (July 7, 1989) – finds constructive knowledge where the employer had reason to know of employee's unauthorized status.

"An employer shall be deemed to have reason to know that an employee is [unauthorized] if it can be shown by a preponderance of the evidence that the employer was in possession of such information as would lead a person exercising reasonable care to acquire knowledge of the fact in question ... or to infer, on the basis of reliable warnings, that such officially questioned employees are not, in fact, authorized to be employed in the United States." at 32.

KEMP SMITH
SINCE 1866

Constructive Knowledge Case Examples

- U.S. v. Collins Foods Int'l, Inc., OCAHO Case No. 89100084, (Jan. 9, 1990) – Employer should have known that the employee was not work authorized because of the delay of the employee in producing a social security card, the misspelling of the employee's name on the social security card, the lamination of the card, the lack of a reference to the United States of America on the card, and the use of two last names on the employee's driver's license and only one last name on the social security card. Due to these issues, the employer was found to have deliberately failed to inquire into the immigration status of the employee in an effort to avoid learning that the employee was not, in fact, work authorized.

KEMP SMITH
SINCE 1866

Constructive Knowledge Case Examples

- U.S. v. Buckingham Limited Partnership, OCAHO Case No. 89100244, (Apr. 6, 1990) – "Federal case law instructs that failure to know what could have been known in the exercise of due diligence amounts to knowledge in the eyes of the law." at 9. In this case, employer was found to have knowingly continued to employ an alien after his work authorization had expired.

KEMP SMITH
SINCE 1866

Constructive Knowledge
Final Rule Effective Sept. 14, 2007
(temporarily enjoined)

- Fails to complete Form I-9

- Improperly completes Form I-9

KEMP SMITH
SINCE 1866

Constructive Knowledge
Final Rule Effective Sept. 14, 2007
(temporarily enjoined)

- Under the final rule, constructive knowledge will also include failure to take reasonable steps to address the following situations:
    1) An employee's request for the employer's sponsorship for a labor certification or visa petition;
    2) Receipt of a no-match letter from the Social Security Administration ("SSA"); and
    3) Receipt of a notice from the Department of Homeland Security ("DHS") that the employment authorization documents presented in connection with the completion of the I-9 form do not match DHS records.

KEMP SMITH
SINCE 1866

Safe Harbor Provisions
SSA No-Match

- Within 30 days of receiving the SSA No-Match Letter the employer <u>must</u> check its records to determine if the discrepancy was caused by clerical error, correct the error with SSA, and verify that the corrected name and social security number now match SSA's records.

- Employer is advised to retain a record of the manner, date, and time of such verification.

- Employer <u>may</u> update the I-9 form relating to the employee <u>or</u> complete a new I-9 (retaining the original <u>but should not</u> perform a new I-9 verification.

KEMP SMITH
SINCE 1866

Safe Harbor Provisions
SSA No-Match

- If the employer determines that the discrepancy is not clerical error, the employer must promptly request that the employee confirm that the name and social security account in the employer's records are correct.

- If the information is incorrect, the employer must make corrections, inform the SSA of the correction and verify a match on the corrected information and make a record of its actions.

KEMP SMITH
SINCE 1866

Safe Harbor Provisions
SSA No-Match

- If the employee confirms that the information on file with the employer is correct, then the employer must promptly advise the employee of the date of receipt of the no-match letter and advise the employee to resolve the discrepancy with SSA no later than 90 days after the receipt date.

KEMP SMITH
SINCE 1866

Safe Harbor Provisions
DHS No-Match

- The employer must contact the local DHS office in accordance with the written notice's instructions and attempt to resolve the question raised by DHS about the immigration status document of employment authorization document

- The specific instructions in the letter may provide less than 30 days for the employer to respond

KEMP SMITH
SINCE 1866

Safe Harbor Provisions
DHS No-Match

- If the employer is unable to verify with DHS within 90 days of receiving the written notice that the immigration status document or employment authorization document is assigned to the employee, the employer must again verify the employee's employment authorization and identity within 3 days by following this verification procedure:
    - The employer completes a new I-9 for the employee, following the same procedure as if the employee was a new hire.
    - The employee must complete Section One and the employer must complete Section Two of the new I-9 form within 93 days of receipt of the notice from DHS.
    - The employer must not accept any document referenced in any written notice from DHS.
    - The employee must present a document that contains a photograph in order to establish identity or both identity and employment authorization.

KEMP SMITH
SINCE 1866

Safe Harbor Provisions

Within 93 days of Receipt of Notice from SSA or DHS

- If the discrepancy cannot be resolved with either SSA or DHS within 90 days of the written communication from either agency, the employer must attempt to re-verify the worker's employment eligibility by completing a new I-9 employment verification form.

- Companies should use the same procedures as when completing an I-9 form at the time of hire with a few exceptions:

KEMP SMITH
SINCE 1866

Safe Harbor Provisions

- The employee must complete Section One and the employer must complete Section Two of the new I-9 form within 93 days of receipt of the notice from DHS or SSA.

- The employer cannot accept any document (or receipt for such a document) referenced in the DHS notification or any document (or receipt for such a document) that contains a social security number that is the subject of the SSA No-Match letter to establish employment eligibility or identity

KEMP SMITH
SINCE 1866

Safe Harbor Provisions

- The employee must present a document that contains a photograph in order to establish identity or both identity and employment authorization.

- The new I-9 form should be retained with the original I-9 form(s).

KEMP SMITH
SINCE 1866

Safe Harbor Provisions

- No safe harbor protocol is available where an employee requests employer sponsorship for a labor certification or visa petition and the employee turns out to be unauthorized.

- The employer may be charged with actual or constructive knowledge of unauthorized status if the employee admits he or she is currently unauthorized to work, or where the information provided to the employer as verification is inconsistent with such a request (e.g. submitted a Resident Alien Card).

KEMP SMITH
SINCE 1866

Penalties

For offenses occurring on or after March 27, 2008

Paperwork
- Not less than $110 and not more than $1,100 per individual

Civil
- First offense: not less than $375, and not to exceed $3,200, for each unauthorized worker.
- Second offense: not less than $3,200, and not to exceed $6,500, for each unauthorized worker.
- More than 2 offenses: not less than $4,300, and not to exceed $16,000, for each unauthorized worker.

KEMP SMITH
SINCE 1866

Temporary Restraining Order and No-Match Letters

- August 31, 2007 the U.S. District Court in northern California granted a temporary restraining order ("TRO"), which has temporarily prohibited DHS from implementing the final no-match rule.

- Also prohibits SSA from issuing No-Match letters which reference DHS.

- On October 1, 2007, a federal judge extended the temporary restraining order for an additional 10 days.

KEMP SMITH
SINCE 1866

SSA No-Match Letter Litigation

- <u>NO MATCH LAWSUIT</u> - The day after Thanksgiving, November 23, the Department of Homeland Security (DHS) announced that it will conduct additional rulemaking proceedings to address the issues raised in the suit filed with the U.S. N.D. California District Court. These actions include preparing a Regulatory Flexibility Act analysis.

- DHS anticipates that the amended rule will "fully address" the Court's concerns. DHS will issue an amended final rule, and then DHS plans to move the Court to vacate the preliminary injunction against the No match letter regulation. DHS stated that it will be able to complete the contemplated rulemaking proceedings by March of 2008. On February 5, 2008, DHS submitted a new version of the proposed No-Match rule to OMB.

- Thus, DHS requested the Court to stay proceedings until March 24, 2008 or until an amended final rule is issued, whichever occurs first. Thus, the no match letter battle continues.

KEMP SMITH
SINCE 1866

Statement by Homeland Security Secretary Michael Chertoff on the No-Match Appeal
Release Date: December 5, 2007

The U.S. Department of Justice filed an appeal on behalf of the Department of Homeland Security (DHS) on the injunction against the No-Match Rule in San Francisco, Calif.

Employers receive a No-Match letter from the Social Security Administration when an employee's name does not match the social security number it has on file. Sometimes there is an innocent explanation for this discrepancy, such as a clerical error. But sometimes the discrepancy reflects the fact that the employee in question is an illegal alien. When employers receive such No-Match letters, they are on notice that the employees in question may not be authorized to work.

Under our No-Match Rule, no employer should terminate an employee based upon a no-match letter alone. But no employer should ignore such a letter or the discrepancy it reveals. The No-Match Rule gives employers and employees 90 days – a full three months – to correct the discrepancy.

If the mismatch is a clerical error, that is a good opportunity to correct the mistake. When the mismatch shows fraud, however, appropriate steps should be taken. Businesses that follow the procedures in the rule will have a safe harbor from enforcement action. Those that ignore no-match letters place themselves at obvious risk and invite suspicion that they are knowingly employing workers who are here illegally.

Far from abandoning the No-Match Rule, we are pressing ahead by taking the district court's order to the Ninth Circuit Court of Appeals. At the same time, we will soon issue a supplement to the rule that specifically addresses the three grounds on which the district court based its injunction. By pursuing these two paths simultaneously, my aim is to get a resolution as quickly as possible so we can move the No-Match Rule forward and provide honest employers with the guidance they need.

The ACLU's lawsuit has put this vital protection on hold. That is bad for immigration enforcement and bad for America's law-abiding employers and their legal workers. The only real beneficiaries of the ACLU's strategy are employers who would rather close their eyes to cheap and profitable illegal labor than obey the laws of our country.

KEMP SMITH
SINCE 1866

Four Goals in Developing a Compliance Program

- **Comprehensive Compliance Policy**
- **Training**
- **Internal Audits**
- **Changing the Corporate Culture**

KEMP SMITH
SINCE 1866

Compliance Checklist

1. Immigration Issues
2. Players
3. Policy Purpose Statement
4. Policy Compliance Manual
5. Verification Procedures
6. Contracts and Sub-contracts
7. Electronic Management Programs
8. Non-discriminatory Practices
9. Management Acceptance
10. Training
11. Periodic Review
12. Internal Investigations
13. Internal Audits
    - I-9 Compliance (Substantive & Technical)
    - Labor Conditions Applications & Public Information Files for H-1B employees
    - PERM Audit Files containing conforming recruitment/results and proof of alien credentials/experience

KEMP SMITH
SINCE 1866

Form I-9 and Revised I-9 Handbook

- New I-9 Form and Revised I-9 Handbook - The November 26, 2007 issue of the *Federal Register* apparently announces the introduction of the newly amended I-9 Employment Eligibility Verification form. As of November 7, 2007, the amended Form I-9 is the only valid version of the I-9 form, BUT DHS will not seek penalties against an employer for using a previous version of the Form I-9 on or before December 26, 2007.

- Employers do not need to fill out new I-9s for current employees based on the issuance of the new form, but the new form must be used for any reverification of employees on or after December 26, 2007. The newly revised "Handbook for Employers, Instructions for Completing the Form I–9, (M–274)" is available online at http://www.uscis.gov. Because of its length, the revised M–274 will not be reprinted in the *Federal Register*. Employers may access the amended Form I–9 (Rev. 06/05/07)N online at http://www.uscis.gov.

KEMP SMITH
SINCE 1866

Form I-9 and Revised I-9 Handbook

- The amended Form I–9 now instructs employees that providing their Social Security number in Section 1 of the form is voluntary, pursuant to section 7 of the Privacy Act (5 U.S.C. 552a note).

- Employees must provide, however, their Social Security number in section 1 of the form, if their employer participates in E-Verify (the employment eligibility verification program formerly known as Basic Pilot or EEV), as provided by section 403(a)(1)(A) of Illegal Immigration Reform and Immigrant Responsibility Act.

- For employees who present their Social Security account number card to their employer as evidence that they are authorized to work in the U.S., the employer must record the Social Security Account number in section 2 of the Form I–9. The amended Form I–9 also includes a clarification that there is no filing fee associated with the Form I–9.

KEMP SMITH
SINCE 1866

Form I-9 and Revised I-9 Handbook

The amended Form I–9 no longer lists the following as List A documents (proof of identity and employment eligibility):

1. Certificate of United States Citizenship (Form N–560 or N–561);
2. Certificate of Naturalization (Form N–550 or N–570);
3. Form I–151, a long out-of-date version of the Alien Registration Receipt Card ("Green Card");
4. Unexpired Reentry Permit (Form I–327); and
5. Unexpired Refugee Travel Document (Form 1–571).

KEMP SMITH
SINCE 1866

Form I-9 and Revised I-9 Handbook

The amended Form I–9 retains four types of acceptable List A documents:

1. U.S. Passport (unexpired or expired);
2. Permanent Resident Card or Alien Registration Receipt Card (Form I–551);
3. Unexpired foreign passport with a temporary I–551 stamp; and
4. Unexpired Employment Authorization Document that contains a photograph (Form I–766, I–688, I–688A, I–688B).
5. The fifth acceptable List A document entitled, "unexpired foreign passport with an attached Form I–94 indicating unexpired employment authorization," has been replaced by "an unexpired foreign passport with an unexpired Arrival-Departure Record, Form I–94, bearing the same name as the passport and containing an endorsement of the alien's nonimmigrant status, if that status authorizes the alien to work for the employer." (Note that there are several nonimmigrant categories (such as B-1, B-2, among others, in which work is not authorized incident to nonimmigrant status). The notice with the I-9 form is attached.

All of these acceptable List A documents were carried over from the previous Form I–9, with the exception of the Form I–766, which is a new addition to List A. The amended Form I-9 also modifies one acceptable List A document, the unexpired foreign passport and I-94, as described.

KEMP SMITH
SINCE 1866

SSA Verification

- http://www.ssa.gov/employer/ssnv.htm

- Verify up to 10 names and SSNs (per screen) online and receive immediate results. This option is ideal to verify new hires. OR

- Upload batch files of up to 250,000 names and SSNs and usually receive results the next government business day. This option is ideal if you want to verify an entire payroll database or if you hire a large number of workers at a time.

KEMP SMITH
SINCE 1866

DHS/SSA E-Verify

The Department of Homeland Security's (DHS) U.S. Citizenship and Immigration Services Bureau (USCIS) and the Social Security Administration (SSA) are jointly conducting E-Verify, formerly known as the Basic Pilot Program/Employment Eligibility Verification Program. E-Verify involves verification checks of the SSA and DHS databases, using an automated system to verify the employment authorization of all newly hired employees.

KEMP SMITH
SINCE 1866

DHS/SSA E-Verify

- According to the White House, each week, 2,000 employers are being added to E-Verify and more than 3.7 Million new hire were processed through E-Verify last year alone.

- To date, E-Verify is helping more than 48,000 companies verify the employment eligibility of their new hires. (January 2008)

KEMP SMITH
SINCE 1866

ICE IMAGE PROGRAM

Employers seeking to participate in IMAGE must first agree to:

- Submit to an I-9 audit by ICE, and

- To ensure the accuracy of their wage reporting, verify the Social Security numbers of their existing labor forces, utilizing the Social Security Number Verification System (SSNVS).

- Upon enrollment and implementation of DHS's best hiring practices, program participants will be deemed "IMAGE Certified"- a distinction DHS believes will become an industry standard.

KEMP SMITH
SINCE 1866

ICE IMAGE PROGRAM

All IMAGE participants gain membership to DHS's Basic Pilot Employment Verification Program, administered by USCIS. Through this employee authorization verification program, employers can verify that newly hired employees are eligible to work in the United States. This Internet-based system is available in all 50 states and is currently free to employers. It provides an automated link to the Social Security Administration database and DHS immigration records. To sign up for participation in the Basic Pilot Employment Verification Program, visit the registration Web site https://www.vis-dhs.com/EmployerRegistration/.

KEMP SMITH
SINCE 1866

ICE BEST HIRING PRACTICES

- Use the Basic Pilot Employment Verification Program for all hiring.

- Establish an internal training program, with annual updates, on how to manage completion of Form I-9 (Employee Eligibility Verification Form), how to detect fraudulent use of documents in the I-9 process, and how to use the Basic Pilot Employment Verification Program.

- Permit the I-9 and Basic Pilot Program process to be conducted only by individuals who have received this training—and include a secondary review as part of each employee's verification to minimize the potential for a single individual to subvert the process.

- Arrange for annual I-9 audits by an external auditing firm or a trained employee not otherwise involved in the I-9 and electronic verification process.

KEMP SMITH
SINCE 1866

ICE BEST HIRING PRACTICES

- Establish a self-reporting procedure for reporting to ICE any violations or discovered deficiencies.

- Establish a protocol for responding to no-match letters received from the Social Security Administration.
- Establish a Tip Line for employees to report activity relating to the employment of unauthorized aliens, and a protocol for responding to employee tip

- Establish and maintain safeguards against use of the verification process for unlawful discrimination.

- Establish a protocol for assessing the adherence to the "best practices" guidelines by the company's contractors/subcontractors.

- Submit an annual report to ICE to track results and assess the effect of participation in the IMAGE program.

KEMP SMITH
SINCE 1866

Office of Special Counsel Immigration for Related Unfair Employment Practices

- The Office of Special Counsel for Immigration-Related Unfair Employment Practices (OSC), in the Civil Rights Division, is responsible for enforcing the anti-discrimination provisions of the Immigration and Nationality Act (INA), 8 U.S.C. § 1324b, which protect U.S. citizens and <u>certain work authorized individuals</u> from employment discrimination based upon citizenship or immigration status discrimination. The INA protects all work authorized individuals from national origin discrimination, unfair documentary practices relating to the employment eligibility verification process, and from retaliation.

KEMP SMITH
SINCE 1866

Office of Special Counsel Immigration for Related Unfair Employment Practices

- Injured parties file discrimination charges directly with OSC's Washington, D.C. office within 180 days of the alleged act of discrimination. OSC may investigate charges for up to 210 days after receipt of the charge. During the final 90-day period, OSC and/or the injured party may file an administrative complaint against the employer.

- http://www.usdoj.gov/crt/osc/

KEMP SMITH
SINCE 1866

Impact of Hoffman Plastic 535 US 137 (2002)

- Undocumented workers not entitled to <u>back pay</u> under collective bargaining law, the National Labor Relations Act (NLRA).

- Workers entitled to be paid for time actually worked regardless of immigration status.

- EEOC – immigration status irrelevant to the EEOC

- DOL – Wage and Hour continues to enforce FLSA and MSPA

KEMP SMITH
SINCE 1866

Impact of Hoffman Plastic 535 US 137 (2002)

- DOL – Wage and Hour continues to enforce Fair Labor Standards Act (FLSA) and Migrant and Seasonal Worker Agricultural Protection Act (MSPA)

- S. 2611 – Kennedy proposed amendment would have legislated around Hoffman

- STRIVE bill has similar provisions.

KEMP SMITH
SINCE 1866

RICO and Harboring

Williams v. Mohawk Industries, Inc., 465 F.3d 1277 (11th Cir. 2006)

Plaintiffs alleged that Mohawk conspired with third-party recruiters to violate federal immigration laws, destroy documentation, and harbor illegal workers. The recruiters were paid for each worker they brought to Mohawk, and some of the recruiters worked closely with Mohawk by offering illegal employees that could be brought to any of Mohawk's facilities on short notice.

District court held that Mohawk's collaboration with the third-party recruiters sufficiently established an "enterprise." Court of Appeals for the Eleventh Circuit affirmed, holding that RICO only requires a "loose or informal" association of entities to establish an enterprise.

KEMP SMITH
SINCE 1866

RICO and Harboring

Civil RICO plaintiff must allege that it was injured in his business or property "by reason of" a violation of RICO's substantive provisions. This "by reason of" language serves as the basis for the proximate cause requirement, established by the Supreme Court in *Holmes v. Securities Investor Trust Protection Corp,* 503 U.S. 258, 268 (1992).

KEMP SMITH
SINCE 1866

CONTACT INFO

Kathleen Campbell Walker
kwalker@kempsmith.com

Edward Rios
erios@kempsmith.com

915-433-5563

KEMP SMITH
SINCE 1866

EMPLOYMENT OF THE UNDOCUMENTED: CRIMINAL AND CIVIL LIABILITY RISKS

*by Mary E. Pivec**

EMPLOYMENT OF THE UNDOCUMENTED: CRIMINAL AND CIVIL LIABILITY RISKS

February 28, 2008

Mary E. Pivec
Keller and Heckman LLP
1001 G Street, NW
Washington, DC 20001
202-434-4212
pivec@khlaw.com
www.khlaw.com

Washington, D.C. • Brussels • San Francisco • Shanghai

---

* **Mary E. Pivec**, a partner with Keller and Heckman, LLP, in Washington, D.C., has extensive experience in representing employers in labor, employment, and immigration matters. She lectures on issues such as union avoidance techniques for supervisors and managers, defeating union representation elections, employer sanctions and I-9 compliance, developing effective employee handbooks, investigating and defending sexual harassment claims, and complying with the Family and Medical Leave Act, the Americans with Disabilities Act, and the Fair Labor Standards Act. Prior to her legal practice, Ms. Pivec worked as a business agent and handled collective bargaining and grievance and arbitration disputes in the public sector. In 2007 she was named by *Super Lawyers* as an outstanding attorney in Washington, D.C., in the fields of employment/labor and immigration law, and has also been named in *The Best Lawyers in America* since 1990 in the area of immigration law.

IRCA Misdemeanor Violations

- **Pattern or Practice, 8 USC §1324a(f)**
  - Knowledge – Actual or Constructive
  - Conduct – Hire (direct or through contract), Referral for Fee, Continuing Employment
  - Good Faith/Affirmative Defense – I-9 completion

- **Maximum Penalties: $3000@UA/6 mos.**

Felony Hiring Violation 8 USC §1324(a)(3)

- **Elements**
  - Actual knowledge that illegals smuggled into the U.S. in violation of law
  - Actual knowledge of illegal status at time of hire
  - At least 10 individuals in 12-month period

- **Maximum imprisonment – 5 years**

- **Maximum Fines – greater of $250,000 or 2x financial gain**

Felony Harboring Violation
8 USC §1324(a)(1)(A)(iii)

- **Required Elements**
  - Knowledge – Actual or constructive (reckless disregard) that a person has come to, entered, or remains in the U.S. in violation of law
  - Conduct – Harboring, concealing, or shielding from detection said person – thereby "substantially facilitating" the alien remaining in the U.S. illegally
  - Intent – To evade or avoid detection by law enforcement (*Susnjar v. United States*, 27 F.2d 223 (6th Cir. 1928))

- **Maximum Imprisonment – 5 yr./10 yr. (commercial advantage/financial gain)**

Employment "Plus" = Potential Felony Harboring Charges

- Housing and transporting workers with actual or constructive knowledge of illegal status
- Warning workers of ICE raid activity
- Counseling workers to use fake documents
- Paying illegal workers off the books
- Transferring illegal workers between job sites to avoid detection
- Assisting illegal workers to complete I-9 forms with fake documents

Conspiracy to Harbor
8 USC §1324(a)(1)(A)(v)(I)

- **Required Elements**
  - Agreement with at least one other person
  - Harbor at least one unauthorized alien
  - One act furthering goal of conspiracy

- **Maximum Imprisonment** – 10 years @ violation

- **Maximum Fines** – greater of $250,000 or 2x gain

Felony Money Laundering
18 U.S.C. §1957

- Requires proof of a financial transaction conducted in the proceeds of "specified unlawful activity"
- 18 USC §1956(c)(7) predicate crimes include harboring, attempting to harbor, aiding and abetting harboring and conspiracy to harbor
- Prosecutors love charge – greed evidence
- Pending controversy over what constitutes "proceeds"
- Maximum Imprisonment – 10 years @ violation

Aiding and Abetting Aggravated Identity Theft, 18 U.S.C. §1028A

- Requires proof of knowingly transferring, possessing, or using a means of personal identification of another without lawful authority during commission of specified felonies, including false personation of citizenship, fraud, and false statements

Criminal Asset Forfeiture for Felony Convictions 18 U.S.C. §982(a)(6)(a)

- Separate Count Considered by Jury
- Types Of Property Subject To Seizure Upon Conviction
  - Vehicles
  - Plant and Equipment
  - Bank Accounts
- Use In Plea Bargaining
  - Heavy price exacted for pleading to a lesser charge

Who Can Be Charged

- Individuals
  - Plant Managers and Supervisors
  - Human Resource Personnel
  - Union Stewards
  - Intermediate and Senior Corporate Officials
  - Accountants

- The Employing Entity

The Civil RICO Risk
18 USC §1962

- Elements of Civil RICO Cause of Action
- Predicate Immigration Crimes – motivated by financial gain
  - 8 USC §1324(a)(3) – Felony Hiring
  - 8 USC §1324(a)(1)(A)(iii), (iv) – Felony Harboring, Transporting
- Damage Theories
- Causality Issues

Debarment From Participation in Federal Procurement Programs

- Automatic inclusion on web-based GSA Excluded Parties List System (EPLS) upon judicial notice of felony conviction, forcing contracting agency to demonstrate that there is a compelling reason to retain excluded contractor

- Assumes convicted entity poses substantial risk of non-performance of contract obligations

- Reinstatement of contractor eligibility to compete for future contacts and task orders involves protracted negotiations and requires mea culpa, detailed corporate compliance plan, and regular self-audits and reporting

Elements of an Effective Corporate Compliance Program

- Standards and procedures reasonably capable of reducing risk of criminal acts, with compliance responsibility vested at highest corporate level
- Due diligence/checks and balances built into system
- Universal corporate compliance training – boardroom to shop floor
- Detailed written guidelines for managers and supervisors
- Effective auditing and monitoring procedures
- Hot line mechanism for reporting alleged violations anonymously and without fear of retaliatory action
- Prompt investigation of all complaints, followed by prompt remediation action
- Strong disciplinary action for intentional violations

Thank you!

Mary E. Pivec
Partner
Keller and Heckman LLP
1001 G Street, NW
Washington, DC 20001
202-434-4212
pivec@khlaw.com

www.khlaw.com

Washington, D.C. • Brussels • San Francisco • Shanghai

PRACTICAL POINTERS IN CONDUCTING INVESTIGATIONS AFTER ICE WORKSITE RAIDS

by Josie Gonzalez[*]

In the aftermath of a raid, U.S. Immigration and Customs Enforcement (ICE) will be interviewing detainees at length to secure material witnesses and their testimony, reviewing every piece of evidence seized, and making additional plans to further document the case against the employer. Under the direction of legal counsel, the employer should immediately take steps to assess remaining records, ensure current compliance, and discover what evidence ICE has gathered.

- At the first opportunity, a private investigator should interview those who were arrested, as well as supervisors and managers, in order to determine:
  - Where employees were arrested—during raid, at home, etc.
  - What other contact the arrested employees may have previously had with ICE
  - What questions were asked or what assertions were made by ICE
  - What answers were given
  - Which employees/supervisors were discussed
  - If there was a pattern of questions asked of detainees—if specific managers or supervisors were targeted
  - What the employee's history was with the company—who hired him or her, who completed the I-9, who referred him or her to the company for hire, what documents were used to complete the I-9, what discussions took place at the time of hire
  - If there is additional information about other employees, managers, or document sources that was not shared with ICE
  - If the names of any former employees were included in discussions with ICE
  - If promises of an employment authorization document or permanent residency were offered in exchange for testimony or undercover work as an informant; or if threats of criminal prosecution were made by ICE
  - How long employees were kept in detention and what the detention conditions were

---

[*] **Josie Gonzalez** is the managing partner of Gonzalez & Harris, and has represented employers in all aspects of immigration law for more than 25 years. She recently represented a major corporation facing federal criminal charges for hiring undocumented workers. Ms. Gonzalez has published numerous articles for legal and trade journals on the topic of employer sanctions. Her background as a former criminal defense attorney and employer sanctions expert makes her uniquely qualified to address issues such as RICO and other criminal charges against employers, the future of employer sanctions, and how to develop and implement immigration corporate compliance materials. She currently chairs AILA's Worksite Enforcement Conference Committee.

- The attorney must analyze the investigator's report, cross referencing information provided by several sources to determine consistencies/inconsistencies, corroboration, and the weight of the evidence obtained by ICE, and charges that may be brought against the employer and/or individual managers as a result.
- In order to avoid a possible conflict of interest, the attorney should not be actively involved in questioning arrested employees, or, at a minimum, never question potential witnesses alone.
- Management should not engage in any actions that may later be construed as interfering in the investigation or suborning perjury. (For example, management should not counsel employees on how to answer questions, or destroy documents.)
- ICE investigations will continue after the raid with the use of undercover informants in order to solidify the case against an employer.
- Copies of seized records should be requested of ICE immediately. Employers should expect a delay in being granted permission to gain access to these records, and should consider the following:
  - ICE will not copy these records or incur any associated costs: the employer will have to make arrangements have records copied in the ICE office or the U.S. Attorney's office.
  - Records are likely to be in a state of chaos, as boxed when seized. ICE will not want to leave a clear trail as to which documents it has reviewed.
  - When copying, employers should copy all I-9s and supporting documents, all personnel files with applications and W-2s, and any additional file documents that may pertain to targeted employees and supervisors/managers, as well as any written policies or memoranda pertaining to hiring procedures or practices.
  - Records should be returned to their original order so that files targeted for copying by the employer are not highlighted for ICE.
  - Determine if the seized records contain copies of "no-match" letters from the Social Security Administration and any related material.
  - Limit discussions with ICE during this process to ensure nothing is said that may later be misrepresented.
  - Once items are identified for copying, one may hire professional copy services, which may need to spend days taking copying machines on site and making copies. Copies may be scanned for later easy retrieval of data.
- The employer should search existing computer and hardcopy personnel and payroll files not seized that may pertain to the employees arrested or others targeted in the course of the investigation.
- While investigations are underway, the attorney should be proactive in working with management to develop a corporate compliance program that will enable

the company to attract, verify, and retain legal workers. This will include an assessment of current practices and procedures, and training of all those involved in the hiring process and completion of I-9s.

- Since I-9s will have been seized and may not be returned or copied for some time, the employer may choose to complete new I-9s for all current employees, ensuring that training has taken place and the new I-9s will be properly completed. These can later be coupled with original I-9s.

- Once the investigation is completed and all available evidence has been examined, the attorney will review the findings with senior management to discuss the company's position, possible actions on the part of ICE, and possible courses of action by the company and counsel.

A Mini-Primer on I-9s
& Related Resource Materials

by Josie Gonzalez

A MINI-PRIMER ON I-9S:

HOW TO REPRESENT AN EMPLOYER IN AN I-9 INSPECTION

by Josie Gonzalez[*]

Table of Contents

1. Summary of Key Issues Related to Representing an Employer in an I-9 Inspection 437
2. I-9 Inspections Outline 443
3. Ethical Considerations in Conducting Immigration Investigations 445
4. Questions for the Company Executive Officer 449
5. Questions for the Hiring Manager 453
6. Preliminary I-9 Inspections Instructions to Client 455
7. I-9 Inspections Checklist 457
8. I-9 Audit Report (Attorney-Client Work Product—Privileged and Confidential) 459
9. Work Authorization Tracking 461
10. Sample ICE Notice of Inspection 463
11. Sample ICE Second Notice of Inspection 465
12. How to Prepare for an ICE Business Inspection 467
13. ICE Business Entity Questionnaire 469
14. ICE Employee Information Certification Form 471
15. Sample ICE Subpoena 473
16. Subpoena and Custody Receipt for Seized Property 475
17. Sample ICE Notice of Suspect Documents 479
18. Sample ICE Notice of Unauthorized Aliens 481
19. Sample Notice of Intent to Fine 483

---

[*] **Josie Gonzalez** is the managing partner of Gonzalez & Harris, and has represented employers in all aspects of immigration law for more than 25 years. She recently represented a major corporation facing federal criminal charges for hiring undocumented workers. Ms. Gonzalez has published numerous articles for legal and trade journals on the topic of employer sanctions. Her background as a former criminal defense attorney and employer sanctions expert makes her uniquely qualified to address issues such as RICO and other criminal charges against employers, the future of employer sanctions, and how to develop and implement immigration corporate compliance materials. She currently chairs AILA's Worksite Enforcement Committee.

SUMMARY OF KEY ISSUES RELATED TO REPRESENTING AN EMPLOYER IN AN I-9 INSPECTION

by Josie Gonzalez

In the last several months of 2007, we witnessed a change in U.S. Immigration and Customs Enforcement (ICE) enforcement tactics. In addition to worksite raids, ICE is once again conducting I-9 inspections in major cities throughout the United States. During the late 1980s and through 1996, these inspections were popular vehicles to gather evidence about the degree of employer compliance with the Immigration Reform and Control Act of 1986 (IRCA).[1] Sometimes the results of the inspections formed the bases to conduct a raid in order to arrest undocumented workers and pursue criminal investigations. However, generally, these inspections merely resulted in civil "paperwork" fines under INA §274A(b) for improper completion of the I-9 and sometimes more substantive fines for either knowingly hiring or knowingly continuing the employment of unauthorized workers under §§274A(a)(1)(A) and 274A(a)(2).

The return of this enforcement component may be based on the fact that ICE can target more employers via the I-9 inspection vehicle, because conducting criminal investigations can be labor intensive. It takes time to conduct undercover operations, set up informants, and conduct wiretaps. Further, one needs the cooperation of a local U.S. attorney, who may be pressed with the prosecution of other crimes perceived as more serious and injurious to the public. With an infusion of congressional funding for worksite enforcement, many ICE officers have been hired and can now be enlisted to assist in I-9 worksite enforcement.

Unquestionably, given the current climate of enhanced criminal enforcement of immigration laws, today's I-9 inspections will be the vehicle for the initiation of criminal investigations. This sober reality must be realized by employers. They now must engage the advice of competent immigration and perhaps criminal counsel to guide them through the minefield of I-9 inspection compliance. This summary of key issues and accompanying practice aids will serve as a tool for the attorney to bravely mine through an I-9 inspection without setting off any explosives.

Do I Have the Skills and Resources to Represent the Employer?

It takes a team consisting of an attorney and trained paralegals or human resources (HR) personnel or consultants to represent a large employer that is served with an inspection notice. The attorney must focus on the big picture and spend considerable time interviewing executive officers and hiring managers in order to assess whether any civil or criminal liability exists. Specifically, has the company's managerial staff knowingly—on a constructive or actual knowledge basis—hired or continued the employment of unauthorized aliens, either directly or through subcontractors? While

---

[1] Pub. L. No. 99-603, 100 Stat. 3359.

the attorney is making this determination, a team of paralegals should be auditing the I-9s in order to report their findings to the supervising attorney, who will make recommendations to management for corrective action. Time is of the essence, as I-9 inspections can move quickly. The employer may have only three days to surrender the I-9s.

Why Is ICE Knocking on My Door?

One must assume that ICE is omniscient and that the company's every word, deed, and action are known to the government. ICE is not knocking on doors randomly. Its investigation will be "lead" driven, based on information garnered from an informant, a competitor, local or state agencies, disgruntled current and former employees, or from many other sources. Therefore, it is imperative that one attempt to know as much about the company's immigration hiring practices as does ICE. How does one gain this information? One learns where the company's Achilles heel lies, primarily through interviewing corporate executives and hiring managers. While I-9s can divulge some suspect trends, they are only a piece of the puzzle. One should be cognizant of potential conflict-of-interest issues that arise when one represents an employer and determines through the questioning of managers that each entity—the corporation and the managers—need their own counsel. However, at the inception, one cannot make that determination without some basic information.

Probative questions for both the company executive officer and the hiring managers are included in these materials. For the corporate executive, one wants to learn more about the company's background and any labor-related challenges that might have impacted its hiring practices. Other questions relate to the company's immigration training of its hiring managers and the corporation's immigration policies and practices. Additional questions are designed to determine the reason why ICE has targeted the company.

For the hiring managers, although the question might be viewed as potentially offensive, one must determine their immigration status. If they only possess permanent resident status, they will be very vulnerable in an ICE investigation, as they can be threatened with loss of permanent residency and removal from the United States. As recent immigrants themselves, they may have information about how one buys false documents, and how to detect a false document. They may have divided, mixed loyalties toward their *"compañeros de trabajo"* (fellow workers) and management. As the successful immigrant who can hire workers, they may be tempted to give jobs to unauthorized workers and relatives. The enclosed questions for the hiring managers seek to elicit answers that will reveal an understanding of what they perceive their immigration responsibilities to be—how they conduct interviews, and how they complete the I-9. The focus is not merely on the time of hire but throughout the employment relationship, because knowledge gained of unlawful status after the time of hire can be damaging to the corporation under the "knowingly continuing to employ" provision of IRCA.

An I-9 Inspection Outline

Notifying the Workforce?

The I-9 inspection outline lists 13 steps that one can follow in handling an inspection. There are many thorny issues—a crucial one is whether the workforce should be notified that an ICE inspection is occurring. In order to conduct a comprehensive audit of the I-9s and address deficiencies such as expired documents and missing signatures and attestations, one must communicate to the workers that their I-9s are being reviewed. There are no secrets in the workforce; word spreads that ICE agents have gone to the plant to serve the company with a notice. Since confidential employee data may be divulged to ICE, labor counsel and other experts share the belief that the workforce should be informed. Undoubtedly, news of the I-9 inspection and the reality that their I-9s and the documents they presented at the time of hire will be reviewed will trigger some resignations. It's best that the employer lose these employees now and commence immediately replenishing its workforce with legal replacements rather than lose them suddenly during an ensuing raid of the facility.

Compounding the dilemma of whether to advise workers of the impending I-9 inspection, ICE now inserts the following notice in its subpoenas issued in connection with the inspection:

> "You are not to disclose the existence of this request for an **indefinite** period of time. Any such disclosure could impede the inspection and thereby interfere with the enforcement of the law."

Note that the ICE subpoena is not a judicial order, so a contempt of court citation or worse tragedy will not befall one for failure to abide by its dictates. While ICE may believe that notification to the employees is an attempt to somehow conceal the discovery of undocumented workers from ICE, the company has many good reasons for notifying the workforce. These reasons are legitimate and are not intended to obstruct or interfere with ICE's investigation. Disclosure of employee terminations is data that is available to ICE, and the home address of the alien is noted on the I-9 itself.

Conducting an I-9 Audit and Addressing I-9 Deficiencies

Ideally, one should conduct a comprehensive audit to identify all I-9 deficiencies; however, one might not have sufficient time to do so. The enclosed practice aids include basic instructions to the employer related to providing the I-9s and payroll data in an "audit-friendly" format for quick action. Thereafter is a checklist for one's audit team to follow. When pressed for time, the five important deficiencies that one must cure are:

(1) No I-9;

(2) No employee status attestation in section 1;

(3) No employee signature;

(4) No completion of data in the three columns in section 2 (unless copies of documents are attached); and

(5) No employer signature.

Note that under §411 of the Illegal Immigration Reform and Immigrant Responsibility Act of 1996,[2] which added subsection (6) to INA §274A(b) [8 USC § 1324a(b)], ICE cannot fine an employer for procedural or technical deficiencies that occurred after September 30, 1986, unless it has provided a notice of deficiency giving 10 days to cure the errors. A list of the deficiencies that are considered "technical" or "procedural" are provided in guidelines that were issued by the agency in March 1997.[3] Included are items such as failure to record documents in section 2, unless copies of documents are attached to the I-9; failure to date the I-9 if such failure happened after September 30, 1996; and failure to record the date of hire in section 2.

On occasion, an I-9 is missing for an employee who now refuses to complete one because he or she is aware that an ICE audit is underway and now admits to lacking the lawful right to work. How should one handle this dilemma? Actually, both the HR manager and the employee cannot sign the I-9 and attest that (1) the employee is authorized to work; (2) the manager believes that the documents are genuine and that the employee is authorized to work. *It is better to have no I-9 than to make a false attestation?* One might partially fill out the top portion of section 1, and then note boldly that the employee refuses to sign because he or she acknowledges that he or she isn't authorized to work, and that employment was terminated. Thus, one has an I-9, but it's incomplete, and a civil fine can be assessed because the existence of this type of I-9 is not a procedural or technical deficiency.

Lastly, the practice aids include a format for noting I-9 deficiencies and corrective action that is required. Invariably, work authorization expirations are not updated, so a grid is included that notes expiration dates with call-up reminders.

The ICE Notice of Inspection

The ICE notice of inspection must provide for three days to surrender the I-9s. Notices are served either in person or sent certified mail. Generally, one can easily seek more time, one to two weeks or more, to surrender them. The surrender of the I-9s can occur at the company or at ICE's office. If they are surrendered at the company, it is important to know that ICE is not authorized, without the employer's explicit consent, to roam the premises or to interview employees. It is advisable not to allow any further intrusion into the worksite.

The notice of inspection is coupled with "Instructions on How to Prepare for an ICE Business Inspection." You must exercise your judgment on how many of these items you wish to surrender to ICE. The regulations provide for just the surrender of the I-9s. However, ICE does have subpoena authority under 8 CFR §287.4 to collect

---

[2] Pub. L. No. 104-208, div. C, §411, 110 Stat. 3009, 3009-666.

[3] INS Memorandum, P. Virtue, "Interim Guidelines: Section 274A(b)(6) of the Immigration & Nationality Act Added by Section 411 of the Illegal Immigration Reform & Immigrant Responsibility Act of 1996" (Mar. 6, 1997), *published on* AILA InfoNet at Doc. No. 97030691 (*posted* Mar. 6, 1997), and reprinted in this book.

evidence that is relevant to its investigation. Often the inspection notice and the supplemental instructions also are accompanied by a subpoena compelling the production of these items as well as any Social Security "no-match" letters received over the past several years. An ICE subpoena is not self-enforcing. ICE must seek enforcement in federal court. Would a federal court likely enforce such a subpoena? There is a strong likelihood that it would; however, the effort to seek enforcement may be too laborious for ICE. On the other hand, the employer should be alerted about this possibility and be able to fund a legal challenge in federal court.

With the surrender of I-9s demonstrating the possible existence of unauthorized workers, there may be probable cause for ICE to secure a search warrant and seize all relevant documents. Generally, the very same things that are listed in its instruction sheet are also noted in the search warrant. It is clear, however, that ICE cannot compel an employer to compile lists and create specific headings such as dates of hire and termination. In lieu of the creation of such a list, ICE asks that one surrender payroll information that contains this data.

In lieu of surrendering all items listed, one can negotiate and provide select data that isn't burdensome for the employer. Note, however, that one must ensure, at a minimum, that I-9s are surrendered within the requisite timeframe agreed upon.

The instructions also ask for the completion of a business entity questionnaire, which solicits financial-related information and other data such as a listing of all company locations, work shifts, whether I-9s were inherited from a predecessor company, names of who completes I-9s, and names of company officers. Divulging some of this information is intrusive and burdensome. Again, one must assess the degree of cooperation that the employer desires and also attempt to limit the scope of the request.

The practice aids also include a copy of a notice of suspect documents, advising that if the employees feel that there is an error, they must present new valid proof of work authorization. Such documents will be reverified by ICE. In the interim, the employee may continue to work. Lastly, the practice aids include a notice of intent to fine, listing violations and fine assessments.

Conclusion

This summary of key issues with the accompanying practice aids can serve as a roadmap for the attorney and the employer faced with an ICE I-9 inspection. If one successfully navigates this minefield, the end result may be a notice of compliance with no fine assessment and a decision not to pursue a criminal prosecution. However, the facts that gave rise to the selection of the company for an inspection may be considered by ICE too egregious to net such a favorable outcome. At a minimum, this roadmap will serve to heighten one's awareness of the pejorative factors that triggered the inspection and to address such factors in a positive, rehabilitative manner in the hopes of lessening or mitigating the deleterious consequences that might ensue.

I-9 Inspections Outline

1. Review scope of I-9 inspection notice

2. Determine if workforce will be notified of I-9 inspection

3. Assess state of employer's I-9s. Conduct audit, identify deficiencies, and correct.

4. Staff and conduct review; employer/employee corrections

    - Identify qualified personnel to assist
    - Establish links to managers and employees for correction requests
    - Confidentiality issues

5. Address steps to be taken to replenish workforce and hire legal replacements

6. Interview executives

7. Interview hiring managers

8. Identify areas of strength and weakness and develop theme to defend, including strategy to improve future immigration compliance

9. Engage criminal defense counsel, if needed

10. Prepare for possible ICE raid

11. Review and analyze ICE civil assessment and outline challenges to ICE fine determinations; alternatively, determine criminal defense strategy

12. Settle fines and penalties, or engage in pre-indictment criminal or plea negotiations

13. Seek civil administrative appeal or criminal jury trial

ETHICAL CONSIDERATIONS IN CONDUCTING IMMIGRATION INVESTIGATIONS

by Josie Gonzalez

Conducting internal investigations can be a potential minefield. Ideally, the immigration attorney should conduct these investigations as a member of a team that includes a white collar criminal defense attorney and corporate counsel. At the outset, one needs to understand the scope of the investigation. There should be clarity regarding how to handle the conflicts of interest that will undoubtedly surface during the course of the investigation. This outline will merely highlight some of the relevant issues that counsel must consider. To gain a better understanding of this thorny topic, the reader is provided with a list of recommended articles at the conclusion.

Advising Corporate Employees of Potential Conflicts

Before interviewing corporate employees, they must be advised that: (1) you are the company's counsel and that you do not represent them;[1] (2) that what they say may be privileged, but that the corporation, not them, holds the privilege and may waive it.[2] Some courts and, indeed, ethical rules of conduct suggest that corporate employees fully understand that: the discovery of improper conduct may be punished; improper conduct may have to be disclosed to the government; one is not providing any legal advice to the employee; and if their interests are adverse to those of the employer, they should seek separate legal counsel.[3] Regarding the need for separate counsel, many corporations pay for the cost of such representation and view it as their obligation to provide outside counsel for any target employee.

The failure to explain that one is representing the company and not the employee could have the unintended consequence of the employee believing that you also rep-

---

[1] ABA Model Rules of Profession Conduct, Rule 4.3 provides: In dealing on behalf of a client with a person who is not represented by counsel, a lawyer shall not state or imply that the lawyer is disinterested. When the lawyer knows or reasonably should know that the unrepresented person misunderstands the lawyer's role in the matter, the lawyer shall make reasonable efforts to correct the misunderstanding.

[2] The seminal case involving attorney client privilege in the context of internal investigations of corporate misconduct is *Upjohn Co. v. United States*, 449 U.S. 383 (1981). In *Upjohn*, a pharmaceutical company retained private counsel to investigate whether its overseas subsidiary engaged in misconduct. The intent of the investigation was so that Upjohn could better understand its legal obligations and ensure corporate integrity. The IRS sought counsel's interview notes and the questionnaires that the employees had completed. The U.S. Supreme Court ruled that the employees' communications with counsel were privileged and that the privilege exists in order to encourage candid communication that will enable the lawyer to give "sound and informed advice."

[3] *In re Grand Jury Subpoena: Under Seal*, 415 F.3d 333 (4th Cir.2005), cert denied, 126 S. Ct.1114 (2006); Rule 1.13 of the ABA Model Rules of Professional Conduct provides: In dealing with an organization's directors, officers, employees, members, shareholders or other constituents, a lawyer shall explain the identity of the client when the lawyer knows or reasonably should know that the organization's interests are adverse to those of the constituents with whom the lawyer is dealing.

resent his or her interests, thus creating an "attorney-client" relationship. For example, if a rogue supervisor is selling immigration documents or hiring relatives or friends that he knows to be lacking proper work authorization, the corporation, in order to protect its interest, may have to assert that this supervisor was acting outside the scope of his duties and was acting to only benefit his interest—directly contrary to company policies. One's failure to provide such clarification may even result in a malpractice action against the lawyer for violating an implied attorney-client relationship.[4] In *United States v. International Brotherhood of Teamsters*,[5] a lawyer was hired to investigate rumors of improper fundraising activities. The lawyer interviewed a campaign manager who later attempted to assert attorney-client privilege regarding his communications with the attorney. The court rejected the privilege but criticized the attorney for failing to clarify that he represented the corporation solely and not the campaign manager.

After conducting employee interviews, it is important to record that one provided the above warnings. It is generally advisable to also record the substance of the interview including the nature of any questions posed and responses given. This memo should be marked, "Attorney-client privileged – Confidential work-product."

If it appears likely that ICE intends to conduct a full-blown investigation of the company, it will undoubtedly attempt to interview corporate employees who were in a position to know about the company's immigration policies—Human Resource managers, supervisors, corporate recruiters, and production managers. In an excellent discussion regarding, "Getting your message to the employees before the government agents get theirs," Ashish S. Joshi counsels distributing a memo to employees that contains the following information:

> "(a) that the government is conducting an investigation of certain matters; (b) that government investigators may wish to interview employees in connection with the investigation; (c) that the company has retained outside counsel to represent it in connection with the investigation; (d) that the company also has arranged for an attorney to be available to provide advice to those employees who wish to consult with counsel; (e) that the role of separate counsel would be to advise employees as to whether it is in the employees' interest to be interviewed, and the appropriate conditions for such interview; (f) that as the matters at issue occurred during the employee's tenure as an employee, the company has agreed to be responsible for advancing fees and related expenses for the employee's legal representation in connection with the investigation;
>
> (g) that while the company recommends that the employee consult with counsel prior to consenting to any interview, it is the employees' prerogative to de-

---

[4] In *Innes v. Howell Corp*, 76 F.3d 702 (6th Cir. 1996), an attorney, on behalf of Howell Corporation was retained to conduct an investigation as to whether Innes had accepted alleged kickbacks. When the lawyer divulged his conversation with Innes to the corporation, Innes sued the attorney claiming that he had a duty of confidentiality that was breached when he communicated the results of his conversation to the corporation.

[5] 119 F.3d 210 (2d Cir. 1997).

cide whether to do so; (h) that should the employee consent to an interview, it is essential that the employee be truthful in responding to questions at any interview; and (i) that the company requests that the employee promptly advise it of any contacts or communications with government investigators whether or not the employee elects to speak with separate counsel. By using such a memorandum, company counsel can document the propriety of the advice given to the employees, minimize the confusion on their part and preserve the advice to avoid any allegation that the company and/or its counsel attempted to tamper with or improperly influence a potential witness or to otherwise obstruct the government's inquiry."[6]

Note that the guidance provided by the above author is directed at the corporate employees who have acted on behalf of the corporation in performing their duties; it is not directed at a workforce that might comprise employees working unlawfully in the United States. The type of guidance provided to such a workforce is outside the scope of these guidelines, but it, too, is a minefield entangled by thorny ethical considerations.

Recommended Reading

1. A. Joshi, "Corporate Counsel, Internal Investigation and the Government Investigation: A Brief Primer in Making Your Way Through a Potential Minefield," *Bus. & Corp. Litig. Newsl.* (ABA Committee on Business and Corporate Litigation, Fall 2007).

2. G. Lin, "The Thompson and McNulty Memoranda: Waiver of the Attorney-Client Privilege and Corporate Counsel's Role in Health Care Fraud Investigations," 20 *Geo. J. Legal Ethics* 793 (Summer 2007).

3. P. Joy & K. McMunigal, "Corporate Privilege Waivers in Plea Negotiations," 21 *Crim. Just.* 42 (ABA Criminal Justice Section, Summer 2006).

4. B. Green, "Interviewing Corporate Client Officers and Employees: Ethical Considerations," *Prof. Liability Litig. Alert* (ABA Section of Litigation, Professional Liability Litigation Committee, vol. 3, no. 1, Winter 2005).

5. D. Purdom, "Conducting Internal Corporate Criminal Investigations," *DCBA Brief* (May 1997).

6. R. Litt, "Inherent Conflicts in Joint Representation," 14 *Crim. Just. Sec. Newsl.* 2, (ABA Criminal Justice Section, Winter 2006).

7. R. Juceam, "Safeguarding Against Criminal Prosecution and Malpractice in Immigration Law—An Outline of Key Topics," *Ethics in a Brave New World—Professional Responsibility, Personal Accountability, & Risk Management for Immigration Practitioners* 57 (AILA 2004), available from AILA Publications, (800) 982-2839, *www.ailapubs.org*.

---

[6] A. Joshi, "Corporate Counsel, Internal Investigation and the Government Investigation: A Brief Primer in Making Your Way Through a Potential Minefield," *Bus. & Corp. Litig. Newsl.* (ABA Committee on Business and Corporate Litigation, Fall 2007).

QUESTIONS FOR THE COMPANY EXECUTIVE OFFICER

1. What jobs make up your workforce and in what kinds of positions are the majority of workers? What is the salary range? What is the percentage of workers that are foreign-born or non–English speaking? Describe your company, the industry, and any particular labor-related challenges that you face.

2. Who completes the I-9s? Describe their background—ethnicity, education, tenure with the company.

3. How much immigration training have they received?

4. How do you recruit for workers?

5. Do you have any policy regarding the employment of relatives?

6. Are Social Security numbers checked?

7. Have you ever received Social Security no-match letters either for individuals or an SSA letter providing a group listing? If so, how many such letters and what have you done? Are any of the listed employees still working at the company? Have any employees returned to work with new and different identity and work authorization documents? Ask to review those I-9s.

8. Have you ever filed any applications on behalf of employees through the Department of Labor, via a labor certification? If yes, provide all details—for whom, when, result; and request a copy of the application and the I-9 for those individuals.

9. Have you ever received any request from any government agency, *e.g.*, State Child Alimony Unit, the IRS or State Unemployment Office questioning the identity and employment of any worker? If so, describe actions taken.

10. Have you ever received any tips—either from within the workforce or outside—that certain employees were not authorized to work? If so, describe actions taken.

11. Have you laid off or fired any workers in the last 12 months? If so, describe who and what positions they held.

12. Have you had any audits by any other agencies such as Wage and Hour?

13. Are you aware of any employees that have been arrested for DUI or any other offense? If so, provide details and request to see those I-9s.

14. Are temporary work authorization documents tracked?

15. Are there any I-9-related problems that you've encountered (*e.g.*, heavy production surge requiring lots of volume hiring; inability to find workers, etc.)?

16. Do you conduct internal audits? Are there any checks and balances to ensure that your managers are complying with immigration laws?

17. Do you keep copies of documents?

18. Do you ever purge your old I-9s?

19. Have you ever had any contact with immigration, such as prior visits or audits? If so, describe results.

20. Do you have any idea why ICE is investigating your company?

QUESTIONS FOR THE HIRING MANAGER

Manager: _____ Location: _____

1. What is your understanding of your immigration responsibilities—start with describing what the immigration law is all about; what are your I-9 responsibilities—from interviewing to I-9 completion.

2. Describe how an I-9 is completed—step by step. Do you follow up when work authorization documents expire?

3. Do you ever complete Section One yourself because you can do it faster or the new hire can't read or understand the form?

4. Do you ever have any reason to doubt the information you are recording on the form?

5. What do you normally feel about the quality of the documents? Can you tell a good card from a phony one?

6. Do any job applicants ever admit to being illegal but plead for a job or does anyone joke about the documents they are presenting?

7. How would you react to these situations?

8. Have you heard of any employees having problems/contact with immigration or the police? For example, someone is afraid to go home to visit relatives for fear of not being able to return? Someone got arrested returning from the border? Arrested for DUI?

9. Has an employee ever asked you to sponsor him for a green card? Do you know if such paperwork has ever been signed or filed?

10. Have you ever had any reports or complaints about workers being illegal, or using another person's Social Security number?

11. Have you ever heard any rumors about anyone selling false documents to job applicants?

12. Has any employee ever requested to change their immigration documents to a different name and number?

13. After someone is hired, have any employees ever confided in you that they are not legal? If so, provide the details.

14. What is your immigration status and how did you immigrate?

15. Why do you think immigration officials happened to target this company?

PRELIMINARY I-9 INSPECTIONS INSTRUCTIONS TO CLIENT

1. Download current employee list to Excel spreadsheet and include columns for the following:
   - ❑ Employee name (Last name, first name)
   - ❑ Date of Hire
   - ❑ Social Security Number
2. Arrange I-9s in alpha order
3. Attach any supporting documents to the I-9s
4. Have terminated I-9s accessible if included in scope of audit
5. Collect any related documents for review, *e.g.*, temporary document tracking reports, notices issued to employees when documents are going to expire, internal I-9 policies, etc.

I-9 Inspections Checklist

AUDIT

- [ ] Instruct employer to provide Excel spreadsheet containing the name, Social Security number, and date of hire for each active employee.
- [ ] Upon obtaining spreadsheet, edit to meet your needs for audit review, *e.g.*, add columns for checking status of I-9 (present, missing, etc.), temporary work authorization expiration dates, and comments (see attached sample).
- [ ] With I-9s organized in alphabetical order, review forms for completeness, filling in the required fields on the spreadsheet for each employee.
- [ ] Comments column should include information regarding corrections to be made, expired documents, etc.
- [ ] List any I-9s presented for employees who do not appear on the list.
- [ ] Provide a legend to explain any abbreviations used.

REPORTING

- [ ] Prepare an audit report that summarizes the spreadsheet information, including such topics as missing I-9s, tracking of temporary work authorization documents, completion of I-9s for foreign nationals, H-1 portability, acceptance and recording of receipts, etc.
- [ ] Prioritize topics, highlighting major areas of concern, *e.g.*, missing I-9s, expired work authorization documents, missing attestations, missing signatures.
- [ ] Instruct employer to correct deficiencies and follow up to ensure corrections are made.

TRACKING

- [ ] If not already established, set up a tracking report for employees with temporary work authorization.

I-9 AUDIT REPORT (ATTORNEY-CLIENT WORK PRODUCT—PRIVILEGED AND CONFIDENTIAL)

I-9 AUDIT REPORT (ATTORNEY CLIENT WORK PRODUCT - PRIVILEGED AND CONFIDENTIAL)
By: BEST LAW FIRM FOR THE SECURE CORPORATION

CURRENT EMPLOYEES
(Fictitious names and SSNs used)

#	I-9	NAME	HIRE DATE	SSN	EXPIRED WORK AUTH.	CURRENT EAD/NIV	COMMENTS / CORRECTIONS
1	✓	Alby, Edward	01/28/04	607-39-7462			Sec. 2: Blank. View original documents, sign & date, or complete new I-9. Note in margin "per audit" by current date.
2	✓	Aronson, James	12/11/00	625-61-6846		L-1 1/20/2010	Sec. 2, List A: Document should be Passport, Issuing authority - UK, Exp. Date. Then I-94 # & L-1 exp. date. Need copy of primary page from passport, not travel visa. Make edits, initial & date, or complete new I-9.
3	✓	Bentfield, Laura	10/20/97	454-59-3178			Sec. 2, List C: No document recorded or copied. View & copy original document, record, initial & date, "per audit"
4	M	Caraway, Miles	04/30/07	554-29-1834			**Missing I-9: Complete new I-9 using current date, if unable to locate original**
5	✓	Dangerfield, Lynda	09/24/07	558-02-4523			Sec. 2, List C: Record issuing authority (SSA), initial & date
6	✓	Gao, Hua Grace	06/13/07	424-55-1345		H-1 5/22/2010	H-1 Portability: H-1 was approved in July, and I-9 was updated to show exp. of 5/22/10. However, initial auth. to begin work 6/13 is based on change of H-1 employer & filing of petition for Secure, so filing receipt should have been used in List C to document auth. to work, in combination with List B identity doc. Record List B doc & see attached instructions for recording filing receipt in List C. Initial & date, "per audit"
7	✓	Hurtado, Miguel	04/30/96	458-55-9756			1996 & 1998 I-9s: Evidently transferred to CA in '98. No need for 2nd I-9; just need original.
8	✓	Lawson, David	06/16/97	624-34-9190			Sec. 1: Employee needs to enter A# after box 2, initial & date
9	✓	Maya, Jose	06/25/90	456-99-8943	8/23/2007		**Priority - Expired EAD: Does not have current work authorization. Must not continue to work if unable to present current work authorization.**
10	GF	Williams, Lyle	06/15/86	567-67-9876			Grandfathered - I-9 is not required
11	✓	Yang, Min	12/17/01	226-71-1187			Sec. 2, List A: foreign passport recorded with F-1 student I-94 (not work authorization). Now has PR - complete new I-9 and attach to old.

Legend: Abbreviations
- ✓   I-9 in file
- GF   Grandfathered: Hired prior to 11/7/86 & does not require an I-9
- M   Missing: Unable to locate I-9
- EAD   Employment Authorization Document: temporary work permit
- I-551   Greencard - permanent resident
- NIV   Nonimmigrant (H-1/L-1)

WORK AUTHORIZATION TRACKING

The spreadsheet presented here is used to keep track of employees with temporary work authorization and the employer's duties of notice to them. Names and other data in this example are fictitious.

WORK AUTHORIZATION EXPIRATIONS and NOTIFICATION TO EMPLOYEES

EMPLOYEE NAME	DOCUMENT TYPE	EXPIRATION DATE	90 DAY NOTICE DUE	NOTICE ISSUED	30 DAY NOTICE DUE	NOTICE ISSUED	COMMENTS / RESULTS
Smith, Karen	EAD	04/10/08	01/10/08	01/10/08	02/10/08		
Flores, Miguel	H-1B I-94	06/18/08	N/A				H-1 extension filed 1/31/2008
Chan, Jared	EAD	08/15/08	05/15/08				

SAMPLE ICE NOTICE OF INSPECTION

C   of Investigations
U.S. Department of Homeland Security

NOTICE OF INSPECTION

Dear Sir or Madam:

Section 274A of the Immigration and Nationality Act, as amended by the Immigration Reform and Control Act of 1986, requires employers to hire only United States citizens and aliens who are authorized to work in the United States. Employers must verify employment eligibility of persons hired after November 6, 1986, using the Employment Eligibility Verification Form I-9.

U.S. Immigration and Customs Enforcement (ICE) regulations require the provision of three days notice prior to conducting a review of an employer's I-9 forms. This letter serves as advance notice that ICE has scheduled a review of your forms for **Tuesday November 13, 2007 at 10:00 am**. You may, however, waive the three-day period, should you wish to do so, by annotating and signing the bottom of this letter and advising this office of your decision. ICE will require all I-9 forms and a list of current and past employees including dates of hire and termination, payroll records and W-2 reports. If the scheduled time is inconvenient, please contact this office to make arrangements for another time.

During the review, Special Agent _____ will discuss the requirements of the law with you and inspect your I-9 forms. The purpose of this review is to assess your compliance with the provisions of the law. ICE will make every effort to conduct the review of records in a timely manner so as not to impede your normal business routine.

Sincerely,

Group Supervisor

I wish to waive the three-day notice to which I am entitled by regulation.

_____   _____   _____
(Name)   (Signature)   (Date)

Notice of Inspection:
Page 2

CERTIFICATE OF SERVICE

DATE: _____

METHOD OF SERVICE: In Person

SERVING OFFICIAL: _____
(SIGNATURE)   (DATE)

PERSON SERVED:

_____   _____
(PRINTED NAME)   (TITLE/POSITION)

_____   _____
(SIGNATURE)   (DATE)

SAMPLE ICE SECOND NOTICE OF INSPECTION

Office of Investigations

U.S. Department of Homeland Security

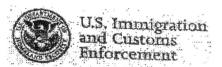

SECOND NOTICE OF INSPECTION

Dear Sir or Madam:

Section 274A of the Immigration and Nationality Act, as amended by the Immigration Reform and Control Act of 1986, requires employers to hire only United States citizens and aliens who are authorized to work in the United States. Employers must verify employment eligibility of persons hired after November 6, 1986, using the Employment Eligibility Verification Form I-9.

U.S. Immigration and Customs Enforcement (ICE) regulations require the provision of three days notice prior to conducting a review of an employer's I-9 forms. This letter serves as advance notice that ICE has scheduled a review of your forms for <u>Monday, January 14, 2008 at 10:00 am</u>. You may, however, waive the three-day period, should you wish to do so, by annotating and signing the bottom of this letter and advising this office of your decision. If the scheduled time is inconvenient, please contact this office to make arrangements for another time.

On _____, provided nineteen (19) Forms I-9 of current employees. With the exception of the nineteen (19) Forms I-9 that have already been presented, ICE is requesting all Forms I-9 from <u>November 8, 2004 to November 8, 2007</u>. In addition, we are requesting a list of all employees from November 8, 2004 to November 8, 2007. The list must include: the employees full name, date of birth, Social Security number, date of hire and date of termination (if applicable).

Should you have any questions you may contact Special Agent _____.

Sincerely,

Group Supervisor

I wish to waive the three-day notice to which I am entitled by regulation.

_____   _____   _____
(Name)   (Signature)   (Date)

CERTIFICATE OF SERVICE

DATE: _____

METHOD OF SERVICE: In Person

SERVING OFFICIAL:

_____   _____
(SIGNATURE)   (DATE)

PERSON SERVED:

_____   _____
(PRINTED NAME)   (TITLE/POSITION)

_____   _____
(SIGNATURE)   (DATE)

HOW TO PREPARE FOR AN ICE BUSINESS INSPECTION

Craig Porter
Special Agent

U.S Department of Homeland Security
300 N. Los Angeles Street
Los Angeles, CA 90012

213-830-5596 tel
213-894-0409 fax

Craig.Porter@DHS.Gov

U.S. Immigration and Customs Enforcement

U.S. Immigration and Customs Enforcement

INSTRUCTIONS ON HOW TO PREPARE FOR AN ICE BUSINESS INSPECTION

It is the intention of the Department of Homeland Security, U. S. Immigration and Customs Enforcement (ICE), to conduct an efficient and non-imposing inspection of your business. Please take a few minutes to read the following instructions on preparing for an Employment Eligibility Verification (Form I-9) Inspection.

Forms I-9: The Agent conducting the inspection will need true and correct originals of all Form I-9 for all current employees hired after November 6, 1986 along with copies of supporting documents (i.e. passports, drivers license, social security card, birth certificate, permanent resident card, etc.) maintained in the normal course of business. To facilitate this in an orderly and efficient manner, please:

- Alphabetize all originals of the Form I-9 for current employees hired after November 6, 1986.
- Please also make one copy of all the Form I-9 for ICE. You may also want to make one additional copy for the company to maintain while ICE has the company's original Form I-9.
- At the end of the inspection, the Agent conducting your inspection will take the originals and one copy of all the Form I-9 back to the office for further review.

Company Payroll: The Agent conducting the inspection will request a copy of the most current payroll. This should show:

- The full name of each employee and the amount of each employee's paycheck and withholding tax deducted (alphabetized in order). If possible, please provide this in an electronic format (i.e. Excel Spreadsheet).

Employee Information Certification Form: An alphabetized list of all current employees hired after November 6, 1986 should be provided; indicating the date of hire, termination date, if applicable, and date of birth for each employee. The Agent will provide the Employee Information Certification Form to you.

- If your company already maintains a similar record, please ask the agent if you may submit that document in lieu of completing the Employee Information Certification. If possible, please provide this in an electronic format (i.e. Excel Spreadsheet).
- You will be requested to certify that the information provided is true, complete and correct to the best of your knowledge.
- Should you wish to use the Employee Information Certification provided, you may want to make copies of the form before beginning.

Business Entity Questionnaire/Employer Information Certification Form: The Agent conducting the inspection will request you to submit a fully completed Business Entity Questionnaire. The Agent will provide the Form to you. Should you have any questions on how to complete this form, please contact the Agent conducting your inspection.

Form DE-6 (Quarterly Wage and Withholding Report): The Agent conducting the inspection will request that you furnish him/her a copy of Form DE-6 Quarterly Wage and Withholding Report for the most recent fiscal year.

ICE Business Entity Questionnaire

Office of Investigations
U.S. Department of Homeland Security
600 Las Vegas Blvd South, Suite 660
Las Vegas, Nevada 89101

U.S. Immigration
and Customs
Enforcement

BUSINESS ENTITY QUESTIONNAIRE

PURSUANT TO AN INSPECTION OF EMPLOYMENT ELIGIBILITY FORMS (SEC. 274A OF THE INA)

1. NAME OF BUSINESS: _____
2. TRADE NAME OF DBA: _____
3. ADDRESS: _____
4. TELEPHONE / FAX#: PHONE (____) _____ FAX (____) _____
5. NATURE OF OWNERSHIP: _____ STATE IN WHICH RECORDED _____
   NAMES OF OWNERS / PARTNERS: _____
6. TYPE OF INDUSTRY OR SERVICE: _____
7. EMPLOYER I.D. # / SSN: _____ NUMBER OF EMPLOYEES: _____
8. GROSS OR NET INCOME: _____ DATE STARTED BUSINESS: _____
9. CHECK BOX WHICH APPLIES-IF YOU STARTED BUSINESS AFTER NOVEMBER 6, 1986, DID YOU:
   ☐ START WITH A WORKFORCE FROM A PREVIOUS BUSINESS WHICH WAS IN OPERATION PRIOR TO 11/6/86; OR
   ☐ START BY HIRING WORKERS WITHOUT TRANSFERRING OVER THE WORKFORCE OF A PREVIOUS/PREDECESSOR COMPANY
10. NUMBER OF DIVISIONS OR SITES: _____ # OF SHIFTS _____
    SHIFT TIMES: _____
    ADDRESS OF OTHER DIVISIONS OR SITES: _____
11. NAME OF PARENT COMPANY: _____
12. IS THIS BUSINESS UNDER ANY BANKRUPTCY PROCEEDINGS AT THIS TIME? ☐ YES ☐ NO
13. WHO HAS THE HIRE AUTHORITY FOR THE COMPANY: _____
14. WHO DOES THE FORM I-9: _____
15. HOW ARE THE EMPLOYEES PAID: _____

CERTIFICATION

The above information is true and correct to the best of my knowledge.

SIGNATURE: _____ PRINT NAME: _____

TITLE: _____ DATE: _____ SSN/ID#: _____

ICE Employee Information Certification Form
Employee Information Certification Form

#	Employee Name	Date of Hire	Date of Termination	Date of Birth
1.				
2.				
3.				
4.				
5.				
6.				
7.				
8.				
9.				
10.				
11.				
12.				
13.				
14.				
15.				
16.				
17.				
18.				
19.				
20.				
21.				
22.				
23.				
24.				
25.				
26.				
27.				
28.				
29.				
30.				

Name of Person Preparing Form

Date

Title of Person Preparing Form

Signature

Page ____ of ____

SAMPLE ICE SUBPOENA

Office of Investigations

U.S. Department of Homeland Security

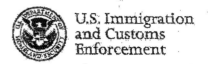
U.S. Immigration and Customs Enforcement

December 21, 2007

Office of Origin:

SUBPOENA

To: Custodian of Records

You are hereby commanded to appear before Senior Special Agent _____ or other designated agent, at your above place of business on <u>December 28, 2007 at 11:00 AM</u> to give testimony in connection with an investigation being conducted under the authority of the Immigration and Nationality Act, relating to your compliance with the employment and verification requirements of Section 274A of the Immigration and Nationality Act, as amended [Title 8, United States Code, Section 1324(a)].

You are further commanded to bring with you the following <u>original</u> books, papers, and documents, viz:

All Social Security Administration "Employer Correction Requests" and "Request for Employee Information" letters that the company has received in calendar years 2005 – 2006 (tax years 2004 – 2005); corresponding payroll records.

_____

Group Supervisor

RETURN OF SERVICE OF SUBPOENA

I certify that on the 21st day of December 2007, the above subpoena was served on the witness named above, or his/her designee, via, <u>in person</u> by:

_____

Senior Special Agent

SUBPOENA AND CUSTODY RECEIPT FOR SEIZED PROPERTY

UNITED STATES OF AMERICA
DEPARTMENT OF JUSTICE
IMMIGRATION AND NATURALIZATION SERVICE

Office of Origin:
Office of the Assistant Special Agent in Charge, Orange County
34 Civic Center Plaza, 4th Floor
Santa Ana, California 92701

Date: November 28, 2007

SUBPOENA

In re: Review of Employment Eligibility Verification Forms (Form I-9)

To:

Phone Number:
Fax Number:

You are hereby commanded to appear before Senior Special Agent Edmund Estrada (SS/A Estrada) at 34 Civic Center Plaza, 4th Floor, Santa Ana, California 92701 on November 30, 2007, at 4:00 p.m., to give testimony in connection with an inspection being conducted under authority of Section 287(b) of the Immigration and Nationality Act, and Section 287.4 of Title 8 of the Code of Federal Regulations, concerning a review of your Employment Eligibility Verification forms (Form I-9).

You are further commanded to bring with you the following documents, viz: **(Please see attached)**

You are not to disclose the existence of this request for an **indefinite** period of time. Any such disclosure could impede the inspection and thereby interfere with the enforcement of the law.

The requirements of this subpoena will be met if copies of the requested documentation are available for pickup, by SS/A Estrada, by, or prior to, November 30, 2007, at 4:00 p.m. If any portion of the requested documentation is available in electronic format, it is requested that you forward the documentation to SS/A Estrada at electronic mail address edmund.estrada1@dhs.gov. Should you have any questions, you may contact SS/A Estrada at telephone number 714-972-4110.

[SEAL]

Signature
Joseph Macias
Name
Assistant Special Agent in Charge
Title

RETURN ON SERVICE OF SUBPOENA

I hereby certify that on the _____ day of _____, 20_____, I served the above subpoena on the witness named above by _____

Name

Title

Form I-138
(Rev.11-5-70) Y

U.S. CUSTOMS SERVICE

NO. 2344834

CUSTODY RECEIPT FOR SEIZED PROPERTY AND EVIDENCE

Handbook 5200-09

1. FPF No.
2. Incident No.
3. Investigative Case No.
4. Prior Detention? Yes ☐ No ☐ If yes, CF 6051D No. _____
5. Date Seized (mm/dd/yyyy): 11/30/2007
6. Time Seized (Use 24 Hrs): 10:10 AM
7. FDIN/Misc.
8. Seized From:
   Name:
   Address:
   Telephone No.
9. Entry No.
10. Seal or Other ID Nos.
11. Remarks:
12. Send Correspondence to:

13. PROPERTY (By Line Item) Attach CF 58 if conveyance

a. Line Item No.	b. Description	c. Packages Number	Type	d. Measurements Qty. UM	e. Est. Dom. Value
1	FORM I-9 AND SUPPORTING DOCUMENTS	29	PAGES EA		$ ORIGINALS
2	FORM I-9 AND SUPPORTING DOCUMENTS	29	PAGES EA		$ COPIES
3	PAYROLL LOG ENDING 11/15/2007	3	PAGES EA		$
4	PAYROLL LOG ENDING 11/30/2007	3	PAGES EA		$
5	PAYROLL REGISTER 11/15/2007	3	PAGES EACH		$
6	CERTIFICATION FORM AND TR 28015 EMPLOYEE LIST	2	PAGES EA		$

14. Seizing Officer
Print Name: EDMUND ESTRADA
Signature: _____
Date: 11/30/2007

15. ACCEPTANCE/CHAIN OF CUSTODY

a. Line Item No.	b. Description	c. Print Name/Title/Organization	d. Signature	e. Date
1-6	DOCUMENTS	ESTRADA/SRM/ICE	_____	11/30/07

CF 6051A Continuation Sheet Attached? Yes ☐ No ☐

Customs Retains Original

Customs Form 6051S (11/01)

SUBPOENA AND CUSTODY RECEIPT FOR SEIZED PROPERTY

CUSTODY RECEIPT FOR DETAINED OR SEIZED PROPERTY
Handbook 5200-09

Continuation Sheet

1. Page __2__ of __2__
2. CF 6051S or D No. __2344834__

3. FPF No.

4. Investigative Case No. or IA File No.

5. PROPERTY (By Line Item) Attach CF 58 if conveyance

a. Line Item No.	b. Description	c. Packages Number	c. Packages Type	d. Measurements Qty.	d. Measurements UM	e. Est. Dom. Value	f. Samples sent to the Customs Lab Yes or No	Date
7	BUSINESS QUESTIONNAIRE	2	PAGES EA			$	Yes☐ No☐	/ /
8	FDD DE 6	127	PAGES EA			$	Yes☐ No☐	/ /
9	EMPLOYEE CORRECTION REQUEST 02/17/2006	4	PAGES EA			$	Yes☐ No☐	/ /
10	EMPLOYEE CORRECTION REQUEST 03/24/2005	4	PAGES EA			$	Yes☐ No☐	/ /
11	NOTICE OF COMPLIANCE 02/03/1997	2	PAGES EA			$	Yes☐ No☐	/ /
12	BLANK SAMPLED NEW HIRE APPROVAL FORM	4	PAGES EA			$	Yes☐ No☐	/ /

6. ACCEPTANCE/CHAIN OF CUSTODY

a. Line Item No.	b. Description	c. Print Name/Title/Organization	d. Signature	e. Date
7-12	DOCUMENTS	FONTANA / SIA / ICE	[signature]	11/30/2007

Customs Retains Original

Customs Form 6051A (11/01)

SAMPLE ICE NOTICE OF SUSPECT DOCUMENTS

Office of Investigations

U.S. Department of Homeland Security
[Address]
[Address]

NOTICE OF SUSPECT DOCUMENTS

Dear Sir/Madam:

On _____ agents from U.S. Immigration and Customs Enforcement (ICE) conducted an inspection of _____ to determine compliance with Section 274A of the Immigration and Nationality Act. During that inspection, the requirements of the law were discussed and I-9 Forms were inspected.

This letter is to inform you that, according to the records checked by the ICE, the following individuals appear, at the present time, not to be authorized to work in the United States. The documents submitted to you were found to pertain to other individuals, or there was no record of the alien registration numbers being issued, or the documents pertain to the individuals but the individuals are not employment authorized or their employment authorization has expired. Accordingly, the documentation previously provided to you for these employees does not satisfy the I-9 Form employment eligibility verification requirements of the Immigration and Nationality Act.

SUBJECT: Notice of Suspect Documents
Page 2

PREVIOUS EMPLOYEES

Unless the above employees present valid identification and employment eligibility documentation acceptable for completing the I-9 Form, other than the documentation noted above, they are considered by the ICE to be unauthorized to work in the United States. If you continue to employ these individuals without valid documentation, you may be subject to a civil money penalty ranging from $275 to $2,200 per unauthorized alien for a first violation. Higher penalties can be imposed for a second or subsequent violation. Further, criminal charges may be brought against any person or entity which engages in a pattern or practice of knowingly hiring or continuing to employ unauthorized aliens. This is a very serious matter that requires your immediate attention.

If you or the employees feel that this determination is in error and the employees are authorized to work, immediately call *Special Agent* _____. The ICE agent will re-verify the information provided about the employees, including any new information provided by you or the employees. You will then be notified of the employees' status in writing. In these instances, do not terminate the employees whose status is in question until you receive written notification from ICE. If you or the employees have any other questions, please call the ICE contact noted above.

Sincerely,

SAMPLE ICE NOTICE OF UNAUTHORIZED ALIENS

U.S. Department of Homeland Security

U.S. Immigration and Customs Enforcement

NOTICE OF UNAUTHORIZED ALIENS

Case Number:

Dear Sir/Madam

You or a representative of,   employed the following individuals at your place of business,   . These individuals have been deemed by ICE to be unauthorized to work in the United States.

   XXXXXXXXXX
   XXXXXXXXXX

Unless they present valid identification and employment eligibility documentation acceptable for completing the I-9 Form, other than the documents previously presented, they are unauthorized to work in the United States.

Any continued employment of the individuals without satisfying the employment eligibility verification requirements may subject you to civil penalties for knowingly continuing to employ unauthorized aliens in violation of Section 274A(a)(2) of the Immigration and

Nationality Act. A civil money penalty ranging from $275 to $2,200 per unauthorized alien. Higher monetary penalties can be imposed for a second or subsequent violation. Further, criminal charges may be brought against any person or entity which engages in a pattern or practice of knowingly hiring or continuing to employ unauthorized aliens. This is a very serious matter that requires your immediate attention.

If you or the employees feel that this determination is in error and the employees are authorized to work, or if you or the employees have any questions, you or the employees may call **Special Agent**

Sincerely,

TYPE OF SERVICE: In Person

(date)

SAMPLE NOTICE OF INTENT TO FINE

RECEIVED
OCT 0 4 2007

Department of Justice
Immigration and Naturalization Service

Notice of Intent to Fine Pursuant to Section 274A
of the Immigration and Nationality Act

NOTICE OF INTENT TO FINE

United States of America

Office Address:

File Number:

In the matter of:	
Address:	

Upon inquiry conducted by the Department of Homeland Security, it is alleged that:

See attachment A

Wherefore, pursuant to Section 274A of the Immigration and Nationality Act and Part 274a, Title 8, Code of Federal Regulations, it is the intention of the Department of Homeland Security to order you to pay a fine in the amount of $67,480.00

Signature of District Counsel or Designee:	Signature of Issuing Officer:
Name of District Counsel or Designee:	Name of Issuing Officer: Gabriela Haskell
Title of District Counsel or Designee: Assistant Chief Counsel	Title of Issuing Officer: Special Agent
Date: September 28, 2007	Date: September 28, 2007

I. You have the right to contest this Notice. If you desire to contest this Notice you must:

    1. Submit a written request for a hearing before an Administrative Law judge within 30 days from the service of this Notice. The hearing will be conducted pursuant to Title 5, United States Code, Sections 554 - 557.

    2. Submit the written request for a hearing either in person or by certified mail to the following address:

II. You may submit to the Service, a written answer responding to each allegation listed in this Notice either in person or by certified mail, at the above address.

III. If a written request for a hearing is not received timely, the Service will issue (within 45 days) a final and unappealable order directing you to pay a fine in the amount specified in this Notice. If the charge specifies violation(s) of subsection 274A(a)(1)(A) or subsection 274A(a)(2) of the Act, the order will also require that you cease and desist from such violation(s).

IV. You have a right to representation by counsel of your choice at no expense to the government.

V. Any statement given may be used against you in these proceedings.

Certificate of Service

Served by (print name): _____

Date served: _____

Method of service: _____

Person or entity served: _____

Place of service: _____

Signature of employee or officer: _____

Name and title of employee or officer: _____

SAMPLE NOTICE OF INTENT TO FINE 485

ATTACHMENT "A"

UPON inquiry conducted by the Department of Homeland Security, Immigration and Customs Enforcement, it is alleged that:

COUNT I

1. You hired the following fourteen (14) individuals for employment in the United States:

EMPLOYEE NAME:

2. You hired the individuals listed in allegation #1 after November 6, 1986 and before October 25, 2006.

3. On September 25, 2006, an agent of the Department of Homeland Security, Immigration and Customs Enforcement, requested that you present for inspection, on October 16, 2006, later changed to October 25, 2006 by mutual consent, all Employment Eligibility Verification Forms, Forms I-9, prepared for your employees.

4. On October 25, 2006, you failed to present and make the Forms I-9 available for inspection, pursuant to the referenced request, for each of the individuals listed in allegation #1.

WHEREFORE, it is charged that you are in violation of section 274A(a)(1)(B) of the Immigration and Nationality Act (the Act), 8 U.S.C. section 1324a(a)(1)(B), which renders it unlawful, after November 6, 1986, for a person or other entity to hire, for employment in the United States, an individual without complying with the requirements of section 274A(b)(3) of the Act, 8 U.S.C. 1324a(b)(3), and 8 C.F.R. section 274a.2(b)(2)(ii).

The civil monetary penalty assessed for COUNT I is $14,000, ($1,000 for each violation).

COUNT II

5. You hired the ninety-two (92) individuals identified in Atttachment "B" for employment in the United States.

6. You hired the individuals listed in Attachment "B" after November 6, 1986 and before October 25, 2206.

7. On September 25, 2006, an agent of the Department of Homeland Security, Immigration and Customs Enforcement, requested that you present for inspection, on October 16, 2006, later changed to October 25, 2006 by mutual consent, all Employment Eligibility Verification Forms (Forms I-9), prepared for your employees.

8. Forms I-9 were presented, as requested, for the referenced ninety-two (92) individuals. However, none of the Forms I-9, for each of the employees identified in Attachment "B", were properly completed.

9. You failed to properly complete section 1 and/or section 2 of the Employment Eligibility Verification Form, Form I-9, for the ninety-two (92) individuals listed in Attachment "B".

10. Attachment "B" identifies the violations and individual fine assessed for each I-9, for each of the identified employees.

WHEREFORE, it is charged that you are in violation of section 274A(a)(1)(B) on the Immigration and Nationality Act (the Act), 8 U.S.C. section 1324a(a)(1)(B), which renders it unlawful, after November 6, 1986, for a person or other entity to hire, for employment in the United States, an individual without complying with the requirements of Section 274A(b)(1) and (2) of the Act, 8 U.S.C. section 1324a(b)(1) and (2), and 8 C.F.R. section 274a.2(b)(1)(i) and (ii).

The civil monetary penalty assessed for these violations is $53,480.00.

WHEREFORE, pursuant to section 274A of the Immigration and Nationality Act (the Act), and Part 274a, Title 8, Code of Federal Regulations, it is the intention of the Department to order you to pay a total fine in the amount of $67,480.00 (Sixty-seven Thousand, Four hundred-eighty Dollars) for COUNTS I and II.

NAME	I-9 REVIEW	FINE AMOUNT
	Certification in Section 2 not timely completed	$550.00
	Section 1 undated. Certification in Section 2 not timely completed.	$550.00
	Section 2 not completed. No documents identified. Certification in Section 2 not timely completed. No signature and undated.	$640.00
	Certification in Section 2 not timely completed.	$550.00
	Section 1 undated.	$550.00
	Certification in Section 2 not timely completed.	$550.00
	No list "C" document. Certification in Section 2 not timely completed. Section 2 unsigned.	$640.00
	Section 2 not completed. Certification in Section 2 not timely completed.	$640.00
	Section 1 undated. Section 2 not completed. Certification in Section 2 not timely completed. Section 2 unsigned and undated.	$640.00
	Section 1 undated. Section 2 not completed. Certification in Section 2 not timely completed. Section 2 unsigned and undated.	$640.00
	Certification in Section 2 not timely completed.	$550.00
	Certification in Section 2 not timely completed.	$550.00
	Section 1 unsigned and undated.	$550.00
	Section 1 undated. Section 2 not completed. Certification in Section 2 not timely completed. Section 2 unsigned and undated.	$640.00
	Certification in Section 2 not timely completed.	$550.00
	Certification in Section 2 not timely completed.	$550.00

Section 1 attestation not completed. Section 1 unsigned and undated.	$550.00
Section 1 undated.	$550.00
Date of commencement of employment not completed in the certification.	$550.00
List "C" document number not listed.	$550.00
Section 1 undated.	$550.00
Section 1 not timely completed. Certification in Section 2 not timely completed.	$550.00
Section 1 undated. Certification in Section 2 not timely completed.	$550.00
Section 2 not completed. Certification in Section 2 not timely completed. Not signed or dated.	$640.00
Section 2 undated.	$550.00
Section 2 not completed. Certification in Section 2 not timely completed. Unsigned and undated.	$640.00
Section 1 undated.	$550.00
Certification in Section 2 not timely completed.	$550.00
Section 1 attestation not completed. Section 1 undated. Certification in Section 2 not timely completed.	$640.00
Section 2 undated.	$550.00
No list "C" document identified. Certification in Section 2 not timely completed.	$640.00
Section 1 undated.	$550.00
Section 2 not completed. Certification in Section 2 not timely completed. Unsigned and undated.	$640.00
No attestation in Section 1.	$550.00

Section 1 not timely completed. Section 2 not completed. Certification in Section 2 not timely completed. Unsigned and undated.	$640.00
No list "C" document identified.	$550.00
Certification in Section 2 not timely completed.	$550.00
Section 1 not timely completed. Section 2 not completed. Certification in Section 2 not timely completed. Unsigned and undated.	$640.00
Section 2 not completed. Certification in Section 2 not timely completed. Unsigned and undated.	$640.00
Section 1 not timely completed. Certification in Section 2 not timely completed.	$550.00
Section 1 not timely completed. Section 2 not completed. Certification in Section 2 not timely completed. Unsigned and undated.	$640.00
Section 1 undated.	$550.00
Section 1 undated.	$550.00
Section 1 not timely completed. Section 2 not completed. Certification in Section 2 not timely completed. Unsigned and undated.	$640.00
Section 1 not timely completed.	$550.00
Section 1 not timely completed. Section 2 not completed. Certification in Section 2 not timely completed. Unsigned and undated.	$640.00
Section 1 undated.	$550.00
Section 2 not completed. Certification in Section 2 not timely completed. Unsigned and undated.	$640.00
Section 1 undated.	$550.00

No attestation in section 1. Certification in Section 2 not timely completed.	$550.00
Section 1 not timely completed. Certification in Section 2 not timely completed.	$550.00
Section 2 not completed. Certification in Section 2 not timely completed.	$550.00
No attestation in section 1.	$550.00
Section 1 undated. Section 2 not completed. Certification in Section 2 not timely completed. Unsigned and undated.	$640.00
Section 1 not timely completed. Section 2 not completed. Certification in Section 2 not timely completed. Unsigned and undated.	$640.00
Section 2 not completed. Certification in Section 2 not timely completed. Unsigned and undated.	$640.00
Section 1 not timely completed. Certification in Section 2 not timely completed.	$550.00
Section 1 not timely completed. Certification in Section 2 not timely completed.	$550.00
Section 1 not timely completed.	$550.00
Section 1 not dated. Section 2 not completed.	$640.00
Section 1 not dated. Certification in Section 2 not timely completed.	$640.00
Section 1 not dated.	$550.00
Section 1 not timely completed.	$550.00
Certification in Section 2 not timely completed.	$550.00
Section 1 not dated.	$550.00
Section 1 not timely completed.	$550.00
Section 1 not dated.	$550.00

Section 1 not timely completed. Section 2 not completed. Certification in Section 2 not timely completed. Unsigned and undated.	$640.00
Section 1 not timely completed. Certification in Section 2 not timely completed.	$550.00
Section 1 not timely completed. Certification in Section 2 not timely completed.	$550.00
No attestation in Section 1. Section 1 not dated.	$550.00
Section 1 not timely completed. Section 2 not completed. Certification in Section 2 not timely completed. Unsigned and undated.	$640.00
Section 1 not timely completed. Section 2 not completed. Certification in Section 2 not timely completed. Unsigned and undated.	$640.00
Section 1 not timely completed.	$550.00
Section 1 not timely completed. Certification in Section 2 not timely completed.	$550.00
Section 1 not timely completed. Certification in Section 2 not timely completed.	$550.00
Section 2, List "C" document not listed. Section 1 not dated.	$550.00
Section 1 not timely completed. Certification in Section 2 not timely completed.	$550.00
Section 1 not timely completed. Section 2 not completed. Certification in Section 2 not timely completed. Unsigned and undated.	$640.00
Section 1 not timely completed. Section 2 not completed. Certification in Section 2 not timely completed.	$640.00

Section 1 not timely completed. Section 2 not completed. Certification in Section 2 not timely completed. Unsigned and undated.	$640.00
Section 1 not timely completed. Certification in Section 2 not timely completed.	$550.00
Section 1 not timely completed. Section 2 not completed. Certification in Section 2 not timely completed. Unsigned and undated.	$640.00
Section 1 not timely completed. Section 2 list "B" document not identified. Certification in Section 2 not timely completed.	$640.00
Section 1 not dated.	$550.00
Section 1 not timely completed. Certification in Section 2 not timely completed.	$550.00
Section 1 not timely completed. Certification in Section 2 not timely completed.	$550.00
Section 1 not timely completed. Section 2, no list "C" document. Certification in Section 2 not timely completed.	$640.00
Section 1 not timely completed. Certification in Section 2 not timely completed.	$550.00
Section 1 not timely completed. Certification in Section 2 not timely completed.	$550.00

EMPLOYEES WITH NO FORM I-9.

NAME	FINE AMOUNT
	$1000.00
	$1000.00
	$1000.00
	$1000.00

$1000.00

$1000.00

$1000.00

$1000.00

$1000.00

$1000.00

$1000.00

$1000.00

$1000.00

$1000.00

Government Resources & Court Documents

HANDBOOK FOR EMPLOYERS—INSTRUCTIONS ON COMPLETING THE FORM I-9

U.S. Department of Homeland Security
U.S. Citizenship and Immigration Services
www.uscis.gov

Official Business
Penalty for Private Use $300
Bulk Rate
Carrier Route Presort
Postage and Fees Paid
Department of Homeland Security
Service Permit No. G-78

M-274 (Rev. 11/01/2007) N

Handbook for Employers

Instructions for Completing the Form I-9
(Employment Eligibility Verification Form)

Contents

Obtaining Forms I-9 and the M-274
See Page 2

Part One – Why Employers Must Verify Employment Eligibility of New Employees
See Page 3

Part Two – Completing the Form I-9
See Page 5

Part Three – Photocopying and Retaining the Form I-9
See Page 12

Part Four – Unlawful Discrimination and Penalties for Prohibited Practices
See Page 15

Part Five – Instructions for Recruiters and Referrers for a Fee
See Page 19

Part Six – E-Verify: The Web-based Verification Companion to the Form I-9
See Page 20

Part Seven – Some Questions You May Have About the Form I-9
See Page 21

Part Eight – Acceptable Documents for Verifying Employment Eligibility
See Page 31

Form I-9, Employment Eligibility Verification

Obtaining Forms I-9 and the M-274

This Handbook includes one copy of the Form I-9, which can be photocopied. To order more forms or handbooks, call the U.S. Citizenship and Immigration Service (USCIS) toll-free number at 1-800-870-3636. Individuals also can order them by phoning the USCIS National Customer Service Center at 1-800-375-5283, or download PDF versions from the USCIS website at www.uscis.gov.

HANDBOOK FOR EMPLOYERS: INSTRUCTIONS FOR COMPLETING THE I-9

Part One
Why Employers Must Verify Employment Eligibility of New Employees

In 1986, Congress reformed U.S. immigration laws. These reforms, the result of a bipartisan effort, preserved the tradition of legal immigration while seeking to close the door to illegal entry. The employer sanctions provisions, found in Section 274A of the Immigration and Nationality Act, were added by the Immigration Reform and Control Act of 1986 (IRCA). These provisions further changed with the passage of the Immigration Act of 1990 and the Illegal Immigration Reform and Immigrant Responsibility Act of 1996. References to "the Act" in this Handbook refer to the Immigration and Nationality Act (INA), as amended.

Employment is often the magnet that attracts individuals to reside in the United States illegally. The purpose of the employer sanctions law is to remove this magnet by requiring employers to hire only individuals who may legally work here: citizens and nationals of the United States, lawful permanent residents, and aliens authorized to work. To comply with the law, you must verify the identity and employment eligibility of each person you hire, complete and retain a Form I-9 for each employee, and refrain from discriminating against individuals on the basis of national origin or citizenship. (See Part Four for more information on unlawful discrimination.)

The Form I-9 helps employers to verify individuals who are authorized to work in the United States. You should complete a Form I-9 for every new employee you hire after November 6, 1986. The law requires you as an employer to:

1. Ensure that your employees fill out Section 1 of the Form I-9 when they start to work;

2. Review document(s) establishing each employee's identity and eligibility to work;

3. Properly complete Section 2 of the Form I-9;

4. Retain the Form I-9 for 3 years after the date the person begins work or 1 year after the person's employment is terminated, whichever is later; and

5. Upon request, provide Forms I-9 to authorized officers of the Department of Homeland Security (DHS), the U.S. Department of Labor (DOL), or the Office of Special Counsel for Immigration Related Unfair Employment Practices (OSC) for inspection.

   NOTE: This does not preclude DHS or DOL from obtaining warrants based on probable cause for entry onto the premises of suspected violators without advance notice.

These requirements apply to all employers, including:

1. Agricultural associations, agricultural employers or farm labor contractors who employ, recruit or refer people for a fee; and

2. Those who employ anyone for domestic work in their private home on a regular basis (such as every week).

If you are self-employed, you do not need to complete a Form I-9 on yourself unless you are also an employee of a business entity, such as a corporation or partnership, in which case the business entity is required to complete a Form I-9 on you.

This Handbook will explain how to properly complete the Form I-9, and answer frequently asked questions about the law as it relates to the Form I-9.

Developments in the Law and Changes to the Form I-9

Congress enacted the Illegal Immigration Reform and Immigrant Responsibility Act of 1996 (IIRIRA), Pub. L. 104-208, on September 30, 1996. Section 412(a) of IIRIRA mandated a reduction in the number of documents that employers may accept from newly hired employees during the employment verification process. On September 30, 1997, the former Immigration and Naturalization Service (INS), published an Interim Designation of Acceptable Documents for Employment Verification that implemented the changes required by IIRIRA. See 62 FR 51001-51006 ("1997 interim rule"). However, the Form I-9 was not amended at that time to reflect the changes made by the 1997 interim rule. For this reason, DHS has updated the Form I-9 to bring it into compliance with the 1997 interim rule. DHS has also updated this Handbook for Employers as a companion to the new version of the Form I-9.

In the supplementary information accompanying the 1997 interim rule, the INS stated that it would exercise prosecutorial discretion not to penalize violations resulting from the changes made by that interim rule as a temporary transitional measure until a new Form I-9 was released in the context of a broader final rulemaking. While DHS still intends to pursue other changes to the Form I-9 in a future update, it decided to update the Form I-9 to bring it in compliance with existing law before making any further changes. Therefore, the Form I-9 has been amended to reflect those changes made by the 1997 regulations, but any changes that would have required the drafting of a new regulation are being saved for a future update of the Form I-9. Employers who do not comply with the current regulatory requirements as indicated on the new Form I-9, for example, by accepting documents no longer listed on the Form I-9 List of Acceptable Documents, may be subject to penalties under section 274A of the Immigration and Nationality Act.

The most significant change to the Form I-9 is a reduction in the acceptable List A documents identified on the form. Five documents are no longer listed as documents acceptable for establishing both identity and employment eligibility under List A: (1) the Certificate of United States Citizenship (Form N-560 or N-561); (2) the Certificate of Naturalization (Form N-550 or N-570); (3) the Form I-151, a long out-of-date version of the Alien Registration Receipt Card ("green card"); (4) the Unexpired Reentry Permit (Form I-327); and (5) the Unexpired Refugee Travel Document (Form 1-571).

The amended Form I-9 retains four types of acceptable List A documents: (1) the U.S. Passport (unexpired or expired); (2) an unexpired Permanent Resident Card or Alien Registration Receipt Card (Form I-551); (3) an unexpired foreign passport with a temporary I-551 stamp; and (4) an unexpired Employment Authorization Document that contains a photograph (Form I-766, I-688, I-688A, I-688B). In addition, the amended Form I-9 modifies one acceptable List A document, replacing the "unexpired foreign passport with an attached Form I-94 indicating unexpired employment authorization" with "an unexpired foreign passport with an unexpired Arrival-Departure Record, Form I-94, bearing the same name as the passport and containing an endorsement of the alien's nonimmigrant status, if that status authorizes the alien to work for the employer." All of these acceptable List A documents were carried over from the previous Form I-9, with the exception of the Form I-766, which is a new version of the Employment Authorization Document that has been added to List A. The order and organization of List A also have been revised for ease of use. For example, the various Employment Authorization Documents are listed together as one category, and the unexpired foreign passport with temporary I-551 stamp is a separate entry from the unexpired passport with Form I-94 indicating an employer-specific work-authorized nonimmigrant status.

This updating of List A on the Form I-9 will help streamline the hiring process by providing employers a better means to conform their document acceptance practices to the requirements of the law. As discussed above, the 1997 regulatory List A on the Form I-9 was not enforced pursuant to the prosecutorial discretion policy described in the supplementary information to the interim rule. With a Form I-9 now available that includes the correct List A, the prosecutorial discretion policy is no longer necessary, and Immigration and Customs Enforcement (ICE) has confirmed that it will no longer be in effect 30 days following publication of the Federal Register Notice.

The amended Form I-9 also informs employees that providing their Social Security number is voluntary, pursuant to section 7 of the Privacy Act (8 U.S.C. 552a(note)). However, employees must provide their Social Security number if their employer participates in E-Verify (the employment eligibility verification program formerly known as Basic Pilot Program or Electronic Employment Verification (EEV)), as provided by Section 403(a)(1)(A) of IIRIRA. The Form I-9 also includes changes to its organization and formatting that are more consistent with standard DHS practices, such as including a clarification that there is no filing fee associated with the Form I-9.

The Homeland Security Act

The Homeland Security Act of 2002 created an executive department combining numerous federal agencies with a mission dedicated to homeland security. On March 1, 2003, the authorities of the former INS were transferred to three new agencies in the Department of Homeland Security: U.S. Citizenship and Immigration Services (USCIS), U.S. Customs and Border Protection (CBP), and U.S. Immigration and Customs Enforcement (ICE). The two DHS immigration components most involved with the matters discussed in this Handbook are USCIS and ICE. USCIS is responsible for most documentation of alien work authorization, for the Form I-9 itself, and for the E-Verify employment eligibility verification program. ICE is responsible for enforcement of the penalty provisions of section 274A of the Act, and for other immigration enforcement within the United States.

Under the Homeland Security Act, the Department of Justice retained certain important responsibilities related to the Form I-9 as well. In particular, the Office of Special Counsel for Immigration Related Unfair Employment Practices (OSC) in the Civil Rights Division is responsible for enforcement of the anti-discrimination provisions in section 274B of the Act, while the Executive Office for Immigration Review (EOIR) is responsible for the administrative adjudication of cases under sections 274A, 274B, and 274C (civil document fraud) of the Act.

HANDBOOK FOR EMPLOYERS: INSTRUCTIONS FOR COMPLETING THE I-9

Part Two
When You Must Complete the Form I-9

You must complete the Form I-9 every time you hire any person to perform labor or services in return for wages or other remuneration. This requirement applies to everyone hired after November 6, 1986.

Ensure that the employee fully completes Section 1 of the Form I-9 at the time of the hire - when the employee begins work. Review the employee's document(s) and fully complete Section 2 of the Form I-9 within 3 business days of the hire.

If you hire a person for less than 3 business days, Sections 1 and 2 of the Form I-9 must be fully completed at the time of the hire – when the employee begins work.

You DO NOT need to complete a Form I-9 for persons who are:

1. Hired before November 7, 1986, who are continuing in their employment and have a reasonable expectation of employment at all times;

2. Employed for casual domestic work in a private home on a sporadic, irregular, or intermittent basis;

3. Independent contractors; or

4. Providing labor to you who are employed by a contractor providing contract services (e.g., employee leasing or temporary agencies).

NOTE: You cannot contract for the labor of an alien if you know the alien is not authorized to work in the United States.

Completing the Form I-9

Section 1

Have the employee complete Section 1 at the time of the hire (when he or she begins to work) by filling in the correct information and signing and dating the form. Ensure that the employee prints the information clearly.

If the employee cannot complete Section 1 without assistance or if he or she needs the Form I-9 translated, someone may assist him or her. The preparer or translator must read the form to the employee, assist him or her in completing Section 1, and have the employee sign or mark the form in the appropriate place. The preparer or translator must then complete the Preparer/Translator Certification block on the Form I-9.

You are responsible for reviewing and ensuring that your employee fully and properly completes Section 1.

NOTE: Providing a Social Security number on the Form I-9 is voluntary for all employees unless you are an employer participating in the USCIS E-Verify Program, which requires an employee's Social Security number for employment eligibility verification. You may not, however, ask an employee to provide you a specific document with his or her Social Security number on it, to avoid unlawful discrimination. For more information on the E-Verify Program, see Part Six. For more information on unlawful discrimination, see Part Four.

Figure 1: *Instructions for Completing Section 1: Employee Identification and Verification*

1. Employee enters full name and maiden name, if applicable.
2. Employee enters current address and date of birth.
3. Employee enters his or her city, state and Social Security number. Entering the Social Security number is optional unless the employer verifies employment eligibility through the USCIS E-Verify Program.
4. Employee reads warning and attests to immigration status.
5. Employee signs and dates the form.
6. If the employee uses a preparer or translator to fill out the form, that person must certify that he or she assisted the employee by completing this signature block.

Section 2

The employee must present to you an original document or documents that establish identity and employment eligibility within 3 business days of the date employment begins. Some documents establish both identity and employment eligibility (List A). Other documents establish identity only (List B) or employment authorization only (List C). The employee can choose which document(s) he or she wants to present from the List of Acceptable Documents. This list appears in the Appendix and on the last page of the revised Form I-9, dated June 5, 2007.

Examine the original document or documents the employee presents and then fully complete Section 2 of the Form I-9. You must examine one document from List A, or one from List B and one from List C. Record the title, issuing authority, number, and expiration date (if any) of the document(s); fill in the date of hire and correct information in the certification block; and sign and date the Form I-9. You must accept any document(s) from List of Acceptable Document presented by the individual which reasonably appear on their face to be genuine and to relate to the person presenting them. You may not specify which document(s) an employee must present.

NOTE: If you participate in the E-Verify Program, you may only accept List B documents that bear a photograph.

In certain circumstances, employers, recruiters and referrers for a fee must accept a receipt in lieu of a List A, List B, or a List C document if one is presented by an employee. A receipt indicating that an individual has applied for initial work authorization or for an extension of expiring work authorization is NOT acceptable proof of employment eligibility on the Form I-9. Receipts are never acceptable if employment lasts less than 3 business days.

Receipts and other documents that serve as proof of temporary employment eligibility that employers can accept are:

1. Receipts for the application of a replacement document where the document was lost, stolen, or destroyed, which can be a List A, List B, or List C document. The employee must present the replacement document within 90 days from the date of hire.

HANDBOOK FOR EMPLOYERS: INSTRUCTIONS FOR COMPLETING THE I-9

2. The arrival portion of a Form I-94 with an attached photo and a temporary I-551 stamp, which is a receipt for a List A document. When the stamp expires, or if the stamp has no expiration, one year from date of issue, the employee must present the Form I-551 Permanent Resident Card.

3. The departure portion of the Form I-94 with a refugee admission stamp, which is a receipt for a List A document. The employee must present, within 90 days from date of hire, Form I-766, or a List B document and an unrestricted Social Security card.

When the employee provides an acceptable receipt, the employer should record the document title in Section 2 of the Form I-9 and write the word "receipt" and any document number in the "Document #" space. When the employee presents the actual document, the employer should cross out the word "receipt" and any accompanying document number, insert the number from the actual document presented, and initial and date the change.

Figure 2: *Section 2: Employer Review and Verification*

1.
2.
3.

1. Employer records document title(s), issuing authority, document number, expiration date from original documents supplied by employee. See Part Eight for the List of Acceptable Documents.
2. Employer enters date of hire (i.e. first day of work).
3. Employer attests to examining the documents provided by filling out the signature block.

Minors (Individuals under Age 18)

If a minor – a person under the age of 18 – cannot present a List A document or an identity document from List B, the Form I-9 should be completed in the following way:

1. A parent or legal guardian must complete Section 1 and write "Individual under age 18" in the space for the employee's signature;
2. The parent or legal guardian must complete the "Preparer/Translator Certification" block;
3. You should write "Individual under age 18" in Section 2, List B, in the space after the words "Document #"; and
4. The minor must present a List C document showing his or her employment eligibility. You should record the required information in the appropriate space in Section 2.

Figure 3: *Completing the Form I-9 for Minors*

1. A parent or legal guardian of a minor employee completes Section 1 and writes, "Individual under age 18" in signature space.
2. A parent or legal guardian completes the Preparer and/or Translator block.
3. Employer enters "Individual under age 18" under List B and records the List C document the minor presents.

HANDBOOK FOR EMPLOYERS: INSTRUCTIONS FOR COMPLETING THE I-9

Employees with Disabilities (Special Placement)

If a person with a disability, who is placed in a job by a nonprofit organization or as part of a rehabilitation program, cannot present a List A document or an identity document from List B, the Form I-9 should be completed in the following way:

1. A representative of the nonprofit organization, a parent or a legal guardian must complete Section 1 and write "Special Placement" in the space for the employee's signature;

2. The representative, parent or legal guardian must complete the "Preparer/Translator Certification" block;

3. You should write "Special Placement" in Section 2, List B, in the space after the words "Document #"; and

4. The employee with a disability must present a List C document showing his or her employment eligibility. You should record the required information in the appropriate space in Section 2.

Figure 4: *Completing the Form I-9 for Employees with Disabilities (Special Placement)*

1. A representative of a nonprofit organization, parent or legal guardian of an individual with a disability completes Section 1 and writes, "Special Placement" in signature space.
2. The representative, parent or legal guardian completes the Preparer and/or Translator block.
3. Employer enters "Special Placement" under List B and records the List C document the employee with a disability presents.

Future Expiration Dates

Future expiration dates may appear on the employment authorization documents of aliens, including, among others, permanent residents and refugees. USCIS includes expiration dates even on documents issued to aliens with permanent work authorization. The existence of a future expiration date:

1. Does not preclude continuous employment authorization;
2. Does not mean that subsequent employment authorization will not be granted; and
3. Should not be considered in determining whether the alien is qualified for a particular position.

Considering a future employment authorization expiration date in determining whether an alien is qualified for a particular job may constitute employment discrimination. (See Part Four.) However, as described below, you may need to reverify the employee's eligibility to work upon the expiration of certain List A or List C documents.

Reverifying Employment Authorization for Current Employees

When an employee's work authorization expires, you must reverify his or her employment eligibility. You may use Section 3 of the Form I-9, or, if Section 3 has already been used for a previous reverification or update, use a new Form I-9. If you use a new form, you should write the employee's name in Section 1, complete Section 3, and retain the new form with the original. The employee must present a document that shows either an extension of the employee's initial employment authorization or new work authorization. If the employee cannot provide you with proof of current work authorization (e.g. any document from List A or List C, including an unrestricted Social Security card), you cannot continue to employ that person.

NOTE: List B identity documents, such as a driver's license, should not be reverified when they expire.

To maintain continuous employment eligibility, an employee with temporary work authorization should apply for new work authorization at least 90 days before the current expiration date. If USCIS fails to adjudicate the application for employment authorization within 90 days, then the employee will be authorized for employment on Form I-766 for a period not to exceed 240 days.

NOTE: You must reverify an employee's employment eligibility on the Form I-9 not later than the date the employee's work authorization expires.

Reverifying or Updating Employment Authorization for Rehired Employees

When you rehire an employee, you must ensure that he or she is still authorized to work. You may do this by completing a new Form I-9 or you may reverify or update the original form by completing Section 3.

If you rehire an employee who has previously completed a Form I-9, you may reverify on the employee's original Form I-9 (or on a new Form I-9 if Section 3 of the original has already been used) if:

1. You rehire the employee within three years of the initial date of hire; and
2. The employee's previous grant of work authorization has expired, but he or she is currently eligible to work on a different basis or under a new grant of work authorization than when the original Form I-9 was completed.

To reverify, you must:

1. Record the date of rehire;
2. Record the document title, number and expiration date (if any) of any document(s) presented;
3. Sign and date Section 3; and
4. If you are reverifying on a new Form I-9, write the employee's name in Section 1.

If you rehire an employee who has previously completed a Form I-9, you may update on the employee's original Form I-9 or on a new Form I-9 if:

1. You rehire the employee within three years of the initial date of hire; and
2. The employee is still eligible to work on the same basis as when the original Form I-9 was completed.

To update, you must:

1. Record the date of rehire;
2. Sign and date Section 3; and
3. If you are updating on a new Form I-9, write the employee's name in Section 1.

Employers always have the option of completing Sections 1 and 2 of a new Form I-9 instead of completing Section 3 when rehiring employees.

HANDBOOK FOR EMPLOYERS: INSTRUCTIONS FOR COMPLETING THE I-9

Figure 5: *Reverification of Employment Eligibility for Current Employees and Rehires*

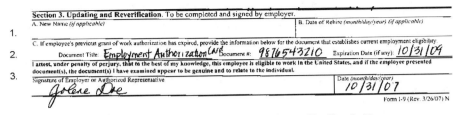

1. Record the employee's new name, if applicable, and date of rehire, if applicable
2. Record the document title, number, and expiration date (if any) of document(s) presented
3. Sign and date

NOTE: You may also fill out a new Form I-9 in lieu of filling out this section.

Part Three
Photocopying and Retaining the Form I-9

Employers must retain completed Forms I-9 for all employees for 3 years after the date they hire an employee or 1 year after the date employment is terminated, whichever is later. These forms can be retained in paper, microfilm, microfiche, or, more recently, electronically.

To store Forms I-9 electronically, you may use any electronic recordkeeping, attestation, and retention system that complies with DHS standards, which includes most off-the-shelf computer programs and commercial automated data processing systems. However, the system must not be subject to any agreement that would restrict access to and use of it by an agency of the United States. (See Electronic Retention of Forms I-9 below.)

Paper Retention of Forms I-9

The Form I-9 can be signed and stored in paper format. Simply reproduce a complete, blank Form I-9, and ensure that the employee receives the instructions for completing the form.

When copying or printing the paper Form I-9, you may reproduce the two-sided form by making either double-sided or single-sided copies.

You may retain completed paper forms onsite, or at an off-site storage facility, for the required retention period, as long as you are able to present the Forms I-9 within 3 days of an audit request from DHS, OSC, or DOL officers.

Microform Retention of Forms I-9

You may store Forms I-9 on microfilm or microfiche. To do so:

1. Select film stock that will preserve the image and allow accessibility and usability for the entire retention period, which in certain circumstances could be upward of 20 years, depending on the employee and your business.

2. Use well-maintained equipment to create and view microfilms and microfiche that provides a high degree of legibility and readability, and has the ability to reproduce legible and readable paper copies. DHS officers must have immediate access to clear, readable documents should they need to inspect your forms.

3. We suggest that you place the required indexes either in the first frames of the first roll of film or in the last frames of the last roll of film of a series. For microfiche, place them in the last frames of the last microfiche or microfilm jacket of a series.

Remember: Forms I-9 must be stored for 3 years after the date you hire an employee or 1 year after the date you or the employee terminates employment, whichever is later. For example, if an employee retires from your company after 15 years, you will need to store his or her Form I-9 for a total of 16 years.

Electronic Forms I-9

USCIS provides a Portable Document Format fillable-printable Form I-9 from its website, www.uscis.gov. The Form I-9 can also be electronically generated or retained, provided that:

1. The resulting form is legible;

2. No change is made to the name, content, or sequence of the data elements and instructions;

3. No additional data elements or language are inserted;

4. The employee receives the Form I-9 instructions; and

5. The standards specified under 8 CFR 274a.2(e) are met.

Electronic Retention of Forms I-9

Employers may complete or retain the Form I-9 in an electronic generation or storage system that includes:

1. Reasonable controls to ensure the integrity, accuracy and reliability of the electronic storage system;

2. Reasonable controls designed to prevent and detect the unauthorized or accidental creation of, addition to, alteration of, deletion of, or deterioration of an electronically completed or stored Form I-9, including the electronic signature if used;

3. An inspection and quality assurance program evidenced by regular evaluations of the electronic generation or storage system, including periodic checks of electronically stored Forms I-9, including the electronic signature if used;

4. A retrieval system that includes an indexing system that permits searches by any data element; and

5. The ability to reproduce legible and readable hardcopies.

Remember, Forms I-9 must be stored for 3 years after the date you hire an employee or 1 year after the date you or the employee terminates employment, whichever is later, which can result in a long retention period.

HANDBOOK FOR EMPLOYERS: INSTRUCTIONS FOR COMPLETING THE I-9

Retaining Copies of Form I-9 Documentation

You may choose to copy or scan documents presented by an employee, which you must retain with his or her Form I-9. Retaining copies of documentation does not relieve you from the requirement to fully complete section 2 of the Form I-9. If you choose to retain copies of employee documentation, you may not just do so for employees of certain national origins or citizenship statuses, or you may be in violation of anti-discrimination laws.

Electronic Signature of Forms I-9

You may choose to fill out a paper Form I-9 and scan and upload the signed Form to retain it electronically. Once you have securely stored the Form I-9 in electronic format, you may destroy the original paper Form I-9.

If you complete Forms I-9 electronically using an electronic signature, you must implement a system for capturing electronic signatures that allows signatories to acknowledge that they read the attestation; and can associate an electronic signature with an electronically completed Form I-9. In addition, the system must:

1. Affix the electronic signature at the time of the transaction;
2. Create and preserve a record verifying the identity of the person producing the signature; and
3. Provide a printed confirmation of the transaction, at the time of the transaction, to the person providing the signature.

NOTE: If you choose to use electronic signature to complete Form I-9, but do not comply with these standards, DHS will determine that you have not properly completed the Form I-9, in violation of Section 274A(a)(1)(B) of the Act.

System Documentation

For each electronic generation or storage system used, you must maintain, and make available upon request, complete descriptions of:

1. The electronic generation and storage system, including all procedures relating to its use;
2. The indexing system, which permits the identification and retrieval for viewing or reproducing of relevant records maintained in an electronic storage system; and
3. The business processes that create, modify, and maintain the retained Forms I-9, and establish the authenticity and integrity of the Forms, such as audit trails.

Note: Insufficient or incomplete documentation is a violation of section 274A(a)(1)(B) of the Act (8 CFR Part 274a.2(f)(2)).

Security

If you retain Forms I-9 electronically, you must implement a records security program that:

1. Ensures that only authorized personnel have access to electronic records;
2. Provides for backup and recovery of records to protect against information loss;
3. Ensures that employees are trained to minimize the risk of unauthorized or accidental alteration or erasure of electronic records; and
4. Ensures that whenever an individual creates, accesses, views, updates, or corrects an electronic record, the system creates a secure and permanent record that establishes the date of access, the identity of the individual who accessed the electronic record, and the particular action taken.

Note: If an employer's action or inaction results in the alteration, loss, or erasure of electronic records, and the employer knew, or reasonably should be known, that the action or inaction could have that effect, the employer is in violation of Section 274A(a)(1)(B) of the Act.

Inspection

DHS, OSC and DOL give employers three day's notice prior to inspecting retained Forms I-9. The employer must make Forms I-9 available upon request at the location where DHS, OSC or DOL requests to see them.

If you store Forms I-9 at an off-site location, inform the inspecting officer of the location where you store them, and make arrangements for the inspection. The inspecting officers can perform your inspection at an office of an authorized agency of the United States if previous arrangements are made. Recruiters or referrers for a fee who designate an employer to complete employment verification procedures may present a photocopy or printed electronic image of the Form I-9 at an inspection. If you refuse or delay an inspection, you will be in violation of DHS retention requirements.

At the time of an inspection, you must:

1. Retrieve and reproduce only the Forms I-9 electronically retained in the electronic storage system and supporting documentation specifically requested by the inspecting officer. This documentation includes associated audit trails that show who has accessed a computer system and

the actions performed within or on the computer system during a given period of time.

2. Provide the inspecting officer with appropriate hardware and software, personnel, and documentation necessary to locate, retrieve, read, and reproduce any electronically stored Forms I-9, any supporting documents, and their associated audit trails, reports, and other data used to maintain the authenticity, integrity, and reliability of the records.

3. Provide the inspecting officer, if requested, any reasonably available or obtainable electronic summary file(s), such as a spreadsheet, containing all of the information fields on all of the electronically stored Forms I-9.

Part Four
Unlawful Discrimination and Penalties for Prohibited Practices

Unlawful Discrimination

General Provisions

The anti-discrimination provision of the Act, as amended, prohibits four types of unlawful conduct: (1) citizenship or immigration status discrimination; (2) national origin discrimination; (3) unfair documentary practices during the Form I-9 process (document abuse); and (4) retaliation. The Office of Special Counsel for Immigration-Related Unfair Employment Practices (OSC), part of the United States Department of Justice Civil Rights Division, enforces the anti-discrimination provision of the INA. Title VII of the Civil Rights Act of 1964 (Title VII), as amended, also prohibits national origin discrimination, among other types of conduct. The United States Equal Employment Opportunity Commission (EEOC) enforces Title VII.

As discussed further below, OSC and EEOC share jurisdiction over national origin discrimination charges. Generally, the EEOC has jurisdiction over larger employers with 15 or more employees, whereas OSC has jurisdiction over smaller employers with between 4 and 14 employees. OSC's jurisdiction over national origin discrimination claims is limited to intentional acts of discrimination with respect to hiring, firing, and recruitment or referral for a fee, but the EEOC's jurisdiction is broader. Title VII covers both intentional and unintentional acts of discrimination in the workplace, including discrimination in hiring, firing, recruitment, promotion, assignment, compensation, and other terms and conditions of employment. OSC has exclusive jurisdiction over citizenship or immigration status discrimination claims against all employers with four or more employees. Similarly, OSC has jurisdiction over all document abuse claims against employers with four or more employees.

Types of Employment Discrimination Prohibited Under the INA

Document Abuse

Discriminatory documentary practices related to verifying the employment eligibility of employees and the Form I-9 process are called document abuse. Document abuse occurs when employers treat individuals differently on the basis of national origin or citizenship status in the Form I-9 process. Document abuse can be broadly categorized into four types of conduct: 1) improperly requesting that employees produce more documents than are required by the Form I-9 to establish the employee's identity and work authorization; 2) improperly requesting that employees produce a particular document, such as a "green card," to establish identity or work eligibility; 3) improperly rejecting documents that reasonably appear to be genuine and belong to the employee presenting them; 4) improperly treating groups of applicants differently when completing the Form I-9, such as requiring certain groups of employees that look or sound "foreign" to produce particular documents the employer does not require other employees to produce. These practices may constitute unlawful document abuse and should be avoided when verifying employment eligibility. All work authorized individuals are protected against this type of discrimination. The INA's prohibition against document abuse covers employers with 4 or more employees.

Citizenship Status Discrimination

Citizenship or immigration status discrimination occurs when an employer treats employees differently based on their citizenship or immigration status in regard to hiring, firing, or recruitment or referral for a fee. U.S. citizens, recent permanent residents, temporary residents under the IRCA legalization program, asylees, and refugees are protected. An employer must treat all of these groups the same. Subject to limited exceptions, the INA's prohibition against citizenship or immigration status discrimination covers employers with 4 or more employees.

National Origin Discrimination

This form of discrimination occurs when an employer treats employees differently based on their national origin in regard to hiring, firing, or recruitment or referral for a fee. An employee's national origin relates to the employee's place of birth, country of origin, ancestry, native language, accent, or because he or she is perceived as looking or sounding "foreign." All work-authorized individuals are protected from national origin discrimination. The INA's prohibition against intentional national origin discrimination generally covers employers with 4 to 14 employees.

Retaliation

Retaliation occurs when an employer or other covered entity intimidates, threatens, coerces, or otherwise retaliates against an individual because the individual has filed an immigration-related employment discrimination charge or complaint; has testified or participated in any immigration-related employment discrimination investigation, proceeding, or hearing; or otherwise asserts his or her rights under the INA's anti-discrimination provision.

Types of Discrimination Prohibited by Title VII

As noted above, Title VII also prohibits employment discrimination on the basis of national origin, as well as race, color, religion, and sex. Title VII covers employers that employ 15 or more employees for 20 or more weeks in the preceding or current calendar year, and prohibits discrimination in any aspect of employment, including: hiring and firing; compensation, assignment, or classification of employees; transfer, promotion, layoff, or recall; job advertisements; recruitment; testing; use of company facilities; training and apprenticeship programs; fringe benefits; pay, retirement plans, and leave; or other terms and conditions of employment.

Avoiding Discrimination in Recruiting, Hiring and the Form I-9 Process

In practice, employers should treat employees equally when recruiting and hiring, and when verifying employment eligibility and completing the Form I-9. Employers should not:

1. Set different employment eligibility verification standards or require that different documents be presented by employees because of their national origin and citizenship status. For example, employers cannot demand that non-U.S. citizens present DHS-issued documents.

    Each employee must be allowed to choose the documents that he or she will produce from the lists of acceptable Form I-9 documents. For example, both citizens and work authorized aliens may produce a driver's license (List B) and an unrestricted Social Security card (List C) to establish identity and employment eligibility.

2. Request to see employment eligibility verification documents before hire and completion of the Form I-9 because someone looks or sounds "foreign," or because someone states that he or she is not a U.S. citizen.

3. Refuse to accept a document, or refuse to hire an individual, because a document has a future expiration date.

4. Request that, during reverification, an employee present a new unexpired employment authorization document (EAD) if he or she presented an EAD during initial verification. For reverification, each employee must be free to choose to present any document either from List A or from List C. Refugees and asylees may possess EADs, but they are authorized to work based on their status, and may possess other documents that prove work authorization from List A or List C to show upon reverification, such as an unrestricted Social Security card.

5. Limit jobs to U.S. citizens unless U.S. citizenship is required for the specific position by law; regulation; executive order; or federal, state, or local government contract. On an individual basis, an employer may legally prefer a U.S. citizen or national over an equally qualified alien to fill a specific position, but may not adopt a blanket policy of always preferring citizens over non-citizens.

Procedures for Filing Charges of Employment Discrimination

OSC

Discrimination charges may be filed by an individual who believes he or she is the victim of employment discrimination, a person acting on behalf of such an individual, or a DHS officer who has reason to believe that discrimination has occurred. Discrimination charges must be filed with OSC within 180 days of the alleged discriminatory act. Upon receipt of a complete discrimination charge, OSC will notify the employer within 10 days that a charge has been filed and commence its investigation. If OSC has not filed a complaint with an administrative law judge within 120 days of receiving a charge of discrimination, it will notify the charging party of its determination not to file a complaint. The charging party (other than a DHS officer) may file a complaint with an administrative law judge within 90 days after receiving the notice from OSC. In addition, OSC may still file a complaint within this 90-day period. The administrative law judge will conduct a hearing and issue a decision. OSC may also attempt to settle a charge or the parties may enter into settlement agreements resolving the charge.

EEOC

A charge must be filed with EEOC within 180 days from the date of the alleged violation, in order to protect the charging party's rights. This 180-day filing deadline is extended to 300 days if the charge also is covered by a state or local anti-discrimination law.

Employers Prohibited from Retaliating against Employees

An employer cannot take retaliatory action against a person who has filed a charge of discrimination with OSC or the EEOC, was a witness or otherwise participated in the investigation or prosecution of a discrimination complaint, or otherwise asserts his or her rights under the INA's anti-discrimination provision and/or Title VII. Such retaliatory action may constitute a violation of the INA's anti-discrimination provision and/or Title VII.

Additional Information

For more information about the anti-discrimination provision of the INA and the procedures of OSC, call 1-800-255-7688 (worker hotline) or 1-800-255-8155 (employer hotline); or 1-800-237-2515 (TDD for hearing impaired); or visit OSC's website at http://www.usdoj.gov/crt/osc

For more information on Title VII and policies and procedures of the Equal Employment Opportunity Commission, call 1-800-USA-EEOC; or 1-800-669-6820 (TTY for hearing impaired); or visit EEOC's website at http://www.eeoc.gov.

Penalties for Prohibited Practices

A. UNLAWFUL EMPLOYMENT

1. Civil Penalties

The Department of Homeland Security (DHS) may impose penalties if an investigation reveals that an employer has knowingly hired or knowingly continued to employ an unauthorized alien, or has failed to comply with the employment eligibility verification requirements, with respect to employees hired after November 6, 1986. DHS will issue a Notice of Intent to Fine (NIF) when it intends to impose penalties. Employers who receive a NIF may request a hearing before an administrative law judge. If an employer's request for a hearing is not received within 30 days, DHS will impose the penalty and issue a Final Order, which cannot be appealed.

a. Hiring or continuing to employ unauthorized aliens

DHS may order employers it determines to have knowingly hired unauthorized aliens (or to be continuing to employ aliens knowing that they are or have become unauthorized to work in the United States) to cease and desist from such activity, and pay a civil money penalty as follows:

1. First Offense: Not less than $275 and not more than $2,200 for each unauthorized alien;
2. Second offense: Not less than $2,200 and not more than $5,500 for each unauthorized alien; or
3. Subsequent Offenses: Not less than $3,300 and not more than $11,000 for each unauthorized alien.

DHS will consider an employer to have knowingly hired an unauthorized alien if, after November 6, 1986, the employer uses a contract, subcontract or exchange, entered into, renegotiated or extended, to obtain the labor of an alien and knows the alien is not authorized to work in the United States. The employer will be subject to the penalties set forth above.

b. Failing to comply with the Form I-9 requirements

Employers who fail to properly complete, retain, and/or make available for inspection Forms I-9 as required by law may face civil money penalties in an amount of not less than $110 and not more than $1,100 for each individual with respect to whom such violation occurred.

In determining the amount of the penalty, DHS will consider:

1. The size of the business of the employer being charged;
2. The good faith of the employer;
3. The seriousness of the violation;
4. Whether or not the individual was an unauthorized alien; and
5. The history of previous violations of the employer.

c. Enjoining pattern or practice violations

If the Attorney General has reasonable cause to believe that a person or entity is engaged in a pattern or practice of employment, recruitment or referral in violation of section 274A(a)(1)(A) or (2) of the Act, the Attorney General may bring civil action in the appropriate U.S. District Court requesting relief, including a permanent or temporary injunction, restraining order or other order against the person or entity, as the Attorney General deems necessary.

d. Requiring indemnification

Employers found to have required a bond or indemnity from an employee against liability under the employer sanctions laws may be ordered to pay a civil money penalty of $1,000 for each violation and to make restitution, either to the person who was required to pay the indemnity, or, if that person cannot be located, to the U.S. Treasury.

e. Good faith defense

If the employer can show that he or she has in good faith complied with the Form I-9 requirements, then the employer has established a "good faith" defense with respect to a charge of knowingly hiring an unauthorized alien, unless the government can show that the employer had actual knowledge of the unauthorized status of the employee.

A good faith attempt to comply with the paperwork requirements of Section 274A(b) of the Act may be adequate notwithstanding a technical or procedural failure to comply, unless the employer has failed to correct the violation within 10 days after notice from DHS, or the employer is engaging in a pattern or practice of violations.

2. Criminal Penalties

a. Engaging in a pattern or practice of knowingly hiring or continuing to employ unauthorized aliens

Persons or entities who are convicted of having engaged in a pattern or practice of knowingly hiring unauthorized aliens (or continuing to employ aliens knowing that they are or have become unauthorized to work in the United States) after November 6, 1986, may face fines of up to $3,000 per employee and/or six months imprisonment.

b. Engaging in fraud or false statements, or otherwise misusing visas, immigration permits and identity documents

Persons who use fraudulent identification or employment eligibility documents or documents that were lawfully issued to another person, or who make a false statement or attestation for purposes of satisfying the employment eligibility verification requirements, may be fined, or imprisoned for up to five years, or both. Other federal criminal statutes may provide higher penalties in certain fraud cases.

B. UNLAWFUL DISCRIMINATION

If an investigation reveals that an employer has engaged in unfair immigration-related employment practices under the INA, the Office of Special Counsel for Immigration-Related Unfair Employment Practices (OSC) may take action. An employer will be ordered to stop the prohibited practice and may be ordered to take one or more corrective steps, including:

1. Hire or reinstate, with or without back pay, individuals directly injured by the discrimination;

2. Post notices to employees about their rights and about employers' obligations;

3. Educate all personnel involved in hiring and in complying with the employer sanctions and antidiscrimination laws about the requirements of these laws.

The court may award attorney's fees to prevailing parties, other than the United States, if it determines that the losing parties' argument is without foundation in law and fact.

Employers who commit citizenship status or national origin discrimination in violation of the anti-discrimination provision of the INA may also be ordered to pay a civil money penalty as follows:

1. First Offense: Not less than $275 and not more than $2,200 for each individual discriminated against;

2. Second Offense: Not less than $2,200 and not more than $5,500 for each individual discriminated against;

3. Subsequent Offenses: Not less than $3,300 and not more than $11,000 for each individual discriminated against.

Employers who commit document abuse in violation of the anti-discrimination provision of the INA may similarly be ordered to pay a civil money penalty as follows:

1. Not less than $110 and not more than $1,100 for each individual discriminated against.

If an employer is found to have committed national origin discrimination under Title VII of the Civil Rights Act of 1964 (Title VII), it may be ordered to stop the prohibited practice and to take one or more corrective steps, including:

1. Hire, reinstate or promote with back pay and retroactive seniority;
2. Post notices to employees about their rights and about the employer's obligations; and/or
3. Remove incorrect information, such as a false warning, from an employee's personnel file.

Under Title VII, compensatory damages may also be available where intentional discrimination is found. Damages may be available to compensate for actual monetary losses, for future monetary losses, and for mental anguish and inconvenience. Punitive damages may be available if the employer acted with malice or reckless indifference.

The employer may also be required to pay attorneys' fees, expert witness fees and court costs.

C. CIVIL DOCUMENT FRAUD

If a DHS investigation reveals that an individual has knowingly committed or participated in acts relating to document fraud (See Part One), DHS may take action. DHS will issue a Notice of Intent to Fine (NIF) when it intends to impose penalties. Persons who receive a NIF may request a hearing before an administrative law judge. If DHS does not receive a request for a hearing within 30 days, it will impose the penalty and issue a Final Order, which is final and cannot be appealed.

Individuals found by DHS or an administrative law judge to have violated Section 274C of the Act may be ordered to pay a civil money penalty as follows:

To cease and desist from such behavior; and

To pay a civil penalty as follows:

a. First offense: Not less than $275 and not more than $2,200 for each fraudulent document that is the subject of the violation; or

b. Subsequent offenses: Not less than $2,200 and not more than $5,500 for each fraudulent document that is the subject of the violation.

Part Five
Instructions for Recruiters and Referrers for a Fee

Under the Immigration and Nationality Act (INA), as amended, it is unlawful for an agricultural association, agricultural employer, or farm labor contractor to hire, or to recruit or refer for a fee, an individual for employment in the United States without complying with the employment eligibility verification requirements. This provision applies to those agricultural associations, agricultural employers, and farm labor contractors who recruit persons for a fee and those who refer persons or provide documents or information about persons to employers in return for a fee.

This limited class of recruiters and referrers for a fee must complete the Form I-9 when a person they refer is hired. The Form I-9 must be fully completed within three business days of the date employment begins, or, in the case of an individual hired for less than three business days, at the time employment begins.

Recruiters and referrers for a fee may designate agents, such as national associations or employers, to complete the verification procedures on their behalf. If the employer is designated as the agent, the employer should provide the recruiter or referrer with a photocopy of the Form I-9. However, recruiters and referrers are still responsible for compliance with the law and may be found liable for violations of the law.

Recruiters and referrers for a fee must retain the Form I-9 for three years after the date the referred individual was hired by the employer. They must also make Forms I-9 available for inspection by a DHS, DOL, or OSC officer.

NOTE: This does not preclude DHS or DOL from obtaining warrants based on probable cause for entry onto the premises of suspected violators without advance notice.

The penalties for failing to comply with the Form I-9 requirements and for requiring indemnification, as described in Part Four, apply to this limited class of recruiters and referrers for a fee.

NOTE: All recruiters and referrers for a fee are still liable for knowingly recruiting or referring for a fee aliens not authorized to work in the United States.

Part Six
E-Verify: The Web-based Verification Companion to the Form I-9

Since verification of the employment eligibility of new hires became law in 1986, the Form I-9 has been the foundation of the verification process. To improve the accuracy and integrity of this process, USCIS operates an electronic employment eligibility verification system called E-Verify.

E-Verify provides an automated link to federal databases to help employers determine the employment eligibility of new hires. E-Verify is free to employers and is available in all 50 states, as well as U.S. territories except for American Samoa and the Commonwealth of the Northern Mariana Islands.

Employers who participate in the E-Verify Program complete the Employment Eligibility Verification Form (Form I-9) for each newly hired employee as is required of all employers in the United States. E-Verify employers may accept any document or combination of documents acceptable on the Form I-9, but if the employee chooses to present a List B and C combination, the List B (identity only) document must have a photograph.

After completing the Form I-9 for a new employee, E-Verify employers must submit an electronic query that includes information from Sections 1 and 2 of the Form I-9. After submitting the query, the employer will receive an automated response from the E-Verify system regarding the employment eligibility of the individual. In some cases, E-Verify will provide a response indicating a tentative nonconfirmation of the employee's employment eligibility. This does not mean that the employee is necessarily unauthorized to work in the United States. Rather, it means that the system is unable to instantaneously confirm that employee's eligibility to work. In the case of a tentative nonconfirmation, the employer and employee must both take steps specified by E-Verify in an effort to resolve the status of the query.

Employers are also required to follow certain procedures when using E-Verify that were designed to protect employees from unfair employment actions. Employers may not verify selectively and must verify all new hires, both U.S. citizens and non-citizens. Employers may not prescreen applicants for employment; check employees hired before the company became a participant in E-Verify; or reverify employees who have temporary work authorization. Employers may not terminate or take other adverse action against employees based on a tentative nonconfirmation.

E-Verify, along with the Form I-9, protects jobs for authorized U.S. workers, improves the accuracy of wage and tax reporting, and helps U.S employers maintain a legal workforce.

Employers can register online for E-Verify at https://www.vis-dhs.com/EmployerRegistration, which provides instructions for completing the registration process. For more information about E-Verify, please contact USCIS at 1-888-464-4218.

HANDBOOK FOR EMPLOYERS: INSTRUCTIONS FOR COMPLETING THE I-9

Part Seven
Some Questions You May Have About the Form I-9

Questions about the Verification Process

1. **Q. Where can I obtain the Form I-9 and the M-274, Handbook for Employers?**

    A. Both the Form I-9 and the Employer Handbook are available as downloadable PDFs at www.uscis.gov. Employers with no computer access can order USCIS forms by calling our toll-free number at 1-800-870-3676. Individuals can also get USCIS forms and information on immigration laws, regulations and procedures by calling our National Customer Service Center toll-free at 1-800-375-5283.

2. **Q. Do citizens and nationals of the United States need to prove they are eligible to work?**

    A. Yes. While citizens and nationals of the United States are automatically eligible for employment, they too must present the required documents and complete a Form I-9. U.S. citizens include persons born in Puerto Rico, Guam, the U.S. Virgin Islands, and the Northern Mariana Islands. U.S. nationals include persons born in American Samoa, including Swains Island.

3. **Q. Do I need to complete a Form I-9 for everyone who applies for a job with my company?**

    A. No. You should not complete Forms I-9 for job applicants. You only need to complete Forms I-9 for people you actually hire. For purposes of this law, a person is "hired" when he or she begins to work for you.

4. **Q. If someone accepts a job with my company but will not start work for a month, can I complete the Form I-9 when the employee accepts the job?**

    A. Yes. The law requires that you complete the Form I-9 only when the person actually begins working. However, you may complete the form earlier, as long as the person has been offered and has accepted the job. You may not use the I-9 process to screen job applicants.

5. **Q. I understand that I must complete a Form I-9 for anyone I hire to perform labor or services in return for wages or other remuneration. What is "remuneration"?**

    A. Remuneration is anything of value given in exchange for labor or services rendered by an employee, including food and lodging.

6. **Q. Do I need to fill out Forms I-9 for independent contractors or their employees?**

    A. No. For example, if you contract with a construction company to perform renovations on your building, you do not have to complete Forms I-9 for that company's employees. The construction company is responsible for completing Forms I-9 for its own employees. However, you must not knowingly use contract labor to circumvent the law against hiring unauthorized aliens.

7. **Q. What should I do if the person I hire is unable to provide the required documents within three business days of the date employment begins?**

    A. If an employee is unable to present the required document or documents within three business days of the date employment begins, the employee must produce an acceptable receipt in lieu of a document listed on the last page of the Form I-9. There are three types of acceptable receipts. See Question 23 below for a description of each receipt and the procedures required to fulfill Form I-9 requirements when an employee presents a receipt.

    By having checked an appropriate box in Section 1, the employee must have indicated on or before the time employment began that he or she is already eligible to be employed in the United States.

    NOTE: Employees hired for less than three business days must produce the actual document(s) and the Form I-9 must be fully completed at the time employment begins.

8. **Q. Can I fire an employee who fails to produce the required documents within three business days?**

    A. Yes. You can terminate an employee who fails to produce the required document or documents, or a receipt for a document, within three business days of the date employment begins. However, you must apply these practices uniformly to all employees.

9. **Q. What happens if I properly complete a Form I-9 and DHS discovers that my employee is not actually authorized to work?**

    A. You cannot be charged with a verification violation. You will also have a good faith defense against the imposition of employer sanctions penalties for knowingly hiring an unauthorized alien, unless the government can show you had knowledge of the unauthorized status of the employee, if you have done the following:

a. Ensured that the employee fully and properly completed Section 1 of the Form I-9 at the time employment began;

b. Reviewed the required documents which should have reasonably appeared to have been genuine and to have related to the person presenting them;

c. Fully and properly completed Section 2 of the Form I-9, and signed and dated the employer certification;

d. Retained the Form I-9 for the required period of time; and

e. Made the Form I-9 available upon request to a DHS, DOL, or OSC officer.

Questions about Documents

10. Q. May I specify which documents I will accept for verification?

    A. No. The employee can choose which document(s) he or she wants to present from the lists of acceptable documents. You must accept any document (from List A) or combination of documents (one from List B and one from List C) listed on the Form I-9 and found in the Appendix of this Handbook that reasonably appear on their face to be genuine and to relate to the person presenting them. To do otherwise could be an unfair immigration-related employment practice in violation of the anti-discrimination provision of the INA. Individuals who look and/or sound foreign must not be treated differently in the recruiting, hiring or verification process.

    NOTE: An employer participating in the E-Verify Electronic Employment Eligibility Verification Program can only accept a List B document with a photograph.

11. Q. If an employee writes down an Alien Number or Admission Number when completing Section 1 of the Form I-9, can I ask to see a document with that number?

    A. No. Although it is your responsibility as an employer to ensure that your employees fully complete Section 1 at the time employment begins, the employee is not required to present a document to complete this section.

    When you complete Section 2, you may not ask to see a document with the employee's Alien Number or Admission Number or otherwise specify which document(s) an employee may present.

12. Q. What is my responsibility concerning the authenticity of document(s) presented to me?

    A. You must examine the document(s) and if they reasonably appear on their face to be genuine and to relate to the person presenting them, you must accept them. To do otherwise could be an unfair immigration-related employment practice. If the document(s) do not reasonably appear on their face to be genuine or to relate to the person presenting them, you must not accept them.

13. Q. Why are certain documents listed in both List B and List C? If these documents are evidence of both identity and employment eligibility, why aren't they found in List A?

    A. Three documents can be found in both List B and List C: the U.S. citizen identification card and the U.S. resident citizen identification card – acceptable as identification cards in List B – and a Native American tribal document. Although these documents are evidence of both identity and employment eligibility, they are not found in List A because List A documents are limited to those designated by Congress in the law. An employee can establish both identity and employment eligibility by presenting one of these documents. You should record the document title, issuing authority, number, and expiration date (if any) for that document in the appropriate spaces for both List B and List C.

14. Q. An employee has attested to being a U.S. citizen or national on section 1 of the Form I-9, but has presented me with a DHS Form I-551 "green card". Another employee has attested to being a lawful permanent resident alien but has presented a U.S. passport. Should I accept these documents?

    A. In these situations, the employer should first ensure that the employee understood and properly completed the section 1 attestation of status. If the employee made a mistake and corrects the attestation, he or she should initial and date the correction, or complete a new Form I-9. If the employee confirms the accuracy of his or her initial attestation, the

HANDBOOK FOR EMPLOYERS: INSTRUCTIONS FOR COMPLETING THE I-9

employer should not accept a "green card" from a U.S. citizen or a U.S. passport from an alien. Although employers are not expected to be immigration law experts, both documents in the question are directly and facially inconsistent with the status attested to and are therefore not documents that reasonably relate to the person presenting them.

15. Q. May I accept an expired document?

    A. Yes, in limited circumstances. An employer may accept an expired U.S. passport. An employer may also accept an expired document from List B to establish identity. Also, as explained in Question 23, an employer may accept an expired EAD from a Temporary Protected Status (TPS) recipient where DHS has granted an automatic extension. However, the document must reasonably appear on its face to be genuine and to relate to the person presenting it. An employer cannot accept any other expired documents.

16. Q. How can I tell if a DHS-issued document has expired?

    A. Some DHS-issued documents, such as older versions of the Alien Registration Receipt Card (Form I-551), do not have expiration dates. However, the 1989 revised version of the Resident Alien Card (Form I-551), which is rose-colored with computer readable data on the back, features a 2-year or 10-year expiration date. Other DHS-issued documents, such as the Employment Authorization Document (Form I-766 or I-688B) also have expiration dates. These dates can be found either on the face of the document or on a sticker attached to the back of the document.

17. Q. Some employees are presenting me with Social Security cards that have been laminated. May I accept such cards as evidence of employment eligibility?

    A. It depends. You may not accept a laminated Social Security card as evidence of employment eligibility if the card states on the back "not valid if laminated." Lamination of such cards renders them invalid. Metal or plastic reproductions of Social Security cards are not acceptable.

18. Q. Some employees have presented Social Security Administration printouts with their name, Social Security number, date of birth and their parents' names as proof of employment eligibility. May I accept such printouts in place of a Social Security card as evidence of employment eligibility?

    A. No. Only a person's official Social Security card is acceptable.

19. Q. What should I do if an employee presents a Social Security card marked "NOT VALID FOR EMPLOYMENT," but states that he or she is now authorized to work?

    A. You should ask the employee to provide another document to establish his or her employment eligibility, since such Social Security cards do not establish this. Such an employee should go to the local SSA office with proof of their lawful employment status to be issued a Social Security card without the "NOT VALID FOR EMPLOYMENT" legend.

20. Q. May I accept a photocopy of a document presented by an employee?

    A. No. Employees must present original documents. The only exception is that an employee may present a certified copy of a birth certificate.

21. Q. I noticed on the Form I-9 that under List A there are two spaces for document numbers and expiration dates. Does this mean I have to see two List A documents?

    A. No. One of the documents found in List A is an unexpired foreign passport with an attached DHS Form I-94, bearing the same name as the passport and containing endorsement of the alien's nonimmigrant status, if that status authorizes the alien to work for the employer. The Form I-9 provides space for you to record the document number and expiration date for both the passport and the DHS Form I-94.

22. Q. When I review an employee's identity and employment eligibility documents, should I make copies of them?

    A. The law does not require you to photocopy documents. However, if you wish to make photocopies, you should do so for all employees, and you should retain each photocopy with the Form I-9. Photocopies must not be used for any other purpose. Photocopying documents does not relieve you of your obligation to fully complete Section 2 of the Form I-9 nor is it an acceptable substitute for proper completion of the Form I-9 in general.

23. **Q. When can employees present receipts for documents in lieu of actual documents establishing employment eligibility?**

   A. The "receipt rule" is designed to cover situations in which an employee is employment authorized at the time of initial hire or reverification, but he or she is not in possession of a document listed on page 4 of the Form I-9. Receipts showing that a person has applied for an initial grant of employment authorization, or for renewal of employment authorization, are not acceptable.

   An individual may present a "receipt" in lieu of a document listed on the Form I-9 to complete Section 2 of the Form I-9. The receipt is valid for a temporary period. There are three different documents that qualify as receipts under the rule.

   The first type of receipt that an employee may present (described above in the answer to question 7) is a receipt for a replacement document when the document has been lost, stolen, or damaged. The receipt is valid for 90 days, after which the individual must present the replacement document to complete the Form I-9. Note that this rule does not apply to individuals who present receipts for new documents following the expiration of their previously held document.

   The second type of receipt that an employee may present is a Form I-94 containing a temporary I-551 stamp and a photograph of the individual, which is considered a receipt for the Form I-551, Permanent Resident Card. The individual must present the Form I-551 by the expiration date of the temporary I-551 stamp, or within one year from the date of issuance of the Form I-94 if the I-551 stamp does not contain an expiration date.

   The third type of receipt that an employee may present is a Form I-94 containing an unexpired refugee admission stamp. This is considered a receipt for either an Employment Authorization Document (i.e., Form I-766 or I-688B) or a combination of an unrestricted Social Security card and List B document. The employee must present acceptable documentation to complete the Form I-9 within 90 days after the date of hire or, in the case of reverification, the date employment authorization expires.

   DHS regulations provide that if it does not adjudicate an application for employment authorization within 90 days, it will grant an employment authorization document valid for a period not to exceed 240 days. To receive an interim employment authorization document, the individual should contact his or her local USCIS office.

   Individuals under the Temporary Protected Status (TPS) Program whose EADs are subject to an automatic extension may continue to work with expired EADs during the automatic extension period specified in the Federal Register Notice announcing the extension.

24. **Q. My employee's DHS-issued employment authorization document expired and the employee now wants to show me a Social Security card. Do I need to see a current DHS document?**

   A. No. During both initial verification and reverification, an employee must be allowed to choose what documentation to present from the Form I-9 lists of acceptable documents. If an employee presents an unrestricted Social Security card upon reverification, the employee does not also need to present a current DHS document. However, if an employee presents a "restricted" Social Security card upon reverification, the employer must reject the restricted Social Security card, since it is not an acceptable Form I-9 document and ask the employee to choose different documentation from List A or List C of the Form I-9. A restricted Social Security card may state "not valid for employment" or "valid for work only with DHS authorization."

25. **Q. Can DHS double-check the status of an alien I hired, or "run" his or her number (typically an A Number or Social Security Number) and tell me whether it's good?**

   A. DHS can not double-check a number for an employer, unless the employer participates in E-Verify, which provides employers a way to confirm the employment eligibility of their newly hired employees. For more information about this program, see Part Six. You may also call DHS at 1-888-464-4218 or visit https://www.vis-dhs.com/employerregistration/.

   An employer also may contact DHS if he or she has strong and articulable reason to believe documentation may not be valid, in which case ICE may investigate the possible violation of law.

26. **Q. My employee presented me with a document issued by INS rather than DHS. Can I accept it?**

HANDBOOK FOR EMPLOYERS: INSTRUCTIONS FOR COMPLETING THE I-9

27. **A.** Effective March 1, 2003, the functions of the former Immigration and Naturalization Service (INS) in the U.S. Department of Justice were transferred to three agencies within the new DHS: USCIS, U.S. Customs and Border Protection (CBP), and U.S. Immigration and Customs Enforcement (ICE). Most immigration documents acceptable for Form I-9 use are issued by USCIS. Some documents issued by the former INS before March 1, 2003, such as Permanent Resident Cards, may still be within their period of validity. If otherwise acceptable, a document should not be rejected because it was issued by INS rather than DHS. It should also be noted that INS documents may bear dates of issuance after March 1, 2003, as it took some time in 2003 to modify document forms to reflect the new DHS identity.

27. **Q. What should I do if an employee presents a Form I-20 and says the document authorizes her to work?**

    A. The Form I-20 is evidence of employment eligibility in two specific situations:

    - The employee works on the campus of the school where he or she is an F-1 student for an employer that provides direct student services, or at an off-campus location that is educationally affiliated with the school's established curriculum or related to contractually funded research projects at the post-graduate level where the employment is an integral part of the student's educational program.

    - The employee is an F-1 student who has been authorized by the Designated School Official (DSO) to participate in a curricular practical training program that is an integral part of an established curriculum (e.g., alternative work/study, internship, cooperative education, or other required internship offered by sponsoring employers through cooperative agreements with the school). The Form I-20 must be endorsed by the DSO for curricular practical training, and list the employer offering the practical training, and the dates the student will be employed.

    In both situations, the Form I-20 must accompany a valid Form I-94 or I-94A indicating F-1 status. When combined with an unexpired foreign passport, the documentation is acceptable for List A of Form I-9.

28. **Q. May I accept Form DS-2019 as proof of employment eligibility?**

    A. The Form DS-2019 can be used only by a J-1 exchange visitor for employment when such employment is part of his or her program. For J-1 students, the Responsible Officer of the school may authorize employment in writing. The Form DS-2019 must accompany a valid Form I-94 or I-94A. When combined with an unexpired, foreign passport, the documentation is acceptable for List A of Form I-9.

Questions about Completing and Retaining the Form I-9

29. **Q. When do I fill out the Form I-9 if I hire someone for less than three business days?**

    A. You must complete both Sections 1 and 2 of Form I-9 at the time of the hire. This means the Form I-9 must be fully completed when the person starts to work.

30. **Q. What should I do if I rehire a person who previously filled out a Form I-9?**

    A. If the employee's Form I-9 is the version dated June 5, 2007 or a subsequent version, you rehire the person within three years of the date that the Form I-9 was originally completed, and the employee is still authorized to work, you may reverify the employee in Section 3 of the original Form I-9.

    If you used a version of the Form I-9 dated before June 5, 2007 when you initially verified the employee, you must complete a new Form I-9 upon rehire.

31. **Q. What should I do if I need to update or reverify a Form I-9 for an employee who filled out an earlier version of the form?**

    A. To update the June 5, 2007, version of the Form I-9, you may line through any outdated information and initial and date any updated information. You may also choose, instead, to complete a new Form I-9.

    If you used a version of the Form I-9 dated before June 5, 2007 when you originally verified the employee, the employee must provide any document(s) he or she chooses from the current List of Acceptable Documents, which you must enter in Section 3 of the latest version of the Form I-9.

32. Q. **Do I need to complete a new Form I-9 when one of my employees is promoted within my company or transfers to another company office at a different location?**

A. No. You do not need to complete a new Form I-9 for employees who have been promoted or transferred.

33. Q. **What do I do when an employee's work authorization noted in either Section 1 or 2 of the Form I-9 expires?**

A. You will need to reverify on the Form I-9 to continue to employ the person. Reverification must occur no later than the date that work authorization expires. The employee must present a document from either List A or List C that shows either an extension of his or her initial employment authorization or new work authorization. You must review this document and, if it reasonably appears on its face to be genuine and to relate to the person presenting it, record the document title, number, and expiration date (if any), in the Updating and Reverification Section (Section 3), and sign in the appropriate space.

If you used a version of the Form I-9 that predates the June 5, 2007, version for the employee's original verification, you must complete Section 3 of the latest Form I-9 upon reverification.

You may want to establish a calendar call-up system for employees whose employment authorization will expire in the future.

NOTE: You should not reverify an expired U.S. passport or an Alien Registration Receipt Card/Permanent Resident Card, Form I-551, or a List B document that has expired.
NOTE: You cannot refuse to accept a document because it has a future expiration date. You must accept any document (from List A or List C) listed on the Form I-9 and in the Appendix of this Handbook that on its face reasonably appears to be genuine and to relate to the person presenting it. To do otherwise could be an unfair immigration-related employment practice in violation of the anti-discrimination provision of the INA.

NOTE: If an employee's EAD expires before the employee receives a new EAD, the employee may take the application receipt to a local USCIS office to receive temporary employment authorization IF it has been more than 90 days since the employee applied for the new EAD.

34. Q. **Can I avoid reverifying an employee on the Form I-9 by not hiring persons whose employment authorization has an expiration date?**

A. You cannot refuse to hire persons solely because their employment authorization is temporary. The existence of a future expiration date does not preclude continuous employment authorization for an employee and does not mean that subsequent employment authorization will not be granted. In addition, consideration of a future employment authorization expiration date in determining whether an alien is qualified for a particular job may be an unfair immigration-related employment practice in violation of the anti-discrimination provision of the INA.

35. Q. **As an employer, do I have to fill out all the Forms I-9 myself?**

A. No. You may designate someone to fill out Forms I-9s for you, such as a personnel officer, foreman, agent or anyone else acting in your interest. However, you are still liable for any violations of the employer sanctions laws.

36. Q. **Can I contract with someone to complete Forms I-9 for my business?**

A. Yes. You can contract with another person or business to verify employees' identities and work eligibility and to complete Forms I-9 for you. However, you are still responsible for the contractor's actions and are liable for any violations of the employer sanctions laws.

37. Q. **As an employer, can I negotiate my responsibility to complete Forms I-9 in a collective bargaining agreement with a union?**
A. Yes. However, you are still liable for any violations of the employer sanctions laws. If the agreement is for a multi-employer bargaining unit, certain rules apply. The association must track the employee's hire and termination dates each time the employee is hired or terminated by an employer in the multi-employer association.

38. Q. **What are the requirements for retaining Forms I-9?**

A. If you are an employer, you must retain Forms I-9 for three years after the date employment begins or one year after the date the person's employment is terminated, whichever is later. If you are an agricultural association, agricultural employer, or farm labor contractor, you must retain Forms I-9 for

HANDBOOK FOR EMPLOYERS: INSTRUCTIONS FOR COMPLETING THE I-9

three years after the date employment begins for persons you recruit or refer for a fee.

39. Q. Will I get any advance notice if a DHS or DOL officer wishes to inspect my Forms I-9?

A. Yes. The officer will give you at least three days (72 hours) advance notice before the inspection. If it is more convenient for you, you may waive the 3-day notice. You may also request an extension of time to produce the Forms I-9. The DHS or DOL officer will not need to show you a subpoena or a warrant at the time of the inspection.

NOTE: *This does not preclude DHS or DOL from obtaining warrants based on probable cause for entry onto the premises of suspected violators without advance notice.*

Failure to provide Forms I-9s for inspection is a violation of the employer sanctions laws and could result in the imposition of civil money penalties.

40. Q. How does OSC obtain information necessary to determine whether an employer has committed an unfair immigration-related employment practice under the anti-discrimination provision of the INA?

A. OSC notifies employers in writing about the initiation of all investigations, and requests in writing information and documents. If an employer refuses to cooperate, OSC can obtain subpoenas to compel production of the information requested.

41. Q. Do I have to complete Forms I-9 for Canadians or Mexicans who entered the United States under the North American Free Trade Agreement (NAFTA)?
A. Yes. You must complete Forms I-9 for all employees. NAFTA entrants must show identity and employment eligibility documents just like all other employees.

42. Q. If I acquire a business, can I rely on Forms I-9 completed by the previous owner/employer?

A. Yes. However, you also accept full responsibility and liability for all Forms I-9 completed by the previous employer relating to individuals who are continuing in their employment.

43. Q. If I am a recruiter or referrer for a fee, do I have to fill out Forms I-9 on persons whom I recruit or refer?

A. No, with three exceptions: Agricultural associations, agricultural employers, and farm labor contractors are still required to complete Forms I-9 on all individuals who are recruited or referred for a fee. However, all recruiters and referrers for a fee must still complete Forms I-9 for their own employees hired after November 6, 1986. Also, all recruiters and referrers for a fee are still liable for knowingly recruiting or referring for a fee aliens not authorized to work in the United States and must comply with federal anti-discrimination laws.

44. Q. Can I complete Section 1 of the Form I-9 for an employee?

A. Yes. You may help an employee who needs assistance in completing Section 1 of the Form I-9. However, you must also complete the "Preparer/Translator Certification" block. The employee must still sign the certification block in Section 1.

45. Q. If I am a business entity (corporation, partnership, etc.), do I have to fill out Forms I-9 on my employees?

A. Yes, you must complete Forms I-9 for all of your employees, including yourself.

46. Q. I have heard that some state employment agencies can certify that people they refer are eligible to work. Is that true?

A. Yes. State employment agencies may elect to provide persons they refer with a certification of employment eligibility. If one of these agencies refers potential employees to you with a job order or other appropriate referral form, and the agency sends you *a* certification within 21 business days of the referral, you do not have to check documents or complete a Form I-9 if you hire that person. However, you must review the certification to ensure that it relates to the person hired and observe the person sign the certification. You must also retain the certification as you would a Form I-9 and make it available for inspection, if requested. You should check with your state employment agency to see if it provides this service and become familiar with its certification document.

Questions about Avoiding Discrimination

47. Q. How can I avoid discriminating against certain employees while still complying with this law?

A. Employers should:

1. Treat employees equally when recruiting, hiring, and terminating employees, and when verifying employment eligibility and completing the Form I-9.

2. Allow all employees, regardless of national origin or immigration status, to choose which document or combination of documents they want to present from the list of acceptable documents on the back of the Form I-9. For example, an employer may not require an employee to present an employment authorization document issued by DHS if he or she chooses to present a driver's license and unrestricted Social Security card.

Employers should NOT:

1. Set different employment eligibility verification standards or require that different documents be presented by employees because of their national origin or citizenship status. For example, employers cannot demand that non-U.S. citizens present DHS-issued documents like "green cards".

2. Ask to see a document with an employee's Alien or Admission Number when completing Section 1 of the Form I-9.

3. Request to see employment eligibility verification documents before hire or completion of the I-9 Form because someone looks or sounds "foreign," or because someone states that he or she is not a U.S. citizen.

4. Refuse to accept a valid employment eligibility document, or refuse to hire an individual, because the document has a future expiration date.

5. Reverify the employment eligibility of a lawful permanent resident ("LPR") whose "green card" has expired after the LPR is hired.

6. Request that, during reverification, an employee present a new unexpired employment authorization document. For reverification, employees are free to choose any document either from List A or from List C of the I-9 Form, including an unrestricted Social Security card.

7. Limit jobs to U.S. citizens unless U.S. citizenship is required for the specific position by law, regulation, executive order, or federal, state or local government contract.

NOTE: On an individual basis, an employer may legally prefer a U.S. citizen over an equally qualified alien to fill a specific position, but may not adopt a blanket policy of always preferring citizens over non-citizens.

48. **Q. Who is protected from discrimination on the basis of citizenship status or national origin under the anti-discrimination provision of the INA?**

    A. All U.S. citizens, permanent residents, temporary residents, asylees and refugees are protected from citizenship status discrimination, except for those lawful permanent residents who have failed to make a timely application for naturalization after they become eligible.

    An employer cannot discriminate against any work-authorized individual in hiring, firing, or recruitment because of his or her national origin.

    Similarly, work-authorized individuals are protected from document abuse with the purpose or intent of discriminating on the basis of national origin or citizenship status in the case of a protected individual (e.g. discrimination during the Form I-9 process).

49. **Q. Can I be charged with discrimination if I contact DHS about a document presented to me that does not reasonably appear to be genuine and relate to the person presenting it?**

    A. No. An employer who is presented with documentation that does not reasonably appear to be genuine or to relate to the employee cannot accept that documentation. While you are not legally required to inform DHS of such situations, you may do so if you choose. However, DHS is unable to provide employment eligibility verification services to employers other than through its E-Verify program. Employers who treat all employees the same and do not single out employees who look or sound foreign for closer scrutiny cannot be charged with discrimination.

50. **Q. I recently hired someone who checked box three on Section 1 of the Form I-9, indicating that he is an alien. However, he informed me that he does not have an employment authorization**

HANDBOOK FOR EMPLOYERS: INSTRUCTIONS FOR COMPLETING THE I-9

expiration date, which appears to be required by the form. What should I do?

A. Refugees and asylees, as well as some other classes of alien such as certain nationals of the Federated States of Micronesia, the Marshall Islands, and Palau, are authorized to work incident to status. Some such aliens may not possess an employment authorization document (I-766 or I-688B) issued by DHS, yet can still establish employment eligibility and identity by presenting other documentation, including a driver's license and an unrestricted Social Security card or Form I-94 indicating their work-authorized status. Such individuals should write "N/A" in Section 1 next to the alien box. The refusal to hire work-authorized aliens because of their immigration status, or because they are unable to provide an expiration date on the Form I-9, may violate the anti-discrimination provision in the INA.

51. Q. What should I do if I have further questions regarding the INA's anti-discrimination provision and the Form I-9 Verification Process?

A. Employers should call OSC's employer hotline with questions:
1-800-255-8155
1-800-362-2735 (TDD); or
Visit the OSC website,
http://www.usdoj.gov/crt/osc/, for more information.

52. Q. What if someone believes they have experienced discrimination under the INA's anti-discrimination provision?

A. Call the Office of Special Counsel for Immigration Related Unfair Employment Practices (OSC) employee hotline:
1-800-255-7688
1-800-237-2515 (TDD); or
Visit the OSC website,
http://www.usdoj.gov/crt/osc/, for more information and to download a charge form.

53. Q. What if someone believes he or she has experienced discrimination under Title VII of the Civil Rights Act of 1964?

A. Call the Equal Employment Opportunity Commission (EEOC):
1-800-USA-EEOC
1-800-669-6820 (TTY); or
Visit EEOC's website at http://www.eeoc.gov.

Questions about Employees Hired Before November 6, 1986

54. Q. Does this law apply to my employees if I hired them before November 7, 1986?

A. No. You are not required to complete Forms I-9 for employees hired before November 7, 1986.

NOTE: This "grandfather" status does not apply to seasonal employees, or to employees who change employers within a multi-employer association.

55. Q. What if an employee was hired before November 7, 1986, but has taken an approved leave of absence?

A. You do not need to complete a Form I-9 for that employee if the employee is continuing in his or her employment and has a reasonable expectation of employment at all times. However, if that employee has quit or been terminated, or is an alien who has been removed from the United States, you will need to complete a Form I-9 for that employee.

56. Q. Will I be subject to employer sanctions penalties if an employee I hired before November 7, 1986, is an illegal alien?

A. No. You will not be subject to employer sanctions penalties for retaining an illegal alien in your workforce if the alien was hired before November 7, 1986. However, the fact that an illegal alien was on your payroll before November 7, 1986, does not give him or her any right to remain in the United States. Unless the alien obtains permission from DHS to remain in the United States, he or she is subject to apprehension and removal.

Questions about Changes to Form I-9

57. Q. Why was the Form I-9 updated?

A. In 1997, an interim regulation was published that removed five documents from List A on the List of Acceptable Documents and added one document to List A. Although the law changed in 1997, the Form I-9 itself was never updated to reflect those changes. The 2007 version of the Form I-9, bearing an edition date of June 5, 2007 now reflects existing regulations. Further revisions may be needed, so DHS may release another update to the Form I-9 in the future.

58. Q. What is the difference between the June 5, 2007 version of the Form I-9 and previous versions?

A. Five documents have been removed from List A acceptable documents:
a) Certificate of U.S. Citizenship (Form N-560 or N-561)
b) Certificate of Naturalization (Form N-550 or N-570)
c) Alien Registration Receipt Card (I-151)
d) Unexpired Reentry Permit (Form I-327)
e) Unexpired Refugee Travel Document (Form I-571)

One document was added to List A acceptable documents:
f) Unexpired Employment Authorization Document (I-766)

All the Employment Authorization Documents with photographs have been consolidated as one item on List A:
g) I-688, I-688A, I-688B, I-766

One document on List A was modified as follows:

- Unexpired foreign passport with an Arrival-Departure Record, Form I-94, bearing the same name as the passport and containing an endorsement of the alien's nonimmigrant status if that status authorizes the alien to work for the employer is incident to that status.

Instructions on Section 1 of the Form I-9 now indicate that the employee is not obliged to provide the Social Security Number in Section 1 of the Form I-9, unless he or she is employed by an employer who participates in the USCIS E-Verify Program

A section on Photocopying and Retaining the Form I-9 has been added, which gives employers guidance on providing the form to employees, how long the forms must be retained and the regulations for electronic signatures and retention.

The estimated reporting burden under the Paperwork Reduction Act has been changed in keeping with the latest estimates.

59. **Q. Can I accept documents that were on previous editions of the Form I-9 but aren't now?**

A. No. Employers may only accept documents listed on the Acceptable Documents list on the June 5, 2007 or any subsequent version of the Form I-9. When reverifying employees, employers also should ensure that they use the most recent version of the form

60. **Q. Is the Form I-9 available in different languages?**

A. The Form I-9 is available in English and Spanish. However, only employers in Puerto Rico may use the Spanish version to meet the verification and retention requirements of the law. Employers in the 50 states may use the Spanish version as a translation guide for Spanish-speaking employees, but the English version must be completed and retained in the employer's records. Employees may also use or ask for a translator/preparer to assist them in completing the form.

61. **Q. Are employers in Puerto Rico required to use the Spanish version of the Form I-9?**

A. No. Employers in Puerto Rico may use either the Spanish or the English version of the June 5, 2007 or any subsequent version of the Form I-9 to verify new employees.

62. **Q. May I continue to use earlier versions of the Form I-9?**

A. No, employers must use the June 5, 2007 or a subsequent version of the Form I-9. All previous editions of the Form I-9, in English or Spanish, are no longer valid. The 1988 version of the Form I-9 in Spanish expired in 1991, and those employers using it will incur fines and penalties for continued use.

HANDBOOK FOR EMPLOYERS: INSTRUCTIONS FOR COMPLETING THE I-9

Part Eight
Acceptable Documents for Verifying Employment Eligibility

The following documents have been designated for determining employment eligibility by the Act. A person must present a document or documents that establish identity and employment eligibility. A comprehensive list of acceptable documents can be found on the next page of this Handbook and on the back of the Form I-9. Samples of many of the acceptable documents appear on the following pages.

To establish both identity and employment eligibility, a person can present a U.S passport, a Permanent Resident Card or Alien Registration Receipt Card, or one of the other documents from List A.

If a person does not present a document from List A, he or she must present one document from List B, which establishes identity, and one document from List C, which establishes employment eligibility.

To establish identity only, a person must present a document from List B, such as a state-issued driver's license, a state-issued identification card, or one of the other documents listed.

To establish employment eligibility only, a person must present a document from List C, such as a Social Security card, a U.S. birth certificate, or one of the other documents listed.

If a person is unable to present the required document(s) within three business days of the date employment begins, he or she must present (within 3 business days) a receipt. The person then must present the actual document when the receipt period ends. The person must have indicated on or before the time employment began, by having checked an appropriate box in Section 1 that he or she is already eligible to be employed in the United States. Receipts showing that a person has applied for an initial grant of employment authorization, or for renewal of employment authorization, are not acceptable.

LIST A

Documents That Establish Both Identity and Employment Eligibility

a. U.S. Passport (unexpired or expired)

b. Permanent Resident Card or Alien Registration Receipt Card (Form I-551)

c. Unexpired foreign passport with a temporary I-551 stamp

d. An unexpired Employment Authorization Document that contains a photograph (Form I-766, I-688, I-688A, I-688B)

e. Unexpired foreign passport with an unexpired Arrival-Departure record, Form I-94, bearing the same name as the passport and containing an endorsement of the alien's nonimmigrant status, if that status authorizes the alien to work for the employer

LIST B

Documents That Establish Identity

For individuals 18 years of age or older:

a. Driver's license or ID card issued by a state or outlying possession of the United States, provided it contains a photograph or information such as name, date of birth, gender, height, eye color and address

b. ID card issued by federal, state or local government agencies or entities, provided it contains a photograph or information such as name, date of birth, gender, height, eye color and address

c. School ID card with a photograph

d. Voter's registration card

e. U.S. military card or draft record

f. Military dependent's ID card

g. U.S. Coast Guard Merchant Mariner Card

h. Native American tribal document

i. Driver's license issued by a Canadian government authority

For persons under age 18 who are unable to present a document listed above:

a. School record or report card

b. Clinic, doctor or hospital record

c. Day-care or nursery school record

LIST C

Documents That Establish Employment Eligibility

a. U.S. Social Security card issued by the Social Security Administration (other than a card stating it is not valid for employment)

NOTE: This must be a card issued by the Social Security Administration: A copy (such as a metal or plastic reproduction) is not acceptable.

b. Certification of Birth Abroad issued by the Department of State (Form FS-545 or Form DS-1350)

c. Original or certified copy of a birth certificate issued by a state, county, municipal authority or outlying possession of the United States bearing an official seal

d. Native American tribal document

e. U.S. Citizen ID Card (USCIS Form I-197)

f. ID Card for Use of Resident Citizen in the United States (USCIS Form I-179)

g. Unexpired employment authorization document issued by DHS (other than those listed under List A)

List A
Documents that Establish Both Identity and Employment Eligibility

The following illustrations in this Handbook do not necessarily reflect the actual size of the documents.

U.S. Passport
Issued by the U.S. Department of State to U.S. citizens and nationals. There are several different versions that are currently valid that vary from the latest version shown here.

Permanent Resident Card (I-551)
The latest version of the Permanent Resident Card, Form I-551, began being issued in November 2004. The card shows the seal of the Department of Homeland Security and contains a detailed hologram on the front of the card. Each card is personalized with an etching showing the bearer's photo, name, signature, date of birth, alien registration number, card expiration date, and card number.

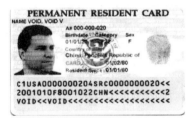

Resident Alien Card (I-551)

These cards are no longer issued, but are valid indefinitely, or until their expiration date. Recipients of this card are lawful permanent residents. This card is commonly referred to as a "green card" and is the replacement for the Form I-151.

Unexpired Foreign Passport with I-551 Stamp

HANDBOOK FOR EMPLOYERS: INSTRUCTIONS FOR COMPLETING THE I-9

Employment Authorization Card I-766

Issued by USCIS to aliens granted temporary employment authorization in the United States. The expiration date is noted on the face of the card

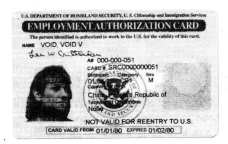

Temporary Resident Card I-688

Issued by USCIS to aliens granted temporary resident status under the Legalization or Special Agricultural Worker program. It is valid until the expiration date stated on the face of the card or on the sticker(s) placed on the back of the card.

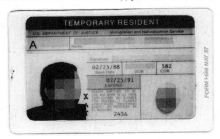

Employment Authorization Card I-688A

Issued by USCIS to applicants for temporary resident status after their interview for Legalization or Special Agricultural Worker status. It is valid until the expiration date stated on the face of the card or on the sticker(s) placed on the back of the card.

Employment Authorization Card I-688B

Issued by USCIS to aliens granted temporary employment authorization in the United States. The card has gold, interlocking lines across the front. The expiration date is noted on the face of the card.

I-94/I-94A Arrival/Departure Record

Arrival-departure record issued by DHS to nonimmigrant aliens and other alien categories. This document indicates the bearer's immigration status, the date that the status was granted, and when the status expires.

List B
Documents that Establish Identity Only

The following illustrations in this Handbook do not necessarily reflect the actual size of the documents.

Sample Driver's License

A driver's license issued by any state or territory of the United States (including the District of Columbia, Puerto Rico, the U.S. Virgin Islands, Guam, the Northern Mariana Islands, and American Samoa) or by a Canadian government authority is acceptable if it contains a photograph or other identifying information such as name, date of birth, sex, height, color of eyes, and address.

Sample State Identification Card

An identification card issued by any state (including the District of Columbia, Puerto Rico, the U.S. Virgin Islands, Guam, and the Northern Mariana Islands) or by a local government is acceptable if it contains a photograph or other identifying information such as name, date of birth, sex, height, color of eyes, and address.

List C
Documents That Establish Employment Eligibility Only

The following illustrations in this Handbook do not necessarily reflect the actual size of the documents.

U.S. Social Security card

Issued by the Social Security Administration, other than a card stating it is not valid for employment. There are many versions of this card.

Certifications of Birth Issued by the Department of State

FS-545
Issued by U.S. embassies and consulates overseas to U.S. citizens born abroad.

DS-1350
Issued by the U.S. Department of State to U.S. citizens born abroad

Handbook for Employers: Instructions for Completing the I-9

Sample Birth Certificates

U.S. Citizen Identification Card I-197

Issued by INS to naturalized U.S. citizens. Although this card has not been issued since 1983, it is valid indefinitely.

Identification Card for Use of Resident Citizen in the United States I-179

Issued by INS to U.S. citizens who are residents of the United States. Although this card is no longer issued, it is valid indefinitely.

I-20 ID Card Accompanied by a Form I-94

Form I-94 for F-1 nonimmigrant students must be accompanied by an I-20 Student ID endorsed with employment authorization by the Designated School Official for off-campus employment or curricular practical training. USCIS will issue Form I-766 (Employment Authorization Document) to all students (F-1 and M-1) authorized for a post-completion practical training period. (See page 37 for Form I-94/I-94A.)

Front

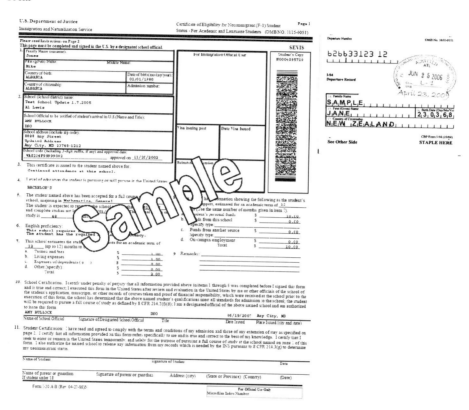

Back

Page 3

IF YOU NEED MORE INFORMATION CONCERNING YOUR F-1 NONIMMIGRANT STUDENT STATUS AND THE RELATING IMMIGRATION PROCEDURES, PLEASE CONTACT EITHER YOUR FOREIGN STUDENT ADVISOR ON CAMPUS OR A NEARBY IMMIGRATION AND NATURALIZATION SERVICE OFFICE.

FAMILY NAME: Jones   FIRST NAME: Mike

SEVIS
Student's Copy
N0004095710

Student Employment Authorization:
Employment Status: Type:
Duration of Employment - From (Date): To (Date):
Employer Name:
Employer Location:

Comments:

Event History
Event Name: Event Date:
Registration   03/12/2007

Current Authorizations: Start Date: End Date:

This page when properly endorsed, may be used for reentry of the student to attend the same school after a temporary absence from the United States. Each certification signature is valid for one year.

Name of School:
AMY BULLOCK   DSO   06/19/2007   Any City, MD
Name of School Official Signature of Designated School Official Title Date Issued Place Issued (city and state)

Name of School Official Signature of Designated School Official Title Date Issued Place Issued (city and state)

Name of School Official Signature of Designated School Official Title Date Issued Place Issued (city and state)

Name of School Official Signature of Designated School Official Title Date Issued Place Issued (city and state)

Form I-20 A-B (Rev. 04-27-88)N

DS-2019 Accompanied by a Form I-94

Nonimmigrant exchange visitors (J-1) must have an I-94 accompanied by an unexpired DS-2019, specifying the sponsor and issued by the U.S. Department of State. J-1 students working outside the program indicated on the DS-2019 also need a letter from their responsible school officer. (See page 37 for Form I-94/I-94A.)

HANDBOOK FOR EMPLOYERS: INSTRUCTIONS FOR COMPLETING THE I-9

REMEMBER:

a. Hiring employees without complying with the employment eligibility verification requirements is a violation of the employer sanctions laws.

b. This law requires employees hired after November 6, 1986, to present documentation that establishes identity and employment eligibility, and employers to record this information on Forms I-9.

c. Employers may not discriminate against employees on the basis of national origin or citizenship status.

Department of Homeland Security
U.S. Citizenship and Immigration Services

Form I-9, Employment
Eligibility Verification

Instructions
Please read all instructions carefully before completing this form.

Anti-Discrimination Notice. It is illegal to discriminate against any individual (other than an alien not authorized to work in the U.S.) in hiring, discharging, or recruiting or referring for a fee because of that individual's national origin or citizenship status. It is illegal to discriminate against work eligible individuals. Employers CANNOT specify which document(s) they will accept from an employee. The refusal to hire an individual because the documents presented have a future expiration date may also constitute illegal discrimination.

What Is the Purpose of This Form?

The purpose of this form is to document that each new employee (both citizen and non-citizen) hired after November 6, 1986 is authorized to work in the United States.

When Should the Form I-9 Be Used?

All employees, citizens and noncitizens, hired after November 6, 1986 and working in the United States must complete a Form I-9.

Filling Out the Form I-9

Section 1, Employee: This part of the form must be completed at the time of hire, which is the actual beginning of employment. Providing the Social Security number is voluntary, except for employees hired by employers participating in the USCIS Electronic Employment Eligibility Verification Program (E-Verify). **The employer is responsible for ensuring that Section 1 is timely and properly completed.**

Preparer/Translator Certification. The Preparer/Translator Certification must be completed if **Section 1** is prepared by a person other than the employee. A preparer/translator may be used only when the employee is unable to complete Section 1 on his/her own. However, the employee must still sign **Section 1** personally.

Section 2, Employer: For the purpose of completing this form, the term "employer" means all employers including those recruiters and referrers for a fee who are agricultural associations, agricultural employers or farm labor contractors.

Employers must complete **Section 2** by examining evidence of identity and employment eligibility within three (3) business days of the date employment begins. If employees are authorized to work, but are unable to present the required document(s) within three business days, they must present a receipt for the application of the document(s) within three business days and the actual document(s) within ninety (90) days. However, if employers hire individuals for a duration of less than three business days, **Section 2** must be completed at the time employment begins. **Employers must record:**

1. Document title;
2. Issuing authority;
3. Document number;
4. Expiration date, if any; and
5. The date employment begins.

Employers must sign and date the certification. Employees must present original documents. Employers may, but are not required to, photocopy the document(s) presented. These photocopies may only be used for the verification process and must be retained with the Form I-9. **However, employers are still responsible for completing and retaining the Form I-9.**

Section 3, Updating and Reverification: Employers must complete **Section 3** when updating and/or reverifying the Form I-9. Employers must reverify employment eligibility of their employees on or before the expiration date recorded in **Section 1**. Employers CANNOT specify which document(s) they will accept from an employee.

A. If an employee's name has changed at the time this form is being updated/reverified, complete Block A.

B. If an employee is rehired within three (3) years of the date this form was originally completed and the employee is still eligible to be employed on the same basis as previously indicated on this form (updating), complete Block B and the signature block.

C. If an employee is rehired within three (3) years of the date this form was originally completed and the employee's work authorization has expired **or** if a current employee's work authorization is about to expire (reverification), complete Block B and:

1. Examine any document that reflects that the employee is authorized to work in the U.S. (see List A **or** C);
2. Record the document title, document number and expiration date (if any) in Block C, and
3. Complete the signature block.

Form I-9 (Rev. 06/05/07) N

Handbook for Employers: Instructions for Completing the I-9

What Is the Filing Fee?

There is no associated filing fee for completing the Form I-9. This form is not filed with USCIS or any government agency. The Form I-9 must be retained by the employer and made available for inspection by U.S. Government officials as specified in the Privacy Act Notice below.

USCIS Forms and Information

To order USCIS forms, call our toll-free number at **1-800-870-3676**. Individuals can also get USCIS forms and information on immigration laws, regulations and procedures by telephoning our National Customer Service Center at **1-800-375-5283** or visiting our internet website at **www.uscis.gov**.

Photocopying and Retaining the Form I-9

A blank Form I-9 may be reproduced, provided both sides are copied. The Instructions must be available to all employees completing this form. Employers must retain completed Forms I-9 for three (3) years after the date of hire or one (1) year after the date employment ends, whichever is later.

The Form I-9 may be signed and retained electronically, as authorized in Department of Homeland Security regulations at 8 CFR § 274a.2.

Privacy Act Notice

The authority for collecting this information is the Immigration Reform and Control Act of 1986, Pub. L. 99-603 (8 USC 1324a).

This information is for employers to verify the eligibility of individuals for employment to preclude the unlawful hiring, or recruiting or referring for a fee, of aliens who are not authorized to work in the United States.

This information will be used by employers as a record of their basis for determining eligibility of an employee to work in the United States. The form will be kept by the employer and made available for inspection by officials of U.S. Immigration and Customs Enforcement, Department of Labor and Office of Special Counsel for Immigration Related Unfair Employment Practices.

Submission of the information required in this form is voluntary. However, an individual may not begin employment unless this form is completed, since employers are subject to civil or criminal penalties if they do not comply with the Immigration Reform and Control Act of 1986.

Paperwork Reduction Act

We try to create forms and instructions that are accurate, can be easily understood and which impose the least possible burden on you to provide us with information. Often this is difficult because some immigration laws are very complex. Accordingly, the reporting burden for this collection of information is computed as follows: **1)** learning about this form, and completing the form, 9 minutes; **2)** assembling and filing (recordkeeping) the form, 3 minutes, for an average of 12 minutes per response. If you have comments regarding the accuracy of this burden estimate, or suggestions for making this form simpler, you can write to: U.S. Citizenship and Immigration Services, Regulatory Management Division, 111 Massachusetts Avenue, N.W., 3rd Floor, Suite 3008, Washington, DC 20529. OMB No. 1615-0047.

EMPLOYERS MUST RETAIN COMPLETED FORM I-9
PLEASE DO NOT MAIL COMPLETED FORM I-9 TO ICE OR USCIS

Department of Homeland Security
U.S. Citizenship and Immigration Services

OMB No. 1615-0047; Expires 06/30/08
Form I-9, Employment Eligibility Verification

Please read instructions carefully before completing this form. The instructions must be available during completion of this form.

ANTI-DISCRIMINATION NOTICE: It is illegal to discriminate against work eligible individuals. Employers CANNOT specify which document(s) they will accept from an employee. The refusal to hire an individual because the documents have a future expiration date may also constitute illegal discrimination.

Section 1. Employee Information and Verification. *To be completed and signed by employee at the time employment begins.*

Print Name: Last	First	Middle Initial	Maiden Name
Address *(Street Name and Number)*		Apt. #	Date of Birth *(month/day/year)*
City	State	Zip Code	Social Security #

I am aware that federal law provides for imprisonment and/or fines for false statements or use of false documents in connection with the completion of this form.

I attest, under penalty of perjury, that I am (check one of the following):
☐ A citizen or national of the United States
☐ A lawful permanent resident (Alien #) A _____
☐ An alien authorized to work until _____
(Alien # or Admission #) _____

Employee's Signature _____ Date *(month/day/year)* _____

Preparer and/or Translator Certification. *(To be completed and signed if Section 1 is prepared by a person other than the employee.) I attest, under penalty of perjury, that I have assisted in the completion of this form and that to the best of my knowledge the information is true and correct.*

Preparer's/Translator's Signature	Print Name
Address *(Street Name and Number, City, State, Zip Code)*	Date *(month/day/year)*

Section 2. Employer Review and Verification. To be completed and signed by employer. Examine one document from List A OR examine one document from List B and one from List C, as listed on the reverse of this form, and record the title, number and expiration date, if any, of the document(s).

List A	OR	List B	AND	List C
Document title:				
Issuing authority:				
Document #:				
Expiration Date *(if any)*:				
Document #:				
Expiration Date *(if any)*:				

CERTIFICATION - I attest, under penalty of perjury, that I have examined the document(s) presented by the above-named employee, that the above-listed document(s) appear to be genuine and to relate to the employee named, that the employee began employment on *(month/day/year)* _____ and that to the best of my knowledge the employee is eligible to work in the United States. (State employment agencies may omit the date the employee began employment.)

Signature of Employer or Authorized Representative	Print Name	Title
Business or Organization Name and Address *(Street Name and Number, City, State, Zip Code)*		Date *(month/day/year)*

Section 3. Updating and Reverification. To be completed and signed by employer.

A. New Name *(if applicable)*	B. Date of Rehire *(month/day/year) (if applicable)*

C. If employee's previous grant of work authorization has expired, provide the information below for the document that establishes current employment eligibility.

Document Title: _____ Document #: _____ Expiration Date (if any): _____

I attest, under penalty of perjury, that to the best of my knowledge, this employee is eligible to work in the United States, and if the employee presented document(s), the document(s) I have examined appear to be genuine and to relate to the individual.

Signature of Employer or Authorized Representative _____ Date *(month/day/year)* _____

Form I-9 (Rev. 06/05/07) N

HANDBOOK FOR EMPLOYERS: INSTRUCTIONS FOR COMPLETING THE I-9

LISTS OF ACCEPTABLE DOCUMENTS

LIST A Documents that Establish Both Identity and Employment Eligibility	LIST B Documents that Establish Identity	LIST C Documents that Establish Employment Eligibility
OR		AND
1. U.S. Passport (unexpired or expired)	1. Driver's license or ID card issued by a state or outlying possession of the United States provided it contains a photograph or information such as name, date of birth, gender, height, eye color and address	1. U.S. Social Security card issued by the Social Security Administration *(other than a card stating it is not valid for employment)*
2. Permanent Resident Card or Alien Registration Receipt Card (Form I-551)	2. ID card issued by federal, state or local government agencies or entities, provided it contains a photograph or information such as name, date of birth, gender, height, eye color and address	2. Certification of Birth Abroad issued by the Department of State *(Form FS-545 or Form DS-1350)*
3. An unexpired foreign passport with a temporary I-551 stamp	3. School ID card with a photograph	3. Original or certified copy of a birth certificate issued by a state, county, municipal authority or outlying possession of the United States bearing an official seal
4. An unexpired Employment Authorization Document that contains a photograph (Form I-766, I-688, I-688A, I-688B)	4. Voter's registration card	4. Native American tribal document
	5. U.S. Military card or draft record	5. U.S. Citizen ID Card *(Form I-197)*
5. An unexpired foreign passport with an unexpired Arrival-Departure Record, Form I-94, bearing the same name as the passport and containing an endorsement of the alien's nonimmigrant status, if that status authorizes the alien to work for the employer	6. Military dependent's ID card	6. ID Card for use of Resident Citizen in the United States *(Form I-179)*
	7. U.S. Coast Guard Merchant Mariner Card	
	8. Native American tribal document	7. Unexpired employment authorization document issued by DHS *(other than those listed under List A)*
	9. Driver's license issued by a Canadian government authority	
	For persons under age 18 who are unable to present a document listed above:	
	10. School record or report card	
	11. Clinic, doctor or hospital record	
	12. Day-care or nursery school record	

Illustrations of many of these documents appear in Part 8 of the Handbook for Employers (M-274)

Guide to Selected U.S. Travel and Identity Documents

This guide has been prepared to assist those tasked with examining travel and employment authorization documents. This guide contains color photographs of the most commonly used documents but it is not comprehensive. There are earlier valid revisions of some illustrated documents and other less common documents that are not illustrated here.

Because the attachments are reproductions, the exact size and color may deviate from the original. Do not make identifications based on size and/or color alone.

For any questions regarding the authenticity of the documents shown in this guide, please contact the nearest office of U.S. Immigration and Customs Enforcement.

GENERAL INFORMATION CONCERNING ALIEN STATUS

In accordance with the 14th amendment to the U.S. Constitution, any person born in and subject to the jurisdiction of the United States is a citizen of the U.S. at birth. U.S. citizenship may also be acquired through **DERIVATION** from a U.S. citizen parent when children are born abroad or through **NATURALIZATION** after meeting the necessary residency requirements. All persons not citizens or nationals of the U.S. are aliens, which generally are classified as **PERMANENT RESIDENTS** ("Immigrants"), **NON-IMMIGRANTS**, or **UNDOCUMENTED ALIENS**.

PERMANENT RESIDENT ALIENS enjoy almost all of the same rights as U.S. citizens. This status may be obtained through a number of different procedures and, unless taken away administratively, is granted for life. Aliens with permanent residency must carry evidence of their status.

NON-IMMIGRANT ALIENS are admitted to the U.S. for a temporary period of time and for a specific purpose, most often as a tourist. There are different categories of non-immigrants, and they are identified through letter/number symbols (e.g. B-2). Non-immigrants are also required to present evidence of their lawful status in the U.S. to officers of U.S. Immigration and Customs Enforcement (ICE). This will usually consist of a passport containing a visa and an Arrival/Departure Record (Form I-94 or CBP I-94A).

UNDOCUMENTED ALIENS are those who may have crossed the border illegally and/or been smuggled into the interior of the U.S., or those who have violated their non-immigrant status by accepting unauthorized employment, remaining longer than permitted, or committing some other violation. Some of these aliens purchase counterfeit documents or assume another person's identity by using fraudulently obtained genuine documents.

UNITED STATES PASSPORT

A **UNITED STATES PASSPORT** is a document that is issued by the State Department to persons who have established citizenship in the United States by birth, naturalization or derivation. The primary purpose of the passport is to facilitate travel to foreign countries by establishing U.S. citizenship and acting as a vehicle to display any appropriate visas and/or entry/exit stamps that may be necessary.

Passports are also very reliable documents that may be used within the United States to establish citizenship, identity and employment authorization.

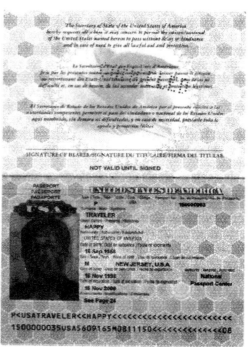

NOTE: There are several different versions of the U.S. passport that are currently valid and vary from the 1998 version illustrated above.

Although there have been many different revisions of the **CERTIFICATE OF NATURALIZATION**, there are two main versions issued by the INS. The more recent bears a gold embossed Great Seal of the United States in the top center portion. Earlier versions had gray or beige background designs and did not contain the embossed seal. Regardless, all certificates of naturalization were printed on watermarked paper. The watermark design of the Department of Justice seal and the letters "USA" becomes visible when this version of the document is held up to a strong light.

(Watermark)

The current revision of the **CERTIFICATE OF NATURALIZATION** is similar to the previous version. It too contains a gold embossed Great Seal of the United States in the top center portion. However, the watermark design has been changed to the emblem of the Department of Homeland Security (DHS). U.S. Citizenship and Immigration Services (USCIS) now issues these certificates.

(Watermark)

ALIEN REGISTRATION RECEIPT CARDS

Forms I-151 and I-551 are issued to aliens who have been granted permanent resident status in the United States. They retain this status while in this country. The bearer is required to have this card in his/her possession at all times.

The first **ALIEN REGISTRATION RECEIPT CARD**, Form I-151, was introduced in 1946. Through 18 years of various revisions, it remained primarily green in color, causing it to become known as a "Green Card". This term is still used commonly, although the cards have not been "Green" since 1959. The I-151 cards contained no expiration date and were only required to be renewed if the recipient was under the age of 14 at the time of issuance, or if the card was lost or stolen.

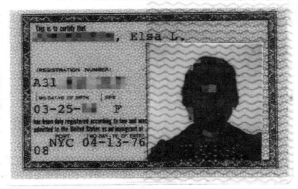

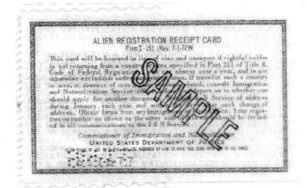

NOTE: As of March 20, 1996, the Form I-151 is no longer acceptable as evidence of permanent residence.

The **RESIDENT ALIEN CARD**, Form I-551, was introduced in January 1977 and phased in over a period of time. In addition to the photograph, the I-551 contains the bearer's signature and fingerprint. As with the older I-151 cards, this version I-551 generally does not contain an expiration date.

Form I-551

The **RESIDENT ALIEN CARD**, Form I-551, was revised in August 1989. This version was the first Alien Registration Card to contain an expiration date on every card. These cards were usually valid for ten years from the date of issue. The expiration date indicates when the card expires and must be renewed. It does **NOT** indicate that the alien's status has expired. The card was modified in January 1992 when a white box was added behind the fingerprint.

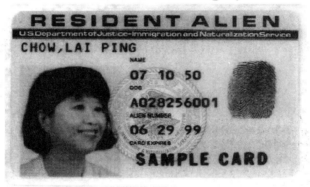

Form I-551 (August 1989)

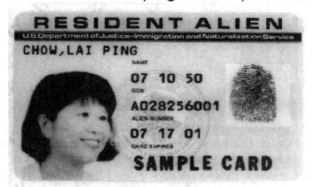

Form I-551 (January 1992)

Reverse

The **PERMANENT RESIDENT CARD**, Form I-551, was introduced in December 1997. Noticeable differences on the front of the card include a change of card title from **RESIDENT ALIEN CARD** to **PERMANENT RESIDENT CARD**, a three-line machine readable zone and the addition of a hologram.

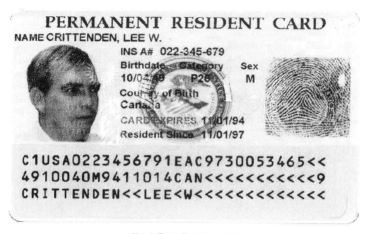

PHOTO SIDE

REVERSE

The Optical Memory Stripe on the reverse contains encoded cardholder information as well as a personalized etching which depicts the bearer's photo, name, signature, date of birth, alien registration number, card expiration date and card number.

The latest version of the **PERMANENT RESIDENT CARD**, Form I-551, was introduced in November 2004. It retains many of the same features of the previous version while updating the design. The card now shows the seal of the Department of Homeland Security and contains a more detailed hologram on the front of the card.

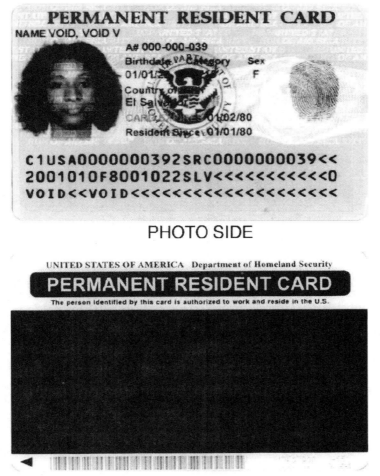

PHOTO SIDE

REVERSE

The Optical Memory Stripe on the reverse retains the same features as the previous card version. The stripe contains encoded cardholder information on the card bearer. Each card is personalized with an etching showing the bearer's photo, name, signature, date of birth, alien registration number, card expiration date and card number.

This **EMPLOYMENT AUTHORIZATION DOCUMENT**, Form I-688B, was introduced in November 1989 and is issued to aliens who have been granted permission to be employed in the U.S. for a specific period of time. The card was produced originally with a Polaroid process and has interlocking gold lines across the front.

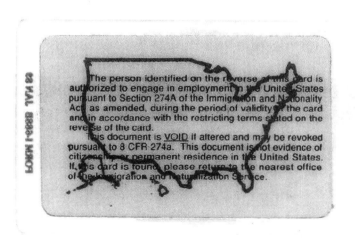

Form I-688B

In January 1997, INS began issuing a new **EMPLOYMENT AUTHORIZATION CARD**, Form I-766. This version is a credit card-sized document. The front of the card bears the photograph, fingerprint and signature of the rightful holder. The reverse contains a standard bar code, magnetic strip, and a two-dimensional bar code which contains unique card, biographic and biometric data.

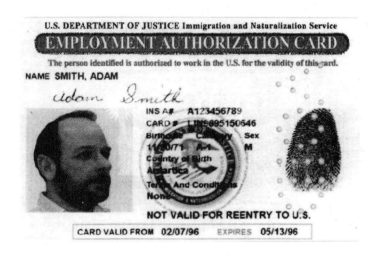

Form I-766 (January 1997)

An updated **EMPLOYMENT AUTHORIZATION CARD**, Form I-766, was introduced in May 2004. The new card is similar in appearance to the previous revision, with some modifications to the card design. The front of the document continues to show the photograph, fingerprint and signature of the bearer beneath a holographic film, but now displays the DHS seal. The reverse has a standard bar code, magnetic strip, and a two-dimensional bar code containing encoded data.

Form I-766 (May 2004)

A **REENTRY PERMIT**, Form I-327, is issued to a permanent resident alien. The document allows the bearer to reenter the United States and is valid for a period of two years. It is not renewable.

The reentry permit contains a digitized photograph and many of the security features of a passport. Visas and entry/exit stamps may be applied to the blank pages.

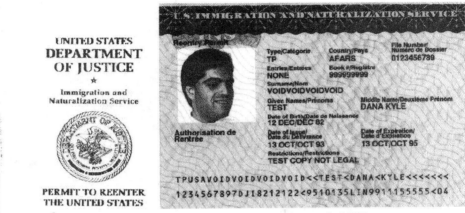

Form I-327

A **REFUGEE TRAVEL DOCUMENT**, Form I-571, is similar to the Reentry Permit, but it is used by aliens who have been classified as refugees or asylees. The security features are the same as those in the Reentry Permit, but the Refugee Travel Document is usually valid for only one year.

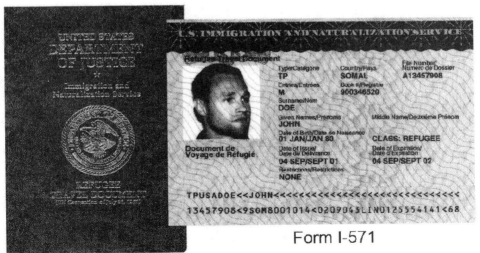

Form I-571

The **TRAVEL DOCUMENT** was introduced in September 2003 and replaces the separate Reentry Permit Form I-327 and Refugee Travel Document Form I-571 with a single booklet used for both. Notations above and below the photo indicate the document type.

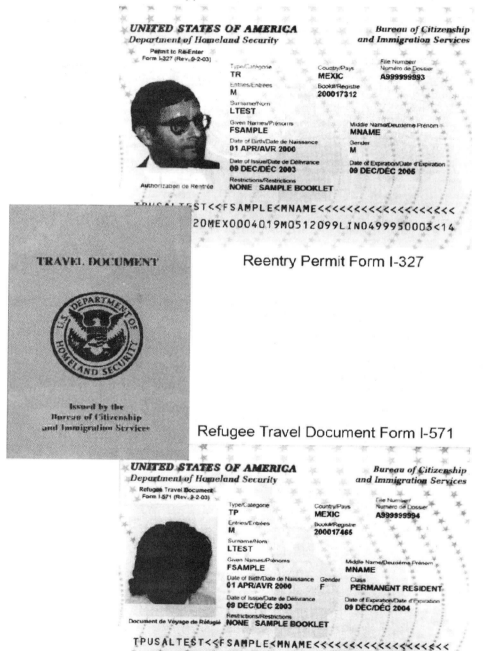

There are four types of **NON-IMMIGRANT VISAS**. The non-machine readable visa is printed with a multicolored ribbon while the machine readable visas are stickers which are applied to the passport page. Visas are used for entry purposes and must be valid on the date of entry into the U.S. It is **not** necessary for the visa to be valid after entry.

IMMIGRANT VISAS are used by people coming to live in the United States. Older versions of the immigrant visa were collected at the time entry, and the immigrants were given a rubber **ADIT STAMP** ("Processed for I-551...") to serve as evidence of permanent residence until they received their residence cards.

In 2003 the Department of State began to issue immigrant visas on the same foils used for non-immigrant visas. These foils remain in the bearer's passport after entry. Initial versions were endorsed with an ADIT stamp.

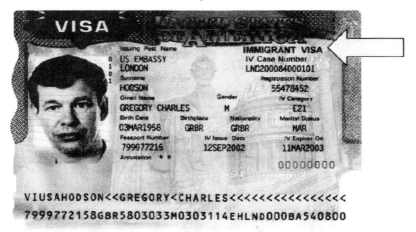

Later versions contain the endorsement printed directly onto the visa foil. The validity begins on the date the person enters the United States.

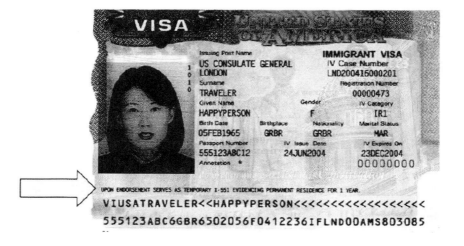

Guide to Selected U.S. Travel and Identity Documents

When an alien has been granted admission into the U.S. by a U.S. Customs and Border Protection (CBP) Inspector at an authorized Port of Entry, he/she will be issued an **ARRIVAL/DEPARTURE RECORD**, Form I-94, the bottom portion of which is stapled to a page in the alien's passport. This document explains how long the bearer may remain in the U.S. and the terms of admission.

Departure Number
742831632 01

Immigration and Naturalization Service
I-94 Departure Record

U.S. IMMIGRATION
WAS 2003
ADMITTED

NOV 2 1 2002

CLASS B-2
UNTIL May 20, 2003

14 Family Name
POE
15 First (Given) Name
John
16 Birth Date (Day, Mo, Yr)
01 01 91
17 Country of Citizenship
ENGLAND

See Other Side   STAPLE HERE

Warning - A nonimmigrant who accepts unauthorized employment is subject to deportation.
Important - Retain this permit in your possession; *you must surrender it when you leave the U.S.* Failure to do so may delay your entry into the U.S. in the future.
You are authorized to stay in the U.S. only until the date written on this form. To remain past this date, without permission from immigration authorities, is a violation of the law.
Surrender this permit when you leave the U.S.:
- By sea or air, to the transportation line;
- Across the Canadian border, to a Canadian Official;
- Across the Mexican border, to a U.S. Official.
Students planning to reenter the U.S. within 30 days to return to the same school, see "Arrival-Departure" on page 2 of Form I-20 prior to surrendering this permit.

Record of Changes

Port: Departure Record
Date:
Carrier:
Flight #/Ship Name:

For sale by the Superintendent of Documents, U.S. Government Printing Office
Washington, D.C. 20402

Form I-94

Many ports of entry along the land borders with Canada and Mexico began using a modified **Form CBP I-94A** in late 2004. The new form is computer generated, with both the bearer's personal information and the terms of admission printed onto the form instead of written by hand.

Form CBP I-94A

The U.S. Department of State introduced a new **BORDER CROSSER CARD**, Form DSP-150 in May 1998. The front of the card has a three line machine readable zone and a hologram. Bearers of this card are **not entitled to work** in the U.S.

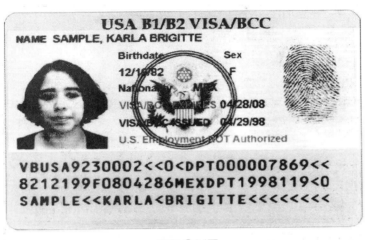

FRONT

REVERSE

The Optical Memory Stripe contains encoded cardholder information as well as a personalized etching which depicts the bearer's photo, name, date of birth, and card expiration date.

SOCIAL SECURITY CARDS

Although **SOCIAL SECURITY CARDS** are not immigration documents, they are mentioned here because they are often used as identification and to establish employment authorization.

Social Security cards have been issued since 1936 and have been revised more than 20 times. Originally, the seal on the social security card read Department of Health, Education, and Welfare. In May 1980, it was changed to the Department of Health and Human Services. In April 1995 it was changed again to read Social Security Administration. Some counterfeiters have failed to notice these changes.

In October 1983, security features were added to the card. All social security cards issued since October 1983 have been printed with raised (intaglio) printing and the signature line consists of microline printing of the words "**SOCIAL SECURITY ADMINISTRATION**" in a repeating pattern.

Do not laminate this card.

This card is invalid if not signed by the number holder unless health or age prevents signature.

Improper use of this card and/or number by the number holder or any other person is punishable by fine, imprisonment or both.

This card is the property of the Social Security Administration and must be returned upon request. If found, return to:
SSA-ATTN: FOUND SSN CARD
P.O. Box 17087 Baltimore Md. 21203
Contact your local Social Security office for any other matter regarding this card.

Department of Health and Human Services
Social Security Administration
Form OA-702 (1-88)   C25000035

To order additional copies of Form M-396 "A Guide to Selected U.S. Travel and Identity Documents", please contact the CBP National Distribution Center at:

Customs and Border Protection
National Distribution Center
P.O. Box 68912
Indianapolis, IN 46268

Fax (317) 290-3046

For government requests, please use Form CF-3039. All other requests should use Form CF-262. These forms can be obtained from the "Resources" section of the ICE website www.ice.gov.

GOOD-FAITH GUIDELINES MEMORANDUM

HQIRT 50/5.12

Date: March 6, 1997
To: Management Team
    Regional Directors
    District Directors
    Chief Patrol Agents
    Officers in Charge
    Regional Counsels
    District Counsels
From: Office of Programs
Subject: Interim Guidelines: Section 274A(b)(6) of the Immigration & Nationality Act Added by Section 411 of the Illegal Immigration Reform & Immigrant Responsibility Act of 1996.

Section 411 of the Illegal Immigration Reform and Immigrant Responsibility Act of 1996 (IIRAIRA), signed into law on September 30, 1996, significantly changed enforcement of the verification requirements of section 274A(b) of the Immigration and Nationality Act (Act). The provisions of section 411 of IIRAIRA took effect upon the signing of the bill; implementing regulations are currently being drafted. Until implementing regulations are in place, the following interim guidelines shall apply to INS field officers and INS attorneys assigned to employer sanctions cases.

A. SECTION 411 OF IIRAIRA: THE GOOD FAITH COMPLIANCE PROVISION

1. Summary of the Good Faith Compliance Provision

The Good Faith Compliance Provision of section 411 of IIRAIRA amends section 274A(b) of the Immigration and Nationality Act (Act) by adding a new paragraph: section 274A(b)(6). The language of this section applies to failures occurring on or after September 30, 1996. See IIRAIRA Section 411(b). Under section 274A(b)(6)(A) of the Act, a person or entity is considered to have complied with a requirement of section 274A(b) of the Act notwithstanding a technical or procedural failure to meet such requirement where the person or entity made a good faith attempt to comply with the requirement. There are two exceptions to the applicability of section 274A(b)(6)(A) of the Act. These are stated in sections 274A(b)(6)(B) and (C) of the Act. First, a person or entity will not be considered to have complied with the requirement in question if the INS or another enforcement agency has explained to the person or entity the basis for the failure, and the person or entity has been provided a period of not less than ten business days beginning after the date of the explanation within which to correct the failure, and the person or entity has not corrected the failure within such period. Second, a person or entity will not be considered to have complied with the requirement in question if the person or entity is engaging in a pattern or practice of violations of the knowing hire or continuing to employ provisions of sections 274A(a)(1)(A) or 274A(a)(2) of the Act.

2. Applicability of Section 274A(b)(6) of the Act: General Overview of Procedures

Section 274A(b)(6) of the Act applies to cases arising from I-9 inspections conducted on or after September 30, 1996.

1 This requires that technical or procedural failures to meet a requirement of section 274A(b) of the Act discovered during an I-9 inspection conducted on or after September 30, 1996 not be included in a NIF unless and until certain notification procedures are followed.

It is within the discretion of the Supervisory INS officer to decide whether the NIF will include technical or procedural failures.

2 If the Supervisory INS officer decides to include these technical or procedural failures in the NIF, issuance of the NIF must be deferred until the employer is given notice of the failures and at least ten business days to correct the failures consistent with this guidance. After review of the corrected failures, the NIF should include any knowing hire/continuing to employ counts, verification counts and uncorrected technical or procedural failures.

If the Supervisory INS officer decides not to include technical or procedural failures in the NIF, a NIF excluding these failures can be issued without the necessity of providing the employer with notice of the failures and a correction period. However, in cases where the NIF will not include technical or procedural failures, the Supervisory INS officer may decide that notification to the employer of the technical or procedural failures is nevertheless appropriate. If an employer has been specifically notified by the INS 3 of the technical or procedural failures and provided an opportunity to correct the failures, yet commits the same type of failure in the future, the employer will be found not to have made a good faith attempt to comply with the verification requirement related to that type of failure at a reinspection. In such a case, the employer cannot benefit from section 274A(b)(6) of the Act with respect to that type of failure.

In cases where no unauthorized aliens are found at a worksite and only failures to meet the verification requirements of section 274A(b) of the Act are discovered, INS policy encourages that a Warning Notice be issued in lieu of a NIF.

3. Meaning of Terms

a. Substantive Verification Failures

4
Section 274A(b)(6) of the Act is applicable only to those verification failures that are designated as "technical or procedural." It has been determined that verification failures that are NOT "technical or procedural" include the following:

    Failure of the person or entity to:

(A) prepare or present the Form I-9;

(B) in Section One of the Form I-9:

(1)   ensure that the individual
5 provides his or her printed name in section 1 of the Form I-9;

(2)   ensure that the individual checks a box in section 1 of the Form I-9 attesting to whether he or she is a citizen or national of the United States, a Lawful Permanent Resident or an alien authorized to work until a specified date;

(3)   ensure that the individual provides his or her A number on the line next to the phrase in section 1 of the Form I-9, "A Lawful Permanent Resident," but only if the A number is not provided in Sections 2 or 3 of the Form I-9 (or on a legible copy of a document retained with the Form I-9 and presented at the I-9 inspection);

(4)   ensure that the individual provides the Alien number or Admission number on the line provided under the phrase in section 1 of the Form I-9, "An alien authorized to work until," but only if the Alien number or Admission number is not provided in Sections 2 or 3 of the Form I-9 (or on a legible copy of a document retained with the Form I-9 and presented at the I-9 inspection);

(5) ensure that the individual signs the attestation in section 1 of the Form I-9; or
(6) ensure that the individual dates section 1 of the Form I-9 at the time of hire if the date of hire occurred before September 30, 1996;
(C) in Section Two of the Form I-9:
(1) review and verify a proper List A document or proper List B and List C documents in section 2 of the Form I-9;
(2) provide the document title, identification number(s) and/or expiration date(s) of a proper List A document or proper List B and List C documents in section 2 of the Form I-9, unless a legible copy of the document(s) is retained with the Form I-9 and presented at the I-9 inspection;
(3) sign the attestation in section 2 of the Form I-9; or
(4) date section 2 of the Form I-9 within three business days of the date the individual is hired or, if the individual is hired for three business days or less, at the time of hire if the date that section 2 was to be completed occurred before September 30, 1996;
(D) in Section Three of the Form I-9:
(1) review and verify a proper List A document or proper List B and List C documents in section 3 of the Form I-9;
(2) provide the document title, identification number(s) and/or expiration date(s) of a proper List A document or proper List B and List C documents in section 3 of the Form I-9, unless a legible copy of the document(s) is retained with the Form I-9 and presented at the I-9 inspection;
(3) sign section 3 of the Form I-9;
(4) date section 3 of the Form I-9; or
(5) date section 3 of the Form I-9 not later than the date that the work authorization of the individual hired or recruited or referred for a fee expires.

A person or entity that has committed one or more of the above failures has violated the verification requirements of section 274A(b) of the Act. The notification and correction period requirements of section 274A(b)(6)(B) of the Act do not apply to these failures.

b. "Technical or Procedural" Verification Failures 6

Until final regulations are in place, it has been determined that verification failures that ARE "technical or procedural" include the following:

Failure of the person or entity to:
(A) in Section One of the Form I-9:
(1) ensure that an individual provides his or her maiden name, address or birth date in section 1 of the Form I-9;
(2) ensure that an individual provides his or her A number on the line next to the phrase in section 1 of the Form I-9, "A Lawful Permanent Resident," but only if the A number is provided in Sections 2 or 3 of the Form I-9 (or on a legible copy of a document retained with the Form I-9 and presented at the I-9 inspection);
(3) ensure that an individual provides his or her Alien number or Admission number on the line provided under the phrase in section 1 of the Form I-9, "An alien authorized to work until," but only if the Alien number or Admission number is provided in Sections 2 or 3 of the Form I-9 (or on a legible copy of a document retained with the Form I-9 and presented at the I-9 inspection);
(4) ensure that an individual dates section 1 of the Form I-9;

(5) ensure that an individual dates section 1 of the Form I-9 at the time of hire if the time of hire occurred on or after September 30, 1996; or

(6) ensure that a preparer and or translator provides his or her name, address, signature or date;

(B) in Section Two of the Form I-9:

(1) provide the document title, identification number(s) and/or expiration date(s) of a proper List A document or proper List B and List C documents in section 2 of the Form I-9 but only if a legible copy of the document(s) is retained with the Form I-9 and presented at the I-9 inspection;

(2) provide the title, business name and business address in section 2 of the Form I-9;

(3) provide the date of hire in the attestation portion of action 2 of the Form I-9;

(4) date section 2 of the Form I-9; or

(5) date section 2 of the Form I-9 within three business days of the date the individuals hired or, if the individual is hired for three business days or less, at the time of hire if the date on which section 2 had to be completed occurred on or after September 30, 1996;

(C) in Section Three of the Form I-9:

(1) provide the document title, identification number(s) and/or expiration date(s) of a proper List A document or proper List B and List C documents in section 3 of the Form I-9 but only if a legible copy of the document(s) is retained with the Form I-9 and presented at the I-9 inspection; or

(2) provide the date of rehire in section 3 of the Form I-9.

c. Good Faith Attempt to Comply With a Requirement of Section 274A(b) of the Act. A person or entity will be considered to have made a good faith attempt to comply with a requirement of section 274A(b) of the Act notwithstanding a technical or procedural failure to meet such requirement unless:

(1) the technical or procedural failure was committed with the intent to avoid a requirement of the Act, as demonstrated by the totality of circumstances including but not limited to the substantial presence of unauthorized aliens hired by the employer and a pattern of repeated failures in the completion of the Forms I-9;

(2) the technical or procedural failure was committed in knowing reliance on section 274A(b)(6) of the Act;

(3) the employer corrected or attempted to correct the technical or procedural failure with knowledge or in reckless disregard of the fact that the correction or the attempted correction contains a false, fictitious, or fraudulent statement or material misrepresentation, or has no basis in law or fact;

(4) the employer or recruiter or referrer for a fee prepared the Form I-9 with knowledge or in reckless disregard of the fact that the Form I-9 contains a false, fictitious, or fraudulent statement or material misrepresentation, or has no basis in law or fact; or

(5) the type of failure was previously the subject of a Warning Notice issued by the INS, Notice of Intent to Fine or Notification of Technical or Procedural Failures Letter (see Appendix E attached).

d. Correction of Technical or Procedural Verification Failures

An employer or recruiter or referrer for a fee who is provided with at least ten business days to correct technical or procedural failures after notification of such failures and

Good-Faith Guidelines Memorandum

corrects the failures within the designated time period is deemed to have complied with the requirements of section 274A(b) of the Act. An employer or recruiter or referrer for a fee will be subject to civil money penalties for uncorrected failures, unless the uncorrected failures could not reasonably be corrected.

To be deemed to have corrected technical or procedural failures that reasonably can be corrected, the employer or recruiter or referrer for a fee must:

(1) in the case of a failure in section 1 of the Form I-9 ensure that the individual and/or preparer and/or translator:
- corrects the failure on the Form I-9;
- initials the correction; 7 and
- dates the correction;

(2) in the case of a failure in sections 2 or 3 of the Form I-9:
- correct the failure on the Form I-9;
- initial the correction;

8 and
- date the correction.

Situations will arise where the employer will not reasonably be able to correct the failures within the time frame provided. The following are examples of when a failure reasonably could not have been corrected:

the individual is no longer employed by the employer; 9

the individual is on medical leave, leave of absence or vacation during the time provided for correction; 10

the preparer and/or translator reasonably cannot be located; or

the failure relates to timeliness. 11

Examples of how timeliness failures should be processed are contained in Appendix C at the end of these guidelines.

For technical or procedural failures that reasonably cannot be corrected, the employer or recruiter or referrer for a fee must provide the INS officer with a brief explanation of why the failures reasonably cannot be corrected. At the discretion of the INS officer, this may be accomplished orally or in writing. If the INS officer determines that the explanation is reasonable, the technical or procedural failure will not be considered a violation.

4. Timeliness Failures Contained on Forms I-9 Obtained From I-9 Inspections Conducted on or After September 30, 1996

The notification and correction period requirements of section 274A(b)(6) of the Act do not apply to timeliness failures in Sections 1 or 2 of the Form I-9 unless the date that the particular section should have been completed falls on or after September 30, 1996.

Unlike all other failures, timeliness failures do not continue after they are first committed. Examples of how timeliness failures should be processed are contained in Appendix C at the end of these guidelines.

5. Forms I-9 That Contain Both Technical or Procedural Failures and Failures That Are Not Technical or Procedural

Where a particular Form I-9 contains technical or procedural failures as well as failures that are not technical or procedural, the notification and correction period requirements of section 274A(b)(6) of the Act apply to only those violations that stem from failures that are technical or procedural. No notice and correction period is required for those violations not considered technical or procedural. Examples of this principle are located in Appendix D at the end of these guidelines.

B. INTERIM PROCEDURES

Until implementing regulations are in place, current practices and procedures must be modified to ensure compliance with section 274A(b)(6) of the Act. Cases resulting form I-9 inspections conducted prior to September 30, 1996 do not fall under section 274A(b)(6) of the Act and, therefore, can proceed to the issuance of a NIF. However, section 274A(b)(6) of the Act does apply to reinspections conducted on or after September 30, 1996.

Each INS field officer and attorney should review cases arising from inspections or reinspections conducted on or after September 30, 1996 in accordance with the following procedures:

1. Where the only violations discovered consist of violations of sections 274A(a)(1)(A) or 274A(a)(2) of the Act or failures to meet section 274A(b) verification requirements that are not technical or procedural, a NIF should be issued as usual.

2. Where a pattern or practice of violations of sections 274A(a)(1)(A) or 274A(a)(2) of the Act is encountered as the result of an I-9 inspection, regardless of whether criminal charges have been brought against the employer, a NIF charging violations of sections 274A(a)(1)(A), 274A(a)(2) or 274A(b) of the Act can be issued as before and can include violations that stem from technical or procedural failures to meet the requirements of section 274A(b) of the Act without regard to the procedures specified in paragraph 4 below.

3. Where no unauthorized aliens are discovered during an I-9 inspection and only verification failures are found, a Warning Notice notifying the employer of verification failures may be issued in lieu of a NIF in accordance with current INS policy. Warning Notices may include technical or procedural verification failures in addition to substantive verification failures without regard to the notification and correction period requirements of section 274A(b)(6) of the Act. However, upon service of a Warning Notice, the INS officer should return the original Forms I-9 to the employer, circling in ink the technical or procedural failures found. A general list of technical or procedural failures must accompany the Warning Notice and Forms I-9. (See Appendix F).

4. Where failures to meet the requirements of section 274A(b) of the Act that include technical or procedural failures are encountered at an I-9 inspection, if the decision is made to include the technical or procedural failures in a NIF, the NIF cannot be issued unless and until the following procedures are followed:
12

a. The employer must be notified of the applicable technical or procedural verification failures. To accomplish this notification, a notification packet must be prepared. This packet must include: a Notification of Technical or Procedural Failures Letter (see Appendix E attached), copies of the Forms I-9 originally presented by the employer that contain technical or procedural failures and copies of any documents originally retained with these Forms I-9.

(1) An INS officer must identify the technical or procedural failures on the copy of each Form I-9 included in the notification packet. To identify the technical or procedural

failures, the INS officer must circle in ink, initial and date each technical or procedural failure. The original Forms I-9 should be maintained in the investigative file.

(2) The Notification of Technical or Procedural Failures Letter must include: the date of issuance; the name and address of the employer; the file number; the date of the inspection; the number of Forms I-9 included in the notification packet; the date by which corrections to the Forms I-9 must be completed and ready for review; the name and telephone number of the immigration contact person; and the signature, name and title of the INS officer issuing the letter. The date by which corrections on the Form I-9 must be completed and ready for review must be at least 10 business days after the date that the Notification of Technical or Procedural Failures Letter is served on the employer. For notification packets served by certified mail, allow at least 15 business days after the date that the notification packet is served on the employer for receipt. INS officers that are authorized to sign the Notification of Technical or Procedural Failures Letter are Immigration Agents, Special Agents. Supervisory Special Agents, Border Patrol Agents and all officers authorized to sign NIFs (see 8 C.F.R. sections 274a.9(c) & 242.1).

b. The notification packet is to be served on the employer either personally or by certified mail, return receipt requested.

c. Prior to service of the notification packet, a complete copy of the notification packet must be made and included in the investigative file. A Form G-166C indicating the date and means of service of the notification packet, the number of the Forms I-9 returned to the employer and the date that the notification packet is to be ready for review should precede the copy of the notification packet in the investigative file.

d. If it is determined, within the exercise of discretion, that the Forms I-9 in the notification packet will NOT be retrieved from the employer and reviewed by an INS officer, a NIF that contains only knowing hire, continuing to employ or substantive verification violations may be issued any time after the date the notification packet is to be ready for review as stated on the Notification of Technical or Procedural Failures Letter.

e. If it is determined, within the exercise of discretion, that the Forms I-9 in the notification packet WILL be retrieved from the employer and reviewed by an INS officer, the notification packet is to be retrieved from the employer on the date specified in the Notification of Technical or Procedural Failures Letter and by the means chosen by the INS officer (certified mail or personal visit to the employer's business).

f. Once the notification packet is retrieved, the INS officer is to review the retrieved Forms I-9 to determine whether the employer corrected the verification failures identified where such corrections reasonably could have been made. This review is a continuation of the original I-9 inspection; it is not a new inspection. This review is limited to a review of the technical or procedural failures identified on he Forms I-9 that were contained in the notification packet provided to the employer. [If evidence of failures to meet the verification requirements of section 274A(b) of the Act for new hires should arise during this stage of the inspection, such evidence can only be considered in he context of a new inspection.]

g. The INS officer reviewing the retrieved Forms I-9 must determine whether the employer corrected the failures identified in the notification packet. This determination must be documented on a Form G-166C and placed in the investigative file. For those technical or procedural failures that the employer has properly corrected, the employer shall be deemed to be in compliance with section 274A(b) of the Act, and these corrected failures are not considered violations. For those identified technical or procedural failures that the employer has not properly corrected where such corrections could reasonably have been made, the employer is deemed to be not in compliance with section 274A(b) of the Act. These failures are considered violations and can be charged in the NIF. For technical or procedural failures that reasonably could not have been corrected, these failures will not be considered violations if the employer provided a reasonable explanation for not correcting the failures. Where the INS officer determines that the explanation is reasonable, an oral explanation may be accepted. An INS officer's acceptance for the employer's oral explanation must be documented on a Form G-166C. Where the INS officer determines that the explanation is not reasonable, the INS officer must request the employer to submit a written explanation that is signed and dated by the employer.

h. Upon completion of the Form I-9 review, the case may proceed to the issuance of a NIF. The NIF may charge all violations encountered during the I-9 inspection, including violations of sections 274A(a)(1)(A), 274A(a)(2) and 274A(b) of the Act. In counts that include uncorrected technical or procedural verification failure, additional allegations must be stated in the count. See Appendix G for a list of these allegations. In calculating the civil money penalty, factor 5 cannot be aggravated on the basis of the Notification of Technical or Procedural Failures packet.

5. If a reinspection is conducted at a later date, the same procedures listed in paragraph 4 must be followed. These procedures are only applicable to those types of technical or procedural verification failures that were not the type of failures that were the subject of a previous Notification of Technical or Procedural Failures Letter. An employer that commits the same type of failures as were indicated in a previous Notification of Technical or Procedural Failures Letter has not demonstrated a good faith attempt to comply with the verification requirements with respect to those types of failures and, therefore, cannot benefit from section 274A(b)(6) of the Act.

6. Cases resulting from I-9 inspections conducted on or after September 30, 1996 where a NIF has been issued and served on the employer without adherence to the notification procedures outlined in paragraph 4 above may require additional action.

a. If the case is in settlement negotiations, INS attorneys are to either, at the discretion of the District Director or Chief patrol Agent: (1) remove the technical or procedural verification failures charged in the NIF, reduce the civil money penalty accordingly and proceed with the case on the remaining charges or (2) cancel the NIF through a letter prepared by the INS attorney and signed by the District Director or Chief Patrol Agent which explains the reason for the cancellation of the NIF and informs the employer of a forthcoming Notification of Technical or Procedural Failures Letter; the investigative file should then be returned to the agent who must follow the procedures outline in paragraph 4 above before a new NIF is issued.

b. In cases where a complaint has been filed with the Chief Administrative Hearing Officer, the complaint should be amended, removing technical or procedural failures that were listed as violations.

c. In cases where a hearing was not timely requested after the NIF was served, either: (1) a Final Order may be issued stating a fine amount that is reduced by those technical or procedural verification failures charged in the NIF that could not be charged absent compliance with the notification procedures outlined in paragraph 4 or (2) in order to allow the technical or procedural failures to be charged in the NIF, cancel the NIF through a letter signed by the District Director or Chief Patrol Agent explaining the reason for the cancellation and that a Notification of Technical or Procedural Failures packet will be prepared. If the second option is chosen, a new NIF may be issued that includes technical or procedural verification failures only after compliance with the procedures outlined in paragraph 4.

These guidelines are effective immediately.

Paul W. Virtue
Acting Executive Commissioner Programs

cc: Official File copy
    HQOPS
    HQCOU
    HQPGM
    HQENF
    HQBOR
    HQINV
    RQUIN Log
    MMETCALF Log
    RSAVIV Log
    JBEDNARZ Log

FORM I-9 SUBSTANTIVE VERIFICATION FAILURE CHECKLIST

No I-9 prepared or presented

FAILURES IN SECTION ONE OF THE FORM I-9

Employee's name not printed on the Form I-9

No check mark in indicating whether employee attests to being a United States Citizen, Lawful Permanent Resident of alien authorized to work

No A number next to the phase, "A Lawful Permanent Resident" where A number is not in sections 2 or 3 of the Form I-9 (or on a legible copy of a document retained with the Form I-9 and presented at the I-9 inspection)

No Alien or Admission number next to the phrase, "An alien authorized to work until" where Alien or Admission number is not provided in sections 2 or 3 of the Form I-9 (or on a legible copy of a document retained with the Form I-9 and presented at the I-9 inspection)

No employee signature

Employee attestation not completed at the time of hire where employee was hired before 9/30/96

FAILURES IN SECTION TWO OF THE FORM I-9

Improper List A, B or C documents reviewed or verified

No document title; identification number; or expiration date of a List A, B or C Document and a legible copy of document(s) is not retained with the Form I-9 and presented at the I-9 inspection

No attestation signature

Employer attestation not completed within 3 business days of the hire or, if the employee is hired for 3 business days or less, at the time of hire where § the date section 2 had to be completed is before 9/30/96

FAILURES IN SECTION THREE OF THE FORM I-9

Improper List A, B or C documents reviewed or verified

No document title; identification number; or § expiration date of a List A, B or C document and a legible copy of document(s) is not retained with the Form I-9 and presented at the I-9 inspection

No signature

No signature date

Section 3 is dated after the date that work authorization expired.

Appendix A

Form I-9 Technical or Procedural Verification Failure Checklist

FAILURES IN SECTION ONE OF THE FORM I-9

No employee: maiden name; address; birthrate

No A number next to the phrase, "A Lawful Permanent Resident" where A number is in sections 2 or 3 of the Form I-9 (or on a legible copy of a document retained with the Form I-9 and presented upon inspection)

No alien or Admission number next to the phrase, "An alien authorized to work until" where: Alien or Admission number is in sections 2 or 3 of the I-9 (or on a legible copy of a document retained with the Form I-9 and presented at the I-9 inspection)

No employee attestation date

Employee attestation not completed at the time of hire where: employee was hired on or after 9/30/96

No preparer and/or translator: name; address; signature

No date in the preparer and/or translator certification box

FAILURES IN SECTION TWO OF THE FORM I-9

No document title; identification number; or expiration date of a List A, B or C document and a legible copy of document(s) is retained with the Form I-9 and presented at the I-9 inspection

No business title; name; address

No date of hire

No employer attestation date

Employer attestation not completed with 3 business days of the hire or, if the employee is hired for 3 business days or less, at the time of hire where: the date section 2 had to be completed falls on or after 9/30/96

FAILURES IN SECTION THREE OF THE FORM I-9

No document title; identification number; or expiration date of a List A,B or C document and a legible copy of comment(s) is retained with the Form I-9 and presented at the I-9 inspection

No date of rehire

Appendix B

FORM I-9 TECHNICAL OR PROCEDURAL VERIFICATION FAILURE CHECKLIST

FAILURES IN SECTION ONE OF THE FORM I-9

- No employee; maiden name; address; birth date

- No A number next to the phrase, "A Lawful Permanent Resident" where A number is in sections 2 or 3 of the I-9 (or on a document retained on the Form I-9 and presented at the I-9 inspection)
- No alien or Admission number next to the phrase, "An alien authorized to work until" where Alien or Admission number is in sections 2 or 3 of the I-9 (or on a document retained on the Form I-9 and presented at the I-9 inspection)
- No employee attestation date
- Employee attestation not completed at the time of hire where the employee was hired on or after 9/30/96
- No preparer and/or translator; name; address; signature
- No date in the preparer and/or translator certification box

FAILURES IN SECTION TWO OF THE FORM I-9

- No document title; identification number; or expiration date of a List A, B or C document and a copy of document(s) is retained with the Form I-9 and presented at the I-9 inspection
- No business tittle; name; address
- No date of hire
- No employer attestation date
- Employer attestation not completed within 3 business days of the hire or, if the employee is hired for 3 business days or less, at the time of hire where the date section 2 had to be completed falls on or after 9/30/96

FAILURES IN SECTION THREE OF THE FORM I-9

- No document title; identification number; or expiration date of a List A,B or C document and a copy of document(s) is retained with the Form I-9 and presented at the I-9 inspection
- No date of rehire

E-VERIFY FACT SHEET

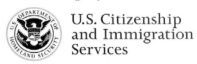

Office of Communications

U.S. Citizenship and Immigration Services

Fact Sheet

February 12, 2008

E-VERIFY

Strengthening the Employment Eligibility Document Review Process for the Nation's Employers

- E-Verify (formerly known as the Basic Pilot/Employment Eligibility Verification Program) is an Internet-based system operated by the Department of Homeland Security (DHS) in partnership with the Social Security Administration (SSA) that allows participating employers to electronically verify the employment eligibility of their newly hired employees. U.S. Citizenship and Immigration Services (USCIS) administers the program.

- E-Verify is free and voluntary and is the best means available for determining employment eligibility of new hires and the validity of their Social Security Numbers. The program provides participating employers an automated Internet-based resource to verify the employment eligibility of newly hired employees. Employment eligibility verification queries authorization checks on all newly hired employees, including U.S. citizens and non-U.S. citizens, can be run against SSA and DHS databases. Through this process, E-Verify assists employers in maintaining a legal workforce and protects jobs for authorized U.S. workers.

- USCIS began testing a photo screening tool enhancement to EEV and formally launched it on Sept. 17, 2007. The tool allows a participating employer to check the photos on Employment Authorization Documents (EAD) or Permanent Resident Cards (green card) against images stored in USCIS databases. The goal of the photo tool is to help employers determine whether the document presented reasonably relates to the individual and contains a valid photo. The former program did not include this identity fraud component.

- More than 52,000 employers are currently using the E-Verify program to verify that their new hires are authorized to work in the United States. There is no charge to participate. The President's FY2009 budget request includes $100 million to expand and improve E-Verify.

- Employers can register for E-Verify on-line at www.uscis.gov/E-Verify. The site provides instructions for completing the Memorandum of Understanding (MOU) needed to officially register for the program.

- Once registered, employers use E-Verify by entering information captured on the Employment Eligibility Verification form (I-9). E-Verify compares employee information against more than 425 million records in the SSA database and more than 60 million records stored in the DHS database. Currently, 93 percent of an employer's queries are instantly verified as work authorized.

- *The Illegal Immigration Reform and Immigrant Responsibility Act of 1996* (IIRIRA) first authorized the program. The *Basic Pilot Extension and Expansion Act of 2003* extended E-Verify until November 2008. Employers can obtain additional information about E-Verify by visiting www.uscis.gov/E-Verify.

E-VERIFY Q&A FOR EMPLOYERS

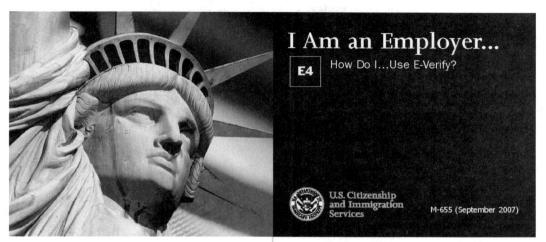

Formerly referred to as the Basic Pilot Program, E-Verify is an Internet-based system operated by U.S. Citizenship and Immigration Services (USCIS), part of the Department of Homeland Security (DHS), in partnership with the Social Security Administration (SSA). E-Verify is currently free to employers. E-Verify provides an automated link to Federal databases to help employers determine employment eligibility of new hires and the validity of their Social Security numbers.

Why should I consider participating in E-Verify?

E-Verify is currently the best means available for employers to verify electronically the employment eligibility of their newly hired employees. E-Verify virtually eliminates Social Security mismatch letters, improves the accuracy of wage and tax reporting, protects jobs for authorized U.S. workers, and helps U.S employers maintain a legal workforce. For more information about the process for using **Form I-9**, *Employment Eligibility Verification*, please see **Customer Guide E-3**, *I Am an Employer...How Do I...Complete Form I-9, Employment Verification*.

Am I required to participate?

No. E-Verify is voluntary for all employers with very limited exceptions. (Some Federal Government employers and violators of certain immigration laws may be ordered to participate.)

How do I register for participation in E-Verify?

You can register online for E-Verify at **https://www.vis-dhs.com/EmployerRegistration**, which provides instructions for completing the registration process. At the end of the registration process, you will be required to sign a Memorandum of Understanding (MOU) that provides the terms of agreement between you as the employer, the SSA, and DHS. An employee who has signatory authority for the employer can sign the MOU. Employers can use their discretion in identifying the best method by which to sign up their locations for E-Verify.

For example, an employer may choose to designate one site to perform the verification queries for newly hired employees on behalf of the entire company. Only one MOU would need to be signed for this option. An employer may also choose which sites to enroll in E-Verify and to have each site perform its own verification queries. This option requires each site performing verification queries to register and to submit an MOU to participate in the program.

Our company has several hiring sites interested in participating in E-Verify. Each site will be conducting the verification process for its newly hired employees. How should these sites register?

Each site that will perform the employment verification queries must go through the registration process and sign an individual MOU.

I am an employer with multiple hiring sites. Can one site verify everyone? How?

Yes, one site may verify new hires at all sites. When registering, the individual at the site that will be verifying new hires should select "multiple site registration" and give the number of sites per State it will be verifying.

If I sign one MOU, can I use a controlled rollout to implement E-Verify across the organization?

Yes, you can choose which sites to enroll. However, each site that has signed an MOU must verify the status of **all** new hires for that site. A new MOU is required only for a new site performing verification queries. If a central location, which is already registered, does the verification queries, then the company would only need to amend the number of hiring sites.

What is an E-Verify Designated Agent?

An E-Verify Designated Agent is a liaison between E-Verify and employers wishing to participate, but who choose to outsource submission of employment eligibility verification queries for newly hired employees. E-Verify Designated Agents conduct the verification process for other employers or clients. An E-Verify Designated Agent must register online and sign an MOU with SSA and DHS. Once the MOU is approved, the E-Verify Designated Agent can then begin registering employers and clients who have designated it to perform the company's verification services. Each employer/client will also be required to sign an MOU and will have a unique E-Verify client number.

What is an E-Verify Corporate Administrator?

An employer has the option to designate an employee as a Corporate Administrator. A Corporate Administrator is someone who has management oversight authority of the employer's hiring sites that participate in the program, but generally does not perform employment eligibility verification queries. The Corporate Administrator role enables oversight of all company sites participating in E-Verify. To become a Corporate Administrator, an individual only needs to register and does not need to sign an MOU. Once registered, this individual will be able to register company sites, add and delete users at company sites, and view reports generated by company sites. The Corporate Administrator, however, does not submit queries for verification.

After an employer registers, how does E-Verify work?

Using an automated system, the program involves verification checks of SSA and DHS databases. The E-Verify MOU, User Manual, and Tutorial contain instructions and other related materials on E-Verify procedures and requirements. Once the user has completed the tutorial, he or she may begin using the system to verify the employment eligibility of all newly hired employees.

What information is required to conduct an E-Verify initial verification?

After hiring a new employee and completing the **Form I-9** required for all new hires (regardless of E-Verify participation), the employer or agent must submit a query that includes information from sections 1 and 2 of the Form I-9, including:

- Employee's name and date of birth,
- Social Security Number (SSN),
- Citizenship status he or she attests to,
- An A number or I-94 number, if applicable,
- Type of document provided on the Form I-9 to establish work authorization status, and
- Proof of identity, and its expiration date, if applicable.

Response to the initial query is sent within seconds of submitting the query. Documents presented for Form I-9 identification only purposes (documents from "List B") to E-Verify employers must have a photograph.

When may an employer initiate a query under E-Verify?

The earliest the employer may initiate a query is after an individual accepts an offer of employment and after the employee and employer complete the Form I-9. The employer must initiate the query no later than the end of 3 business days after the new hire's actual start date.

An employer may initiate the query before a new hire's actual start date; however, it may not pre-screen applicants and may not delay training or an actual start date based upon a tentative non-confirmation or a delay in the receipt of a confirmation of employment authorization. An employee should not face any adverse employment consequences based upon an employer's use of E-Verify unless a query results in a final non-confirmation. In addition, an employer cannot use an employment authorization response to speed up an employee's start date. This would be unfair treatment to use E-Verify results to accelerate employment for this employee compared to another who may have received a tentative non-confirmation.

For example, Company X always assigns a start-date to new employees that is 2 weeks after the employee has completed an approved drug test. After the employee has accepted a job with Company X and after the employee and Company X complete the Form I-9, the company can initiate the E-Verify query. However, the company cannot speed up or delay the employee's start-date based upon the results of the query (unless the program issues a final non-confirmation, in which case the employee should not be further employed).

Employers must verify employees in a non-discriminatory manner and may not schedule the timing of queries based upon the new hire's national origin, citizenship status, race, or other characteristic that is prohibited by U.S. law.

What is the required timeframe for conducting an employment eligibility check on a newly hired employee?

Employers must make verification inquiries within 3 business days of an employee starting work.

Which employees should be verified through the system?

As a participant in E-Verify, employers are required to verify all newly hired employees, both U.S. citizens and non-citizens. Employers may not verify selectively and must verify all new hires while participating in the program. The program may not be used to prescreen applicants for employment, go back and check employees hired before the company signed the MOU, or re-verify employees who have temporary work authorization.

Can I verify the immigration status of a new hire that is not a U.S. citizen?

No. E-Verify only verifies a new hire's employment eligibility, not his or her immigration status.

If I am an employer who would like to run an employee's Form I-9 information through E-Verify, but that employee does not yet have a Social Security Number, what should I do?

E-Verify cannot be used for employees who do not yet have a Social Security Number (SSN). If you are an employer with such an employee, you should complete the Form I-9 process with him or her and wait to run an E-Verify query on that individual until you have received his or her SSN. You should note on the I-9 form why you have not yet run an E-Verify query. Your employee should get his or her number to you quickly, and then you may run a query on that individual. In the meantime, you will have completed the Form I-9 Employment Eligibility Verification process with your employee and verified his or her work authorization so that your employee will be allowed to work temporarily without a SSN.

I would like to use electronic Form I-9s for my employees. Does USCIS offer a system that would automatically generate E-Verify queries from the electronic Form I-9s?

Currently, USCIS does not offer this service, but several private companies do.

Is there a "batch access" method in the system?

Yes, it is called "Web Services," and it is a real-time batch method. It requires a company to develop an interface between its personal system or electronic Form I-9 system and the E-Verify database. For more information and help with design specifications, please contact USCIS at **1-800-741-5023**.

E-Verify Q&A for Employers

Can I terminate my participation in E-Verify at any time?

Yes, you may choose to leave E-Verify at any time.

Does participation in E-Verify provide safe harbor from worksite enforcement?

No. Participation in E-Verify does not provide protection from worksite enforcement. However, an employer who verifies work authorization under E-Verify is presumed to have not knowingly hired an unauthorized alien.

How can I find out more about E-Verify?

To find out more about E-Verify, please visit **www.dhs.gov /e-verify** or contact USCIS at **1-888-464-4218**.

Key Information

Key Forms Referenced in This Guide	Form #
Employment Eligibility Verification	I-9
Application for Employment Authorization	I-765
Employer Handbook	M-274

How to Contact USCIS

- **On the Internet at: www.uscis.gov**
  For more copies of this guide, or information about other citizenship and immigration services, please visit our website. You can also download forms, e-file some applications, check the status of an application, and more. It's a great place to start! If you don't have Internet access at home or work, try your local library. If you can't find what you need, please call Customer Service.
- **Customer Service: 1-800-375-5283**
- Hearing Impaired TDD Customer Service: 1-800-767-1833

Disclaimer: This guide provides basic information to help you become generally familiar with our rules and procedures. For more information, or the law and regulations, please see our website. Immigration law can be complex, and it is impossible to describe every aspect of every process. You may wish to be represented by a licensed attorney or by a nonprofit agency accredited by the Board of Immigration Appeals.

Other U.S. Government Services—Click or Call		
General Information	www.firstgov.gov	1-800-333-4636
U.S. Department of State	www.state.gov	1-202-647-6575

Social Security Number Verification Service (SSNVS) Handbook

Social Security Administration
Office of Systems Electronic Services
6401 Security Boulevard
Baltimore, Maryland 21235

Revised September 2007

CONTACT INFORMATION

Social Security Number Verification Service (SSNVS)

www.ssa.gov/bso/bsowelcome.htm

Employer Reporting Assistance
For help with registering or annual wage reporting, call
1-800-772-6270 (toll free)
or 1-410-965-4241
Monday - Friday
7:00 a.m. to 7:00 p.m. Eastern Standard Time
Or e-mail Social Security at Employerinfo@ssa.gov

> TDD/TYY call 1-800-201-7165 (toll free)
>
> ***BSO Technical Assistance***
> For technical help with using BSO, call
> **1-888-772-2970** (toll free)
> Monday - Friday
> 8:30 a.m. to 4:00 p.m. Eastern Standard Time
>
> Fax: 1-410-597-0237
> E-mail: bso.support@ssa.gov
> *Caution: Social Security recommends that you not include private information, such as your Social Security Number, in Internet e-mail messages.*
>
> ***General Information***
> For information about Social Security programs and benefits, call
> **1-800-772-1213** (toll free)
> Monday - Friday
> 7:00 a.m. to 7:00 p.m. Eastern Standard Time
>
> For General Information TDD/TTY, call 1-800-325-0778 (toll free)

WHAT IS SSNVS AND BSO?

The Social Security Number Verification Service (SSNVS) is one of the services offered by Social Security Administration's (SSA) Business Services Online (BSO). It allows registered users (employers and certain third-party submitters) to verify the names and Social Security Numbers (SSNs) of employees against SSA records.

With SSNVS, you may:

- Verify up to 10 names and SSNs online and receive immediate results. There is no limit to the number of times the *SSN Verification* web page may be used within a session.

- Upload electronic files of up to 250,000 names and SSNs and usually receive results the next government business day.

In addition to SSNVS, the BSO suite consists of Registration Services and Employer Services. Registration Services offer a User Identification Number (User ID) assignment, password selection and various registration maintenance functions. Employer Services offer W-2 file upload, W-2 and W-2c online key-in functions (no special software or forms required) and the ability to track files and view processing results and notices.

THE IMPORTANCE OF CORRECT SSNs

SSA can post employee wages correctly only when employers and submitters report employee wages under the correct name and SSN. Recording names and SSNs correctly is the key to successful processing of annual wage reports. It saves the employer and the administration processing costs and allows SSA to properly credit your employees' earnings record. Credits to your employees' earnings record are important in determining their future eligibility and payment of SSA's retirement, disability and survivor benefits.

PROPER USE OF SSNVS

SSNVS should only be used for the purpose for which it is intended.

- SSA will verify SSNs and names solely to ensure that the records of current or former employees are correct for the purpose of completing Internal Revenue Service (IRS) Form W-2 (Wage and Tax Statement).

- It is illegal to use the service to verify SSNs of potential new hires or contractors or in the preparation of tax returns.

- Company policy concerning the use of SSNVS should be applied consistently to all workers; for example:

    o If used for newly hired workers, verify information on all newly hired workers.
    o If used to verify information on other workers, verify the information for all other workers.

- Third-party use of SSNVS is strictly limited to organizations that contract with employers to either handle the wage reporting responsibilities or perform an administrative function directly related to annual wage reporting responsibilities of hired employees. It is suggested that contracts between the third-party and the employer stipulate that the functions being performed by the third-party contractor adhere to the proper use of SSNVS. It is not proper to use SSNVS for non-wage reporting purposes such as identity, credit checks, mortgage applications, etc.

- Anyone who knowingly and willfully uses SSNVS to request or obtain information from SSA under false pretenses violates Federal law and may be punished by a fine, imprisonment or both.

- SSA may ban you and/or the company you represent from the use of SSNVS if SSA determines there has been misuse of the service.

- SSA returns all names and SSNs submitted. If the name and SSN does not match our records, SSA advises the following:

- o This response does not imply that you or your employee intentionally provided incorrect information about the employee's name or SSN.
- o This response does not make any statement about your employee's immigration status.
- o This response is not a basis, in and of itself, to take any adverse action against the employee, such as laying off, suspending, firing or discriminating against the employee.

NOTE: If you rely only on the verification information SSA provides to justify adverse action against a worker, you may violate State or Federal law and be subject to legal consequences.

THIRD-PARTY VERIFICATIONS

If an employer has hired you to handle his/her company's annual wage reporting responsibilities, a fee-based approach can be used when offering SSNVS to your clients. However, caution should be taken. SSA offers services such as SSNVS free of charge. Some companies in the private sector offer those same services for a fee and develop misleading brochures and advertisements. To discourage the use of misleading mailings about Social Security and Medicare, Congress enacted specific prohibitions in Section 312 of the Social Security Independence and Program Improvements Act of 1994 that broadened the existing deterrents. The prohibitions are listed in Title 42 of the U.S. Code, Section 1320b-10. To ensure that you conform to these legal requirements, be careful to adhere to the following:

- Be cautious not to suggest to your clients that this service is only available through you,

- Advise all customers that this service is available at no cost from SSA and that this service is not a unique or exclusive arrangement between SSA and your company, and

- Be sure not to give any impression when describing your SSN verification service to your clients that your company has an arrangement that allows direct access to SSA databases, program software, etc.

NEW USERS

If you are a new employee or newly self-employed, you will not be able to complete the online registration process if:

- Your current employer did not file a Form W-2 for you with SSA for Tax Year 2006, or

- You are currently self-employed but did not submit self-employment earnings to the IRS for Tax Year 2006.

If either of the above statements applies to you, begin the online registration

SOCIAL SECURITY NUMBER VERIFICATION SERVICE (SSNVS) HANDBOOK

process as described in the REGISTRATION section of this handbook. BSO will display a message asking you to call the Employer Reporting Assistance number at 1-800-772-6270. Call this number to complete the registration process and receive your User ID.

There are several steps that must be completed before you can use SSNVS. You must:

1. *Register for BSO*
2. *Login to BSO*
3. *Request access to SSNVS*
4. *Receive an Activation Code (mailed to your employer)*
5. *Login to BSO*
6. *Activate access*

Every BSO user must register separately. You may not register on behalf of another person.

SYSTEM REQUIREMENTS

To use SSNVS, you will need:

- Internet access,

- A web browser, such as Internet Explorer, FireFox or Netscape Navigator. Your browser version must allow 'cookies' (files stored temporarily on your computer) and have 128-bit encryption.

> *NOTE: In order to use BSO, your browser version must be set to accept cookies and support 128-bit encryption. This is the default setting for most browsers. If you receive a request to store a file on your computer, select Yes. BSO cookies will be deleted when you close your browser.*

- Adobe Acrobat Reader (version 5.0 or higher is recommended). You will need this software to view and print your forms. For a free copy of Acrobat Reader go to www.adobe.com.

SECURITY

SSNVS and all applications within the BSO Suite of Services use Secure Sockets Layer (SSL) communications protocol and 128-bit line encryption to protect your privacy. These technologies prevent eavesdropping and ensure the security of data transmitted over the Internet.

These security features do not apply to Internet e-mail. SSA recommends that you not include private information, such as your SSN, in Internet e-mail messages.

SSNVS / BSO AVAILABILITY

SSNVS normally operates during the following hours, including holidays and may be available at other times as well:

SSNVS Hours of Operation

Day	Time
Monday - Friday	5:00 a.m. to 1:00 a.m. Eastern Standard Time
Saturday	5:00 a.m. to 11:00 p.m. Eastern Standard Time
Sunday	8:00 a.m. to 11:30 p.m. Eastern Standard Time

> **NOTE:** SSNVS/BSO is not available when SSA is in the process of implementing changes to their system. This usually occurs around the end of the calendar year. Advance notice is provided on the BSO website. Also, during website down times, informational messages are displayed when a user attempts to access the system.

REGISTRATION

INFORMATION NEEDED TO REGISTER

> **NOTE**: Self-employed BSO users may use SSNVS only if they provided an Employer Identification Number (EIN) at the time of registration. To apply for an EIN, go to the IRS website: www.irs.gov/businesses/small.

The information you provide when you register allows SSA to confirm your identity before issuing a User ID or to contact you, if necessary. You will be asked to provide the following:

- Type of employer/employee,
- Company EIN,
- Company or business name,
- Company phone number,
- Indication if you are a third-party submitter registering to do business on behalf of another company,
- Name as it appears on your Social Security card,

SOCIAL SECURITY NUMBER VERIFICATION SERVICE (SSNVS) HANDBOOK

- SSN,
- Date of birth,
- Your preferred mailing address,
- Work phone number,
- Fax number (optional), and
- E-mail address.

You will also be asked to enter a unique password of your choice.

Your full name, SSN, date of birth, and EIN will be verified against SSA records.

If you have been hired on behalf of an employer, you should provide information about your own company when you register through BSO for SSNVS.

If you have a reason to use BSO but are not a citizen of the United States (and you live outside the United States), leave the U.S. SSN field blank. You will be allowed to continue without providing this information. If you register without providing a United States SSN, additional authentication will be required before you can use BSO services.

REGISTERING

When you have the above information ready, follow these steps to register online:

1. Go to the BSO Welcome web page.

   > **NOTE**: *Do not use your browser's Back, Forward, or Refresh buttons while completing the registration form. This could clear the form unintentionally.*

2. Select the *Register* button on the *BSO Welcome* web page. This will open the *Registration Attestation* web page, an important user certification statement.

3. Select the *I Accept* button to indicate that you have read and understand the user certification statement and agree to its contents. This will open the registration form.

4. Provide the requested information on the registration form. Assistance and tips for completing the registration form can be found by clicking the *BSO Help* button.

   > **NOTE:** *The SSN and EIN fields cannot be updated. You must re-register to enter new information in these fields.*

5.
6. Select the *Register* button when you have completed the registration form. BSO will verify your identity against SSA records and display your User ID.

> **NOTE:** *Make a note of your User ID because you will need it to log in to BSO.*

7.

Immediately after registering, you will be able to maintain/update your registration information, request access to BSO services, and contact SSA electronically.

YOUR BSO PASSWORD

At the time of registration, you must enter a unique password of your choice. Your password must contain a combination of eight (8) letters and numbers (e.g., 9580859A or frog2828). Passwords are NOT case sensitive. No special characters are allowed. Secure your password and do not share it with anyone. Your User ID and password are required to log in to BSO.

> **NOTE:** *Here is a list of password instructions:*
>
> - *Your password must be eight (8) characters long and must be a combination of letters and numbers.*
> - *There must be at least one letter and at least one number in your password.*
> - *Passwords are NOT case sensitive.*
> - *Do not use special characters.*
> - *You must change your password at least once every 365 days to prevent your User ID from expiring.*

CHANGING YOUR PASSWORD

It is mandatory to change your password at least once every 365 days to keep your User ID from expiring. If your User ID expires, you will need to re-register.

The email address you provided during registration allows SSA to send you a notice when it is time to change your password. In addition, you will receive *BSO News* which provides important wage and tax reporting updates.

IF YOU FORGET YOUR PASSWORD

If you forget your password, you may request a new one by following these steps:

1. Select the *Forgot Your Password* link on the *Business Services Online Login* web page. This will open a password request form.

2. Type your First and Last Name, SSN, Date of Birth and EIN.

3. Select the *Request New Password* button. BSO will display a message indicating that your password has been reissued successfully. SSA will mail you a temporary password, usually within two (2) weeks.

After you request a new password, your old password will no longer be valid. You will not be able to use BSO until you receive your temporary password in the mail.

When you have logged in with your temporary password, you will be prompted to enter a unique password of your choice. Your password must contain a combination of eight (8) letters and numbers (e.g., 9580859A or frog2828). Passwords are NOT case sensitive.

> ***NOTE:*** *Your password is for your use only and may not be disclosed to anyone else, including other employees. Exercise caution in disclosing your User ID. Your User ID is the equivalent of your electronic signature and is assigned to you personally - not generically to your company. You are responsible for all actions taken using your User ID.*

COMPLETE YOUR PHONE REGISTRATION

New users may have to complete their online registration by speaking with an Employer Reporting Branch (ERB) representative. After speaking with an ERB your next step would be to select the *Complete Your Phone Registration* button from the *BSO Welcome* web page and enter the following information:

- User Identification Number (User ID) provided by ERB personnel,

- First and Last Name,

- SSN (if applicable),

- Date of Birth,

- EIN, and

- Password (For more information, see "Your BSO Password" section above).

Once your personal and company information has been authenticated against SSA records, you can request access to SSNVS.

ACCESS TO SSNVS

Before you can verify names and SSNs, you will need to request access to SSNVS. Once access has been requested you will receive an activation code from SSA. You are required to enter the SSNVS activation code prior to your first use.

REQUEST ACCESS TO SSNVS

> **NOTE:** *Self-employed BSO users may use SSNVS only if they provided an Employer Identification Number (EIN) at the time of registration. To apply for an EIN, go to the IRS website: www.irs.gov/businesses/small.*

To request access to SSNVS, after you have registered to use BSO, complete the following steps:

1. Login to BSO.

2. From the *BSO Main Menu*, select *Account Maintenance* and then select *Request Access to BSO Services*. The *Request Access to BSO Services* web page will open with a description of the available suites of services.

3. Check the *Electronic Wage Reporting Service* box and select the *Next* button.

4. Continue navigating through the wizard by selecting the *Next* button until the *Verify Social Security Numbers Online* web page displays. Click on the *Yes* button to request access to this function.

5. Select the *Next* button until reaching the *Request Summary* web page and then select the *Confirm* button to view the *Request Access to BSO Services Confirmation* web page.

SSA will mail an activation code for SSNVS to your employer at the address the IRS has on file from the Form 941, Employer's Federal Tax Return or SS-4, Application for Employer Identification Number.

If you are already registered to use BSO services, you may request access to SSNVS by selecting *Account Maintenance* from the *BSO Main Menu* web page and then selecting the *Request Access to BSO Services* link.

ACTIVATION CODE

The activation code is an alphanumeric code sent by SSA to the employer or registered User ID holder when access to certain services are requested. This code must be entered on the *Activate Access to BSO Services* web page in order to grant the user access to the requested service.

The activation code mailed to your employer is usually received within two (2) weeks. The letter to your employer with the activation code instructs him or her to provide you with the activation code. The activation code is an added layer of security. You will not have access to SSNVS until you have activated the service by entering the activation code.

ACTIVATE ACCESS TO SSNVS

SSNVS requires the activation code that was mailed to your employer to be entered to activate your access to the SSNVS service prior to your first use.

Once you have received your activation code from your employer:

1. Login to BSO.

2. From the *BSO Main Menu*, select *Account Maintenance* and then select *Activate Access to BSO Services* link. The *Activate Access to BSO Services* web page will open.

3. Enter the activation code.

4. Select the *Activate* button. A *Confirmation* web page will display indicating that SSA has approved your request.

You may then begin using your SSNVS services immediately.

RE-REQUEST ACTIVATION CODE

> **NOTE:** *The activation code for SSNVS is sent directly to your employer. Please check with your employer to verify that the activation code has been received.*

If it has been 10 days or more since you requested access to SSNVS and your employer has not received your activation code from SSA:

1. From the *BSO Main Menu*, select *Account Maintenance* and then select the *Re-Request Activation Codes* link. The *Re-Request Activation Codes* web page will open.

2. Check the *box* corresponding to SSNVS.

3. Select the *Re-Request* button. A *Re-Request Activation Codes Confirmation* web page will display confirming SSA received your request.

Restrictions:

- If it has been 60 days or more since you requested access:

    o Your activation code is invalid.

    o You may not re-request an activation code.

    o You must request access to SSNVS again using the *Request Access to BSO Services* web page.

> **NOTE:** *Once an activation code has been re-requested, the original activation code is de-activated and is no longer valid.*

REMOVE ACCESS TO SSNVS

1. From the *BSO Main Menu*, select *Account Maintenance* and then select the *Remove Access to BSO Services* link. The *Remove Access to BSO Services* web page will open.

2. Check the box *Verify Social Security Numbers Online*.

3. Select the *Remove* button. A *Confirmation* web page will display indicating that SSA has approved your request.

If you remove access to any service(s) in error, you must re-request access via the *Request Access to BSO Services* web page.

LOGGING INTO SSNVS

To access SSNVS, you must first log in to BSO:

- Open the BSO Welcome web page.

- Select *Login* on the *BSO Welcome* web page. This will open the *General Login Attestation* web page containing an important user certification statement.

> **NOTE:** *If your browser does not support 128-bit encryption, an authorization error message will be displayed when you select the Login link. See the SYSTEM REQUIREMENTS section of this handbook for system requirements.*

-
- Select the *I Accept* button to indicate that you have read the user certification statement and agree to its contents. This will open the

SOCIAL SECURITY NUMBER VERIFICATION SERVICE (SSNVS) HANDBOOK

Business Services Online Login web page.

- Enter your User ID and password.

    o Enter your User ID and password.

    o If you have received a temporary password in the mail, log in with your User ID and temporary password. You will then need to change your temporary password. When the *BSO Change Password* web page is displayed, enter the temporary password and then enter your own unique password twice.

    o If you registered for BSO with the ERB personnel by telephone, but have not yet selected your password, select the *Complete Your Phone Registration* link from the *Business Services Online Login* web page. This will open the *BSO Registration* web page. For more information, see the Complete Your Phone Registration section of this handbook.

- Select the *Login* button from the *Business Services Online Login* web page. This will open the *BSO Main Menu* web page. The *BSO Main Menu* web page is your point of entry for SSNVS and all other BSO services.

> **NOTE:** *The use of the browser's Back, Forward and Refresh buttons may unintentionally log you out of BSO.*

> **NOTE:** *If you forgot your password, please refer to Your BSO Password section of this handbook under* REGISTRATION.

USING SSNVS

SSNVS allows you to submit names and SSNs for verification both online and through electronic file submission.

REQUEST ONLINE SSN VERIFICATION

The *SSN Verification* web page enables you to submit up to 10 names and SSNs for verification and obtain immediate results. There is no limit to the number of times the *SSN Verification* web page may be used within a session.

The *SSN Verification* web page contains the following data entry fields:

Employer Identification Number (EIN) - The EIN of the employer under which wages are to be reported for the names and SSNs being verified.

- The Employer's EIN field is mandatory.
- The Employer's EIN must be nine (9) numerical characters only.
- Spaces, alphabetic characters, hyphens, slashes or any other special characters are not allowed.

Social Security Number (SSN)

- The SSN field is mandatory.
- The SSN must be nine (9) numerical characters only.
- Spaces, alphabetic characters, hyphens, slashes or any other special characters are not allowed.

First Name

- The First Name field is mandatory.
- The First Name must be between one (1) and 10 characters in length.
- If the First Name is longer than 10 characters, enter the first 10 characters of the First Name.
- Enter the First Name using alphabetic characters only.
- Spaces, numbers, hyphens, slashes or any other special characters are not allowed.

Middle Name

- The Middle Name field is optional.
- If entered, the Middle Name must be between one (1) and seven (7) characters in length.
- If the Middle Name is longer than seven (7) characters, enter the first seven (7) characters of the Middle Name.
- Enter the Middle Name using alphabetic characters only.
- Spaces, numbers, hyphens, slashes or any other special characters are not allowed.

Last Name

- The Last Name field is mandatory.
- The Last Name must be between one (1) and 13 characters in length.
- If the Last Name is longer than 13 characters, enter the first 13 characters of the Last Name.
- Enter the Last Name using alphabetic characters only.
- Spaces, numbers, hyphens, slashes or any other special characters are not allowed.

Suffix

- The Suffix field is optional.

SOCIAL SECURITY NUMBER VERIFICATION SERVICE (SSNVS) HANDBOOK

- If entered, the Suffix must be Jr, Sr, or a Roman Numeral I through X.
- Numbers, hyphens, slashes or any other special characters are not allowed.

Date of Birth (DOB)

- The DOB field is optional.
- If entered, the DOB must contain eight (8) digits.
- Enter the employee's DOB using the format MMDDYYYY where:
    - MM is the month; enter a value of 01 through 12.
    - DD is the day; enter a value of 01 through 31.
    - YYYY is the year; enter the first two (2) digits of the century followed by a value of 00 through 99.
- Spaces, letters, hyphens, slashes or any other special characters are not allowed.
- The DOB cannot be before 1800 or after the current date.

Gender

- The Gender field is optional.
    - F = Female
    - M = Male

> **NOTE:** SSA may not be able to process your request if you enter identical SSNs or identical First and Last Names multiple times.

The First, Middle and Last Name fields provide links to the help guide for entering complex names. To access the *SSNVS Help* web page, you must be logged into SSNVS. The *Help* button is in the left-hand corner of each SSNVS web page and opens in a new browser window.

> **NOTE:** If data entry errors are found, you will be prompted to correct your errors.

UPLOAD AN ELECTRONIC FILE FOR VERIFICATION

SSNVS allows you to request name and SSN verifications via electronic file submissions.

1. The *Submit a File for SSN Verification - Before You Start* web page contains the following information.

    - **Review your file** for correct formatting to ensure that the file is error-free. A properly formatted file will avoid rejection. See the Submission File Format section of the handbook for the correct file format. Files containing more than 100 records are scanned for format errors. If more than 50% of the records contain format errors, the file is not processed.

- o **Excel Users** To ensure that your electronic file submission processes successfully, the file must NOT be in an *.xls format. If you are using Excel, you must save the file in the appropriate format.

    To properly save an Excel file for processing:

    1. On the File Menu, select Save As.
    2. In the Save As dialog box, select the drop-down box Save as type.
    3. Select Formatted text (Space delimited) (*.prn).
    4. Insert your filename and click Save.

    Once you have saved your file, check your file against the Submission File Format. Please ensure that the record length is 130 characters and all fields are properly placed in their respective positions.

- **Zip your file** if you have over 500 name and SSN verification requests or you have a slow connection. The transmission time required will be substantially reduced if the file is zipped (compressed).

When the file is ready for upload, select the *Continue* button.

2. The *Submit a File for SSN Verification - Submit Your File* web page contains the following data entry fields.
    - ***Employer's EIN***

        The EIN of the employer under which wages are to be reported for the names and SSNs being verified.

    - ***Select File***

        - o If you know the name of the file you wish to upload, type the file name in the *Select File* data entry field.

            or

        - o Select a file from your local or network directory by selecting the *Browse* button. When the file submission box appears, select the location and name of the file you want to upload. When you select *OK* and return to *Submit a File for SSN Verification - Submit Your File* web page, the file name is automatically entered in the *Select File* data entry field.

Social Security Number Verification Service (SSNVS) Handbook

- o Once the *Select File* data entry field is complete, select the *Submit* button to begin uploading your file. Your file submission is complete when the *Submit a File for SSN Verification - Confirmation* web page is displayed.

- o After the *Submit* button has been selected, you will see a dialog box showing the process of your file being uploaded. When the file upload is complete, you will receive a pop-up box stating "Your file submission was successful" and a recommendation to save or print the acknowledgement.

Submission times depend on many factors. SSA allows up to four (4) hours for a single file submission. If your connection is lost during file submission, you will have to submit the file again.

> **NOTE:** *Please do not exit SSNVS or log out until you receive your confirmation number.*

3. The *Submit a File for SSN Verification - Confirmation* web page contains the following information.

   This web page acknowledges that your file was received and provides other submitted related information.

   - Confirmation number, a 16-position alphanumeric number, assigned by SSA, that you will need to retrieve the results of your submission. Make a note of this number; you need it to check the status of your file.
   - Date of submission,
   - Time of submission,
   - Your file name (For information only, not to be used for tracking the status of your file.),
   - File size,
   - What you should do next and
   - What to expect.

Once a file is successfully submitted and you have noted its confirmation number, you can process more files by selecting the *Submit Another File* button; this returns you to the *Submit a File for SSN Verification - Submit Your File* web page.

SUBMISSION FILE FORMAT

To ensure your electronic file submission processes successfully, the file must be a text file (.txt) in the following format:

> *NOTE: Record delimiters are not to be used (i.e., do not place a comma or any other character after any field).*
>
> *NOTE: If a field marked "May not be left blank." does not contain an entry, the item is automatically considered a non-verified record.*
>
> *NOTE: In order to sort the return file to your specifications, we recommend using the User Control Data field to create a unique identifier for each record. This unique identifier would be placed in positions 90-103 in your submission file and returned to you in positions 84-97 in the return file.*

Field Name	Instruction	Position	Field Size	Field Type
SOCIAL SECURITY NUMBER	• Must include all 9 digits including lead zeros. • May not be left blank.	1-9	9	Numeric
ENTRY CODE "TPV"	• Must insert "TPV." • May not be left blank.	10-12	3	Alpha
PROCESSING CODE 214	• Must insert "214." • May not be left blank.	13-15	3	Numeric
LAST NAME	• Do not use hyphens, apostrophes, spaces, periods, suffixes (Jr) or prefixes (Dr). • Must contain at least one character. • May not be left	16-28	13	Alpha

SOCIAL SECURITY NUMBER VERIFICATION SERVICE (SSNVS) HANDBOOK

	blank.			
FIRST NAME	• Do not use hyphens, apostrophes, spaces, periods, suffixes (Jr) or prefixes (Dr). • Must contain at least one character. • May not be left blank.	29-38	10	Alpha
MIDDLE NAME / INITIAL	• Do not use hyphens, apostrophes, spaces, periods, suffixes (Jr) or prefixes (Dr). • Optional	39-45	7	Alpha
DATE OF BIRTH (MMDDYYYY)	• If unknown, leave blank. • Optional	46-53	8	Numeric

GENDER CODE	• Must contain one of the following:
	   o M=Male or
	   o F=Female
	• Optional
		54	1	Alpha

BLANK	SSA use only.	55-89	35	Blanks
USER CONTROL DATA	Free form text for employer.	90-103	14	Alphanumeric
BLANK	SSA use only.	104-123	20	Blanks
REQUESTER IDENTIFICATION CODE	• Enter OEVS. • May not be left blank.	124-127	4	Alpha
MULTIPLE REQUEST INDICATOR	• Must insert "000". • May not be left blank.	128-130	3	Numeric

RETURNED FILE FORMAT

The returned text file is formatted as defined in the following table:

Field Name	Instruction	Position	Field Size	Field Type
SOCIAL SECURITY NUMBER	For security reasons, if the record has a verification code of 2, 3, 4, 6 or is blank, the first five (5) positions will be masked with an "X."	1-9	9	Alphanumeric
LAST NAME	Data identical to input provided by the requester.	10-22	13	Alpha
FIRST NAME	Data identical to input provided by the requester.	23-32	10	Alpha
MIDDLE NAME/INITIAL	Data identical to input provided by the requester.	33-39	7	Alpha
DATE OF BIRTH (MMDDYYYY)	Data identical to input provided by the requester.	40-47	8	Numeric
GENDER CODE	Data identical to input provided by the requester.	48	1	Alpha
CONFIRMATION OR	16-position number assigned to a file submitted after 08/25/07	49-83	35	Alphanumeric

TRACKING NUMBER	or Eight (8)-position number assigned to a file submitted prior to 08/25/07.			
USER CONTROL DATA	Data identical to input provided by the requester.	84-97	14	Alphanumeric
VERIFICATION CODE	Blank = Verified. 1 = SSN not in file (never issued). 2 = Name and DOB match; gender code does not match. 3 = Name and gender code match; DOB does not match. 4 = Name matches; DOB and gender code do not match. 5 = Name does not match; DOB and gender code not checked. 6 = SSN did not verify; other reason.	98	1	Blank or Numeric
PROCESSING CODE 214	Data identical to input provided by the requester.	99-101	3	Numeric
REQUESTER IDENTIFICATION	Data identical to input provided	102-105	4	Alphanumeric

CODE	by the requester.			
MULTIPLE REQUEST INDICATOR	Data identical to input provided by the requester.	106-108	3	Numeric
BLANK	SSA use only.	109-120	12	Blanks
DEATH INDICATOR	Y = SSA records indicate the number holder is deceased. N = SSA records indicate the number holder is not deceased.	121	1	Alpha
BLANK	SSA use only.	122-130	9	Blanks

SSN VERIFICATION RESULTS

On the *SSN Verification Results* web page, a table is displayed with the results for name and SSN verification requests submitted online. In addition, a tally is displayed showing the total number of:

- Records submitted,
- Failed,
- Deceased and
- Verified.

VERIFIED

The SSN submitted for verification matches SSA's records.

- A "blank" *Verification Results* field = a verified SSN.

For security reasons, if the record has a "blank" *Verification Results* field, the first five (5) positions of the SSN will be masked with an "X."

FAILED VERIFICATION

For security reasons, if the record has a verification code of 2, 3, 4 or 6, the first five (5) positions of the SSN will be masked with an "X."

Verification Results Code - The following is the list of FAILED verification codes.

SOCIAL SECURITY NUMBER VERIFICATION SERVICE (SSNVS) HANDBOOK

- 1 = SSN not in file (never issued).

- 2 = Name and DOB match; gender code does not match.

- 3 = Name and gender code match; DOB does not match.

- 4 = Name matches; DOB and gender code do not match.

- 5 = Name does not match; DOB and gender code not checked.

- 6 = SSN did not verify; other reason.

DECEASED (PER SSA RECORDS)

The SSN submitted for verification matches SSA's records, but our records indicate that the individual is deceased.

STATUS AND RETRIEVAL OPTIONS

To view the *Status and Retrieval* web page, select the *View Status and Retrieval Information* link on the *BSO Main Menu* web page. The *Status and Retrieval* web page enables users to view the status of electronic files submitted for overnight processing.

There are three (3) options for checking file status:

Option 1: Confirmation or Tracking Number

To view the status of an individual file:

- Type the 16-position alphanumeric confirmation number or the eight (8)-position alphanumeric tracking number you received when your file was submitted.

- Select the *Submit* button.

Option 2: Date Range

To view the status of all files you submitted within a date range:

- Type the beginning and ending dates into the Range Start Date and Range End Date fields.

    The Date Range must:

    - Contain eight (8) digits in the MMDDYYYY format, where:
        - MM is the month; enter a value 01 through 12.
        - DD is the day; enter a value 01 through 31.
        - YYYY is the year; enter the first two (2) digits of the century followed by a value of 00 through 99.
    - Be within two (2) years of the current date.
    - Not be later than the current date.

- Select the *Submit* button.

Option 3: All Submissions

To view the status of the most recent 100 submissions within the last two (2) years, select the *Submit* button.

If the file you are searching for is not displayed, focus your search by using Option 1 or 2.

STATUS AND RETRIEVAL RESULTS

When your file has been processed, you may download and/or view the results on the *Status and Retrieval Results* web page.

The status and retrieval results are displayed in a table; for a full explanation of each column, click on the column header. This opens a new browser to the *SSNVS Help* web page, which is only accessible when logged into SSNVS.

- For 10 or less SSNs submitted, the results may be downloaded or viewed online.

- For more than 10 SSNs submitted, the results may be downloaded only.

> **NOTE:** *For security reasons, if the record has a verification code of 2, 3, 4, 6 or if the Verification Results field is "blank", the first five (5) positions of the SSN will be masked with an "X".*

If the file is in process or was not processed due to a format error or failed unzip, the *Record Submitted* and *Available Through* fields will be blank.

STATUS	EXPLANATION
AVAILABLE	The file is ready for viewing or downloading.
DOWNLOADED	The file is available and already has been downloaded.
FORMAT OR SURFACE ERRORS	The file was rejected. At least one (1) record in the file did not have the correct length of 130 characters *or* more than 50% of the Name and SSN records in the file failed edits.
FAILED UNZIP	The file either was not compatible with PKZip or contained multiple files.
IN PROCESS	Except for peak submission periods, file results will usually be available the next government business day.
NOT AVAILABLE	The file is more than 30 days old and can no longer be viewed or downloaded. See Available Through explanation below.
UNABLE TO PROCESS- RESUBMIT	The file could not be processed and must be resubmitted.
VIEWED	The file is available and has already been viewed.

Depending on the number of results returned, select the *Download* or *View* link in the *Retrieval Option(s)* column.

RETRIEVAL OPTION(S)	EXPLANATION
DOWNLOAD	Select to download your file results. **IMPORTANT:** You may have to associate the downloaded file with your default text editor *or* save the downloaded file as a text file.
VIEW	Select to view your file results.

| | **NOTE:** This option is available only if there are 10 or less SSNs submitted for verification. |

AVAILABLE THROUGH- Users are able to view or download the results for 30 days from the day they become available. After 30 days and up to two (2) years, users can only view the status of their files. During the period files are available, users can download or view them an unlimited number of times.

Other links that appear on this screen allow you to display context-related help.

WHAT TO DO IF AN SSN FAILS TO VERIFY

Follow these steps for each SSN that failed verification:

1. Compare the failed SSN with your employment records. If you made a typographical error, correct the error and resubmit the corrected data.

2. If your employment records match your submission, ask your employee to check his/her Social Security card and inform you of any name or SSN difference between your records and his/her card. If your employment records are incorrect, correct your records and resubmit the corrected data.

3. If your employment record and the employee's Social Security card match, ask the employee to check with any local SSA Office to resolve the issue. Once the employee has contacted the SSA Office, he/she should inform you of any changes. You should correct your records accordingly and resubmit the corrected data.

4. If the employee is unable to provide a valid SSN, you are encouraged to document your efforts to obtain the correct information. (Documentation should be retained with payroll records for a period of three (3) years.)

5. If you are unable to contact the employee, you are encouraged to document your efforts.

6. If you have already sent a Form W-2 with an incorrect name and/or SSN, then submit a Form W-2c (Corrected Wage and Tax Statement) to correct the mismatch. W-2c services are available through BSO Wage Reporting. There is no need to re-register for your BSO User ID.

Remember
• A mismatch is not a basis, in and of itself, for you to take any adverse action against an employee, such as laying off, suspending, firing or

> discriminating.
>
> - Company policy should be applied consistently to all workers.
>
> - Any employer that uses the failure of the information to match SSA records to take inappropriate adverse action against a worker may violate State or Federal law.
>
> - The information you receive from SSNVS does not make any statement regarding a worker's immigration status.

LOGGING OUT

To log out of SSNVS:

- Select the *Logout* link at the top or bottom of any SSNVS web page.

- The *BSO Logout* web page will display.

- Select *Yes* to exit and return to the *BSO Welcome* web page.

SSNVS NEWS

The SSNVS News web page provides important updates and information regarding SSN verification.

GETTING HELP

HELP LINK

To access the *SSNVS Help* web page, you must be logged into SSNVS. The Help button is in the left hand corner of each SSNVS web page and opens in a new browser window.

CONTACT SSA

You may either speak with or e-mail an SSA representative. To speak with a representative, refer to the Contact Information section at the beginning of this handbook. To e-mail a representative:

- Select the *Contact SSA* link at the top or bottom of any SSNVS web page. This will open the *Contact SSA* web page in a new browser window.

- Select "*Social Security Number Verification Service Support Team*" from the drop-down menu of the Recipient field.

- Enter your message in the Message field. Please be as specific as possible, and include:
    o The question or problem,
    o Web page details (e.g., title, URL, etc.),
    o Any error messages received,
    o A telephone number where we may contact you, and
    o Any other relevant information.

EMPLOYER REPORTING INFORMATION

Visit the Employer Reporting Instructions & Information web page for additional information. Select the *Business Services Online Tutorial* link for an online tour of BSO. You need Adobe Acrobat Reader (version 5.0 or higher recommended) to view the BSO Tutorial. For a free copy of Acrobat Reader, go to www.adobe.com.

MAINTAINING YOUR REGISTRATION INFORMATION

Use the *Account Maintenance* link on the *BSO Main Menu* web page to:

- Update your contact information,

- Change your password, and

- Deactivate your User ID.

These features are described below.

UPDATING YOUR CONTACT INFORMATION

Select the *Update your Registration Information* link on the *Account Maintenance* web page to change or add to the contact information you provided during registration. The e-mail address you provided during registration allows SSA to send you an e-mail notice when it is time to change your password. In addition,

SSA you will receive *BSO News*, which provides important wage and tax reporting updates.

> *NOTE:* The SSN and EIN fields cannot be updated. You must re-register to enter new information in these fields.

CHANGING YOUR PASSWORD

For information on how to change your password, see the section "Changing Your Password" under the REGISTRATION section of this handbook.

DEACTIVATING YOUR USER ID

Select the *Deactivate Your User ID* link from the *Account Maintenance* web page to deactivate your User ID in the event that you leave the company, your User ID is disclosed to an unauthorized party or for any other reason. The prompt User ID deactivation helps to ensure the security of the information you provide to SSA.

If you require help with deactivating your User ID, or if you wish to deactivate an obsolete User ID belonging to another person, call the Employer Reporting Assistance number at the beginning of this handbook.

Deactivating your own User ID does not prevent you from obtaining a new User ID.

GLOSSARY OF TERMS

Activation Code - an alphanumeric value code sent by SSA to the employer or registered User ID holder when access to certain services is requested. This code must be entered on the *Activate Access to BSO Services* web page the first time the user attempts access to the requested service.

Authentication - the act of proving the identity of an individual.

BSO - Business Services Online; a suite of Internet services for businesses and employers to exchange information with SSA.

BSO News - an electronic newsletter that provides important updates and information regarding SSA Business Services Online.

Business Services Online Tutorial - an online training lesson that instructs the user on how to use BSO. It is for employers and submitters who would like to explore the business services available through BSO.

Confirmation Number - a 16-position alphanumeric number used to uniquely identify each name and SSN verification request submitted after 8/25/07.

EIN - Employer Identification Number; a nine (9)-digit number the IRS assigns to an entity to identify businesses as taxpayers.

Electronic File - a specifically formatted file submitted electronically for overnight processing via the *Submit a File for SSN Verification - Submit Your File* web page.

Employer's EIN - the Employer Identification Number of the employer under which wages are to be reported for the names and SSNs being verified.

Employer Reporting Branch (ERB) personnel - SSA employees who serve as the primary telephone answering point for general inquiries received from employers and third-party payroll service providers.

Employee Verification Service (EVS) - EVS matches your record of current or former employee names and SSNs with SSA's records.

IRS - Internal Revenue Service; a United States government agency responsible for tax collection and tax law.

IRES - Integrated Registration Services; the SSA Internet registration application for BSO.

Masking - de-identifying confidential data to safeguard the privacy of client data.

Mismatch - a name and SSN verification request that does not match SSA's records.

Password - a unique combination of eight (8) letters and numbers that must be entered to gain access to BSO.

SSA - Social Security Administration; an independent agency of the United States government that manages the United States' insurance programs, consisting of retirement, disability, survivor benefits and Supplemental Security Income.

SSN - Social Security Number; a unique nine (9)-digit number assigned by SSA to identify an individual when reporting wages, paying taxes and collecting benefits.

SSNVS - Social Security Number Verification Service; an online service provided by SSA that allows registered users to verify employee names and SSNs against SSA's records.

SSNVS News - Provides important updates and information regarding SSN verification.

Third-Party - strictly limited to organizations that contract with employers to either handle the wage reporting responsibilities or perform an administrative function

SOCIAL SECURITY NUMBER VERIFICATION SERVICE (SSNVS) HANDBOOK

directly related to annual wage reporting responsibilities of hired employees.

Tracking Number - an eight (8)-position alphanumeric number used to uniquely identify each name and SSN verification request submitted before 8/25/07.

User Certification Statement - a statement to which a BSO registered user must attest, certifying they have read, understood and agreed to the terms of use for BSO.

User ID - User Identification Number; a unique value issued by SSA to the user at BSO registration that identifies the individual. This value must be entered to gain access to BSO.

Verification - the act or process of establishing the truth, accuracy or reality of something.

APPENDIX A

ADDITIONAL VERIFICATION OPTIONS

Employee Verification Service (EVS)

> **NOTE:** *SSA no longer accepts EVS requests on diskette, cartridge or tape.*

The following instructions are for employers and third-party submitters who wish to submit SSN verification requests to SSA via paper or telephone. EVS requests can be submitted at any time and are processed within 24 hours.

There are three (3) EVS methods to choose from based on the number of employee names/SSNs that you want to verify:

- **1 to 5 Name/SSN Requests**
  - Call our toll-free number for employers, 1-800-772-6270 or the general SSA number at 1-800-772-1213. Both numbers are open for service weekdays from 7:00 a.m. to 7:00 p.m., Eastern Standard Time.
  - You must have the following information for each verification request.
    - Social Security Number
    - Last Name, First Name, Middle Initial
    - Date of Birth (MMDDYYYY)
    - Gender Code (M-Male; F-Female)

- **1 to 50 Name/SSN Requests**
    - Submit on paper to your local SSA office. Your local office will provide you with format and submission instructions. Some offices accept faxed listings. Go to <u>Local Office Search</u> to find your local SSA Office.
    - This listing may be formatted across the web page in a columnar format, such as:

Social Security Number	Last Name	First Name	Middle Initial	Date of Birth	Gender Code

- **50 to 300 Name/SSN Requests**
    - A simple registration process is required for verification requests of more than 50 names/SSNs.
        - Below are the EVS registration instructions for both individual employers and third-party submitters:
            1. Complete the <u>EVS registration form</u>. The company's address should show a street address, city, state and ZIP code. A P.O. Box may be included in the address, but a P.O. Box alone will not be accepted. The registration form must be signed by a manager or authorized official of the company. The title of the signer must follow the signature.
            2. There are two Federal privacy act statements included - one for <u>individual employers</u> and one for <u>third-party submitters</u>. Sign and date the appropriate form. **Keep a copy of your privacy act statement**. You will need to send a copy of the statement with each listing you want verified.
            3. Mail or fax both the registration form and privacy act statement to:
            Social Security Administration
            OCO, DES, EVS
            300 N. Greene Street, 5-E-10 North Building
            Baltimore, Maryland 21290-0300
            Fax (410) 966-3366 or (410) 966-9439
        - Once SSA has processed your registration request, we will mail you a Requester Identification Code. This code

EVS correspondence with SSA concerning a change in address, contact person or telephone number. EVS correspondence should be sent to the address or fax number shown above. If you misplace your Requester Identification Code, call the EVS information line at (410) 965-7140.

o   Instructions for submitting paper listings to SSA for EVS verification.

1. Format your listing to include the following data:

Social Security Number
Last Name, First Name, Middle Initial
Date of Birth (MMDDYYYY)
Gender Code (M-Male; F-Female)

This listing may be formatted across the page in a columnar format, such as:

Social Security Number	Last Name	First Name	Middle Initial	Date of Birth	Gender Code

2. Send the paper listing, your 4-digit Requester Identification Code and **a signed copy of your privacy act statement to**:

Social Security Administration
Wilkes-Barre Data Operations Center
P.O. Box 6500
Wilkes-Barre, PA 18767-6500

> **NOTE:** *Do not send paper listings to Baltimore or your local office with your registration form. Paper listings with 50 to 300 SSNs must be sent to the Wilkes-Barre address above.*

> **NOTE:** *For 300 or more verification requests, please use the Social Security Number Verification Service (SSNVS). For more information see <u>What is SSNVS and BSO?</u> section of this handbook.*

Call the EVS information line, 410-965-7140, if you have questions or need additional information.

What to Do If an SSN Fails to Verify

Each SSN sent in the file will be returned to you with a verification code. If the verification code is blank, the record agrees with SSA's data file. Please annotate your records that this SSN has been verified.

If the verification code is not blank, follow these steps:

3. Ask to see the employee's Social Security card to ensure that the SSN and name were correctly shown on the file.

4. Check to see whether you made a typographical error. If so, correct the data and resend to SSA in a subsequent file. Please resend only the corrected data.

5. If the SSN shown on the card and the file match, ask the employee to check with any SSA Office or call 1-800-772-1213 to determine and correct the problem. Ask the employee to give you the corrected name for your payroll records.

TARRASCO INDICTMENT: INDUCEMENT AND FALSE STATEMENTS

UNITED STATES DISTRICT COURT
FOR THE NORTHERN DISTRICT OF MISSISSIPPI
GREENVILLE DIVISION

UNITED STATES OF AMERICA

V.

CRIMINAL NO. 4:07CR 140
8 U.S.C. § 1324(a)(1)(A)(iv)
18 U.S.C. § 1001

JOSE SANTOS GONZALEZ and
TARRASCO STEEL COMPANY, INC.

INDICTMENT

The Grand Jury charges that:

I.

At all times relevant to this indictment, JOSE SANTOS GONZALEZ and TARRASCO STEEL COMPANY, INC., were engaged in commercial construction. JOSE SANTOS GONZALEZ and TARRASCO STEEL COMPANY, INC., entered into several contracts which had been let under the provisions of the Davis-Bacon Act and subject to supervision by the United States Department of Labor. The Defendants were subcontractors on the construction of critical infrastructure facilities used in interstate commerce, including but not limited to the new Mississippi River bridge at Greenville, Mississippi. Because more than $2,000.00 in federal funds were obligated under that contract, JOSE SANTOS GONZALEZ and TARRASCO STEEL COMPANY INC. were required to submit weekly certified payrolls (Department of Labor Form WH-347 or equivalent) to their prime contractors in order to demonstrate compliance with the Davis-Bacon Act, under the supervision of the Mississippi Department of Transportation and the United States Department of Labor. That certified payroll was required to contain, among other things, the name and address and social security number of each person the defendants employed as a construction worker on the above-mentioned project (designated as "employees" on the form), and, for each worker, the correct work classification, hourly rate of pay, number of daily and weekly hours worked, deductions made, and actual wages paid for the week..

JOSE SANTOS GONZALEZ, and TARRASCO STEEL COMPANY, INC., defendants herein, did in a matter within the jurisdiction of the executive branch of the United States, knowingly and willfully make and use false writings and documents, knowing the same to contain materially false and fraudulent statements and entries. As president of TARRASCO STEEL COMPANY, INC., JOSE SANTOS GONZALEZ signed and certified payrolls knowing that they contained materially false and fraudulent entries, using false and fraudulent social security numbers to conceal the fact that JOSE SANTOS GONZALEZ and TARRASCO STEEL COMPANY, INC., were employing illegal aliens rather than lawfully documented (resident) aliens or United States citizens.

COUNT ONE

From on or about January 1, 2003, until on or about March 29, 2007, in the Northern District of Mississippi, and elsewhere, JOSE SANTOS GONZALEZ and TARRASCO STEEL COMPANY, INC., defendants herein, encouraged and induced illegal aliens to reside in the United States, knowing and in reckless disregard of the fact that such residence was in violation of the law, all for the commercial advantage and private financial gain of the defendants, in that JOSE SANTOS GONZALEZ and TARRASCO STEEL COMPANY, INC., provided employment to a number of illegal aliens, knowing and having reasonable cause to know that as a result of that employment that they would be remaining and residing illegally in the United States, in violation of Title 18 United States Code Section 1324 (a)(1)(A)(iv).

COUNT TWO

The allegations contained in paragraph One are incorporated and alleged herein as if fully set forth herein. On or about March 10, 2007, in the Northern District of Mississippi, JOSE SANTOS GONZALEZ as president of TARRASCO STEEL COMPANY, INC., prepared and signed a certified payroll for submission to Hill Brothers Construction, a prime contractor on the Greenville bridge project. Certifying under penalty of law wages paid to employees for the period of March 4 through March 10, 2007, said certified payroll containing materially false and fraudulent social security numbers to conceal the fact that JOSE SANTOS GONZALES and TARRASCO STEEL COMPANY, INC., were employing illegal aliens rather than lawfully documented (resident) aliens or United States citizens in violation of Title 18 United States Code § 1001.

COUNT THREE

The allegations contained in paragraph One are incorporated and alleged herein as if fully set forth herein. On or about March 17, 2007, in the Northern District of Mississippi, JOSE SANTOS GONZALEZ, as president of TARRASCO STEEL COMPANY, INC., prepared and signed a certified payroll for submission to Hill Brothers, a prime contractor on the Greenville bridge project. Certifying under penalty of law wages paid to employees for the period of March 11 through March 17, 2007, said certified payroll containing materially false and fraudulent social security numbers to conceal the fact that JOSE SANTOS GONZALES and TARRASCO STEEL COMPANY, INC., were employing illegal aliens rather than lawfully documented (resident) aliens or United States citizens in violation of Title 18 United States Code § 1001.

COUNT FOUR

The allegations contained in paragraph One are incorporated and alleged herein as if fully set forth herein. On or about March 10, 2007, in the Northern District of Mississippi, JOSE SANTOS GONZALEZ as president of TARRASCO STEEL COMPANY, INC., prepared and signed a certified payroll for submission to GC Constructors, a prime contractor on the Greenville bridge project. Certifying under penalty of law wages paid to employees for the period of March 4 through March 10, 2007, said certified payroll containing materially false and fraudulent social security numbers to conceal the fact that JOSE SANTOS GONZALES and TARRASCO STEEL COMPANY, INC., were employing illegal aliens rather than lawfully documented (resident) aliens or United States citizens in violation of Title 18 United States Code § 1001.

COUNT FIVE

The allegations contained in paragraph One are incorporated and alleged herein as if fully set forth herein. On or about March 17, 2007, in the Northern District of Mississippi, JOSE SANTOS GONZALEZ as president of TARRASCO STEEL COMPANY, INC., prepared and signed a certified payroll for submission to GC Constructors, a prime contractor on the Greenville bridge project. Certifying under penalty of law wages paid to employees for the period of March 11 through March 17, 2007, said certified payroll containing materially false and fraudulent social security numbers to conceal the fact that JOSE SANTOS GONZALES and TARRASCO STEEL COMPANY, INC., were employing illegal aliens rather than lawfully documented (resident) aliens or United States citizens in violation of Title 18 United States Code § 1001.

COUNT SIX

The allegations contained in paragraph One are incorporated and alleged herein as if fully set forth herein. On or about March 10, 2007, in the Northern District of Mississippi, JOSE SANTOS GONZALEZ as president of TARRASCO STEEL COMPANY, INC., prepared and signed a certified payroll for submission to Jensen Construction, a prime contractor on the Greenville bridge project. Certifying under penalty of law wages paid to employees for the period of March 4 through March 10, 2007, said certified payroll containing materially false and fraudulent social security numbers to conceal the fact that JOSE SANTOS GONZALES and TARRASCO STEEL COMPANY, INC., were employing illegal aliens rather than lawfully documented (resident) aliens or United States citizens in violation of Title 18 United States Code § 1001.

COUNT SEVEN

The allegations contained in paragraph One are incorporated and alleged herein as if fully set forth herein. On or about March 17, 2007, in the Northern District of Mississippi, JOSE SANTOS GONZALEZ as president of TARRASCO STEEL COMPANY, INC., prepared and signed a certified payroll for submission to Jensen Construction, a prime contractor on the Greenville bridge project. Certifying under penalty of law wages paid to employees for the period of March 11 through March 17, 2007, said certified payroll containing materially false and fraudulent social security numbers to conceal the fact that JOSE SANTOS GONZALES and TARRASCO STEEL COMPANY, INC., were employing illegal aliens rather than lawfully documented (resident) aliens or United States citizens in violation of Title 18 United States Code § 1001.

COUNT EIGHT

The allegations contained in paragraph One are incorporated and alleged herein as if fully set forth herein. On or about March 17, 2007, in the Northern District of Mississippi, JOSE SANTOS GONZALEZ as president of TARRASCO STEEL COMPANY, INC., prepared and signed a certified payroll for submission to Austin Bridge, a prime contractor on the Greenville bridge project. Certifying under penalty of law wages paid to employees for the period of March 11 through March 17, 2007, said certified payroll containing materially false and fraudulent social security numbers to conceal the fact that JOSE SANTOS GONZALES and TARRASCO STEEL COMPANY, INC., were employing illegal aliens rather than lawfully documented (resident) aliens or United States citizens in violation of Title 18 United States Code § 1001.

COUNT NINE

The allegations contained in paragraph One are incorporated and alleged herein as if fully set forth herein. On or about March 17, 2007, in the Northern District of Mississippi, JOSE SANTOS GONZALEZ as president of TARRASCO STEEL COMPANY, INC., prepared and signed a certified payroll for submission to Huey P. Long, a prime contractor on the Greenville bridge project. Certifying under penalty of law wages paid to employees for the period of March 11 through March 17, 2007, said certified payroll containing materially false and fraudulent social security numbers to conceal the fact that JOSE SANTOS GONZALES and TARRASCO STEEL COMPANY, INC., were employing illegal aliens rather than lawfully documented (resident) aliens or United States citizens in violation of Title 18 United States Code § 1001.

COUNT TEN

The allegations contained in paragraph One are incorporated and alleged herein as if fully set forth herein. On or about March 10, 2007, in the Northern District of Mississippi, JOSE

SANTOS GONZALEZ as president of TARRASCO STEEL COMPANY, INC., prepared and signed a certified payroll for submission to Massman Construction, a prime contractor on the Greenville bridge project. Certifying under penalty of law wages paid to employees for the period of March 4 through March 10, 2007, said certified payroll containing materially false and fraudulent social security numbers to conceal the fact that JOSE SANTOS GONZALES and TARRASCO STEEL COMPANY, INC., were employing illegal aliens rather than lawfully documented (resident) aliens or United States citizens in violation of Title 18 United States Code § 1001.

FORFEITURE PROVISION

[18 U.S.C. § 982 (a) (6)]

Upon conviction of one or more of the offenses alleged in Count One of this Indictment, defendant(s) JOSE SANTOS GONZALEZ and TARRASCO STEEL COMPANY INC. shall forfeit to the United States pursuant to 18 U.S.C. § 982(a)(6), all conveyances used in the commission of the violation, all property, real and personal, that constitutes or is derived from or is traceable to proceeds obtained directly or indirectly from the commission of the offense, and all property, real or personal, that was used to facilitate, or was intended to be used to facilitate the commission of the offense, including but not limited to the following:

A. **MONEY JUDGMENT**

A sum of money equal to $2,960,227.67 in United States currency, representing the amount of proceeds obtained by defendants from January 1, 2005 to March 29, 2007 as a result of the offenses of bringing in and harboring aliens as prohibited by 8 U.S.C. § 1324 for which the defendants are jointly and severally liable.

B. REAL PROPERTY

Real property located at 190 Oak Drive, Greenville, Washington County Mississippi, which includes all appurtenances and hereditaments thereto, and all improvements, buildings, structures and fixtures thereon, and any proceeds therefrom, described as follows:

1.815 acres, more or less, lying in Section 33, Township 18 North, Range 8 West, Washington County, Mississippi, and more particularly described as follows:

Commencing at the Southwest corner of Section 33, Township 18 North, Range 8 West, Washington County, Mississippi; thence North 00 degrees 30 minutes West 875.0 feet along the West boundary of Section 33 to the **Point of Beginning**; thence continue North 00 degrees 30 minutes West 275.0 feet; thence North 82 degrees East 267.55 feet to the West side of public road; thence South 09 degrees 52 minutes East 272.8 feet along the West side of public road; thence South 82 degrees West 312.35 feet to the **Point of Beginning**.

C. CURRENCY/CHECKS

(1) $169,573.44 seized pursuant to a Seizure Warrant from Regions Bank Account Number 90-0150-3608 held in the name of TARRASCO STEEL COMPANY, INC.;

(2) $26,657.36 seized pursuant to a Seizure Warrant from Regions Bank Account Number 69-0233-3308 held in the name of TARRASCO STEEL COMPANY INC.;

(3) $34,365.29 seized pursuant to a Seizure Warrant from Regions Bank Account Number 69-0238-3402 held in the name of JOSE SANTOS GONZALEZ;

(4) $13,779.30 seized pursuant to a Seizure Warrant from Hill Bros. due to TARRASCO STEEL COMPANY, INC.;

(5) $1,945.93 seized pursuant to a Seizure Warrant from Hill Bros. due to TARRASCO STEEL COMPANY, INC.;

(6) $155,756.22 seized pursuant to a Seizure Warrant from Austin Bridge & Road due to TARRASCO STEEL COMPANY, INC.;

(7) $42,139.59 seized pursuant to a Seizure Warrant from Traylor/Massman due to TARRASCO STEEL COMPANY, INC.;

(8) $13,150.39 seized pursuant to a Seizure Warrant from Jensen Construction due to TARRASCO STEEL COMPANY, INC.

If any of the above-described forfeitable property, as a result of any act or omission of the defendants:

(a) cannot be located upon the exercise of due diligence;

(b) has been transferred or sold to, or deposited with, a third party;

© has been placed beyond the jurisdiction of the court;

(d) has been substantially diminished in value; or

(e) has been commingled with other property which cannot be divided without difficulty;

It is the intent of the United States, pursuant to 18 U.S.C. § 982(b)(1) and 21 U.S.C. § 853(p), to seek forfeiture of any other property of said defendants up to the value of the forfeitable property described above.

A TRUE BILL

/s/ SIGNATURE REDACTED
FOREMAN

UNITED STATES ATTORNEY

WOLNITZEK INFORMATION:
HARBORING FOR COMMERCIAL ADVANTAGE

UNITED STATES DISTRICT COURT
EASTERN DISTRICT OF KENTUCKY
NORTHERN/~~CENTRAL~~ DIVISION
COVINGTON

UNITED STATES OF AMERICA

V. INFORMATION NO. 07-85-DCR

JEFFREY W. WOLNITZEK
and SPECTRUM INTERIORS, INC.

* * * * *

THE ATTORNEY GENERAL CHARGES:

COUNT 1
8 U.S.C. § 1324(a)(1)(A)(v)(I)

On or about May 5, 2006, in Kenton County, in the Eastern District of Kentucky,

JEFFREY W. WOLNITZEK

and others, conspired to conceal, harbor, and shield aliens from detection in any place, knowing and in reckless disregard of the fact that such aliens had come to, entered, and remained in the United States in violation of the law, for the purpose of commercial advantage and private financial gain in violation of 8 U.S.C. §§ 1324(a)(1)(A)(iii) and (A)(1)(B)(I), all in violation of 8 U.S.C. § 1324(a)(1)(A)(v)(I).

COUNT 2
8 U.S.C. § 1324(a)(1)(A)(iii)

From on or about August 2002 through on or about November 28, 2006, in Boone and Kenton Counties, in the Eastern District of Kentucky, and elsewhere

SPECTRUM INTERIORS, INC.

and others, aiding and abetting each other, did conceal, harbor, and shield aliens from detection in any place, knowing and in reckless disregard of the fact that such aliens had come to, entered, and remained in the United States in violation of the law, for the purpose of commercial advantage and private financial gain in violation of 8 U.S.C. § 1324(a)(1)(B)(I), all in violation of 8 U.S.C. §§ 1324(a)(1)(A)(iii) and (a)(1)(A)(v)(II).

COUNT 3
8 U.S.C. § 1324(b)

In committing the violations alleged in Counts 1 and 2, the defendants,

**JEFFREY W. WOLNITZEK, JR.
and SPECTRUM INTERIORS, INC.**

shall forfeit to the United States, all right, title, and interest, in the following assets:

MONEY JUDGMENT:

$2,000,000.00 (Two Million Dollars) in United States currency, in that such sum in aggregate is property which constitutes, or is derived from or is traceable to the proceeds obtained directly or indirectly from the commission of the offenses, for which the defendants are joint and severally liable.

By virtue of the commission of the felony offenses charged in Counts 1 and 2 of this information, any and all interest the defendants have in the above-described property is vested in the United States and hereby forfeited to the United States pursuant to 8 U.S.C. § 1324(b).

Substitute Assets

If any of the above-described forfeitable property, as a result of any act or omission of the defendants,

> (1) cannot be located upon the exercise of due diligence;
>
> (2) has been transferred or sold to, or deposited with, a third person;
>
> (3) has been placed beyond the jurisdiction of the Court;
>
> (4) has been substantially diminished in value; or
>
> (5) has been commingled with other property which cannot be subdivided without difficulty:

it is the intent of the United States, pursuant to 21 U.S.C. § 853(p) as incorporated in 28 U.S.C. § 2461, to seek forfeiture of any other property of said defendants up to the value of the above forfeitable property.

AMUL R. THAPAR
UNITED STATES ATTORNEY

PEREYRA-GABINO ORDER: CONCEALING/SHIELDING

IN THE UNITED STATES DISTRICT COURT
FOR THE SOUTHERN DISTRICT OF IOWA

UNITED STATES OF AMERICA,	)	
	)	Criminal No. 4:07-CR-088
Plaintiff,	)	
	)	
vs.	)	
	)	ORDER
BRAULIO PEREYRA-GABINO,	)	
	)	
Defendant.	)	

THE COURT HAS BEFORE IT defendant Braulio Pereyra-Gabino's second motion to dismiss, filed November 8, 2007, and third motion to dismiss filed November 9, 2007. The United States resisted both motions on November 21, 2007.[1] The motions are now considered fully submitted.

I.   BACKGROUND

Defendant Braulio Pereyra-Gabino is charged under the present indictment with one count of concealing and shielding from detection and attempting to conceal and shield from detection aliens who defendant knew or acted with reckless disregard of the fact were in the United States in violation of 8 U.S.C. §1324(a)(1)(A)(iii) and (v)(II) and (B).

On August 2, 2007, Pereyra-Gabino filed his first motion to dismiss, arguing that the

---

[1] An *Amicus Curiae* Brief was filed by the United Food and Commercial Workers International Union in Support of Pereyra-Gabino's Third Motion to Dismiss on December 12, 2007.

present indictment was (1) duplicitous in violation of the Due Process Clause of the Fifth Amendment and the right to a unanimous jury verdict under the Sixth Amendment of the United States Constitution; and (2) impermissibly vague in violation of the Due Process Clause of the Fifth Amendment of the United States Constitution. On September 28, 2007, this Court denied Pereyra-Gabino's first motion and ordered the Government to produce a bill of particulars identifying each alien that is at issue. On October 5, 2007 the Government produced a bill of particulars in response to the Court's Order.

In his second motion to dismiss, Pereyra-Gabino: (1) renews his argument that the present indictment is duplicitous in violation of the Due Process Clause of the Fifth Amendment and the right to a unanimous jury verdict under the Sixth Amendment; and (2) argues that the Indictment fails to ensure defendant will be prosecuted only on the basis of the crime charged by the grand jury in violation of the Fifth Amendment. In his third motion to dismiss, Pereyra-Gabino argues that the Government's theory of prosecution in this case violates his right to freedom of speech under the First Amendment. Each argument is considered below.

II. APPLICABLE LAW AND DISCUSSION

A. Aiding and abetting liability under 8 U.S.C. §1324(a)(1)(A)(v)(ii)

As a preliminary matter, the Court finds it necessary to first address the issue of whether Pereyra-Gabino has been properly charged as an aider and abettor under 8 U.S.C. § 1324 (a)(1)(A)(v)(ii).[2] On its face, the indictment charges Pereyra-Gabino as both a principal (under

---

[2] While the issue has not been explicitly raised by the parties, it is clearly a point of dispute and confusion. Pereyra-Gabino argues that "Mr. Pereyra is charged as a principal, not under a theory of aiding and abetting," Def. Br. at 3-4 (D.I. 25), while the Government has

§1324(a)(1)(A)(iii)) and as an aider and abettor (under §1324(a)(1)(A)(v)(ii)). As discussed below, the Court is concerned with the charge itself, and with the Government's characterization of the charge in its pleadings.

For example, in its Bill of Particulars the Government states:

> The government restates that defendant is also charged as aiding and abetting the concealment of identity under Title 8, United States Code § 1324(a)(1)(A)(iii) and (v)II. *The Spanish language workers would be those defendant would be aiding and abetting.*

Bill of Particulars at 1 (emphasis added). Along the same lines, neither the indictment nor the Government's pleadings have identified a person(s) who Pereyra-Gabino aided and abetted in the act of concealment. Judging from these facts, it appears to this Court that Pereyra-Gabino has been charged with aiding and abetting the alleged criminal conduct of *the illegal aliens themselves.* While such a charge may be warranted, the Government is cautioned that 8 U.S.C. § 1324, the only statute under which Pereyra-Gabino is charged, *does not permit such a charge.*

8 U.S.C. § 1324(a)(1)(A)(iii) extends criminal liability to any person who "conceals, harbors, or shields [an illegal alien] from detection." It is clear from the language of the statute that this provision (and the statute in general) seeks to punish the conduct of a person who somehow assists an illegal alien(s), *not the conduct of the illegal alien(s) himself.* Under the terms of the statute, an illegal alien cannot harbor, conceal, or shield himself from detection. *See United States v. One 48 Ft. White Colored Sailboat Named Libertine*, 24 F. Supp. 2d 174, 180 (D.P.R. 1998) (interpreting 8 U.S.C. §1324(a)(1)(A)(I), noting that "one cannot 'bring' oneself in within the meaning of the statute."). It logically follows that, *under the statute at issue*, a

---

repeatedly emphasized that Pereyra-Gabino is charged as both a principal *and* as an aider and abettor.

person cannot be guilty of aiding and abetting the conduct of the illegal alien(s) either.[3] If that is the Government's theory, it is charged incorrectly and the Government is cautioned that it faces the prospect of having this portion of the indictment dismissed.[4]

B. The Government's Bill of Particulars

In its September 28, 2007 Order, this Court declined to dismiss the indictment and ordered the Government "to provide Pereyra-Gabino with a bill of particulars identifying *each alien* that he is charged with shielding or attempting to shield from detection." September 28, 2007 Order at 5 (emphasis added). The Government responded by producing a bill of particulars on October 5, 2007.

As Pereyra-Gabino points out, the Government's bill of particulars is not a model of clarity. Attached to its bill, the Government included a list of participants at the August 21, 2006 orientation process at the Swift plant in Marshalltown, Iowa. It identifies the named "Spanish language workers" on that list as the aliens with respect to whom the Government will offer evidence. The bill further states that "several individual aliens" have "cooperated with the government regarding their Swift employment and the activity of Pereyra-Gabino." Bill of Particulars at 2. According to the bill, this group "includes" seven individuals who are identified

---

[3] 8 U.S.C. § 1324(a)(1)(A)(v)(ii) extends the same criminal liability to any person who "aids and abets the commission of any of the *preceding acts*." Liability for "aiding and abetting" under the statute is, therefore, very specific. In this case, the "preceding acts" at issue would be the act of harboring, concealing, or shielding from detection, acts which *cannot* be committed by the alien(s) himself. The Government did not charge Pereyra-Gabino with general aiding and abetting under 18 U.S.C. §2.

[4] In the alternative, of course, the Government can voluntarily dismiss the charge of aiding and abetting under 8 U.S.C. § 1324(a)(1)(A)(v)(ii).

by name. *Id.* Finally, the bill states that "[v]arious individual workers would . . . rent apartments from Pereyra-Gabino," yet names only Jorge Talavera-Lopez as such an individual. *Id.*

While the Government has complied in spirit with the Court's September 28, 2007 Order, its bill of particulars is drafted in such a way to permit being read as exemplary and not restrictive. The Court's September 28, 2007 Order was clear however (identify "each alien"), and the Government's list of aliens has to "meaningfully restrict the government in order to fulfill the purpose of the bill of particulars." *United States v. Germain*, 33 Fed. Appx. 565, 566 (2nd Cir. 2002). Accordingly, for purposes of the trial, the aliens at issue are limited to those individuals identified by name on the orientation list and those specifically named in the bill. *See id.* (once the Government has responded with a bill of particulars it is "strictly limited to proving what it has set forth in it.").[5]

C. Second Motion to Dismiss

1. Duplicity

Pereyra-Gabino renews his argument that the indictment remains duplicitous and vague, as it fails to designate a specific alien that the defendant shielded or attempted to shield. Def. Br. at 2 (D.I. 25). As stated in the Court's previous Order, a duplicitous count does not necessarily

---

[5] While the Government may need only to prove illegal conduct with respect to one alien in order to prove the offense charged, *see United States v. Calhelha*, 456 F. Supp. 2d 350, 366 (D. Conn. 2006), in the event that Pereyra-Gabino is convicted, the Government can attempt to establish at sentencing that his offense involved a larger number of aliens than the number identified in the bill of particulars. *See United States v. Shan Wei Yu*, 484 F.3d 979, 986 (8th Cir. 2007) (upholding the upward departure in sentencing based on district court's factual conclusion that the offense involved "substantially more than 100 illegal aliens.").

render an indictment defective. *See* Order at 2-3 and accompanying case law. The Government has identified a finite number of individuals in its bill of particulars, and its proof at trial is limited to those persons. As the Court has already counseled, it "will draft the verdict forms in such a manner as to ensure that Mr. Pereyra-Gabino's right to a unanimous jury verdict is adequately protected." *Id.* at 3.[6]

2. Fifth Amendment right to be charged by Grand Jury

Pereyra-Gabino argues that "[t]he indictment with Bill of Particulars fails to ensure Defendant will not be prosecuted for a crime other than what was charged by the grand jury." Def. Br. at 3 (D.I. 25). In addition, Pereyra-Gabino argues that identification at this point of the alien(s) who were concealed and/or shielded from detection amounts to a constructive amendment of the indictment. This Court disagrees.

"Typically an indictment is not sufficient only if an essential element of the offense is omitted from it." *United States v. Hance*, 501 F.3d 900, 906(8th Cir. 2007) (internal citation omitted). As noted in the Court's previous order, the "essential elements" of a violation of 8 U.S.C. §1324(a)(1)(A)(iii) are that the defendant: (1) harbored, concealed, or shielded from detection (2) an illegal alien (3) with knowledge of or with reckless disregard for the alien's unlawful presence in the United States. *United States v. Wang*, 964 F.2d 811, 813-14 (8th Cir.

---

[6] The Court finds that Pereyra-Gabino's concerns with adequate notice and double jeopardy have been adequately addressed by the indictment and the Government's bill of particulars. *See* Order at 4-5. From a practical perspective, this case is peculiar and a reverse from what is typical. Pereyra-Gabino is effectively asking the Government to re-indict him with a *multiple count* indictment naming each individual alien rather than proceed with the indictment as it currently exists as a single count indictment.

1992). Each of these elements are contained in the present indictment. The identity of the alien(s) at issue *is not* an essential element of the offense under 8 U.S.C. §1324(a)(1)(A)(iii). *United States v. Calhelha*, 456 F. Supp. 2d 350, 364 (D. Conn. 2006) ("[T]he statutory provisions at issue do not require specific identification of aliens."); *United States v. Powell*, 498 F.2d 890, 892 (9th Cir. 1974) ("Nothing in the statute requires identification by name."). The indictment reflects that the Grand Jury found probable cause to believe that Pereyra-Gabino had concealed and/or shielded an illegal alien (in this case illegal aliens) from detection.[7]

"A constructive amendment occurs when the *essential elements* of the offense as charged in the indictment are altered in such a manner - often through the evidence presented at trial or the jury instructions - that the jury is allowed to convict the defendant of an offense different from or in addition to the offenses charged in the indictment." *United States v. Whirlwind Soldier*, 499 F.3d 862, 870 (8th Cir. 2007) (emphasis added). Similar to the discussion above, the Government's identification of the aliens for which it will offer evidence does not alter the essential elements of the offense.[8] Pereyra-Gabino's second motion to dismiss is denied.

---

[7] In the alternative, the Government could have charged Pereyra-Gabino with concealing and shielding from detection an unnamed "alien" as opposed to "aliens." In that case, Pereyra-Gabino would be in the same situation he finds himself - that is, claiming that he does not know who that alien is or whether the grand jury considered facts related to that alien.

[8] It would perhaps be a different scenario if the Government had chosen to identify the aliens at issue in the indictment itself. If that were the case, then naming aliens *in addition* to those named in the indictment would broaden the indictment beyond that which the Grand Jury considered, even though the identity of the alien would not otherwise be an element of the offense. *See United States v. Robles-Vertiz*, 155 F.3d 725, 729 (5th Cir. 1998). Pereyra-Gabino's real argument is that the indictment itself is too broad, not that the Government or the Court somehow broadened the indictment beyond what was charged. This Court addressed the breadth of the charging document in its September 28, 2007 Order and ordered a bill of particulars, in part, to "to inform the defendant of the nature of the charges against him and to prevent or minimize the element of surprise at trial."

D. Third Motion to Dismiss Indictment

In his Third Motion to Dismiss, Pereyra-Gabino argues that "the Government's theory of prosecution in this case, based on the protected speech of the Defendant, violates Mr. Pereyra's Right to Freedom of Speech, as guaranteed by the First Amendment." Def. Mot. at 2 (D.I. 26). The Court finds it unnecessary, at this stage in the litigation, to discuss the merits of the parties' positions on this issue other than to note that it agrees with Pereyra-Gabino that there are significant First Amendment concerns raised by this indictment and the record thus far. The Court finds, however, that it is inappropriate to rule on the motion until the Government's evidence has been presented. Pereyra-Gabino's third motion to dismiss, therefore, is denied.[9]

---

[9] Pereyra-Gabino can, of course, renew his motion to dismiss on First Amendment grounds at the close of the evidence, at which point the full parameters of his conduct can be understood. The *Amicus Brief* filed in Support of Pereyra-Gabino's motion, while scholarly and well-researched, was ill-timed as the record has not been fully developed.

III. CONCLUSION

For the reasons outlined above, Pereyra-Gabino's second and third motions to dismiss are denied.

IT IS ORDERED.

Dated this 21th day of December, 2007.

RONALD E. LONGSTAFF, Senior Judge
United States District Court

SUBJECT-MATTER INDEX

A

acquisitions, *see* Mergers and acquisitions

adjustment of status
unauthorized employment, consequences of, 27

antidiscrimination provisions, *see* Discrimination

Arizona legislation
employment verification and related laws, 233, 282–83, 296, 398

Arkansas legislation
affecting government contractors, 274–75, 287

asylees
employment verification, 221–22

attorneys
ethical issues in representing employer
ICE worksite investigations, 49–56
internal investigations, 445–48

audits, internal, *see* I-9 form and compliance

B

B-1 / B-2 nonimmigrants
risks of improper classification, 219

background checks
I-9 compliance, 242

Basic Pilot Program, *see* E-Verify Program

best practices
checklists and bullet points, 322–30
IMAGE, *see* IMAGE program
Wal-Mart model, 339–40
consent decree, 333–38

Bono Amendment
correction of technical infractions and "good-faith compliance" defense, 212–15

C

citizenship discrimination, *see* Discrimination

civil fines, *see* Sanctions

civil RICO actions, *see* Racketeer Influenced and Corrupt Organizations Act

Colorado legislation
employment verification and related laws, 64–66, 233, 275–76, 279, 281–82, 288, 293, 297, 396

compliance, *see* I-9 form and compliance

constructive knowledge
Generally, 374, 399–403
appearance or accent, impermissible inference, 272
bases for ICE investigation, 181–82
case examples, 400–402
DHS final rule, 402–03
E-Verify program, concerns raised by, 18
independent contractors, 31, 58–59
interpretation under IRCA, 5–6
labor certification, filing of, 50–52
personal liability of corporation's agent, 72–73
Social Security no-match letters, 8–9, 62–64, 188, 190–91, 193–94, 196, 197–98, 373
subcontractors, 399
unlawful hiring, constructive knowledge sufficient for RICO predicate act, 303–04

criminal penalties
Generally, 101–11, 211–12, 377, 392
false statements
on I-9 form, 26–27
Tarrasco indictment, 621–29
forfeiture, 107–08, 425
good faith, 109–10
harboring, 101–05, 423–24
case law examples, 393–94
Pereyra-Gabino order on motion to dismiss indictment, 635–43
as RICO predicate act, 103, 302–03, 418–19
Tarrasco indictment, 621–29
Wolnitzek information, 631–33
identity theft, aiding and abetting, 425
IRCA misdemeanor violations, 422
misdemeanors under INA §274A, 108–09
money laundering, 105–07, 424
prosecutorial discretion, 109
punitive aspects of civil enforcement, difficult to distinguish from criminal enforcement, 168–76
summary of penalties, 70–74
trend toward criminal sanctions, 13–15, 317
unlawful hiring, 422
as RICO predicate act, 303–04
who can be charged, 426

D

databases
see also E-Verify program; IMAGE program; Social Security Number Verification System
merger of immigration and criminal databases, unreliability of data, 145–50
National Crime Information Center (NCIC) database, 146

debarment
from federal procurement programs, 427
from H-1B or PERM program, 51, 245–46
for violation of Missouri law, 276, 290

discrimination *(citizenship- or national origin–based)*
August 2007 no-match regulation, concerns, 196–97
burden of proof, 217–18
contact information, 33
employer sanctions as cause, GAO report, 38
IRCA antidiscrimination provisions, 10–11, 272
Office of Special Counsel responsibilities, 416
pre-employment inquiries, 220–21
procedures for filing complaint, 417

documentation, *see* I-9 form and compliance

driver's licenses
REAL ID Act, generally, 24–25
state legislation, 25

due diligence, *see* Mergers and acquisitions

E

E-Verify program
Generally, 16–17, 129–31, 222–23, 231–38, 378–79, 413–14
compared to SSNVS, 29
considerations before using, 235
contact information, 32
emerging issues, 235–37
judicial analysis, 237
political aspects
expiration and extension, 238
future of program, 21
push for enrollment, 233–35
Yale-Loehr congressional testimony, 39–40
procedure, 17–18, 231–32
state-level requirements, 233
timeliness and accuracy, 18–19
USCIS publications
Fact Sheet, 581
Q & A for employers, 583–85
weaknesses, 20

employees
see also Independent contractors and subcontractors
centralization of authority to verify employment, 218
definition of, 206–07, 271
personal liability, 12, 70–73

employment authorization
see also I-9 form and compliance; Verification of employment authorization
expiration, 360–62
interim authorization for H-1Bs and L-1s, 220
internal tracking, sample spreadsheet, 461

employment verification, *see* Verification of employment authorization

enforcement, *see* Worksite enforcement

ethics, *see* Attorneys

F

false statements, *see* Criminal penalties
fines, *see* Criminal penalties; Sanctions
forfeiture
civil, *see* Sanctions
criminal, *see* Criminal penalties

Fourth Amendment
defective warrants, litigation, 150–60
privacy expectations and immigration raids, 113–77

Fresh Del Monte Produce
worksite enforcement action, 59

G

Garcia Labor Companies
worksite enforcement action, 61, 395

George's Processing Inc.
worksite enforcement action, 59–60

Georgia legislation
employment verification and related laws, 22, 64–66, 233, 275–76, 289, 396

Getahun v. OCAHO
employment verification of asylees, 221–22

Golden State Fence Company
worksite enforcement action, 90, 395

good faith, *see* I-9 form and compliance

H

H-1B nonimmigrants
  classification as independent contractors improper, 219
  interim employment authorization
    240- and 90-day rules, 220
    porting employees, 220, 363

handbooks
  Guide to Selected U.S. Travel and Identity Documents (ICE), 545–67
  Handbook for Employers: Instructions for Completing the Form I-9 (USCIS)
    full text, 497–543
    summary, 381–86, 411–12
  Social Security Number Verification System Handbook (SSA), 587–620

harboring, *see* Criminal penalties

Hazelton (PA) ordinances
  challenges, 160–68

Hoffman Plastic
  impact, 417–18

HV CONNECT, Inc.
  worksite enforcement action, 60

I

I-9 form and compliance
  Generally, 199–200, 203–24, 270–73
  basic requirements, 206–07, 226–27
  checklist for compliance, 410
  completing form
    common mistakes, 68–70
    corrections, 372
  documentation
    expired documents, 366
    lost documents, presentation of receipts, 207–08, 368–70
    number and type required, 215–17, 351, 365–66, 381–82, 527–28
      illustrations and descriptions, 352–56, 529–38, 545–67
      photocopying and scanning documents, 210, 227
  electronic I-9s, *see subhead:* Storage and retention *[in this heading]*
  elements of a compliance program, 206–12, 225, 427
  FAQs for employers, 28–32, 360–62, 364–71, 381–86
  goals in developing compliance program, 410
  good faith, 9, 74, 205, 212–15
    avoiding criminal prosecution, 109–10
    Bono Amendment, 212–15
    substantive vs. technical/procedural failures, comparison chart, 387
    USCIS interim guidelines, 569–79
  inspections (ICE), *see* Worksite enforcement
  internal audits
    advisability, 30–31, 97–98, 200, 222
    checklist, 341–48
    ethical obligations of counsel, 52–53
    sample report, 459
    sample spreadsheet, 461
    structure and practice tips, 66–68, 68–70
  internal investigations, *see* Investigations
  introduction under IRCA, 4–5, 203–04
  mergers and acquisitions, *see* Mergers and acquisitions
  misrepresentations
    effect on continued employment, 29–30
    as violations of law, 26–27
  penalties and fines, *see* Criminal penalties; Sanctions
  practice pointers, 218–22, 349–79
  recruiter obligations, 32
  rehires, 210
  reverification obligation, 6–7, 208, 219–20
  revision of form by DHS, 12–13, 350–51, 381–86
  staffing, centralization of authority to verify employment, 218
  storage and retention, 208–09, 371
    centralization of storage, 219
    electronic I-9 storage, 15–16, 33, 209, 228–31
  tools for compliance, 227–44
    background checks, 242
    citizenship requirements, 242–43
    E-Verify, *see* E-Verify program
    electronic I-9s, *see subhead:* Storage and retention *[in this heading]*
    IMAGE, *see* IMAGE program
    Social Security number trace services, 242
    SSNVS, *see* Social Security Number Verification System
  transferred employees, 208
  USCIS's *Handbook for Employers: Instructions for Completing the Form I-9*
    full text, 497–543
    summary, 381–86, 411–12

ICE Mutual Agreement between Government and Employers, *see* IMAGE program

ICE raids
  see Worksite enforcement

Idaho legislation
employment verification and related laws, 396

identity documents
see also I-9 form and compliance, *subhead:* Documents
Guide to Selected U.S. Travel and Identity Documents (ICE), 545–67

identity theft, *see* Criminal penalties

IFCO Systems
worksite enforcement action, 7, 27, 61

Illinois legislation
employment verification and related laws, 282–84, 297, 398

IMAGE program
Generally, 22–23, 131–32, 222–23, 238–43, 414–15
best hiring practices, 239–41, 415–16
contact information, 33

Immigration Reform and Control Act of 1986 (IRCA)
Generally, 3–33, 203–04
employee issues, 24–27
employer responsibilities under IRCA, 4–12
FAQs from employers, 28–32
misdemeanor violations, *see* Criminal penalties
personal liability, 12
recent developments, 12–24
Yale-Loehr congressional testimony, 36–37

independent contractors and subcontractors
Generally, 31
contract language, 98
determination of, 271
due diligence questions for acquiring companies, 260
vs. employees, 58–59
good-faith compliance efforts, 109–10
"knowing" hiring violations through contract, 210–11, 399
risks of mislabeling, 219
Wal-Mart best practices model, 339–40
consent decree, 333–38

interim employment authorization, *see* Employment authorization

internal audits, *see* I-9 form

investigations, internal
see also Worksite enforcement, *subhead:* Investigations (ICE)
ethical considerations, 445–48
post–ICE raid investigations, practical pointers, 429–31

questions for company executive officer, 449–51
questions for hiring manager, 453–54

IRCA, *see* Immigration Reform and Control Act of 1986

J

Jones Industrial Network
worksite enforcement action, 60

Jordan Commission
Yale-Loehr congressional testimony, 38–39

K

Katz v. U.S.
privacy expectations and immigration raids, 113–77

Kentucky Limited Liability Corporations
worksite enforcement action, 61

"knowing" employment
interpretation under IRCA, 5–6

Koch Foods
worksite enforcement action, 59, 394

L

L nonimmigrants
classification as independent contractors improper, 219
interim employment authorization, 220

labor certifications
ethical issues, 49–52

local laws, *see* State and local legislation; Worksite enforcement; *specific localities*

Louisiana legislation
verification of employment authorization, 282–84, 298

M

mergers and acquisitions
basics of corporate transactions, 254
due diligence
definition, 245
identification of immigration compliance issues, 245–52, 256–57
post–due diligence options and considerations, 257–59
I-9 compliance issues, generally, 253–61
questionnaire and checklists, 262–67
retention of I-9s, potential liability, 32, 371
target company, representation of, 260

Michael Bianco, Inc.
worksite enforcement action, 60, 395

Missouri legislation
affecting government-aid recipients, 279–81, 294
affecting government contractors, 276–77, 290

Mohawk Industries
RICO litigation, 307–09

money laundering, *see* Criminal penalties

N

National Crime Information Center (NCIC), *see* Databases

National Fugitive Operations Program (NFOP)
establishment of ICE program, 145–50

national origin discrimination, *see* Discrimination

"no match" letters
Generally, 7–9, 132–33, 187–201
August 2007 safe harbor rule (72 FR 45611)
   discrimination concerns, 196–97
   employer obligations and procedures, 8, 31–32, 62–64, 190–96, 374–75, 403–07
   litigation against rule, 8–9, 63–64, 193–96, 205, 373, 409
   penalties, 408
use of SSN Verification System, 198–99

O

Oklahoma legislation
employment verification and related laws, 233, 276–78, 291, 397

"Operation Return to Sender"
home ICE raids, 144–60

"Operation Wagon Train," *see* Swift & Company

P

penalties, *see* Criminal penalties; Sanctions

Pennsylvania legislation
affecting government-aid recipients, 278–79, 295

Pereyra-Gabino
order on motion to dismiss harboring indictment, 635–43

privacy expectations
ICE raids, 113–77

Q

Quality Service Integrity, Inc.
worksite enforcement action, 60, 394

R

Racketeer Influenced and Corrupt Organizations Act (RICO)
applicability to immigration offenses, 95–97, 301–11, 426
harboring as predicate act, 103, 302–03, 418–19
precautions when conducting internal audit, 341
unlawful hiring as predicate act, 303–04

raids, *see* Worksite enforcement, *subhead:* ICE raids

REAL ID Act
driver's license applications, 24–25
state legislation in response to, 25

recruiters
I-9 obligations, 32
vs. smugglers, 73

reverification, *see* I-9 form and compliance

RICO, *see* Racketeer Influenced and Corrupt Organizations Act

Rosenbaum-Cunningham International
worksite enforcement action, 60

S

safe harbor, *see* "No match" letters, *subhead:* August 2007 DHS rule

sanctions
civil fines, 13–14, 211–12, 372
civil forfeiture, 107–08
cooperative efforts between businesses and government, caveats, 77–99
criminal penalties, *see* Criminal penalties
debarment, *see* Debarment
personal liability of agent, 12, 70–73
precautions when conducting internal audit, 341
Yale-Loehr congressional testimony, 35–47
   Basic Pilot Program, 39–40
   history of sanctions, 36–39
   recommendations, 43–46
   systemic problems, 40–43

Sarbanes-Oxley Act
due diligence issues, 247

Social Security Administration (SSA)
  contact information, 33
  E-Verify, *see* E-Verify program
  information sharing with ICE, 7–8
  Social Security numbers (SSNs)
    "no match" letters, *see* "No match" letters
    not required for employment, 30, 199, 383
    SSN Verification System, *see* Social Security Number Verification System
    trace searches, 242

Social Security Number Verification System (SSNVS)
  Generally, 23–24, 241–43, 413
  alternatives, 242–43
  compared to E-Verify, 29
  limitations on use, 241
  penalties for misuse, 242
  SSNVS Handbook (SSA), 587–620
  timing, 29
  usage in light of August 2007 no-match safe-harbor regulation, 198–99

state and local legislation
  see also specific states and localities
  employment eligibility verification, 64–66, 269–300, 396–98
    E-Verify implementation, 21–22, 233
    government-aid recipients, state law affecting, 278–81, 293–95
    government contractors, state law affecting, 274–78, 287–92
  future of local immigration raids, 160–68
  joint resolution opposing REAL ID Act, 25
  local ordinances, list of, 269

Stucco Design, Inc.
  worksite enforcement action, 61

subcontractors, *see* Independent contractors and subcontractors

successor corporations, *see* Mergers and acquisitions

Sun Drywall and Stucco, Inc.
  worksite enforcement action, 395

Swift & Company
  worksite enforcement actions (Operation Wagon Train), 4, 20, 60, 91, 124–44

T

Tarrasco Steel
  indictment, 621–29
  worksite enforcement action, 60

temporary protected status (TPS)
  automatic extensions, 367

Tennessee legislation
  employment verification and related laws, 233, 276–78, 282–83, 292, 299, 398

Texas legislation
  timeline, 392–93
  verification of employment authorization affecting government-aid recipients, 278–79, 295

travel documents
  see also I-9 form and compliance, *subhead:* Documents
  Guide to Selected U.S. Travel and Identity Documents (ICE), 545–67

Tyson Foods
  RICO litigation, 305–06, 309–11
  worksite enforcement action, 85–89

U

unfair employment practices, *see* Discrimination

unlawful hiring, *see* Criminal penalties

U.S. Immigration and Customs Enforcement (ICE)
  see also Worksite enforcement
  ICE Mutual Agreement between Government and Employers, *see* IMAGE program
  information sharing with SSA, 7–8

Utah legislation
  driver's licenses, 25

V

verification of employment authorization
  see also I-9 form and compliance
  Generally, 16–24
  asylees, 221–22
  E-Verify, *see* E-Verify program
  IMAGE, *see* IMAGE program
  independent contractors, *see* Independent contractors and subcontractors
  Jordan Commission, 38–39
  legislation, *see* State and local legislation; *specific states and localities*
  recommendations, Yale-Loehr congressional testimony, 43–47
  SSN Verification System, *see* Social Security Number Verification System
  technical and procedural infractions, 212–15
    comparison chart, 387

Visa Waiver nonimmigrants
risks of improper classification, 219

W

Wal-Mart
best practices model, 339–40
consent decree, 333–38
worksite enforcement action, 88–89

West Virginia legislation
employment verification and related laws, 282–84, 300, 397

Wolnitzek and Spectrum Interiors
harboring for commercial advantage, criminal information, 631–33

work authorization, *see* Employment authorization; I-9 form and compliance; Verification of employment authorization

worksite enforcement
Generally, 57–75
April 2006 ICE initiative, 58–62
businesses' cooperation with government, caveats, 77–99
ICE raids
Generally, 179–85
counseling employers and/or workers, 184–85
ethical considerations, 53–55
criticisms, 27
home ICE raids, "Operation Return to Sender," 144–60
post-raid internal investigation, 429–31
as pretext for criminal enforcement, 138–40, 157–59
privacy expectation, 113–77
warrants and scope of ICE powers, 133–44, 182–83
inspections, 52–53, 208–09
ICE forms and sample notices
Business Entity Questionnaire, 469
Employee Information Certification Form, 471
How to Prepare for an ICE Business Inspection, 467
Notice of Inspection, 463–64, 465–66
Notice of Intent to Fine, 483–94
Notice of Suspect Documents, 479–80
Notice of Unauthorized Aliens, 481–82
subpoenas, 473, 475–77
representing employers
checklist, 457
instructions to client, 455
key issues, 437–41
outline, 443–44
investigations (ICE), 179–82
see also Investigations, internal
ethical issues in representing employers, 49–56
internal investigations, *see* Investigations
local immigration raids, future of, 160–68
practice tips for employers, 61–62
punitive aspects of civil enforcement, difficult to distinguish from criminal enforcement, 168–76
specific enforcement actions, 4, 7, 20, 27, 59–61, 84–91, 124–44, 394–95
state and local legislation, *see* State and local legislation; *specific states and localities*
statistics, 376–77, 390–91

Y–Z

Yale-Loehr, Stephen
congressional testimony on employer sanctions and employment verification, 35–47

Zirkle Fruit Company
RICO litigation, 304–05